THE ESSENCE OF
FRIEDMAN

THE ESSENCE OF

F·R·I·E·D·M·A·N

EDITED BY KURT R. LEUBE

FOREWORD BY W. GLENN CAMPBELL

INTRODUCTION BY ANNA J. SCHWARTZ

HOOVER INSTITUTION PRESS

STANFORD UNIVERSITY, STANFORD, CALIFORNIA

www.hoover.org

Hoover Institution Press Publication No. 366
Hoover Institution at Leland Stanford Junior University,
Stanford, California 94305

Frontispiece and cover photograph by Bachrach.

First printing, 1987
23 22 21 20 19 18 17 16 15   15 14 13 12 11 10 9 8 7

Manufactured in the United States of America
The paper used in this publication meets the minimum requirements of American National Standard for Information Sciences—Permanence of Paper for Printed Library Materials, ANSI Z39.48–1992. ♾

Library of Congress Cataloging-in-Publication Data
Friedman, Milton, 1912–2006
The essence of Friedman.
        p.   cm. — (Hoover Institution Press publication series ; 366)
Bibliography: p.
Includes index.
ISBN 978-0-8179-8661-2 (cloth: alk. paper)
ISBN 978-0-8179-8662-9 (paperback: alk. paper)
ISBN 978-0-8179-8666-7 (epub)
ISBN 978-0-8179-8667-4 (mobi)
ISBN 978-0-8179-8668-1 (PDF)
1. Economics.   2. Monetary policy.   I. Leube, Kurt R.
II. Title   III. Series: Hoover Institution Press publication ; 366.
HB171.F774   1987   330.1   87-4003
                                                  CIP

DEDICATED WITH ADMIRATION AND GRATITUDE TO
PROFESSOR MILTON FRIEDMAN
—IN APPRECIATION OF HIS WISDOM AND FORESIGHT—
ON THE OCCASION OF HIS 75TH BIRTHDAY

CONTENTS

PART TWO: ECONOMIC METHODOLOGY

PART THREE: ECONOMIC THEORY

PART FOUR: MONETARY ANALYSIS

PART FIVE: MONETARY POLICY

FOREWORD

This collection of essays has been assembled and is being published to honor one of the most distinguished and influential economists of our century on the occasion of his 75th birthday. Milton Friedman is a rare individual who possesses special talents and who has had a profound impact on the outlook of countless people in numerous walks of life. He commands the highest respect from his fellow economists for his technical writings and draws attention from the more general public for his sensible philosophy on the role of markets and government in an economy. His ability to clearly convey economic principles is envied by all. His contributions to economic science earned him a Nobel Prize in 1976. On the other side of the spectrum, his columns in *Newsweek* represented one of his many successful forums for influencing ideas and public opinion, an activity that ran for nearly twenty years. An indication of his vast general appeal is evident with his appearance on the cover of *Time* in 1969— no economist has ever been in the public eye as Milton Friedman has.

The Essence of Friedman represents a skillfully selected sample of Milton Friedman's scholarly and popular writings. I am grateful to Kurt R. Leube for making the selections and editing the volume. A special sense of gratitude goes to Anna J. Schwartz, Milton's long-time friend and co-author, who has contributed a valuable introduction to this particular collection of essays. Finally, and most important, I salute Rose D. Friedman, Milton's wife and co-author, for her significant role in the professional contributions of Milton Friedman.

When he retired from the University of Chicago in 1977, Milton Friedman became a senior research fellow at the Hoover Institution and has been with us ever since. He continues to be as prolific and influential as ever in the world of economics and public policy, and offers much to the development and professional growth of the Institution's Domestic Studies Program. His wise counsel has been invaluable, and we look forward to a continuing association for many more years to come. On behalf of my colleagues, I extend warm birthday greetings to him, along with the wish that he and his wife enjoy continued good health and vitality.

W. GLENN CAMPBELL
Director, Hoover Institution

PREFACE

The Hoover Institution is publishing these selected essays of Milton Friedman to honor him on his 75th birthday.

The world knows Milton Friedman, presidential economic adviser, Nobel Prize winner, *Newsweek* columnist—but few know the background career of the man who has developed new and challenging theories in economics. A brief biography gives some insight into the life experiences that helped shape his career and world view.

Milton Friedman was born on July 31, 1912, in Brooklyn, New York, youngest of four children and the only son in an immigrant family from Carpatho-Rumania. When Milton was one year old, his family moved to Rahway, New Jersey, a small industrial town about 20 miles south of New York. The family income was always small and uncertain and when Milton was only fifteen years old and a senior in high school his father died, leaving his mother and his sisters to provide for the family.

Inspired by one of his high school teachers, Milton developed a keen interest in mathematics. In 1928, financed by a variety of odd jobs and the award of a scholarship, he entered Rutgers University, from which he graduated with a bachelor's degree in mathematics and economics.

At Rutgers, Friedman met two extraordinary men, Arthur F. Burns and Homer Jones, who had a major impact on his life, introducing him to rigorous economic theory and the highest scientific standards. On Jones's recommendation Friedman was offered a tuition scholarship from the department of economics at the University of Chicago. He was also offered a scholarship in applied mathematics from Brown University. After considerable soul-searching, he accepted the Chicago scholarship and devoted himself to economics.

The stimulating intellectual climate at the University of Chicago, where such great scholars as Frank Knight, Jacob Viner, Henry Schultz, and Henry Simons taught, left an impression on Friedman that determined his career. Viner's course in theory opened up a new world for Friedman. Equally important, he met Rose Director, a fellow student whom he was to marry six years later and who, from that time, became an active partner in his professional development. At Chicago he joined a coterie of brilliant graduate students whose friendship and vibrant intellectual spirit Friedman has cherished throughout his career. In 1933 he received a master's degree in economics.

Awarded a fellowship, Friedman spent the year 1934 at Columbia University where Harold Hotelling, Wesley C. Mitchell, and John M. Clark exposed him to mathematical economics and an institutional and empirical approach that differed sharply from the Chicago tradition, which strongly emphasizes theory. Friedman's technical work reflects the combination of these influences from Chicago and Columbia.

During the summer of 1935, Friedman joined the National Resources Committee in Washington, D.C., where he worked on the design of an extensive empirical consumer budget study. This effort clearly anticipated one of the two principal components of his theory of the consumption function, which he later developed fully.

In the fall of 1937 he left Washington to work at the National Bureau of Economic Research in New York. Simon Kuznets, another future Nobel laureate, hired him to work on a study dealing with professional income structures, which resulted in their jointly published *Income from Independent Professional Practice*. This study, which served as the basis for his Ph.D. dissertation at Columbia University in 1946, was completed in 1940. However, its publication was delayed for some five years due to a controversy caused by the authors' conclusion that the medical profession had monopolistic powers that enabled it to raise medical incomes above a competitive level. The book includes pioneering work by Friedman on the theory of human capital and the theory of income distribution. Here, for the first time, Friedman introduced the important distinction between "permanent" and "transitory" income: the second principal component of Friedman's consumption theory, later developed fully in his book *A Theory of the Consumption Function* (1957).

In 1938 Friedman and Rose Director were married. For the now nearly 50 years since, they have been active intellectual partners, co-authoring several influential books in political economics. The Friedmans have two children, Janet, a lawyer, and David, a professor of economics, currently at the University of Chicago.

From 1941 to 1943, Friedman worked as an economist at the U.S. Treasury on wartime tax measures, including the introduction of withholding at source for the personal income tax. From 1943 to 1945, he worked as a mathematical statistician at the Statistical Research Group, a subsidiary located at Columbia University of the wartime Office of Scientific Research and Development. The Group provided statistical assistance to the military on a wide variety of projects.

Friedman's two different occupations during World War II had a major influence on his scientific work and to some extent helped to shape his distinctive views about the nature and purpose of intellectual inquiry. The one gave him direct experience at a high level with the making of government economic policy; the other deepened his understanding of the relation between the approaches used in physical and social sciences.

Friedman spent 1945–1946 teaching at the University of Minnesota, and then, in 1946, moved to the University of Chicago to teach economic theory, filling what had been Jacob Viner's position. Chicago has been his intellectual home ever since. In 1962 he was appointed the Paul Snowden Russell Distinguished Service Professor of Economics.

In 1947 Friedman participated in a meeting, organized by Friedrich A. von Hayek, at Mont Pelerin in Switzerland. The participants, called together to discuss the worldwide threat to a free society, included classical liberal scholars, journalists, and politicians from all over the world. The Mont Pelerin Society, formed at this meeting, has been highly successful in promoting the basic principles of free markets and free institutions. Friedman served as president of this society in 1970–1972.

At Arthur F. Burns's invitation, Friedman undertook responsibility for the National Bureau of Economic Research's (NBER) empirical research on the role of money in the trade cycle. The combination of theoretical development at the University of Chicago with empirical studies at the NBER in collaboration with economic historian Anna J. Schwartz proved highly productive, yielding three major volumes and a number of important articles. *A Monetary History of the United States, 1867–1960*, published in 1963, is a comprehensive examination of monetary experience in the United States over nine decades, documenting the importance of the supply of money and its relationship to prices and incomes. *Monetary Statistics of the United States*, published in 1970, is a compendium of basic monetary data as well as an analysis of the various meanings assigned to the concept of "money." *Monetary Trends in the United States and the United Kingdom: Their Relation to Income, Prices, and Interest Rates, 1867–1975*, published in 1982, is an econometric counterpart to the narrative account of the *Monetary History*.

As a consultant for a U.S. government agency administering the Marshall Plan, Friedman spent the autumn of 1950 in Paris. His work on the Schumann

Plan served as the basis for his essay, "The Case for Flexible Exchange Rates," included in his first collection, *Essays in Positive Economics* (1953). This book contains most of his theoretical writings of the preceding decade. During the 1953–1954 academic year, Friedman was a Fulbright visiting professor at Gonville and Caius College, Cambridge University.

The growing threat to the free market from the growth of government inspired Milton and Rose D. Friedman to write *Capitalism and Freedom* (1962), based on a series of lectures given by Friedman. This provocative book received little attention when it was first published. Yet, it has sold about a half million copies over the past quarter century, and has been translated into more than ten foreign languages, including Russian. In it the Friedmans examine the case for competitive capitalism, criticize many forms of government intervention, and offer private alternatives.

Since the early 1960s, Friedman has increasingly been drawn into the public arena. In 1964 he served as an informal economic adviser to Senator Goldwater in his unsuccessful campaign for the presidency; in 1968, to Richard Nixon in his successful run, and subsequently to Ronald Reagan in his 1980 campaign. He was a member of the President's Commission on an All-Volunteer Armed Force (1969–1970) and the President's Commission on White House Fellows (1971–1973), and is currently a member of the President's Economic Policy Advisory Board, a group of nongovernmental experts appointed in early 1981 by President Reagan. But Friedman's primary interest always has been and continues to be his scholarly work. In consequence, he has consistently refused any offer of a full-time government position.

In 1966 Friedman began to write a column for *Newsweek* that appeared once every three weeks until early 1984. Many of these brief, self-contained commentaries on current affairs have been reprinted in the three overlapping volumes: *An Economist's Protest: Columns on Political Economy* (1972); *There's No Such Thing as a Free Lunch* (1975); and *Bright Promises, Dismal Performance* (1983).

Friedman was elected president of the American Economic Association in 1967. His presidential address, "The Role of Monetary Policy," has become one of his most widely cited and influential contributions. In 1969 he published his second collection of essays, *The Optimum Quantity of Money and Other Essays*, which contains much of his theoretical work on money written over almost two decades.

On October 14, 1976, Friedman was awarded the Nobel Prize in economic science "for his achievements in the fields of consumption analysis, monetary history and theory, and for his demonstration of the complexity of stabilization policy." As on other occasions, Friedman was unawed by the award. He made it quite clear that he was more interested in "what his academic colleagues thought of him than the opinion of the Swedish jurors."

Since his official retirement from the University of Chicago in 1977, Friedman has been a senior research fellow at Stanford University's Hoover Institution.

Friedman's deep concern with the decline of personal freedom led him and his wife to co-author their work *Free to Choose* (1980), which is probably their most popular and influential book. Published in the spring of 1980, it immediately caught the attention of the general public and made its way to the best-seller list, becoming the best-selling nonfiction book in the United States for the year 1980. It was translated into most major languages the same year. The book was based on a ten-part television series of the same name that has given the Friedmans' ideas a wide audience internationally.

Four years after the publication of *Free to Choose*, Milton and Rose D. Friedman jointly published *Tyranny of the Status Quo* (1984), in which they analyze the common tendency in government to reverse the declared policies of politicians. This book was also complemented by a three-part television series of the same name in which Friedman discusses a broad range of topics with seven university students of widely varying views.

Milton Friedman is one of the most influential economists of our time, unsurpassed as an academic teacher, persuasive as a public adviser, and path-breaking as a scholar and scientist. His scientific fame rests primarily on his permanent income theory, his theory of the consumption function, his contributions to monetary theory, especially to the restatement of the quantity theory of money, and his natural rate of unemployment hypothesis. His methodology has established a whole school of thought. Friedman's work in the field of political economics has produced classics in the literature of liberty and is a rich source of seminal ideas and market alternatives.

◆ ◆ ◆ ◆

It has been a difficult task to distill the essence from an oeuvre as extensive as that of Professor Friedman. As John Burton put it, "It is like trying to catch the Niagara Falls in a pint pot."[1] However, I have exercised my subjective judgment in selecting for this collection the most representative of Professor Friedman's works. Although numerous worthwhile essays have been reluctantly omitted due to limitations of space, I am glad that my final choices received Professor Friedman's approval. I wish to thank him for his patience and cooperation.

I am grateful to Anna J. Schwartz for preparing the introduction to this

---

1. John Burton, "Positively Milton Friedman," in J. R. Shackleton and Gareth Locksley, eds., *Twelve Contemporary Economists* (London: Macmillan, 1981), p. 53.

book. She is probably the best authority to appreciate Friedman's place in the history of economic thought. She has given us a succinct and lucid summary of Friedman's work and a personal and unique view of him as economist, colleague, and friend.

Without the assistance of the Hoover Institution and its director, W. Glenn Campbell, Principal Associate Director John F. Cogan, and Associate Director John Raisian, this volume could not have been published. I am especially thankful for their support.

My special thanks are given to Gloria Valentine, Professor Friedman's administrative assistant, for her great help. Gloria prepared Milton Friedman's first comprehensive bibliography, which I have included in this volume.

My thanks are also due to the fine Hoover Institution Press staff for their diligent work and their patience.

KURT R. LEUBE

INTRODUCTION

◆ ANNA J. SCHWARTZ ◆

The twenty-six chapters assembled in this book are a small sample drawn from the body of work that Milton Friedman has published since 1935. Three-fifths of the selections were originally published in the 1950s and 1960s, the remainder in the period since. Friedman's productivity at seventy-five shows no sign of diminution. The well is deep and has not run dry.

The five parts in which the book has been divided suggest the breadth of Friedman's range. His fame among professional economists rests first on his distinctive contributions to economic theory. Parts Two and Three give examples of these contributions. The chapters on monetary analysis (Part Four) are of equal importance in assessing Friedman's influence on professional economists, as well as on a broader worldwide audience. This analysis laid the ground for the counterattack he led on the doctrine of the unimportance of monetary policy that characterized Keynesian economics until the 1970s. Friedman's monetary policy recommendations are the complement of his monetary analysis. To see which recommendations have remained unaltered and which have changed over time is fascinating in its own right (Part Five).

As is well known, Friedman did not confine himself to scholarly activities in the classroom or to professional meetings. After the New Deal era and especially after World War II, in a climate which regarded enlarging the responsibilities of government as a social norm, he sought a public hearing for his novel and unorthodox views on limiting government intervention. An intellectual heir of nineteenth-century liberalism, he championed such concepts as individual freedom from government compulsion; the virtues of a market economy, free trade, and free capital movements; and the value of a stable price level achieved by stable policies and not by price controls of any kind (Part One). These positions currently may not appear to be particularly radical. However, since the time Friedman first made his views on these matters known in his journal articles, popular books, and TV and radio appearances—views derived from evidence in professional studies—experience has taught the world lessons that he had underscored years earlier. In addition, he combined criticism of existing institutions with innovative suggestions to make them more efficient and consistent with a society of individuals enjoying freedom of choice.

The chapters thus center attention on different roles that Friedman has filled: economic scientist, monetary counterrevolutionary, exponent of individual freedom. The selected examples of his work give us a glimpse of how he played these roles.

Economic Scientist

Friedman is first and foremost an economic scientist. Friedman's conception of the goal of economic science is presented in Chapter 11. The question this essay deals with is the purpose of theory in a science. Widely regarded as a classic, even though often reviewed negatively, and the subject of many contentious sessions on methodology at annual meetings of associations of economists, the essay has had a profound influence.

Friedman begins by drawing a distinction—one he often refers to in other contexts—between positive and normative economics. Positive economics is concerned with the effects of changes in circumstances, including policy actions taken to solve an economic problem. Normative economics is concerned with the way economic problems *should* be solved. Positive economics separates questions of what is from normative economic questions of what ought to be.

The continuing wrangle over Friedman's views has been occasioned by his analysis of the role of theory in positive economics—particularly his belief that the realism of assumptions underlying a theory is irrelevant. In fact, he argues, the more significant the theory, the more unrealistic its assumptions. The correct test of a theory or hypothesis is its fruitfulness and success in yielding predictions about phenomena not yet observed—predictions that are capable of being contradicted but are not. He challenges the procedures of those economists who evaluate theories by the realism of their assumptions. They would replace a theory that they regard as unacceptable because of its assumptions with an alternative theory that they regard as acceptable because of more realistic assumptions. Friedman is not mealymouthed in dismissing their work as vacuous because it generates no testable predictions. In particular, he attacks such examples as the theory of monopolistic competition. He has not endeared himself to the affected members of the profession by this stricture, which may partly explain the furor the essay on methodology created.

Friedman has not merely preached the requirement that theories undergo empirical tests; he has practiced it. The concluding chapter of *A Theory of the Consumption Function*, reprinted here in Chapter 12, is a masterly treatment of the relationship between theory and data. The theory that Friedman proposed was that the fraction of their income that people spend on consumption depends on permanent income—his coinage, meaning the present value of all expected future flows of income from both human and nonhuman capital— and that permanent consumption does not change because of transitory increases or decreases in income. He tested the theory by examining family budget and time series data, which confirmed the predictions of the theory. He showed, on one hand, that savings as a fraction of income were much higher at high than at low incomes in the budget data because consumption and income as measured in those data combine permanent and transitory components. On the other hand, time series data, which are closer approximations to permanent consumption and permanent income, showed that savings in the United States were a roughly constant fraction of national income, despite the secular rise in real income. (Incidentally, contrast the theory that Friedman proposed and tested with the consumption function in Keynesian economics that was defined as a stable function of current disposable income—without any methodological concerns.)

Friedman's emphasis on formulating scientific hypotheses that are capable of being subjected to empirical tests of their predictions is further illustrated by the subject matter of Chapters 13 and 14. The hypothesis in Chapter 13 concerns the choices individuals make in the presence of uncertainty, buying insurance to hedge against large losses and engaging in gambling at unfair odds. The hypothesis is that individuals behave as if they were trying to maximize the expected value of a quantity called their utility or their income. The conclusion is that direct evidence in favor of the hypothesis is limited, but that confidence in the validity of the hypothesis rests on its coherence with the body of economic theory. An offshoot of that hypothesis is concerned with the personal distribution of income. The hypothesis Friedman advances in Chapter 14 is that existing inequality may reflect individual tastes and preferences for risk, different choices being made by individuals from the same set of alternatives, with random events having an impact subsequent to the choice. He notes similarities between features of observed distributions of wealth and income and the theory under consideration, but recognizes the need for further tests.

These three illustrations of Friedman's approach to the role of theory in positive economics can be summarized by quoting the concluding sentences from Chapter 11. They are an apt description of Friedman's talent.

> The construction of hypotheses is a creative act of inspiration, intuition, invention; its essence is the vision of something new in familiar material. The process must be discussed in psychological, not logical, categories; studied in autobiographies and biographies, not treatises on scientific method; and promoted by maxim and example, not by syllogism or theorem.

Finally, Chapter 15 is didactic. How does a society determine the amount of capital—the sources of productive services—it wishes to maintain? The theory of capital is elegantly analyzed, showing the relation between the stock and the use of flows to add to or subtract from the stock, and how the interest rate acts as the price that gives owners of capital an incentive to maintain it or alter it. Friedman was a teacher for the greater part of his career and this chapter is a simulacrum of the instruction provided in his classroom.

Monetary Counterrevolutionary

The Keynesian revolution transformed economic thought. Its central message was that government can cure depression and unemployment by fiscal policy that increases government spending minus tax receipts. Keynesian doctrine assigned a negligible role to money, asserting that it had little influence on total spending, consumption, or prices, except indirectly through interest rates. However, interest rates were largely ineffective. Reductions induce little or no increase in investment demand. Only such an increase would generate a net increase in spending that a multiplier would magnify into an expansion of income. In addition, since interest rates could not fall below zero, beyond some point, injections of money into the system would be held passively, with no inducement to shift out of money into other assets.

The Keynesian revolution was an attack on the ability of a market economy to achieve full employment and price stability by automatic tendencies. It swept the economics profession and government bureaucracies. The textbooks indoctrinated a generation of students in the view that the quantity theory of money had been rendered obsolete by the Keynesian income-expenditure theory. Friedman's counterargument, initially regarded with disbelief, was strongly supported by the subsequent course of events. The combination of his argument and events in time compelled Keynesians to modify their doctrines and led to wide acceptance of Friedman's views.

The final section of Chapter 15—a discussion of the effect on capital theory of the existence of money—digresses to dispute some Keynesian propositions that depend on a fixed-price level. Once the price level associated with the quantity of money, or the rate of price change associated with a changing quantity of money is allowed for, those propositions are invalid. The digression provides a link to the central position of monetary analysis in Friedman's intellectual history, the basis for his opposition to Keynesian doctrine.

The monetary analysis that Friedman developed began with his seminal restatement of the quantity theory of money (Chapter 16). He presented it as a theory about the demand for money implicit in traditional formulations of the theory that emphasized money as the determinant of prices and nominal income. The novelty in Friedman's restatement was, first, the conception of the budget constraint as a broad measure of wealth, including human as well as real and financial capital, all of which might be substitutes for money in the household balance sheet. Hence, the relative yields of the various possible substitutes for money were relevant. Second, his inclusion of a variable measuring the expected depreciation of the purchasing power of money was clairvoyant, given the onset of inflation a decade after the restatement.

The key prediction of the quantity theory, contrary to Keynesian doctrine, is that the demand for money, although not necessarily stable in a numerical sense, is a stable function of a small number of variables, such as those Friedman specified. That prediction has been tested innumerable times by a host of economists, including Friedman and his students. The tests have involved fitting different functional forms to observations for different countries, time periods, frequency of data points, and variables. Earlier work gave strong support to the prediction. More recent empirical work has yielded some puzzles that undoubtedly will be clarified as experience casts up new observations for further tests.

The historical experience of the United States, from the Civil War until 1960, with respect to the relations between changes in money and changes in prices and output and their sum—changes in nominal income—provided the evidence on which Friedman based four analytical propositions (Chapters 17 and 18):

1. To achieve price stability, noninflationary growth of the money stock is essential.

2. Provided price changes are moderate and predictable, economic growth is achievable with either rising or falling prices.

3. The relations between changes in money and changes in the variables money affects have been unchanging, despite differences in the influences affecting money growth.

4. The dominant channel of influence has been from changes in money to changes in income, not the reverse.

The finding that had the greatest impact on professional views regarding the potency of money was the documentation in the historical study that the severity of the depression of 1929–1933, far from supporting the Keynesian interpretation, was the consequence of inept monetary policy. The Federal Reserve's failure to prevent a succession of banking panics led to the destruction of one-third of the money stock and the ensuing drastic decline in prices and output.

In his Nobel lecture (Chapter 19), Friedman resumed analysis of a question he had dealt with in Chapter 17 on the relation between prices and output, examining not only the long-term, as in the earlier case, but also the short-term relation, and restating the question in terms the profession had come to use: the trade-off between inflation and unemployment. Estimated Phillips curves, with the unemployment rate on the horizontal axis and the inflation rate on the vertical, seemed to be negatively sloped. Economists in the Keynesian camp came to regard the trade-off in the 1960s as a stable relationship, offering the policymaker a choice between the combination of a lower unemployment rate and a higher inflation rate or a higher unemployment rate and lower inflation rate.

On theoretical grounds, Friedman challenged the validity of a stable Phillips curve (Chapter 21). What mattered for unemployment, he pointed out, is not inflation itself but unanticipated inflation. Only unanticipated inflation can lead to temporarily lower unemployment. Once employers realize that there has been no increase in relative demand for their output but only an increase in the general price level, and workers realize that they have been fooled with respect to the purchasing power of nominal wages, unemployment returns to the level at which it stood before the unanticipated price rise. Unemployment can be kept below that level only by bigger and bigger doses of unanticipated inflation.

In the Nobel lecture, Friedman stressed the concept of the natural rate of unemployment—his coinage, again, of nearly a decade earlier—as the level of voluntary unemployment determined by institutional and legislative arrangements in a given economy. The natural rate is the lowest unemployment rate that is sustainable without accelerating or unanticipated inflation. In the long run the natural rate or expectations-adjusted Phillips curve is not negatively sloping but vertical. The unemployment rate can be permanently lowered only by modifying the determinants of the natural rate—the age and sex composition of the labor force, the ratio of unemployment benefits to nominal wages, minimum wage laws, union strength, and so on. Friedman noted that in the mid-1970s the Phillips curve had become positively sloped, with both unemployment and inflation simultaneously increasing, but regarded the phenomenon as a transitional one that would change depending on the future behavior of inflation.

Friedman's conjectures about the formation of expectations by employers and workers in his analysis of the Phillips curve influenced the development by younger economists of the rational-expectations hypothesis (Chapter 20). It stated that economic agents form their expectations by using efficiently the information available to them, and understanding the interrelationships among the variables. Expectations may be mistaken because of random unpredictable shocks, but errors are not systematic. A highly controversial variant of the theory implies that no announced systematic government policy can influence real variables like the unemployment rate. No verdict on this implication has as yet been reached. Friedman notes that the formulation of the theory is still in process and its empirical underpinnings have still to be established.

Friedman concludes the chapter by summarizing a variety of empirical findings concerning the relationship between changes in the quantity of money and the level of prices and findings concerning long-term and cyclical effects of monetary changes. This summary particularly merits the reader's attention.

An important by-product of the empirical findings is the set of monetary policy views that they led Friedman to espouse. Chapters 21 through 26 represent works originally published over the span of a quarter century. All along, his chief aim was to recommend monetary arrangements for a free society that would assign responsibility for money to government yet limit government's power so that it would not be used in ways that would weaken a free society.

Some constants in Friedman's approach to monetary policy may be noted. He has been a gradualist. Mistakes in the conduct of monetary policy, he believes, should be corrected in a gradual manner, over a period of years, not at one fell swoop. He has consistently opposed the use of monetary policy to fine-tune the economy. He has always taught that there are things that monetary policy cannot do—such as pegging the real interest rate, the rate of unemployment, the level of the real quantity of income, the real quantity of money, or the rate of growth of the latter—and things that it can do—controlling nominal quantities or their rate of growth, including the rate of inflation or deflation (Chapter 21). Finally, he has repeatedly urged monetary authorities to avoid sharp swings in policy.

One possible change in current domestic institutional arrangements that Friedman has advocated several times—not as an ideal but still an improvement—is subordinating the Federal Reserve to the Treasury, to achieve a single locus of power over monetary and fiscal policy (Chapters 22 and 23). Concerning two sets of international monetary arrangements, Friedman's appraisal has been unvarying. One is the gold standard, the other the exchange-rate system. Friedman is firm in the belief that the possibility of restoring a gold standard that would constrain monetary authorities to take actions in line with movements in their gold holdings is illusory. In any event, he opposes a gold standard that would require governments to fix the price of gold (Chapter 24). Friedman has favored a floating exchange-rate system from the time that the Bretton Woods system was first established (Chapter 25). The present floating rate system is subject to government intervention so does not fully realize the benefits that he outlined, but at least the change has been in the direction that he approves.

Having commented on Friedman's policy recommendations that have not changed over the years, one should also note those that have undergone change. One concerns the effects on policy of particular personalities being in charge of domestic monetary arrangements, implying that outcomes would have been different with different individuals at the top (Chapter 22). Friedman's initial adoption of that view was based on the impressive intellectual force of Benjamin Strong, governor of the Federal Reserve Bank of New York, 1914–1928. His untimely death the year before the Great Depression suggested that, had he lived, more appropriate policy decisions would have been made by the Federal Reserve System. Experience with greater and lesser lights at the helm of the Federal Reserve since 1951 has not changed his view of what Strong's presence might have accomplished, but has impressed him with the way the institution molds the personalities, so that little difference among them emerges in respect of the Federal Reserve's operations.

A more substantive change in Friedman's thinking about the way to conduct domestic monetary policy to provide a stable monetary framework reflects his frustration with the lack of success of the recommendation that he has long made that a legislated rule be imposed on the Federal Reserve, specifying a target for monetary growth. In 1975, when Congress required the Federal Reserve to specify explicit numerical targets, a milestone appeared to have been reached. However, the Federal Reserve does not achieve the targets it sets for itself, and yet escapes accountability for its failures. Friedman has since proposed a constitutional amendment as a substitute for a legislated rule, and limiting the growth rate of high-powered money—the non-interest-bearing obligations of the U.S. government—rather than a broader monetary aggregate (Chapter 22). Still more recently, Friedman has proposed that, after a transition period, high-powered money be frozen at a fixed amount, as the most effective way of ending the arbitrary power of the Federal Reserve. The total quantity of different money assets would be determined by market interactions of financial institutions and individual money holders.

Chapter 26 is a retrospective on some early views by Friedman justifying government intervention in money matters. He sees no economic reason why the determination of a unit of account and provision of high-powered money could not be left to the market, but is skeptical that a system in which governments have historically intervened in these areas can easily be replaced by a strictly private system. He welcomes deregulation of financial intermediaries but is uncertain whether government must continue to serve as a lender of last resort. He concludes with the question whether the world fiat monetary system will degenerate into a runaway inflation, as it has in the past in fiat monetary systems in individual countries. In that eventuality, Friedman argues, it is currently important to explore alternative monetary reforms that might be invoked to replace the existing system.

The reader comes away with the impression that Friedman was more optimistic a quarter century ago than he is at present about the prospects of a stable monetary framework. His counterrevolution has produced significant alterations in professional thinking about the importance of money in the functioning of the economy. It has not, however, persuaded mainstream economists that a central bank cannot control real variables. Indeed, to some extent, his success has backfired, since economists, in particular the Keynesians, now regard the central bank as a more potent instrument for controlling the economy than they had earlier believed. The fact that Friedman has made little headway in convincing the profession that discretionary management of money is responsible for both instability of the price level and the real economy is an indication that at least one item of the agenda of the monetary counterrevolution is yet to be accomplished.

Exponent of Individual Freedom

The essays in Part One introduce the reader to the broad sweep of issues Friedman has analyzed for their impact on a free society. In such a society individual freedom flourishes. For him, private enterprise and political freedom are the two pillars of a free society. Central to Friedman's vision of private enterprise is the part that the market plays in promoting voluntary associations among individuals. In stereotypes of a free-enterprise economy, selfish, atomistic individuals are its characteristic feature. In Friedman's vision, at its heart is cooperation through market exchange that benefits all. The prevailing disdain for the market and for profit is allied with an aversion for capitalism. Competitive capitalism, which gives fullest scope to market exchange and political freedom, earns three cheers in these essays.

The first five chapters deal in one way or another with "the role of the market as a device for the voluntary cooperation of many individuals in the establishment of common values" (Chapter 1). The remaining chapters are critical of various U.S. institutions. They also suggest how the institutions might be reshaped to improve their efficiency while enhancing the values of a free society. Some of these suggestions have in part or in whole been adopted.

In discussing the market, Friedman has in mind exchange transactions that are broader than the narrowly economic (Chapter 1). In the marketplace for ideas, free speech—a special case of free exchange—provides a mutual benefit for participants with differing opinions. Free exchange has produced modern scientific knowledge, the structure of common law, and the development of language, each emerging as the result of voluntary cooperation of individual human beings in their search for common values.

In Friedman's view, there is no distinction between freedom of speech and economic freedom. He gives numerous examples showing that intellectuals in general and the judiciary in particular are inconsistent, being solicitous of preserving freedom of speech, no matter what costs are imposed on third parties, but justifying restrictions on economic freedom on the basis of even trivial third-party effects (Chapter 2). His own position is consistent, since he regards both freedom of speech and economic freedom as of equal importance in maintaining a free society. A strong presumption would have to exist before he would support restriction of either area to avoid third-party effects. Friedman notes that the inconsistency extends beyond speech to a supposed distinction, which he rejects, between political freedom and economic freedom.

Friedman treats the subject of the market in a different context in discussing two leading methods for giving market mechanisms a greater role in a centrally planned society—requiring state-owned enterprises to play at free-market capitalism, and constructing a restricted and modified form of capitalism (Chapter 3). He concludes that "even allegedly command economies will find it desirable to use free markets over as wide an area as is politically and economically possible." However, he is dubious that in the absence of markets with divisible and transferable property rights, it is possible to reproduce in any significant respect the functioning of competitive private enterprise.

Friedman relates the problems that arise in trying to introduce effective market elements into command economies to the failure of prices to function there in the three ways that they function in market economies. The first function is to provide information about tastes, resource availability, and productive possibilities, about goods availability today versus tomorrow. A second function is to provide an incentive to adopt the least costly methods of production and to use resources for the most highly valued uses. The third function is to determine the distribution of income. In a command economy, prices are prevented from affecting the distribution of income, hence the information that prices convey carries no incentive to act on the information.

Friedman notes that, since the expansion of the role of government during the past half century in predominantly market economies, an attempt has been made to separate the third function from the other two functions of prices, by making the incomes people receive independent of the prices at which they can sell their services. However, prices that are not permitted to affect the distribution of income cannot serve as the means of transmitting information and creating incentives to act on that information. In that event, the price system will have to be replaced by authoritarian decisions about what should be produced in what quantities, and who should be assigned to what job.

Probably no point of view that Friedman has expressed has been greeted with more outrage by those on the opposite side than his analysis of the reasons it is harmful to a free society to urge businessmen to be socially responsible (Chapter 4). On a recent radio program a dean of the Harvard Business School excoriated Friedman for his view.

Friedman regards businessmen's willingness to involve the corporations they serve in activities that are hailed as socially responsible as spending money that is not theirs but rightfully belongs to stockholders, customers, or employees. By such activities, businessmen in effect impose taxes and decide how the taxes should be spent. They become, as it were, civil servants, although not selected through an explicit political process and although no explicit political mechanism guides the way they assess the taxes and use the proceeds.

Friedman notes that corporations often cloak self-serving actions as exercises of social responsibility. One example is the provision of amenities to the community in which they are located to garner recognition that has positive effects on sales or employee relations.

Friedman objects to social responsibility activities, whatever their motivation, because they reinforce the view that pursuit of profits is immoral and must be mitigated by acts of social responsibility, and rely on political rather than market mechanisms to determine the way business allocates scarce resources among competing uses.

The market mechanism operates on the basis of unanimity. No individual can coerce another, cooperation is voluntary, and, unless all benefit, the parties need not participate. There are no social values or responsibilities other than the shared values and responsibilities of individuals in their voluntary cooperative transactions. By contrast, the political mechanism operates on the basis of conformity. The individual may have a vote but if overruled must conform. He must contribute to a general social purpose whether or not he so wishes. The political mechanism, however, is sometimes necessary because unanimity is not always feasible and conformity is sometimes unavoidable.

A sociological investigation provides another occasion for Friedman to discuss capitalism, the market, and political freedom. He asks how one can reconcile the benefits that Jews have received from a competitive economy under capitalism with their disproportionately anti-capitalist views (Chapter 5). Competitive capitalism permitted them to flourish economically and culturally because it prevented anti-Semites from imposing their values on others, and from discriminating against Jews.

Friedman dismisses the common explanations—that the anti-capitalism of the Jews is a reflection of values derived from the Jewish religion and culture; that intellectuals, including Jewish intellectuals, are disposed to embrace collectivist views; and that capitalism is responsible for the evils of anti-Semitism.

He finds more fundamental the explanation that Jews supported the Left from the time of the French Revolution because it was only on the Left that a place for Jews in public life was possible—on the Right, the Christian religion remained a prerequisite for political participation. A complementary explanation is that Jews came to accept the values of the larger society that money-making and moneylending, with which Jews were identified, were contemptible. So they attacked the market system with its reliance on monetary values and impersonal transactions and glorified the political process in which an ideal state run by well-meaning people produced benefits for their fellowmen.

The ideology of the Jews is opposed to their self-interest. No conflict emerged in the West so long as Jews could reap the benefits of capitalism, where laissez faire prevailed, while approving socialism as an ideal. The conflict has become real where government has grown and collectivist ideas have become generally acceptable. Friedman suggests that the reality of the conflict may weaken the paradox.

Among the institutions criticized in these pages is the existing grab-bag of welfare programs that dispense payments in kind based on the circumstances of the recipients (Chapter 6). Instead of such programs, Friedman proposes the use of the mechanism by which the bulk of taxes is now collected—the personal income tax—as the device for helping the poor. It would substitute payments in money and a single numerical means test by supplementing the income of the poor with a fraction of their unused income tax exemptions and deductions. Friedman coined the name, the negative income tax, for his proposal, and discusses five advantages and six objections. He notes that, although it is objectionable that the negative income tax operates outside the market and reduces the incentive of those helped to help themselves, nevertheless, it does not entirely eliminate the incentive, as would a system supplementing incomes up to a fixed minimum, as present measures do. The advantages include offering a way to eliminate existing programs gradually, and removing the possibility of adding new programs. It is no doubt the tyranny of the status quo, to use a cliché that Friedman has found descriptive, that accounts for the status of the negative income tax as an idea that has not yet been implemented.

Friedman has been a consistent opponent of conscription as a method of manning the military and is in favor of volunteer armed forces (Chapter 7). In this area he has contributed to that result by his trenchant analysis of the cost of conscription compared to the cost of volunteers. He showed that, although volunteer forces might raise the apparent money cost to the government, they would lower the real cost to the nation. The real cost of conscription to a conscript is measured by the difference between the amount he would need to be paid to serve willingly and the military pay he actually receives. This difference is an implicit tax in kind that must be added to explicit taxes imposed on the nation to calculate the real cost of the armed forces. Volunteer forces, on the other hand, would attract those for whom service was the career they chose and who would require the lowest sums of money to induce them to serve. In his usual thorough canvassing of all angles, Friedman then pointed to possible offsets to the monetary costs of volunteer forces: volunteers would serve longer terms; a higher fraction would re-enlist and have a higher level of skill, so the waste of man-hours in training would be reduced; and better pay to volunteers might lessen the political appeal of veterans' benefits now granted after service. He also examined three objections, the racial composition, flexibility, and possible political danger of volunteer forces, and found them not convincing or no worse a problem for volunteer than for conscripted forces. Friedman's powers of persuasion were clearly peerless in this instance.

Friedman's case against U.S. foreign economic aid has thus far not won the day, although at the start of the Reagan administration he might have had reason for optimism. He builds the case on two propositions (Chapter 8): first, centralized government control and planning hinders rather than promotes economic development; second, foreign aid strengthens the government relative to the private sector and thereby not only contributes to policies that retard or prevent economic development but also has political effects that are adverse to freedom and democracy. Aid may add to the capital available to a country but also leads to economically wasteful projects, mainly because aid is extended to governments not to private enterprises. Underdeveloped countries are not too poor to save and provide capital for themselves. Given proper incentives, even the poor save, and foreign capital will be attracted if property is secure. Government must provide law and order and security to person and property and may promote progress by providing such services as roads and education, but detailed control of investment, far from being a requisite for progress, is a hindrance. Government officials are less flexible, less adaptive than private individuals raising and spending their own funds. The only effective route to economic development is to provide individuals a maximum of opportunity to operate in a free capital market without central planning.

Friedman proposes instead that the United States abolish all tariffs, quotas, and other restrictions on trade over a defined period and thereafter maintain complete free trade. Underdeveloped countries would then have confidence in a market for their products, and elimination of trade barriers would also stimulate foreign investment in those countries. He advocates giving a generous terminal grant to each recipient country, on which each could draw as it wished. The objectives of foreign aid would be achieved by a program of free trade and free enterprise, not by centralized and comprehensive economic planning.

Another problem institution that Friedman would reform is the public school system, particularly schools located in large urban areas (Chapter 9). He has long advocated a voucher plan for elementary and secondary schools to correct problems in the educational system. He proposes that vouchers be made available that would be redeemable for a sum of money good only for educational expense at any private or public school willing to enroll the student. Parents would thus enjoy a wider choice of schools for their children.

His response to objections to the voucher plan is as follows: (1) Vouchers would be given to parents, not to schools, so their use to pay tuition at parochial schools would not violate the First Amendment. (2) Vouchers need not raise total public expenditures if the amount of the voucher is kept below the current cost per public school child. (3) The possibility of fraud would be minimized by limiting spending of the voucher to approved schools. (4) Rather than exacerbating racial and class conflict, vouchers would eliminate divisive forced busing and, by giving black parents control over their children's schooling, would deprive black political leaders of the political patronage and power they now exercise over schools. (5) Public schools in large cities now foster residential stratification, but under the voucher plan schools would be heterogeneous by attracting students from a wide variety of residential areas. Even if parents chose to add sums to the amount of the voucher, there is no evidence that unrestricted vouchers would result in economic segregation. Poor as well as affluent parents might well add on as a means of improving their children's schooling. (6) No reason exists to doubt that new schools would be established, because the voucher plan would open a vast market that could attract many entrants, both those with profit and nonprofit incentives. (7) If the public school system today were in fact the cornerstone of our democracy, parents would not use their vouchers at nongovernmental competitive schools. There would be no reason then to fear that competition would destroy the public school system.

Despite the opposition of the educational bureaucracy to the introduction of market competition in schooling—the key obstacle to a voucher plan—Friedman is confident that vouchers or their equivalent will soon be accepted. Greater parental choice is the only available alternative that would reduce rising discontent with the school system.

With respect to higher education, Friedman finds the dual problems of quality and equity there as in elementary and secondary education, but altered by the absence of compulsory attendance. The quality difference arises from the existence of government institutions with low tuition fees and a high dropout rate, whereas at private institutions, with high tuition fees, the dropout rate is much lower because both the college and the student have a strong incentive to serve one another. The equity question is related to the use of tax money to finance higher education. So-called social benefits that are said to justify the use of tax money have never been identified. The benefits accrue to students themselves. There is no more reason for government to subsidize human capital than there is for it to subsidize physical capital. The other justification of the use of tax money is said to be the promotion of equal educational opportunity. Since the subsidies have benefited largely middle and upper income families who send children to colleges and universities to a far greater extent than do lower income groups, the justification is without substance. Yet Friedman concludes that the elimination of taxpayer subsidization of higher education is not currently politically feasible. So the poor will continue to pay taxes to subsidize the rich.

Friedman proposes reducing the harm done by taxpayer subsidization of higher education by the introduction of either a contingent loan financing system or a voucher plan. Either one would promote equality of educational opportunity and greater equity in the distribution of subsidies.

The final chapter in Part One is a selection of eleven of the many columns Friedman has written for *Newsweek* magazine. Most deal succinctly with the harmful effects of government programs, although in every case the motivations for the interventions were high-minded: rent controls, urban renewal programs, education programs such as bilingualism, price and wage controls, regulatory commissions, licensing of occupations, prohibition of drugs, welfare programs, government control of airports, the Post Office. The exclusive role of government, Friedman emphasizes in one column, is to design general rules and adjudicate disputes about the rules, not to determine the outcome of individual activities. Its only real power is to take money from some and give it to—or spend it on behalf of—others. In a column on Chile, he foresees that economic freedom is not assured there in the absence of political freedom. A column on Brazil, written in 1974, approves the use of purchasing-power escalator clauses as a second-best solution to cope with inflation. The journalism Friedman has pursued distills and communicates the lessons of his scientific findings.

The Essence of Friedman

Milton Friedman is a composite of a dispassionate intellectual and a passionate reformer. In this regard he is unique among present-day economists. Some predecessors have been reformers but as economists did not match his stature. Although he often admonishes that the best is the enemy of the good, he has a taste for the absolute where his moral fervor is at stake.

Teaching and research in great part have occupied Milton Friedman's life.

His scholarly attainments are unquestionable, but they are not generally known to the worldwide public that recognizes his name. Yet no one who reads his work, whether for a popular or a scientific audience, can fail to be impressed by the orderly mind that is in evidence. He invariably brings fresh insight to any problem that has seized him. His creativity is exceptional, as is his generosity in giving students and colleagues the benefit of his suggestions for investigating a subject.

Unlike some of his critics who caricature his viewpoints, Friedman gives a fair account of analytic approaches others have proposed that he finds unsatisfactory. In presenting his own approach, he not only marshals doctrinal or empirical support for it, he is scrupulous in examining possible weaknesses or contradictions that may be raised.

Friedman's extracurricular activities have been devoted to the cause of freeing Western society from dependence on centralized authority. Since the 1950s, his lectures on campuses here and abroad, public debates, books, journalism, and radio and TV appearances have won him influence and attention, favorable and unfavorable, on a scale that is extraordinary for a college professor who has never held public office. And they have been remarkably successful in spreading his ideas.

Friedman is a controversial figure because he dissents from dominant opinion in the media and academic life. He takes a mordant view of standard "liberal" attitudes. What particularly arouses his critics is the corollary of his advocacy of individual freedom—his belief in limited government. To extol the market and to question government beneficence is for the critics a heresy. Some have portrayed Friedman as an apologist for business interests, despite his scathing denunciations of business leaders for seeking government subsidies and guarantees. He is evenhanded in opposing all special interests that enlist political influence to obtain government largesse. When wage restraint was urged to curb inflation, against the interest of union members, he observed that union leaders in this country were more courageous than business leaders in objecting to government interference with market mechanisms. Moreover, urging wage restraint, when inflation is a monetary phenomenon, is the kind of folly that Friedman is expert at skewering.

The promise of the man and his work is conveyed not in an introduction but in the main text. The essence of Friedman is captured there.

ESSAYS IN
POLITICAL ECONOMICS

◆

◆ PART ◆ ONE ◆

VALUE JUDGMENTS
IN ECONOMICS

· 1 ·

I have been impressed by the tendency at this symposium for the philosophers and the economists to speak at cross-purposes. The philosophers, I am sure, have somewhat the impression that the economists are avoiding what they regard as the basic issue, namely, the value judgments that affect and enter into private and public policy. And by value judgments, the philosophers do not mean relative exchange value. They mean "moral" or "ethical" values. The philosophers in my opinion are correct. To help explain why we have been avoiding "their" issue and to contribute a little to bridge the gap, I shall discuss three points: (1) The basic reason for the avoidance is that there are no value judgments in economics; (2) The appearance to the contrary arises partly from the tendency to use alleged differences in value judgments as an evasion in explaining differences in policy conclusions; (3) The market itself, broadly conceived, is a mechanism for the development and not merely the reflection of value judgments.

1. *The absence of value judgments in economics.* This point has been made by Professor Nagel in his comment and I am fully in agreement with him. In principle, economics as a special discipline is concerned with the consequences of changes in circumstances on the course of events, with prediction

Reprinted by permission of New York University Press from *Human Values and Economic Policy* edited by Sidney Hook. Copyright 1967 by New York University. Originally appeared as a symposium comment on a paper by Professor Kenneth Boulding.

and analysis, not with evaluation. It has something to say about whether specified objectives can be achieved and if so, how, but not, strictly speaking, with whether they are good or bad objectives.

Yet economics has something to say about value judgments. In the first place, no objectives are really fully defined. They are partly revealed in their consequences. In the second place, we never really know all our values. As my revered teacher Frank H. Knight is wont to say, though we all repeat *de gustibus non est disputandum*, in practice we spend our time arguing about little else. And such discussion is relevant and fruitful. Its aim is to see what the implications of our value judgments are, whether they are internally consistent. This is the contribution of Arrow's important and fundamental work and of much of what is called welfare economics.

Further, economists are not solely that but also human beings, and their own values undoubtedly affect their economics. A *wert-frei* economics is an ideal and like most ideals often honored in the breach. The economist's value judgments doubtless influence the subjects he works on and perhaps also at times the conclusions he reaches. And, as already suggested, his conclusions react on his value judgments. Yet this does not alter the fundamental point that, in principle, there are no value judgments in economics, despite the title of this session.

2. *The resort to alleged value judgments as evasions.* I have been much impressed, in the course of much controversy about issues of economic policy, that most differences in economic policy in the United States do not reflect differences in value judgments, but differences in positive economic analysis. I have found time and again that in mixed company—that is, a company of economists and noneconomists such as is here today—the economists present, although initially one would tend to regard them as covering a wide range of political views, tend to form a coalition vis-à-vis the noneconomists, and, often much to their surprise, to find themselves on the same side. They may argue among themselves on the fine points, but these differences disappear when they confront the lay world.

But even within the profession, the same point applies. Paul Samuelson and I have often disagreed in recent years about the relative weight to be put on monetary and fiscal policy. This difference does not reflect—as I trust Paul Samuelson will agree—any difference in our basic or even reasonably proximate objectives. It reflects a difference in the tentative hypotheses we accept about the relation between monetary and fiscal changes on the one hand and economic changes on the other.

An example I have often used that brings out the same point is the minimum wage rate. If we leave aside those who have special interests in the issue, the difference between those who favor and those who oppose minimum wage rates is not about the objective but about the effect. Both groups would like to see poverty reduced. Those who, like myself, are opposed to minimum-wage laws predict that the effect of the laws will be to render people unemployed and hence to increase poverty; those who favor them predict that the effect will be to reduce poverty. If they agreed on effects they would agree on policy. The difference is not a moral one but a scientific one, in principle capable of being resolved by empirical evidence.

The reason why, in my opinion, apparent differences in policy judgments between people in the same culture are largely of this kind is the point raised in the discussion of Arrow's paper and in Boulding's paper: the need for agreement on basic values to avoid the "impossibility" theorem. Differences in opinion among people from different cultures would probably more frequently reflect "real" differences in value judgments.

The fact—or what I allege to be a fact—that differences about policy reflect mostly differences in predictions is concealed by the widespread tendency to attribute policy differences to differences in value judgments. This tendency arises because it is often so much easier to question a man's motives than to meet his arguments or counter his evidence. We can shortcut the hard process of analysis and collection of evidence, and at the same time bring the support of indignation and moral fervor to our views, by regarding the man who differs with us as a "bad" man who wants to achieve "bad" objectives. I was particularly impressed by the seductiveness of this approach during the 1964 presidential election, when most of the intellectuals, of all people, largely cut off the possibility of rational discussion by refusing to recognize the possibility that Senator Goldwater might have much the same objectives as they and simply differ in his judgment about how to achieve them.

To avoid misunderstanding, let me emphasize that I am not asserting that all policy differences are attributable to differences in positive analysis. Some clearly do reflect differences in value judgments. But I submit, the cause of reaching rational agreement will be furthered if we leave that explanation as a last resort rather than using it as the first.

Let me also note that there undoubtedly is a relation between men's value judgments and their presumptions about matters of fact. There is a subtle and complex relation that needs further study but on which I have nothing but platitudes to offer.

3. *Role of market in developing value judgments.* My third point is more closely related to Boulding's paper. Boulding takes as the essence of economic exchange the "nicely calculated less or more." His position on the limitations of economic exchange is very similar to that which J. M. Clark so felicitously summarized in his famous remark that "an irrational passion for dispassionate rationality takes the joy out of life." Boulding ends by discussing the integrative system that is necessary to complement market exchange narrowly conceived.

Valid and important as Boulding's comments are, they are confined to only one dimension of the relation between economic analysis and value judg-ments. Another, and a very different dimension, is the role of the market as a device for the voluntary cooperation of many individuals in the establishment of common values, whether these be ratios of exchange in the market or the components of the integrative system to which Boulding refers. In this dimen-sion, "exchange" and the "market" cover a far broader range than the narrowly economic. The aim of my comments is to direct attention to the broader relevance of what seem at first like narrowly economic constructs.

Boulding emphasizes the quid pro quo character of market exchange. This characteristic is precisely the requirement for an exchange to be voluntary. Unless each participant receives something he values more than what he gives up, he will not enter into a transaction—if the transaction is to take place, he will have to be coerced. In a "free" market, he must be "persuaded," which is the same as "bribed."

For exchange to take place, the values of the participants must differ. If Mr. A has X and Mr. B has Y and both agree that X is to be preferred to Y, no exchange of X for Y can take place. Exchange of X for Y only takes place if Mr. A values Y more than X and Mr. B values X more than Y. In that case, both A and B benefit from the exchange of X for Y and the exchange will take place, unless prevented by some third party. As this trivial example illustrates, the essence of exchange is the reconciliation of divergent values; of achievement of unanimity without conformity. If, instead of the one act of exchanging all of X for all of Y, we conceive of X and Y as divisible magnitudes and of exchange proceeding piecemeal, then exchange between Mr. A and Mr. B will continue until, *at the margin*, both attach the same relative value to a little more of X or of Y. In this sense they have been brought to agreement about value through exchange. Yet this agreement is only at the remaining point of contact between them. Both can be well satisfied with the prior exchanges even though that leaves Mr. A, say, having most of the Y and Mr. B having most of the X. Introduce other participants, and the process of achieving unanimity without conformity is broadened: throughout the whole market, all participants will come to have common values at the margin. It takes a difference of opinion to make a horse race, as the saying goes, and the opportunity to wager on the outcome enables the difference of opinion to be a source of mutual satisfaction rather than an occasion for conflict.

The same analysis applies immediately to free speech and free discussion. Here again, the freedom to speak does not imply having an audience, just as the freedom to sell does not mean having a buyer, only the opportunity to seek one. Only if speaker and listener can mutually benefit will transactions take place in the market for ideas. And, again, it will generally require a difference of opinions for the transaction to be consummated. Few experiences are duller than communicating with someone with whom you are in complete agreement on everything—though that concept is clearly a nonexistent ideal type. None of us even agrees completely with himself.

The essence of free speech as of free exchange is the mutual benefit to the participants. The hope is that it will enable us to reconcile our differences while each of us gains in the process. Indeed, I should not say "of free speech as of free exchange," for free speech is a special case of free exchange.

Similarly, consider academic freedom or freedom to pursue the bent of one's intellectual interests in research and writing. If intellectuals applied to this area the kind of analysis they bring to the market in goods and services, many or perhaps most would have to oppose such freedom. They would be led to deplore the "chaos" involved in letting each man decide for himself what is important, the "duplication" and "wastes of competition" involved in different scholars studying the same problems, the lack of "social priorities" in determining which are the important problems to be studied. They would be led to call for central planning, with a governmental body to decide what topics most need investigation, to assign scholars to the areas in which they could, as judged by that body, contribute most, to see to it that there is no wasteful duplication of effort, and so on.

Because this comes close to home, intellectuals know better. They know that if there were complete agreement on values and on knowledge in this area, such central planning would be harmless—and also unnecessary. But with the present extent of disagreement and of ignorance, they prefer the "wastes" of a free competitive market to the coercion of central planning, and they reinforce their preference by the rationalization, which conforms to my prejudices, too, that this is a surer way to add to our knowledge than reliance on a few chosen agents. Unfortunately, they do not recognize their inconsistency in applying wholly different standards to the market for goods.

Boulding emphasizes that "the economist tends to regard the price system with an almost superstitious awe" and to marvel at "the subtle order that is revealed in the making and interaction of human decisions." These same sentiments are evoked by the more generalized application of free exchange. The whole wondrous body of modern scientific knowledge has been built up by free exchange in the market place for ideas. Or consider another example, the development of language. Here is a complex interrelated structure capable of gradual evolution. Yet no one planned it that way. It just grew through the voluntary cooperation of millions of individuals coordinated by free verbal exchange. The structure of common law is yet another splendid example.

Which brings me full circle to the point made by Boulding that set me off: the need for an integrative system, which I interpret to mean the need for a common set of values that must be unthinkingly accepted by the bulk of the people the bulk of the time in order for any stable society to exist. How have these values developed and changed and come to be accepted? What is a desirable mechanism for the preservation of such a set of values, which yet retains the possibility for change?

Here is where I suggest that economic analysis can contribute most to the political scientist and the philosopher. For it brings out how such a structure can emerge and develop from the spontaneous and voluntary cooperation of individual human beings and need not be imposed or constructed or legislated by philosopher-kings or aristocrats or presidents or legislators, though all of these have much to contribute to its development. In many ways, this is the basic role of the free market in both goods and ideas—to enable mankind to cooperate in this process of searching for and developing values.

Needless to say, the process of social evolution of values does not guarantee that the integrative system that develops will be consistent with the kind of society that you or I with our values would prefer—indeed, the evidence of experience suggests that it is most unlikely to. Most of mankind at all times has lived in misery and under tyranny. One of the urgent questions requiring investigation is, indeed, what integrative system will be consistent with the kind of society we value, what circumstances contribute to the development of such a system, and to what extent the key element is the process itself—such as free discussion—or the substantive content of the integrative system.

Each of us, as he attempts to influence the values of his fellows, is part of this process of development of integrative systems. Each of us, also, is proceeding, as he must, on the basis of tentative answers to the questions just suggested. So in such sessions as these we are simultaneously actor and audience, observer and observed, teacher and student.

THE ECONOMICS OF
FREE SPEECH

· 2 ·

The structure of law that is appropriate for the maintenance of a free society cannot be determined without examining its economic implications. They are intimately related. I am going to try to illustrate this connection for a particular problem in law, the maintenance of free speech; in some ways the most fundamental of all the freedoms in our society.

At the extreme, there is a clear and direct relationship between economic arrangements, on the one hand, and free speech, on the other. For example, the restrictions on Alexander Solzhenitsyn's free speech when he was in the Soviet Union were significantly affected by the character of the economic system, and not merely by the particular way in which the Soviet Union chose to use that economic system. Suppose you could stretch your imagination so far as to suppose that a totalitarian centralized system such as the Soviet Union was by some miracle dedicated to trying to preserve free speech. Consider the economic problems that would be involved in doing so. The real test of free speech is the ability of a minority to express its view. Suppose a small group in the Soviet Union would like to propagandize for capitalism. In order to propagandize, it has to rent a hall. Whom can it rent a hall from? All halls are owned by the government. In order to propagandize by putting out leaflets, it has to get a printing press. Where does it get a printing press? They're all owned

© Milton Friedman, 1978. Based on a talk given at dedication of court room, University of San Diego Law School, San Diego, California, November 7, 1977.

by the government. It has to buy paper from a government-owned company. It has to have it printed by a government-owned printing shop. It would take an extraordinary degree of dedication to the principle of free speech for each and every one of these people along the line to be willing to make their facilities available, but even suppose they were willing to do so. Where would the money come from to finance these activities in a society in which the major sources of funds are governmental? There are some wealthy people in Russia, but they are not wealthy in the sense in which they can provide out of their own resources substantial sums of money for campaigns. On the contrary, to finance such activities would require a government fund for the propagation of subversive doctrine. Suppose such a fund existed. It's clear that the demand would exceed the supply—that would be a pretty attractive way to make a living! So with the best of will it would be literally impossible to maintain free speech in a full-fledged collectivist, socialist state.

We seldom recognize the enormous importance of diversified sources of financial and economic support in making it possible for a "nut" to have his say. You know, today's nut may be tomorrow's prophet. The essence of free speech is to preserve the opportunity for nuts to turn into prophets.

The relation between economic arrangements and free speech is close long before you get to a full-fledged socialist state. I want to illustrate how close that relationship is in terms of the situation in this country, and in other countries in the West, which we would say are predominantly free societies. Consider, for example, the restrictions that have been imposed in the United States particularly in the course of the past 40 or 50 years on various groups in our society. One group in the United States that has been denied free speech in practice, not in principle, are businessmen. Recently, I received a letter from an executive vice president of an oil and gas association. I won't mention the name of the person or of the oil and gas association but I will only read what he said:

As you know, the real issue more so than price per thousand cubic feet [this was with respect to energy legislation] is the continuation of the First Amendment of the Constitution, the guarantee of freedom of speech. With increasing regulation, as big brother looks closer over our shoulder, we grow timid against speaking out for truth and our beliefs against falsehoods and wrongdoings. Fear of IRS audits, bureaucratic strangulation or government harassment is a powerful weapon against freedom of speech.

In the October 31st edition of the U.S. News & World Report, the Washington Whisper section noted that, "Oil industry officials claim that they have received this ultimatum from Energy Secretary James Schlesinger: 'Support the Administration's proposed tax on crude oil or else face tougher regulation and a possible drive to break up the oil companies.'"

Let me give you another, more subtle example of the restrictions on free speech imposed on businessmen. I am sure all of you, like me, have received from your banks a little piece of paper printed by the U.S. Department of the Treasury which urges you to buy U.S. savings bonds. If that piece of paper were published by a private commercial concern, the Federal Trade Commission might very well castigate it as misleading and inaccurate advertising. I have often said that the U.S. savings bond campaign has been one of the greatest bucket-shop operations in history. The government tells people, "You buy these bonds and it will assure your future. This is the way to save and to provide income for your children's education and your retirement." Then it turns around and produces inflation that erodes the value of those bonds so that anybody who has bought a bond during the past fifteen or twenty years has ended up getting back a sum that has less purchasing power, that will buy fewer goods and services, than the amount he originally paid. And, to add insult to injury, he has had to pay taxes on the so-called interest, interest that doesn't even compensate for the inflation produced by the federal government that sells him the bonds and makes those promises.

You may not agree with me. You may think the bonds are a good investment, but I introduced this example for a very different purpose. Do you suppose the bankers who send you this piece of paper believe it? Do what I've done. I've asked quite a number of bankers, "Do you think that savings bonds are a good investment for your customers?" They uniformly answer, "No, it's a terrible investment." I say to them, "Why do you send this piece of paper around to your customers? Why are you participating in what I believe is fundamentally a bucket-shop operation?" They all give me the same answer: "The Treasury would be very unhappy if we didn't. There's great pressure from the Treasury."

Not long since I talked in Salt Lake City with a middle-management executive of a large enterprise who was telling me how terrible he thought the savings bond campaign was. In the next breath he told me how much time he had to spend promoting it among his employees because of pressure from higher-ups who in turn were reflecting pressure from the U.S. Treasury. Do those bankers, or these executives, have effective free speech?

Of course, occasionally there are courageous bankers, courageous businessmen who, despite the cost, express themselves freely. But the public statements of business leaders are almost always bland. They talk in general terms about the evils of government regulation and about the importance of free enterprise, but when it comes down to cases, they are very careful not to be too specific. Again there are some noble exceptions.

You may say, "That doesn't matter, those are only businessmen; after all, businessmen have enough to do making money, they don't have to worry about free speech." Let's turn to my own field, to academics and ask, "What has happened to the freedom of speech of academics?" Consider my colleagues at the University of Chicago in the medical school, most of whom are supported in their research by grants from the National Institute of Health. Which of them wouldn't think three times before he made an impassioned speech against national health insurance? I don't blame them, don't misunderstand me. I'm not criticizing anybody. I'm only trying to discuss the relationship between the economic arrangements we adopt on the one hand and free speech on the other. People ought to bear a cost for free speech. However, the cost ought to be reasonable and not disproportionate. There ought not to be, in the words of a famous Supreme Court decision, "A chilling effect" on freedom of speech. Yet there is little doubt that the extent to which people in the academic world are being financed by government has a chilling effect on their freedom of speech.

What is true for the medical people is equally true for my own colleagues in economics departments who are receiving grants from the National Science Foundation. I happen to think that the National Science Foundation ought not to exist, that it is an inappropriate function of government. Not very many of my colleagues would be willing to endorse that statement in public, certainly not those who have grants from the NSF. In fact, I've often said that about the only academic who in this day and age has freedom of speech is a tenured professor at a private university who's on the verge of, or has already, retired. That's me.

Let's go from the academics and these chilling effects on freedom of speech and look at the relationship between economic arrangements and freedom of the press in a more direct and immediate fashion. There was a story some time back about the *London Times*, a great newspaper in Britain, "The Great Thunderer" as it used to be called. It was prevented from publishing one day by a union, I believe typographers, though it may have been another of the technical mechanical unions. Why did they close it down? Because *The Times* was scheduled to run an article about the union's attempt to influence what was printed in the paper. That's as clear and straightforward a violation of the freedom of press as you can think of. You may say, "Well, that one didn't involve government." Of course it did! Because no union can gain so dominant a position without the aid and backing of the government.

Another example from Great Britain is equally pertinent. There is now a National Union of Journalists in Great Britain which is pushing for a closed shop of journalists writing in British papers—and there is a bill pending in Parliament to facilitate this outcome. The union is threatening to boycott papers that employ nonmembers of the National Union of Journalists who are not willing to join and accept their declaration of principles. And all this in Great Britain, the home of our liberties, from whence came the Magna Carta.

To turn more directly to the courts, judges, like intellectuals in general, have shown a kind of schizophrenia as between different areas of free speech. The courts have tended to draw a sharp line between what they designate as political or cultural speech on the one hand and what they designate as commercial speech on the other. Thanks to the tutoring that Professor Bernard Siegan has given me, I realize that the Supreme Court recently has taken some timid steps toward extending First Amendment rights to commercial speech. They have done so in connection with a Virginia law that would have prevented pharmacists from advertising, an Arizona law that would have prevented attorneys from advertising, and a New Jersey local law that would have prevented people from putting "For Sale" signs on their property. The Supreme Court has declared all these laws unconstitutional. But in each decision, they have been very timid and have continued to insist that there is a sharp line between the two kinds of speech and that the First Amendment gives absolute protection only to political speech, and not to commercial speech.

While I welcome these recent moves, the difference in attitude toward political and commercial speech is still extreme. For example, a court in Ohio threatened to close down a pornographic magazine, *The Hustler*, and sentenced the proprietor and publisher to jail. A prestigious list of intellectuals signed a petition objecting strenuously to what they interpreted as a violation of free speech and an act of censorship. Personally, I do not see much difference between *The Hustler* case, as a restriction of freedom of speech, and the legal prohibition of radio and TV advertising of cigarettes. Yet no distinguished, or for that matter undistinguished, intellectuals signed a petition in behalf of the freedom of enterprises to advertise cigarettes—though one, namely myself, did write a *Newsweek* column to that effect. In its decision on the Virginia advertising case, the Supreme Court explicitly said its decision did not render it invalid for the government to require advertising to bear a warning label such as the warning label on cigarettes, "The Surgeon General has determined that smoking may be bad for your health." Congress has now passed a new law which is going to require all saccharin to bear a similar label. I have yet to see any intellectuals object to that infringement on free speech. Yet suppose a law were passed requiring *The Hustler* magazine to carry a warning: "Reading this magazine may be dangerous to the moral health of children, other immature people, and even some mature people." Is there any doubt that such a law would produce an uproar, and that it would be overturned by the first court to hear the case? You cannot maintain that this difference in reaction is because somehow the contents of *The Hustler* are more noble or uplifting than the smoking of cigarettes or the use of saccharin. The difference simply reflects what is fundamentally an arbitrary distinction between certain kinds of speech.

To give an even more dramatic example, we have no hesitancy in saying that requiring tobacco companies to put a warning label on cigarettes doesn't infringe on their freedom of speech. There is little doubt that far more human lives have been lost over the past century as a result of Karl Marx's *Das Kapital* than from smoking cigarettes. Would it therefore be appropriate to require every copy of Marx's *Das Kapital* to carry a warning label saying, "Reading this book may be dangerous to social and personal health?"

Everyone would agree that's a violation of free speech. Why the one and not the other? Personally, I think it's terrible to smoke cigarettes. I quit twenty years ago and so obviously I want everybody else to quit. Personally, I think Marx's *Das Kapital* is a pernicious and dangerous book. But that does not mean that I believe it is desirable to restrict advertising for either cigarettes or *Das Kapital*. On the contrary, I favor the avoidance of legal restrictions on either the one or the other.

The schizophrenia of intellectuals in general, of courts in particular, extends far beyond regarding commercial speech as somehow very different from political speech. It goes to the whole problem of the supposed distinction between political freedom on the one hand and economic freedom on the other, to the difference in the way that the courts have interpreted the free speech clause and the due process clause. We've seen in the extreme case of Russia, and in less extreme cases as well, that you cannot have political freedom without a very large measure of economic freedom. A large measure of economic freedom is a necessary condition for political freedom—but more to the present point, there is no really sharp line between the two.

Economic and political freedom are not different in kind and it is frequently not easy to distinguish between them. Let me illustrate. Russia does not permit free speech. Everybody agrees that's a violation of political freedom. Russia does not permit emigration. Is that a violation of economic freedom or of political freedom? Russia does not permit those people it lets go out as emigrants to take more than their bare personal possessions with them. Is that a violation of economic freedom or is it a violation of political freedom? Great Britain permits its citizens to emigrate and it permits free speech but it does not permit emigrants to take their property out with them. Is that a violation of economic freedom or of political freedom?

Recently, as it happened, I received another letter that illustrates this relation. This was a letter from Pakistan. It was from an academic at a Pakistan university who had studied at the London School of Economics and who was now back in Pakistan. He wrote, "I have been delving into the political philosophy of liberalism and individualism and have read whatever little on the subject is available in our libraries... It has been my great misfortune that your highly popular work, *Capitalism and Freedom*, is not present in the libraries of this country... Exchange control regulations in this country prevent me from buying it from a publisher in the U.S." Is that a restriction of his economic freedom or of his political freedom or of his intellectual freedom?

Take something closer to home yet. Freedom of choice about where you live is surely more important to most people than free speech as it has been typically defined. Yet the courts have routinely upheld zoning and land-use legislation that seriously interferes with freedom. Not to mention the kind of emigration requirements that I was just speaking about, a recent article in the *Los Angeles Times* illustrates the difficulty in drawing the line between economic and political freedom. The story is about a student at a high school in Iowa who is from Nicaragua and who is living in this country on a visa to attend high school. Unfortunately for him, he wanted to be self-supporting so he got a paper route that pays him nine dollars a week. The immigration services found out about that and they now tell him that he will have to leave the country unless he quits his job. Are they interfering with his economic freedom? Or are they interfering with his human and political and personal freedom?

When a city legislates zoning ordinances that prevent people within that city from making voluntary transactions with people outside the city to buy or sell property imposing great costs on one or the other or both, are they interfering with economic freedom or human, political freedom?

The line is a difficult one to draw. All of these cases, particularly the housing and the zoning cases, raise third-party effects, neighborhood effects as they are sometime called. An agreement between two people to buy a piece of land or build a house affects neighbors who look on it. The point I want to emphasize is that those same effects are present in all the free speech cases. There's no distinction on that ground.

Consider, for example, the recent case in which an American Nazi group wanted to have a march in a mostly Jewish suburb of Chicago. That was a clear free speech case, yet there is no doubt that it involved serious third-party effects in the way of a possible riot, imposing costs on residents or bystanders not directly involved, let alone the police costs of enforcing order.

Take such a simple thing as permitting a parade down a main street of a city. That may impose heavy costs on businesses along the way through the loss of custom.

Consider still a different third-party effect. A political candidate campaigns for office by riding around in a truck with a loudspeaker on top, blaring into houses along the way. If a commercial truck advertising, let's say, soap or perfume or detergent, were to try to blare out its message on the same streets, at the same volume, there's little doubt that that would be regarded as a serious violation of the freedom of others. But is the message the one is delivering really more important, more reliable and more trustworthy than the message the other is imparting?

I am myself a liberal in the true original sense of the term, namely, belief in freedom. So I favor both free speech and economic freedom. And I would lean over backwards very far indeed with respect to third-party effects in order to preserve both. But that is not my main point in the present context.

My main point is to demonstrate that there is a basic and fundamental inconsistency in the attitude of intellectuals in general, and the judiciary in particular, to the two areas of freedom. I can understand how someone would be willing, in order to protect third parties, to restrict both free speech and economic freedom. That's a consistent position. I obviously can understand how someone would take the position I do—that the social objective of maintaining a free society is so important that a very strong presumption must exist before freedom in either area is restricted to avoid third-party effects. What I cannot understand is the schizophrenic position that almost any costs may be imposed on third parties in order to protect one kind of freedom, namely freedom of speech, but that almost any third-party effect, however trivial, justifies restricting another kind of freedom, namely, economic freedom. That seems to me to be a wholly inconsistent position which no reasonably logical, consistent man who understands what is involved can hold.

Summary

The relation between economic arrangements and freedom of speech is clear in the extreme cases of totalitarian economic systems such as the Soviet system. But it is extremely close even in the modern mixed economies. Businessmen, heavily dependent on government for contracts, or subject to regulation by one or another government agency, or subject to investigation with respect to taxes, will individually be reluctant to exercise their right to free speech in ways that might bring down governmental retaliation or harassment. Academics, dependent on government finance for support of their research, will likewise experience "a chilling effect" on their freedom of speech. It is appropriate that individuals bear a cost for exercising free speech—but the cost should not be disproportionate.

Freedom of the press, like freedom of speech, is affected by economic arrangements. Strong unions, gaining their strength from government support, are in a position to affect what the newspapers, magazines, and other media will publish.

Judges, like intellectuals in general, have shown a kind of schizophrenia in drawing a sharp line between "political or cultural speech" and "commercial speech." This distinction cannot be defended. Freedom to publish pornography is not fundamentally different from freedom to advertise cigarettes; requiring or using labels about health on cigarette packages is not fundamentally different from requiring or using a label on Marx's *Das Kapital* saying "Reading this book may be dangerous to social and personal health."

The schizophrenia extends far beyond speech—to a supposed distinction between political freedom and economic freedom. They are not different in kind and it is not easy to distinguish between them. Are Russia's restrictions on emigration a restraint of political freedom but Britain's restrictions on the property an emigrant may take with him solely a restraint of economic freedom?

There is a basic inconsistency in the attitude of intellectuals in general to the two areas of freedom. I can understand how someone would be willing, in order to protect third parties, to restrict both free speech and economic freedom. I naturally understand my own position—that the social objective of maintaining a free society is so important that a very strong presumption must exist before freedom in either area is restricted to avoid third-party effects. I cannot understand the schizophrenic position that almost any costs may be imposed on third parties to protect one kind of freedom, freedom of speech, but that almost any third-party effect, however trivial, justifies restricting another kind of freedom, economic freedom.

MARKET MECHANISMS AND CENTRAL ECONOMIC PLANNING

· 3 ·

The subject that I am going to talk about—the possibility of introducing market arrangements in centrally planned economies—is one that was very close to Warren Nutter's interests throughout much of his life. Some of his most important work dealt with the Soviet economy and with an understanding of its performance.

COMMAND VERSUS MARKET ECONOMIES

We should begin by drawing a contrast between two kinds of arrangements for organizing economic activity. They are commonly designated by the terms "command economy" and "market economy." The ideal type of command economy is one in which individuals who act do so not as principals but as agents for someone else. They are carrying out an order, doing what they are told. The ideal type of market economy is one in which individuals act as principals in pursuit of their own interests. If any individual serves as an agent for someone else, he does so on a voluntary, mutually agreed upon basis.

In practice, there can be no pure command economy. Such an economy would be composed of robots who had no separate volition, no separate

©1981 American Enterprise Institute for Public Policy Research, Washington, D.C. Originally delivered as a G. Warren Nutter Lecture in Political Economy. Reprinted with permission.

interests. This approach is reflected in Tennyson's "Theirs not to reason why, Theirs but to do and die." Even in the most extreme case of a command economy—an army battalion on the march—even, I suspect, in a case such as the charge of the Light Brigade, no human being really acts as a pure robot. How wholeheartedly he carries out commands, the degree of venturesomeness and courage he displays—in these respects he acts as a principal in response to his own interests.

A pure market economy is at least conceivable. The economist's favorite example of a market economy is Robinson Crusoe, but even that is modified somewhat by the presence of the man Friday. A Robinson Crusoe without a man Friday would constitute a market economy in which he is acting as a principal in pursuit of his own interests.

For society, there are no pure command or market economies, either as ideals or in practice. Even in the most extreme version of the anarchist-libertarian ideal of a market economy, families exist; and within a family there are command elements. Children sometimes behave in response to orders and not of their own volition as principals, a fact that is equally true of other members of the family. Similarly, as I have already suggested, the most obvious and extreme case of a command economy is an army in which the general supposedly gives an order to the colonel, the colonel to the major, the major to the captain, the captain to the lieutenant, and so on down to the buck private. At every stage the individuals who are responding to those orders have volitions of their own and interests of their own, and they react in part in accordance with these. At every stage in that process they have some element of discretion; they know things about the immediate local circumstances that the general at the top could not conceivably know. Thus actual societies are always mixtures. Only in very small groups such as families can command be even the principal, much less the exclusive, method of organizing economic activities.

Consider the most extreme command economies currently in existence—the Soviet Union and mainland China. I suspect that in the Soviet Union and even in China, if you could only find some way to quantify it, you would discover that most resources are organized through the principle of the market, of voluntary cooperation by people pursuing their own interests, rather than through the elaborate structure of direct command. An obvious example is the private agricultural plots in Russia, which are said to occupy 3 percent of the arable land and to contribute between a quarter and a third of the country's total agricultural output. But let us go beyond that example.

In the Soviet Union's labor market, people are hired and people are fired. Individuals have some freedom to choose where they are going to work and to accept or reject a job. This freedom is not absolute by any manner of means; some people do not have that choice. My wife and I often recall an instance during the trip we made to the Soviet Union. We were being driven from one airport to another, accompanied by the inevitable tourist guide, a young man who was just about to graduate from Moscow University. He was interested, I may say, in American literature. When we asked him who his favorite American author was, no one in this room would guess that it was Howard Fast. We asked him what he was going to do after he graduated from Moscow University; and he said, "Well I don't know. They haven't told me yet." That is the essence of a command economy; yet most laborers, most workers, in the Soviet Union are not in our guide's position. They are hired, and they are fired, with the result that most labor is ultimately allocated through market arrangements.

In a pure command economy, goods and services would be allocated directly to individuals. Each person would get from the central authority a basket of goods, and he would have no choice concerning the content of that basket of goods. If we look at the way goods and services are distributed in the Soviet Union, we will find that they are sold through stores. True, a person may have to stand in long lines or queues to buy things, but the method of distribution is fundamentally a market mechanism of setting prices on goods and having people buy them. In some cases people need more than one kind of money: ration coupons as well as paper money. Nonetheless, the method is in large measure a market method. Again, gray markets spring up everywhere in such a country. If a Soviet citizen's electricity goes haywire, he is much more likely to try to get a private individual to come and fix it for a cash fee than he is to call the government agency assigned the task of fixing his electricity, because he will have little confidence that anyone would arrive from the government agency within a reasonable period of time.

With respect to intrafamily behavior, one notes that, while the family is in some ways the ideal type of command economy, it also has very large elements of voluntary exchange and market reaction. In Warren Nutter's marvellous little book *The Strange World of Ivan Ivanov*,[1] which was developed and compiled from a series of newspaper articles he published, he describes in great detail the daily life of a family in the Soviet Union and contrasts it with the life of an American family. There are enormous differences; and yet as you go through the book you are struck by how large a fraction of the activities can be characterized and described as operating through the market. It is a very distorted market, but it is a market nonetheless.

We were very much impressed with the same phenomena in China. Despite recent easing, command elements are more important in the Chinese economy than in the Russian economy. For example, the allocation of labor is dictated much more by command elements. In all the factories that we visited, we kept inquiring what would happen if they needed to employ five more people. "We'd ask the people downtown and they would send us five people." "Would you have a choice about hiring the five?" "Oh no, no, they are the people we would have to employ." We tried to find out whether there was any possibility that a worker at one plant could arrange a transfer if he believed that he would be better off at another plant. "Oh yes," they told us. If he believed that he could be more useful in another factory, all he would have to do is tell his supervisor, and his supervisor would tell his superior, and so on up to the top. Then the top man would communicate with his counterpart at the other factory, and he in turn would send the message down the line. In that way it would be possible for the worker to transfer. I kept asking whether they knew of any such cases. No, they had not come across any such cases—with one exception, which had to do not with a factory but with a scientific institute.

Despite the ubiquitous command element in the Chinese economy, there are also pervasive market elements. The Chinese have recently started to introduce private agricultural plots in the communes. We were taken to the most prosperous commune in the most prosperous county in the most prosperous province in China. About a year and a half earlier, they had introduced private plots. According to their figures, private plots accounted for 2.5 percent of the arable land of the commune but were already producing 10 percent of the income from crops. Similarly, there are many stores, both specialty shops and department stores, not to mention food markets. Goods and services are distributed by purchase and sale rather than by direct allocation. It is limited, but there is still some gray market activity and so on.

A question that is typically asked in connection with central economic planning is how extensively market elements can be introduced in a command economy. I believe that this way of putting it is upside down. The real question is how far one can go in introducing command elements into a market economy. I believe that it would be literally impossible for any large-scale economy to be operated on a strictly command basis. Fundamentally, what enables a country such as China or the Soviet Union to function at all is the market elements that are either deliberately introduced or are inadvertently permitted to operate.

When I speak of market elements being introduced into command economies such as China's and the Soviet Union's, I am not speaking of free markets; they are highly distorted markets. That is why those countries have such low standards of living; that is why they are so inefficient.

We all know the key insight that Adam Smith brought to this subject, which underlies the possibility of markets operating to coordinate economic activity. That key insight is that if exchange is voluntary—if two people engage in any exchange on a voluntary basis—the exchange will occur only if both sides benefit. Economic activity is not a "zero-sum game," to use the term that Lester Thurow recently adopted as the title of a book. It is an activity in which everybody can benefit. That, as I say, was Adam Smith's key insight, and it produced his corollary of the invisible hand; that is, a person who seeks to promote only his own interest is "led by an invisible hand to promote an end which was no part of his intention." We are all familiar with this proposition.

If we are to understand the problems that arise in trying to introduce effective market elements into command economies, it is important that we examine in more detail the functions that prices serve in the operation of the invisible hand and the coordination of economic activity.

THE FUNCTIONS OF PRICES

Fundamentally, prices serve three functions in such a society. First, they transmit information. We find out very quickly that it is necessary to conserve energy because that information is transmitted in the form of higher prices of oil. The crucial importance of this function tended to be neglected until Friedrich Hayek published his great article on "The Use of Knowledge in Society" in the *American Economic Review* in 1945. This function of prices is essential, however, for enabling economic activity to be coordinated. Prices transmit information about tastes, about resource availability, about productive possibilities. They transmit a very wide range of information. They transmit information about the availability of goods today versus tomorrow through futures markets, and so on. A second function that prices perform is to provide an incentive for people to adopt the least costly methods of production and to use available resources for the most highly valued uses. They perform that function because of their third function, which is to determine who gets what and how much—the distribution of income.

The reason it is essential to stress these three functions and to show their interrelation is that, in my opinion, essentially all of the problems in central economic planning arise from trying to separate the functions from one another. As we can readily see, prices give people an incentive only because they are used to distribute income. If what a person gets for his activity does not depend in any way on what he does, if prices do not serve the third function of distributing income, then there is no reason for him to worry about the information that prices are transmitting, and there is no incentive for him to act in accordance with that information. If his income does depend on what he does, on the difference between the prices that he receives for selling his services and the prices he has to pay for items he buys—if it depends on the difference between receipts and costs from the point of view of a business enterprise, or wages and costs for a worker, and so on—then he has a very strong incentive to try to ensure that he sells his services in the best market for the highest price, that he produces products at the least cost, that he produces those products for which other people are willing to pay the most. The real beauty, and I use the word "beauty" advisedly, of a price system is precisely the way in which the incentive to act on information accompanies the information that is transmitted. This is not true in a command economy. Information is transmitted from one level of a command economy to another, but that information does not carry with it any incentive to act in accordance with it. There must be some kind of supplementary means of seeing to it that people act on the information.

In every society the distribution of income is a major source of dissatisfaction. That is true in a command economy, and it is true in a market economy; every person always knows that he deserves more than he is getting and that the other fellow deserves less. That is a natural human instinct. I am reminded of a remark made by Alvin Johnson many years ago when he was conducting a study of incomes in different occupations. He found that physicians complained that lawyers were getting more than physicians, and lawyers complained that physicians were getting more than lawyers; carpenters complained that plumbers were getting more than carpenters, and plumbers complained that carpenters were getting more than plumbers; and so on down the line. Johnson finally concluded that life was an underpaid occupation.

In predominantly market economies, a very large fraction of all government activity, particularly the enormous expansion in government activity over the past 50 years, has been directed toward trying to separate the distribution of income from market determination, trying to separate the third function of prices from the other two functions, trying to make the amount that people get independent of the prices at which they can sell their services. It is impossible to accomplish this goal and still preserve the other functions of prices. You have to compromise.

However much we might wish it to be otherwise, it simply is not possible to use prices to transmit information and to provide an incentive to act on that information without also using prices to affect, even if not to determine completely, the distribution of income. If a person's income will be the same whether he works hard or not, why should he work hard? Why should he make the effort to search out the buyer who values most highly what he has to sell if he will not get any benefit from doing so, and so on down the line? I need not spell that out in detail.

If prices are prevented from affecting the distribution of income, even if they do not completely determine it, they cannot be used for other purposes. The only alternative is command. Some authority would have to decide who should produce what and how much. That authority would have to decide who should sweep the streets and who manage the factory, who should be the policeman and who the physician.

It is tempting to think that a desire to render social service to benefit the community can replace the incentive provided by the price system. The result has been repeated attempts by leaders—both in countries that rely primarily on the market and in collectivist countries—to exhort their citizens to work harder or to economize or to hold down prices or wages or to engage in other supposedly desirable activities, all in the name of patriotism or the national interest. Such exhortation has an unbroken record of failing to solve the problems that called them forth. The reason is not because people are unresponsive to appeals to their patriotism or to the national interest or to their sense of social cohesion. Those are very powerful sentiments, and they do lead people to make extraordinary exertions. Just look at the way people react to appeals to their patriotism in times of war and the extent to which they are willing to sacrifice their lives for objectives that have very little or nothing to do with their immediate self-interest.

The reason why exhortation fails is much more fundamental. It is because exhortation can seldom be accompanied by the information that is relevant for the response to achieve the desired objective. That is possible when the exhortation, for example, is to enlist in an army. It is almost never possible when the exhortation is directed at behavior designed to promote social or economic coordination. How can the individual judge what is socially desirable or what actions he can take that will benefit the community? His vision is necessarily limited; he cannot envisage the more distant effects of his action. He is as likely to do harm as good when he acts in ignorance under the incentive to aid the "national interest" or to perform "social service." The great virtue of the incentive transmitted through the price system is not that it is necessarily stronger than other types of incentives or that it is "nobler" but simply that it is automatically accompanied by the information that is relevant to the effective operation of the incentive.

When centrally planned economies have tried to use the market, the major obstacle to their success has been their desire to separate the function of prices in distributing income from the function of prices in transmitting information and providing incentives. The attempt to do so and yet preserve the virtues of the free market has produced an extensive literature on alternative devices.

LANGE AND LERNER "PLAYING AT CAPITALISM"

As economists should know very well, the most famous treatment of this subject in modern times, and certainly in the West, was by Oskar Lange, a Polish economist, first in two articles and then in slightly revised form in a book that also included an earlier essay by Fred M. Taylor,[2] and by Abba P. Lerner in a series of articles and later in a book.[3] Lange and Lerner tried to explain how a socialist society could be organized through the market. A very similar approach was presented around the same time by the English econo-mist James Meade in his book on *Planning and the Price Mechanism.*[4]

Essentially, the Lange-Lerner solution requires enterprises owned by the state to play at free-market capitalism. The idea is to formulate the end-results of the operation of a free competitive market and to translate those results into instructions to managers of state enterprises about how to run those enter-prises. In a free competitive market, for example, price tends to equal marginal cost, that is, the cost of producing an extra unit. Accordingly, Lange and Lerner would have the authorities instruct managers of state-run enterprises to set the price of each of their products equal to marginal cost or, alternatively, if the authorities themselves set the price, to adjust the volume of production so that marginal cost equals price. In calculating marginal cost, they would have the managers of enterprises use the closest possible approximation to the wages, the interest rates, the cost of raw materials, *et cetera*, that would arise in a free market. This was, however, to be "playing at" capitalism because, in their scheme, the incomes received by individuals would not necessarily be those that would result from an actual free market. Managers of state enterprises would receive wages and not the "profits" from the enterprise, although perhaps they might receive payments geared to profits. There might be incentive payments. The managers would not be the owners of the enterprise; the state would own the enterprise. When the managers invested capital, they would not be investing their own funds or the funds of identifiable persons for whom they were operating as agents. They would be investing state funds. The risks they would be taking would not be risks for themselves or for identifiable principals but for the state. Similarly, the incomes of the workers would not necessarily be equal to the notional wages that the entrepreneurs would include in calculating how much to produce.

This is a small sample of the ingenious analysis in the Lange-Lerner book. It is an admirable book that has much to teach about the operation of a free market; indeed, much more, I believe, than about their actual objective, how to run a socialist state. It is unnecessary to go into great detail about their analysis, because what seems to me to be the basic flaw in this analysis has little to do with the sophisticated parts of their discussion. Let me emphasize that their approach has a great deal of merit. It forces planners in a society to try to estimate what the results would have been in a free market and therefore to take into account the truly relevant considerations in achieving efficient production. It specifies the principles that the planners in such a society should follow in the trial-and-error process of adjusting prices to experience; that is, to adjust the quantity demanded to the available supply in the short run, and the available supply to the quantity demanded at a price equal to marginal cost in the long run.

I may say that the principles that Lange and Lerner outline are very much neglected in our own society. Let me digress for a moment to give a current example from the British experience. One of the problems that Mrs. Thatcher's government has faced arose out of a commitment that she made during the campaign to accept the findings of a commission comparing salaries in government service with those in private industry. The commission concluded that the salaries of government servants should be raised by 28 percent to make them comparable with private salaries. If the planners in England had read—and absorbed—Lange and Lerner, they would have known what the right principle was: a job is overpaid if there are many applicants for few jobs; a job is underpaid if there are few applicants for many jobs. There is no doubt about what the situation in Britain was: there were altogether too many government servants; but at the same time, there were a great many applicants for each new job available in the civil service. Obviously the civil servants were being overpaid and not underpaid. Had the Commission followed Lange and Lerner's book, they could never have reached the conclusion that government salaries were too low.

Various forms of the Lange-Lerner system have been tried on a smaller or a larger scale in many countries—in Lange's native land, Poland, where the success of those ventures is not exactly apparent; in Czechoslovakia; in Hungary; and in Romania. Although the results have often been superior to those achieved earlier, they have also uniformly disappointed the hopes of the sponsors of reform.

In 1968 Warren Nutter pointed out the key difficulty in the system in an important article entitled "Markets without Property: A Grand Illusion," from which I quote:

> If we now come full circle and return to Lange's model of socialism, we see how empty his theoretical apparatus is. Markets without divisible and transferable property rights are a sheer illusion. There can be no competitive behavior, real or simulated, without dispersed power and responsibility. And it will not do to disperse the one without the other. If all property is to be literally collectivized and all pricing literally centralized, there is no scope left for a mechanism that can reproduce in any significant respect the functioning of competitive private enterprise.[5]

A more pungent summary of exactly the same point was made by an English financial journalist, Samuel Brittan, in an article published in *Encounter* in January 1980:

> To publish a set of rules asking the managers of state enterprises to behave "*as if*" they were profit-maximizing entrepreneurs in competitive private industry ignores the actual personal motivations faced by these men . . . You do not make a horse into a zebra merely by painting stripes on its back.[6]

The fundamental problem with this approach is how to monitor performance. To state the central feature of a free-market system in a different way, it is a system under which each individual monitors his own performance and has an incentive to monitor it properly, a point that Thomas Sowell has developed with great insight in his recent book, *Knowledge and Decisions*.[7] The person who is using his own labor to produce goods for himself has a strong motivation to work hard and efficiently—as do those people tilling private plots in the Soviet Union and China. The person risking his own property has an incentive to make the best use of it. If he is using his property to hire others to produce a product or render a service, he has a strong incentive to monitor their labor; and, knowing that he is doing so and can reward or discharge them, the workers have a strong incentive to work efficiently. The consumer spending his own money has a strong incentive to spend it carefully. And so on.

Conversely, in a system in which managers of state enterprises are told to behave as if they were profit-making entrepreneurs, what incentive do they have to monitor themselves? Government officials will seek to monitor them, but what incentives do those officials have to monitor them properly? And how can they obtain the information to monitor the managers?

This problem can be brought out most clearly not by examining the routine, day-to-day, repetitive operations of an enterprise, but rather by examining what in many ways is the most important single activity from the point of view of producing growth, development, and change, namely, innovation—deciding what new products to produce, what new methods to use in producing products, what new capital investment to undertake, and so on. Take a specific example. A person has an idea which, in his best judgment, has only one chance in ten of being successful. If successful, however, the financial return in the form of the value of the extra product produced or of the saving in production expenses would be, let us say, a hundred times the cost of introducing the idea. It is clearly desirable that this activity be undertaken. It is a good bet. If many such bets are taken, the end-result will be highly favorable; the winners will more than make up for the losers.

In a market system in which the individual who makes the decision to undertake that venture receives all or a large fraction of the additional returns, he has an incentive to undertake it. He knows that there are nine chances out of ten that he will lose his money; yet the gain he will receive in the one case out of ten when his idea works is big enough to justify taking the risk.

Consider the same situation in a state-run enterprise. How can the manager of that enterprise persuade the people under whom he works that the odds and potential returns are what he believes them to be? He may have great confidence in his own judgment; yet he may have very great difficulty in persuading his superiors. In addition, the reward structure is likely to be very different. If the venture is successful, he will no doubt receive some extra compensation; he may be awarded a medal, receive kudos and honors, become a hero of the nation. If, however, the venture is a failure, as it will be in nine cases out of ten, he will almost surely be reprimanded and may lose his position and perhaps even his life and liberty. The reward in the case of success does not compensate for the loss in case of failure. His natural tendency is to avoid such risky enterprises, to play it safe, to undertake investments that are almost certain to yield returns. Who can blame such a manager? Considering the circumstances under which such managers operate, that is the reasonable, rational, human way to behave. For society as a whole, however, that kind of behavior is the road to stagnation and rigidity, and that in fact has been the outcome in collectivist societies.

YUGOSLAV WORKER COOPERATIVES

A very different approach has been adopted in Yugoslavia, and it is the other main variant I want to discuss. The Yugoslav approach involves not playing at capitalism but establishing a restricted form of capitalism. This form operates on two different levels: strict capitalist private ownership and operation, that is, a real market; and worker cooperatives, a kind of halfway capitalist market.

Between 80 and 90 percent of the arable land in Yugoslavia is in strict private ownership. The peasant proprietors produce for the market. This sector of agriculture is comparable to the private plots that farmers in the Soviet Union or in China are permitted to cultivate.

Apart from agriculture, Yugoslavia permits—or at least it did when I was there some years back (I have not been there in recent years)—strict private ownership of all enterprises that employ fewer than five people other than family members. As I say, the exact numbers may be different now but something like that is permitted. Although this keeps private enterprises relatively small, the cooperation of enterprises conducted by different members of the same family enables some to be fairly extensive while still remaining within the formal limits. Such enterprises have been particularly important in the tourist industry, where they have played a major role in providing Yugoslavia with a productive and financially rewarding industry.

For larger enterprises, Yugoslavia has adopted a form of worker cooperative in which the enterprises, instead of being explicitly owned by the state, supposedly are owned by the workers in the enterprises. I say "explicitly" and "supposedly" because the cooperatives involve the same mixture of collectivism and capitalism as do U.S. corporations. Who owns a U.S. corporation? The stockholders? Or is the owner the government, which receives 46 percent of the profits and bears 46 percent of the losses of all but relatively small corporations? Once when I was in Yugoslavia, I calculated that the difference between the degree of socialism in Yugoslavia and in the United States at that time was, if my memory is right, 14 percentage points. In the United States, the corporate income tax was then 52 percent, and so the government owned 52 percent of every enterprise. In Yugoslavia, the central government was taking about 66 percent of the profits of the worker cooperatives. Thus there was only a 14-percentage-point difference in the degree of socialism. Just as we think of our enterprises as privately owned and operated, and this view contains an important element of validity, so in Yugoslavia these cooperative enterprises are regarded by the workers as being owned by the workers, a view that also contains a considerable element of validity.

This approach was adopted some decades ago after Yugoslavia had experimented with the rigid central planning methods of the Soviet Union. Those methods were very unsuccessful; and at about the same time that Yugoslavia broke politically with the Soviet Union, it abandoned them in favor of the worker cooperatives. The worker cooperatives have been far more successful than was rigid central planning. At the same time, they have been far less successful than a more nearly full-fledged free-market system. The first time we were in Yugoslavia, which was nearly twenty years ago, we were very much impressed by the contrast between our reaction and that of some other foreigners whom we met there. We went to Yugoslavia from the Soviet Union, and Yugoslavia struck us as a fairly prosperous and relatively open society. People we met there, however, who had gone to Yugoslavia from Austria, thought that Yugoslavia was a very backward and unfree society.

It is worth examining more closely the problems with this approach because it seems very attractive. There has been much discussion in the West about the desirability of converting enterprises into worker-owned enterprises, and there have been a few examples in which such conversions have taken place. As you may know, when North West Industries owned the Chicago & North Western Railroad, which was losing money very rapidly, they found a profitable way to get rid of it by giving it to the workers, thereby establishing substantial tax reductions. As a result, the Chicago & North Western Railroad became a worker-owned enterprise, but not in the Yugoslav way because the workers actually had stock in the enterprise that they could dispose of and sell. In the Yugoslav case, workers do not have such shares.

The major defect of the Yugoslav approach arises from this difference in the linkage of property rights to employment status. Yugoslav workers have no separable or transferable rights to the productive enterprise. Workers are owners only as long as they are workers. If they terminate their employment, they no longer have any property rights or any rights to the income from the enterprise. As a result, a real capital market cannot exist. In line with the quotation that I read from Warren Nutter's article, both power and responsibility are dispersed; but there are no fully divisible and transferable property rights. The absence of such property rights rules out not only a capital market but also the possibility that private individuals can venture and innovate on anything but a minor scale, risking their own funds and reaping the rewards, without necessarily providing labor power themselves. That is possible in Yugoslavia on a very small scale, but nothing beyond that.

A few examples will show how this feature reduces the effectiveness of the system. Consider, for example, how workers are allocated among enterprises. Let us take an enterprise that happens to be highly successful. It is producing a product for which there is a good market; its receipts greatly exceed its costs. It is in the social interest that the enterprise be expanded, that it hire more workers. Each worker's reward consists not only of the value of the labor services that he contributes but also of his pro rata share of the returns attributable to the capital in the enterprise, whether that capital is in the tangible form of buildings and machines or in the intangible form of know-how and consumer goodwill. We can well understand that existing workers in such an enterprise will be reluctant to consent to the hiring of more workers because they will recognize that hiring additional workers would dilute the share of property income that each worker receives. As a result, successful enterprises are prevented from expanding. Workers who are not fortunate enough to be employed in such a successful enterprise must find employment in enterprises where their productive contribution is less. As an aside, we were fascinated to learn that one way in which managers of such enterprises have tried to offset this effect is by promoting nepotism; that is, when hiring additional workers, they give preference to the wives or the children of existing workers. In this way, they try to identify the incentives of the enterprise with the incentives of the workers.

Another aspect of the same problem is the absence of the right incentive for a worker to labor at the activity at which he is most productive. Consider a worker who could contribute more to the output of firm A, let us say, than to the output of firm B. Suppose, however, that firm A has little capital and earns little from its capital, whereas firm B has a great deal of capital and earns much that way. In consequence, if the worker can manage to work in firm B, he will have a higher income than if he works in firm A because he will share in a higher amount of property income, which will more than offset the lower value of the labor that he contributes. If he already works in firm B, he clearly has no incentive to shift to firm A, although that would be socially desirable.

A similar problem arises with respect to the use of the current profits of enterprises. A major decision that must be made by every enterprise is how to use its current profits, how much to devote to payments to its owners (in this case the workers), how much to set aside for investment and for building for the future. Under the Yugoslav system, current workers may not directly benefit from investment made for the future. That is especially true for older workers, and they are the ones who are likely to have achieved the greatest influence in the workers' councils. Who are the people who are elected to the workers' councils? They are not the young workers; they are the older workers. They are only going to work for a few more years, and so they are unlikely to favor investments that will not pay off for ten or fifteen years. As a result, workers have a strong incentive to press for the use of as large a fraction as possible of current profits for current benefits to current workers—in the form of direct bonuses, worker housing, or other benefits. Here again, one method that managers have tried to use to overcome this bias is nepotism. That is to say, enlisting the children of workers and the children's children in the enterprise provides the workers in the workers' council with an incentive to be concerned about the more distant future. That is far from a fully effective mechanism, however. The only fully effective mechanism would be to separate ownership from employment by giving the workers, or anyone else for that matter, transferable rights to the productive enterprise: that is, by making it a real, honest-to-God capitalist form of separable property right. Investment would then add to the value of these rights, and individuals could benefit currently from such investment.

Exactly the same problem limits the availability of risk capital. In general, investments in risky activities will pay off in the future and not in the present. Hence the bias against an investment in the future leads to a bias against investment of risk capital. Moreover, it is one thing for an individual by himself, or even for a few individuals who have common tastes and can join together, to undertake a major gamble. It is a very different thing for a large group of workers through a bureaucratic mechanism to justify engaging in risky activities. If one looks at Western capitalist societies, one sees that risky ventures have seldom been financed through banks; they have seldom been financed through major bureaucratic organizations, including the government—except, I should add, for some risky ventures that are almost sure to fail but that have strong political appeal. Risky ventures that seem to hold good promise of success but that are also very uncertain have almost invariably been financed by a small group of individuals risking their own funds or the funds of their relatives and friends.

The Yugoslavs have used banks and bank loans as a means of distributing capital. This arrangement does help; it does facilitate capital mobility and enable funds from a successful enterprise to be transferred to some extent to other enterprises that have promise of success but do not have the funds available. It is only a very partial substitute for a fully effective capital market, nonetheless. After all, the banks themselves are also worker cooperatives, and their employees have the same kinds of incentives to avoid risk as do the other bureaucratic enterprises.

SOME CONCLUSIONS

Let me now try to draw some conclusions from these comments about the operation of the market and about what I think are the two leading methods proposed for giving market mechanisms a greater role in a centrally planned society—trying to have the enterprises play at capitalism, and trying to construct a restricted and modified form of capitalism.

Basically, the conclusion is that there is no really satisfactory substitute for a full-scale use of a free market. It does not follow, however, that it may not be desirable to depart from a completely free market. In the first place, efficiency in production is not the only goal that people have. All of us are willing to sacrifice some efficiency for other goals. In the second place, the market is simply incapable of doing some things. The market cannot provide national defense. For that purpose, it is essential to depart from the market, which also involves further interference with the market through the effects of the methods used for raising funds to finance national defense. Third, as we are all aware, the market operates defectively in those cases in which an important part of the effects of any transaction—either benefits or costs—impinges on parties other than those directly involved in the transaction, parties whom it is difficult to identify. This third factor, which has been labeled "neighborhood effects" or "externalities," is particularly troublesome because government attempts to deal with such externalities have typically turned out to do more harm than good. In principle, nonetheless, we cannot deny that there is a case for that kind of intervention.

There are no completely pure systems; every system is something of a mixed system that, on the one hand, includes command elements and, on the other, relies predominantly on voluntary cooperation. The problem is one of proportion, of keeping command elements to a minimum and, where they are introduced, of doing so in a way that interferes as little as possible with the operation of the market while achieving the objectives other than productive efficiency that are being sought.

I believe that the most important implication of this analysis is that even allegedly command economies will find it desirable to use free markets over as wide an area as is politically and economically possible. In particular, even for such collectivist societies as China, Russia, Yugoslavia, that area clearly includes much of agriculture and of retail trade, as well as small enterprises in manufacturing, mining, transportation, and communication. All three countries already practice this policy to some extent, but to a far smaller extent than would be feasible even while retaining centralized political control. Of course, every move in this direction does set up some sources of power independent of the central political authority, which is no doubt why collectivist countries have been so reluctant to move in this direction.

Second, insofar as the objective is to affect the distribution of income rather than to achieve particular production targets, the lesson of history is that it is better to do so through general taxes and subsidies rather than through interfering with the price system. That lesson applies to predominantly market economies such as our own as well as to command economies. In using taxes and subsidies, it is desirable to keep the marginal rates as low as possible. Countries in the West—the United States among others—have resorted to highly graduated rates; but although the rates are graduated on paper, they are not effective in practice. The millions of taxpayers, each seeking to reduce the taxes he must pay, have found effective ways to offset and evade the graduated rates.

The same principle applies to subsidization. Insofar as the political authorities want to assist particular groups of people, they should give them money rather than making available to them goods and services at artificially low prices. The groups will benefit more, and the system will be interfered with less. I may say that this point has been raising particular problems for China in the past year or two because their price structure is absurd, partly because they have tried to keep some prices of so-called necessities and the like very low. They have had great difficulty in trying to follow the Lange-Lerner advice to let those prices rise to more nearly what they would be in a free market. Their limited success in doing so has given rise to great complaints about inflation, a phenomenon with which we are all too familiar. If subsidies are given in money instead of in goods and services at artificially low prices, the recipients will benefit more, and the productive system will be interfered with less.

Third, for enterprises that remain state enterprises, the Lange-Lerner rule, although it cannot be fully effective because it cannot be properly monitored, nonetheless indicates the right direction for policy to take. Enterprises should be made responsible for their own behavior; their targets should be set in generalized terms of profits or money rather than in terms of specific physical outcomes. Let the enterprises bid separately for the resources they need, and let the prices be determined at a level that will equate demand and supply.

As I have already noted, the chief defect of all alternatives to an extensive use of free markets will be in the area of innovation, change, and progress, as we in the United States have been learning to our cost in recent years. Unfortunately or fortunately, depending on your point of view, in that area there is no effective substitute for permitting the private market really to flourish.

Finally, the major lesson that has impressed me as I have studied the economic policies and practices in various countries—whether fully capitalist, or mixed, or primarily collectivist—is that there is a difference between

rhetoric and reality, between intentions and results. The prating in the collectivist economies about introducing market elements is mostly rhetoric. In
China, we were enormously impressed by the contrast between rhetoric and
reality. We read the pronouncements by Chairman Hua Guofeng about the
plans for introducing greater market elements into the Chinese economy,
about how enterprises were going to have greater freedom in distributing their
products and in deciding what to invest, what to produce, and so on. In every
factory we visited, we asked the people whom we interviewed—most were
public relations people rather than the people who were really running the
factory—"Do you know about the new economic policy that your government
is proposing?" Yes, they all knew about it, and they were all able to describe it to
me in great detail. Then I would ask the next question: "Tell me, how has that
affected your particular firm?" "Oh," they would say, "it hasn't had a chance to
affect us yet."

As the famous English writer Samuel Johnson put it two centuries ago,
"the road to Hell is paved with good intentions." Or, if I may use one of my
favorite quotations, as a deputy from Nemours at the French National Assembly at the time of the French Revolution put it in 1790 (I may add that deputy's
name was Pierre S. du Pont):

> Gentlemen, it is a disagreeable custom to which one is easily led by the
> harshness of the discussions, to assume evil intentions. It is necessary to be
> gracious as to intentions; one should believe them good, and apparently they
> are; but we do not have to be gracious at all to inconsistent logic or to absurd
> reasoning. Bad logicians have committed more involuntary crimes than bad
> men have done intentionally.

Notes

1. G. Warren Nutter, *The Strange World of Ivan Ivanov* (New York and Cleveland:
World Publishing Co., 1969).

2. Oskar Lange, "On the Economic Theory of Socialism," *Review of Economic
Studies* 4 (October 1936): 53–71, and 4 (February 1937): 123–42. A revised version was
subsequently published in Oskar Lange and Fred M. Taylor, *On the Economic Theory of
Socialism*, Benjamin E. Lippencott, ed. (Minneapolis: University of Minnesota Press,
1938), pp. 55–142.

3. Abba P. Lerner, "Economic Theory and Socialist Economy," *Review of Economic
Studies* 2 (October 1934): 51–61; idem, "A Note on Socialist Economics," *Review of
Economic Studies* 4 (October 1936): 72–76; idem, "Statics and Dynamics in Socialist
Economics," *Economic Journal* 47 (June 1937): 253–70; and idem, *The Economics of
Control* (New York: Macmillan, 1944).

4. James E. Meade, *Planning and the Price Mechanism: The Liberal-Socialist Solution* (London: G. Allen & Unwin, 1948).

5. G. Warren Nutter, "Markets without Property: A Grand Illusion," in Nicholas A. Beadles and L. Aubrey Drewry, Jr., eds., *Money, the Market, and the State: Economic Essays in Honor of James Muir Waller* (Athens: University of Georgia Press, 1968), pp. 137–45 (quotation is from pp. 144–45).

6. Samuel Brittan, "Hayek, the New Right, & the Crisis of Social Democracy," *Encounter* (January 1980): 30–46 (quotation is from p. 38).

7. Thomas Sowell, *Knowledge and Decision* (New York: Basic Books, 1980).

THE SOCIAL RESPONSIBILITY
OF BUSINESS

· 4 ·

When I hear businessmen speak eloquently about the "social responsibilities of business in a free enterprise system," I am reminded of the wonderful line about the Frenchman who discovered at the age of 70 that he had been speaking prose all his life. The businessmen believe that they are defending free enterprise when they declaim that business is not concerned "merely" with profit but also with promoting desirable "social" ends; that business has a "social conscience" and takes seriously its responsibilities for providing employment, eliminating discrimination, avoiding pollution, and whatever else may be the catchwords of the contemporary crop of reformers. In fact they are—or would be if they or anyone else took them seriously—preaching pure and unadulterated socialism. Businessmen who talk this way are unwitting puppets of the intellectual forces that have been undermining the basis of a free society these past decades.

The discussions of the "social responsibilities of business" are notable for their analytical looseness and lack of rigor. What does it mean to say that "business" has responsibilities? Only people can have responsibilities. A corporation is an artificial person and in this sense may have artificial responsibilities, but "business" as a whole cannot be said to have responsibilities, even in this vague sense. The first step toward clarity in examining the doctrine of the social responsibility of business is to ask precisely what it implies for whom.

The New York Times Magazine, September 13, 1970, pp. 33, 122–26. ©1970 by The New York Times Company. Reprinted by permission.

Presumably, the individuals who are to be responsible are businessmen, which means individual proprietors or corporate executives. Most of the discussion of social responsibility is directed at corporations, so in what follows I shall mostly neglect the individual proprietor and speak of corporate executives.

In a free enterprise, private property system, a corporate executive is an employee of the owners of the business. He has direct responsibility to his employers. That responsibility is to conduct the business in accordance with their desires, which generally will be to make as much money as possible while conforming to the basic rules of the society, both those embodied in law and those embodied in ethical custom. Of course, in some cases his employers may have a different objective. A group of persons might establish a corporation for an eleemosynary purpose—for example, a hospital or a school. The manager of such a corporation will not have money profit as his objective but the rendering of certain services.

In either case, the key point is that, in his capacity as a corporate executive, the manager is the agent of the individuals who own the corporation or establish the eleemosynary institution, and his primary responsibility is to them.

Needless to say, this does not mean that it is easy to judge how well he is performing his task. But at least the criterion of performance is straightforward, and the persons among whom a voluntary contractual arrangement exists are clearly defined.

Of course, the corporate executive is also a person in his own right. As a person, he may have many other responsibilities that he recognizes or assumes voluntarily—to his family, his conscience, his feelings of charity, his church, his clubs, his city, his country. He may feel impelled by these responsibilities to devote part of his income to causes he regards as worthy, to refuse to work for particular corporations, even to leave his job, for example, to join his country's armed forces. If we wish, we may refer to some of these responsibilities as "social responsibilities." But in these respects he is acting as a principal, not an agent; he is spending his own money or time or energy, not the money of his employers or the time or energy he has contracted to devote to their purposes. If these are "social responsibilities," they are the social responsibilities of individuals, not of business.

What does it mean to say that the corporate executive has a "social responsibility" in his capacity as businessman? If this statement is not pure rhetoric, it must mean that he is to act in some way that is not in the interest of his employers. For example, that he is to refrain from increasing the price of the product in order to contribute to the social objective of preventing inflation, even though a price increase would be in the best interests of the corporation.

Or that he is to make expenditures on reducing pollution beyond the amount that is in the best interests of the corporation or that is required by law in order to contribute to the social objective of improving the environment. Or that, at the expense of corporate profits, he is to hire "hard-core" unemployed instead of better qualified available workmen to contribute to the social objective of reducing poverty.

In each of these cases, the corporate executive would be spending someone else's money for a general social interest. Insofar as his actions in accord with his "social responsibility" reduce returns to stockholders, he is spending their money. Insofar as his actions raise the price to customers, he is spending the customers' money. Insofar as his actions lower the wages of some employees, he is spending their money.

The stockholders or the customers or the employees could separately spend their own money on the particular action if they wished to do so. The executive is exercising a distinct "social responsibility," rather than serving as an agent of the stockholders or the customers or the employees, only if he spends the money in a different way than they would have spent it.

But if he does this, he is in effect imposing taxes, on the one hand, and deciding how the tax proceeds shall be spent, on the other.

This process raises political questions on two levels: principle and consequences. On the level of political principle, the imposition of taxes and the expenditure of tax proceeds are governmental functions. We have established elaborate constitutional, parliamentary, and judicial provisions to control these functions, to assure that taxes are imposed so far as possible in accordance with the preferences and desires of the public—after all, "taxation without representation" was one of the battle cries of the American Revolution. We have a system of checks and balances to separate the legislative function of imposing taxes and enacting expenditures from the executive function of collecting taxes and administering expenditure programs and from the judicial function of mediating disputes and interpreting the law.

Here the businessman—self-selected or appointed directly or indirectly by stockholders—is to be simultaneously legislator, executive, and jurist. He is to decide whom to tax by how much and for what purpose, and he is to spend the proceeds—all this guided only by general exhortations from on high to restrain inflation, improve the environment, fight poverty, and so on and on.

The whole justification for permitting the corporate executive to be selected by the stockholders is that the executive is an agent serving the interests of his principal. This justification disappears when the corporate executive imposes taxes and spends the proceeds for "social" purposes. He becomes in effect a public employee, a civil servant, even though he remains in name an employee of a private enterprise. On grounds of political principle, it is intolerable that such civil servants—insofar as their actions in the name of social responsibility are real and not just window-dressing—should be selected as they are now. If they are to be civil servants, then they must be selected through a political process. If they are to impose taxes and make expenditures to foster "social" objectives, then political machinery must be set up to guide the assessment of taxes and to determine through a political process the objectives to be served.

This is the basic reason why the doctrine of "social responsibility" involves the acceptance of the socialist view that political mechanisms, not market mechanisms, are the appropriate way to determine the allocation of scarce resources to alternative uses.

On the grounds of consequences, can the corporate executive in fact discharge his alleged "social responsibilities"? On the one hand, suppose he could get away with spending the stockholders' or customers' or employees' money. How is he to know how to spend it? He is told that he must contribute to fighting inflation. How is he to know what action of his will contribute to that end? He is presumably an expert in running his company—in producing a product or selling it or financing it. But nothing about his selection makes him an expert on inflation. Will his holding down the price of his product reduce inflationary pressure? Or, by leaving more spending power in the hands of his customers, simply divert it elsewhere? Or, by forcing him to produce less because of the lower price, will it simply contribute to shortages? Even if he could answer these questions, how much cost is he justified in imposing on his stockholders, customers, and employees for this social purpose? What is his appropriate share and what is the appropriate share of others?

And, whether he wants to or not, can he get away with spending his stockholders', customers', or employees' money? Will not the stockholders fire him? (Either the present ones or those who take over when his actions in the name of social responsibility have reduced the corporation's profits and the price of its stock.) His customers and his employees can desert him for other producers and employers less scrupulous in exercising their social responsibilities.

This facet of "social responsibility" doctrine is brought into sharp relief when the doctrine is used to justify wage restraint by trade unions. The conflict of interest is naked and clear when union officials are asked to subordinate the interest of their members to some more general social purpose. If the union officials try to enforce wage restraint, the consequence is likely to be wildcat strikes, rank-and-file revolts, and the emergence of strong competitors for their jobs. We thus have the ironic phenomenon that union leaders—at least in the United States—have objected to government interference with the market far more consistently and courageously than have business leaders.

The difficulty of exercising "social responsibility" illustrates, of course, the great virtue of private competitive enterprise—it forces people to be responsible for their own actions and makes it difficult for them to "exploit" other people for either selfish or unselfish purposes. They can do good—but only at their own expense.

Many a reader who has followed the argument this far may be tempted to remonstrate that it is all well and good to speak of government's having the responsibility to impose taxes and determine expenditures for such "social" purposes as controlling pollution or training the hard-core unemployed, but that the problems are too urgent to wait on the slow course of political processes, that the exercise of social responsibility by businessmen is a quicker and surer way to solve pressing current problems.

Aside from the question of fact—I share Adam Smith's skepticism about the benefits that can be expected from "those who affected to trade for the public good"—this argument must be rejected on grounds of principle. What it amounts to is an assertion that those who favor the taxes and expenditures in question have failed to persuade a majority of their fellow citizens to be of like mind and that they are seeking to attain by undemocratic procedures what they cannot attain by democratic procedures. In a free society, it is hard for "good" people to do "good," but that is a small price to pay for making it hard for "evil" people to do "evil," especially since one man's good is another's evil.

I have, for simplicity, concentrated on the special case of the corporate executive, except only for the brief digression on trade unions. But precisely the same argument applies to the newer phenomenon of calling upon stockholders to require corporations to exercise social responsibility (the recent G.M. crusade, for example). In most of these cases, what is in effect involved is some stockholders trying to get other stockholders (or customers or employees) to contribute against their will to "social" causes favored by the activists. Insofar as they succeed, they are again imposing taxes and spending the proceeds.

The situation of the individual proprietor is somewhat different. If he acts to reduce the returns of his enterprise in order to exercise his "social responsibility," he is spending his own money, not someone else's. If he wishes to spend his money on such purposes, that is his right, and I cannot see that there is any objection to his doing so. In the process, he, too, may impose costs on employees and customers. However, because he is far less likely than a large corporation or union to have monopolistic power, any such side effects will tend to be minor.

Of course, in practice the doctrine of social responsibility is frequently a cloak for actions that are justified on other grounds rather than a reason for those actions.

To illustrate, it may well be in the long-run interest of a corporation that is a major employer in a small community to devote resources to providing amenities to that community or to improving its government. That may make it easier to attract desirable employees, it may reduce the wage bill or lessen losses from pilferage and sabotage or have other worthwhile effects. Or it may be that, given the laws about the deductibility of corporate charitable contributions, the stockholders can contribute more to charities they favor by having the corporation make the gift than by doing it themselves, since they can in that way contribute an amount that would otherwise have been paid as corporate taxes.

In each of these—and many similar—cases, there is a strong temptation to rationalize these actions as an exercise of "social responsibility." In the present climate of opinion, with its widespread aversion to "capitalism," "profits," the "soulless corporations," and so on, this is one way for a corporation to generate goodwill as a byproduct of expenditures that are entirely justified in its own self-interest.

It would be inconsistent of me to call on corporate executives to refrain from this hypocritical window-dressing because it harms the foundations of a free society. That would be to call on them to exercise a "social responsibility"! If our institutions, and the attitudes of the public make it in their self-interest to cloak their actions in this way, I cannot summon much indignation to denounce them. At the same time, I can express admiration for those individual proprietors or owners of closely held corporations or stockholders of more broadly held corporations who disdain such tactics as approaching fraud.

Whether blameworthy or not, the use of the cloak of social responsibility, and the nonsense spoken in its name by influential and prestigious businessmen, does clearly harm the foundations of a free society. I have been impressed time and again by the schizophrenic character of many businessmen. They are capable of being extremely far-sighted and clear-headed in matters that are internal to their businesses. They are incredibly short-sighted and muddle-headed in matters that are outside their businesses but affect the possible survival of business in general. This short-sightedness is strikingly exemplified in the calls from many businessmen for wage and price guidelines or controls or income policies. There is nothing that could do more in a brief period to destroy a market system and replace it by a centrally controlled system than effective governmental control of prices and wages.

The short-sightedness is also exemplified in speeches by businessmen on social responsibility. This may gain them kudos in the short run. But it helps to strengthen the already too prevalent view that the pursuit of profits is wicked and immoral and must be curbed and controlled by external forces. Once this view is adopted, the external forces that curb the market will not be the social consciences, however highly developed, of the pontificating executives; it will be the iron fist of government bureaucrats. Here, as with price and wage controls, businessmen seem to me to reveal a suicidal impulse.

The political principle that underlies the market mechanism is unanimity. In an ideal free market resting on private property, no individual can coerce any other, all cooperation is voluntary, all parties to such cooperation benefit or they need not participate. There are no "social" values, no "social" responsibilities in any sense other than the shared values and responsibilities of individuals. Society is a collection of individuals and of the various groups they voluntarily form.

The political principle that underlies the political mechanism is conformity. The individual must serve a more general social interest—whether that be determined by a church or a dictator or a majority. The individual may have a vote and a say in what is to be done, but if he is overruled, he must conform. It is appropriate for some to require others to contribute to a general social purpose whether they wish to or not.

Unfortunately, unanimity is not always feasible. There are some respects in which conformity appears unavoidable, so I do not see how one can avoid the use of the political mechanism altogether.

But the doctrine of "social responsibility" taken seriously would extend the scope of the political mechanism to every human activity. It does not differ in philosophy from the most explicitly collectivist doctrine. It differs only by professing to believe that collectivist ends can be attained without collectivist means. That is why, in my book *Capitalism and Freedom*,[1] I have called it a "fundamentally subversive doctrine" in a free society, and have said that in such a society, "there is one and only one social responsibility of business—to use its resources and engage in activities designed to increase its profits so long as it stays within the rules of the game, which is to say, engages in open and free competition without deception or fraud."

NOTE

1. Milton Friedman, *Capitalism and Freedom* (Chicago: University of Chicago Press, 1962).

CAPITALISM AND THE JEWS: CONFRONTING A PARADOX

· 5 ·

My aim is to examine a particular case of an historical and political paradox—the attitude of Jews toward capitalism. Two propositions can be readily demonstrated: first, the Jews owe an enormous debt to free enterprise and competitive capitalism; second, for at least the past century the Jews have been consistently opposed to capitalism and have done much on an ideological level to undermine it. How can these propositions be reconciled?

I was led to examine this paradox partly for obvious personal reasons. I am accustomed to being a member of an intellectual minority, to being accused by fellow intellectuals of being a reactionary or an apologist or plain nuts. But those of us who are also Jewish are even more embattled, being regarded not only as intellectual deviants but also as traitors to a supposed cultural and national tradition.

This personal interest was reinforced by the hope that study of this special case might offer a clue to a more general paradox—typified by postwar West Germany and its flourishing capitalism where Jews play a minor role, yet where the intellectual climate is largely collectivist. Unfortunately, that hope has not been fulfilled. I believe that I can explain to a very large extent the anti-capitalist tendency among Jews, but the most important elements of the explanation are peculiar to the special case and cannot readily be generalized. I trust that others will be more successful.

From *Encounter* 63, no. 1 (June 1984). Reprinted with permission. Initially delivered as presidential address at 1972 Mont Pelerin Society meeting.

The Benefit Jews Have Derived from Capitalism

Let me start by briefly documenting the first proposition: that the Jews owe an enormous debt to capitalism. The feature of capitalism that has benefited the Jews has of course been competition.[1] Wherever there is monopoly, whether it be private or governmental, there is room for the application of arbitrary criteria in the selection of the beneficiaries of the monopoly—whether these criteria be color of skin, religion, national origin, or whatnot. Where there is free competition, only performance counts. The market is color-blind. No one who goes to the market to buy bread knows or cares whether the wheat was grown by a Jew, Catholic, Protestant, Muslim, or atheist; by whites or blacks. Any miller who wishes to express his personal prejudices by buying only from preferred groups is at a competitive disadvantage, since he is keeping himself from buying from the cheapest source. He can express his prejudice, but he will have to do so at his own expense, accepting a lower monetary income than he could otherwise earn.

A personal experience illuminates sharply the importance of competition. A dozen years ago I attended the International Monetary Conference held in Montreal. The persons there consisted, on the one hand, of members of the conference, who include the two top executives of the major commercial banks throughout the world; on the other, of persons like myself invited as speakers or participants in panel discussions. A conversation with an American banker present who recounted a tale of anti-Semitism in American banking led me to estimate roughly the fraction of the two groups who were Jewish. Of the first group—the bankers proper—I estimated that about 1 percent were Jewish. Of the much smaller second group, the invited participants in the program, roughly 25 percent were Jewish.

Why the difference? Because banking today is everywhere monopolistic in the sense that there is not free entry. Government permission or a franchise is required. On the other hand, intellectual activity of the kind that would recommend persons for the program is a highly competitive industry with almost completely free entry.

This example is particularly striking because banking is hardly a field, like, say, iron and steel, in which Jews have never played an important role. On the contrary, for centuries Jews were a major if not dominant element in banking and particularly in international banking. But when that was true, banking was an industry with rather free entry. Jews prospered in it for that reason and also because they had a comparative advantage arising from the Church's views on usury, the dispersion of Jews throughout the world, and their usefulness to ruling monarchs precisely because of the isolation of the Jews from the rest of the community.[2]

The anecdote illuminates much history. Throughout the nearly two thousand years of the Diaspora, Jews were repeatedly discriminated against, restricted in the activities they could undertake, on occasion expelled en masse, as in 1492 from Spain, and often the object of the extreme hostility of the peoples among whom they lived. They were able nonetheless to exist because of the absence of a totalitarian state, so that there were always some market elements, some activities open to them to enter. In particular, the fragmented political structure and the numerous separate sovereignties meant that international trade and finance in particular escaped close control, which is why Jews were so prominent in this area. It is no accident that Nazi Germany and Soviet Russia, the two most totalitarian societies in the past 2,000 years (modern China perhaps excepted), also offer the most extreme examples of official and effective anti-Semitism.

If we come to more recent times, Jews have flourished most in those countries in which competitive capitalism had the greatest scope: Holland in the sixteenth and seventeenth centuries, and Britain and the United States in the nineteenth and twentieth centuries, Germany in the late nineteenth and twentieth centuries—a case that is particularly pertinent when that period is compared with the Hitler period.[3] Moreover, within those countries, Jews have flourished most in the sectors that have the freest entry and are in that sense most competitive. Compare the experience of the Jews in banking, that I have referred to, with their experience in retail trade, which has been almost a prototype of the textbook image of perfect competition and free entry. Or compare their minor role in large industry with their prominence in the professions such as law, medicine, accountancy, and the like.[4] Though there were barriers to entry in the professions too, once past the initial barriers there is a large measure of free competition for custom. Even the differences within the professions illustrate my theme. In the United States, for which I know the details, there was for a long time a major difference between medicine and law in the extent to which state licensure was an effective bar to entry. For reasons that are not relevant here, there was significant restriction of entry in medicine, relatively little in law. And Jews were proportionately much more numerous in law than in medicine.

The movie industry in the United States was a new industry and for that reason open to all. Jews became a major factor and this carried over to radio and television when they came on the scene. But now that government control and regulation have become more and more important, I am under the impression that the Jewish role in radio and television is declining.

A rather different example of the benefits Jews have derived from competitive capitalism is provided by Israel, and this in a dual sense.

First, Israel would hardly have been viable without the massive contributions that it received from world Jewry, primarily from the United States, secondly from Britain and other western capitalist countries. Suppose these countries had been socialist. The hypothetical socialist countries might conceivably have contributed, but if so they would have done so for very different reasons and with very different conditions attached. Compare Soviet aid to Egypt or official U.S. aid to Israel with private contributions. In a capitalist system, any group, however small a minority, can use its own resources as it wishes, without seeking or getting the permission of the majority.

Second, within Israel, despite all the talk of central control, the reality is that rapid development has been primarily the product of private initiative. After my first extended visit to Israel several decades ago, I concluded that two traditions were at work in Israel: an ancient one, going back nearly two thousand years, of finding ways around governmental restrictions; a modern one, going back a century, of belief in "democratic socialism" and "central planning." Fortunately for Israel, the first tradition has proved far more potent than the second.

To summarize: Except for the sporadic protection of individual monarchs to whom they were useful, Jews have seldom benefited from governmental intervention on their behalf. They have flourished when and only when there has been a widespread acceptance by the public at large of the general doctrine of nonintervention, so that a large measure of competitive capitalism and of tolerance for all groups has prevailed. They have flourished then despite continued widespread anti-Semitic prejudice because the general belief in nonintervention was more powerful than the specific urge to discriminate against the Jews.

THE ANTI-CAPITALIST MENTALITY OF THE JEWS

Despite this record, for the past century, the Jews have been a stronghold of anti-capitalist sentiment. From Karl Marx through Leon Trotsky to Herbert Marcuse, a sizable fraction of the revolutionary anti-capitalist literature has been written by Jews. Communist parties in all countries, including the party that achieved revolution in Russia but also present-day communist parties in western countries, and especially in the United States, have been run and manned to a disproportionate extent by Jews—though I hasten to add that only a tiny fraction of Jews have ever been members of the communist party.[5] Jews have been equally active in the less-revolutionary socialist movements in all countries, as intellectuals generating socialist literature, as active participants in leadership, and as members.

Coming still closer to the center, in Britain the Jewish vote and participation is predominantly in the Labour Party; in the United States, in the left wing of the Democratic Party. The party programs of the so-called right-wing parties in Israel would be regarded as "liberal," in the economic sense, almost everywhere else. These phenomena are so well known that they require little elaboration or documentation.[6]

WHY THE ANTI-CAPITALIST MENTALITY?

How can we reconcile my two propositions? Why is it that despite the historical record of the benefits of competitive capitalism to the Jews, despite the intellectual explanation of this phenomenon that is implicit or explicit in all liberal literature from at least Adam Smith on, the Jews have been disproportionately anti-capitalist?

We may start by considering some simple yet inadequate answers. Lawrence Fuchs, in a highly superficial analysis of *The Political Behavior of American Jews*, argues that the anti-capitalism of the Jews is a direct reflection of values derived from the Jewish religion and culture. He goes so far as to say (p. 197):

> if the communist movement is in a sense a Christian heresy, it is also Jewish orthodoxy—not the totalitarian or revolutionary aspects of world communism, but the quest for social justice through social action.

Needless to say—a point I shall return to later in a different connection—Fuchs himself is a liberal in the American sense. He regards the political liberalism of the Jews in this sense as a virtue, and hence is quick to regard such liberalism as a legitimate offspring of the Jewish values of learning, charity, and concern with the pleasures of this world. He never even recognizes, let alone discusses, the key question whether the ethical end of "social justice through social action" is consistent with the political means of centralized government.

This explanation can be dismissed out of hand. Jewish religion and culture date back over two millennia; the Jewish opposition to capitalism and attachment to socialism, at the most, less than two centuries. Only after the Enlightenment, and then primarily among the Jews who were breaking away from the Jewish religion, did this political stance emerge. Werner Sombart, in his important and controversial book *The Jews and Modern Capitalism* (first published in 1911), makes a far stronger case that Jewish religion and culture implied a capitalist outlook than Fuchs does that it implied a socialist outlook. Sombart wrote:

> Throughout the centuries, the Jews championed the cause of individual liberty in economic activity against the dominating views of the time. The individual was not to be hampered by regulations of any sort... I think that the Jewish religion has the same leading ideas as capitalism... The whole

religious system is in reality nothing but a contract between Jehovah and his chosen people...God promises something and gives something, and the righteous must give Him something in return. Indeed, there was no community of interest between God and man which could not be expressed in these terms—that man performs some duty enjoined by the Torah and receives from God a quid pro quo.

Sombart goes on to discuss the attitude toward riches and poverty in the Old and New Testaments.

You will find a few passages [in the Old Testament and the Talmud] wherein poverty is lauded as something nobler and higher than riches. But on the other hand you will come across hundreds of passages in which riches are called the blessing of the Lord, and only their misuse or their dangers warned against.

By contrast, Sombart refers to the famous passage in the New Testament, "it is easier for a camel to go through the eye of a needle than for a rich man to enter into the kingdom of God," and remarks,

as often as riches are lauded in the Old Testament, they are damned in the New...The religion of the Christians stands in the way of their economic activities...The Jews were never faced with this hindrance.

He concludes:

Free trade and industrial freedom were in accordance with Jewish law, and therefore in accordance with God's will."[7]

Sombart's book, I may say, has in general had a highly unfavorable reception among both economic historians in general and Jewish intellectuals in particular, and indeed, something of an aura of anti-Semitism has come to be attributed to it. Much of the criticism seems valid but there is nothing in the book itself to justify any charge of anti-Semitism though there certainly is in Sombart's behavior and writings several decades later. Indeed, if anything I interpret the book as philo-Semitic. I regard the violence of the reaction of Jewish intellectuals to the book as itself a manifestation of the Jewish anti-capitalist mentality. I shall return to this point later.

A more balanced judgment than either Fuch's or Sombart's, and one with which I am in full accord, is rendered by Nathan Glazer, who writes,

It is hard to see direct links with Jewish tradition in these attitudes. . . One thing is sure: it is an enormous oversimplification to say Jews in Eastern Europe became socialists and anarchists because the Hebrew prophets had denounced injustice twenty-five hundred years ago. . . The Jewish religious tradition probably does dispose Jews, in some subtle way, toward liberalism and radicalism, but it is not easy to see in present-day Jewish social attitudes the heritage of the Jewish religion.[8]

A second simple explanation is that the Jewish anti-capitalist mentality simply reflects the general tendency for intellectuals to be anti-capitalist plus the disproportionate representation of Jews among intellectuals. For example, Nathan Glazer says,

The general explanations for this phenomenon [the attachment of the major part of the intelligentsia to the Left] are well known. Freed from the restraints of conservative and traditional thinking, the intelligentsia finds it easier to accept revolutionary thinking, which attacks the established order of things in politics, religion, culture, and society. . . Whatever it is that affected intellectuals, also affected Jews.[9]

Glazer goes on, however, to qualify greatly this interpretation by citing some factors that affected Jews differently from other intellectuals. This explanation undoubtedly has more validity than Fuchs's simpleminded identification of anti-capitalism with Jewish religion and culture. As the West German example mentioned earlier suggests, non-Jewish intellectuals are capable of becoming dominantly collectivist. And there is no doubt that the intellectual forces Glazer refers to affected Jewish intellectuals along with non-Jewish. However, the explanation seems highly incomplete in two respects. First, my impression is that a far larger percentage of Jewish intellectuals than of non-Jewish have been collectivist. Second, and more important, this explanation does not account for the different attitudes of the great mass of Jews and non-Jews who are not intellectuals. To explain this difference we must dig deeper.

A third simple explanation that doubtless has some validity is the natural tendency for all of us to take the good things that happen to us for granted but to attribute any bad things to evil men or an evil system. Competitive capitalism has permitted Jews to flourish economically and culturally because it has prevented anti-Semites from imposing their values on others, and from discriminating against Jews at other people's expense. But the other side of that coin is that it protects anti-Semites in the expression of their anti-Semitism in their personal behavior so long as they do it at their own expense. Competitive capitalism has therefore not eliminated social anti-Semitism. The free competition of ideas that is the natural companion of competitive capitalism might in time lead to a change in tastes and values that would eliminate social anti-

Semitism, but there is no assurance that it will. As the New Testament puts it, "In my Father's house are many mansions."

No doubt, Jews have reacted in part by attributing the residual discrimination to "the System." But that hardly explains why the part of the "System" to which the discrimination has been attributed is "Capitalism." Why not, in nineteenth-century Britain, to the Established Church and the aristocracy; in nineteenth- and twentieth-century Germany, to the bureaucracy; and in the twentieth-century United States, to the social rather than economic establishment? After all, Jewish history surely offers more than ample evidence that anti-Semitism has no special connection with a market economy. So this explanation, too, is unsatisfactory.

I come now to two explanations that seem to me much more fundamental. The first explanation, which has to do with the particular circumstances in Europe and in the nineteenth century, I owe to the extremely perceptive analysis of Werner Cohn in his unpublished Ph.D. thesis on the "Sources of American Jewish Liberalism."[10] Cohn points out that:

> Beginning with the era of the French revolution, the European political spectrum became divided into a "Left" and a "Right" along an axis that involved the issue of secularism. The Right (conservative, monarchical, "clerical") maintained that there must be a place for the Church in the public order; the Left (democratic, liberal, radical) held that there can be no (public) Church at all . . .
>
> The axis separating Left from Right also formed a natural boundary for the pale of Jewish political participation. It was the Left, with its new secular concept of citizenship, that had accomplished the Emancipation, and it was only the Left that could see a place for the Jews in public life. No Conservative party in Europe—from the bitterly hostile Monarchists in Russia through the strongly Christian *noines* in France to the amiable Tories in England—could reconcile itself to full Jewish political equality. Jews supported the Left, then, not only because they had become unshakeable partisans of the Emancipation, but also because they had no choice; as far as the internal life of the Right was concerned, the Emancipation had never taken place, and the Christian religion remained a prerequisite for political participation.

Note in this connection that the only major leaders of conservative parties who were of Jewish origin—Benjamin Disraeli in England, Friedrich Julius Stahl in Germany—were both professing Christians (Disraeli's father was converted, Stahl was baptized at the age of nineteen).

Cohn goes on to distinguish between two strands of Leftism: "rational" or "intellectual" and "radical." He remarks that:

Radical Leftism... was the only political movement since the days of the Roman empire in which Jews could become the intellectual brethren of non-Jews... While intellectual Leftism was Christian at least in the sense of recognizing the distinction between "religious" and "secular," radical Leftism—eschatological socialism in particular—began to constitute itself as a new religious faith in which no separation between the sacred and the profane was tolerated... [intellectual Leftism] offered [the Jews] a wholly rational and superficial admission to the larger society, [radical Leftism] a measure of real spiritual community.

I share Glazer's comment on these passages: "I do not think anyone has come closer to the heart of the matter than has the author of these paragraphs." Cohn's argument goes far to explain the important role that Jewish intellectuals played in the Marxist and socialist movement, the almost universal acceptance of "democratic socialism" by the European Jews in the Zionist movement (particularly those who emigrated to Palestine), and the socialist sentiment among the German-Jewish immigrants to the United States of the mid-nineteenth century and the much larger flood of East European Jews at the turn of the century.

Yet by itself it is hard to accept Cohn's point as the whole explanation for the anti-capitalist mentality of the Jews. In the United States, from the beginning, the separation of church and state was accepted constitutional doctrine. True, the initial upper class was Christian and Protestant, but that was true of the population as a whole. Indeed, the elite Puritan element was, if anything, pro-Semitic. As Sombart points out in reconciling his thesis about the role of Jews in capitalist development with Max Weber's about the role of "the Protestant Ethic" in capitalist development, the Protestants (and the Puritans especially) went back to the Old Testament for their religious inspiration and patterned themselves on the ancient Hebrews. Sombart asserts: "Puritanism *is* Judaism." Cohn too emphasizes this phenomenon, pointing to Puritan tolerance toward Jews in the colonial era, despite their general intolerance toward other religious sects.[11]

To come down to more recent times in the United States, Theodore Roosevelt was highly popular among the Jews partly because of his willingness to object publicly to Russian pogroms. Outside of the closely knit socialist community in New York most Jews probably were Republicans rather than Democrats until the 1920s, when first Al Smith and then Franklin Delano Roosevelt produced a massive shift to the Democrats from both the Right and the Left. The shift from the Left betokened a weakening of the European influence, rather than being a manifestation of it. Yet despite that weakening influence, the American Jewish community, which now consists largely of second- and third- (and later) generation Americans, retains its dominant leftish cast.

The final explanation that suggests itself is complementary to Cohn's yet not at all identical with it. To justify itself by more than the reference to the alleged role of the Jews in Christ's crucifixion, anti-Semitism produced a stereotype of the Jew as primarily interested in money, as a merchant or moneylender who put commercial interests ahead of human values, who was money-grasping, cunning, selfish and greedy, who would "jew" you down and insist on his pound of flesh. Jews could have reacted to this stereotype in two ways: first, by accepting the description but rejecting the values that regarded these traits as blameworthy; second, by accepting the values but rejecting the description. Had they adopted the first way, they could have stressed the benefits rendered by the merchant and by the moneylender. They could have recalled, perhaps, Bentham's comment that

> the business of a moneylender. . . has nowhere nor at any time been a popular one. Those who have the resolution to sacrifice the present to the future are natural objects of envy to those who have sacrificed the future to the present. The children who have eaten their cake are the natural enemies of the children who have theirs. While the money is hoped for, and for a short time after it has been received, he who lends it is a friend and benefactor: by the time the money is spent, and the evil hour of reckoning is come, the benefactor is found to have changed his nature, and to have put on the tyrant and the oppressor. It is oppression for a man to reclaim his own money; it is none to keep it from him."[12]

Similarly, Jews could have noted that one man's selfishness is another man's self-reliance; one man's cunning, another's wisdom; one man's greed, another's prudence.

But this reaction was hardly to be expected. None of us can escape the intellectual air we breathe, can fail to be influenced by the values of the community in which we live. As Jews left the closed ghetto and *shtetl* and came into contact with the rest of the world, they inevitably came to accept and share the values of that world, the values that looked down on the "merely" commercial, that regarded moneylenders with contempt. They were led to say to themselves: if Jews are like that, the anti-Semites are right.

The other possible reaction is to deny that Jews are like the stereotype, to set out to persuade oneself (and incidentally the anti-Semites) that far from being money-grasping, selfish, and heartless, Jews are really public-spirited, generous, and concerned with ideals rather than material goods. How better to do so than to attack the market with its reliance on monetary values and impersonal transactions and to glorify the political process, to take as an ideal a state run by well-meaning people for the benefit of their fellow men?

I was first led to this explanation of the anti-capitalist mentality of the Jews by my experience in Israel. After several months there, I came to the conclusion that the quickest way to reach a generalization in any area about values in Israel was to ask what was true of the Jews in the Diaspora and reverse it.

Jews in the Diaspora were urban dwellers engaged in commercial pursuits and almost never in agriculture; in Israel, agriculture has much higher prestige than commerce.

Jews in the Diaspora shunned every aspect of military service; Israelis value the military highly and have demonstrated extraordinary competence.

These two reversals are readily explained as the children of necessity, but let me continue.

Yiddish or Ladino was the language of the Jews in the Diaspora; both are looked down on in Israel, where Hebrew is the national language.

Jews in the Diaspora stressed intellectual pursuits and rather looked down on athletics; there is tremendous emphasis on athletics in Israel.

And for what may seem like an irrelevant clincher: Jews in the Diaspora were reputed to be excellent cooks; cooking in Israel is generally terrible, in homes, hotels, and restaurants.

Can this record not be interpreted as an attempt, no doubt wholly subconscious, to demonstrate to the world that the commonly accepted stereotype of the Jew is false?

I interpret in the same way the evidence assembled by Wilson and Banfield that Jews (and "Yankees") tend to adopt a "community-serving conception" of the public interest, and to vote against their own immediate self-interest, in larger proportions than most other groups.[13]

I interpret also in this way the attempt by Fuchs to trace Jewish "liberalism" to Jewish values and the negative reaction of Jewish critics to Sombart's book. If, like me, you regard competitive capitalism as the economic system that is most favorable to individual freedom, to creative accomplishments in technology and the arts, and to the widest possible opportunities for the ordinary man, then you will regard Sombart's assignment to the Jews of a key role in the development of capitalism as high praise. You will, as I do, regard his book as philo-Semitic. On the other hand, if you are trying your level best to demonstrate that Jews are dedicated to selfless public service in a socialist state, that commerce and moneylending were activities forced on them by their unfortunate circumstances and were wholly foreign to their natural bent, then you will regard Sombart as an anti-Semite simply reinforcing the stereotype against which you are battling. In this vein, the *Universal Jewish Encyclopaedia* says in its article on Sombart: "He *accused* the Jews of having created capitalism" (my italics).

The complementary character of the final two explanations is, I trust, clear. Whence comes the value structure that puts service to the general public above concern for oneself and one's close family—government employment above private business—political activity above commercial activity—love of mankind in general above concern for men in particular—social responsibility above individual responsibility? Very largely from the collectivist trend of thought to which Jews contributed so much for the reasons advanced by Cohn.

Consider, for a moment, the reaction to the anti-Semitic stereotype by a nineteenth-century English philosophical radical steeped in Benthamite utilitarianism—by a David Ricardo, James Mill, even Thomas Malthus. Could one of them ever have termed the allegation that Jews created capitalism an *accusation?* They would have termed it high praise. They would have regarded widespread emphasis on rational profit calculation as just what was needed to promote "the greatest good of the greatest number," emphasis on the individual rather than the society as a corollary of belief in freedom, and so on.

CONCLUSION

I conclude then, that the chief explanations for the anti-capitalist mentality of the Jews are (1) the special circumstances of nineteenth-century Europe which linked pro-market parties with established religions and so drove Jews to the Left; and (2) the subconscious attempt by Jews to demonstrate to themselves and the world the fallacy of the anti-Semitic stereotype. No doubt these two main forces were reinforced, and the views of the Jews altered in detail, by their historical and cultural heritage, which made them especially sensitive to injustice and especially committed to charity. They were reinforced also by whatever the forces are that predispose intellectuals towards the Left.

Whether or not this explanation is a satisfactory resolution of the paradox which was my starting point, it remains true that the ideology of the Jews has been and still is opposed to their self-interest. Except behind the Iron Curtain, this conflict has been mostly potential rather than real. In the West, so long as a large measure of laissez-faire capitalism prevailed, the economic drive of the Jews to improve their lot, and to move upward in the economic and social scale, was in no way hindered by the preaching of socialism as an ideal. They could enjoy the luxury of reacting against the anti-Semitic stereotype, yet benefit from the characteristics that that stereotype caricatured. On a much more subtle and sophisticated level, they were in the position of the rich parlor-socialists—of all ethnic and religious backgrounds—who bask in self-righteous virtue by condemning capitalism while enjoying the luxuries paid for by their capitalist inheritance.

As the scope of government has grown, as the collectivist ideas have achieved acceptance and affected the structure of society, the conflict has become very real. I have already stressed the conflict in Israel that has led to giving a far greater role to market forces than the ideology of the early leaders envisioned. I have been struck more recently in the United States with the emergence of the conflict in reaction to some of the proposals by Senator McGovern in his ill-starred presidential candidacy. His early proposal (later rescinded) to set a top limit on inheritances produced an immediate reaction from some of those who might have been expected to be and were his strongest supporters. It came home to them that his measures—completely consistent with their professed ideology—would greatly hamper the upward social and economic mobility of which they had been the beneficiaries.

Perhaps the reality of the conflict will end, or at least weaken, the paradox that has been the subject of my essay. If so, it will be a small silver lining in the dark cloud of encroaching collectivism.

NOTES

1. The only other writer I have come across who explicitly stresses the benefits Jews have derived from capitalism is Ellis Rivkin, *The Shaping of Jewish History* (New York, 1971). Unfortunately, Rivkin's interesting analysis is marred by misconceptions about the nature and operation of capitalism. He takes the accumulation of capital rather than free entry as its distinguishing feature.

2. See, for example, Hannah Arendt, *The Origins of Totalitarianism* (1951), on "court Jews"; also Werner Sombart, *The Jews and Modern Capitalism* (tr. 1913).

3. Sombart argues that the relation is the reverse: that capitalism flourished where it did because Jews were given a considerable measure of freedom. But he would not have denied that the relation is reciprocal. And his version has been seriously questioned by economic historians. See introduction by Bert F. Hoselitz to American edition of Sombart's book, *Jewish Contributions to Civilization* (1919), chap. viia, pp. 247–67.

4. See Nathaniel Weyl, *The Creative Elite in America* (1966), particularly the tables in Appendix III giving results for different "elite rosters."

5. For the United States, see Nathan Glazer, *The Social Basis of American Communism* (1961), pp. 85, 130, 132. See also Jacob L. Talmon's essay on "Jews between Revolution and Counter-Revolution" in his *Israel among the Nations* (1970), pp. 26–81.

6. For the American record, see Werner Cohn, *Sources of American Jewish Liberalism—A Study of the Political Alignments of American Jews* (unpublished Ph.D. thesis, New School for Social Research, June 1956); Lawrence Fuchs, *The Political Behavior of American Jews* (1956); Nathan Glazer, *American Judaism* (1957); Nathan Glazer and Daniel Patrick Moynihan, *Beyond the Melting Pot* (2d ed. 1970).

7. Sombart, *The Jews and Modern Capitalism*, pp. 153, 205, 209, 216, 221–22, 248.

8. Glazer, *American Judaism*, pp. 135–36, 139.

9. Glazer, *The Social Basis of American Communism*, pp. 166–67.

10. See also, in *Encounter*, Werner Cohn's "The 'Aryans' of Jean-Paul Sartre" (December 1981).

11. However, according to Abba Eban, *My People* (1968): "Jews were refused admittance into Massachusetts and Connecticut by the Puritans, whose idea of religious liberty was linked to their own brand of faith. However, in liberal Maryland and in Rhode Island, where freedom of conscience was an unshakable principle, they found acceptance."

12. Jeremy Bentham, *In Defence of Usury* (1787).

13. James Q. Wilson and Edward C. Banfield, "Public-Regardingness as a Value Premise in Voting Behavior," *American Political Science Review* 58, no. 4 (December 1964): 876–87; "Political Ethos Revisited," *American Political Science Review* 65, no. 4 (December 1971): 1048–62. The similarity between the Jews and the Yankees in some of the characteristics examined by Wilson and Banfield is some evidence, if rather weak evidence, for the influence of religion and culture in view of the connection between Puritanism and Judaism.

THE CASE FOR THE
NEGATIVE INCOME TAX

· 6 ·

The direct relief and aid to dependent children programs are only the tip of the welfare iceberg. There is a maze of detailed governmental programs that have been justified on welfare grounds—though typically their product is illfare: public housing, urban renewal, old age and unemployment insurance, job training, the host of assorted programs under the mislabeled "war on poverty," farm price supports, and so on at incredible length.

THE NEGATIVE INCOME TAX

There is a far better way to guarantee a minimum annual income to all than our present grab bag of programs. That way is to use the mechanism by which we collect the bulk of our taxes, namely, the personal income tax. At one time, citizens were required to contribute to the support of the commonwealth by payments in kind—forced collections of food or timber or forced labor on public projects. That is still the rule in many backward areas and is widely practiced in all totalitarian countries. Both freedom and efficiency were fostered by substituting taxes in money for taxes in kind.

In our welfare programs, we are back in the earlier era, dispensing largess in

Excerpted from Melvin R. Laird, ed., *Republican Papers* (Garden City, N.Y.: Doubleday & Co., 1968). Reprinted with permission.

TABLE 6.1

EXAMPLE OF INCOME TAX INCORPORATING
50 PERCENT RATE ON NEGATIVE TAXABLE INCOME
(FAMILY OF FOUR; EXISTING EXEMPTIONS AND STANDARD DEDUCTION;
EXISTING RATES ON POSITIVE INCOME)

Total Income before Tax	Exemptions and Deductions	Taxable Income	Tax Rate	Tax	Income after Tax
0	$3,000	$−3,000	50%	$−1,500	$1,500
1,000	3,000	−2,000	50%	−1,000	2,000
2,000	3,000	−1,000	50%	− 500	2,500
3,000	3,000	0			3,000
4,000	3,000	+1,000	14%	+ 140	3,860

kind, or trying to, and examining the detailed physical circumstances of the recipient. Here, too, the route to progress is to substitute payments in money for payments in kind and the single numerical means test of income for the ambiguous means tests we now use.

I have termed this device for helping the poor a *negative income tax* in order to stress its identity in concept and operation with the present income tax. The essential idea is to extend the income tax by supplementing the income of the poor by a *fraction* of their unused income tax exemptions and deductions.

Under present law, a family of four is entitled to exemptions and deductions of not less than $3,000 (precisely this sum if the family uses the standard deduction). If such a family has a total income of $3,000 it pays no tax. If it has a total pre-tax income of $4,000 (and uses the standard deduction), it has a positive taxable income of $1,000. At the current tax rate for that bracket of 14 percent, it pays $140 a year in taxes, leaving it with $3,860 in income after taxes (see table). If such a family had a total pre-tax income of $2,000, it would have unused exemptions and deductions of $1,000, or in other words, it would have a negative taxable income of $1,000 [$2,000–$3,000]. Under present law, it gets no benefit from those unused exemptions and deductions. Under a negative income tax, it would be entitled to receive a payment, the amount depending on the tax rate.

If the tax rate were the same as for the first bracket of positive income, or 14 percent, it would be entitled to receive $140, leaving it with a post-tax income of $2,140. If the tax rate were 50 percent, the highest rate that seems to me at all feasible, and the one I have used for illustrative purposes, it would be entitled to receive $500, leaving it with a post-tax income of $2,500.

If the family had a zero pre-tax income, it would have a negative taxable income of $3,000. With a 50 percent rate, it would be entitled to receive $1,500 leaving it with a post-tax income of $1,500.

For each size of family, this plan defines *two* incomes: the *break-even* income, at which the family pays no tax and receives no payment—in the example, $3,000—and the *minimum guaranteed* income—in the example, $1,500.[1] For different sizes of families, these incomes are different, both the break-even income and the minimum guaranteed income being higher, the larger the size of the family.[2]

As a practical matter, payments under the negative income tax could not wait for an accurate determination of the amount due, since that would mean postponing payments until after the end of the year. Here again, the situation is precisely the same as under our present personal income tax and the same devices would be used. Wage earners now have taxes deducted at source throughout the year. Recipients of other incomes now file advance estimates of anticipated income and make advance payments of estimated taxes. Both groups reconcile payments with amounts due after the end of the year. Similarly, under a negative income tax, wage earners who are entitled to payments because they receive wages less than the break-even amount would receive their extra payments along with their wages. Others would file estimates of anticipated income and anticipated amounts to which they are entitled, and would receive their payments at regular intervals—weekly or biweekly or monthly—throughout the year. Again, there would be a reconciliation at the end of the year.

To facilitate advance estimates, and revisions of estimates, use could be made of local post offices or perhaps social security offices to supplement internal revenue offices. However, the whole program would be administered by the Internal Revenue Service as part and parcel of its administration of the regular personal income tax.

In effect, the addition of the negative income tax would require everyone to file an income tax return. This universal filing requirement would have the incidental advantage that it would improve the administration of the positive income tax, making it easier to check evasion of the tax.[3]

There are many other details that would have to be worked out in an operating negative income tax—definition of the family unit, treatment of items like charitable receipts and welfare payments in computing negative taxable income, and so on. All these are problems that now arise under the positive tax. The general rule should be to follow precisely the same rules in computing negative as in computing positive taxable incomes. There appear to be no special problems peculiar to the negative income tax.[4]

ADVANTAGES OF THE NEGATIVE INCOME TAX

The negative income tax would guarantee a minimum income while at the same time avoiding most of the defects of present welfare programs.

1. *It concentrates public funds on the poor.* By comparison with the host of present programs, the negative income tax has the great virtue that it would concentrate public funds on supplementing the incomes of the poor—not distribute funds broadside in the hope that some will trickle down to the poor. It would help people because they are poor, not because they are old or disabled or unemployed or farmers or tenants of public housing. No doubt, these characteristics are often associated with poverty, but the association is very far from perfect.

2. *It treats indigent as responsible individuals, not incompetent wards of the state.* By giving help in the form of money by the objective impersonal criterion of income, the negative income tax would give the indigent responsibility for their own welfare, and thereby promote the development of habits of independence and self-reliance.

3. *It gives indigent an incentive to help themselves.* Present direct assistance programs in effect embody a 100 percent tax rate on additional income of people receiving assistance: for every dollar earned, their assistance payments are reduced by one dollar. There has come to be wide recognition of the serious disincentive effects of this arrangement and numerous suggestions have been made to avoid this effect. For example, New York City is experimenting with a program whereby welfare recipients will be permitted to keep a flat amount of outside earnings plus a fraction of earnings above that flat amount without reducing their welfare benefits. All such proposals linked to present direct assistance programs have a fatal defect: two individuals holding the same job at the same salary may have different total incomes because one was on welfare before getting the job, while the other was employed throughout. The first will be getting welfare payments to add to his income; the second will not. This is highly inequitable and is likely to be productive of much justifiable objection on the part of low income people who have managed to support themselves.

The negative income tax with a fractional rate is the only way so far proposed that treats all equally while at the same time maintaining an incentive for the indigent to help themselves by small and gradual steps. At the 50 percent rate used for illustration, recipients of aid would keep 50 cents out of every additional dollar earned. This is less of an incentive, of course, than if they could keep the whole dollar, but far more of an incentive than exists at present when they can keep nothing. For incentive purposes, it would be desirable to have as low a rate as possible, but this objective has to be balanced against the need to provide a tolerable level of income maintenance. Under present income tax exemptions, any rate very much lower than 50 percent would cut negative income tax payments to so low a level that they would not provide a major alternative to present assistance programs.[5]

4. *It would cost less than present programs yet help indigent more.* Because the negative income tax is directed specifically at poverty, it would both help the indigent more and yet cost far less than our present collection of programs. We are now spending over $50 billion a year on all welfare programs of which some $7 to $8 billion is going for public assistance (direct relief, aid to dependent children, old age assistance, aid to the blind, and to the permanently and totally disabled). The gross cost of the 50 percent plan outlined above would be somewhat greater than the amount we are now spending on direct assistance programs but only about a fifth of the total amount that we are now spending on all welfare programs.[6] Clearly, the elimination of public assistance plus only a modest reduction in other programs would be enough to finance that particular negative income tax with no net cost. Yet that plan would make most of the needy better off than they are under present programs.

Moreover, these figures greatly overestimate the net cost. They make no allowance for the effect of the greater incentive to earn income on either the number of the needy or the amount of income subject to positive tax. And they make no allowance for the increased receipts under the positive income tax from the reduction of evasion as a result of universal filing of tax returns.

5. *It eliminates bureaucracy and political slush fund.* The negative income tax would enable us to eliminate almost entirely the cumbrous and expensive welfare bureaucracy that is required for present programs. The worthy people who now staff that bureaucracy could devote their talents to more useful activity. The possibility of using the bureaucracy for political patronage would be eliminated. A related advantage is that the negative income tax cannot be used as a political slush fund, as so many current programs—notably in the war on poverty—can be and have been used.

OBJECTIONS TO THE NEGATIVE INCOME TAX

A number of objections have been raised to the negative income tax—by both the Left and the Right. Most of these seem to me to arise either from misunderstanding or utopianism.

1. *The negative income tax removes a means test.* One frequent objection is that, by making the receipt of payments a matter of right, the negative income tax eliminates any means test and introduces a new principle in the relation between citizens and the government.

This is simply a misunderstanding. The negative income tax retains a means test, but the test is the single straightforward numerical test of income not the present complex test. It uses the same means test for deciding who shall receive assistance as we now use to decide who shall pay the expenses of government.

Similarly, the negative income tax introduces no new principle. As noted at the outset, we now have in fact, though not always in law, a governmentally guaranteed minimum.

2. *The negative income tax destroys incentive.* Some proponents of a guaranteed annual income have proposed in effect a negative income tax at a rate of 100 percent. They have proposed that the government fill the gap between some specified income level and the actual income of each family, thereby making the break-even income and the minimum guaranteed income identical. Such plans would indeed destroy incentive. They retain the worst feature of the present direct assistance program but would be far more costly because they eliminate the features of present programs that discourage applicants for welfare. I regard such plans as thoroughly irresponsible, undesirable, and impractical.

Though superficially similar to a negative income tax, such a plan is in fact radically different—just as a positive income tax levied at a 100 percent rate differs radically from one levied at a fractional rate.

A negative income tax at a fractional rate, as already stressed, gives greater incentives to earn income than our present programs, which mostly have an implicit 100 percent rate. Compared with a hypothetical world in which there are no government welfare programs at all, the negative income tax, even at a fractional rate, would indeed weaken incentive. But, whether desirable or not, that is not our world and there is not the remotest chance that it will be in the foreseeable future. Those, like myself, who would like to see the role of government reduced, only harm our own cause by evaluating a program by such an unreal standard.

3. *The negative income tax cannot be adjusted to the specific needs of each indigent family.* This is of course entirely true. The question is whether it is an objection. A federal negative income tax is being proposed as a general nationwide program to set a floor under the incomes of the disadvantaged. But conditions differ widely from state to state and even within states. Prices vary, so that it requires different sums of money to purchase the same level of living. Average income varies, so does the level of living that is regarded as a poverty level, and so also the economic capacity of the communities to assist the less fortunate. These variations are reflected now in the wide differences among states in the levels of assistance given under present programs—differences that seem to me much too wide. The negative income tax with a 50 percent rate would establish a nationwide minimum standard well above the level now achieved in many, probably most, states. It would be well below the level now achieved in some of the wealthier states.

However, it is designed to provide a nationwide program. There is nothing to prevent states from supplementing the benefits paid under the negative income tax out of state funds, and there is every reason to encourage them to do so. The best way for them to do so, I believe, would be to enact a supplementary state negative income tax, just as they now have supplementary state positive income taxes. They could have different exemptions and different rates but they could, as many now do under the positive income tax, coordinate state enforcement with federal enforcement.

Undoubtedly, there would also be special problems within each city or state. Being general and impersonal, the negative income tax cannot be adapted to cases of special hardship, and no doubt such cases would exist. However, by providing a basic minimum, it would reduce such cases to a manageable number, which could be taken care of by supplementary state programs or, preferably, by private charity. One of the great costs of the proliferation of governmental welfare programs is the elimination of a basic role for private charity, with its flexibility, diversity, and adaptability. An indirect advantage of the negative income tax is that it would provide an important place for private charity to serve precisely that function which private agencies can serve best—handling the special case.

4. *The negative income tax would be divisive.* The objection has sometimes been made that, by dividing the community into those who receive checks from the government and those who send checks, the negative income tax would fragment the community. Clearly, this objection has no force at all if the negative income tax is compared with present programs. They are far worse in this respect. However, the objection is raised mostly by proponents of family allowances.[7] They argue that giving a straight cash subsidy to parents of all children in proportion to the number of children would unify the community by comparison with a negative income tax. Yet, they say, the economic effect would be similar, since, if the family allowance is included in taxable income, much of it would be recovered from higher income families in the form of additional taxes.

A negative income tax is partly a family allowance, since large families have higher exemptions under the income tax than small families and so would receive larger benefits for any given family income. However, it gives a family allowance only to families defined as needy, not to all families.

In principle, there always exists a universal subsidy (sometimes called a "social dividend") plus a tax system that would produce identically the same results as a negative income tax. For example, consider the illustrative 50 percent negative income tax plan. The equivalent universal subsidy (or family allowance plan) would be a subsidy to each family equal to the break-even income under that plan, inclusion of the subsidy in taxable income, elimination of the present minimum exemptions and deductions under the income tax, and a tax rate of 50 percent on an initial bracket equal to the break-even income. Each and every family would be in the same position as under the negative income tax plan when the extra tax is deducted from the subsidy.[8]

The problem in practice is that this system involves mailing out checks to 200 million people in order to help 20 or 40 million, and then having the 160 or 180 million others mail back checks. This is highly inefficient. Equally important, it is complex and confusing politically. It is not clear what is being done. Both administratively and politically, it seems to me far better to net out the payments and extra taxes.

The apparent budgetary cost of even small children's allowances is extremely high because checks are being sent to ten families in order really to help one or two. The reverse flow through higher taxes is disguised and uncertain. Hence, any children's or family allowance is likely to be so small as not to permit the elimination of any substantial part of the present welfare programs. The end result would be to add another rag to the bag while retaining the present highly divisive welfare programs. Universal family allowances therefore seem to me undesirable.

5. *The negative income tax would be another rag in the bag.* I have urged the negative income tax as a substitute for existing programs. But, it is said, in practice the negative income tax would simply be piled on other programs and not be a substitute for them, so that the argument I have just made against family allowances applies equally to the negative income tax.

This objection clearly cannot be dismissed out of hand and is, indeed, in my opinion, the most weighty of those I have listed. There is a tendency in government for old programs never to die, or even to fade away, but simply to be continued, whatever their success in meeting the problem for which they were enacted. If they are failures, the only effect is that still more programs are enacted.

One not very satisfactory answer to this objection is that it is a counsel of despair. If those of us who regard governmental programs in any area as bad do not fight for better programs as a substitute, but simply engage in delaying actions, then the objection is certain to be valid. That course of action makes it a self-fulfilling prophecy.

In the present instance, as it happens, I believe there is a more satisfactory answer to the objection than this general answer. While the negative income tax is unlikely to be adopted as a substitute for *all* welfare programs—as I should prefer—it does seem to me highly likely to be accepted as a substitute for the direct public assistance programs. There are two reasons why this seems to me so. The first is that the defects of those programs—particularly direct relief and aid to dependent children—are so great, so glaring, and so widely recognized, that there is a desire in every part of the political spectrum to find a substitute for them. The second is that the usual bastion of an existing program—the pressure group formed by the bureaucracy administering it and by the people who can use it for patronage—is less potent in this instance than usual. It is less potent because the mass of jobs are so unattractive that it is hard to fill them. The turnover is high and there are few patronage plums.

Despite these favorable conditions, the negative income tax may not be introduced as a complete substitute for the direct public assistance programs. But even then, it is likely to be used as a partial substitute and it is almost certain to be a substitute for other additions to the program. The political reality may be that the programs will be expanded in one way or another. If so, far better that it be in this way.

Finally, we must look to the future. Whatever may be the original intent, I believe that a negative income tax will be so much more effective than current programs that, in the course of time, it would increasingly replace them, in the process diminishing the problem toward which all of the programs are directed.

6. *The negative income tax will foster political irresponsibility.* If we adopt an open and aboveboard program for supplementing the incomes of people below some specified level, will there not be continued political pressure for higher and higher break-even incomes, for higher and higher rates on negative income? Will the demagogues not have a field day appealing to the have-nots to legislate taxes on the haves for transfer to them?

Clearly these dangers exist. But, like the incentive question, they must be evaluated in terms of the world as it is, not in terms of a dream world in which there are no governmental welfare measures. The relevant political question is whether the negative income tax is more susceptible to these dangers than alternative programs of the kind we now have or are likely to get.

When I first proposed in print the negative income tax, I wrote that it might well be more susceptible to these dangers than other programs.[9] As I have thought further about the subject, and have participated in the public discussion of the proposal, I have been led to change this opinion. I now believe that there are strong reasons to believe that the negative income tax is less susceptible than other proposals to the political dangers.

Because the negative income tax is intimately linked with the general income tax structure, there is no way to raise the break-even incomes without raising the exemption for tax purposes, which clearly requires a higher rate on incomes above the exemption. The cost of the payments is in one lump sum that can be calculated and that will be painfully obvious to every taxpayer. It will be obvious that every rise in the rate applied to negative taxable income raises the cost. Finally, the negative income tax does not, as do other welfare programs, generate a large bureaucracy that has an interest in expanding the program and it cannot be used as a political slush fund.

Conclusion

The problem we face in the welfare area is to halt the proliferation of the bad programs we now have and ultimately to dismantle them. But while these programs are on the whole bad, more or less incidentally they do help some people who are disadvantaged. Can we in good conscience mount a political attack on them unless we can provide an alternative way to achieve the small amount of help they do provide the disadvantaged? Can we be effective, unless we have a satisfactory answer to the inevitable charge that we are heartless and want to let the poor starve? And would we not be guilty of the charge, if we had no alternative? Most of these programs should never have been enacted. But they have been enacted and they now must be dismantled gradually, both to promote social stability and because the government has a responsibility to meet commitments it has entered into.

The negative income tax offers a way to replace the existing programs gradually. As a proposal, it offers a platform from which an effective political attack can be launched on existing undesirable programs. Once in operation, it would assure assistance to the needy now getting help under present programs, and so make it feasible to repeal them or permit them to wither away as current commitments are met. Once in operation, too, it would remove the specious excuse now offered for every suggested expansion of the federal authority—that it is "needed" to help one or another disadvantaged group.

These are the negative advantages, as it were, of the negative income tax. The positive case for it is no less strong. "It is directed specifically at the problem of poverty. It gives help in the form most useful to the individual, namely, cash. It is general and could be substituted for the host of special measures now in effect. It makes explicit the cost borne by society. It operates outside the market. Like any other measure to alleviate poverty, it reduces the incentives of those helped to help themselves, but it does not eliminate the incentive entirely, as a system of supplementing incomes up to some fixed minimum would,"[10] and it reduces incentives less than other measures that are now in operation or that have been suggested. Finally, it treats all members of the community alike, with a single impersonal means test for all, the same for those who in a particular year pay taxes and for those who in that year receive benefits.

Notes

1. Note that under present laws, negative taxable income could be more than $3,000, since a taxpayer who uses actual rather than standard deductions could have

exemptions plus deductions of more than $3,000. This is a point that deserves much more attention than it has received. On the one hand, it offers the possibility of introducing a desirable flexibility into the program. For example, it would offer a far better way than medicare or socialized medicine to finance by tax funds abnormal medical costs: simply permit such costs to continue, as now, to be a deduction in computing income. On the other hand, this point gives still more importance to undesirable deductions and exclusions under the present income tax. Such deductions and exclusions mean that a family with high income from tax-exempt sources or with large deductions could not only avoid tax as it now does but could also qualify for subsidies.

2. With a 50 percent rate on negative taxable income, and present law with respect to exemptions and standard deductions, these are as shown in Table 6.2.

TABLE 6.2

Family size	Guaranteed minimum income	Break-even income
1	$ 450	$ 900
2	800	1,600
3	1,150	2,300
4	1,500	3,000
5	1,850	3,700
6	2,200	4,400

3. It is interesting to note that in the 1930s, when Pierre S. du Pont was tax commissioner of the State of Delaware and was subsidizing the office out of his own pocket, he introduced universal filing solely for the purpose of reducing evasion of the state income tax.

4. Many of these problems are discussed in detail in Christopher Green, *Negative Taxes and the Poverty Problem* (The Brookings Institution, 1967).

5. I would prefer much higher exemptions and a lower rate, but that would require major reform of the positive income tax. Though desirable in its own right, that is a separate issue.

6. Christopher Green estimated for 1964 that the cost of the 50 percent plan would be $7 to $9 billion (if public assistance payments are excluded from the income base used in calculating taxable income), compared with public assistance payments in that year of $5.1 billion. Op. cit.

7. It was brought to my attention by Daniel P. Moynihan in oral comments at a recent conference on problems of social welfare.

8. To illustrate, a family of four with no other income would receive $3,000 as a social dividend, giving it a taxable income of $3,000 subject to a tax rate of 50 percent. Its tax would be $1,500, leaving it with an after-tax income of $1,500, just as under the illustrative negative income tax.

9. See Milton Friedman, *Capitalism and Freedom* (Chicago: University of Chicago Press, 1962), p. 192.

10. Quoted from Friedman, *Capitalism and Freedom*, p. 192.

AN ALL-VOLUNTEER ARMY

· 7 ·

The present legal authority for conscripting men into the armed services expires June 30. It is no accident that it expires in an odd-numbered year. That was deliberately contrived to make sure that renewal of the draft would come up when neither congressional nor presidential elections were pending. Hitherto this stratagem has worked like a charm—the draft was renewed in 1955, 1959, and 1963 with hardly a ripple of public concern or opposition and with only perfunctory congressional hearings.

This year the committees with primary responsibility—the armed services committees headed in the Senate by Senator Richard Russell and in the House by Representative Mendel Rivers—have been, as always, holding hearings, but this time their hearings have been more than a pro forma endorsement of General Lewis B. Hershey and the Selective Service System. President Johnson has suggested major changes in the operation of the draft—that we take the youngest men first, cut student deferments, and introduce a lottery selection system. But everyone seems to want to get in on the draft act.

Senator Edward Kennedy has chaired a labor and public welfare subcommittee that has held hearings on the effect of the draft on manpower problems. The Joint Economic Committee, headed by Senator William Proxmire, has touched on the same subject in its hearings on the effect of Vietnam on the

The New York Times Magazine, May 14, 1967. ©1967 by The New York Times Company. Reprinted by permission.

economy. Senator Mark O. Hatfield has introduced a bill that provides for the early transition to a fully voluntary system of manning the armed forces. Representatives Donald Rumsfeld and Thomas Curtis have introduced a bill calling for a congressional study of the feasibility of terminating the draft soon. A Council for a Volunteer Military, sponsored by individuals covering the political spectrum from right to left, has just been formed. And so on and on.

The passions engendered by Vietnam clearly explain why the renewal of the draft is not a routine matter in this odd year of 1967. But the interesting thing is that a man's position about the draft cannot be inferred from his position about the war. Both men who favor stronger military action and men who favor a bombing pause in the North or even complete withdrawal have come out in favor of terminating the draft and relying on volunteers to man the armed forces. In the past several months Barry Goldwater has devoted three of the columns he writes to urging that conscription be ended and that it be ended now. Norman Thomas and James Farmer have both taken the same position. John Kenneth Galbraith, new head of Americans for Democratic Action, has long been an articulate and effective opponent of the draft. Fortunately, belief in personal freedom is a monopoly of neither Republicans nor Democrats, of neither conservatives nor liberals.

There is by now wide agreement that the present system of conscription is defective and must be changed—even General Hershey has given in. Highly placed voices—including those of Sargent Shriver and Willard Wirtz; more ambiguously, Robert McNamara and, most surprisingly, anthropologist Margaret Mead—have urged a system of universal national service, in which all young men (and, if Miss Mead has her way, all young women as well) would be conscripted and assigned to a variety of tasks, one being to serve in the military.

There is far less recognition that while the president's proposals would improve the operation of conscription, *no system relying on compulsion can remove the basic defects of the present draft.* In current circumstances only a minority of young men are needed to man the armed forces. Short of letting men decide for themselves, there is no equitable way of determining which young man should serve and which two or three should not. Short of making the armed forces offer conditions that attract the men it needs, there is no way of avoiding waste and misuse of men in the armed forces, or the use of men in the military who would contribute far more in civilian activities.

And, of course, any system involving compulsion is basically inconsistent with a free society. A lottery would only make the arbitrary element in the present system overt. Universal national service would compound the evil— regimenting all youth to camouflage the regimentation of some.

The continued use of compulsion is undesirable and unnecessary. We can and should man our armed forces with volunteers. This is the method the United States has traditionally used except in major wars. The past two decades are the only exception. It is time that we brought that exception to an end.

THE ADVANTAGES OF A VOLUNTARY ARMY

Even in strictly military terms, a voluntary force would be more effective. It would be manned by people who had chosen a military career, rather than partly by reluctant conscripts anxious only to serve out their term. It would have much lower turnover, freeing men for military service who are now spending their time training others or being trained. Intensive training, a higher average level of skill, the use of more and better equipment would permit military strength to be raised while the number of men in the services was reduced. Not least of the advantages of a volunteer force is its effect on morale. Military service is now demeaned, treated as a necessary but degrading duty that men have to be dragooned into performing. A voluntary army would restore a proper sense of pride, of respect for the important, dangerous and difficult task that the armed forces perform.

The elimination of compulsion would enhance the freedom of all of us. The young would be free to decide whether to serve or not to serve. Members of draft boards would be relieved of the awful task of arbitrarily deciding how a young man shall spend several of the most important years of his life—let alone whether his life shall be risked in warfare. The tormenting and insoluble problem now posed by the conscientious objector would disappear. We could immediately dispense with investigating the innermost values and beliefs of those who claim to be conscientious objectors—a process entirely repugnant to a society of free men.

Conscription has been used as a weapon—or thought by young men to have been so used—to discourage freedom of speech, assembly, and protest. The freedom of young men to emigrate or to travel abroad has been limited by the need to get the permission of a draft board (if they are not to put themselves inadvertently in the position of being a lawbreaker). Uncertainty about the draft has affected the freedom of young men to plan their schooling, their careers, their marriages, and their families in accordance with their own long-run interests.

Manning the armed forces with volunteers would have other real advantages for the country at large. Colleges and universities could pursue their proper educational function, freed alike from the incubus of young men—probably numbering in the hundreds of thousands—who would prefer to be at work rather than at school, but who now continue their schooling in the hope of avoiding the draft; and from controversy about issues strictly irrelevant to their educational function. We certainly need controversy in the universities—but about intellectual and educational issues, not whether to rank students or not to rank.

The community would benefit from a reduction in unwise early marriages contracted at least partly under the whip of the draft, as well as from the associated decline in the birth rate. Industry and government would benefit from being able to hire young men on their merits, not their deferments. Not least, the level and tone of public discussion might be raised—though this is perhaps simply an expression of my innate optimism.

Some of these advantages would also result from substituting a lottery for present methods of selection—but only in part, and only for those who are clearly selected out.

Is a Voluntary Army Feasible?

Is it not simply wishful thinking to suppose that we can abandon conscription when a hot war is raging in Vietnam, when we must maintain armed forces exceeding 3 million men in total? Men are now free to volunteer, yet the number who do so is clearly inadequate and, moreover, many volunteer only because they expect to be drafted. The number of "true" volunteers is clearly much too small to man armed forces of our present size. This undoubted fact is repeatedly cited as evidence that a voluntary army is unfeasible.

It is evidence of no such thing. It is evidence rather that we are now grossly underpaying our armed forces. The starting pay for young men who enter the armed forces is less than $45 a week—and that sum includes not only cash pay and allotments, but also the value of clothing, food, housing, and other items furnished in kind. The starting pay is virtually the same now as in 1950—but prices are higher, so in terms of goods and services the man who enlists gets considerably less now than he did then. All of the pay raises since then have gone to officers and to enlisted men with longer terms of service. They have to be induced to stay in service. Fresh recruits can be conscripted—so why raise the pay?

Little wonder that volunteers are so few. Most young men can earn twice as much in civilian jobs.

To attract more volunteers, we would have to improve conditions of service. This means higher entering salaries. But it also means better housing facilities and improved amenities in other respects. The existence of conscription means that the military need pay little attention to the wants of the enlisted men—if not enough volunteer, press the button and General Hershey will raise draft calls. Indeed, it is a tribute to the humanitarianism of the military—and the effectiveness of indirect pressures via the political process—

that service in the armed forces is not made even less attractive than it now is. But ask any ex-GI how attractive that is.

Money is not the only, or even the major, factor young men consider in choosing their careers. Military service has many nonmonetary attractions to young men—the chance to serve one's country, adventure, travel, opportunities for training, and so on. Today these attractions are offset not only by low pay but also by the very existence of compulsion. Military service is now synonymous with enforced incarceration. And the presence of young men who are in the armed forces only because they are forced to serve hardly contributes to a spirit of pride within the service.

Improved pay, better conditions of service, and imaginative personnel policies, both in attracting men and using them, could change drastically the whole image which the armed services present to young men. The Air Force, because it has relied so heavily on "real" volunteers, perhaps comes closest to demonstrating what could be done.

The coming of age of the young men born in the postwar baby boom has provided a steadily increasing number of persons eligible for military service. The best estimates are that, to man voluntary armed services of our present effectiveness, only about one-quarter or less of all young men would have to see some military service. This percentage is much lower than the corresponding percentage at the time of Korea, when low birth rates of the depression years were making themselves felt. It is also much lower than the percentage who must see service under conscription, because volunteers serve longer terms on the average.

A recent poll of college students—brought to my attention by Senator Edward Kennedy when I was testifying before his committee earlier this spring—showed a large majority who favored a voluntary army, but an even larger majority who said they would not themselves volunteer. Is this not, the Senator in effect asked, evidence that a volunteer army is not feasible?

The answer is no. The young men are answering in terms of conditions as they now are. And, of course, at present terms and conditions, their answer is correct—and who can blame them? They do not know how they would behave if conditions were different, if service in the armed forces were made much more attractive.

The question of how much more we would have to pay to attract sufficient volunteers has been scrutinized intensively in a Department of Defense study of military recruitment. Based on a variety of evidence collected in that study, Professor Walter Oi of the University of Washington, who worked on the study, has estimated that a starting pay (again including pay in kind as well as in cash) of something like $4,000 a year—about $80 a week—would suffice. This is surely not an unreasonable level of pay. Oi estimates that the total extra payroll costs (after allowing for the savings in turnover and men employed in training) would be about $3 billion to $4 billion a year for armed forces equivalent to 2.7 million men under present methods of recruitment, and not more than $8 billion a year for armed forces equivalent to the present higher number of men (3.1 to 3.2 million).

Using the same evidence, the Defense Department has come up with estimates as high as $17.5 billion. This is an incredible figure—it would mean that the pay of every man in the armed service from the newly enlisted man to the top general could be *raised* by $6,000 a year. But even that absurd estimate is not unfeasible in the context of total federal government expenditures of more than $170 billion a year, and military expenditures of over $70 billion.

In any event, we do not need precise estimates of what it will take to attract enough men. Out of simple justice, we should raise the pay and improve the living conditions of enlisted men. If we did so, the number of "real" volunteers would increase, even while conscription continued. Experience could then show how responsive volunteers are to the terms offered, and by how much the terms would have to be improved to end conscription.

A Volunteer Army Would Cost Less

The need to raise pay to attract volunteers leads many to believe that a volunteer army would cost more. The fact is that it would cost less to man the armed forces by volunteers than it now costs to man them by compulsion—*if cost is properly calculated*. The cost listed in the federal budget might be higher—though even that is not certain. But the real cost to the community would be far lower.

The real cost of conscripting a soldier who would not voluntarily serve on present terms is not his pay and the cost of his keep. It is the amount of money for which he would be willing to serve. Compare, for example, the real cost to a star professional football player and to an unemployed worker. Both might have the same attitudes toward the army and like—or dislike—a military career equally. But because the one has so much better alternatives than the other, it would take a much higher sum to attract him. When he is forced to serve, we are in effect imposing on him a tax in kind equal in value to the difference between what it would take to attract him and the military pay he actually receives. This implicit tax in kind must be added to the explicit taxes imposed on the rest of us to get the real cost of our armed forces.

If this is done, it will be seen at once that abandoning conscription would almost surely reduce the real cost—because the armed forces would then be manned by men for whom soldiering was the best available career, and hence who would require the lowest sums of money to induce them to serve. It might raise the apparent money cost to the government but only because it would substitute taxes in money for taxes in kind.

The implicit tax in kind is not a light one. If it were proposed that we impose a special income tax of 50 percent on enlisted men in the armed services, there would be cries of outrage. Yet that is what we are now doing in concealed form. Abolishing conscription would have the great merit of imposing those taxes on the rest of us, where they belong, not on the young men in uniform.

There are some important offsets even on the level of budgetary costs. Volunteers would serve longer terms, a higher fraction would re-enlist, and they would have a higher average level of skill. The armed services would waste fewer manhours in training and being trained. Because manpower is cheap to the military, it now tends to waste it, using enlisted men for tasks badly suited to their capacities or for tasks that could be performed by civilians or machines, or eliminated entirely. Again, ask any ex-GI for evidence.

Better pay at the time to volunteers also might lessen the political appeal of veterans' benefits that we now grant after the event. These now cost $6 billion a year or one-third as much as current annual payroll costs for the active armed forces—and they will doubtless continue to rise under present conditions.

THE RACIAL COMPOSITION OF VOLUNTEER FORCES

One objection that has been voiced against volunteer forces is that they would be staffed predominantly by Negroes because a military career would be so much more attractive than the other alternatives open to them.

There is first a question of fact. This tendency is present today in exaggerated form—the present levels of pay are *comparatively* more attractive to Negroes than the higher levels of pay for voluntary forces would be. And this shows up in a much higher rate of re-enlistment by Negroes than by whites. Yet the fraction of persons in the armed forces who are Negro is roughly the same as in the population at large. It has been estimated that even if every qualified Negro who does not now serve were to serve, whites would still constitute a substantial majority of the armed forces. And this is a wholly unrealistic possibility. The military services require a wide variety of skills and offer varied opportunities. They have always appealed to people of different classes and backgrounds and they will continue to do so. Particularly if pay and amenities were made more attractive, there is every reason to expect that they would draw from all segments of the community.

The Negroes in the forces tend to have lower skills than the whites. As a result, they constitute a larger fraction of the combat units than of the armed forces in general. The fraction of the men in combat in Vietnam who are Negro is decidedly higher than their proportion in the population. Yet even there, they are a small minority of the fighting men. More important, most of them are there by choice: because they voluntarily chose to enlist or re-enlist.

This raises the basic question of principle. Clearly, it is a good thing not a bad thing to offer better alternatives to the currently disadvantaged. The argument to the contrary rests on a political judgment: that a high ratio of Negroes in the armed services would exacerbate racial tensions at home and provide in the form of ex-soldiers a militarily trained group to foment violence. Perhaps there is something to this. My own inclination is to regard it as the reddest of red herrings. Our government should discriminate neither in the civil nor in the military services. We must handle our domestic problems as best we can and not use them as an excuse for denying Negroes opportunities in the military service. We should be proud of the armed forces for the fine job they have done in providing opportunities to the disadvantaged—not discriminate against the Negroes in manning the armed forces because we have done so much less well in civilian life.

The Flexibility of Voluntary Forces

Another argument that has been made against voluntary forces is that they lack flexibility—and that world conditions may change and call for larger or smaller armed forces. With conscription, draft calls can be rapidly stepped up, and conversely.

This is a real problem—but can easily be overrated. Emergencies must be met with forces in being, however they are recruited. Many months now elapse between an increase in draft calls, and the availability of additional trained men.

The key question is how much flexibility is required. Recruitment by voluntary means can provide considerable flexibility—at a cost. The way to do so is to make pay and conditions of service more attractive than necessary. There will then be an excess of volunteers—queues. If the number of men required increases, the queues can be shortened, and conversely.

The change in scale involved in total war is a very different matter. If the military judgment is that, in such a contingency, there would be time and reason to expand the armed forces manifold, either universal military training to provide a trained reserve force, or standby provisions for conscription could be justified. Both are very different from the use of conscription to man the standing army in time of peace or brush-fire wars like that in Vietnam which require recruiting only a minority of young men.

The flexibility provided by conscription has another side. It means that, at least for a time, the administration and the military services can proceed fairly arbitrarily in committing U.S. forces. The voluntary method provides a continuing referendum of the public at large. The popularity or unpopularity of the activities for which the armed forces are used will clearly affect the ease of recruiting men. This is a consideration that will be regarded by some, including myself, as an advantage of the voluntary method, by others as a disadvantage.

ARE VOLUNTARY FORCES A POLITICAL DANGER?

A final objection that has been raised against a volunteer army is that it would endanger political freedom. There is a real danger, but it arises from the existence of large armed forces plus the industrial complex required to support them, not from the method of recruiting enlisted men. Our free institutions would certainly be safer if the conditions of the world permitted us to maintain smaller armed forces. But they are not made safer by using compulsion rather than free choice to fill the ranks.

The military coup just engineered in Greece was by an army manned by conscripts. So was the recent military takeover in Argentina. Napoleon and Franco rose to power at the head of conscripts. Britain and the United States have maintained freedom while relying primarily on volunteers; Switzerland and Sweden, while using conscription. It is hard to find any relation historically between the method of recruiting enlisted men and the political threat from the armed forces.

The danger to liberty comes from the officers, who are now and always have been a professional corps of volunteers. However we recruit enlisted men, it is essential that we adopt practices that will guard against the political danger of creating a military officers corps with loyalties of its own and out of contact with the broader body politic. Fortunately, we have so far largely avoided this danger. The broad basis of recruitment to the military academies, by geography as well as social and economic factors, the ROTC programs in the colleges, the recruitment of officers from enlisted ranks, and similar measures, have all contributed to this result.

For the future, we need to continue such a broad recruitment policy. We need also to foster lateral recruitment into the officers corps from civilian activities—rather than rely primarily on promotion from within. The military services no less than the civil service need and will benefit from in-and-outers. For the political gain, we should willingly pay the higher financial costs involved in fairly high turnover and rather short average terms of service for officers. We should follow personnel policies that will continue to make at least a period of military service as an officer attractive to young men from many walks of life.

There is no way of avoiding the political danger altogether. But it can be minimized as readily with a volunteer as with a conscripted army.

CONCLUSION

The case for abolishing conscription and recruiting our armed forces by voluntary methods seems to me overwhelming.

We should at once raise the pay of enlisted men, improve conditions of service, and stimulate more efficient use of manpower by the services. We should continue to raise the pay until the number of "true" volunteers is large enough so that the lash of compulsion can be eliminated. And to avoid procrastination by the military, who will be tempted to continue to rely on the crutch of conscription, we should set a definite termination date for conscription.

Foreign Economic Aid: Means and Objectives

· 8 ·

Foreign economic aid is widely regarded as a weapon in the ideological war in which the United States is now involved. Its assigned role is to help win over to our side those uncommitted nations that are also underdeveloped and poor. According to this view, these nations are determined to develop economically. They will seek to do so, with or without our help. If we do not help them, they will turn to Russia. It is, therefore, in our own interest to help them to achieve their aims. And the way to help them is to make capital and technical assistance available largely free of charge, the cost to be borne by the United States and, we hope, those of its allies who are in a comparable stage of development.

    This argument confuses two very different issues. One is the *objectives* toward which United States policy should be directed. The other is the *means* that are appropriate for the achievement of those objectives. I share fully the views of the proponents of foreign economic aid about objectives. It is clearly in our national interest that the underdeveloped nations choose the democratic rather than the totalitarian way of life. It is clearly in our national interest that they satisfy their aspirations for economic development as fully as possible in a democratic framework. And our national interest coincides with our humanitarian ideals: our fundamental objective is a world in which free men can peaceably use their capacities, abilities, and resources as effectively as

From *The Yale Review* 47 (Summer 1958). ©Yale University. Reprinted with permission.

possible to satisfy their aspirations. We cannot long hope to maintain a free island in a totalitarian world.

But this agreement about objectives does not settle the question of means. Is foreign economic aid as it has been administered, or as it is proposed that it should be administered, well adapted to secure these great objectives? This question is begged in most current discussion. Once the objectives are stated, it is generally simply taken for granted that foreign economic aid is an appropriate means, if not indeed the only appropriate means, to achieve these objectives. This conclusion seems to me fundamentally mistaken. Though foreign economic aid may win us some temporary allies, in the long run it will almost surely retard economic development and promote the triumph of communism. It is playing into our enemies' hands, and should be abolished. Instead we should concentrate on promoting worldwide economic development through means that are consonant with the American tradition itself—strengthening of free market domestic economies in the less-developed nations, the removal of obstacles to private international trade, and the fostering of a climate favorable to private international investment.

To avoid confusion, it will be well to emphasize at the outset that this article is concerned solely with one particular category of U.S. expenditures on foreign aid—economic aid—and with one class of arguments for such expenditures—their value in promoting the economic development of other countries. To readers of *The Yale Review*, it may supplement Irving Kristol's penetrating analysis of "The Ideology of Economic Aid" in the Summer 1957 issue, which deals with some of the other issues connected with economic aid as well as some of the ambiguities and complexities in the general objectives I have simply taken for granted.

The sum listed in the federal budget as spent for economic aid is only a small part of the total recorded expenditures for foreign aid. In the fiscal year ending June 30, 1957, total expenditures for foreign aid were nearly four billion dollars. Of this total, nearly two and a half billion dollars was for so-called military aid—primarily the transfer of military equipment to various U.S. allies. Another billion went for so-called defense support—expenditures in or payments to other countries (notably South Korea, Nationalist China, and South Vietnam) to finance activities that are regarded as contributing to their military effort. In addition, the president is empowered to make payments to certain countries, principally in the Middle East, the purpose of which is to induce the recipient countries to support particular policies that are thought to be in our interest—these are, in essence, straight military or political subsidies. Finally, about half a billion dollars went for so-called economic aid which includes both technical assistance (Point IV help) and funds for the economic development of recipient countries to which no direct military or political strings are attached.

At first glance, one may wonder why this relatively small budget category stirs up so much controversy. Part of the answer is that the figures cited are somewhat misleading. The generally more favorable attitude of Congress toward direct and indirect military aid understandably leads the administration to classify as much as possible under these two headings. In addition, what in form is straight military aid may in effect be equivalent to economic aid, and it is often difficult to distinguish between the two. If country A would in any event have devoted a given sum to the purchase of military equipment and the United States pays for it instead, the country has available that sum for other purposes; the effect may be precisely the same as if the corresponding sum had been granted country A in straight economic aid. But more than this: it is on the enlargement of economic aid that advocates of greater public spending have concentrated their attention. In article and speech, enlargement has been pressed by such men as Chester Bowles, Paul Hoffman, Walter Reuther, and Adlai Stevenson. In their recent book *A Proposal*, Professors Millikan and Rostow of the Massachusetts Institute of Technology have urged that the United States should commit itself over a five-year period to put up some ten billion dollars for world economic development. And there is powerful support in the United Nations for setting up a special fund, SUNFED, for this purpose. In short, economic aid is neither so small nor so unimportant as current budgeted expenditures on it might suggest. On the contrary, it is the storm center of the whole debate about how this country can help other countries develop.

The case for military aid and defense support clearly rests on a very different range of considerations than the case for economic aid. Military aid and defense support are to be attacked or defended in terms of their contribution, first, to our effective military strength and, second, to the achievement of our direct political objectives. I can see no objection to them in principle; any criticism of them, or defense of their expansion, must rest on the severely practical grounds that, dollar for dollar, they yield less, or more, strength than alternative modes of expenditure. The one serious danger of confusion between these categories and economic aid is that the argument for economic aid which this article considers is sometimes used as a rationalization to permit straight military or political subsidies to be made under a different label. We shall be concerned with neither these types of expenditure nor this use of the argument for economic aid.

Economic aid proper raises much broader and certainly very different issues. These issues deserve far more public debate than they are getting. We are on the verge of committing ourselves to a policy which in my view can only have disastrous consequences for our country and our way of life. And we are doing so not after thoughtful and thorough consideration of the issues in-volved, but almost by inadvertence, by proceeding along what seems the line of least resistance.

Two questions must be answered in judging government economic aid. First, is it likely in fact to promote the economic development of the countries to whom aid is granted? Second, do its political effects in those countries promote democracy and freedom?

The second question, though not much discussed, is easy to answer and admits of little dispute. As it has so far been administered, our aid program has consisted predominantly of grants or loans or provision of personnel or mate-rial directly to the governments of recipient countries for specified projects regarded as contributing to economic development. It has thereby tended to strengthen the role of the government sector in general economic activity relative to the private sector. Yet democracy and freedom have never been either attained or maintained except in communities in which the bulk of economic activity is organized through private enterprise.

This problem has of course been recognized and partly explains why some grants or loans have been made to private enterprises in the recipient countries rather than directly to governments. Last year John B. Hollister, on the occasion of his retirement as head of the International Cooperation Adminis-tration, proposed that a much enlarged fraction of total funds be channeled to private enterprises. This modification, which aroused strong opposition and is not likely to be carried far, would reduce the tendency of the aid program to strengthen the government sector. It would, however, not eliminate it. We are hardly likely to make funds available to enterprises in poor standing with their governments or for projects opposed by governments. The final result will therefore be much the same.

Many proponents of foreign aid recognize that its long-run political effects are adverse to freedom and democracy. To some extent, they plead special extenuating circumstances. For example, the group in power in a particular country may for the time being be in a shaky political position, yet its overthrow may mean the assumption of power by antidemocratic forces. And economic aid may help such a government over its temporary political crisis. Their main reply, however, is that economic progress is a prerequisite to freedom and democracy in underdeveloped countries, and that economic aid will contribute to this outcome and thereby on balance promote political freedom. This makes the crucial question, even for political effects, the first, namely, the economic effects of economic aid.

The belief that foreign aid effectively promotes economic development rests in turn on three basic propositions: first, that the key to economic development is the availability of capital; second, that underdeveloped countries are too poor to provide the capital for themselves; third, that centralized and comprehensive economic planning and control by government is an essential requisite for economic development.

All three propositions are at best misleading half-truths. Additional capital is certainly essential for development. And of course the more capital the better, other things being the same. But the way in which capital is provided will affect other things. The pharaohs raised enormous sums of capital to build the pyramids; this was capital formation on a grand scale; it certainly did not promote economic development in the fundamental sense of contributing to a self-sustaining growth in the standard of life of the Egyptian masses. Modern Egypt has under government auspices built a steel mill; this involves capital formation; but it is a drain on the economic resources of Egypt, not a contribution to economic strength, since the cost of making steel in Egypt is very much greater than the cost of buying it elsewhere; it is simply a modern equivalent of the pyramids except that maintenance expenses are higher. Such modern monuments are by no means the exception; they are almost certain to be the rule when funds are made available directly or indirectly to governments that are inevitably under pressure to produce the symbols of modern industrialism. There is hardly an underdeveloped country that does not now waste its substance on the symbol of a government-owned or government-subsidized international airline. And there is hardly one that does not want its own steel mill as yet another potent symbol.

Some monuments are inevitable in the course of economic development and may indeed be politically desirable as tangible and dramatic signs of change. If the appetite for monuments were at once so intense as to make them the first claim on a country's resources and yet so limited and satiable that their extent was independent of the resources available, monument-building might be a costly fact of life but would have little relevance to foreign economic aid. Unfortunately, this is hardly the case. The appetite grows by what it feeds on. The availability of resources at little or no cost to the country in question inevitably stimulates monument-building. Thus while foreign aid grants may in the first instance add to the capital available to a country, they also lead to a notable increase in the amount of capital devoted to economically wasteful projects.

Cannot, it will be asked, these problems be solved by our exercising control over the use of the capital we make available to governments? And would they not be avoided even more directly if we adopted the proposal to make funds available directly to private enterprises? Aside from the political problems raised by any attempt at close control of even the funds we give, the answer is no. In the first place, there is a purely technical difficulty. Our grants are only part of the total capital available to a country and of the funds available to the government. It will do no good to control the use of the one part while exercising no control over the other; the effect would simply be to alter the bookkeeping—whatever we regarded as appropriate projects would be treated as financed with our funds, and the monuments would be built with local funds. Effective control would thus require us to control the whole of the capital investment of the country, a result that is hardly feasible on political grounds. But even if it were, the problem would by no means be solved. We would simply be substituting one central planning group for another. This leads to the third proposition: that central planning by government is essential to economic development.

Before turning to this issue, it will be well to consider the assertion that the underdeveloped countries are too poor to save and provide capital for them-selves. Here, too, the alleged fact is most dubious. Currently developed countries were once underdeveloped. Whence came their capital? The key problem is not one of possibility but of incentive and of proper use. For generations, India was a "sink" for the precious metals, as the writers on money always put it. There was much saving, but it took the unproductive form of accumulation of specie. In Africa, natives on the very margin of subsistence have, given a market demand for their produce, extended greatly the area under cultivation, an activity involving the formation of capital, though seldom entering into recorded figures on savings. Domestic capital can be supplemented by foreign capital if the conditions are right—which means if property is secure against both private and public seizure. Many low income countries cannot of course attract foreign capital; in most of these, in fact, locally owned capital is invested abroad, and for the same reason—because there is not an environment favorable to private property and free enterprise. And in this respect, too, government-to-government grants are likely to be adverse to economic development. They strengthen the government sector at the expense of the private sector, and reduce the pressure on the government to maintain an environment favorable to private enterprise. We may and do seek to counteract this effect by using our grants to get "concessions" from the government favorable to private enterprise. But this is seldom anything like a complete offset—the change in the objective power of the government sector is likely ultimately to outweigh by far the imposed restraint on how for the time being it uses that power. The final result of our grants is therefore likely to be a reduction in the amount of capital available from other sources both internally and from the outside.

In short, if any generalization is valid, it is that the availability of capital while an important problem is a subsidiary one—if other conditions for economic development are ripe, capital will be readily available; if they are not, capital made available is very likely to be wasted.

Let us turn now to the proposition that economic development requires centralized governmental control and planning, that it requires a coordinated "development program." This proposition, too, contains an element of truth. Government certainly has an important role to play in the process of development. It must provide a stable legal framework; it must provide law and order, security to person and property. Beyond this, it has an important role in promoting certain basic services, such as elementary education, roads, and a monetary system; it can make an important contribution by extension activities which help to spread knowledge of new and improved techniques. And numerous other activities of the same sort come to mind.

But none of these activities calls for a centralized program for economic development or detailed control of investment. And such a centralized program is likely to be a hindrance, not a help. Economic development is a process of changing old ways of doing things, of venturing into the unknown. It requires a maximum of flexibility, of possibility for experimentation. No one can predict in advance what will turn out to be the most effective use of a nation's productive resources. Yet the essence of a centralized program of economic development is that it introduces rigidity and inflexibility. It involves a central decision about what activities to undertake, and the use of central force and authority to enforce conformity with that decision.

It may well be that in many underdeveloped countries existing or potential government officials are as competent both to judge what lines of activity will be profitable and to run particular plants as existing or potential private businessmen. There is yet a crucial advantage in letting private business do as much as possible. Private individuals risk their own funds and thus have a much stronger incentive to choose wisely and well. They can be more numerous and they have much detailed information about specific situations that cannot possibly be available to governmental officials. Even more important, however wisely the decisions are made, there are bound to be mistakes. Progress requires that these be recognized, that unsuccessful ventures be abandoned. There is at least some chance that unsuccessful private ventures will be allowed to fail. There is almost none that public ones will be—unless the failure is as flagrant as the British ground nuts venture. The mistake will simply be concealed by subsidy or tariff protection or prohibition of competition. If anything is clear from widespread experience with governmental economic activity, it is that a governmental venture, once established, is seldom abandoned. And surely it is almost as clear that governmental officials are less experimental, less flexible, less adaptive, than private individuals risking their own funds.

What is required in the underdeveloped countries is the release of the energies of millions of able, active, and vigorous people who have been chained by ignorance, custom, and tradition. Such people exist in every underdeveloped country. If it seems otherwise, it is because we tend to seek them in our own image in "big business" on the western model rather than in the villages and on the farms and in the shops and bazaars that line the streets of the crowded cities of many a poor country. These people require only a favorable environment to transform the face of their countries. Instead there is real danger that the inherited set of cultural and social restraints will simply be replaced by an equally far-reaching imposed set of political and economic controls, that one straitjacket will be substituted for another. What is required is rather an atmosphere of freedom, of maximum opportunity for individuals to experiment, and of incentive for them to do so in an environment in which there are objective tests of success and failure—in short, a vigorous, free, capitalistic market.

Thus central control would be a poor way to promote economic development even if the central authorities chose individual projects as wisely as private individuals and with the same end in view. In fact, as we have already seen, the government is almost sure to promote other ends—the national and personal prestige that can be attained through monument-building—so that the case against centralized control is even stronger.

The issues we have been discussing are strikingly illustrated in a report submitted in December 1956 by the MIT Center for International Studies to the special Senate committee to study the foreign aid program. The report studies the problem of how to judge whether a country should be given additional aid. The answer is that the criterion should be whether the country is making an "additional national effort" toward economic development. Two, and only two, rules of thumb are given for deciding whether this is the case: "one index that national effort is being mobilized for development is the launching of measures to capture a good fraction of increases in income for the purpose of further investment"; another "measure of national effort. . . is the degree to which a country's leaders have worked out an overall development program."

Here are two of the basic propositions we started with. And the striking thing is that by these tests the United States would never have qualified as a country making an "additional national effort" toward economic development! We have never had explicit "measures to capture a good fraction of increases in income for the purpose of further investment." Nor have our "leaders" ever "worked out an overall development program." And what is true of the United States is true of every other free nation that has achieved economic development. The only possible exceptions are the economic programs worked out after the Second World War by Britain and some other European countries, and these were largely abandoned because they were failures.

The only countries that satisfy the tests suggested by the MIT report are the communist countries—these all have measures "to capture a good fraction of increases in income for the purpose of further investment" and all have an "overall development program." And none of these has in fact achieved economic development in the sense of a self-sustaining rise in the standard of living of the ordinary man. In the satellite countries, the standard of living of the ordinary man has quite clearly fallen. Even in Russia, the ordinary man is by no means clearly better off now than before the Communists took over, and, indeed, may be worse off even in terms solely of material comforts. While education and health services have clearly improved, food, shelter, and clothing have all apparently deteriorated for the masses. The achievements of which Russia justifiably boasts are to be found elsewhere: in its heavy industries, its military output, and its space satellites—achievements that from the point of view of the consumer classify strictly as monument-building.

It thus seems clear that a free market without central planning has, at least to date, been not only the most effective route to economic development but the only effective route to a rising standard of life for the masses of the people. And it is eminently clear that it has been the only route consistent with political freedom and democracy. Yet the MIT report and most other writings on the subject simply take the opposite for granted, without even noting that in doing so they are going against the whole of the evidence to date, and without offering a shred of evidence of their own. This is modern mythology with a vengeance.

What is involved here is no less than another phase of the ideological war in which we are engaged. A central premise of the communist ideology is that the state must exercise comprehensive control and direction over the economic activities of its citizens; a central premise of western liberalism is that free men operating in a free market can promote their own objectives without the necessity for an all-powerful state.

Foreign economic aid implicitly accepts this premise of the communist ideology; yet it is intended as a weapon against communism. Many who favor it as applied abroad would be horrified at the idea of applying its principles at home. If they accept it, it is because they do not understand what it implies or because they take the word of the "experts" that it is the "only" way to win friends abroad. They, and the experts, are in the state of the man who discovered that he had been speaking prose all his life. Loyal Americans that they are, they have unthinkingly accepted a basic premise of the communist ideology without recognizing it for what it is and in the face of the available evidence. This is a measure of the success of Marxist thought, which is most dangerous precisely when its products lose their labels.

Despite the intentions of foreign economic aid, its major effect, insofar as it has any effect at all, will be to speed the communization of the underdeveloped world. It may, for a time, keep some of these countries nominally on our side. But neutral or even hostile democracies are less of a threat to the preservation of a free world than ostensibly friendly totalitarian countries.

An effective program to promote a free and prosperous world must be based on our own ideology, not on the ideology we are fighting. What policy would be consistent with our ideology?

The aim should be to promote free markets throughout the world and maximum reliance by all countries on free enterprise in an environment favorable to competition and to individual initiative. We cannot do this by telling other governments what to do or by bribing them to go against their own natures any more than we can force men to be free. What we can do is to set an example and to help establish an international climate favorable to economic and political freedom; we can make it easier for other countries to take the path of freedom if they wish to.

The most important area in which we can do this is foreign trade. Here, in particular, our policies belie our professions. We profess to believe in free competition and free markets, yet we have erected barriers to "protect" domestic producers from competition; we profess to believe in minimal government interference with economic activity, yet our government imposes quotas on imports and dumps exports abroad because of a policy of government support of farm prices. True, we have also reduced tariffs and barriers to trade in many areas, and these actions, ably supplemented by the unintended effects of inflation, have reduced our trade restrictions to their lowest level in many decades. Yet those that remain, as well as the fresh restrictions that have been imposed, particularly on agricultural products, have, I believe, done far more harm to our foreign relations than any good we have done even temporarily by our economic aid. The rest of the world regards us as hypocrites, and they are at least partly right.

Entirely aside from the problem of foreign relations, these policies do us direct economic harm. They prevent us from using our resources as effectively as we might both at home and abroad; they hurt us as well as the rest of the world. A free trader like myself would like to see them abolished for this reason alone—in order to enable us to have a higher standard of living. But this is only part of the case for free trade, and, in the present context, the lesser part.

A major factor pushing underdeveloped countries in the direction of central planning and of autarchy is their lack of confidence in a market for their products. Suppose, they argue, we do follow the route of free enterprise and free trade, concentrate on producing those things we can produce most cheaply, and count on getting the goods we want to consume through international trade. Is not success likely simply to produce increases in import barriers by the United States and other countries so that we find ourselves all dressed up with a fine export industry and nowhere to go? And, under present circumstances, can one say with any confidence that they are wrong? Ask the Swiss watchmakers and English bicycle producers.

It is not often recognized how widespread are the implications of the restrictions on trade and, in particular, the uncertainty about them. We do not, it will be said, offer a market for the potential products of most underdeveloped countries so that our trade barriers do not affect them. But this is clearly wrong. It is a major virtue of free international trade that it is multilateral not bilateral. Were we to import more from, say, Western Europe, Western Europe would be able to import more from still other countries, and so on in endless chain, so that our own greater exports might go to very different countries than those from whom we purchased products.

Or to take yet another facet of the problem—the effect on foreign investment. In part, such investment is stimulated by trade barriers: if India will not permit the import of complete cars, an automobile company may set up an assembly plant. But this investment is wasted from the point of view of world productivity: it is used simply to do in one country what could be done more efficiently elsewhere. Productive foreign investment is hindered by trade barriers, both directly and indirectly. It is hindered directly because trade barriers distort the incentives to investment and also make it more difficult for the investor to receive the return on his investment in the currency he wants—a country can earn foreign currency to pay him only by exports. It is hindered indirectly because business and trade relations among nations are a major channel for the spread of information about investment opportunities and the establishment of contacts that make them possible. Commissions of VIPs assigned the task of finding "investment opportunities" are a poor substitute for the day-to-day contact of numerous individuals engaged in earning their daily living by selling goods and rendering services in a foreign country.

Or again, look for the sources of American influence on foreign attitudes and cultures and where will one find them? Not in the literature disseminated by USIS, useful though that may be, but in the activities of International Harvester, Caterpillar Tractor, Singer Sewing Machine, Coca-Cola, Hollywood, and so on. Channels of trade are by all odds the most effective means of disseminating understanding and knowledge of the United States.

British maintenance of free trade—whatever its motives—was surely a major factor knitting the nineteenth-century world together and promoting the rapid and effective development of many then underdeveloped countries. And trade barriers, currency controls, and other economic restrictions are surely a major factor dividing the twentieth-century world and impeding the effective development of the currently underdeveloped countries.

Suppose we were to announce to the world that we committed ourselves to abolish all tariffs, quotas, and other restrictions on trade by a specified date— say, in five or ten years—and that thereafter we would maintain complete free trade. Can there be any doubt that the effects on our international position— both immediately through the announcement effects and ultimately through the long-run economic effects—would be vastly more favorable than those achievable by any conceivable program of foreign economic aid even if one assigns to that aid all the virtues claimed by its proponents? We would be playing from our strength. We would be offering an opportunity to free men to make effective use of their freedom rather than contributing chains to enslave men.

It would, of course, be better if such action were taken by many nations. But it would be a serious mistake for us to link our actions to that of others; the result would be to slow the movement toward free trade to the pace desired by the most recalcitrant member. Far better to move unilaterally. We would benefit economically and politically from a unilateral move, and we might have far more effect on other countries through example than over the conference table.

A movement toward free trade would affect adversely many particular individuals and concerns—those who have invested talent and capital in "protected" industries. But our mobility and adaptability are such that a gradual movement—over the course of, say, ten years—would give the affected individuals ample opportunity to adjust to the new circumstances with little if any loss. The new opportunities afforded by the expansion of world trade, and the more efficient use of our resources involved therein, would benefit many more than were harmed. After all, the transition to free trade over ten years would have far less of an impact than the technological changes that occur decade after decade and that we take in our stride.

As of the moment, we have a bear by the tail in our foreign economic policy—and, unfortunately, it is not the Russian Bear. We get little if any political kudos for continuing economic aid—the recipient countries have come to take it for granted and even to regard it as their right. Yet for this very reason, the sudden cessation of aid would be regarded as an unfriendly and hostile act and would arouse great hostility toward the United States. Thus even if one accepts the arguments of the preceding sections, there remains the problem how to achieve the transition from our present policy to the alternative.

The simplest and least undesirable way seems to me to be to make a final terminal grant to each recipient country. The grant should be fairly generous, say something like two to three times the annual grants we have been making to the country. It should be completely unrestricted and preferably made in the form of a dollar—or even better a Swiss franc—balance on which the recipient country can draw as it wishes. In this way, our own involvement in central planning by other countries could be terminated at once, and the government of the recipient country would attach the greatest value to the grant.

The cost of such a termination program would be sizeable in the year of termination. But it would be a once-for-all cost rather than the steady and growing drain to which we appear to be on the verge of committing ourselves.

SUMMARY

Foreign economic aid needs to be sharply distinguished from direct military aid and defense support even though it may be hard to classify any particular expenditure. Foreign economic aid consists of grants or loans from our government to other governments or to enterprises in other countries for specified projects regarded as contributing to economic development. It includes both technical assistance and grants or loans of money.

The objectives of foreign economic aid are commendable. The means are, however, inappropriate to the objectives. Foreign economic aid, far from contributing to rapid economic development along democratic lines, is likely to retard improvement in the well-being of the masses, to strengthen the government sector at the expense of the private sector, and to undermine democracy and freedom. The proponents of foreign aid have unwittingly accepted a basic premise of the communist ideology that foreign aid is intended to combat. They have accepted the view that centralized and comprehensive economic planning and control by government is an essential requisite for economic development. This view is contradicted by our own experience and the experience of every other free country.

An effective program must be based on our own ideology, not on the ideology we are fighting. Such a program would call for eliminating the inconsistency between the free trade and free enterprise policies we preach and the protectionist and interventionist policies we at least partly practice. An effective and dramatic program would be to commit ourselves unilaterally to achieving complete free trade by a specified and not too distant date. This would do much to promote an environment and international climate favorable to the rapid development of the uncommitted world along free and democratic lines. It would be an act of truly enlightened self-interest.

WHAT'S WRONG
WITH OUR SCHOOLS?

· 9 ·

Education has always been a major component of the American dream. In Puritan New England, schools were quickly established, first as an adjunct of the church, later taken over by secular authorities. After the opening of the Erie Canal, the farmers who left the rocky hills of New England for the fertile plains of the Middle West established schools wherever they went, not only primary and secondary schools, but also seminaries and colleges. Many of the immigrants who streamed over the Atlantic in the second half of the nineteenth century had a thirst for education. They eagerly seized the opportunities available to them in the metropolises and large cities where they mostly settled.

At first, schools were private and attendance strictly voluntary. Increasingly, government came to play a larger role, first by contributing to financial support, later by establishing and administering government schools. The first compulsory attendance law was enacted by Massachusetts in 1852, but attendance did not become compulsory in all states until 1918. Government control was primarily local until well into the twentieth century. The neighborhood school, and control by the local school board, was the rule. Then a so-called reform movement got under way, particularly in the big cities, sparked by the wide differences in the ethnic and social composition of

From Chapter 6 of *Free to Choose*, copyright 1980 by Milton Friedman and Rose D. Friedman. Reprinted by permission of Harcourt Brace Jovanovich, Inc.

different school districts and by the belief that professional educators should play a larger role. That movement gained additional ground in the 1930s along with the general tendency toward both expansion and centralization of government.

We have always been proud, and with good reason, of the widespread availability of schooling to all and the role that public schooling has played in fostering the assimilation of newcomers into our society, preventing fragmentation and divisiveness, and enabling people from different cultural and religious backgrounds to live together in harmony.

Unfortunately, in recent years our educational record has become tarnished. Parents complain about the declining quality of the schooling their children receive. Many are even more disturbed about the dangers to their children's physical well-being. Teachers complain that the atmosphere in which they are required to teach is often not conducive to learning. Increasing numbers of teachers are fearful about their physical safety, even in the classroom. Taxpayers complain about growing costs. Hardly anyone maintains that our schools are giving the children the tools they need to meet the problems of life. Instead of fostering assimilation and harmony, our schools are increasingly a source of the very fragmentation that they earlier did so much to prevent.

At the elementary and secondary level, the quality of schooling varies tremendously: outstanding in some wealthy suburbs of major metropolises, excellent or reasonably satisfactory in many small towns and rural areas, incredibly bad in the inner cities of major metropolises.

"The education, or rather the *un*education, of black children from low income families is undoubtedly the greatest disaster area in public education and its most devastating failure. This is doubly tragic for it has always been the official ethic of public schooling that it was the poor and the oppressed who were its greatest beneficiaries."[1]

Public education is, we fear, suffering from the same malady as are so many of the programs discussed in the preceding and subsequent chapters. More than four decades ago Walter Lippmann diagnosed it as "the sickness of an over-governed society," the change from "the older faith. . . that the exercise of unlimited power by men with limited minds and self-regarding prejudices is soon oppressive, reactionary, and corrupt, . . . that the very condition of progress was the limitation of power to the capacity and the virtue of rulers" to the newer faith "that there are no limits to man's capacity to govern others and that, therefore, no limitations ought to be imposed upon government."[2]

For schooling, this sickness has taken the form of denying many parents control over the kind of schooling their children receive either directly, through choosing and paying for the schools their children attend, or indirectly, through local political activity. Power has instead gravitated to professional educators. The sickness has been aggravated by increasing centraliza-tion and bureaucratization of schools, especially in the big cities.

Private market arrangements have played a greater role at the college and university level than at the elementary and secondary level. But this sector has not been immune from the sickness of an overgoverned society. In 1928 fewer students were enrolled in government institutions of higher education than in private institutions; by 1978 close to four times as many were. Direct govern-ment financing grew less rapidly than government operation because of tuition charges paid by students, but even so, by 1978 direct government grants accounted for more than half of the total expenditures on higher education by all institutions, government and private.

The increased role of government has had many of the same adverse effects on higher education as on elementary and secondary education. It has fostered an atmosphere that both dedicated teachers and serious students often find inimical to learning.

ELEMENTARY AND SECONDARY EDUCATION: THE PROBLEM

Even in the earliest years of the republic, not only the cities but almost every town and village and most rural districts had schools. In many states or localities, the maintenance of a "common school" was mandated by law. But the schools were mostly privately financed by fees paid by the parents. Some supplementary finance was generally also available from the local, county, or state government, both to pay fees for children whose parents were regarded as unable to do so and to supplement fees paid by parents. Though schooling was neither compulsory nor free, it was practically universal (slaves, of course, excepted). In his report for 1836, the superintendent of common schools of the state of New York asserted: "Under any view of the subject it is reasonable to believe, that in the common schools, private schools and academies, the number of children actually receiving instruction is equal to the whole number between five and sixteen years of age."[3] Conditions doubtless varied from state to state, but by all accounts schooling was widely available to (white) children from families at all economic levels.

Beginning in the 1840s, a campaign developed to replace the diverse and largely private system by a system of so-called free schools, i.e., schools in which parents and others paid the cost indirectly by taxes rather than directly by fees. According to E. G. West, who has studied extensively the development of government's role in schooling, this campaign was not led by dissatisfied parents, but "mainly by teachers and government officials."[4] The most famous crusader for free schools was Horace Mann, "the father of American public education," as he is termed in the Encyclopaedia Britannica article on his life.[5]

Mann was the first secretary of the Massachusetts State Board of Education established in 1837, and for the next twelve years he conducted an energetic campaign for a school system paid for by government and controlled by professional educators. His main arguments were that education was so important that government had a duty to provide education to every child, that schools should be secular and include children of all religious, social, and ethnic backgrounds, and that universal, free schooling would enable children to overcome the handicaps of the poverty of their parents. "In his secretarial reports to the Massachusetts Board of Education, Mann proclaimed repetitively . . . that education was a good public investment and increased output."[6] Though the arguments were all pitched in terms of the public interest, much of the support of teachers and administrators for the public school movement derived from a narrow self-interest. They expected to enjoy greater certainty of employment, greater assurance that their salaries would be paid, and a greater degree of control if government rather than parents were the immediate paymaster.

"Despite vast difficulties and vigorous opposition . . . the main outlines of" the kind of system urged by Mann "were achieved by the middle of the nineteenth century."[7] Ever since, most children have attended government schools. A few have continued to attend so-called private schools, mostly schools operated by the Catholic Church and other religious denominations.

The United States was not unique in moving from a mostly private to a mostly governmental system of schools. Indeed, one authority has described "the gradual acceptance of the view that education ought to be a responsibility of the state" as the "most significant" of the general trends of the nineteenth century "that were still influencing education in all western countries in the second half of the twentieth century."[8] Interestingly enough, this trend began in Prussia in 1808, and in France, under Napoleon, about the same time. Britain was even later than the United States. "[U]nder the spell of laissez faire [it] hesitated a long time before allowing the state to intervene in educational affairs," but finally, in 1870, a system of government schools was established, though elementary education was not made compulsory until 1880, and fees were not generally abolished until 1891.[9] In Britain, as in the United States, schooling was almost universal before the government took it over. Professor West has maintained persuasively that the government takeover in Britain, as in the United States, resulted from pressure by teachers, administrators, and well-meaning intellectuals, rather than parents. He concludes that the government takeover reduced the quality and diversity of schooling.[10]

Education is still another example, like social security, of the common element in authoritarian and socialist philosophies. Aristocratic and authoritarian Prussia and Imperial France were the pioneers in state control of education. Socialistically inclined intellectuals in the United States, Britain, and later Republican France were the major supporters of state control in their countries.

The establishment of the school system in the United States as an island of socialism in a free market sea reflected only to a very minor extent the early emergence among intellectuals of a distrust of the market and of voluntary exchange. Mostly, it simply reflected the importance that was attached by the community to the ideal of equality of opportunity. The ability of Horace Mann and his associates to tap that deep sentiment enabled them to succeed in their crusade.

Needless to say, the public school system was not viewed as "socialist" but simply as "American." The most important factor determining how the system operated was its decentralized political structure. The U.S. Constitution narrowly limited the powers of the federal government, so that it played no significant role. The states mostly left control of schools to the local community, the town, the small city, or a subdivision of a large city. Close monitoring of the political authorities running the school system by parents was a partial substitute for competition and assured that any widely shared desires of parents were implemented.

Before the Great Depression the situation was already changing. School districts were consolidated, educational districts enlarged, and more and more power was granted to professional educators. After the depression, when the public joined the intellectuals in an unbridled faith in the virtues of government, and especially of central government, the decline of the one-room school and the local school board became a rout. Power shifted rapidly from the local community to broader entities—the city, the county, the state, and, more recently, the federal government.

In 1920 local funds made up 83 percent of all revenues of public schools, federal grants less than 1 percent. By 1940 the local share had fallen to 68 percent. Currently it is less than one-half. The state provided most of the rest of the money: 16 percent in 1920, 30 percent in 1940, and currently more than 40 percent. The federal government's share is still small but growing rapidly: from less than 2 percent in 1940 to roughly 8 percent currently.

As professional educators have taken over, control by parents has weakened. In addition, the function assigned to schools has changed. They are still expected to teach the three Rs and to transmit common values. In addition, however, schools are now regarded as means of promoting social mobility, racial integration, and other objectives only distantly related to their fundamental task.

In Chapter 4 [of *Free to Choose*] we referred to the theory of bureaucratic displacement that Dr. Max Gammon had developed after studying the British National Health Service: in his words, in "a bureaucratic system . . . *increase in expenditure* will be matched by *fall in production* . . . Such systems will act rather like 'black holes' in the economic universe, simultaneously sucking in resources, and shrinking in terms of 'emitted' production."[11]

His theory applies in full force to the effect of the increasing bureaucratization and centralization of the public school system in the United States. In the five years from school year 1971–1972 to school year 1976–1977, total professional staff in all U.S. public schools went up 8 percent, cost per pupil went up 58 percent in dollars (11 percent after correction for inflation). *Input clearly up*.

The number of students went *down* 4 percent, the number of schools went *down* 4 percent. And we suspect that few readers will demur from the proposition that the quality of schooling went *down* even more drastically than the quantity. That is certainly the story told by the declining grades recorded on standardized examinations. *Output clearly down*.

Is the decline in output per unit of input due to increasingly bureaucratic and centralized organization? As some evidence, the number of school districts went down by 17 percent in the seven-year period from 1970–1971 to 1977–1978—continuing the longer-term trend to greater centralization. As to bureaucratization, for a somewhat earlier five-year period for which data are available (1968–1969 to 1973–1974), when the number of students went up 1 percent, the total professional staff went up 15 percent, and teachers 14 percent, *but supervisors went up 44 percent.*[12]

The problem in schooling is not mere size, not simply that school districts have become larger, and that, on the average, each school has more students. After all, in industry, size has often proved a source of greater efficiency, lower cost, and improved quality. Industrial development in the United States gained a great deal from the introduction of mass production, from what economists call the "economies of scale." Why should schooling be different?

It isn't. The difference is not between schooling and other activities but between arrangements under which the consumer is free to choose and arrangements under which the producer is in the saddle so the consumer has little to say. If the consumer is free to choose, an enterprise can grow in size only if it produces an item that the consumer prefers because of either its quality or its price. And size alone will not enable any enterprise to impose a product on the consumer that the consumer does not consider is worth its price. The large size of General Motors has not prevented it from flourishing. The large size of W. T. Grant & Co. did not save it from bankruptcy. When the consumer is free to choose, size will survive only if it is efficient.

In political arrangements size generally does affect consumers' freedom to choose. In small communities the individual citizen feels that he has, and indeed does have, more control over what the political authorities do than in large communities. He may not have the same freedom to choose that he has in deciding whether to buy something or not, but at least he has a considerable opportunity to affect what happens. In addition, when there are many small communities, the individual can choose where to live. Of course, that is a complex choice, involving many elements. Nonetheless, it does mean that local governments must provide their citizens with services they regard as worth the taxes they pay or either be replaced or suffer a loss of taxpayers.

The situation is very different when power is in the hands of a central government. The individual citizen feels that he has, and indeed he does have, little control over the distant and impersonal political authorities. The possibility of moving to another community, though it may still be present, is far more limited.

In schooling, the parent and child are the consumers, the teacher and school administrator the producers. Centralization in schooling has meant larger size units, a reduction in the ability of consumers to choose, and an increase in the power of producers. Teachers, administrators, and union officials are no different from the rest of us. They may be parents, too, sincerely desiring a fine school system. However, their interests as teachers, as administrators, as union officials are different from their interests as parents and from the interests of the parents whose children they teach. Their interests may be served by greater centralization and bureaucratization even if the interests of the parents are not—indeed, one way in which those interests are served is precisely by reducing the power of parents.

The same phenomenon is present whenever government bureaucracy takes over at the expense of consumer choice: whether in the post office, in garbage collection, or in the many examples in other chapters.

In schooling, those of us who are in the upper income classes retain our freedom to choose. We can send our children to private schools, in effect paying twice for their schooling—once in taxes to support the public school system, once in school fees. Or we can choose where to live on the basis of the quality of the public school system. Excellent public schools tend to be concentrated in the wealthier suburbs of the larger cities, where parental control remains very real.[13]

The situation is worst in the inner cities of the larger metropolises—New York, Chicago, Los Angeles, Boston. The people who live in these areas can pay twice for their children's schooling only with great difficulty—though a surprising number do so by sending their children to parochial schools. They cannot afford to move to the areas with good public schools. Their only recourse is to try to influence the political authorities who are in charge of the public schools, usually a difficult if not hopeless task, and one for which they are not well qualified. The residents of the inner cities are probably more disadvantaged in respect of the level of schooling they can get for their children than in any other area of life with the possible exception of crime protection—another "service" that is provided by government.

The tragedy, and irony, is that a system dedicated to enabling all children to acquire a common language and the values of U.S. citizenship, to giving all children equal educational opportunity, should in practice exacerbate the stratification of society and provide highly unequal educational opportunity. Expenditures on schooling per pupil are often as high in the inner cities as in even the wealthy suburbs, but the quality of schooling is vastly lower. In the suburbs almost all of the money goes for education; in the inner cities much of it must go to preserving discipline, preventing vandalism, or repairing its effects. The atmosphere in some inner city schools is more like that of a prison than of a place of learning. The parents in the suburbs are getting far more value for their tax dollars than the parents in the inner cities.

A VOUCHER PLAN FOR
ELEMENTARY AND SECONDARY SCHOOLING

Schooling, even in the inner cities, does not have to be the way it is. It was not that way when parents had greater control. It is not that way now where parents still have control.

The strong American tradition of voluntary action has provided many excellent examples that demonstrate what can be done when parents have greater choice. One example at the elementary level is a parochial school, St. John Chrysostom's, that we visited in one of the poorest neighborhoods in New York City's Bronx. Its funds come in part from a voluntary charitable organization, New York's Inner City Scholarship Fund, in part from the Catholic Church, in part from fees. The youngsters at the school are there because their parents chose it. Almost all are from poor families, yet their parents are all paying at least some of the costs. The children are well behaved, eager to learn. The teachers are dedicated. The atmosphere is quiet and serene.

The cost per pupil is far less than in public schools even after account is taken of the free services of those teachers who are nuns. Yet on the average, the children are two grades ahead of their peers in public school. That's because teachers and parents are free to choose how the children shall be taught. Private money has replaced tax money. Control has been taken away from bureaucrats and put back where it belongs.

Another example, this one at the secondary level, is in Harlem. In the 1960s Harlem was devastated by riots. Many teenagers dropped out of school. Groups of concerned parents and teachers decided to do something about it. They used private funds to take over empty stores and they set up what became known as storefront schools. One of the first and most successful was called Harlem Prep, designed to appeal to youngsters for whom conventional education had failed.

Harlem Prep had inadequate physical facilities. Many of its teachers did not have the right pieces of paper to qualify for certification to teach in public schools. But that did not keep them from doing a good job. Though many students had been misfits and dropouts, they found the sort of teaching they wanted at Harlem Prep.

The school was phenomenally successful. Many of its students went to college, including some of the leading colleges. But unfortunately, this story has an unhappy ending. After the initial period of crisis had passed, the school ran short of cash. The Board of Education offered Ed Carpenter (the head of the school and one of its founders) the money, provided he would conform to their regulations. After a long battle to preserve independence, he gave in. The school was taken over by bureaucrats. "I felt," commented Mr. Carpenter, "that a school like Harlem Prep would certainly die, and not prosper, under the rigid bureaucracy of a Board of Education . . . We had to see what was going to happen. I didn't believe it was going to be good. I am right. What has happened since we have come to the Board of Education is not all good. It is not all bad, but it's more bad than good."

Private ventures of this kind are valuable. However, at best they only scratch the surface of what needs to be done.

One way to achieve a major improvement, to bring learning back into the classroom, especially for the currently most disadvantaged, is to give all parents greater control over their children's schooling, similar to that which those of us in the upper income classes now have. Parents generally have both greater interest in their children's schooling and more intimate knowledge of their capacities and needs than anyone else. Social reformers, and educational reformers in particular, often self-righteously take for granted that parents, especially those who are poor and have little education themselves, have little interest in their children's education and no competence to choose for them. That is a gratuitous insult. Such parents have frequently had limited opportunity to choose. However, U.S. history has amply demonstrated that, given the opportunity, they have often been willing to sacrifice a great deal, and have done so wisely, for their children's welfare.

No doubt, some parents lack interest in their children's schooling or the capacity and desire to choose wisely. However, they are in a small minority. In any event, our present system unfortunately does little to help their children.

One simple and effective way to assure parents greater freedom to choose, while at the same time retaining present sources of finance, is a voucher plan. Suppose your child attends a public elementary or secondary school. On the average, countrywide, it cost the taxpayer—you and me—about $2,000 per year in 1978 for every child enrolled. If you withdraw your child from a public school and send him to a private school, you save taxpayers about $2,000 per year—but you get no part of that saving except as it is passed on to all taxpayers, in which case it would amount to at most a few cents off your tax bill.

You have to pay private tuition in addition to taxes—a strong incentive to keep your child in a public school.

Suppose, however, the government said to you: "If you relieve us of the expense of schooling your child, you will be given a voucher, a piece of paper redeemable for a designated sum of money, if, and only if, it is used to pay the cost of schooling your child at an approved school." The sum of money might be $2,000, or it might be a lesser sum, say $1,500 or $1,000, in order to divide the saving between you and the other taxpayers. But whether the full amount or the lesser amount, it would remove at least a part of the financial penalty that now limits the freedom of parents to choose.[14]

The voucher plan embodies exactly the same principle as the GI bills that provide for educational benefits to military veterans. The veteran gets a voucher good only for educational expense and he is completely free to choose the school at which he uses it, provided that it satisfies certain standards.

Parents could, and should, be permitted to use the vouchers not only at private schools but also at other public schools—and not only at schools in their own district, city, or state, but at any school that is willing to accept their child. That would both give every parent a greater opportunity to choose and at the same time require public schools to finance themselves by charging tuition (wholly, if the voucher corresponded to the full cost; at least partly, if it did not). The public schools would then have to compete both with one another and with private schools.

This plan would relieve no one of the burden of taxation to pay for schooling. It would simply give parents a wider choice as to the form in which their children get the schooling that the community has obligated itself to provide. The plan would also not affect the present standards imposed on private schools in order for attendance at them to satisfy the compulsory attendance laws.

We regard the voucher plan as a partial solution because it affects neither the financing of schooling nor the compulsory attendance laws. We favor going much farther. Offhand, it would appear that the wealthier a society and the more evenly distributed is income within it, the less reason there is for government to finance schooling. The parents bear most of the cost in any event, and the cost for equal quality is undoubtedly higher when they bear the cost indirectly through taxes than when they pay for schooling directly— unless schooling is very different from other government activities. Yet in practice, government financing has accounted for a larger and larger share of total educational expenses as average income in the United States has risen and income has become more evenly distributed.

We conjecture that one reason is the government operation of schools, so that the desire of parents to spend more on schooling as their incomes rose found the path of least resistance to be an increase in the amount spent on government schools. One advantage of a voucher plan is that it would encourage a gradual move toward greater direct parental financing. The desire of parents to spend more on schooling could readily take the form of adding to the amount provided by the voucher. Public financing for hardship cases might remain, but that is a far different matter than having the government finance a school system for 90 percent of the children going to school because 5 or 10 percent of them might be hardship cases.

The compulsory attendance laws are the justification for government control over the standards of private schools. But it is far from clear that there is any justification for the compulsory attendance laws themselves. Our own views on this have changed over time. When we first wrote extensively a quarter of a century ago on this subject, we accepted the need for such laws on the ground that "a stable democratic society is impossible without a minimum degree of literacy and knowledge on the part of most citizens."[15] We continue to believe that, but research that has been done in the interim on the history of schooling in the United States, the United Kingdom, and other countries has persuaded us that compulsory attendance at schools is not necessary to achieve that minimum standard of literacy and knowledge. As already noted, such research has shown that schooling was well-nigh universal in the United States before attendance was required. In the United Kingdom, schooling was well-nigh universal before either compulsory attendance or government financing of schooling existed. Like most laws, compulsory attendance laws have costs as well as benefits. We no longer believe the benefits justify the costs.

We realize that these views on financing and attendance laws will appear to most readers to be extreme. That is why we only state them here to keep the record straight without seeking to support them at length. Instead, we return to the voucher plan—a much more moderate departure from present practice.

Currently, the only widely available alternative to a local public school is a parochial school. Only churches have been in a position to subsidize schooling on a large scale and only subsidized schooling can compete with "free" schooling. (Try selling a product that someone else is giving away!) The voucher plan would produce a much wider range of alternatives—unless it was sabotaged by excessively rigid standards for "approval." The choice among public schools themselves would be greatly increased. The size of a public school would be determined by the number of customers it attracted, not by politically defined geographical boundaries or by pupil assignment. Parents who organized nonprofit schools, as a few families have, would be assured of funds to pay the costs. Voluntary organizations—ranging from vegetarians to Boy Scouts to the YMCA—could set up schools and try to attract customers. And most important, new sorts of private schools could arise to tap the vast new market.

Let us consider briefly some possible problems with the voucher plan and some objections that have been raised to it.

(1) *The church-state issue.* If parents could use their vouchers to pay tuition at parochial schools, would that violate the First Amendment? Whether it does or not, is it desirable to adopt a policy that might strengthen the role of religious institutions in schooling?

The Supreme Court has generally ruled against state laws providing assistance to parents who send their children to parochial schools, although it has never had occasion to rule on a full-fledged voucher plan covering both public and nonpublic schools. However it might rule on such a plan, it seems clear that the Court would accept a plan that excluded church-connected schools but applied to all other private and public schools. Such a restricted plan would be far superior to the present system, and might not be much inferior to a wholly unrestricted plan. Schools now connected with churches could qualify by subdividing themselves into two parts: a secular part reorganized as an independent school eligible for vouchers, and a religious part reorganized as an after-school or Sunday activity paid for directly by parents or church funds.

The constitutional issue will have to be settled by the courts. But it is worth emphasizing that vouchers would go to *parents, not to schools*. Under the GI bills, veterans have been free to attend Catholic or other colleges and, so far as we know, no First Amendment issue has ever been raised. Recipients of social security and welfare payments are free to buy food at church bazaars and even to contribute to the collection plate from their government subsidies, with no First Amendment question being asked.

Indeed, we believe that the penalty that is now imposed on parents who do not send their children to public schools violates the spirit of the First Amendment, whatever lawyers and judges may decide about the letter. Public schools teach religion, too—not a formal, theistic religion, but a set of values and beliefs that constitute a religion in all but name. The present arrangements abridge the religious freedom of parents who do not accept the religion taught by the public schools yet are forced to pay to have their children indoctrinated with it, and to pay still more to have their children escape indoctrination.

(2) *Financial cost.* A second objection to the voucher plan is that it would raise the total cost to taxpayers of schooling—because of the cost of vouchers given for the roughly 10 percent of children who now attend parochial and other private schools. That is a "problem" only to those who disregard the present discrimination against parents who send their children to nonpublic schools. Universal vouchers would end the inequity of using tax funds to school some children but not others.

In any event, there is a simple and straightforward solution: let the amount of the voucher be enough less than the current cost per public school child to keep total public expenditures the same. The smaller amount spent in a private competitive school would very likely provide a higher quality of schooling than the larger amount now spent in government schools. Witness the drastically lower cost per child in parochial schools. (The fact that elite, luxury schools charge high tuition is no counterargument, any more than the $12.25 charged by the "21" Club for its Hamburger Twenty-One in 1979 meant that McDonald's could not sell a hamburger profitably for 45 cents and a Big Mac for $1.05.)

(3) *The possibility of fraud.* How can one make sure that the voucher is spent for schooling, not diverted to beer for papa and clothes for mama? The answer is that the voucher would have to be spent in an *approved* school or teaching establishment and could be redeemed for cash only by such schools. That would not prevent *all* fraud—perhaps in the forms of "kickbacks" to parents— but it should keep fraud to a tolerable level.

(4) *The racial issue.* Voucher plans were adopted for a time in a number of southern states to avoid integration. They were ruled unconstitutional. Discrimination under a voucher plan can be prevented at least as easily as in public schools by redeeming vouchers only from schools that do not discriminate. A more difficult problem has troubled some students of vouchers. That is the possibility that voluntary choice with vouchers might increase racial and class separation in schools and thus exacerbate racial conflict and foster an increasingly segregated and hierarchical society.

We believe that the voucher plan would have precisely the opposite effect; it would moderate racial conflict and promote a society in which blacks and whites cooperate in joint objectives, while respecting each other's separate rights and interests. Much objection to forced integration reflects not racism but more or less well-founded fears about the physical safety of children and the quality of their schooling. Integration has been most successful when it has resulted from choice, not coercion. Nonpublic schools, parochial and other, have often been in the forefront of the move toward integration.

Violence of the kind that has been rising in public schools is possible only because the victims are compelled to attend the schools that they do. Give them effective freedom to choose and students—black and white, poor and rich, North and South—would desert schools that could not maintain order. Discipline is seldom a problem in private schools that train students as radio and television technicians, typists and secretaries, or for myriad other specialties.

Let schools specialize, as private schools would, and common interest would overcome bias of color and lead to more integration than now occurs. The integration would be real, not merely on paper.

The voucher scheme would eliminate the forced busing that a large majority of both blacks and whites object to. Busing would occur, and might indeed increase, but it would be voluntary—just as the busing of children to music and dance classes is today.

The failure of black leaders to espouse vouchers has long puzzled us. Their constituents would benefit most. It would give them control over the schooling of their children, eliminate domination by both the citywide politicians and, even more important, the entrenched educational bureaucracy. Black leaders frequently send their own children to private schools. Why do they not help others to do the same? Our tentative answer is that vouchers would also free the black man from domination by his own political leaders, who currently see control over schooling as a source of political patronage and power.

However, as the educational opportunities open to the mass of black children have continued to deteriorate, an increasing number of black educators, columnists, and other community leaders have started to support vouchers. The Congress of Racial Equality has made the support of vouchers a major plank in its agenda.

(5) *The economic class issue.* The question that has perhaps divided students of vouchers more than any other is their likely effect on the social and economic class structure. Some have argued that the great value of the public school has been as a melting pot, in which rich and poor, native- and foreign-born, black and white have learned to live together. That image was and is largely true for small communities, but almost entirely false for large cities. There, the public school has fostered residential stratification, by tying the kind and cost of schooling to residential location. It is no accident that most of the country's outstanding public schools are in high income enclaves.

Most children would still probably attend a neighborhood elementary school under a voucher plan—indeed, perhaps more than now do because the plan would end forced busing. However, because the voucher plan would tend to make residential areas more heterogeneous, the local schools serving any community might well be less homogeneous than they are now. Secondary schools would almost surely be less stratified. Schools defined by common interests—one stressing, say, the arts; another, the sciences; another, foreign languages—would attract students from a wide variety of residential areas. No doubt self-selection would still leave a large class element in the composition of the student bodies, but that element would be less than it is today.

One feature of the voucher plan that has aroused particular concern is the possibility that parents could and would "add on" to the vouchers. If the voucher were for, say, $1,500, a parent could add another $500 to it and send his child to a school charging $2,000 tuition. Some fear that the result might be even wider differences in educational opportunities than now exist because low income parents would not add to the amount of the voucher while middle income and upper income parents would supplement it extensively.

This fear has led several supporters of voucher plans to propose that "add-ons" be prohibited.[16]

Coons and Sugarman write that the

> freedom to add on private dollars makes the Friedman model unacceptable to many, including ourselves. . . Families unable to add extra dollars would patronize those schools that charged no tuition above the voucher, while the wealthier would be free to distribute themselves among the more expensive schools. What is today merely a personal choice of the wealthy, secured entirely with private funds, would become an invidious privilege assisted by government. . . This offends a fundamental value commitment—that any choice plan must secure equal family opportunity to attend any participating school.
>
> Even under a choice plan which allowed tuition add-ons, poor families might be better off than they are today. Friedman has argued as much. Nevertheless, however much it improved their education, conscious government finance of economic segregation exceeds our tolerance. If the Friedman scheme were the only politically viable experiment with choice, we would not be enthusiastic.[17]

This view seems to us an example of the kind of egalitarianism discussed in the preceding chapter: letting parents spend money on riotous living but trying to prevent them from spending money on improving the schooling of their children. It is particularly remarkable coming from Coons and Sugarman, who elsewhere say, "A commitment to equality at the deliberate expense of the development of individual children seems to us the final corruption of whatever is good in the egalitarian instinct"[18]—a sentiment with which we heartily agree. In our judgment the very poor would benefit the most from the voucher plan. How can one conceivably justify objecting to a plan, "however much it improved [the] education" of the poor, in order to avoid "government finance of" what the authors call "economic segregation," even if it could be demonstrated to have that effect? And, of course, it cannot be demonstrated to have that effect. On the contrary, we are persuaded on the basis of considerable study that it would have precisely the opposite effect—though we must accompany that statement with the qualification that "economic segregation" is so vague a term that it is by no means clear what it means.

The egalitarian religion is so strong that some proponents of restricted vouchers are unwilling to approve even experiments with unrestricted vouchers. Yet, to our knowledge, none has ever offered anything other than unsupported assertions to support the fear that an unrestricted voucher system would foster "economic segregation."

This view also seems to us another example of the tendency of intellectuals to denigrate parents who are poor. Even the very poorest can—and do—scrape up a few extra dollars to improve the quality of their children's schooling, although they cannot replace the whole of the present cost of public schooling. We suspect that add-ons would be about as frequent among the poor as among the rest, though perhaps of smaller amounts.

As already noted, our own view is that an unrestricted voucher would be the most effective way to reform an educational system that now helps to shape a life of misery, poverty, and crime for many children of the inner city; that it would undermine the foundations of much of such economic segregation as exists today. We cannot present the full basis for our belief here. But perhaps we can render our view plausible by simply recalling another facet of an earlier judgment: is there any category of goods and services—other than protection against crime—the availability of which currently differs more widely among economic groups than the quality of schooling? Are the supermarkets available to different economic groups anything like so divergent in quality as the schools? Vouchers would improve the quality of the schooling available to the rich hardly at all; to the middle class, moderately; to the lower income class, enormously. Surely the benefit to the poor more than compensates for the fact that some rich or middle income parents would avoid paying twice for schooling their children.

(6) *Doubt about new schools.* Is this not all a pipe dream? Private schools now are almost all either parochial schools or elite academies. Will the effect of the voucher plan simply be to subsidize these, while leaving the bulk of the slum dwellers in inferior public schools? What reason is there to suppose that alternatives will really arise?

The reason is that a market would develop where it does not exist today. Cities, states, and the federal government today spend close to $100 billion a year on elementary and secondary schools. That sum is a third larger than the total amount spent annually in restaurants and bars for food and liquor. The smaller sum surely provides an ample variety of restaurants and bars for people in every class and place. The larger sum, or even a fraction of it, would provide an ample variety of schools.

It would open a vast market that could attract many entrants, both from public schools and from other occupations. In the course of talking to various groups about vouchers, we have been impressed by the number of persons who said something like, "I have always wanted to teach [or run a school] but I couldn't stand the educational bureaucracy, red tape, and general ossification of the public schools. Under your plan, I'd like to try my hand at starting a school."

Many of the new schools would be established by nonprofit groups. Others would be established for profit. There is no way of predicting the ultimate composition of the school industry. That would be determined by competition. The one prediction that can be made is that only those schools that satisfy their customers will survive—just as only those restaurants and bars that satisfy their customers survive. Competition would see to that.

(7) *The impact on public schools*. It is essential to separate the rhetoric of the school bureaucracy from the real problems that would be raised. The National Education Association and the American Federation of Teachers claim that vouchers would destroy the public school system, which, according to them, has been the foundation and cornerstone of our democracy. Their claims are never accompanied by any evidence that the public school system today achieves the results claimed for it—whatever may have been true in earlier times. Nor do the spokesmen for these organizations ever explain why, if the public school system is doing such a splendid job, it needs to fear competition from nongovernmental, competitive schools or, if it isn't, why anyone should object to its "destruction."

The threat to public schools arises from their defects, not their accomplishments. In small, closely knit communities where public schools, particularly elementary schools, are now reasonably satisfactory, not even the most comprehensive voucher plan would have much effect. The public schools would remain dominant, perhaps somewhat improved by the threat of potential competition. But elsewhere, and particularly in the urban slums where the public schools are doing such a poor job, most parents would undoubtedly try to send their children to nonpublic schools.

That would raise some transitional difficulties. The parents who are most concerned about their children's welfare are likely to be the first to transfer their children. Even if their children are no smarter than those who remain, they will be more highly motivated to learn and will have more favorable home backgrounds. The possibility exists that some public schools would be left with "the dregs," becoming even poorer in quality than they are now.

As the private market took over, the quality of all schooling would rise so much that even the worst, while it might be *relatively* lower on the scale, would be better in *absolute* quality. And as Harlem Prep and similar experiments have demonstrated, many pupils who are among "the dregs" would perform well in schools that evoked their enthusiasm instead of hostility or apathy.

As Adam Smith put it two centuries ago,

No discipline is ever requisite to force attendance upon lectures which are really worth the attending. . . Force and restraint may, no doubt, be in some degree requisite in order to oblige children. . . to attend to those parts of education which it is thought necessary for them to acquire during that early period of life; but after twelve or thirteen years of age, provided the master does his duty, force or restraint can scarce ever be necessary to carry on any part of education.

Those parts of education, it is to be observed, for the teaching of which there are no public institutions, are generally the best taught.[19]

THE OBSTACLES TO A VOUCHER PLAN

Since we first proposed the voucher plan a quarter century ago as a practical solution to the defects of the public school system, support has grown. A number of national organizations favor it today.[20] Since 1968 the Federal Office of Economic Opportunity and the then Federal Institute of Education encouraged and financed studies of voucher plans and offered to help finance experimental voucher plans. In 1978 a constitutional amendment was on the ballot in Michigan to mandate a voucher plan. In 1979 a movement was under way in California to qualify a constitutional amendment mandating a voucher plan for the 1980 ballot. A nonprofit institute has recently been established to explore educational vouchers.[21] At the federal level, bills providing for a limited credit against taxes for tuition paid to nonpublic schools have several times come close to passing. While they are not a voucher plan proper, they are a partial variant, partial both because of the limit to the size of the credit and because of the difficulty of including persons with no or low tax liability.

The perceived self-interest of the educational bureaucracy is the key obstacle to the introduction of market competition in schooling. This interest group, which, as Professor Edwin G. West demonstrated, played a key role in the establishment of public schooling in both the United States and Great Britain, has adamantly opposed every attempt to study, explore, or experiment with voucher plans.

Kenneth B. Clark, a black educator and psychologist, summed up the attitude of the school bureaucracy:

> It does not seem likely that the changes necessary for increased efficiency of our urban public schools will come about because they should...What is most important in understanding the ability of the educational establish-ment to resist change is the fact that public school systems are protected public monopolies with only minimal competition from private and paro-chial schools. Few critics of the American urban public schools—even severe ones such as myself—dare to question the givens of the present organization of public education...Nor dare the critics question the relevance of the criteria and standards for selecting superintendents, principals, and teachers, or the relevance of all of these to the objectives of public education—producing a literate and informed public to carry on the business of democ-racy—and to the goal of producing human beings with social sensitivity and dignity and creativity and a respect for the humanity of others.

A monopoly need not genuinely concern itself with these matters. As long as local school systems can be assured of state aid and increasing federal aid without the accountability which inevitably comes with aggressive competition, it would be sentimental, wishful thinking to expect any significant increase in the efficiency of our public schools. If there are no alternatives to the present system—short of present private and parochial schools, which are approaching their limit of expansion—then the possibilities of improvement in public education are limited.[22]

The validity of this assessment was subsequently demonstrated by the reaction of the educational establishment to the federal government's offer to finance experiments in vouchers. Promising initiatives were developed in a considerable number of communities. Only one—Alum Rock, California— succeeded. It was severely hobbled. The case we know best, from personal experience, was in New Hampshire, where William P. Bittenbender, then chairman of the State Board of Education, was dedicated to conducting an experiment. The conditions seemed excellent, funds were granted by the federal government, detailed plans were drawn up, experimental communities were selected, preliminary agreement from parents and administrators was obtained. When all seemed ready to go, one community after another was persuaded by the local superintendent of schools or other leading figures in the educational establishment to withdraw from the proposed experiment, and the whole venture collapsed.

The Alum Rock experiment was the only one actually to be carried out, and it was hardly a proper test of vouchers. It was limited to a few public schools and allowed no addition to government funds from either parents or others. A number of so-called mini-schools were set up, each with a different curriculum. For three years, parents could choose which their children would attend.[23]

As Don Ayers, who was in charge of the experiment, said, "Probably the most significant thing that happened was that the teachers for the first time had some power and they were able to build the curriculum to fit the needs of the children as they saw it. The state and local school board did not dictate the kind of curriculum that was used in McCollam School. The parents became more involved in the school. They attended more meetings. Also they had a power to pull their child out of that particular mini-school if they chose another mini-school."

Despite the limited scope of that experiment, giving parents greater choice had a major effect on education quality. In terms of test scores, McCollam School went from thirteenth to second place among the schools in its district.

But the experiment is now over, ended by the educational establishment— the same fate that befell Harlem Prep.

The same resistance is present in Great Britain, where an extremely effective group called FEVER (Friends of the Education Voucher Experiment in Representative Regions) has tried for four years to introduce an experiment in a town in the county of Kent, England. The governing authorities have been favorable, but the educational establishment has been adamantly opposed.

The attitude of the professional educators toward vouchers is well expressed by Dennis Gee, headmaster of a school in Ashford, Kent, and secretary of the local teachers' union: "We see this as a barrier between us and the parent—this sticky little piece of paper [i.e., the voucher] in their hand—coming in and under duress—you will do this or else. We make our judgment because we believe it's in the best interest of every Willie and every little Johnny that we've got—and not because someone's going to say 'if you don't do it, we will do that.' It's this sort of philosophy of the marketplace that we object to."

In other words, Mr. Gee objects to giving the customer, in this case the parent, anything to say about the kind of schooling his child gets. Instead, he wants the bureaucrats to decide.

"We are answerable," says Mr. Gee,

> to parents through our governing bodies, through the inspectorate to the Kent County Council, and through Her Majesty's inspectorate to the Secretary of State. These are people, professionals, who are able to make professional judgments.
>
> I'm not sure that parents know what is best educationally for their children. They know the best environment they can provide at home. But we've been trained to ascertain the problems of children, to detect their weaknesses, to put right those things that need putting right, and we want to do this freely, with the cooperation of parents and not under undue strains.

Needless to say, at least some parents view things very differently. A local electrical worker and his wife in Kent had to engage in a year-long dispute with the bureaucracy to get their son into the school that they thought was best suited to his needs.

Said Maurice Walton,

> As the present system stands, I think we parents have no freedom of choice whatever. They are told what is good for them by the teachers. They are told that the teachers are doing a great job, and they've just got no say at all. If the voucher system were introduced, I think it would bring teachers and parents together—I think closer. The parent that is worried about his child would remove his child from the school that wasn't giving a good service and take it to one that was. . . . If a school was going to crumble because it's got nothing but vandalism, it's generally slack on discipline, and the children aren't learning—well, that's a good thing from my point of view.
>
> I can understand the teachers saying it's a gun at my head, but they've got

the same gun at the parents' head at the moment. The parent goes up to the teacher and says, well, I'm not satisfied with what you're doing, and the teacher can say, well tough. You can't take him away, you can't move him, you can't do what you like, so go away and stop bothering me. That can be the attitude of some teachers today, and often is. But now that the positions are being reversed [with vouchers] and the roles are changed, I can only say tough on the teachers. Let them pull their socks up and give us a better deal and let us participate more.

Despite the unrelenting opposition of the educational establishment, we believe that vouchers or their equivalent will be introduced in some form or other soon. We are more optimistic in this area than in welfare because education touches so many of us so deeply. We are willing to make far greater efforts to improve the schooling of our children than to eliminate waste and inequity in the distribution of relief. Discontent with schooling has been rising. So far as we can see, greater parental choice is the only alternative that is available to reduce that discontent. Vouchers keep being rejected and keep emerging with more and more support.

HIGHER EDUCATION: THE PROBLEMS

The problems of higher education in America today, like those in elementary and secondary education, are dual: quality and equity. But in both respects the absence of compulsory attendance alters the problem greatly. No one is required by law to attend an institution of higher education. As a result, students have a wide range of choice about what college or university to attend if they choose to continue their education. A wide range of choice eases the problem of quality, but exacerbates the problem of equity.

Quality. Since no person attends a college or university against his will (or perhaps his parents'), no institution can exist that does not meet, at least to a minimal extent, the demands of its students.

There remains a very different problem. At government institutions at which tuition fees are low, students are second-class customers. They are objects of charity partly supported at the expense of the taxpayer. This feature affects students, faculty, and administrators.

Low tuition fees mean that while city or state colleges and universities attract many serious students interested in getting an education, they also attract many young men and women who come because fees are low, residential housing and food are subsidized, and above all, many other young people are there. For them, college is a pleasant interlude between high school and going to work. Attending classes, taking examinations, getting passing grades—

these are the price they are paying for the other advantages, *not* the primary reason they are at school.

One result is a high dropout rate. For example, at the University of California at Los Angeles, one of the best regarded state universities in the country, only about half of those who enroll complete the undergraduate course—and this is a high completion rate for government institutions of higher education. Some who drop out transfer to other institutions, but that alters the picture only in detail.

Another result is an atmosphere in the classroom that is often depressing rather than inspiring. Of course, the situation is by no means uniform. Students can choose courses and teachers according to their interest. In every school, serious students and teachers find a way to get together and to achieve their objectives. But again, that is only a minor offset to the waste of students' time and taxpayers' money.

There are good teachers in city and state colleges and universities as well as interested students. But the rewards for faculty and administrators at the prestigious government institutions are not for good undergraduate teaching. Faculty members advance as a result of research and publication; administrators advance by attracting larger appropriations from the state legislature. As a result, even the most famous state universities—the University of California at Los Angeles or at Berkeley, the University of Wisconsin, or the University of Michigan—are not noted for undergraduate teaching. Their reputation is for graduate work, research, and athletic teams—that is where the payoffs are.

The situation is very different at private institutions. Students at such institutions pay high fees that cover much if not most of the cost of their schooling. The money comes from parents, from the students' own earnings, from loans, or from scholarship assistance. The important thing is that the students are the primary customers; they are paying for what they get, and they want to get their money's worth.

The college is selling schooling and the students are buying schooling. As in most private markets, both sides have a strong incentive to serve one another. If the college doesn't provide the kind of schooling its students want, they can go elsewhere. The students want to get full value for their money. As one undergraduate at Dartmouth College, a prestigious private college, remarked, "When you see each lecture costing thirty-five dollars and you think of the other things you can be doing with the thirty-five dollars, you're making very sure that you're going to go to that lecture."

One result is that the fraction of students who enroll at private institutions who complete the undergraduate course is far higher than at government institutions—95 percent at Dartmouth compared to 50 percent at UCLA. The Dartmouth percentage is probably high for private institutions, as the

UCLA percentage is for government institutions, but that difference is not untypical.

In one respect this picture of private colleges and universities is oversimplified. In addition to schooling, they produce and sell two other products: monuments and research. Private individuals and foundations have donated most of the buildings and facilities at private colleges and universities, and have endowed professorships and scholarships. Much of the research is financed out of income from endowments or out of special grants from the federal government or other sources for particular purposes. The donors have contributed out of a desire to promote something they regard as desirable. In addition, named buildings, professorships, and scholarships also memorialize an individual, which is why we refer to them as monuments.

The combination of the selling of schooling and monuments exemplifies the much underappreciated ingenuity of voluntary cooperation through the market in harnessing self-interest to broader social objectives. Henry M. Levin, discussing the financing of higher education, writes, "[I]t is doubtful whether the market would support a Classics department or many of the teaching programs in the arts and humanities that promote knowledge and cultural outcomes which are believed widely to affect the general quality of life in our society. The only way these activities would be sustained is by direct social subsidies," by which he means government grants.[24] Mr. Levin is clearly wrong. The market—broadly interpreted—*has* supported social activities in private institutions. And it is precisely because they provide general benefits to society, rather than serving the immediate self-interest of the providers of funds, that they are attractive to donors. Suppose Mrs. X wants to honor her husband, Mr. X. Would she, or anyone else, regard it as much of an honor to have the ABC Manufacturing enterprise (which may be Mr. X's real monument and contribution to social welfare) name a newly built factory for him? On the other hand, if Mrs. X finances a library or other building named for Mr. X at a university, or a named professorship or scholarship, that will be regarded as a real tribute to Mr. X. It will be so regarded precisely because it renders a public service.

Students participate in the joint venture of producing teaching, monuments, and research in two ways. They are customers, but they are also employees. By facilitating the sale of monuments and research, they contribute to the funds available for teaching, thereby earning, as it were, part of their way. This is another example of how complex and subtle are the ways and potentialities of voluntary cooperation.

Many nominally government institutions of higher learning are in fact mixed. They charge tuition and so sell schooling to students. They accept gifts for buildings and the like and so sell monuments. They accept contracts from government agencies or from private enterprises to engage in research. Many state universities have large private endowments—the University of California at Berkeley, the University of Michigan, the University of Wisconsin, to name only a few. Our impression is that the educational performance of the institution has in general been more satisfactory, the larger the role of the market.

Equity. Two justifications are generally offered for using tax money to finance higher education. One, suggested above by Mr. Levin, is that higher education yields "social benefits" over and above the benefits that accrue to the students themselves; the second is that government finance is needed to promote "equal educational opportunity."

(i) *Social benefits.* When we first started writing about higher education, we had a good deal of sympathy for the first justification. We no longer do. In the interim we have tried to induce the people who make this argument to be specific about the alleged social benefits. The answer is almost always simply bad economics. We are told that the nation benefits by having more highly skilled and trained people, that investment in providing such skills is essential for economic growth, that more trained people raise the productivity of the rest of us. These statements are correct. But none is a valid reason for subsidizing higher education. Each statement would be equally correct if made about physical capital (i.e., machines, factory buildings, etc.), yet hardly anyone would conclude that tax money should be used to subsidize the capital investment of General Motors or General Electric. If higher education improves the economic productivity of individuals, they can capture that improvement through higher earnings, so they have a private incentive to get the training. Adam Smith's invisible hand makes their private interest serve the social interest. It is against the social interest to change their private interest by subsidizing schooling. The extra students—those who will only go to college if it is subsidized—are precisely the ones who judge that the benefits they receive are less than the costs. Otherwise they would be willing to pay the costs themselves.

Occasionally the answer is good economics but is supported more by assertion than by evidence. The most recent example is in the reports of a special commission on higher education established by the Carnegie Foundation. In one of its final reports, *Higher Education: Who Pays? Who Benefits? Who Should Pay?*, the commission summarizes the supposed "social benefits." Its list contains the invalid economic arguments discussed in the preceding paragraph—that is, it treats benefits accruing to the persons who get the education as if they were benefits to third parties. But its list also includes some alleged advantages that, if they did occur, would accrue to persons other than those who receive the education, and therefore might justify a subsidy: "general advancement of knowledge . . . greater political effectiveness of a democratic society . . . greater social effectiveness of society through the resultant better understanding and mutual tolerance among individuals and groups; the more effective preservation and extension of the cultural heritage."[25]

The Carnegie commission is almost unique in at least paying some lip service to possible "negative results of higher education"—giving as examples, however, only "the individual frustrations resulting from the current surplus of Ph.D.'s (which is not a social but an individual effect) and the public unhappiness with past outbreaks of campus disruption."[26] Note how selective and biased are the lists of benefits and "negative results." In countries like India, a class of university graduates who cannot find employment they regard as suited to their education has been a source of great social unrest and political instability. In the United States "public unhappiness" was hardly the only, or even the major, negative effect of "campus disruption." Far more important were the adverse effects on the governance of the universities, on the "political effectiveness of a democratic society," on the "social effectiveness of society through . . . better understanding and mutual tolerance"—all cited by the commission, without qualification, as social benefits of higher education.

The report is unique also in recognizing that "without any public subsidy, some of the social benefits of higher education would come as *side effects* of privately financed education in any case."[27] But here again this is simply lip service. Although the commission sponsored numerous and expensive special studies, it did not undertake any serious attempt to identify the alleged social effects in such a way as to permit even a rough quantitative estimate of their importance or of the extent to which they could be achieved without public subsidy. As a result, it offered no evidence that social effects are on balance positive or negative, let alone that any net positive effects are sufficiently large to justify the many billions of dollars of taxpayers' money being spent on higher education.

The commission contented itself with concluding that "no precise—or even imprecise—methods exist to assess the individual and societal benefits as against the private and public costs." But that did not prevent it from recommending firmly and unambiguously an increase in the already massive government subsidization of higher education.

In our judgment this is special pleading, pure and simple. The Carnegie commission was headed by Clark Kerr, former chancellor and president of the University of California, Berkeley. Of the eighteen members of the commission, including Kerr, nine either were or had been heads of higher educational institutions, and five others were professionally associated with institutions of higher education. The remaining four had all served on the board of trustees or regents of universities. The academic community has no difficulty recognizing and sneering at special pleading when businessmen march to Washington under the banner of free enterprise to demand tariffs, quotas, and other special benefits. What would the academic world say about a steel industry commission, fourteen of whose eighteen members were from the steel industry, which recommended a major expansion in government subsidies to the steel industry? Yet we have heard nothing from the academic world about the comparable recommendation of the Carnegie commission.

(ii) *Equal educational opportunity.* The promotion of "equal educational opportunity" is the major justification that is generally offered for using tax money to finance higher education. In the words of the Carnegie commission, "We have favored. . . [a] larger public. . . share of monetary outlays for education on a temporary basis in order to make possible greater equality of educational opportunity."[28] In the words of the parent Carnegie Foundation, "Higher education is. . . a major avenue to greater equality of opportunity, increasingly favored by those whose origins are in low-income families and by those who are women and members of minority groups."[29]

The objective is admirable. The statement of fact is correct. But there is a missing link between the one and the other. Has the objective been promoted or retarded by government subsidy? Has higher education been a "major avenue to greater equality of opportunity" because of or despite government subsidy?

One simple statistic from the Carnegie commission's own report illustrates the problem of interpretation: 20 percent of college students from families with incomes below $5,000 in 1971 attended private institutions; 17 percent from families with incomes between $5,000 and $10,000; 25 percent from families with incomes over $10,000. In other words, the private institutions provided more opportunity for young men and women at the very bottom as well as the top of the income scale than did the government institutions.[30]

And this is just the tip of the iceberg. Persons from middle and upper income families are two or three times as likely to attend college as persons from lower income groups, and they go to school for more years at the more expensive institutions (four-year colleges and universities rather than two-year junior colleges). As a result, students from higher income families benefit the most from the subsidies.[31]

Some persons from poor families do benefit from the government subsidy. In general, they are the ones among the poor who are better off. They have human qualities and skills that will enable them to profit from higher education, skills that would also have enabled them to earn a higher income without a college education. In any event, they are destined to be among the better off in the community.

Two detailed studies, one for Florida, one for California, underline the extent to which government spending on higher education transfers income from low to high income groups.

The Florida study compared the total benefits persons in each of four income classes received in 1967–1968 from government expenditures on higher education with the costs they incurred in the form of taxes. Only the top income class got a net gain; it got back 60 percent more than it paid. The bottom two classes paid 40 percent more than they got back, the middle class nearly 20 percent more.[32]

The California study, for 1964, is just as striking, though the key results are presented somewhat differently, in terms of families with and without children in California public higher education. Families with children in public higher education received a net benefit varying from 1.5 percent to 6.6 percent of their average income, the largest benefit going to those who had children at the University of California and who also had the highest average income. Families without children in public higher education had the lowest average income and incurred a net cost of 8.2 percent of their income.[33]

The facts are not in dispute. Even the Carnegie commission admits the perverse redistributive effect of government expenditures on higher education—although one must read their reports with great care, and indeed between the lines, to spot the admission in such comments as, "This 'middle class' generally . . . does quite well in the proportion of public subsidies that it receives. Greater equity can be achieved through a reasonable redistribution of subsidies."[34] Its major solution is more of the same: still greater government spending on higher education.

We know of no government program that seems to us so inequitable in its effects, so clear an example of Director's Law, as the financing of higher education. In this area those of us who are in the middle and upper income classes have conned the poor into subsidizing us on the grand scale—yet we not only have no decent shame, we boast to the treetops of our selflessness and public-spiritedness.

HIGHER EDUCATION: THE SOLUTION

It is eminently desirable that every young man and woman, regardless of his or her parents' income, social position, residence, or race, have the opportunity to get higher education—*provided that he or she is willing to pay for it either currently or out of the higher income the schooling will enable him or her to earn.* There is a strong case for providing loan funds sufficient to assure opportunity to all. There is a strong case for disseminating information about the availability of such funds and for urging the less privileged to take advantage of the opportunity. There is no case for subsidizing persons who get higher education at the expense of those who do not. Insofar as governments operate institutions of higher education, they should charge students fees corresponding to the full cost of the educational and other services they provide to them.

However desirable it may be to eliminate taxpayer subsidization of higher education, that does not currently seem politically feasible. Accordingly, we shall supplement our discussion of an alternative to government finance with a less radical reform—a voucher plan for higher education.

Alternative to government finance. Fixed-money loans to finance higher schooling have the defect that there is wide diversity in the earnings of college graduates. Some will do very well. Paying back a fixed-dollar loan would be no great problem for them. Others will end with only modest incomes. They would find a fixed debt a heavy burden. Expenditure on education is a capital investment in a risky enterprise, as it were, like investment in a newly formed small business. The most satisfactory method of financing such enterprises is not through a fixed-dollar loan but through equity investment—"buying" a share in the enterprise and receiving as a return a share of the profits.

For education, the counterpart would be to "buy" a share in an individual's earning prospects, to advance him the funds needed to finance his training on condition that he agree to pay the investor a specified fraction of his future earnings. In this way an investor could recoup more than his initial investment from relatively successful individuals, which would compensate for the failure to do so from the unsuccessful. Though there seems no legal obstacle to private contracts on this basis, they have not become common, primarily, we conjecture, because of the difficulty and costs of enforcing them over the long period involved.

A quarter century ago (1955), one of us published a plan for "equity" financing of higher education through a government body that

> could offer to finance or help finance the training of any individual who could meet minimum quality standards. It would make available a limited sum per year for a specified number of years, provided the funds were spent on securing training at a recognized institution. The individual in return would agree to pay to the government in each future year a specified percentage of his earnings in excess of a specified sum for each $1,000 that he received from the government. This payment could easily be combined with the payment of income tax and so involve a minimum of additional administrative expense. The base sum should be set equal to estimated average earnings without the specialized training; the fraction of earnings paid should be calculated so as to make the whole project self-financing. In this way, the individuals who received the training would in effect bear the whole cost. The amount invested could then be determined by individual choice.[35]

More recently (1967), a panel appointed by President Johnson and headed by Professor Jerrold R. Zacharias of MIT recommended the adoption of a specific version of this plan under the appealing title Educational Opportunity Bank and made an extensive and detailed study of its feasibility and of the terms that would be required in order for it to be self-supporting.[36] No reader of this book will be surprised to learn that the proposal was met by a blast from the Association of State Universities and Land Grant Colleges—a fine example of what Adam Smith referred to as "the passionate confidence of interested falsehood."[37]

In 1970, as recommendation 13 out of thirteen recommendations for the financing of higher education, the Carnegie commission proposed the establishment of a National Student Loan Bank that would make long-term loans with repayment partly contingent upon current earnings. "Unlike the Educational Opportunity Bank," says the commission, ". . . we see the National Student Loan Bank as a means of providing supplementary funding for students, not as a way of financing total educational costs."[38]

More recently still, some universities, including Yale University, have considered or adopted contingent-repayment plans administered by the university itself. So a spark of life remains.

A voucher plan for higher education. Insofar as any tax money is spent to subsidize higher education, the least bad way to do so is by a voucher arrangement like that discussed earlier for elementary and secondary schools.

Have all government schools charge fees covering the full cost of the educational services they provide and so compete on equal terms with non-government schools. Divide the total amount of taxes to be spent annually on higher education by the number of students it is desired to subsidize per year. Give that number of students vouchers equal to the resulting sum. Permit the vouchers to be used at any educational institution of the student's choice, provided only that the schooling is of a kind that it is desired to subsidize. If the number of students requesting vouchers is greater than the number available, ration the vouchers by whatever criteria the community finds most acceptable: competitive examinations, athletic ability, family income, or any of myriad other possible standards. The resulting system would follow in broad outline the GI bills providing for the education of veterans, except that the GI bills were open-ended; their benefits were available to all veterans.

As we wrote when we first proposed this plan:

> The adoption of such arrangements would make for more effective competition among various types of schools and for a more efficient utilization of their resources. It would eliminate the pressure for direct government assistance to private colleges and universities and thus preserve their full independence and diversity at the same time as it enabled them to grow relative to state institutions. It might also have the ancillary advantage of causing scrutiny of the purposes for which subsidies are granted. The subsidization of institutions rather than of people has led to an indiscriminate subsidization of all activities appropriate for such institutions, rather than of the activities appropriate for the state to subsidize. Even cursory examination suggests that while the two classes of activities overlap, they are far from identical.
>
> The equity argument for the alternative [voucher] arrangement is . . .

clear. . . The state of Ohio, for example, says to its citizens: "If you have a youngster who wants to go to college, we shall automatically give him or her a sizable four-year scholarship, provided that he or she can satisfy rather minimal education requirements, and provided further that he or she is smart enough to choose to go to the University of Ohio [or some other state-supported institution]. If your youngster wants to go, or you want him or her to go, to Oberlin College, or Western Reserve University, let alone to Yale, Harvard, Northwestern, Beloit, or the University of Chicago, not a penny for him." How can such a program be justified? Would it not be far more equitable, and promote a higher standard of scholarship, to devote such money as the state of Ohio wished to spend on higher education to scholarships tenable at any college or university and to require the University of Ohio to compete on equal terms with other colleges and universities?[39]

Since we first made this proposal, a number of states have adopted a limited program going partway in its direction by giving scholarships tenable at private colleges and universities, though only those in the state in question. On the other hand, an excellent program of regents scholarships in New York State, very much in the same spirit, was emasculated by Governor Nelson Rockefeller's grandiose plans for a State University of New York modeled after the University of California.

Another important development in higher education has been a major expansion in the federal government's involvement in financing, and even more in regulating both government and nongovernment institutions. The intervention has in large measure been part of the greatly expanded federal activity to foster so-called "affirmative action," in the name of greater civil rights. This intervention has aroused great concern among faculty and administrators at colleges and universities, and much opposition by them to the activities of federal bureaucrats.

The whole episode would be a matter of poetic justice if it were not so serious for the future of higher education. The academic community has been in the forefront of the proponents of such intervention—when directed at other segments of society. They have discovered the defects of intervention—its costliness, its interference with the primary mission of the institutions, and its counterproductiveness in its own terms—only when these measures were directed at them. They have now become the victims both of their own earlier professions of faith and of their self-interest in continuing to feed at the federal trough.

CONCLUSION

In line with common practice, we have used "education" and "schooling" as synonymous. But the identification of the two terms is another case of using persuasive terminology. In a more careful use of the terms, not all "schooling" is "education," and not all "education" is "schooling." Many highly schooled people are uneducated, and many highly "educated" people are unschooled.

Alexander Hamilton was one of the most truly "educated," literate, and scholarly of our founding fathers, yet he had only three or four years of formal schooling. Examples could be multiplied manyfold, and no doubt every reader knows highly schooled people whom he regards as uneducated and unschooled people whom he considers learned.

We believe that the growing role that government has played in financing and administering schooling has led not only to enormous waste of taxpayers' money but also to a far poorer educational system than would have developed had voluntary cooperation continued to play a larger role.

Few institutions in our society are in a more unsatisfactory state than schools. Few generate more discontent or can do more to undermine our liberty. The educational establishment is up in arms in defense of its existing powers and privileges. It is supported by many public-spirited citizens who share a collectivist outlook. But it is also under attack. Declining test scores throughout the country; increasing problems of crime, violence, and disorder at urban schools; opposition on the part of the overwhelming majority of both whites and blacks to compulsory busing; restiveness on the part of many college and university teachers and administrators under the heavy hand of HEW bureaucrats—all this is producing a backlash against the trend toward centralization, bureaucratization, and socialization of schooling.

We have tried in this chapter to outline a number of constructive suggestions: the introduction of a voucher system for elementary and secondary education that would give parents at all income levels freedom to choose the schools their children attend; a contingent-loan financing system for higher education to combine equality of opportunity with the elimination of the present scandalous imposition of taxes on the poor to pay for the higher education of the well-to-do; or, alternatively, a voucher plan for higher education that would both improve the quality of institutions of higher education and promote greater equity in the distribution of such taxpayer funds as are used to subsidize higher education.

These proposals are visionary but they are not impracticable. The obstacles are in the strength of vested interests and prejudices, not in the feasibility of administering the proposals. There are forerunners, comparable programs in operation in this country and elsewhere on a smaller scale. There is public support for them.

We shall not achieve them at once. But insofar as we make progress toward them—or alternative programs directed at the same objective—we can strengthen the foundations of our freedom and give fuller meaning to equality of educational opportunity.

NOTES

1. Leonard Billet, *The Free Market Approach to Educational Reform*, Rand Paper P-6141 (Santa Monica, Calif.: The Rand Corporation, 1978), pp. 27–28.

2. From *The Good Society*, as quoted by W. Allen Wallis in *An Over-Governed Society* (New York: Free Press, 1976), p. viii.

3. Quoted by E. G. West, "The Political Economy of American Public School Legislation," *Journal of Law and Economics* 10 (October 1967): 101–28, quotation from p. 106.

4. Ibid., p. 108.

5. Note the misleading terminology. "Public" is equated with "governmental," though in other contexts, as in "public utilities," "public libraries," and so on, that is not done. In schooling, is there any relevant sense in which Harvard College is less "public" than the University of Massachusetts?

6. Ibid., p. 110.

7. R. Freeman Butts, *Encyclopaedia Britannica*, vol. 7 (1970), p. 992.

8. W. O. L. Smith, *Encyclopaedia Britannica*, vol. 7 (1970), p. 988.

9. Ibid., pp. 988–89.

10. E. G. West, *Education and the State* (London: The Institute of Economic Affairs, 1965).

11. Max Gammon, *Health and Security: Report on Public Provision for Medical Care in Great Britain* (London: St. Michael's Organization, 1976) p. 27.

12. We are indebted to Herbert Lobsenz and Cynthia Savo of Market Data Retrieval for making these data available to us from their Education Data Bank.

13. Indeed, many of these public schools can be regarded as, in effect, tax loopholes. If they were private, the tuition charges would not be deductible for purposes of the federal income tax. As public schools financed by local taxes, the taxes are deductible.

14. One of us first proposed this voucher plan in Milton Friedman, "The Role of Government in Education," in Robert A. Solo, ed., *Economics and the Public Interest* (New Brunswick, N.J.: Rutgers University Press, 1955). A revised version of this article is Chapter 6 of Milton Friedman, *Capitalism and Freedom* (Chicago: University of Chicago Press, 1962).

15. Ibid., p. 86.

16. See Christopher Jencks and associates, *Education Vouchers: A Report on Financing Elementary Education by Grants to Parents* (Cambridge, Mass.: Center for the Study of Public Policy, December 1970); John E. Coons and Stephen D. Sugarman, *Education by Choice: The Case for Family Control* (Berkeley: University of California Press, 1978).

17. Coons and Sugarman, *Education by Choice*, p. 191.

18. Ibid., p. 130.

19. *Wealth of Nations*, vol. II, p. 253 (book V, chap. I).

20. For example, the Citizens for Educational Freedom, the National Association for Personal Rights in Education.

21. Education Voucher Institute, incorporated in May 1979 in Michigan.

22. Kenneth B. Clark, "Alternative Public School Systems," in the special issue on *Equal Educational Opportunity* of the *Harvard Educational Review* 38, no. 1 (Winter 1968): 100–113; passage cited from pp. 110–11.

23. Daniel Weiler, A *Public School Voucher Demonstration: The First Year at Alum Rock*, Rand Report No. 1495 (Santa Monica, Calif.: The Rand Corporation, 1974).

24. Henry M. Levin, "Aspect of a Voucher Plan for Higher Education," Occasional Paper 72–7 (School of Education, Stanford University, July 1972), p. 16.

25. Carnegie Commission on Higher Education, *Higher Education: Who Pays? Who Benefits? Who Should Pay?* (McGraw-Hill, June 1973), pp. 2–3.

26. Ibid., p. 4.

27. Ibid., p. 4.

28. Ibid., p. 15.

29. Carnegie Foundation for the Advancement of Teaching, *More than Survival: Prospects for Higher Education in a Period of Uncertainty* (San Francisco: Jossey Bass Publishers, 1975), p. 7.

30. Carnegie Commission, *Higher Education*, p. 176. We have not calculated the percentages in the text from the Carnegie table but from the source it cited, Table 14, U. S. Census Reports Series P–20 for 1971, no. 241, p. 40. In doing so, we found that the Carnegie report percentages are slightly in error.

The figures we give are somewhat misleading because married students living with their spouses are classified by their own and their spouses' family income rather than by the income of their parents. If married students are omitted, the effect described is even greater: 22 percent of students from families with incomes of less than $5,000 attended private schools, 17 percent from families with incomes between $5,000 and $10,000, and 25 percent from families with incomes of $10,000 and over.

31. According to figures from the U.S. Bureau of the Census, of those persons between eighteen and twenty-four who were enrolled as undergraduates in public colleges in 1971, fewer than 14 percent came from families with incomes below $5,000 a year, although more than 22 percent of all eighteen- to twenty-four-year-olds came from these low income families. And 57 percent of those enrolled came from families with incomes above $10,000 a year, although fewer than 40 percent of eighteen- to twenty-four-year-olds came from these higher income families.

Again, these figures are biased by the inclusion of married students with spouse present. Only 9 percent of other students enrolled in public colleges came from families with incomes below $5,000, although 18 percent of all such eighteen- to twenty-four-year-olds came from these low income families. Nearly 65 percent of students of other marital status enrolled came from families with incomes of $10,000 or more, although only a bit over 50 percent of all such eighteen- to twenty-four-year-olds did.

Incidentally, in connection with this and the preceding note, it is noteworthy that the Carnegie commission, in the summary report in which it refers to these figures, does not even mention that it combines indiscriminately the married and unmarried students, even though doing so clearly biases their results in the direction of understating the transfer of income from lower to higher incomes that is involved in governmental financing of higher education.

32. Douglas M. Windham made two estimates for 1967–1968 for each of four income classes of the difference between the dollar value of the benefits received from public higher education and the cost incurred. The estimates showing the smaller transfer are as follows.

TABLE 9.1

Income Class ($ per year)	Total Benefits	Total Costs	Net Cost (−) or Gain (+)
$ 0– 3,000	$10,419,600	$14,259,360	−$ 3,839,760
3,000– 5,000	20,296,320	28,979,110	− 8,682,790
5,000–10,000	70,395,980	82,518,780	− 12,122,800
10,000 and over	64,278,490	39,603,440	+ 24,675,050

SOURCE: Douglas M. Windham, *Education, Equality and Income Redistribution* (Lexington, Mass.: Heath Lexington Books, 1970), p. 43.

33. [See Table 9.2, p. 126.] W. Lee Hansen and Burton A. Weisbrod, *Benefits, Costs, and Finance of Public Higher Education* (Chicago: Markom Publishing Co., 1969), p. 76, except that line 5 was calculated by us. Note that the taxes in line 3, unlike the costs allowed for in Florida, include all taxes, not simply the taxes going to pay for higher education.

34. Carnegie Commission, *Higher Education*, p. 7.

35. Originally published in Milton Friedman, "The Role of Government in Education," and reprinted in slightly revised form in *Capitalism and Freedom*; quotation from p. 105 of the latter.

36. *Educational Opportunity Bank, a Report of the Panel on Educational Innovation to the U.S. Commissioner of Education and the Director of the National Science Foundation* (Washington, D.C.: U.S. Government Printing Office, August 1967). Supporting material was presented in K. Shell, F. M. Fisher, D. K. Foley, A. F. Friedlaender (in association with J. Behr, S. Fischer, K. Mosenson), "The Educational Opportunity Bank: An Economic Analysis of a Contingent Repayment Loan Program for Higher Education," *National Tax Journal* (March 1968): 2–45, as well as in unpublished documents of the Zacharias panel.

37. For the statement of the association, see National Association of State Universities and Land Grant Colleges, *Proceedings, November 12–15, 1967*, pp. 67–68. For the Smith quotation, *Wealth of Nations*, vol. 1, p. 460 (book IV, chap. III), where the reference is to traders seeking government protection from foreign goods.

38. Carnegie Commission, *Higher Education*, p. 121.

39. Quoted from *Capitalism and Freedom*, pp. 99–100.

TABLE 9.2

	All Families	Families without Children in California Public Higher Education	Families with Children in California Public Higher Education			
			Total	Junior College	State College	University of California
1. Average family income	$8,000	$7,900	$9,560	$8,800	$10,000	$12,000
2. Average higher education subsidy per year	—	0	880	720	1,400	1,700
3. Average total state and local taxes paid	620	650	740	680	770	910
4. Net transfer (line 2 − line 3)	—	−650	+140	+40	+630	+790
5. Net transfer as percent of average income	—	−8.2%	+1.5	+0.5	+6.3	+6.6

Economic Journalism

· *10* ·

Laws That Do Harm

◆　　　◆

There is a sure-fire way to predict the consequences of a government social program adopted to achieve worthy ends. Find out what the well-meaning, public-interested persons who advocated its adoption expected it to accomplish. Then reverse those expectations. You will have an accurate prediction of actual results.

To illustrate on the broadest level, idealists from Marx to Lenin and the subsequent fellow travelers claimed that communism would enhance both freedom and prosperity and lead to the "withering away of the state." We all know the results in the Soviet Union and the People's Republic of China: misery, slavery, and a more powerful and all-encompassing government than the world had ever seen.

Idealists, from Harold Laski to Jawaharlal Nehru, promised the suffering

Indian masses that "democratic economic planning" would abolish famines, bring material prosperity, resolve age-old conflicts between the castes, and eliminate inequality. The result has been continued deprivation for the masses, continued violence between the castes, and widened inequality.

Perverse Results: To come down to less sweeping cases *rent control* has been promoted for millenniums as a way to hold down rents and ensure more housing for the disadvantaged. Wherever it has been adopted, the actual result has been precisely the opposite for all but a few favored tenants. Rent control has encouraged the wasteful use of housing space and has discouraged the building of more housing units. As a result, rents actually paid—whether legally or under the table—by all tenants except those who do not move have skyrocketed. And even the tenants who do not move complain about not being able to.

Over two years ago, when the San Francisco supervisors were contemplating a form of rent control, I republished in a local paper a *Newsweek* column of mine on rent control, prefacing it with the comment that only a "fool or a knave" could support rent control after examining the massive evidence on its effects. Needless to say, that did not prevent the majority of a board of supervisors, consisting of neither fools nor knaves, from enacting the ordinance I objected to. And the lessons of experience have not prevented the adoption of rent control in other cities—or the repetition of that same experience.

Urban renewal programs were urged to cure "urban blight" and improve the housing available to the poor. The result was a "Federal Bulldozer," as Martin Anderson titled his searching examination of urban renewal. More dwelling units were torn down than were constructed. The new units constructed were mostly for middle and upper income classes. Urban blight was simply shifted and made worse by the still higher density created elsewhere by removing the poor from the "renewed" area.

In *education*, professionalization, integration, bilingualism, massive doses of federal assistance—all have been promoted to improve the quality of schooling and reduce racial tension and discrimination. The result was predictable: a drastic lowering of educational performance and an increase in actual segregation of races, at least in the North.

President Nixon introduced *price controls* on August 15, 1971, to eliminate inflation, which at the time was running at about 4 to 5 percent per year. When controls ended in 1974, inflation soared into double digits.

The *Interstate Commerce Commission* was promoted in the 1880s and 1890s by the Ralph Naders of the day to discipline monopolistic railroads and benefit their customers. One group in today's Nader conglomerate has published a devastating study of the ICC demonstrating that it strengthened the monopoly power of the railroads, and later of trucking. The users of transportation have had the dubious privilege of paying higher prices for poorer service.

Name an Exception: Need I go on? I challenge my readers to name a government social program that has achieved the results promised by its well-meaning and public-interested proponents. I keep repeating "well-meaning and public-interested proponents" because they have generally been the dupes of others who had very clear self-interested motives and often did achieve the results that they intended—the railroads in the 1890s for example.

The amazing thing to me is the continued gullibility of intellectuals and the public. I wish someone would explain that to me. Is it simply because no one has given this widely documented generalization a catchy name—like . . . (suggestions welcome)?

FREE MARKETS AND THE GENERALS

◆　◆

The adoption of free-market policies by Chile with the blessing and support of the military junta headed by General Pinochet has given rise to the myth that only an authoritarian regime can successfully implement a free-market policy.

The facts are very different. Chile is an exception, not the rule. The military is hierarchical and its personnel are imbued with the tradition that some give and some obey orders: it is organized from the top down. A free market is the reverse. It is voluntaristic, authority is dispersed; bargaining, not submission to orders, is its watchword; it is organized from the bottom up.

Military juntas in other South American countries have been as authoritarian in the economic sphere as they have been in politics. So were General Franco and the Greek colonels. Some have introduced free-market elements to meet an economic crisis—but so did Russia in the 1920s with its new economic policy and so has China in recent years. However, to the best of my knowledge, none, with the exception of Chile, has supported a fully free-market economy as a matter of principle.

Miracles: Chile is an economic miracle. Inflation has been cut from 700

---

percent a year in mid-1974 to less than 10 percent a year. After a difficult transition, the economy boomed, growing an average of about 8 percent a year from 1976 to 1980. Real wages and employment rose rapidly and unemployment fell. Imports and exports surged after export subsidies were eliminated and tariffs were slashed to a flat 10 percent (except for temporarily higher rates for most automobiles). Many state enterprises have been denationalized and motor transport and other areas deregulated. A voucher system has been put into effect in elementary and secondary education. Most remarkable of all, a social security reform has been adopted that permits individuals to choose between participating in the government system or providing for their own retirement privately.

Chile is an even more amazing political miracle. A military regime has supported reforms that reduce sharply the role of the state and replace control from the top with control from the bottom.

This political miracle is the product of an unusual set of circumstances. The chaos produced by the Allende regime that precipitated the military takeover in 1973 discredited central economic control. In an attempt to rectify the situation, the military drew on a comprehensive plan for a free-market economy that had been prepared by a group of young Chilean economists, most, though not all, of whom had studied at the University of Chicago. For the first two years, the so-called Chicago boys participated in implementing the plan but only in subordinate positions, and there was little progress in reducing inflation. Somewhat in desperation, the junta turned major responsibility over to the Chicago boys. Fortunately, several of them combined outstanding intellectual and executive ability with the courage of their convictions and a sense of dedication to implementing them—and the economic miracle was on its way.

Chile is currently having serious difficulties—along with much of the rest of the world. And the opposition to the free-market policies that had been largely silenced by success is being given full voice—from both inside and outside the military.

This temporary setback will likely be surmounted. But I predict that the free-market policy will not last unless the military government is replaced by a civilian government dedicated to political liberty—as the junta has announced is its intention. Otherwise, sooner or later—and probably sooner rather than later—economic freedom will succumb to the authoritarian character of the military.

Liberty: A civilian government, too, might destroy the free market—after all, Allende was doing so in Chile when he was overthrown by the military. Yet it is no accident that the spread of the free market in the nineteenth century was accompanied by the widening of political liberty and that although politically free societies have moved in the direction of collectivism, none has gone all the way except through the force of arms.

I have long argued that economic freedom is a necessary but not sufficient condition for political freedom. I have become persuaded that this generalization, while true, is misleading unless accompanied by the proposition that political freedom in turn is a necessary condition for the long-term maintenance of economic freedom.

THE USES OF CORRUPTION

♦ ♦

The headlines about under-the-table payments by major corporations scream "corporate corruption." The seldom-noticed fact is that every case so far chronicled involves payments to obtain contracts from governments. There have been no scandals about questionable payments between private enterprises—though of course there have been corrupt activities of other kinds by private enterprises, as in the scandal about Equity Funding.

What the current rash of cases illustrates is that some government officials (who, after all, spend other people's money) are tempted to use their position for personal gain, that private enterprises are tempted to accommodate them, and that those enterprises that resist the temptation may well lose profitable business.

ETHICS AND THE MARKET

The scarcity of payoffs of this kind between private enterprises is a nice illustration of how private cupidity can promote ethical standards. A payoff can only be financed out of the proceeds of sales. But people who spend their own money can hardly be paid off out of what they themselves spend. People who delegate the spending of their money to agents have a strong personal interest to make sure that the agents are honest and reliable and to keep tabs on what they do. This personal interest is diluted in the great impersonal corporations, yet even so is far more effective than in big government. In a village or small town, an individual citizen may be able to keep tabs on his agents; in metropolises, much less the nation, he cannot. In the business world, honesty and fair dealing have a market value. In the political world, the reputation for honesty and fair dealing may have a value, but the fact may be a liability.

Government corruption is of long standing—partly because, however regrettable on an ethical plane, it has its uses. Both aspects are well illustrated by an incident from our early history.

Alexander Hamilton's first major report as our first Secretary of the Treasury proposed the funding of the national debt that had been accumulated during the Revolution and the Confederation, as well as the assumption by the United States of the corresponding debts of the individual states, that is, their repayment in full at par value. This report was termed by one of his early biographers, Senator Henry Cabot Lodge, "The cornerstone of the government of the United States." Most historians to this day agree that adoption of Hamilton's proposal played an important role in promoting the future prosperity of the country.

Hamilton's Tactics in 1790

Yet adoption of the proposal, on August 4, 1790, was achieved only by resort to what must be called corruption. At the time the measure was proposed, the debt in question was selling at a small fraction of its face value. Wrote Thomas Jefferson of Virginia, long afterward: "When the trial of strength had indicated the form in which the bill would finally pass, this being known within doors sooner than without, especially than to those who were in distant parts of the Union, the base scramble began. Couriers and relay-horses by land, and swift-sailing boats by sea, were flying in all directions. Active partners and agents were associated and employed in every state, town and country neighborhood; and this paper was bought for 5 shillings, and even as low as 2 shillings, in the pound, before the holder knew that Congress had already provided for its redemption at par."

Writes a biographer of Hamilton: "Of the 64 members of the House, it was long afterwards brought out, 29 were security holders." Hamilton himself did not personally profit from the speculation connected with this measure but close associates, including his brother-in-law, clearly did.

Even so, not enough members of Congress had a direct personal stake to pass assumption. At the crucial test, Hamilton was still a few votes short. He got those votes by making a deal with Jefferson. Despite his later animadversions, Jefferson provided the votes required to pass assumption in return for

Hamilton's providing the votes needed to transfer the capital of the nation from New York via Philadelphia to an enclave carved out of Maryland and Virginia.

It is not easy to draw a simple moral—from either the present scandals or Alexander Hamilton's triumph.

Good Wealth, Bad Wealth

◆   ◆

Mr. Smith uses savings of $60,000 accumulated over many years to build a factory producing widgets much desired by consumers. Mr. Jones uses savings of $60,000 accumulated over many years to buy a medallion entitling him to operate a taxicab in New York City, rendering services much desired by consumers.

Both Smith and Jones have created private wealth—embodied in a factory in the one case, in a taxicab medallion in the other. Both use their private wealth to serve the public. From a private point of view, their cases are indistinguishable and equally deserving of commendation.

Private vs. Public: From the public point of view, the two cases are radically different. Smith's wealth adds to the total supply of physical capital available to serve the public; it adds to the productive capacity of the community. Jones's does not. It simply transfers wealth from Jones to whoever owned the medallion before. Moreover, the existence of such a category of wealth—a share, as it were, in a governmentally created cartel—harms the community as a whole.

The medallion has a market value only because the sum that customers are willing to pay for the services rendered by the cab exceeds the cost of owning and running the cab, including, of course, the value that Jones attributes to his own labor. In the absence of the cartel, the excess of returns over costs would lead more persons to enter the taxicab business. The fares fixed by local authorities for taxicab service would go down, or cabs would be more easily obtainable, until costs and returns came into balance. Consumers would be better off and so would the additional owners of cabs and all hired drivers of cabs.

I make this comparison not to attack the limitation of taxicab licenses—though that limitation deserves to be attacked—but to illuminate a major source of confusion about the role of government in regulating industry, and a major source of the difficulty in ending undesirable regulation.

To continue with my example, suppose that the numerical limitation on taxicabs were eliminated, and licenses were freely issued. The effect on Jones would be identical to the effect on Smith of government expropriation of his factory without compensation—something specifically prohibited by the Fifth Amendment to the Constitution ("Nor shall private property be taken for public use without just compensation"). It is entirely understandable that Jones would oppose the one measure with the same righteous wrath with which Smith would oppose the other.

Though privately identical, the two actions would have wholly different effects on the public interest: the one eliminates "artificial" wealth that was created by government edict and that harms the public; the other confiscates physical wealth that benefits the public.

Ethics vs. Politics: On an ethical level, Jones is as deserving of compensation for the taking of his wealth as Smith would be for the taking of his wealth—the only qualification being that Jones acquired the medallion in the knowledge that an exclusive privilege granted by government could be withdrawn by government. Yet acting in accordance with that ethical judgment would be disastrous. It would require government to compensate every vested interest in society, however created, for any harm to it as a result of legislation (including the taxpayers providing the funds to pay compensation!). Aside from the impossibility of determining even the rough monetary effects of legislation, such a principle would enshrine the status quo and prevent the correction of past errors. Moreover, its logical counterpart is that government should receive the monetary equivalent of any gains to persons from the legislation—again not only a practical impossibility, but a measure that in principle would drastically change the effect of legislation by eliminating any incentive for persons to take advantage of potential benefits—just as compensating for losses would eliminate any incentive to minimize losses.

My simple comparison has relevance to a wide range of problems—ICC restrictions on trucking and busing, CAB restrictions on airlines, FCC controls on television, radio, and telephones, price ceilings on crude oil and natural gas, licensing of occupations, rent controls, and on and on. All are cases of private wealth created by measures that harm the public. We have in the process created a Frankenstein monster that it will not be easy to subdue.

PROHIBITION AND DRUGS

♦   ♦

"The reign of tears is over. The slums will soon be only a memory. We will turn our prisons into factories and our jails into storehouses and corncribs. Men will walk upright now, women will smile, and the children will laugh. Hell will be forever for rent."

That is how Billy Sunday, the noted evangelist and leading crusader against Demon Rum, greeted the onset of Prohibition in early 1920. We know now how tragically his hopes were doomed. New prisons and jails had to be built to house the criminals spawned by converting the drinking of spirits into a crime against the state. Prohibition undermined respect for the law, corrupted the minions of the law, created a decadent moral climate—but did not stop the consumption of alcohol.

Despite this tragic object lesson, we seem bent on repeating precisely the same mistake in the handling of drugs.

ETHICS AND EXPEDIENCY

On ethical grounds, do we have the right to use the machinery of government to prevent an individual from becoming an alcoholic or a drug addict? For children, almost everyone would answer at least a qualified yes. But for responsible adults, I, for one, would answer no. Reason with the potential addict, yes. Tell him the consequences, yes. Pray for and with him, yes. But I believe that we have no right to use force, directly or indirectly, to prevent a fellow man from committing suicide, let alone from drinking alcohol or taking drugs.

I readily grant that the ethical issue is difficult and that men of goodwill may well disagree. Fortunately, we need not resolve the ethical issue to agree on policy. *Prohibition is an attempted cure that makes matters worse—for both the addict and the rest of us.* Hence, even if you regard present policy toward drugs as ethically justified, considerations of expediency make that policy most unwise.

Consider first the addict. Legalizing drugs might increase the number of addicts, but it is not clear that it would. Forbidden fruit is attractive, particularly to the young. More important, many drug addicts are deliberately made by pushers, who give likely prospects their first few doses free. It pays the pusher to do so because, once hooked, the addict is a captive customer. If drugs were legally available, any possible profit from such inhumane activity would disappear, since the addict could buy from the cheapest source.

Whatever happens to the number of addicts, the individual addict would clearly be far better off if drugs were legal. Today, drugs are both incredibly expensive and highly uncertain in quality. Addicts are driven to associate with criminals to get the drugs, become criminals themselves to finance the habit, and risk constant danger of death and disease.

Consider next the rest of us. Here the situation is crystal clear. The harm to us from the addiction of others arises almost wholly from the fact that drugs are illegal. A recent committee of the American Bar Association estimated that addicts commit one-third to one-half of all street crime in the United States. Legalize drugs, and street crime would drop dramatically.

Moreover, addicts and pushers are not the only ones corrupted. Immense sums are at stake. It is inevitable that some relatively low-paid police and other government officials—and some high-paid ones as well—will succumb to the temptation to pick up easy money.

LAW AND ORDER

Legalizing drugs would simultaneously reduce the amount of crime and raise the quality of law enforcement. Can you conceive of any other measure that would accomplish so much to promote law and order?

But, you may say, must we accept defeat? Why not simply end the drug traffic? That is where experience under Prohibition is most relevant. We cannot end the drug traffic. We may be able to cut off opium from Turkey—but there are innumerable other places where the opium poppy grows. With French cooperation, we may be able to make Marseilles an unhealthy place to manufacture heroin—but there are innumerable other places where the simple manufacturing operations involved can be carried out. So long as large sums of money are involved—and they are bound to be if drugs are illegal—it is literally hopeless to expect to end the traffic or even to reduce seriously its scope.

In drugs, as in other areas, persuasion and example are likely to be far more effective than the use of force to shape others in our image.

Is Welfare a Basic Human Right?

◆   ◆

In a recent *Newsweek* column on poverty, Shana Alexander wrote, "Access to food, clothing, shelter, and medical care is a basic human right."

The heart approves Ms. Alexander's humanitarian concern, but the head warns that her statement admits of two very different meanings, one that is consistent with a free society, and one that is not.

The Right to Work

One meaning is that everyone should be free to use his human capacities to acquire food, clothing, shelter, and medical care by either direct production or voluntary cooperation with others. This meaning is the essence of a free society organized through voluntary cooperation.

This meaning is far from trivial. Indeed, I conjecture that most hardship and misery in the United States today reflect government's interference with this right. You cannot earn your livelihood by becoming a plumber, barber, mortician, lawyer, physician, dentist, or by entering a host of other trades, unless you first are licensed by the government. And the granting of a license is typically in the hands of practitioners of the trade you desire to enter, who find it in their self-interest to restrict entry.

You will have difficulty getting a highly paid job as a carpenter, mason, or electrician unless you can persuade a union to let you join, and that may not be easy if your brother or father or uncle is not a member of the union. It will be especially difficult if you are black and poor, however competent. Like the American Medical Association, the unions can enforce their tight monopoly only with the support of the government.

If you are a black teenager whose services are currently worth only $1.50 an hour, it is illegal for most employers to hire you, even though you are willing to accept that wage.

And I have only scratched the surface of existing restrictions on your basic human right to use your capacities as you wish, provided only that you do not interfere with the right of others to do the same.

But this is not Ms. Alexander's meaning, as is clear from her next sentence: "When lawmakers attempt to convert welfare into workfare . . . this is less conversion than perversion of that basic idea."

Ms. Alexander apparently believes that you and I have a "basic human right" to food, clothing, shelter, and medical care without a quid pro quo. That is a very different matter.

If I have the "right" to food in this sense, someone must have the obligation to provide it. Just who is that? If it is Ms. Alexander, does that not convert her into my slave? Nothing is changed by assigning the "right" to the "poor." Their "right" is meaningless unless it is combined with the power to force others to provide the goods to which Ms. Alexander believes they are entitled.

This is clearly unacceptable. But neither can we rely solely on the "right to access" in the first sense. Protecting that right fully would reduce poverty and destitution drastically. But there would still remain people who, through no fault of their own, because of accidents of birth, or illness, or whatever, were unable to earn what the rest of us would regard as an acceptable minimum income. I believe that the best, though admittedly imperfect, solution for such residual hardship would be voluntary action on the part of the rest of us to assist our less fortunate brethren.

TRANSITION PROGRAMS

But our problem is far more serious. Restrictions on access in the first sense, plus ill-conceived welfare measures, have made millions of people dependent on government for their most elementary needs. It was a mistake to have permitted this situation to develop. But it has developed, and we cannot simply wipe the slate clean. We must develop transition programs that eliminate the welfare mess without unconscionable hardship to present welfare recipients.

That is why, for three decades, I have urged the replacement of our present collection of so-called poverty programs by a negative income tax that would guarantee a minimum to everyone and would encourage recipients to become self-supporting.

I favor a negative income tax not because I believe anyone has a "right" to be fed, clothed, and housed at someone else's expense but because I want to join my fellow taxpayers in relieving distress and feel a special compulsion to do so because governmental policies have been responsible for putting so many of our fellow citizens in the demeaning position in which they now find themselves.

ROOFS OR CEILINGS

◆   ◆

In 1946, George Stigler and I published a pamphlet attacking the legal ceilings that had been imposed on rents during World War II and were then still in effect. We argued that the ceilings, by keeping rents artificially low for those persons who were fortunate enough to live in controlled dwellings, encouraged the waste of housing space and, at the same time, discouraged the construction of additional dwellings. Hence our title, "Roofs or Ceilings."

Nationwide ceilings were subsequently abolished. However, localities were given the option to continue them. New York City—with that unerring instinct for self-destruction that has brought it to its present condition—is the only major city still controlling rents under this option.

A recent article by Richard Stone in *The Wall Street Journal*, "Shortage of Housing in New York Gets Worse Every Day," brought this ancient pamphlet vividly back to mind. At a time when there is so much talk about imposing new price controls, this cautionary tale is worth pondering.

THE NEW YORK STORY

Reports Stone: "The dimensions of the New York shortage are vast. The rental vacancy rate is below 1 percent... Private building is at near-paralysis... Increasing numbers of landlords simply give up, abandoning buildings they can neither afford to maintain nor sell at any price. Tenants, left with no heat, water, or electricity vacate such buildings in a matter of days. When that happens, blight swallows up whole neighborhoods, almost overnight.

"Every day there are fewer housing units available in New York City than the day before.

"New York's archaic rent-control law keeps the marginally poor whose fortune is improving from moving out of slum neighborhoods."

Others go to great lengths to find a rent-controlled apartment, including keeping "track of obituaries to divine what deaths are creating rent-control vacancies."

"Partly because of rent control, rents on private housing built since 1947—housing that doesn't come under the law—skyrocketed over the past decade... After fierce public outcry, the city last summer passed a law holding annual increases to 5 percent. To no one's surprise, several major builders responded by withdrawing from the city."

Or, as we wrote in our 1946 pamphlet: "Rent ceilings cause haphazard and arbitrary allocation of space, inefficient use of space, retardation of new construction. The legal ceilings on rents are the reason there are so few places for rent. Because of the excess of demand over supply, rental property is now rationed [in New York] by various forms of chance and favoritism. As long as the shortage created by rent ceilings remains, there will be a clamor for continued rent controls. This is perhaps the strongest indictment of ceilings on rent. They, and the accompanying shortage of dwellings to rent, perpetuate themselves, and the progeny are even less attractive than the parents."

Housing and Grapefruit

Do not suppose that this sad tale reflects anything special about housing. During World War II, when price control was nearly universal, black markets and rationing by chance, favoritism, and bribery developed in steel, meat, bananas—you name it.

Since World War II, there have been major crises in gold and foreign exchange—because governments have tried to fix the prices of both. When the price of the dollar was fixed too low in terms of other currencies, there was a "dollar shortage"; more recently, when it has been fixed too high, there has been concern about balance-of-payments deficits.

The price system is a remarkably efficient system for bringing buyers and sellers together, for assuring that the quantities some people want to buy will match the quantities other people want to sell. Immobilize the price system and something else—if only chaos and queues—must take its place.

Would you like to see a shortage of grapefruit in New York that will get worse with every day? Let New York impose and effectively enforce a ceiling price on grapefruit below the market price. Let Washington do so, and the shortage will be nationwide. And you can substitute any product you wish for "grapefruit," provided you add the qualification that the ceiling price be "effectively enforced."

That is the direction in which the well-meaning people who are talking about legal price and wage control are pushing us. They should be condemned to hunting for an apartment in New York.

ECONOMIC MIRACLES

♦   ♦

I have just returned from a brief visit to Brazil, the third major nation in recent history to take off on a period of growth so rapid as to justify the term "economic miracle." The explosion is obvious even to the casual visitor. The cars that jam the streets of São Paulo and Rio are almost all new; multistory buildings, both new and still under construction, crowd the sky; cranes are almost as numerous as TV antennas, and the air of bustle and hustle is unmistakably different from the pre-Christmas shopping rush. Many of the men in responsible positions are surprisingly young; clearly a new generation is taking charge. Their confidence, pride, and high expectations are seasoned with just a tinge of uneasiness about the future. "Will it really last?" is a question that no one asks yet that all seem to have at the back of their minds.

The Brazilian miracle dates from 1967, when output started growing at an average rate of approximately 10 percent a year. The other miracles, in Germany and Japan, started nearly two decades earlier, shortly after the end of World War II. Though the three countries differ greatly in history, culture, resources, and technological sophistication, there are striking similarities among the three miracles.

THE SIMILARITIES

1. *All three miracles were preceded by a period of economic disorganization that was produced or intensified by price and wage controls imposed to suppress inflation.*

In Germany and Japan, a productive capacity diminished by war and defeat faced a money supply swollen by wartime spending and postwar fiscal collapse. Wartime price and wage controls were continued by the occupation authorities who enforced them far more rigorously than a native police force could ever have done. The result was economic collapse.

In Brazil, political instability in the late 1950s and early 1960s produced large government deficits financed by a rapid increase in the quantity of money.

Inflation reached a rate of more than 100 percent a year by early 1964. The government attempted to suppress the inflation by measures such as fixing prices and wages, controlling foreign-exchange transactions, and introducing multiple exchange rates. As in Germany and Japan, the controls produced widespread waste, inefficiency, and black markets.

2. *All three miracles were made possible by monetary reforms that ended most government controls over prices and wages and thereby permitted a market-price system to operate.*

In Germany and Japan, the prior economic collapse had been so extreme that the reforms, drastic though they were, were followed almost immediately by recovery and expansion.

In Brazil, where the prior collapse was much less extreme, a tight money policy that reduced the rate of inflation from more than 100 percent to about 30 percent in three years was accompanied by recession and increased unemployment. However, after the initial shock was absorbed, the freeing of markets plus political stability unleashed unsuspected dynamic forces.

MONETARY CORRECTION

3. *All three miracles relied primarily on private enterprise for their motive power.*

In all three countries, government intervened extensively—subsidizing here, taxing there, building roads, ports, and similar facilities, taking over part or all of selected industries. Yet these measures, though highly visible, were the trimming on the cake, not the cake itself. I believe that most of them did more harm than good. The government served best when it interfered least with the driving force of private enterprise coordinated by market prices.

The one major difference among the policies that fostered the three miracles is the tactic adopted to permit the price system to operate.

Germany and Japan followed a monetary policy that, until very recently, all but eliminated inflation. They were therefore under no pressure to control prices and wages and could let the price system operate freely.

Brazil followed a different course. After reducing inflation to about 30 percent per year by 1967, it eased off. Simultaneously, however, it introduced purchasing-power escalator clauses into a wide range of contracts. The term used in Brazil is "monetary correction." If a Brazilian deposits money in a savings bank, the bank not only will pay him a stated interest rate, say 5 percent, but also will periodically credit his account with a monetary correction equal to the rate of inflation over the period. Longer-term business loans, government securities, mortgages, and so on are handled the same way: the borrower pays the lender a stated rate plus a monetary correction.

All wage rates are subject to mandatory adjustment by a similar monetary correction—though in fact most wages have been rising much faster than that. The personal exemptions under the income tax and the tax brackets are adjusted by a monetary correction. So also is the value of fixed business assets for purposes of calculating depreciation allowed under the tax laws. The exchange rate is adjusted frequently to allow for inflation. And so on and on.

The use of the monetary correction in some of these ways is mandated by law; in others, it is voluntary. In practice, its use is sufficiently widespread to remove most of the pressure for price and wage controls.

The monetary correction is an accounting nuisance and it cannot be truly universal. A world of zero inflation would obviously be better. Yet, given the inevitable, if temporary, costs of reducing inflation rapidly without such a measure, the Brazilians have been extremely wise to adopt it. I believe that their miracle would have been impossible without the monetary correction. With it, they have been able to reduce inflation gradually from about 30 percent in 1967 to about 15 percent now without inhibiting rapid growth, and they may be able to succeed in gradually bringing inflation down to near zero. With it, they currently experience less economic distortion from a 15 percent inflation than the United States, without it, experiences from a 9 percent inflation.

A True "Second Best"

Even the most ardent defenders of price and wage controls regard them as at most a "second best," as an expedient to avoid still worse problems. The three major economic miracles—as well as many less dramatic episodes—teach that they are rather a "first worst," a cancer that can destroy an economic system's capacity to function.

The widespread use of purchasing-power escalator clauses as a remedy "for fluctuations of general prices" was proposed by the great British economist Alfred Marshall as long ago as 1887. The Brazilian experience parallels Marshall's proposal with amazing fidelity—by the force of necessity, not design. Theory and practice coincide in demonstrating that a true second best for living with inflation is the widespread use of purchasing-power escalator clauses. It is past time that the United States applied the lesson.

UP IN THE AIR

◆ ◆

This column was begun in a jet that had crossed the Atlantic in six hours but had now been circling Kennedy for an hour, stacked up awaiting permission to land.

What waste. A multimillion dollar jet, a marvel of modern technology, manned by a highly skilled and highly paid crew, occupied by nearly 200 passengers, many spending highly valuable time, serviced by a pleasant and attractive complement of hostesses, guzzling fuel as it circled aimlessly high in the sky. The cost was easily thousands of dollars an hour.

How is it that this waste occurs, not only occasionally, which is no doubt unavoidable, but regularly, so that experienced travelers, let alone the airlines, regard it as a routine matter? How is it that the large financial return from eliminating the waste is not an effective prod?

SOCIALISM VS. CAPITALISM

As I sat in the plane, I reflected that the airplane manufacturers seem to be able to turn out these marvelous mechanical miracles in ample number to meet the demand of the airlines for them. The airlines seem to be able to acquire the highly skilled flight crews in ample number (with a real assist, it is true, from the military services, which train most of them). They seem to be able to hire sufficient stewardesses to woman the cabins. Occasionally, a plane is delayed by mechanical trouble, but the airlines generally have been able to acquire the skilled maintenance and ground men to service the planes, so this is seldom a bottleneck. I have heard no stories of planes being delayed by the inability to get ample airplane fuel, or meals to feed the passengers, or liquor to befuddle them.

How is it that it has been possible to attend to all these matters—and yet not to arrange things on the ground so that planes can generally be landed promptly and without delay? Is it somehow inherently more difficult to arrange space for landing planes than to build them and operate them in the air? That seems very dubious indeed.

I believe the answer to the puzzle is much simpler. Every other activity described is mostly private and highly competitive—private enterprise builds the planes, private (or where governmental, highly competitive) airlines fly them, private firms produce and supply the fuel for man and machine. The airports, on the other hand, are a socialized monopoly—financed and run by government. As a result, there is no effective way that the waste involved in airport delays can be converted into effective pressure to eliminate them. The pressure must make its convoluted way through the FAA, the administration, Congress, and local governments.

There is no reason why this need be so. In the heyday of free enterprise, the railroads built and almost wholly financed their own terminals—even when they were "union" terminals servicing a number of lines—and still operate them. Why should airlines not be required to provide their own landing facilities—not necessarily directly but perhaps by paying fees to other private enterprises that run the airports? The airlines doubtless initially welcomed federal subsidization of landing facilities. I wonder whether they now think they really got a bargain?

President Nixon has proposed a vast expansion of landing facilities to be financed by user charges but to continue to be operated by governmental agencies. The method of finance is the right one. The cost of landing facilities should be borne by those who use them. The method of operation is the wrong one. The right solution is to move toward private operation as well as finance.

Too Pat?

Many a reader will regard my explanation as too pat—as simply a knee-jerk reaction of an economic liberal (in the original sense of that much-abused term). Maybe so—but I urge them to see whether the shoe does not fit, not only here but elsewhere. Where are the long lines of frustrated drivers? At the doors of the automobile dealers selling cars produced by private enterprise—or on the highways and city streets provided by government? What are the problems plaguing education? A shortage of high-quality desks, chairs, and other educational equipment, including books, produced by private enterprise—or the inefficient organization and conduct of public schools? Where is technology backward and primitive? In the privately run telephone industry (albeit the existence of monopoly does occasionally produce delay and inefficiency)—or in the governmentally run Post Office?

FAIR VERSUS FREE

♦ ♦

In presenting his energy program, President Carter stressed "fairness" as an essential ingredient of an acceptable program. The Federal Communications Commission seeks to enforce a "fairness doctrine" on radio and TV stations. We suffered numerous "fair trade" laws, until they were declared unenforceable. One businessman vies with another in proclaiming his faith in competition—provided that it is "fair."

Yet, scrutinize word for word the Declaration of Independence, the Constitution, and the Bill of Rights, and you will not find the word "fair." The First Amendment does not protect the "fair" exercise of religion, but the "free" exercise thereof; it does not restrain Congress from abridging the "fairness" of speech or of the press, but the "freedom" of speech or of the press.

FROM UMPIRE TO BIG BROTHER

The modern tendency to substitute "fair" for "free" reveals how far we have moved from the initial conception of the Founding Fathers. They viewed government as policeman and umpire. They sought to establish a framework within which individuals could pursue their own objectives in their own way, separately or through voluntary cooperation, provided only that they did not interfere with the freedom of others to do likewise.

The modern conception is very different. Government has become Big Brother. Its function has become to protect the citizen, not merely from his fellows, but from himself, whether he wants to be protected or not. Government is not simply an umpire but an active participant, entering into every nook and cranny of social and economic activity. All this, in order to promote the high-minded goals of "fairness," "justice," "equality."

Does this not constitute progress? A move toward a more humane society? Quite the contrary. When "fairness" replaces "freedom," all our liberties are in danger. In *Walden*, Thoreau says: "If I knew for a certainty that a man was coming to my house with the conscious design of doing me good, I should run for my life." That is the way I feel when I hear my "servants" in Washington assuring me of the "fairness" of their edicts.

There is no objective standard of "fairness." "Fairness" is strictly in the eye of the beholder. If speech must be fair, then it cannot also be free; someone must decide what is fair. A radio station is not free to transmit unfair speech— as judged by the bureaucrats at the Federal Communications Commission. If the printed press were subject to a comparable "fairness doctrine," it too would have to be controlled by a government bureau and our vaunted free press would soon become a historical curiosity.

What is true for speech—where the conflict is perhaps clearest—is equally true for every other area. To a producer or seller, a "fair" price is a high price. To the buyer or consumer, a "fair" price is a low price. How is the conflict to be adjudicated? By competition in a free market? Or by government bureaucrats in a "fair" market?

Businessmen who sing the glories of free enterprise and then demand "fair" competition are enemies, not friends, of free markets. To them, "fair" competition is a euphemism for a price-fixing agreement. They are exemplifying Adam Smith's remark that "people of the same trade seldom meet together, even for merriment and diversion, but the conversation ends in a conspiracy against the public, or in some contrivance to raise prices." For consumers, the more "unfair" the competition the better. That assures lowest prices and highest quality.

RULES OR ACTIONS

Is then the search for "fairness" all a mistake? Not at all. There is a real role for fairness, but that role is in constructing general rules and adjudicating disputes about the rules, not in determining the outcome of our separate activities. That is the sense in which we speak of a "fair" game and a "fair" umpire. If we applied the present doctrine of "fairness" to a football game, the referee would be required after each play to move the ball backward or forward enough to make sure that the game ended in a draw!

Our Founding Fathers designed a fair Constitution to protect human freedom. In Thomas Jefferson's ringing phrases from the Declaration of Independence, "Governments are instituted among Men . . . to secure . . . certain unalienable Rights, that among these are Life, Liberty, and the Pursuit of Happiness."

RIGHT AT LAST, AN EXPERT'S DREAM

◆ ◆

The recent plunge in the price of oil has some important lessons to teach. The most important by far is that basic economic forces, like the proverbial mills of God, may "grind slowly, yet they grind exceedingly small." Sooner or later they are more powerful and certain in their operation than the attempts of even the strongest of governments to countermand them.

A related lesson is that it is far easier to judge the direction in which economic forces are tending than the timing of their effects. The third lesson is, be wary of the self-proclaimed "experts."

The OPEC factor: Economists have long been predicting that the Organization of Petroleum Exporting Countries could not last. In a 1974 column for *Newsweek*, I predicted that "the Arabs would have to curtail their output by ever larger amounts. But even if they cut their output to zero, they could not for long keep the world price of crude at $10 a barrel." For that prediction, I was awarded a booby prize by the Association for the Promotion of Humor in International Affairs.

In a 1983 column, I wrote that "before the activation of the OPEC cartel in 1973, the price of crude oil was less than $3 a barrel and for many years had been declining after adjustment for inflation. Since then, prices in general in the United States have somewhat more than doubled. About $7 or $8 a barrel today [$8 to $9, if I had written it in 1986] would be the counterpart of a $3 price then. On purely economic grounds, that would seem to be the *upper limit* of where the price of oil will settle. If this seems incredible, just recall how incredible it seemed in 1973 that the price could go from less than $3 a barrel to more than $34 a barrel. Beware the tyranny of the status quo."

The price of crude oil has finally dropped to a level that, adjusted for inflation, is below the $10 limit of my 1974 column. In current prices, it is still about twice the upper limit in my 1983 column. Hence my title. But I hasten to add that I am far from fully vindicated. Timing, as well as direction, is important. OPEC, with much assistance from the United States, was able to hold the price of oil very close to an inflation-adjusted $10 for five years and then, after the Iranian revolution, was able to hold it at an even higher level for another five years—far longer than seemed to me likely in 1974 or 1983.

Like the oil episode, our experience with inflation over the past quarter of a century also exemplifies these basic economic lessons.

The high and rising rate of monetary growth during the 1960s and 1970s was bound to produce high and rising inflation—but economists, myself included, were often wide of the mark in predicting its precise timing and magnitude.

The sharp reduction in monetary growth from 1980 to 1982 was bound to produce disinflation; and so it did—but sooner and more sharply than most forecasters anticipated.

The recent high rates of monetary growth are bound to produce higher inflation—but just when that will occur and how far it will go are far more difficult to judge.

As to the experts, the inflation of the 1970s did not lead to the hyperinflation that so many "gold bugs" regarded as inevitable. Similarly, the recent disinflation has not produced the economic collapse that devotees of the Kondratieff long cycle, a statistical pattern of economic activity that projects an average life span of 54 years for each swing in the economic cycle, regard as overdue.

The same thing is true for the price of oil. The quintupling of the inflation-adjusted price of oil had serious adverse effects on the United States and the rest of the world. However, it did not produce the worldwide financial and economic disasters that so many purveyors of doom and gloom were forecasting at the time.

Bad and the good: The sharp recent plunge in the price of oil, though highly favorable for the United States and the industrialized world, will have serious adverse effects on some sectors of the American economy and on some countries (already, for example, the economy of oil-producing states like Texas is suffering mightily). But it will produce neither the disastrous effects on the banking and oil-related industries, or on the lesser developed countries, that many of the same "experts" are now forecasting—nor the permanently lower inflation and booming economy that other "experts" are predicting.

Our master Adam Smith—the real one of the eighteenth century and not the current journalistic impostor—deserves to have the last word on basic economic forces. More than two centuries ago a friend told Adam Smith that the surrender of General John Burgoyne at Saratoga Springs during the American Revolution would be the ruination of Britain. Replied Adam Smith calmly: "Be assured, my young friend, that there is a great deal of *ruin* in a nation."

ECONOMIC
METHODOLOGY

◆ ◆

• PART • TWO •

THE METHODOLOGY OF POSITIVE ECONOMICS*

· *11* ·

In his admirable book on *The Scope and Method of Political Economy* John Neville Keynes distinguishes among "a *positive science*. . . [,] a body of systematized knowledge concerning what is; a *normative* or *regulative science*. . . [,] a body of systematized knowledge discussing criteria of what ought to be . . . ; an *art*. . . [,] a system of rules for the attainment of a given end"; comments that "confusion between them is common and has been the source of many mischievous errors"; and urges the importance of "recognizing a distinct positive science of political economy."[1]

This paper is concerned primarily with certain methodological problems that arise in constructing the "distinct positive science" Keynes called for—in particular, the problem how to decide whether a suggested hypothesis or theory should be tentatively accepted as part of the "body of systematized knowledge concerning what is." But the confusion Keynes laments is still so rife and so much of a hindrance to the recognition that economics can be, and

Copyright 1953 by The University of Chicago.

From Milton Friedman, *Essays in Positive Economics* (Chicago: University of Chicago Press, 1953).

* I have incorporated bodily in this article without special reference most of my brief "Comment" in B. F. Haley, ed., *A Survey of Contemporary Economics*, vol. II (Chicago: Richard D. Irwin, Inc., 1952), pp. 455–57.

I am indebted to Dorothy S. Brady, Arthur F. Burns, and George J. Stigler for helpful comments and criticism.

in part is, a positive science that it seems well to preface the main body of the paper with a few remarks about the relation between positive and normative economics.

1. The Relation between
Positive and Normative Economics

Confusion between positive and normative economics is to some extent inevitable. The subject matter of economics is regarded by almost everyone as vitally important to himself and within the range of his own experience and competence; it is the source of continuous and extensive controversy and the occasion for frequent legislation. Self-proclaimed "experts" speak with many voices and can hardly all be regarded as disinterested; in any event, on questions that matter so much, "expert" opinion could hardly be accepted solely on faith even if the "experts" were nearly unanimous and clearly disinterested.[2] The conclusions of positive economics seem to be, and are, immediately relevant to important normative problems, to questions of what ought to be done and how any given goal can be attained. Laymen and experts alike are inevitably tempted to shape positive conclusions to fit strongly held normative preconceptions and to reject positive conclusions if their normative implications—or what are said to be their normative implications—are unpalatable.

Positive economics is in principle independent of any particular ethical position or normative judgments. As Keynes says, it deals with "what is," not with "what ought to be." Its task is to provide a system of generalizations that can be used to make correct predictions about the consequences of any change in circumstances. Its performance is to be judged by the precision, scope, and conformity with experience of the predictions it yields. In short, positive economics is, or can be, an "objective" science, in precisely the same sense as any of the physical sciences. Of course, the fact that economics deals with the interrelations of human beings, and that the investigator is himself part of the subject matter being investigated in a more intimate sense than in the physical sciences, raises special difficulties in achieving objectivity at the same time that it provides the social scientist with a class of data not available to the physical scientist. But neither the one nor the other is, in my view, a fundamental distinction between the two groups of sciences.[3]

Normative economics and the art of economics, on the other hand, cannot be independent of positive economics. Any policy conclusion necessarily rests on a prediction about the consequences of doing one thing rather than another, a prediction that must be based—implicitly or explicitly—on positive economics. There is not, of course, a one-to-one relation between policy conclusions and the conclusions of positive economics; if there were, there would be no separate normative science. Two individuals may agree on the consequences of a particular piece of legislation. One may regard them as desirable on balance and so favor the legislation; the other, as undesirable and so oppose the legislation.

I venture the judgment, however, that currently in the Western world, and especially in the United States, differences about economic policy among disinterested citizens derive predominantly from different predictions about the economic consequences of taking action—differences that in principle can be eliminated by the progress of positive economics—rather than from fundamental differences in basic values, differences about which men can ultimately only fight. An obvious and not unimportant example is minimum-wage legislation. Underneath the welter of arguments offered for and against such legislation there is an underlying consensus on the objective of achieving a "living wage" for all, to use the ambiguous phrase so common in such discussions. The difference of opinion is largely grounded on an implicit or explicit difference in predictions about the efficacy of this particular means in furthering the agreed-on end. Proponents believe (predict) that legal minimum wages diminish poverty by raising the wages of those receiving less than the minimum wage as well as of some receiving more than the minimum wage without any counterbalancing increase in the number of people entirely unemployed or employed less advantageously than they otherwise would be. Opponents believe (predict) that legal minimum wages increase poverty by increasing the number of people who are unemployed or employed less advantageously and that this more than offsets any favorable effect on the wages of those who remain employed. Agreement about the economic consequences of the legislation might not produce complete agreement about its desirability, for differences might still remain about its political or social consequences; but, given agreement on objectives, it would certainly go a long way toward producing consensus.

Closely related differences in positive analysis underlie divergent views about the appropriate role and place of trade unions and the desirability of direct price and wage controls and of tariffs. Different predictions about the importance of so-called economies of scale account very largely for divergent views about the desirability or necessity of detailed government regulation of industry and even of socialism rather than private enterprise. And this list could be extended indefinitely.[4] Of course, my judgment that the major differences about economic policy in the Western world are of this kind is itself a "positive" statement to be accepted or rejected on the basis of empirical evidence.

If this judgment is valid, it means that a consensus on "correct" economic policy depends much less on the progress of normative economics proper than on the progress of a positive economics yielding conclusions that are, and deserve to be, widely accepted. It means also that a major reason for distinguishing positive economics sharply from normative economics is precisely the contribution that can thereby be made to agreement about policy.

2. POSITIVE ECONOMICS

The ultimate goal of a positive science is the development of a "theory" or "hypothesis" that yields valid and meaningful (i.e., not truistic) predictions about phenomena not yet observed. Such a theory is, in general, a complex intermixture of two elements. In part, it is a "language" designed to promote "systematic and organized methods of reasoning."[5] In part, it is a body of substantive hypotheses designed to abstract essential features of complex reality.

Viewed as a language, theory has no substantive content; it is a set of tautologies. Its function is to serve as a filing system for organizing empirical material and facilitating our understanding of it; and the criteria by which it is to be judged are those appropriate to a filing system. Are the categories clearly and precisely defined? Are they exhaustive? Do we know where to file each individual item, or is there considerable ambiguity? Is the system of headings and subheadings so designed that we can quickly find an item we want, or must we hunt from place to place? Are the items we shall want to consider jointly filed together? Does the filing system avoid elaborate cross-references?

The answers to these questions depend partly on logical, partly on factual, considerations. The canons of formal logic alone can show whether a particular language is complete and consistent, that is, whether propositions in the language are "right" or "wrong." Factual evidence alone can show whether the categories of the "analytical filing system" have a meaningful empirical counterpart, that is, whether they are useful in analyzing a particular class of concrete problems.[6] The simple example of "supply" and "demand" illustrates both this point and the preceding list of analogical questions. Viewed as elements of the language of economic theory, these are the two major categories into which factors affecting the relative prices of products or factors of production are classified. The usefulness of the dichotomy depends on the "empirical generalization that an enumeration of the forces affecting demand in any problem and of the forces affecting supply will yield two lists that contain few items in common."[7] Now this generalization is valid for markets like the final market for a consumer good. In such a market there is a clear and sharp distinction between the economic units that can be regarded as demanding the product and those that can be regarded as supplying it. There is seldom much doubt whether a particular factor should be classified as affecting supply, on the one hand, or demand, on the other; and there is seldom much necessity for considering cross-effects (cross-references) between the two categories. In these cases the simple and even obvious step of filing the relevant factors under the headings of "supply" and "demand" effects a great simplification of the problem and is an effective safeguard against fallacies that otherwise tend to occur. But the generalization is not always valid. For example, it is not valid for the day-to-day fluctuations of prices in a primarily speculative market. Is a rumor of an increased excess-profits tax, for example, to be regarded as a factor operating primarily on today's supply of corporate equities in the stock market or on today's demand for them? In similar fashion, almost every factor can with about as much justification be classified under the heading "supply" as under the heading "demand." These concepts can still be used and may not be entirely pointless; they are still "right" but clearly less useful than in the first example because they have no meaningful empirical counterpart.

Viewed as a body of substantive hypotheses, theory is to be judged by its predictive power for the class of phenomena which it is intended to "explain." Only factual evidence can show whether it is "right" or "wrong" or, better, tentatively "accepted" as valid or "rejected." As I shall argue at greater length below, the only relevant test of the *validity* of a hypothesis is comparison of its predictions with experience. The hypothesis is rejected if its predictions are contradicted ("frequently" or more often than predictions from an alternative hypothesis); it is accepted if its predictions are not contradicted; great confidence is attached to it if it has survived many opportunities for contradiction. Factual evidence can never "prove" a hypothesis; it can only fail to disprove it, which is what we generally mean when we say, somewhat inexactly, that the hypothesis has been "confirmed" by experience.

To avoid confusion, it should perhaps be noted explicitly that the "predictions" by which the validity of a hypothesis is tested need not be about phenomena that have not yet occurred, that is, need not be forecasts of future events; they may be about phenomena that have occurred but observations on which have not yet been made or are not known to the person making the prediction. For example, a hypothesis may imply that such and such must have happened in 1906, given some other known circumstances. If a search of the records reveals that such and such did happen, the prediction is confirmed; if it reveals that such and such did not happen, the prediction is contradicted.

The validity of a hypothesis in this sense is not by itself a sufficient criterion for choosing among alternative hypotheses. Observed facts are necessarily finite in number; possible hypotheses, infinite. If there is one hypothesis that is consistent with the available evidence, there are always an infinite number that are.[8] For example, suppose a specific excise tax on a particular commodity produces a rise in price equal to the amount of the tax. This is consistent with competitive conditions, a stable demand curve, and a horizontal and stable supply curve. But it is also consistent with competitive conditions and a positively or negatively sloping supply curve with the required compensating shift in the demand curve or the supply curve; with monopolistic conditions, constant marginal costs, and stable demand curve, of the particular shape required to produce this result; and so on indefinitely. Additional evidence with which the hypothesis is to be consistent may rule out some of these possibilities; it can never reduce them to a single possibility alone capable of being consistent with the finite evidence. The choice among alternative hypotheses equally consistent with the available evidence must to some extent be arbitrary, though there is general agreement that relevant considerations are suggested by the criteria "simplicity" and "fruitfulness," themselves notions that defy completely objective specification. A theory is "simpler" the less the initial knowledge needed to make a prediction within a given field of phenomena; it is more "fruitful" the more precise the resulting prediction, the wider the area within which the theory yields predictions, and the more additional lines for further research it suggests. Logical completeness and consistency are relevant but play a subsidiary role; their function is to assure that the hypothesis says what it is intended to say and does so alike for all users—they play the same role here as checks for arithmetical accuracy do in statistical computations.

Unfortunately, we can seldom test particular predictions in the social sciences by experiments explicitly designed to eliminate what are judged to be the most important disturbing influences. Generally, we must rely on evidence cast up by the "experiments" that happen to occur. The inability to conduct so-called controlled experiments does not, in my view, reflect a basic difference between the social and physical sciences both because it is not peculiar to the social sciences—witness astronomy—and because the distinction between a controlled experiment and uncontrolled experience is at best one of degree. No experiment can be completely controlled, and every experience is partly controlled, in the sense that some disturbing influences are relatively constant in the course of it.

Evidence cast up by experience is abundant and frequently as conclusive as that from contrived experiments; thus the inability to conduct experiments is not a fundamental obstacle to testing hypotheses by the success of their predictions. But such evidence is far more difficult to interpret. It is frequently complex and always indirect and incomplete. Its collection is often arduous, and its interpretation generally requires subtle analysis and involved chains of reasoning, which seldom carry real conviction. The denial to economics of the dramatic and direct evidence of the "crucial" experiment does hinder the adequate testing of hypotheses; but this is much less significant than the difficulty it places in the way of achieving a reasonably prompt and wide consensus on the conclusions justified by the available evidence. It renders the weeding out of unsuccessful hypotheses slow and difficult. They are seldom downed for good and are always cropping up again.

There is, of course, considerable variation in these respects. Occasionally, experience casts up evidence that is about as direct, dramatic, and convincing as any that could be provided by controlled experiments. Perhaps the most obviously important example is the evidence from inflations on the hypothesis that a substantial increase in the quantity of money within a relatively short period is accompanied by a substantial increase in prices. Here the evidence is dramatic, and the chain of reasoning required to interpret it is relatively short. Yet, despite numerous instances of substantial rises in prices, their essentially one-to-one correspondence with substantial rises in the stock of money, and the wide variation in other circumstances that might appear to be relevant, each new experience of inflation brings forth vigorous contentions, and not only by the lay public, that the rise in the stock of money is either an incidental effect of a rise in prices produced by other factors or a purely fortuitous and unnecessary concomitant of the price rise.

One effect of the difficulty of testing substantive economic hypotheses has been to foster a retreat into purely formal or tautological analysis.[9] As already noted, tautologies have an extremely important place in economics and other sciences as a specialized language or "analytical filing system." Beyond this, formal logic and mathematics, which are both tautologies, are essential aids in checking the correctness of reasoning, discovering the implications of hypotheses, and determining whether supposedly different hypotheses may not really be equivalent or wherein the differences lie.

But economic theory must be more than a structure of tautologies if it is to be able to predict and not merely describe the consequences of action; if it is to be something different from disguised mathematics.[10] And the usefulness of the tautologies themselves ultimately depends, as noted above, on the acceptability of the substantive hypotheses that suggest the particular categories into which they organize the refractory empirical phenomena.

A more serious effect of the difficulty of testing economic hypotheses by their predictions is to foster misunderstanding of the role of empirical evidence in theoretical work. Empirical evidence is vital at two different, though closely related, stages: in constructing hypotheses and in testing their validity. Full and comprehensive evidence on the phenomena to be generalized or "explained" by a hypothesis, besides its obvious value in suggesting new hypotheses, is needed to assure that a hypothesis explains what it sets out to explain—that its implications for such phenomena are not contradicted in advance by experience that has already been observed.[11] Given that the hypothesis is consistent with the evidence at hand, its further testing involves deducing from it new facts capable of being observed but not previously known and checking these deduced facts against additional empirical evidence. For this test to be relevant, the deduced facts must be about the class of phenomena the hypothesis is designed to explain; and they must be well enough defined so that observation can show them to be wrong.

The two stages of constructing hypotheses and testing their validity are related in two different respects. In the first place, the particular facts that enter at each stage are partly an accident of the collection of data and the knowledge of the particular investigator. The facts that serve as a test of the implications of a hypothesis might equally well have been among the raw material used to construct it, and conversely. In the second place, the process never begins from scratch; the so-called initial stage itself always involves comparison of the implications of an earlier set of hypotheses with observation; the contradiction of these implications is the stimulus to the construction of new hypotheses or revision of old ones. So the two methodologically distinct stages are always proceeding jointly.

Misunderstanding about this apparently straightforward process centers on the phrase "the class of phenomena the hypothesis is designed to explain." The difficulty in the social sciences of getting new evidence for this class of phenomena and of judging its conformity with the implications of the hypothesis makes it tempting to suppose that other, more readily available, evidence is equally relevant to the validity of the hypothesis—to suppose that hypotheses have not only "implications" but also "assumptions" and that the conformity of these "assumptions" to "reality" is a test of the validity of the hypothesis *different from* or *additional to* the test by implications. This widely held view is fundamentally wrong and productive of much mischief. Far from providing an easier means for sifting valid from invalid hypotheses, it only confuses the issue, promotes misunderstanding about the significance of empirical evidence for economic theory, produces a misdirection of much intellectual effort devoted to the development of positive economics, and impedes the attainment of consensus on tentative hypotheses in positive economics.

In so far as a theory can be said to have "assumptions" at all, and in so far as their "realism" can be judged independently of the validity of predictions, the relation between the significance of a theory and the "realism" of its "assumptions" is almost the opposite of that suggested by the view under criticism. Truly important and significant hypotheses will be found to have "assumptions" that are wildly inaccurate descriptive representations of reality, and, in general, the more significant the theory, the more unrealistic the assumptions (in this sense).[12] The reason is simple. A hypothesis is important if it "explains" much by little, that is, if it abstracts the common and crucial elements from the mass of complex and detailed circumstances surrounding the phenomena to be explained and permits valid predictions on the basis of them alone. To be important, therefore, a hypothesis must be descriptively false in its assumptions; it takes account of, and accounts for, none of the many other attendant circumstances, since its very success shows them to be irrelevant for the phenomena to be explained.

To put this point less paradoxically, the relevant question to ask about the "assumptions" of a theory is not whether they are descriptively "realistic," for they never are, but whether they are sufficiently good approximations for the purpose in hand. And this question can be answered only by seeing whether the theory works, which means whether it yields sufficiently accurate predictions. The two supposedly independent tests thus reduce to one test.

The theory of monopolistic and imperfect competition is one example of the neglect in economic theory of these propositions. The development of this analysis was explicitly motivated, and its wide acceptance and approval largely explained, by the belief that the assumptions of "perfect competition" or "perfect monopoly" said to underlie neoclassical economic theory are a false image of reality. And this belief was itself based almost entirely on the directly perceived descriptive inaccuracy of the assumptions rather than on any recognized contradiction of predictions derived from neoclassical economic theory. The lengthy discussion on marginal analysis in the *American Economic Review* some years ago is an even clearer, though much less important, example. The articles on both sides of the controversy largely neglect what seems to me clearly the main issue—the conformity to experience of the implications of the marginal analysis—and concentrate on the largely irrelevant question whether businessmen do or do not in fact reach their decisions by consulting schedules, or curves, or multivariable functions showing marginal cost and marginal revenue.[13] Perhaps these two examples, and the many others they readily suggest, will serve to justify a more extensive discussion of the methodological principles involved than might otherwise seem appropriate.

3. CAN A HYPOTHESIS BE TESTED BY THE REALISM OF ITS ASSUMPTIONS?

We may start with a simple physical example, the law of falling bodies. It is an accepted hypothesis that the acceleration of a body dropped in a vacuum is a constant—g, or approximately 32 feet per second per second on the earth— and is independent of the shape of the body, the manner of dropping it, etc. This implies that the distance traveled by a falling body in any specified time is given by the formula $s = \frac{1}{2}gt^2$, where s is the distance traveled in feet and t is the time in seconds. The application of this formula to a compact ball dropped from the roof of a building is equivalent to saying that a ball so dropped behaves *as if* it were falling in a vacuum. Testing this hypothesis by its assumptions presumably means measuring the actual air pressure and deciding whether it is close enough to zero. At sea level the air pressure is about fifteen pounds per square inch. Is fifteen sufficiently close to zero for the difference to be judged insignificant? Apparently it is, since the actual time taken by a compact ball to fall from the roof of a building to the ground is very close to the time given by the formula. Suppose, however, that a feather is dropped instead of a compact ball. The formula then gives wildly inaccurate results. Apparently, fifteen pounds per square inch is significantly different from zero for a feather but not for a ball. Or, again, suppose the formula is applied to a ball dropped from an airplane at an altitude of 30,000 feet. The air pressure at this altitude is decidedly less than fifteen pounds per square inch. Yet, the actual time of fall from 30,000 feet to 20,000 feet, at which point the air pressure is still much less than at sea level, will differ noticeably from the time predicted by the formula—much more noticeably than the time taken by a compact ball to fall from the roof of a building to the ground. According to the formula, the velocity of the ball should be gt and should therefore increase steadily. In fact, a ball dropped at 30,000 feet will reach its top velocity well before it hits the ground. And similarly with other implications of the formula.

The initial question whether fifteen is sufficiently close to zero for the difference to be judged insignificant is clearly a foolish question by itself. Fifteen pounds per square inch is 2,160 pounds per square foot, or 0.0075 ton per square inch. There is no possible basis for calling these numbers "small" or "large" without some external standard of comparison. And the only relevant standard of comparison is the air pressure for which the formula does or does not work under a given set of circumstances. But this raises the same problem at a second level. What is the meaning of "does or does not work"? Even if we could eliminate errors of measurement, the measured time of fall would seldom if ever be precisely equal to the computed time of fall. How large must the difference between the two be to justify saying that the theory "does not work"? Here there are two important external standards of comparison. One is the accuracy achievable by an alternative theory with which this theory is being compared and which is equally acceptable on all other grounds. The other arises when there exists a theory that is known to yield better predictions but only at a greater cost. The gains from greater accuracy, which depend on the purpose in mind, must then be balanced against the costs of achieving it.

This example illustrates both the impossibility of testing a theory by its assumptions and also the ambiguity of the concept "the assumptions of a theory." The formula $s = \frac{1}{2}gt^2$ is valid for bodies falling in a vacuum and can be derived by analyzing the behavior of such bodies. It can therefore be stated: under a wide range of circumstances, bodies that fall in the actual atmosphere behave *as if* they were falling in a vacuum. In the language so common in economics this would be rapidly translated into: the formula assumes a vacuum. Yet it clearly does no such thing. What it does say is that in many cases the existence of air pressure, the shape of the body, the name of the person dropping the body, the kind of mechanism used to drop the body, and a host of other attendant circumstances have no appreciable effect on the distance the body falls in a specified time. The hypothesis can readily be rephrased to omit all mention of a vacuum: under a wide range of circumstances, the distance a body falls in a specified time is given by the formula $s = \frac{1}{2}gt^2$. The history of this formula and its associated physical theory aside, is it meaningful to say that it assumes a vacuum? For all I know there may be other sets of assumptions that would yield the same formula. The formula is accepted because it works, not because we live in an approximate vacuum—whatever that means.

The important problem in connection with the hypothesis is to specify the circumstances under which the formula works or, more precisely, the general magnitude of the error in its predictions under various circumstances. Indeed, as is implicit in the above rephrasing of the hypothesis, such a specification is not one thing and the hypothesis another. The specification is itself an essential part of the hypothesis, and it is a part that is peculiarly likely to be revised and extended as experience accumulates.

In the particular case of falling bodies a more general, though still incomplete, theory is available, largely as a result of attempts to explain the errors of the simple theory, from which the influence of some of the possible disturbing factors can be calculated and of which the simple theory is a special case. However, it does not always pay to use the more general theory because the extra accuracy it yields may not justify the extra cost of using it, so the question under what circumstances the simpler theory works "well enough" remains important. Air pressure is one, but only one, of the variables that define these circumstances; the shape of the body, the velocity attained, and still other variables are relevant as well. One way of interpreting the variables other than air pressure is to regard them as determining whether a particular departure from the "assumption" of a vacuum is or is not significant. For example, the difference in shape of the body can be said to make fifteen pounds per square inch significantly different from zero for a feather but not for a compact ball dropped a moderate distance. Such a statement must, however, be sharply distinguished from the very different statement that the theory does not work for a feather because its assumptions are false. The relevant relation runs the other way: the assumptions are false for a feather because the theory does not work. This point needs emphasis, because the entirely valid use of "assumptions" in *specifying* the circumstances for which a theory holds is frequently, and erroneously, interpreted to mean that the assumptions can be used to *determine* the circumstances for which a theory holds, and has, in this way, been an important source of the belief that a theory can be tested by its assumptions.

Let us turn now to another example, this time a constructed one designed to be an analogue of many hypotheses in the social sciences. Consider the density of leaves around a tree. I suggest the hypothesis that the leaves are positioned as if each leaf deliberately sought to maximize the amount of sunlight it receives, given the position of its neighbors, as if it knew the physical laws determining the amount of sunlight that would be received in various positions and could move rapidly or instantaneously from any one position to any other desired and unoccupied position.[14] Now some of the more obvious implications of this hypothesis are clearly consistent with experience: for example, leaves are in general denser on the south than on the north side of trees but, as the hypothesis implies, less so or not at all on the northern slope of a hill or when the south side of the trees is shaded in some other way. Is the hypothesis rendered unacceptable or invalid because, so far as we know, leaves do not "deliberate" or consciously "seek," have not been to school and learned the relevant laws of science or the mathematics required to calculate the "optimum" position, and cannot move from position to position? Clearly, none of these contradictions of the hypothesis is vitally relevant; the phenomena involved are not within the "class of phenomena the hypothesis is designed to explain"; the hypothesis does not assert that leaves do these things but only that their density is the same *as if* they did. Despite the apparent falsity of the "assumptions" of the hypothesis, it has great plausibility because of the conformity of its implications with observation. We are inclined to "explain" its validity on the ground that sunlight contributes to the growth of leaves and that hence leaves will grow denser or more putative leaves survive where there is more sun, so the result achieved by purely passive adaptation to external circumstances is the same as the result that would be achieved by deliberate accommodation to them. This alternative hypothesis is more attractive than the constructed hypothesis not because its "assumptions" are more "realistic" but rather because it is part of a more general theory that applies to a wider variety of phenomena, of which the position of leaves around a tree is a special case, has more implications capable of being contradicted, and has failed to be contradicted under a wider variety of circumstances. The direct evidence for the growth of leaves is in this way strengthened by the indirect evidence from the other phenomena to which the more general theory applies.

The constructed hypothesis is presumably valid, that is, yields "sufficiently" accurate predictions about the density of leaves, only for a particular class of circumstances. I do not know what these circumstances are or how to define them. It seems obvious, however, that in this example the "assumptions" of the theory will play no part in specifying them: the kind of tree, the character of the soil, etc., are the types of variables that are likely to define its range of validity, not the ability of the leaves to do complicated mathematics or to move from place to place.

A largely parallel example involving human behavior has been used elsewhere by Savage and me.[15] Consider the problem of predicting the shots made by an expert billiard player. It seems not at all unreasonable that excellent predictions would be yielded by the hypothesis that the billiard player made his shots *as if* he knew the complicated mathematical formulas that would give the optimum directions of travel, could estimate accurately by eye the angles, etc., describing the location of the balls, could make lightning calculations from the formulas, and could then make the balls travel in the direction indicated by the formulas. Our confidence in this hypothesis is not based on the belief that billiard players, even expert ones, can or do go through the process described; it derives rather from the belief that, unless in some way or other they were capable of reaching essentially the same result, they would not in fact be *expert* billiard players.

It is only a short step from these examples to the economic hypothesis that under a wide range of circumstances individual firms behave *as if* they were seeking rationally to maximize their expected returns (generally if misleadingly called "profits")[16] and had full knowledge of the data needed to succeed in this attempt; *as if*, that is, they knew the relevant cost and demand functions, calculated marginal cost and marginal revenue from all actions open to them, and pushed each line of action to the point at which the relevant marginal cost and marginal revenue were equal. Now, of course, businessmen do not actually and literally solve the system of simultaneous equations in terms of which the mathematical economist finds it convenient to express this hypothesis, any more than leaves or billiard players explicitly go through complicated mathematical calculations or falling bodies decide to create a vacuum. The billiard player, if asked how he decides where to hit the ball, may say that he "just figures it out" but then also rubs a rabbit's foot just to make sure; and the businessman may well say that he prices at average cost, with of course some minor deviations when the market makes it necessary. The one statement is about as helpful as the other, and neither is a relevant test of the associated hypothesis.

Confidence in the maximization-of-returns hypothesis is justified by evidence of a very different character. This evidence is in part similar to that adduced on behalf of the billiard-player hypothesis—unless the behavior of businessmen in some way or other approximated behavior consistent with the maximization of returns, it seems unlikely that they would remain in business for long. Let the apparent immediate determinant of business behavior be anything at all—habitual reaction, random chance, or whatnot. Whenever this determinant happens to lead to behavior consistent with rational and informed maximization of returns, the business will prosper and acquire resources with which to expand; whenever it does not, the business will tend to lose resources and can be kept in existence only by the addition of resources from outside. The process of "natural selection" thus helps to validate the hypothesis—or, rather, given natural selection, acceptance of the hypothesis can be based largely on the judgment that it summarizes appropriately the conditions for survival.

An even more important body of evidence for the maximization-of-returns hypothesis is experience from countless applications of the hypothesis to specific problems and the repeated failure of its implications to be contradicted. This evidence is extremely hard to document; it is scattered in numerous memorandums, articles, and monographs concerned primarily with specific concrete problems rather than with submitting the hypothesis to test. Yet the continued use and acceptance of the hypothesis over a long period, and the failure of any coherent, self-consistent alternative to be developed and be widely accepted, is strong indirect testimony to its worth. The evidence *for* a hypothesis always consists of its repeated failure to be contradicted, continues to accumulate so long as the hypothesis is used, and by its very nature is difficult to document at all comprehensively. It tends to become part of the tradition and folklore of a science revealed in the tenacity with which hypotheses are held rather than in any textbook list of instances in which the hypothesis has failed to be contradicted.

4. The Significance and Role of the "Assumptions" of a Theory

Up to this point our conclusions about the significance of the "assumptions" of a theory have been almost entirely negative: we have seen that a theory cannot be tested by the "realism" of its "assumptions" and that the very concept of the "assumptions" of a theory is surrounded with ambiguity. But, if this were all there is to it, it would be hard to explain the extensive use of the concept and the strong tendency that we all have to speak of the assumptions of a theory and to compare the assumptions of alternative theories. There is too much smoke for there to be no fire.

In methodology, as in positive science, negative statements can generally be made with greater confidence than positive statements, so I have less confidence in the following remarks on the significance and role of "assumptions" than in the preceding remarks. So far as I can see, the "assumptions of a theory" play three different, though related, positive roles: (a) they are often an economical mode of describing or presenting a theory; (b) they sometimes facilitate an indirect test of the hypothesis by its implications; and (c), as already noted, they are sometimes a convenient means of specifying the conditions under which the theory is expected to be valid. The first two require more extensive discussion.

a. The Use of "Assumptions" in Stating a Theory

The example of the leaves illustrates the first role of assumptions. Instead of saying that leaves seek to maximize the sunlight they receive, we could state the equivalent hypothesis, without any apparent assumptions, in the form of a list of rules for predicting the density of leaves: if a tree stands in a level field with no other trees or other bodies obstructing the rays of the sun, then the density of leaves will tend to be such and such; if a tree is on the northern slope of a hill in the midst of a forest of similar trees, then . . . ; etc. This is clearly a far less economical presentation of the hypothesis than the statement that leaves seek to maximize the sunlight each receives. The latter statement is, in effect, a simple summary of the rules in the above list, even if the list were indefinitely extended, since it indicates both how to determine the features of the environment that are important for the particular problem and how to evaluate their effects. It is more compact and at the same time no less comprehensive.

More generally, a hypothesis or theory consists of an assertion that certain forces are, and by implication others are not, important for a particular class of phenomena and a specification of the manner of action of the forces it asserts to be important. We can regard the hypothesis as consisting of two parts: first, a conceptual world or abstract model simpler than the "real world" and containing only the forces that the hypothesis asserts to be important; second, a set of rules defining the class of phenomena for which the "model" can be taken to be an adequate representation of the "real world" and specifying the correspondence between the variables or entities in the model and observable phenomena.

These two parts are very different in character. The model is abstract and complete; it is an "algebra" or "logic." Mathematics and formal logic come into their own in checking its consistency and completeness and exploring its implications. There is no place in the model for, and no function to be served by, vagueness, maybe's, or approximations. The air pressure is zero, not "small," for a vacuum; the demand curve for the product of a competitive producer is horizontal (has a slope of zero), not "almost horizontal."

The rules for using the model, on the other hand, cannot possibly be abstract and complete. They must be concrete and in consequence incomplete—completeness is possible only in a conceptual world, not in the "real world," however that may be interpreted. The model is the logical embodiment of the half-truth, "There is nothing new under the sun"; the rules for applying it cannot neglect the equally significant half-truth, "History never repeats itself." To a considerable extent the rules can be formulated explicitly—most easily, though even then not completely, when the theory is part of an explicit more general theory as in the example of the vacuum theory for falling bodies. In seeking to make a science as "objective" as possible, our aim should be to formulate the rules explicitly in so far as possible and continually to widen the range of phenomena for which it is possible to do so. But, no matter how successful we may be in this attempt, there inevitably will remain room for judgment in applying the rules. Each occurrence has some features peculiarly its own, not covered by the explicit rules. The capacity to judge that these are or are not to be disregarded, that they should or should not affect what observable phenomena are to be identified with what entities in the model, is something that cannot be taught; it can be learned but only by experience and exposure in the "right" scientific atmosphere, not by rote. It is at this point that the amateur is separated from the professional in all sciences and that the thin line is drawn which distinguishes the crackpot from the scientist.

A simple example may perhaps clarify this point. Euclidean geometry is an abstract model, logically complete and consistent. Its entities are precisely defined—a line is not a geometrical figure "much" longer than it is wide or deep; it is a figure whose width and depth are zero. It is also obviously "unrealistic." There are no such things in "reality" as Euclidean points or lines or surfaces. Let us apply this abstract model to a mark made on a blackboard by a piece of chalk. Is the mark to be identified with a Euclidean line, a Euclidean surface, or a Euclidean solid? Clearly, it can appropriately be identified with a line if it is being used to represent, say, a demand curve. But it cannot be so identified if it is being used to color, say, countries on a map, for that would imply that the map would never be colored; for this purpose, the same mark must be identified with a surface. But it cannot be so identified by a manufacturer of chalk, for that would imply that no chalk would ever be used up; for his purposes, the same mark must be identified with a volume. In this simple example these judgments will command general agreement. Yet it seems obvious that, while general considerations can be formulated to guide such judgments, they can never be comprehensive and cover every possible instance; they cannot have the self-contained coherent character of Euclidean geometry itself.

In speaking of the "crucial assumptions" of a theory, we are, I believe, trying to state the key elements of the abstract model. There are generally many different ways of describing the model completely—many different sets of "postulates" which both imply and are implied by the model as a whole. These are all logically equivalent: what are regarded as axioms or postulates of a model from one point of view can be regarded as theorems from another, and conversely. The particular "assumptions" termed "crucial" are selected on grounds of their convenience in some such respects as simplicity or economy in describing the model, intuitive plausibility, or capacity to suggest, if only by implication, some of the considerations that are relevant in judging or applying the model.

b. The Use of "Assumptions" as an Indirect Test of a Theory

In presenting any hypothesis, it generally seems obvious which of the series of statements used to expound it refer to assumptions and which to implications; yet this distinction is not easy to define rigorously. It is not, I believe, a characteristic of the hypothesis as such but rather of the use to which the hypothesis is to be put. If this is so, the ease of classifying statements must reflect unambiguousness in the purpose the hypothesis is designed to serve. The possibility of interchanging theorems and axioms in an abstract model implies the possibility of interchanging "implications" and "assumptions" in the substantive hypothesis corresponding to the abstract model, which is not to say that any implication can be interchanged with any assumption but only that there may be more than one set of statements that imply the rest.

For example, consider a particular proposition in the theory of oligopolistic behavior. If we assume (a) that entrepreneurs seek to maximize their returns by any means including acquiring or extending monopoly power, this will imply (b) that, when demand for a "product" is geographically unstable, transportation costs are significant, explicit price agreements illegal, and the number of producers of the product relatively small, they will tend to establish basing-point pricing systems.[17] The assertion (a) is regarded as an assumption and (b) as an implication because we accept the prediction of market behavior as the purpose of the analysis. We shall regard the assumption as acceptable if we find that the conditions specified in (b) are generally associated with basing-point pricing, and conversely. Let us now change our purpose to deciding what cases to prosecute under the Sherman Antitrust Law's prohibition of a "conspiracy in restraint of trade." If we now assume (c) that basing-point pricing is a deliberate construction to facilitate collusion under the conditions specified in (b), this will imply (d) that entrepreneurs who participate in basing-point pricing are engaged in a "conspiracy in restraint of trade." What was formerly an assumption now becomes an implication, and conversely. We shall now regard the assumption (c) as valid if we find that, when entrepreneurs participate in basing-point pricing, there generally tends to be other evidence, in the form of letters, memorandums, or the like, of what courts regard as a "conspiracy in restraint of trade."

Suppose the hypothesis works for the first purpose, namely, the prediction of market behavior. It clearly does not follow that it will work for the second purpose, namely, predicting whether there is enough evidence of a "conspiracy in restraint of trade" to justify court action. And, conversely, if it works for the second purpose, it does not follow that it will work for the first. Yet, in the absence of other evidence, the success of the hypothesis for one purpose—in explaining one class of phenomena—will give us greater confidence than we would otherwise have that it may succeed for another purpose—in explaining another class of phenomena. It is much harder to say how much greater confidence it justifies. For this depends on how closely related we judge the two classes of phenomena to be, which itself depends in a complex way on similar kinds of indirect evidence, that is, on our experience in other connections in explaining by single theories phenomena that are in some sense similarly diverse.

To state the point more generally, what are called the assumptions of a hypothesis can be used to get some indirect evidence on the acceptability of the hypothesis in so far as the assumptions can themselves be regarded as implications of the hypothesis, and hence their conformity with reality as a failure of some implications to be contradicted, or in so far as the assumptions may call to mind other implications of the hypothesis susceptible to casual empirical observation.[18] The reason this evidence is indirect is that the assumptions or associated implications generally refer to a class of phenomena different from the class which the hypothesis is designed to explain; indeed, as is implied above, this seems to be the chief criterion we use in deciding which statements to term "assumptions" and which to term "implications." The weight attached to this indirect evidence depends on how closely related we judge the two classes of phenomena to be.

Another way in which the "assumptions" of a hypothesis can facilitate its indirect testing is by bringing out its kinship with other hypotheses and thereby making the evidence on their validity relevant to the validity of the hypothesis in question. For example, a hypothesis is formulated for a particular class of behavior. This hypothesis can, as usual, be stated without specifying any "assumptions." But suppose it can be shown that it is equivalent to a set of assumptions including the assumption that man seeks his own interest. The hypothesis then gains indirect plausibility from the success for other classes of phenomena of hypotheses that can also be said to make this assumption; at least, what is being done here is not completely unprecedented or unsuccessful in all other uses. In effect, the statement of assumptions so as to bring out a relationship between superficially different hypotheses is a step in the direction of a more general hypothesis.

This kind of indirect evidence from related hypotheses explains in large measure the difference in the confidence attached to a particular hypothesis by people with different backgrounds. Consider, for example, the hypothesis that the extent of racial or religious discrimination in employment in a particular area or industry is closely related to the degree of monopoly in the industry or area in question; that, if the industry is competitive, discrimination will be significant only if the race or religion of employees affects either the willingness of other employees to work with them or the acceptability of the product to customers and will be uncorrelated with the prejudices of employers.[19] This hypothesis is far more likely to appeal to an economist than to a sociologist. It can be said to "assume" single-minded pursuit of pecuniary self-interest by employers in competitive industries; and this "assumption" works well in a wide variety of hypotheses in economics bearing on many of the mass phenomena with which economics deals. It is therefore likely to seem reasonable to the economist that it may work in this case as well. On the other hand, the hypotheses to which the sociologist is accustomed have a very different kind of model or ideal world, in which single-minded pursuit of pecuniary self-interest plays a much less important role. The indirect evidence available to the sociologist on this hypothesis is much less favorable to it than the indirect evidence available to the economist; he is therefore likely to view it with greater suspicion.

Of course, neither the evidence of the economist nor that of the sociologist is conclusive. The decisive test is whether the hypothesis works for the phenomena it purports to explain. But a judgment may be required before any satisfactory test of this kind has been made, and, perhaps, when it cannot be made in the near future, in which case, the judgment will have to be based on the inadequate evidence available. In addition, even when such a test can be made, the background of the scientists is not irrelevant to the judgments they reach. There is never certainty in science, and the weight of evidence for or against a hypothesis can never be assessed completely "objectively." The economist will be more tolerant than the sociologist in judging conformity of the implications of the hypothesis with experience, and he will be persuaded to accept the hypothesis tentatively by fewer instances of "conformity."

5. Some Implications for Economic Issues

The abstract methodological issues we have been discussing have a direct bearing on the perennial criticism of "orthodox" economic theory as "unrealistic" as well as on the attempts that have been made to reformulate theory to meet this charge. Economics is a "dismal" science because it assumes man to be selfish and money-grubbing, "a lightning calculator of pleasures and pains, who oscillates like a homogeneous globule of desire of happiness under the impulse of stimuli that shift him about the area, but leave him intact";[20] it rests on outmoded psychology and must be reconstructed in line with each new development in psychology; it assumes men, or at least businessmen, to be "in a continuous state of 'alert,' ready to change prices and/or pricing rules whenever their sensitive intuitions . . . detect a change in demand and supply condi-

172 ♦ ECONOMIC METHODOLOGY

tions";[21] it assumes markets to be perfect, competition to be pure, and commodities, labor, and capital to be homogeneous.

As we have seen, criticism of this type is largely beside the point unless supplemented by evidence that a hypothesis differing in one or another of these respects from the theory being criticized yields better predictions for as wide a range of phenomena. Yet most such criticism is not so supplemented; it is based almost entirely on supposedly directly perceived discrepancies between the "assumptions" and the "real world." A particularly clear example is furnished by the recent criticisms of the maximization-of-returns hypothesis on the grounds that businessmen do not and indeed cannot behave as the theory "assumes" they do. The evidence cited to support this assertion is generally taken either from the answers given by businessmen to questions about the factors affecting their decisions—a procedure for testing economic theories that is about on a par with testing theories of longevity by asking octogenarians how they account for their long life—or from descriptive studies of the decision-making activities of individual firms.[22] Little if any evidence is ever cited on the conformity of businessmen's actual market behavior—what they do rather than what they say they do—with the implications of the hypothesis being criticized, on the one hand, and of an alternative hypothesis, on the other.

A theory or its "assumptions" cannot possibly be thoroughly "realistic" in the immediate descriptive sense so often assigned to this term. A completely "realistic" theory of the wheat market would have to include not only the conditions directly underlying the supply and demand for wheat but also the kind of coins or credit instruments used to make exchanges; the personal characteristics of wheat traders such as the color of each trader's hair and eyes, his antecedents and education, the number of members of his family, their characteristics, antecedents, and education, etc.; the kind of soil on which the wheat was grown, its physical and chemical characteristics, the weather prevailing during the growing season; the personal characteristics of the farmers growing the wheat and of the consumers who will ultimately use it; and so on indefinitely. Any attempt to move very far in achieving this kind of "realism" is certain to render a theory utterly useless.

Of course, the notion of a completely realistic theory is in part a straw man. No critic of a theory would accept this logical extreme as his objective; he would say that the "assumptions" of the theory being criticized were "too" unrealistic and that his objective was a set of assumptions that were "more" realistic though still not completely and slavishly so. But so long as the test of "realism" is the directly perceived descriptive accuracy of the "assumptions"— for example, the observation that "businessmen do not appear to be either as avaricious or as dynamic or as logical as marginal theory portrays them"[23] or that "it would be utterly impractical under present conditions for the manager of a multiprocess plant to attempt. . . to work out and equate marginal costs and marginal revenues for each productive factor"[24]—there is no basis for making such a distinction, that is, for stopping short of the straw man depicted in the preceding paragraph. What is the criterion by which to judge whether a particular departure from realism is or is not acceptable? Why is it more "unrealistic" in analyzing business behavior to neglect the magnitude of businessmen's costs than the color of their eyes? The obvious answer is because the first makes more difference to business behavior than the second; but there is no way of knowing that this is so simply by observing that businessmen do have costs of different magnitudes and eyes of different color. Clearly it can only be known by comparing the effect on the discrepancy between actual and predicted behavior of taking the one factor or the other into account. Even the most extreme proponents of realistic assumptions are thus necessarily driven to reject their own criterion and to accept the test by prediction when they classify alternative assumptions as more or less realistic.[25]

The basic confusion between descriptive accuracy and analytical relevance that underlies most criticisms of economic theory on the grounds that its assumptions are unrealistic as well as the plausibility of the views that lead to this confusion are both strikingly illustrated by a seemingly innocuous remark in an article on business-cycle theory that "economic phenomena are varied and complex, so any comprehensive theory of the business cycle that can apply closely to reality must be very complicated."[26] A fundamental hypothesis of science is that appearances are deceptive and that there is a way of looking at or interpreting or organizing the evidence that will reveal superficially disconnected and diverse phenomena to be manifestations of a more fundamental and relatively simple structure. And the test of this hypothesis, as of any other, is its fruits—a test that science has so far met with dramatic success. If a class of "economic phenomena" appears varied and complex, it is, we must suppose, because we have no adequate theory to explain them. Known facts cannot be set on one side; a theory to apply "closely to reality" on the other. A theory is the way we perceive "facts," and we cannot perceive "facts" without a theory. Any assertion that economic phenomena *are* varied and complex denies the tentative state of knowledge that alone makes scientific activity meaningful; it is in a class with John Stuart Mill's justly ridiculed statement that "happily, there is nothing in the laws of value which remains [1848] for the present or any future writer to clear up; the theory of the subject is complete."[27]

The confusion between descriptive accuracy and analytical relevance has led not only to criticisms of economic theory on largely irrelevant grounds but also to misunderstanding of economic theory and misdirection of efforts to repair supposed defects. "Ideal types" in the abstract model developed by economic theorists have been regarded as strictly descriptive categories intended to correspond directly and fully to entities in the real world independently of the purpose for which the model is being used. The obvious discrepancies have led to necessarily unsuccessful attempts to construct theories on the basis of categories intended to be fully descriptive.

This tendency is perhaps most clearly illustrated by the interpretation given to the concepts of "perfect competition" and "monopoly" and the development of the theory of "monopolistic" or "imperfect competition." Marshall, it is said, assumed "perfect competition"; perhaps there once was such a thing. But clearly there is no longer, and we must therefore discard his theories. The reader will search long and hard—and I predict unsuccessfully— to find in Marshall any explicit assumption about perfect competition or any assertion that in a descriptive sense the world is composed of atomistic firms engaged in perfect competition. Rather, he will find Marshall saying: "At one extreme are world markets in which competition acts directly from all parts of the globe; and at the other those secluded markets in which all direct competition from afar is shut out, though indirect and transmitted competition may make itself felt even in these; and about midway between these extremes lie the great majority of the markets which the economist and the businessman have to study."[28] Marshall took the world as it is; he sought to construct an "engine" to analyze it, not a photographic reproduction of it.

In analyzing the world as it is, Marshall constructed the hypothesis that, for many problems, firms could be grouped into "industries" such that the similarities among the firms in each group were more important than the differences among them. These are problems in which the important element is that a group of firms is affected alike by some stimulus—a common change in the demand for their products, say, or in the supply of factors. But this will not do for all problems: the important element for these may be the differential effect on particular firms.

The abstract model corresponding to this hypothesis contains two "ideal" types of firms: atomistically competitive firms, grouped into industries, and monopolistic firms. A firm is competitive if the demand curve for its output is infinitely elastic with respect to its own price for some price and all outputs, given the prices charged by all other firms; it belongs to an "industry" defined as a group of firms producing a single "product." A "product" is defined as a collection of units that are perfect substitutes to purchasers so the elasticity of demand for the output of one firm with respect to the price of another firm in the same industry is infinite for some price and some outputs.[29] A firm is monopolistic if the demand curve for its output is not infinitely elastic at some price for all outputs. If it is a monopolist, the firm is the industry.[30]

As always, the hypothesis as a whole consists not only of this abstract model and its ideal types but also of a set of rules, mostly implicit and suggested by example, for identifying actual firms with one or the other ideal type and for classifying firms into industries. The ideal types are not intended to be descriptive; they are designed to isolate the features that are crucial for a particular problem. Even if we could estimate directly and accurately the demand curve for a firm's product, we could not proceed immediately to classify the firm as perfectly competitive or monopolistic according as the elasticity of the demand curve is or is not infinite. No observed demand curve will ever be precisely horizontal, so the estimated elasticity will always be finite. The relevant question always is whether the elasticity is "sufficiently" large to be regarded as infinite, but this is a question that cannot be answered, once for all, simply in terms of the numerical value of the elasticity itself, any more than we can say, once for all, whether an air pressure of fifteen pounds per square inch is "sufficiently" close to zero to use the formula $s = \frac{1}{2}gt^2$. Similarly, we cannot compute cross-elasticities of demand and then classify firms into industries according as there is a "substantial gap in the cross-elasticities of demand." As Marshall says, "The question where the lines of division between different commodities [i.e., industries] should be drawn must be settled by convenience of the particular discussion."[31] Everything depends on the problem; there is no inconsistency in regarding the same firm as if it were a perfect competitor for one problem, and a monopolist for another, just as there is none in regarding the same chalk mark as a Euclidean line for one problem, a Euclidean surface for a second, and a Euclidean solid for a third. The size of the elasticity and cross-elasticity of demand, the number of firms producing physically similar products, etc., are all relevant because they are or may be among the variables used to define the correspondence between the ideal and real entities in a particular problem and to specify the circumstances under which the theory holds sufficiently well; but they do not provide, once for all, a classification of firms as competitive or monopolistic.

An example may help to clarify this point. Suppose the problem is to determine the effect on retail prices of cigarettes of an increase, expected to be permanent, in the federal cigarette tax. I venture to predict that broadly correct results will be obtained by treating cigarette firms as if they were producing an identical product and were in perfect competition. Of course, in such a case, "some convention must be made as to the" number of Chesterfield cigarettes "which are taken as equivalent" to a Marlborough.[32]

On the other hand, the hypothesis that cigarette firms would behave as if they were perfectly competitive would have been a false guide to their reactions to price control in World War II, and this would doubtless have been recognized before the event. Costs of the cigarette firms must have risen during the war. Under such circumstances perfect competitors would have reduced the quantity offered for sale at the previously existing price. But, at that price, the wartime rise in the income of the public presumably increased the quantity demanded. Under conditions of perfect competition strict adherence to the legal price would therefore imply not only a "shortage" in the sense that quantity demanded exceeded quantity supplied but also an absolute decline in the number of cigarettes produced. The facts contradict this particular implication: there was reasonably good adherence to maximum cigarette prices, yet the quantities produced increased substantially. The common force of increased costs presumably operated less strongly than the disruptive force of the desire by each firm to keep its share of the market, to maintain the value and prestige of its brand name, especially when the excess-profits tax shifted a large share of the costs of this kind of advertising to the government. For this problem the cigarette firms cannot be treated *as if* they were perfect competitors.

Wheat farming is frequently taken to exemplify perfect competition. Yet, while for some problems it is appropriate to treat cigarette producers as if they comprised a perfectly competitive industry, for some it is not appropriate to treat wheat producers as if they did. For example, it may not be if the problem is the differential in prices paid by local elevator operators for wheat.

Marshall's apparatus turned out to be most useful for problems in which a group of firms is affected by common stimuli, and in which the firms can be treated *as if* they were perfect competitors. This is the source of the misconception that Marshall "assumed" perfect competition in some descriptive sense. It would be highly desirable to have a more general theory than Marshall's, one that would cover at the same time both those cases in which differentiation of product or fewness of numbers makes an essential difference and those in which it does not. Such a theory would enable us to handle problems we now cannot and, in addition, facilitate determination of the range of circumstances under which the simpler theory can be regarded as a good enough approximation. To perform this function, the more general theory must have content and substance; it must have implications susceptible to empirical contradiction and of substantive interest and importance.

The theory of imperfect or monopolistic competition developed by Chamberlin and Robinson is an attempt to construct such a more general theory.[33] Unfortunately, it possesses none of the attributes that would make it a truly useful general theory. Its contribution has been limited largely to improving the exposition of the economics of the individual firm and thereby the derivation of implications of the Marshallian model, refining Marshall's monopoly analysis, and enriching the vocabulary available for describing industrial experience.

The deficiencies of the theory are revealed most clearly in its treatment of, or inability to treat, problems involving groups of firms—Marshallian "industries." So long as it is insisted that differentiation of product is essential—and it is the distinguishing feature of the theory that it does insist on this point—the definition of an industry in terms of firms producing an identical product cannot be used. By that definition each firm is a separate industry. Definition in terms of "close" substitutes or a "substantial" gap in cross-elasticities evades the issue, introduces fuzziness and undefinable terms into the abstract model where they have no place, and serves only to make the theory analytically meaningless—"close" and "substantial" are in the same category as a "small" air pressure.[34] In one connection Chamberlin implicitly defines an industry as a group of firms having identical cost and demand curves.[35] But this, too, is logically meaningless so long as differentiation of product is, as claimed, essential and not to be put aside. What does it mean to say that the cost and demand curves of a firm producing bulldozers are identical with those of a firm producing hairpins?[36] And if it is meaningless for bulldozers and hairpins, it is meaningless also for two brands of toothpaste—so long as it is insisted that the difference between the two brands is fundamentally important.

The theory of monopolistic competition offers no tools for the analysis of an industry and so no stopping place between the firm at one extreme and general equilibrium at the other.[37] It is therefore incompetent to contribute to the analysis of a host of important problems: the one extreme is too narrow to be of great interest; the other, too broad to permit meaningful generalizations.[38]

6. Conclusion

Economics as a positive science is a body of tentatively accepted generalizations about economic phenomena that can be used to predict the consequences of changes in circumstances. Progress in expanding this body of generalizations, strengthening our confidence in their validity, and improving the accuracy of the predictions they yield is hindered not only by the limitations of human ability that impede all search for knowledge but also by obstacles that are especially important for the social sciences in general and economics in particular, though by no means peculiar to them. Familiarity with the subject matter of economics breeds contempt for special knowledge about it. The importance of its subject matter to everyday life and to major issues of public policy impedes objectivity and promotes confusion between scientific analysis and normative judgment. The necessity of relying on uncontrolled experience rather than on controlled experiment makes it difficult to produce dramatic and clear-cut evidence to justify the acceptance of tentative hypotheses. Reliance on uncontrolled experience does not affect the fundamental methodological principle that a hypothesis can be tested only by the conformity of its implications or predictions with observable phenomena; but it does render the task of testing hypotheses more difficult and gives greater scope for confusion about the methodological principles involved. More than other scientists, social scientists need to be self-conscious about their methodology.

One confusion that has been particularly rife and has done much damage is confusion about the role of "assumptions" in economic analysis. A meaningful scientific hypothesis or theory typically asserts that certain forces are, and other forces are not, important in understanding a particular class of phenomena. It is frequently convenient to present such a hypothesis by stating that the phenomena it is desired to predict behave in the world of observation *as if* they occurred in a hypothetical and highly simplified world containing only the forces that the hypothesis asserts to be important. In general, there is more than one way to formulate such a description—more than one set of "assumptions" in terms of which the theory can be presented. The choice among such alternative assumptions is made on the grounds of the resulting economy, clarity, and precision in presenting the hypothesis; their capacity to bring indirect evidence to bear on the validity of the hypothesis by suggesting some of its implications that can be readily checked with observation or by bringing out its connection with other hypotheses dealing with related phenomena; and similar considerations.

Such a theory cannot be tested by comparing its "assumptions" directly with "reality." Indeed, there is no meaningful way in which this can be done. Complete "realism" is clearly unattainable, and the question whether a theory is realistic "enough" can be settled only by seeing whether it yields predictions that are good enough for the purpose in hand or that are better than predictions from alternative theories. Yet the belief that a theory can be tested by the realism of its assumptions independently of the accuracy of its predictions is widespread and the source of much of the perennial criticism of economic theory as unrealistic. Such criticism is largely irrelevant, and, in consequence, most attempts to reform economic theory that it has stimulated have been unsuccessful.

The irrelevance of so much criticism of economic theory does not of course imply that existing economic theory deserves any high degree of confidence. These criticisms may miss the target, yet there may be a target for criticism. In a trivial sense, of course, there obviously is. Any theory is necessarily provisional and subject to change with the advance of knowledge. To go beyond this platitude, it is necessary to be more specific about the content of "existing economic theory" and to distinguish among its different branches; some parts of economic theory clearly deserve more confidence than others. A comprehensive evaluation of the present state of positive economics, summary of the evidence bearing on its validity, and assessment of the relative confidence that each part deserves is clearly a task for a treatise or a set of treatises, if it be possible at all, not for a brief paper on methodology.

About all that is possible here is the cursory expression of a personal view.

Existing relative price theory, which is designed to explain the allocation of resources among alternative ends and the division of the product among the cooperating resources and which reached almost its present form in Marshall's *Principles of Economics*, seems to me both extremely fruitful and deserving of much confidence for the kind of economic system that characterizes Western nations. Despite the appearance of considerable controversy, this is true equally of existing static monetary theory, which is designed to explain the structural or secular level of absolute prices, aggregate output, and other variables for the economy as a whole and which has had a form of the quantity theory of money as its basic core in all of its major variants from David Hume to the Cambridge School to Irving Fisher to John Maynard Keynes. The weakest and least satisfactory part of current economic theory seems to me to be in the field of monetary dynamics, which is concerned with the process of adaptation of the economy as a whole to changes in conditions and so with short-period fluctuations in aggregate activity. In this field we do not even have a theory that can appropriately be called *the* existing theory of monetary dynamics.

Of course, even in relative price and static monetary theory there is enormous room for extending the scope and improving the accuracy of existing theory. In particular, undue emphasis on the descriptive realism of "assumptions" has contributed to neglect of the critical problem of determining the limits of validity of the various hypotheses that together constitute the existing economic theory in these areas. The abstract models corresponding to these hypotheses have been elaborated in considerable detail and greatly improved in rigor and precision. Descriptive material on the characteristics of our economic system and its operations have been amassed on an unprecedented scale. This is all to the good. But, if we are to use effectively these abstract models and this descriptive material, we must have a comparable exploration of the criteria for determining what abstract model it is best to use for particular kinds of problems, what entities in the abstract model are to be identified with what observable entities, and what features of the problem or of the circumstances have the greatest effect on the accuracy of the predictions yielded by a particular model or theory.

Progress in positive economics will require not only the testing and elaboration of existing hypotheses but also the construction of new hypotheses. On this problem there is little to say on a formal level. The construction of hypotheses is a creative act of inspiration, intuition, invention; its essence is the vision of something new in familiar material. The process must be discussed in psychological, not logical, categories; studied in autobiographies and biographies, not treatises on scientific method; and promoted by maxim and example, not syllogism or theorem.

NOTES

1. (London: Macmillan & Co., 1891), pp. 34–35 and 46.

2. Social science or economics is by no means peculiar in this respect—witness the importance of personal beliefs and of "home" remedies in medicine wherever obviously convincing evidence for "expert" opinion is lacking. The current prestige and acceptance of the views of physical scientists in their fields of specialization—and, all too often, in other fields as well—derives, not from faith alone, but from the evidence of their works, the success of their predictions, and the dramatic achievements from applying their results. When economics seemed to provide such evidence of its worth, in Great Britain in the first half of the nineteenth century, the prestige and acceptance of "scientific economics" rivaled the current prestige of the physical sciences.

3. The interaction between the observer and the process observed that is so prominent a feature of the social sciences, besides its more obvious parallel in the physical sciences, has a more subtle counterpart in the indeterminacy principle arising out of the interaction between the process of measurement and the phenomena being measured. And both have a counterpart in pure logic in Gödel's theorem, asserting the impossibility of a comprehensive self-contained logic. It is an open question whether all three can be regarded as different formulations of an even more general principle.

4. One rather more complex example is stabilization policy. Superficially, divergent views on this question seem to reflect differences in objectives; but I believe that this impression is misleading and that at bottom the different views reflect primarily different judgments about the source of fluctuations in economic activity and the effect of alternative countercyclical action. For one major positive consideration that accounts for much of the divergence see Milton Friedman, "The Effects of a Full-Employment Policy on Economic Stability: A Formal Analysis," *Essays in Positive Economics* (Chicago: University of Chicago Press, 1953), pp. 117–32. For a summary of the present state of professional views on this question see "The Problem of Economic Instability," a report of a subcommittee of the Committee on Public Issues of the American Economic Association, *American Economic Review* 40 (September 1950): 501–38.

5. Final quoted phrase from Alfred Marshall, "The Present Position of Economics" (1885), reprinted in ed. A. C. Pigou, *Memorials of Alfred Marshall* (London: Macmillan & Co., 1925), p. 164. See also "The Marshallian Demand Curve," in Friedman, *Essays*, pp. 56–57, 90–91.

6. See "Lange on Price Flexibility and Employment: A Methodological Criticism," in Friedman, *Essays*, pp. 282–89.

7. "The Marshallian Demand Curve," in Friedman, *Essays*, p. 57.

8. The qualification is necessary because the "evidence" may be internally contradictory, so there may be no hypothesis consistent with it. See also "Lange on Price Flexibility and Employment," in Friedman, *Essays*, pp. 282–83.

9. See "Lange on Price Flexibility and Employment," in Friedman, *Essays*, passim.

10. See also Milton Friedman and L. J. Savage, "The Expected-Utility Hypothesis and the Measurability of Utility," *Journal of Political Economy* 60 (December 1952): 463–74, esp. 465–67; chapter 13 of this volume.

11. In recent years some economists, particularly a group connected with the Cowles Commission for Research in Economics at the University of Chicago, have placed great emphasis on a division of this step of selecting a hypothesis consistent with known evidence into two substeps: first, the selection of a class of admissible hypotheses from all possible hypotheses (the choice of a "model" in their terminology); second, the selection of one hypothesis from this class (the choice of a "structure"). This subdivision may be heuristically valuable in some kinds of work, particularly in promoting a systematic use of available statistical evidence and theory. From a methodological point of view, however, it is an entirely arbitrary subdivision of the process of deciding on a particular hypothesis that is on a par with many other subdivisions that may be convenient for one purpose or another or that may suit the psychological needs of particular investigators.

One consequence of this particular subdivision has been to give rise to the so-called identification problem. As noted above, if one hypothesis is consistent with available evidence, an infinite number are. But, while this is true for the class of hypotheses as a whole, it may not be true of the subclass obtained in the first of the above two steps—the "model." It may be that the evidence to be used to select the final hypothesis from the subclass can be consistent with at most one hypothesis in it, in which case the "model" is said to be "identified"; otherwise it is said to be "unidentified." As is clear from this way of describing the concept of "identification," it is essentially a special case of the more general problem of selecting among the alternative hypotheses equally consistent with the evidence—a problem that must be decided by some such arbitrary principle as Occam's razor. The introduction of two substeps in selecting a hypothesis makes this problem arise at the two corresponding stages and gives it a special cast. While the class of all hypotheses is always unidentified, the subclass in a "model" need not be, so the problem arises of conditions that a "model" must satisfy to be identified. However useful the two substeps may be in some contexts, their introduction raises the danger that different criteria will unwittingly be used in making the same kind of choice among alternative hypotheses at two different stages.

On the general methodological approach discussed in this footnote see Tryvge Haavelmo, "The Probability Approach in Econometrics," *Econometrica* 12 (1944): supplement; Jacob Marschak, "Economic Structure, Path, Policy, and Prediction," *American Economic Review* 37 (May 1947): 81–84, and "Statistical Inference in Economics: An Introduction," in T. C. Koopmans, ed., *Statistical Inference in Dynamic Economic Models* (New York: John Wiley & Sons, 1950); T. C. Koopmans, "Statistical Estimation of Simultaneous Economic Relations," *Journal of the American Statistical Association* 40 (December, 1945): 448–66; Gershon Cooper, "The Role of Economic Theory in Econometric Models," *Journal of Farm Economics* 30 (February 1948): 101–16. On the identification problem see Koopmans, "Identification Problems in Econometric Model Construction," *Econometrica* 17 (April 1949): 125–44; Leonid Hurwicz, "Generalization of the Concept of Identification," in Koopmans, ed., *Statistical Inference in Dynamic Economic Models*.

12. The converse of the proposition does not of course hold: assumptions that are unrealistic (in this sense) do not guarantee a significant theory.

13. See R. A. Lester, "Shortcomings of Marginal Analysis for Wage-Employment Problems," *American Economic Review* 36 (March 1946): 62–82; Fritz Machlup, "Marginal Analysis and Empirical Research," *American Economic Review* 36 (September 1946): 519–54; R. A. Lester, "Marginalism, Minimum Wages, and Labor Markets," *American Economic Review* 37 (March 1947): 135–48; Fritz Machlup, "Rejoinder to an Antimarginalist," *American Economic Review* 37 (March 1947): 148–54; G. J. Stigler, "Professor Lester and the Marginalists," *American Economic Review* 37 (March 1947): 154–57; H. M. Oliver, Jr., "Marginal Theory and Business Behavior," *American Economic Review* 37 (June 1947): 375–83; R. A. Gordon, "Short-Period Price Determination in Theory and Practice," *American Economic Review* 38 (June, 1948), 265–88.

It should be noted that, along with much material purportedly bearing on the validity of the "assumptions" of marginal theory, Lester does refer to evidence on the conformity of experience with the implications of the theory, citing the reactions of employment in Germany to the Papen plan and in the United States to changes in minimum-wage legislation as examples of lack of conformity. However, Stigler's brief comment is the only one of the other papers that refers to this evidence. It should also be noted that Machlup's thorough and careful exposition of the logical structure and meaning of marginal analysis is called for by the misunderstandings on this score that mar Lester's paper and almost conceal the evidence he presents that is relevant to the key issue he raises. But, in Machlup's emphasis on the logical structure, he comes perilously close to presenting the theory as a pure tautology, though it is evident at a number of points that he is aware of this danger and anxious to avoid it. The papers by Oliver and Gordon are the most extreme in the exclusive concentration on the conformity of the behavior of businessmen with the "assumptions" of the theory.

14. This example, and some of the subsequent discussion, though independent in origin, is similar to and in much the same spirit as an example and the approach in an important paper by Armen A. Alchian, "Uncertainty, Evolution, and Economic Theory," *Journal of Political Economy* 58 (June 1950): 211–21.

15. Milton Friedman and L. J. Savage, "The Utility Analysis of Choices Involving Risk," *Journal of Political Economy* 56 (August 1948): 298. Reprinted in American Economic Association, *Readings in Price Theory* (Chicago: Richard D. Irwin, Inc., 1952), pp. 57–96.

16. It seems better to use the term "profits" to refer to the difference between actual and "expected" results, between *ex post* and *ex ante* receipts. "Profits" are then a result of uncertainty and, as Alchian (op. cit., p. 212), following Tintner, points out, cannot be deliberately maximized in advance. Given uncertainty, individuals or firms choose among alternative anticipated probability distributions of receipts or incomes. The specific content of a theory of choice among such distributions depends on the criteria by which they are supposed to be ranked. One hypothesis supposes them to be ranked by the mathematical expectation of utility corresponding to them (see Friedman and Savage, "The Expected-Utility Hypothesis and the Measurability of Utility," op. cit.). A special case of this hypothesis or an alternative to it ranks probability distributions by the mathematical expectation of the money receipts corresponding to them. The

latter is perhaps more applicable, and more frequently applied, to firms than to individuals. The term "expected returns" is intended to be sufficiently broad to apply to any of these alternatives.

The issues alluded to in this note are not basic to the methodological issues being discussed, and so are largely bypassed in the discussion that follows.

17. See George J. Stigler, "A Theory of Delivered Price Systems," *American Economic Review* 39 (December 1949): 1143–57.

18. See Friedman and Savage, "The Expected-Utility Hypothesis and the Measurability of Utility," pp. 466–67, for another specific example of this kind of indirect test.

19. A rigorous statement of this hypothesis would of course have to specify how "extent of racial or religious discrimination" and "degree of monopoly" are to be judged. The loose statement in the text is sufficient, however, for present purposes.

20. Thorstein Veblen, "Why Is Economics Not an Evolutionary Science?" (1898), reprinted in *The Place of Science in Modern Civilization* (New York, 1919), p. 73.

21. Oliver, "Marginal Theory and Business Behavior," p. 381.

22. See H. D. Henderson, "The Significance of the Rate of Interest," *Oxford Economic Papers* 1 (October 1938): 1–13; J. E. Meade and P. W. S. Andrews, "Summary of Replies to Questions on Effects of Interest Rates," *Oxford Economic Papers* 1 (October 1938): 14–31; R. F. Harrod, "Price and Cost in Entrepreneurs' Policy," *Oxford Economic Papers* 2 (May 1939): 1–11; and R. J. Hall and C. J. Hitch, "Price Theory and Business Behavior," *Oxford Economic Papers* 2 (May 1939): 12–45; Lester, "Shortcomings of Marginal Analysis for Wage-Employment Problems," op. cit.; Gordon, "Short-Period Price Determination," op. cit. See Machlup, "Marginal Analysis and Empirical Research," op. cit., esp. sec. II, for detailed criticisms of questionnaire methods.

I do not mean to imply that questionnaire studies of businessmen's or others' motives or beliefs about the forces affecting their behavior are useless for all purposes in economics. They may be extremely valuable in suggesting leads to follow in accounting for divergencies between predicted and observed results; that is, in constructing new hypotheses or revising old ones. Whatever their suggestive value in this respect, they seem to me almost entirely useless as a means of *testing* the validity of economic hypotheses. See my comment on Albert G. Hart's paper, "Liquidity and Uncertainty," *American Economic Review* 39 (May 1949): 198–99.

23. Oliver, "Marginal Theory and Business Behavior," p. 382.

24. Lester, "Shortcomings of Marginal Analysis for Wage-Employment Problems," p. 75.

25. E.g., Gordon's direct examinations of the "assumptions" leads him to formulate the alternative hypothesis generally favored by the critics of the maximization-of-returns hypothesis as follows: "There is an irresistible tendency to price on the basis of average total costs for some 'normal' level of output. This is the yardstick, the short-cut, that businessmen and accountants use, and their aim is more to earn satisfactory profits and play safe than to maximize profits" (op. cit., p. 275). Yet he essentially abandons this hypothesis, or converts it into a tautology, and in the process implicitly accepts the test by prediction when he later remarks: "Full cost and satisfactory profits may

continue to be the objectives even when total costs are shaded to meet competition or exceeded to take advantage of a sellers' market" (ibid., p. 284). Where here is the "irresistible tendency"? What kind of evidence could contradict this assertion?

26. Sidney S. Alexander, "Issues of Business Cycle Theory Raised by Mr. Hicks," *American Economic Review* 41 (December 1951): 872.

27. Ashley, ed., *Principles of Political Economy* (New York: Longmans, Green & Co., 1929), p. 436.

28. *Principles*, p. 329; see also pp. 35, 100, 341, 347, 375, 546.

29. This ideal type can be divided into two types: the oligopolistic firm, if the demand curve for its output is infinitely elastic at some price for some but not all outputs; the monopolistic firm proper, if the demand curve is nowhere infinitely elastic (except possibly at an output of zero).

30. For the oligopolist of the preceding note an industry can be defined as a group of firms producing the same product.

31. *Principles*, p. 100.

32. Quoted parts from ibid.

33. E. H. Chamberlin, *The Theory of Monopolistic Competition*, 6th ed. (Cambridge: Harvard University Press, 1950); Joan Robinson, *The Economics of Imperfect Competition* (London: Macmillan & Co., 1933).

34. See R. L. Bishop, "Elasticities, Cross-elasticities, and Market Relationships," *American Economic Review* 42 (December 1952): 779–803, for a recent attempt to construct a rigorous classification of market relationships along these lines. Despite its ingenuity and sophistication, the result seems to me thoroughly unsatisfactory. It rests basically on certain numbers being classified as "large" or "small," yet there is no discussion at all of how to decide whether a particular number is "large" or "small," as of course there cannot be on a purely abstract level.

35. Chamberlin, "Monopolistic Competition," p. 82.

36. There always exists a transformation of quantities that will make either the cost curves or the demand curves identical; this transformation need not, however, be linear, in which case it will involve different-sized units of one product at different levels of output. There does not necessarily exist a transformation that will make both pairs of curves identical.

37. See Robert Triffin, *Monopolistic Competition and General Equilibrium Theory* (Cambridge: Harvard University Press, 1940), esp. pp. 188–89.

38. For a detailed critique see George J. Stigler, "Monopolistic Competition in Retrospect," in *Five Lectures on Economic Problems* (London: Macmillan & Co., 1949), pp. 12–24.

ECONOMIC THEORY

◆ ◆ ◆

• PART • THREE •

Consumption and
Permanent Income

· 12 ·

The central theme of this monograph can be illustrated by a simple hypothetical example. Consider a large number of men all earning $100 a week and spending $100 a week on current consumption. Let them receive their pay once a week, the paydays being staggered, so that one-seventh are paid on Sunday, one-seventh on Monday, and so on. Suppose we collected budget data for a sample of these men for one day chosen at random, defined income as cash receipts on that day, and defined consumption as cash expenditures. One-seventh of the men would be recorded as having an income of $100, six-sevenths as having an income of zero. It may well be that the men would spend more on payday than on other days but they would also make expenditures on other days, so we would record the one-seventh with an income of $100 as having positive savings, the other six-sevenths as having negative savings. Consumption might appear to rise with income, but, if so, not as much as income, so that the fraction of income saved would rise with income. These results tell us nothing meaningful about consumption behavior; they simply reflect the use of inappropriate concepts of income and consumption. Men do not adapt their cash expenditures on consumption to their cash receipts, and their cash expenditures on consumption may not be a good index of the value of services consumed—in our simple example, consumption expenditures might well be zero on Sunday.

Chapter 9 of Milton Friedman, A *Theory of the Consumption Function* (Princeton, N.J.: Princeton University Press, 1957).

Lengthening the period of observation from a day to a week would eliminate entirely the error introduced into our simple example by the use of inappropriate concepts of income and consumption. It is the central theme of this monograph that the use of a period as long as a year does not render the error in actual data negligible, let alone eliminate it entirely. The results obtained from such annual data conform in broad outline to those of our simple example: recorded consumption is on the average positive when recorded income is zero, and the fraction of income saved rises with income. If the thesis of this monograph is correct, these results are to be explained in the same way. They too reflect the use of inappropriate concepts of income and consumption.

Our analysis accordingly distinguishes sharply between income as recorded—which we term measured income—and the income to which consumers adapt their behavior—which we term permanent income—and, similarly, between measured consumption and permanent consumption. The concept of permanent income is easy to state in these general terms, hard to define precisely. Permanent income cannot be observed directly, it must be inferred from the behavior of consumer units. And this is equally true of permanent consumption and its relation to permanent income.

The wide range of empirical material examined in this monograph turns out to be consistent with a rather simple relation between permanent consumption and permanent income suggested by purely theoretical considerations, namely, a ratio between permanent consumption and permanent income that is the same for all levels of permanent income but depends on other variables, such as the interest rate, the ratio of wealth to income, and so on. The widespread belief that the ratio of consumption to income declines as income rises can be explained entirely by the considerations stressed in our example.

Our conclusion about the meaning of permanent income cannot be stated so simply. We can think of the factors affecting the consumer's receipts as having a range of time dimensions: some factors affect his receipts only for a day, others for a week, a year, two years, and so on. We have approximated this continuum by a dichotomy. Effects lasting less than a certain time period are considered transitory, those lasting for a longer time, permanent. The length of this time period we call the consumer unit's horizon. A number of different pieces of evidence support the highly tentative conclusion that the horizon so defined is about three years.

On our interpretation of the evidence, the transitory components of a consumer unit's income have no effect on his consumption except as they are translated into effects lasting beyond his horizon. His consumption is determined by longer-range income considerations plus transitory factors affecting consumption directly. The transitory components of income show up primarily in changes in the consumer unit's assets and liabilities, that is, in his measured savings.

This approach to the interpretation of consumption data and the particular hypothesis to which it has led have far-reaching implications. The rest of this chapter states the hypothesis more formally, summarizes the evidence adduced in support of it, lists generalizations about consumer behavior derived from it, and outlines some of its implications for research, economic understanding, and economic policy.

1. SUMMARY STATEMENT OF HYPOTHESIS

The permanent income hypothesis can be summarized in a system of three simple equations for the individual consumer unit:

$$c_p = k(i, w, u)y_p, \qquad (\alpha)$$

$$y = y_p + y_t, \qquad (\beta)$$

$$c = c_p + c_t. \qquad (\gamma)$$

Equation (α) asserts that planned or permanent consumption (c_p) is a fraction (k) of planned or permanent income (y_p) that does not depend on the size of permanent income but does depend on other variables, in particular, the interest rate (i), the ratio of nonhuman wealth to income (w), and other factors affecting the consumer unit's tastes for current consumption versus accumulation of assets (u), such as the degree of uncertainty attached to the receipt of income, the consumer unit's age and its composition, and objective indexes of cultural factors like race or national origin. This is the simplest equation that seems consistent with the pure theory of consumer behavior as presented in chapter II.

Equations (β) and (γ) assert that measured income (y) and measured consumption (c) can each be regarded as the sum of two components: (1) the permanent component that enters into (α), and (2) a transitory component reflecting the influence of factors regarded as chance or random by the consumer unit, as well as errors of measurement. As they stand, these equations have no substantive content; they are purely definitional.

The permanent components of income and consumption can never be observed directly for an individual consumer unit; we can only observe *ex post* what it spends and what it receives. We can, however, make inferences about the permanent components for groups of families from observed data if we accept certain assumptions about the relation between permanent and transitory components. The particular assumptions I have made are that the transitory components of consumption and income can be taken to be uncorrelated with the corresponding permanent components and with each other; these are an essential part of the hypothesis presented in this monograph. In addition, I have on occasion assumed the mean transitory components of consumption and income to be zero. This is not essential to the hypothesis and has been done only for the convenience or simplicity of the particular application.

These assumptions breathe substantive content into equations (β) and (γ). Equations (α), (β), and (γ) then imply an observed regression of measured consumption on measured income for which the ratio of consumption to income declines as measured income increases—as in our simple introductory example and for the same reasons. They imply also a computed elasticity of measured consumption with respect to measured income that is proportional to the fraction of the total variance of income for the group concerned that is contributed by the permanent component (P_y), and a height of the regression that depends on the mean level of the permanent and transitory components of income and consumption and on the variables affecting k. The regression is shifted upward by a rise in mean permanent income and by an increase in k. Thus, changes in neither the elasticity nor the height of the observed regressions need imply any changes in consumer tastes and preferences for current consumption versus accumulation of wealth, or in opportunities for exchanging the one for the other. They may instead reflect simply changes in certain characteristics of the income distribution. The appearance of changing consumer behavior may simply be a disguised reflection of the fact of changing income structure.

For simplicity of exposition, the hypothesis has been described in its arithmetic form. A variant is to retain (α) but to replace (β) and (γ) by similar expressions in the logarithms of the various terms, and to assume zero correlation between the logarithmic transitory components of income and consumption and each of these and the corresponding logarithmic permanent component. This logarithmic variant seems to fit the empirical evidence better than the arithmetic variant and is the one that has been used in most of the empirical work of the preceding chapters. Its implications are essentially the same as those of the arithmetic variant, since the one can be regarded as a first order approximation to the other, and most verbal statements of the implications apply equally to both; its advantage is that the implications hold over a wider range.

The relation between aggregate consumption and aggregate income depends not only on the consumption function for individual consumer units but also on the distribution of consumer units by the variables affecting their behavior. Under simplifying assumptions, however, the aggregate function has the same form as the individual function and can likewise be described by (α), (β), and (γ), with the exception that the variables determining the ratio of permanent consumption to permanent income (designated k^* for aggregate data) are different. They are now the distribution of consumer units by i, w, and u, or such summary measures of these distributions as their means and variances. Given the same assumptions of zero correlation between transitory and permanent components and between transitory components of consumption and income, the hypothesis then has the same implications for the regression of consumption on income computed from aggregate data as for the regression computed from data for individual consumer units. In neither case is stability of the observed regression a necessary consequence of stability in consumer behavior with respect to current consumption and current saving.

The hypothesis has many empirical implications in addition to those already stated about the regression of measured consumption on measured income. For example, it can be used to decompose the dispersion of measured income, and also of measured consumption, into the parts attributable to transitory and permanent components. It implies that if consumer units are classified by the change in income from one year to another, the regressions of consumption on income for such groups will, under plausible conditions, be parallel and differ in height by amounts that can be specified in advance; and that the common slope will be steeper than the slope of the regression for all units combined by an amount that can be calculated from a characteristic of the income distribution for the group as a whole. It can be used to predict the correlation between the ratio of measured saving to measured income of the same units in different years. For aggregate data for a country like the United States that has been experiencing secular growth, it implies that the elasticity of consumption with respect to measured income computed from time series will be higher, the longer the period spanned by the data, and the longer the elementary time unit of observation; that it will also be higher when computed from data on aggregate consumption and income than from per capita data and when computed from data in current prices than from data in constant prices.

2. Evidence on the Acceptability of the Permanent Income Hypothesis

The implications of the permanent income hypothesis explain the major apparent anomalies that arise if the observed regression between measured consumption and measured income is interpreted, as it generally has been, as a stable relation between permanent components—though, of course, this is not the name that has been attached to the measured magnitudes. On such an interpretation the observed regression of consumption on income for a single group of consumer units implies (a) that inequality of income will increase over time—since consumption exceeds income for low income units and is less than income for high income units, so apparently the poor are getting poorer and the rich richer; (b) that savings must have become an increasing fraction of income over time in the United States and similar countries—since real income has been increasing more or less steadily; and (c) that regressions computed from budget studies made at widely spaced dates will not differ systematically. Yet there is ample evidence that (a) inequality of income has, if anything, decreased over time in the United States, (b) savings have been a roughly constant fraction of income over time in the United States, (c) computed regressions have steadily been higher, the later the date of the budget study. All three observations are entirely consistent with the permanent income hypothesis presented in this monograph.

The consistency of the hypothesis with these broad facts is only a small part of the evidence in its favor. In addition, the hypothesis is consistent with numerous detailed findings about consumption behavior that have accumulated from analyses of both budget data for individual consumer units and time series data on aggregate consumption and income; in particular, each of the implications listed in the preceding section has been compared with observation and no serious discrepancy has been found in either qualitative or quantitative elements of the implications. Perhaps the two most striking pieces of evidence for the hypothesis are, first, its success in predicting in quantitative detail the effect of classifying consumer units by the change in their measured income from one year to another; and, second, its consistency with a body of data that have not heretofore been used in analyzing consumption behavior or, indeed, even regarded as relevant to consumption behavior, namely, data on the measured income of individual consumer units in successive years. An estimate of the fraction of the variance of measured income contributed by permanent components (i.e., of P_y) can be made from such data by techniques that I developed much earlier for another purpose, namely, the analysis of the stability of relative income status. On the permanent income hypothesis the measured income elasticity of consumption is also an estimate of this same fraction.[1] These two estimates are derived from two largely independent bodies of data. Comparison of them for a variety of groups of consumer units show that they are highly correlated and approximately of the same order of magnitude.

There is some leeway in the hypothesis in the precise meaning to be assigned to the permanent component of income. The broadest definition would regard this component as attributable to any factors whose influence extends over more than one elementary time unit (a year, in most studies). Successively narrower definitions would include only factors affecting income in three or more years, four or more years, and so on until the narrowest definition would identify the permanent component with expected lifetime income. The comparisons mentioned in the preceding paragraph as well as a number of other pieces of evidence suggest that the empirically appropriate definition is to regard the permanent component as reflecting the influence of factors affecting income for a period of three or more years. But this must still be regarded as a highly tentative conclusion.

A number of hypotheses have been suggested in recent years to explain the contradictions mentioned above between the available evidence and the hypothesis that consumption expenditures are a stable function of absolute income. The chief such hypotheses can be regarded as special cases of the permanent income hypothesis under special conditions. This is true of the hypothesis that the ratio of consumption to income for a consumer unit depends on the relative income position of the consumer unit as measured by either the ratio of its income to the mean income of the group of which it is regarded as a member or its percentile position in the income distribution. It is equally true of the hypothesis that aggregate consumption depends not only on current aggregate income but also on the highest previous income, which has been considered a special case of the relative income hypothesis. Regarded as an alternative theory, the relative income hypothesis has fewer empirical implications than the permanent income hypothesis, so is less fruitful; in addition, such empirical evidence as I have examined, for circumstances when the implications of the two hypotheses differ, favors the permanent income hypothesis rather than the relative income hypothesis.

3. Generalizations about Consumer Behavior Based on the Hypothesis

Empirical evidence has been considered in this study primarily from the standpoint of its consistency with the permanent income hypothesis rather than of its contribution to the understanding of consumer behavior. In the process of using the evidence to test the hypothesis, however, we have necessarily been led to use the hypothesis to extract generalizations from the evidence; these are two sides of the same coin. It may illuminate these tests and this evidence if we summarize here this byproduct, taking for granted that the agreement of the hypothesis with the available evidence is sufficient to justify its tentative acceptance. It should be emphasized that the generalizations that follow are all for personal consumption and personal savings; they do not cover corporate savings or governmental savings.

a. We have found no evidence of any structural change in the behavior of consumer units in the United States with respect to spending and saving over at least the past 60 years. The data for this period all conform to the pattern defined by our hypothesis, including not only the general equations (α), (β), and (γ) but also the more specific assumptions about the lack of correlation between the transitory components of income and of consumption and between each of these and the corresponding permanent component. And they conform to this pattern in the sense not only that the general functional relations apply but also that the parameters of the relations seem to have been unchanged over the period in question. A horizon of about three years seems to have characterized the outlook of consumer units, though it should be noted that the results are not very sensitive to the length of the horizon.

b. Over this period, k, the ratio of permanent consumption to permanent income has been decidedly higher for wage earners than for entrepreneurial groups; from .90 to .95 for wage earners, from .80 to .90 for entrepreneurs, probably close to the lower end of this range for nonfarm entrepreneurs and to the middle or upper end for farmers.

The difference between entrepreneurial and nonentrepreneurial groups in the size of k seems larger and better established than any other we have examined. The value of k is perhaps a trifle higher for Negroes than for whites; this difference, which is small and not well established, is opposite in direction from that which has been inferred from conventional analysis of the data. The value of k is probably higher for large than for small families, but again this cannot be regarded as well established.

c. At least part of the reason why k is lower for entrepreneurial than for nonentrepreneurial groups is the greater uncertainty of income prospects for the former, which makes the need for a reserve against emergencies greater.

For nonentrepreneurial consumer units living in urban communities of at least moderate size, the dispersion of transitory components of income is about 20 to 25 percent of their average income; that is, about two out of three will in any year be within plus or minus 20 or 25 percent of what they regard as their permanent position.

For nonentrepreneurial groups in small cities and villages, it seems likely that the transitory component is even less widely dispersed, though the evidence for this statement is very limited.

For entrepreneurial consumer units, whether farm or nonfarm, the relative dispersion of transitory components of income seems to be upwards of 40 percent, perhaps as high as 50 percent, of average income, or something like twice as great as for nonentrepreneurial groups.

For the various nonfarm groups combined, including entrepreneurs and others, the average relative dispersion of transitory components is about 30 percent.

d. Part of the reason why k is lower for entrepreneurial than for non-entrepreneurial groups may be the ability of the entrepreneurial group to earn a higher rate of return on accumulated capital; a similar difference between nonfarm and farm entrepreneurs may also explain why k is lower for the nonfarm entrepreneurs. However, this conclusion is highly conjectural and cannot be regarded as well established.

e. In terms of permanent income status, farmers are less dispersed than nonfarm groups as a whole, though perhaps about as dispersed as nonfarm wage and clerical workers. Nonfarm entrepreneurial groups are more widely dispersed than either farmers or other nonfarm groups. Our estimates of the size of the dispersion vary from about 60 to 70 percent for farmers to 80 to 90 percent for nonfarm entrepreneurial groups.

f. The variability in permanent income status has accounted for something like 80 to 85 percent of the variability of measured annual income for broad nonfarm groups in the United States; for a much smaller fraction, for farm groups. It has apparently accounted for a larger fraction in Great Britain and Sweden than in the United States. This means that the distribution of annual income exaggerates the inequality of long-run income status by more for farmers than for nonfarmers, and by more for the United States than for Great Britain or Sweden.

g. There is limited evidence that transitory components are much less important for consumption than for income, having a relative dispersion of the order of perhaps 10 percent instead of the 30 percent recorded for income.

h. There is no evidence of a lag in the adjustment of consumer expenditures to changes in circumstances beyond that which is implicit in the idea that consumers adapt their expenditures to longer-run income status as measured by permanent income rather than to their momentary receipts. The effects of changes in measured income on consumer expenditures can all be accounted for in this way.

i. The ratio of aggregate consumption to aggregate income for the United States (k^*) has remained roughly constant for more than half a century at about .88 for a definition of consumption that excludes expenditures on major consumer durable goods and includes their estimated use value. Accumulation of durables has accounted for an increasing fraction of savings, so the ratio of consumption to income would be slightly higher and would show a moderately rising secular trend for measures of consumption that treated expenditures on durables as consumption. These conclusions are supported by both budget data and time series data.

j. The constancy of the numerical value of k^*, though consistent with the permanent income hypothesis, is not required by it, even in the absence of structural change and even when the conditions are satisfied for the aggregate function to be described by equations like (α), (β), and (γ). The constancy of k^* means that the variables determining k and the distribution of consumer units by these variables have been either constant or offsetting in their effects.

Probably the two major offsetting forces have been (1) the declining relative importance of farming, which would tend to raise k^*, and (2) the declining size of family, which would tend to lower k^*. A third major factor, the changing role of the state in the provision of security, has itself had offsetting effects on k^* as it is measured from the available statistics.

k. Permanent income for the community as a whole can be regarded as a weighted average of current and past measured incomes, adjusted upwards by a steady secular trend and with weights declining as one goes farther back in time. The average time span between the measured incomes averaged and current permanent income is about 2.5 years.

The corresponding aggregate consumption function is

$$c^*(T) = k^* \beta \int_{-\infty}^{T} e^{(\beta - \alpha)(t - T)} y^*(t) dt$$

where c^* is aggregate or per capita consumption and y^* aggregate or per capita income, T designates the time unit in question, t designates time in general and is simply a variable of integration that does not appear in the final function, and k^*, α, and β are the parameters of the function. k^* is to be interpreted as the ratio of permanent consumption to permanent income, α as the secular rate of growth of income, and β as the damping coefficient which describes the process of forming estimates of expected or permanent income from current and past measured income; the higher β, the more rapidly the weights decline as one goes back in time, and the shorter the average lag between permanent income and the incomes averaged. For the period 1905 to 1951, and Raymond Goldsmith's data on deflated per capita savings and deflated per capita personal income, the estimated values of the parameters are

$$k^* = .88$$

$$\alpha = .02$$

$$\beta = .40.$$

The values of α and β should be fairly insensitive to the precise data used, whereas k^* will be quite sensitive. The value cited is for a concept of consumption that includes only the use value of major consumer durable goods, treating accumulation in the stock of consumer durables as savings, and that includes additions to social security reserves as personal savings and income.

4. IMPLICATIONS OF THE HYPOTHESIS FOR RESEARCH

The broader implications of acceptance of the permanent income hypothesis affect two very different areas of human effort: (1) research into consumption behavior and income structure and (2) economic understanding and policy.

A major part of the effort in consumption research, both with respect to total consumption and consumption expenditures on particular categories, has been directed toward determining the regression of consumption on income. This emphasis reflects the belief that current income is the major determinant of current consumption expenditures and that comparison of regressions is a way of eliminating the influence of income and so isolating the effects of other factors affecting consumer behavior. This partial correlation approach underlies most of the data collection and presentation; it explains alike why the Study of Consumer Purchases, perhaps the largest and most carefully planned budget study ever undertaken, collected expenditure data from a controlled rather than representative sample; and why measured income is the major, and often the only, variable used to classify consumer units in tabulations of budget data. This partial correlation approach characterizes also the bulk of the analytical research into consumer behavior, from Engel's original enunciation of his famous laws which led to his name being attached to regressions of consumption on income, to current self-consciously complex econometric research; from the examination of data for a small group of consumer units, to the calculation of demand functions from a combination of time series and budget data for a nation as a whole and for many separate commodities. Sophistication has taken the form of adding more and more variables, and of using more refined statistical techniques to estimate their effects and to allow for sampling and measurement errors; it has not changed the basic orientation or direction of the research.

Acceptance of the permanent income hypothesis implies that much or most of this research has been misdirected. What has been held constant is not income in the sense that is relevant to consumption behavior but a more or less arbitrary mixture of income in this sense and accidental elements. Statistical measures that have been taken to reflect the influence of differences in consumer behavior in fact reflect features of the income distribution. In consequence, the discovery of regularities in consumer behavior has been bedeviled by the confounding of such behavior with unrelated though not irrelevant features of the distribution of income. The result has been the introduction of increasing complexity into the analysis in an effort to rationalize the data within the same general framework.

This complexity is frequently pointed to with pride by workers in the field as evidence of the subtlety of their analysis. It is tempting to make a virtue of necessity by asserting that the consumer *is* a complex creature who is influenced by everything under the sun and hence that only an analysis in terms of a large number of variables can hope to extract a consistent pattern from his behavior. In fact, the necessity of introducing many variables is a sign of defeat and not of success; it means that the analyst has not found a truly fruitful way of interpreting or understanding his subject matter; for the essence of such a fruitful theory is that it is simple. The consumption analyst, as it were, has been priding himself on his success in adding yet more epicycles. The possibility of dispensing with these does not, of course, mean that his empirical findings are in error, that the variables he finds related to consumer behavior are not related to it, any more than acceptance of the Copernican view rendered nonexistent the astronomical movements that it was necessary to introduce additional epicycles to explain. What it does mean is that these empirical relations can all be inferred from a much simpler structure, that they can all be regarded as manifestations in different guise of a single and simpler set of forces rather than as the result of largely irreducible ultimate variables.

Acceptance of the permanent income hypothesis means that much less emphasis should be attached to the regressions of consumption on income, especially in the analysis of total consumption and savings. The principal task in this area at the present stage of knowledge is to find the major determinants of k and to measure their influence. The data needed for this purpose, at least for the first attack on the problem, are average consumption and average income for groups of consumer units for which transitory components can largely be expected to average out; for example, communities, or moderately homogeneous occupational groups within cities. I know, myself, of only one study, by Dorothy Brady, which has used the community as the unit of observation and has dealt with relations among averages.[2] We need to determine whether and how the ratio of such averages, which we have been calling the average propensity to consume, is connected with the variables our hypothesis leads us to put into the forefront: the rate of interest, the relative dispersion of transitory components of income and of consumption, the ratio of wealth to income, the age and composition of consumer units. Much can be done along these lines with existing data, though thanks to their different orientation, community averages are either not available for many such data or can be computed only with difficulty. With respect to future collection of data, acceptance of this approach in many ways simplifies the problem, by enabling emphasis to be put almost entirely on samples giving good estimates of means. This can be done with a smaller sample and perhaps a simpler sampling design than is required to get good estimates of multivariate relations including current income of the consumer unit as a major variable.

From the point of view of the permanent income hypothesis, the regression of consumption on income not only should receive much less exclusive emphasis in consumption research than it has heretofore, it also serves a different function and use. Its function is primarily to provide a means to decompose the total variation in income into the parts contributed by permanent and transitory components. The result is useful for consumption research in providing an estimate of one variable that may be expected to influence k, namely, the relative dispersion of transitory components. Its main use, however, is not in consumption research at all but in analyzing the distribution of income. It enables the mass of consumer budget data to be used to interpret data on the distribution of income and to convert them into estimates of the distribution of permanent income status.

Curiously enough, while the hypothesis converts the regression of consumption on income into a tool for analyzing income distribution, it gives the regression of income on consumption, which has heretofore been almost entirely neglected, significance for consumption research. For this regression enables us to decompose the total variation in consumption into the parts contributed by permanent and transitory components and so to estimate the relative dispersion of transitory components of consumption. The regression of income on consumption needs to be computed from any existing data for which it is possible to do so, and in future studies the two regressions should be treated symmetrically.

A final implication of the hypothesis for research that deserves mention is the importance it confers on data on the consumption or income of the same consumer units in different years, especially on such data giving both the consumption and income of the same units. It is likely that data of this kind now exist which have not been exploited, and these are one of the kinds of consumption data that should receive highest priority in future collection of data.

5. Substantive Implications of the Hypothesis

Acceptance of the permanent income hypothesis necessarily has implications for any problem of economic understanding or policy in which the determinants of savings play a significant role. At least in recent years, there have been two main classes or problems of this kind: those connected with the process of economic development, particularly of so-called underdeveloped economies, and those connected with economic fluctuations.

a. Economic Development

Students of economic development tend to give a major role to the availability of resources for capital formation. One source is, of course, domestic savings. Their availability has, in turn, been taken to depend largely on the level of real income, on the one hand, and the inequality of income on the other.

The level of real income has been regarded as playing a dual role. First, the level of income defines the total amount available for consumption and savings; if, by some criterion, the total is low, so is the potential amount available for either purpose. This is, of course, a purely arithmetical truism and is unaffected by the hypothesis accepted about the factors determining the division of the total between consumption and savings. Second, acceptance of the absolute income hypothesis led to the belief that a low real income was unfavorable to savings in the further sense that it made for a relatively low ratio of savings to income.

The relative income hypothesis, which has received increasing acceptance in recent years, removed the direct connection between low real income and a low savings ratio but substituted an indirect connection. True, it argued, in an isolated community, the level of real income would have no effect on the savings ratio. But in a community connected with the rest of the world it would. According to the most widely accepted theoretical justification for the relative income hypothesis, that of Duesenberry, relative income is important within a community because of emulation and the demonstration of the availability and usefulness of superior goods. But these same effects work as well between communities. The "demonstration effect" of the level of consumption in high income countries, or of citizens of high income countries resident in underdeveloped countries, tends, it has been argued, to lead the citizens of the underdeveloped countries to devote an unduly high percentage of their low level of income to current consumption and, especially, to use in that way any increases in income.

Acceptance of the permanent income hypothesis removes both the direct and this particular indirect connection between low real income and a low savings ratio. According to it, the savings ratio is independent of the level of income. Relative income, as measured, is empirically related to the savings ratio within a country not because of emulation or the demonstration effect but because relative measured income is a biased index of relative permanent income status. If the emulation and demonstration effects are not present within a community, there is no reason to expect them to operate between communities. It may be that a country or group with a relatively low real income will also have a low aggregate ratio of savings to income; but it may also have a high ratio, and in either case the explanation is to be sought not in the level of income but in other factors.

Although, on the permanent income hypothesis, a low level of real income does not make for a low savings ratio, a rapid rate of rise in income, whatever the level, may do so. The reason is that a rise expected to continue tends to raise permanent income relative to measured income and so to raise consumption relative to measured income. I conjecture that whether this effect shows itself is likely to depend critically on the source of the rise in real income. If it reflects development financed at least in part from domestic capital in an environment which makes for a high rate of return on domestic capital, the high rate of return to savings is an offset to the high ratio of permanent to current income and may well be more important. On the other hand, if the rise in income reflects primarily an external stimulus that gives little or no role to domestic capital, there may be no offset and one might expect the savings ratio to fall. An example of this second possibility might be the rising income among Okinawan natives as a result of its development as a United States military base, though I know too little about the details to be confident that it is. At any rate, if some examples of the two kinds of developments could be found, they might offer a rather nice test of the present analysis and of the applicability of the permanent income hypothesis across countries.

Thanks to the widespread acceptance not only of the absolute income hypothesis but of a very special form of it, the inequality of the distribution of income has been regarded as a major factor explaining the aggregate savings ratio.[3] Wide inequality of income is thought to tend toward a high savings ratio, and an approach toward equality, toward a low savings ratio. This consideration has frequently been a major argument offered in defense of inequality by people who are in other respects egalitarians: inequality in an underdeveloped country, they say, is a necessary evil since there is no other way to generate the savings needed for economic development.

According to the permanent income hypothesis, the effect of inequality depends critically on the source of the inequality. Insofar as the inequality is attributable to differences in permanent income status, it has no effect on the savings ratio. Insofar as it is attributable to differences in transitory components, it does, because inequality then means uncertainty about income prospects and hence increases the need for a reserve against emergencies. What is favorable to a high savings ratio is not inequality per se but uncertainty, provided, of course, it is uncertainty of a kind that does not reduce the average rate of return on capital—a qualification that is entered to allow for the clearly unfavorable effect on savings of increased uncertainty about the security of property such as might arise from fears of confiscation or close regulation by government.

This distinction beween the sources of inequality seems to me of great importance. If I may speculate on the basis of utterly inadequate knowledge in the hope of provoking further study by better qualified students, it seems to me that the kind of inequality characteristic of many so-called underdeveloped countries is precisely the kind that is irrelevant to the savings ratio. Such countries frequently have rigid social systems, sharp separations between classes, great stability in the membership of classes within generations and from generation to generation; in short, wide inequality in permanent income status. The process of development, of industrialization, breaks down these rigid class distinctions; historically, it tends not only to produce a smaller degree of inequality in measured income but, what is more important for our purposes, also to substitute inequality arising from transitory factors for in-equalities of permanent income status. The reduction of the inequality of permanent income status, whatever its importance in other connections, is neutral with respect to the savings ratio. This kind of inequality, which interestingly is generally the kind that is most distasteful to egalitarians, cannot be defended as required to generate savings. On the other hand, the fluidity introduced into relative income status, the emergence of fresh pos-sibilities of moving from one class to another, of possibilities of large gains and large losses over short periods of time—changes which the egalitarian may welcome as increasing equality of opportunity even if resulting in inequality of outcome—these changes are favorable to the savings ratio.

To continue these speculations outside my own field of competence, I wonder whether undue attention has not been given to the magnitude of the savings ratio at the expense of the form that savings take. Savings may well have been at least as large a fraction of income in the Middle Ages as in modern times; they then in considerable measure, perhaps in major part, took the form of cathedrals, which, however productive of ultimate satisfaction and of social security in more than one sense of that term, were not productive of worldly goods. I understand that budget studies for India, which at first sight seem to give very different results from corresponding studies for the United States, are found largely to duplicate the latter if the category "ornaments" is interpreted as savings or, in the jargon of budget studies, as "net changes in assets and liabilities." The East was for long regarded as a "sink" for the precious metals, surely evidence both of substantial savings and of the particular form that it took. Perhaps the crucial role that has been assigned to the savings ratio in economic development should be assigned instead to the factors determin-ing the form in which wealth is accumulated; to the investment rather than saving process, as it were.

b. Economic Fluctuations

There has been widespread acceptance in recent years of explanations of economic fluctuations that interpret them as primarily a resultant of the interaction of unstable investment and a relatively stable relation between consumption and current income. While I do not myself accept this income-expenditure theory as a valid and tested interpretation of experience, the acceptance of the permanent income hypothesis clearly has important implications for it that are worth recording.

The combination of this interpretation with a belief in a shortage of investment opportunities and in a rising ratio of savings to income as real income rises led, particularly in the United States in the late 1930s, to a fear of "secular stagnation": "mature" economies, it was argued, tend to have limited investment opportunities and high savings ratios at full employment. Acceptance of the permanent income hypothesis removes completely one of the pillars of the "secular stagnation" thesis; there is no reason to expect the savings ratio to rise with a secular rise in real income. In addition, it destroys the case for one proposed remedy. To counter the danger of secular stagnation, it was argued, requires raising the average propensity to consume at a full employment income. Acceptance of a particular version of the absolute income hypothesis led to the belief that one way to do so was to reduce the inequality of income, so the fear of secular stagnation was used as an argument in favor of income redistributive measures. Acceptance of the permanent income hypothesis means that, whatever may be the merits or demerits of raising the consumption ratio, changes in the inequality of income, at least of permanent income, cannot be expected to have this result. Apparently the permanent income hypothesis is evenhanded—if it removes the justification for inequality as a necessary evil to produce required savings, it also removes the justification for reducing inequality as a means of reducing attempted savings.

Postwar expansion and apparently widespread investment opportunities have on occasion led some proponents of the income-expenditure theory to fear "secular exhilaration." Consistency would have required them to favor measures designed to increase inequality as a means of reducing the ratio of consumption to income at full employment and so reducing the danger of inflation. However, to the best of my knowledge, none has done so. Clearly, on the permanent income hypothesis no such conclusion would be justified.

As I have noted, the permanent income hypothesis has relevance not only to these arguments about inequality based on particular empirical judgments, but also to the underlying Keynesian theoretical structure, in both its long-run or structural, and its short-run or cyclical, aspects.

In its long-run aspect, the central analytical proposition of the structure is the denial that the long-run equilibrium position of a free enterprise economy is necessarily at full employment; there may be, it is asserted, no monetary equilibrium at all, unless some deus ex machina such as rigid nominal wage rates is introduced to produce one; and the "real" equilibrium may be at a less than full employment position. Acceptance of the permanent income hypothesis in its most general form does not render these propositions invalid, for they do not depend on the proposition that savings is an increasing ratio of income as income rises and could be valid even if savings were a constant ratio. What does render these analytical propositions invalid is acceptance of the special feature of the hypothesis that w, the ratio of wealth to income, is a significant variable affecting k, the ratio of permanent consumption to permanent income, and that an increase in w tends to raise k.

In its short-run aspect, as an interpretation of cyclical fluctuations, the central role in the income-expenditure theory is played by the relation between consumption and current income. The permanent income hypothesis has, so far as I can see, no implications for the empirical validity or acceptability of this interpretation of cyclical fluctuations; that must be decided by comparing its predictions with the predictions of alternative theories. But it does have important implications for the form of the consumption function and, in consequence, for the cyclical characteristics of an economy for which the income-expenditure explanation of fluctuations holds. The permanent income hypothesis leads to an aggregate consumption function like that presented above in point k of section 3, in which current consumption is largely determined by past incomes. One need not accept this particular form; the general result follows simply from the idea that current consumption is adapted to some measure of longer-run income status rather than to current receipts. The effect is almost certain to be a much smaller estimate of the marginal propensity to consume out of current income than would be obtained from a function that makes consumption dependent on current income alone. To put it in other terms: it means that a much larger part of current consumption is interpreted as autonomous and a much smaller part as dependent on current income and hence, through the multiplier process, on investment. The result is a smaller investment multiplier, and an inherently cyclically more stable system. For the particular consumption function we have estimated from the data, the multiplier of personal disposable income with respect to autonomous expenditures is only about 1.4, and this takes no account of the stabilizing effects of the progressive personal tax structure, corporate taxation and savings, and the like.[4] To avoid misunderstanding, I hasten to repeat that these are not intended to be assertions about the actual empirical characteristics of our economy; they are conditional assertions and dependent for their validity on the prior acceptance of the income-expenditure theory as an explanation of economic fluctuations.

An enumeration of the implications of acceptance of a new hypothesis can never hope to be exhaustive. Indeed, one of the main implications is that it will stimulate people to think in new directions and new ways that cannot possibly be specified in advance. Even though I have ventured in this section well beyond my empirical evidence and the areas of my own competence, I have no doubt omitted more of the ultimate implications of the acceptance of the permanent income hypothesis than I have included. This is at once the appeal and the justification of what we flatter ourselves by calling "pure" research.

Notes

1. If computed from an arithmetically linear regression, at the mean income and for zero mean transitory components of income and consumption.

2. "Family Savings in Relation to Changes in the Level and Distribution of Income," *Studies in Income and Wealth*, vol. 15 (New York: National Bureau of Economic Research, 1952).

3. If consumption is a linear function of absolute income, the aggregate savings ratio depends only on the mean income and not on its distribution, although savings are a larger fraction of income the higher the income, so long as the intercept of the consumption function is positive. For the relation described in the text to hold, the consumption function must be concave downward on the average.

4. A more extended treatment of this point is contained in Milton Friedman and Gary Becker, "A Statistical Illusion in Judging Keynesian Models," *Journal of Political Economy* (February 1957).

THE EXPECTED-UTILITY HYPOTHESIS AND THE MEASURABILITY OF UTILITY[1]

· 13 ·

Renewed attention is currently being devoted to a hypothesis about choices involving risk suggested by Gabriel Cramer and Daniel Bernoulli, employed by Alfred Marshall, and recently revived by von Neumann and Morgenstern: namely, that individuals choose in such circumstances as if they were seeking to maximize the expected value of some quantity. The hypothetical quantity thus defined has, especially recently, been called "utility." This hypothesis, if reasonably valid in a sufficiently wide domain, has far-reaching implications for economic theory.[2] It provides a unified interpretation of two kinds of economic behavior that have traditionally been rationalized on divergent, and largely inconsistent, lines—first, choices among alternatives regarded as certain, rationalized in terms of consistent preferences for the goods in question and deliberative selection of the alternative highest in the scale of preference; second, choices among alternatives involving risk, rationalized in terms of ill-defined preferences for "risk" or "uncertainty," generally regarded as "irrational" in the sense that they admit of no simple and reasonably universal description but can only be determined ad hoc in each individual case. Furthermore, the expected-utility hypothesis has potentially rich empirical content. As we have shown elsewhere, a few simple and widely accepted empirical generalizations about behavior under circumstances involving risk can be used to specialize

Co-authored with L. J. Savage. Copyright 1952 by the University of Chicago Press. Reprinted from *Journal of Political Economy* 60, no. 6 (December 1952).

the hypothesis sufficiently for it to yield significant implications for phenomena that lend themselves much less readily to casual empirical observation.[3] These predictions, in turn, when and if verified, will be both a fruit of the hypothesis and a further test of its validity.

Unfortunately, general understanding of the meaning, relevance, and role of the hypothesis has been greatly obstructed by a twofold error in its earlier use: the belief, first, that a numerical utility, unique except for origin and unit of scale, was necessary for the analysis of choices among alternatives regarded as certain; second, that the expectation of this measurable utility must in the same way govern choices among alternatives involving risk. The discovery by Pareto, Slutsky, and later writers that such a numerical utility is not necessary for analyzing riskless choices was correctly regarded as an important theoretical advance. But, in presence of the idea that a utility measure derived from riskless choices must also govern choices among alternatives involving risk, it diverted attention from the possibility that there might be some function, not derivable from riskless choices, the expected value of which governed choices among alternatives involving risk.

In the light of this background, the writers who have recently revived and reinterpreted the hypothesis should have taken special pains to be unmistakably clear about the sense in which the hypothesis justifies or permits the assignment of a measure unique except for origin and unit of scale to preferences for goods and services and perhaps should have used a new name for this measure rather than the name "utility," with all its unfortunate connotations. Unfortunately, they have done neither the one nor the other. Von Neumann and Morgenstern, in reviving the hypothesis and presenting their enlightening axiomatization of it, failed to guard adequately against misunderstanding and, indeed, by some unguarded statements, probably promoted misunderstanding. Similarly, our own exposition of the relation between the hypothesis and available empirical evidence is inadequate in failing to deal directly with the problem of "measurability"; experience demonstrates that our parenthetical allusions to the problem were not sufficiently clear and that they too may have promoted rather than alleviated misunderstanding.

William Baumol's recent note in the *Journal of Political Economy* provides an excellent occasion for seeking to repair in some measure our earlier failure by an attempt to make clear the grounds on which the acceptance or rejection of the hypothesis must rest and the sense in which its acceptance justifies or permits the treatment of utility as "measurable."[4] Baumol's note is devoted precisely to these questions and states clearly the criticisms of the hypothesis that arise naturally out of the earlier discussions of "measurability."

Baumol objects to the hypothesis on two grounds: (1) that "the Neumann-Morgenstern utility construction may be incompatible with the scale of preferences of the individual" and (2) that "a Neumann-Morgenstern utility index" may be "unjustifiably arbitrary."[5] The first objection raises the general question of the grounds on which the hypothesis should be accepted or rejected (sec. 1); the second, the sense in which the hypothesis "makes" utility "measurable" (sec. 2).

1. Grounds for Accepting or Rejecting the Hypothesis

The function of a scientific hypothesis is to enable us to "predict" phenomena not yet observed, that is, to make statements about phenomena not yet observed that are (a) capable of being contradicted and (b) will not in fact be contradicted. If the statements about unobserved phenomena are not capable of being contradicted, the hypothesis is empty and hence useless for prediction—the hypothesis that a person will choose what he chooses is clearly "correct" and equally clearly "empty," because incapable of contradiction. If the statements about unobserved phenomena are contradicted ("frequently" or more often and more flagrantly than statements suggested by an alternative hypothesis), then the hypothesis is wrong. The wider the range of observable phenomena capable of contradicting the hypothesis, the greater its *potential* fruitfulness, because this is equivalent to greater precision of prediction. The wider the range of occasions on which the hypothesis has successfully withstood the test of contradiction, the greater the confidence in its validity. The desideratum is a hypothesis that yields highly precise predictions (i.e., predictions easily capable of being wrong); that has been used to make many such predictions (i.e., has had many opportunities for contradiction); and that has yielded solely "correct" predictions (i.e., has repeatedly failed to be contradicted).

These trite and oversimplified observations on the basis for choosing among hypotheses are necessary here because their implicit rejection is at the bottom of much of the criticism leveled against the expected-utility hypothesis: the hypothesis is objected to because it is not "empty," because it can be wrong. For example, Baumol says that he can conceive of behavior that would contradict the expected-utility hypothesis and yet would not be clearly "pathological" and that some of the results of the hypothesis "are not introspectively obvious."[6] In part, Baumol is saying that casual observation and introspection suggest that the hypothesis is false. This assertion is relevant evidence against the hypothesis, since it amounts to saying that crudely observed experience contradicts predictions made by the hypothesis. But it is clear from the examples and context that Baumol is also saying something quite different, which he regards as equally relevant evidence against the hypothesis; namely, that the hypothesis is not obviously and inevitably true, that behavior is conceivable that would contradict it, rather than that such behavior has been observed, however crudely. In light of the preceding paragraph, this feature is clearly a virtue of a scientific hypothesis, not a defect—it is a valid objection only to claims that the hypothesis must be true (i.e., is a tautology). The possibility of specifying behavior that would contradict the hypothesis means that the hypothesis is not empty; that such behavior is not clearly "pathological" or "introspectively obvious" means that the hypothesis, *if valid*, would enable us to make more precise predictions than we can without it.[7]

But granted that the expected-utility hypothesis is *potentially* fruitful and that objections to its acceptance like those just cited are largely irrelevant, what positive reasons are there to accept it? Has it repeatedly survived the test of contradictability? Are there any convincing reasons for believing that it will do so or continue to do so? A highly qualified affirmative answer can be given to both these questions, but no more; as things now stand, the hypothesis, despite its respectable age, must be regarded as a promising conjecture deriving its plausibility more from indirect evidence than from direct survival of "critical" experiments.

Much of the readily available evidence on the consistency of the hypothesis with experience, that is, on the failure of its implications to be contradicted by such experience, is summarized in our earlier article, where some of it is used to specialize the hypothesis. We suggested in that article additional possibilities of contradiction, but so far as we know these have not yet been exploited. Some recent experiments by Mosteller and Nogee[8] add to the direct observational evidence and fail to contradict the hypothesis. Yet the evidence of this relatively direct kind now available is far from adequate to justify any real confidence in the validity of the hypothesis; at best, it justifies mild optimism.

The very real appeal of the hypothesis derives, we believe, less from this direct evidence than from indirect evidence rendering it plausible that the hypothesis will continue to fail to be contradicted, at least in some important domains. This indirect evidence is provided in some measure by the coherence of the hypothesis with the rest of economic theory. In much greater measure, it is provided by the plausibility of a set of postulates that are sufficient for the derivation of the hypothesis and are themselves derivable from it and so are an alternative statement of the hypothesis. In saying that these postulates are more plausible than the hypothesis to which they are logically equivalent, we mean that the postulates immediately call to mind a host of implications (or predictions from the hypothesis) susceptible to casual empirical observation. With respect to the class of phenomena to which these implications relate, the hypothesis has had many opportunities for contradiction and has repeatedly failed to be contradicted. The evidence is "indirect," because this is not the class of phenomena we are primarily interested in using the hypothesis to predict. Success of the hypothesis for this class makes it plausible that it will succeed for another, not unrelated, class; it does not, however, justify the same confidence as direct evidence for the latter class.

The important original contribution of von Neumann and Morgenstern is precisely to have provided this indirect evidence through their axiomatization of the hypothesis. Since there is a mistake (adverted to by Baumol in his footnote 16 and called to our attention by Paul A. Samuelson) in the translation of the Neumann-Morgenstern postulates we presented in our earlier paper,[9] and since one of us (Savage) has been doing further work on the postulational base of the hypothesis in another connection, a restatement of the postulational evidence is presented here.[10]

Let us suppose, for simplicity, that the final outcome for an individual of a process of choice is among one of some finite number of possibilities, say the set X with elements $x_1, x_2, \ldots, x_n$. These outcomes, the x_i, can be described as the "incomes" that might possibly accrue to the individual, where income is to be understood in the widest sense, embracing, for example, cash income, schedule of cash income over time, baskets of goods, fate in love and war, etc. The assumption that there are only a finite number of outcomes is obviously without any practical significance; mathematically, it is a blemish that can be removed.

In advance, the alternatives available to the individual consist of a set of probability distributions. Any one alternative, frequently called a "prospect," say, the probability distribution f, consists of a probability f_1 that x_1 will be the final outcome, f_2 that x_2 will be, and so on. It can be interpreted as a gamble or lottery ticket offering the individual the probability f_i of receiving the income x_i for each i.

The postulates refer to the set F of all conceivable probability distributions $f, g, h, \ldots$, on the fixed finite set X defined above. Not all of these, of course, need be available to the individual in any particular case. An element f of F may be expressed in the notation $f=[f_1, f_2, \ldots, f_n]$, where the f_i's are nonnegative numbers adding up to unity.

The expression $f \leq g$ is to be read and interpreted, "The gamble f is not preferred (by the individual) to g," by which is meant that if f and g are the only alternatives available to the individual, he will not systematically choose f.

Though no postulate has yet been introduced, a very important assumption is implicit in the structure thus far defined; namely, that preferences of the person in uncertain situations to which probability applies are governed solely by the probabilities attached to each possible income. This assumption admits and is worthy of some analysis. But this analysis will be passed over here, because we are under the impression that the assumption is, with the usual grain of salt, acceptable to present critics of the utility hypothesis.

Statement of the postulates is facilitated by the notational convention that if $f=[f_1, \ldots, f_n]$, $g=[g_1, \ldots, g_n]$, and $0 \leq \alpha \leq 1$; then $\alpha f+(1-\alpha)g=[\alpha f_1 +$

$(1-\alpha)g_1, \ldots, \alpha f_n + (1-\alpha)g_n]$. Clearly, $\alpha f + (1-\alpha)g$ is itself an element of F, and reduces to f or g when α is 1 or 0, respectively. Quite formally the postulates to be discussed are these.

P1. For all f, g, h (not necessarily distinct) in F:
  1. $f \leq g$, or $g \leq f$.
  2. If $f \leq g$ and $g \leq h$, then $f \leq h$.
P2. If $\alpha f + (1-\alpha)h \leq g$ for all α such that $0 \leq \alpha < 1$, then $f \leq g$.
P3. For $0 < \alpha < 1$, $\alpha f + (1-\alpha)h \leq \alpha g + (1-\alpha)h$, if and only if $f \leq g$.

In the presence of P1–3 the utility hypothesis is rigorously implied as a theorem, namely:

Theorem. There are numbers $c_1, \ldots, c_n$ such that $f \leq g$, if and only if

$$\Sigma f_i c_i \leq \Sigma g_i c_i.$$

Moreover, any two such sequences of numbers c_i and c_i' are connected by an equation

$$c_i' = s + t c_i$$

for some s, t, with $t > 0$.

The proof of this theorem, which is the expected-utility hypothesis, is easy but not appropriate for presentation here.[11] Conversely, it is almost obvious that even the first part of the theorem implies P1–3, verifying an assertion made earlier.

The important question for us is whether the postulates can be expected to correspond reasonably well with observable economic behavior, and this question will now be taken up for the three postulates one by one.

The first postulate states that the individual can be supposed to have a complete and consistent (transitive) ordering of all possible alternatives; that is, one can tell which of two objects the individual prefers or whether he is indifferent between them; and if he does not prefer f to g, and does not prefer g to h, then he does not prefer f to h. These and closely related assumptions have been given much attention by economists. There is widespread agreement that they are introspectively very appealing and that their agreement with experience, though not perfect, is quite good enough to merit continued interest.[12]

The second postulate is a technical assumption of continuity, which seems quite acceptable, though it is not altogether without content. It says, for example, that if a person will not cross the street, no matter how light the traffic, he would not cross even if there were no danger at all.

It is essentially the third postulate that critics of the utility hypothesis seem to find inadequately motivated. But we shall show that this postulate is implied by a principle that we believe practically unique among maxims for wise action in the face of uncertainty, in the strength of its intuitive appeal. The principle is universally known and recognized; and the Greeks must surely have had a name for it, though current English seems not to.

To illustrate the principle before defining it, suppose a physician now knows that his patient has one of several diseases for each of which the physician would prescribe immediate bed rest. We assert that under this circumstance the physician should and, unless confused, will prescribe immediate bed rest whether he is now, later, or never, able to make an exact diagnosis.

Much more abstractly, consider a person constrained to choose between a pair of alternatives, a and b, without knowing whether a particular event E does (or will) in fact obtain. Suppose that, depending on his choice and whether E does obtain, he is to receive one of four (not necessarily distinct) gambles, according to the following schedule.

	EVENT	
Choice	E	not E
a	$f(a)$	$g(a)$
b	$f(b)$	$g(b)$

The principle in sufficient generality for the present purpose asserts: If the person does not prefer $f(a)$ to $f(b)$, and does not prefer $g(a)$ to $g(b)$, then he will not prefer the choice a to b. Further, if the person does not prefer a to b, he will either not prefer $f(a)$ to $f(b)$ or not prefer $g(a)$ to $g(b)$ (possibly both).

We anticipate that if the reader considers this principle, in the light of the illustration that precedes and such others as he himself may invent, he will concede that the principle is not one he would deliberately violate. This in turn we consider to be some reason for supposing that people do actually tend to avoid flagrant violation of the principle.

In the presence of the assumption (already mentioned) that incomes and probabilities alone determine the preference of a given person, P3 is a consequence of the principle now under discussion. To see this, it is necessary only to set $f(a)=f$, $f(b)=g$, $g(a)=g(b)=h$, and to suppose that the probability of E is α. After this specialization, a is the gamble $\alpha f+(1-\alpha)h$, b is $\alpha g+(1-\alpha)h$, and the principle simply states P3.

2. THE "MEASURABILITY" OF UTILITY

Baumol objects to the notion that the expected-utility hypothesis enables "*the true measure*" of utility to be "deduced from . . . the observed behavior of an individual."[13] There is a sense in which this objection is entirely valid. The significance of the objection is, however, rather different from that implied by Baumol. Since this is an issue on which there is currently much confusion and much writing at cross-purposes, it will be well to start from first principles.

Consider a situation in which an individual must choose one among a set of "prospects." An extremely general theory of choice is essentially P1 alone; more precisely, that there exists a consistent and transitive ordering of all possible prospects which has the property that the individual will choose the alternative available to him that is highest in this ordering. Let F stand for the set of all possible prospects $f, g, . . .$; and $U(f)$ for a (numerical valued) function which has the property that the individual

will choose f in preference to g, be indifferent between f and g, or choose g in preference to f, according as $U(f) > U(g)$, $U(f) = U(g)$, or $U(f) < U(g)$.   (1)

Such a function will always exist, under mathematical assumptions of no practical consequence.

$U(f)$ thus gives rise to, or generates, an ordering of prospects and, if desired, may be called *the*, or in some respects better *a*, "utility function" of prospects. The individual may now be said to choose so as to maximize "utility."

On this theory, the choice among the available alternatives depends only on their ordering. If there exists any one function U that is consistent with observed choices, then any other function that gives the same ordering of prospects will be equally consistent with observed choices. Consequently, it can equally well be said that the utility of prospects is given by any member of the family of functions

$$V[U(f)],   (2)$$

where V is an entirely arbitrary, strictly monotonic function, in particular any function such that dV/dU is positive (so that all members of the family order the prospects in the same direction).

This is the central element of validity in Baumol's position. No one member of (2) has any more right to be called "the" utility function than any other member. In this sense, utility is not "measurable" no matter what may be the precise meaning of a prospect, or the class of prospects considered.

This "general" theory of choice is almost completely empty. It is not quite empty, because it requires consistency and transitivity, and very little more, and behavior is conceivable that would contradict these requirements; but it is so close to being empty that it is relatively useless for predicting behavior. A "special" theory consists in specifying more precisely the characteristics of $V[U(f)]$ or, equivalently, the ordering among the prospects. Let discussion be restricted to prospects that can be considered as probability combinations of elementary objects, and, for simplicity, consider the elementary objects to be amounts of income per unit time. Then a prospect is to be regarded as a set of alternative incomes, together with the associated probability that each income will be realized.[14] The "special" theory under discussion is that there exists a function of income, say, $C(I)$, such that its expected value gives an ordering of prospects with property (1); that is, its expected value is *one* member of the family (2). Let us call this member U. Then, the special theory is that

$$U(f) = \overline{C}(I_f) \qquad (3)$$

satisfies (1), where the bar over the C indicates expected value, and the subscript to the I indicates that the expected value is computed for the prospect f.[15]

If there exists any such function $C(I)$, then it is unique except for origin and unit of scale; that is, the only transformations of C that yield the same ordering of prospects consisting of more than one possible income with nonzero probability are of the form

$$D[C(I)] = s + tC(I), \qquad (4)$$

with s arbitrary and $t > 0$.

This theory is by no means empty; indeed, if it were valid, knowledge of an individual's choices among some prospects each containing only one or two possible incomes would permit prediction of his choices among all other prospects, no matter how complex.

If the theory is valid—that is, if it correctly predicts behavior—then there exists a function $C(I)$ unique except for origin and unit of scale. This function contains all the information that is relevant for predicting behavior. The way to use it is to calculate its expected value for alternatives under consideration and to predict that the alternative with the highest expected value will be chosen. It is conventional, but only conventional, to describe this process as the maximization of expected utility. If the hypothesis is valid, the expected value of $C(I)$ is one member of the family of functions defined by $V[U(f)]$.

Admittedly, however, it is only one member. Any other member could be used: the cube, or fifth, power of the expected value of $C(I)$ will give the same ordering of the prospects as the expected value itself, and either could be termed "the" utility of prospects involving risk.

In our earlier article, which deals primarily with the consistency of this special theory with observed behavior, we, like others writing on this subject, called $D[C(I)]$, the family of functions given by (4), the "utility function of certain incomes." If, however, one regards any member of (2) other than $\bar{C}(I)$ (or a linear transformation of it), say $V[\bar{C}(I)]$, as giving "the" utility of uncertain prospects, it is not valid to regard $C(I)$ as "the" utility of the certain income I; "the" utility of the certain income I is then $V[C(I)]$. Our terminology was therefore misleading without more explanation than we gave and doubtless promoted confusion between the functions $D[C(I)]$ and the utility functions of prospects $V[U(f)]$. This confusion is manifest in Baumol's note when he remarks: "If we . . . accept the view that any index obtained from a valid index by a monotone transformation is also valid, those of the Friedman-Savage results mentioned at the end of the preceding section, which refer to the shape of the income marginal utility curve, lose all their meaning."[16] This is a non sequitur: the results mentioned relate to the funtions $D[C(I)]$; interpreted as referring to these functions, they retain all their meaning; they are essential for the content of the theory; but of course they are not directly relevant to any member of the family of functions $V[U(f)]$ other than the members given by $D[\bar{C}(I)]$.

What justification, then, is there for calling the particular members of $V[U(f)]$ given by $D[\bar{C}(I)]$, "the" utility of prospects involving risk and hence for speaking of utility as "measurable" rather than for calling the whole family of functions $V[U(f)]$ "the" utility of such prospects and hence speaking of utility as "ordinal" and not "measurable"? The justification is that, if the hypothesis is accepted, the former mode of speaking is far more convenient than the latter. Convenience may seem a slender justification; it is in fact an extremely important one. As Baumol correctly remarks, "In a sense any scale of measurement is arbitrary. Thus, aside from inconvenience, need anything be wrong with the use of a measure of distance which varies as the square . . . of the metric scale?"[17] There is nothing wrong, aside from inconvenience; but inconvenience is not to be brushed aside so lightly. Aside from "inconvenience," need anything be wrong with the use of Roman rather than Arabic numerals; or with dropping numerical nomenclature entirely, replacing it by extemporaneous circumlocutions? Of course, the inconvenience of not using the metric scale cannot seriously be compared in magnitude with the inconvenience of not using mathematics in science at all, but this is only because measurements of length are just one among many kinds of measurements in science, not because of any difference in kind. And, even so, everyone in a country where the square of length as ordinarily measured was the official measure of "length" would suffer serious inconvenience indeed, for calculations like $(\sqrt{x}+\sqrt{y})^2$ and $(\sqrt{x}+\sqrt{y}+\sqrt{z})^2$ would have to be performed many times each day. All this computing of squares and square roots would be a pointless and heavy complication of empirical regularities that have been discovered in nature (only inadequately compensated by some convenience in dealing with right triangles).

If the expected-utility hypothesis is accepted, there is the same justification for calling "utility" "measurable," and $\bar{C}(I)$ its "measure," as there is for calling length and temperature "measurable," and the word "measurable" has precisely the same meaning in all three cases. Is it seriously being suggested by Baumol and those who share his views that the word now be redefined so as to apply to none of the three cases?

At the moment the "convenience" gained by adopting the convention of calling $D[\bar{C}(I)]$ "the" measure of utility is nothing like so clear or great as that involved in calling the ordinary sort of length "the" measure of length. This is partly because the hypothesis that makes the utility convention convenient is not firmly established, and partly because most discussion of the hypothesis is still at a highly abstract level at which there is no great inconvenience in using a broad rather than a narrow set of functions. The argument from convenience will be far stronger when, and if, repeated failures of the hypothesis to be contradicted strengthen confidence in its validity, and when, and if, it is sufficiently specialized to be useful in concrete applications. And if this hypothesis should be rejected because an alternative is found that is "better," in the sense of being equally fruitful and less frequently contradicted, then convenience may lead to the acceptance of a radically different "measure" of utility, or whatever new concept may replace it. The significant problem for positive economics is precisely to bring about such developments for this and alternative or supplementary hypotheses; to promote the construction of hypotheses about economic behavior that will enable predictions to be made about some behavior from the observation of other behavior. In this work, it will frequently be convenient to describe such a hypothesis in terms of some function with assigned properties and belonging to some class. "Measurability" is used to refer to the narrowness of the class. While this is only a convenient way of speaking, of describing a collection of rules for prediction, it is an important convenience, and economists should not be urged to forego its use simply because others may suppose that such statements refer to "reality" in an awesome spirit that is really nonsense. Economists can and should, like other scientists, recognize the relativity of their tools to the state of their science.

An excellent example for present purposes is provided by the attempts of Irving Fisher and Ragnar Frisch to measure utility referred to by Baumol.[18] In its simplest form, for example, Fisher's method rests on a particular hypothesis about behavior, namely, that the ordering of various combinations of goods in the individual's scale of preferences can be reproduced by the sum of one-variable functions, each containing as a variable the quantity of a particular good. This hypothesis is by no means empty. If it were accepted, it would justify calling the sum of the one-variable functions (say, U) "the" utility function and would provide a "measurable" utility. Of course, it would nonetheless be true that any monotonic increasing function of U would give the same ordering of bundles of goods; however, only a linear one would be expressible as the sum of one-variable functions. But this particular hypothesis—of universal "independence" of goods in this sense—has as one implication that no good is an "inferior" good (i.e., that all income elasticities are positive), and this implication is contradicted by a great deal of evidence, which, indeed, is reasonably consistent with almost the opposite—that all goods, if narrowly defined, are "inferior" for some ranges of income. In consequence, the hypothesis of universal independence must be rejected. Less sweeping hypotheses requiring only limited "independence" can be formulated that would also provide a "measurable" utility. The difficulty is that an indefinitely large number can be formulated and that no one seems to have discovered a particular one that has fruitful empirical implications capable of being contradicted, yet not contradicted when submitted to test.

The failure of these experiments should be interpreted neither as a consequence of the nonmeasurability of utility in some absolute sense nor as showing that utility is not measurable. They were simply experiments that failed to produce empirical hypotheses acceptable to the authors themselves or to their colleagues in light of the available evidence. It may be that future experiments along the same general lines will be more successful.

If the issue in question has seemed important, it is, we believe, largely because of a failure to distinguish sharply between "positive" economics and welfare economics. The discovery—if such it be—that a class of individual behavior can be predicted by supposing individuals to act as if they were maximizing the expected value of a function unique except for origin and unit of scale has, in and of itself, no welfare implication at all; and none is added by adopting the convention of calling the expected value of that function "utility." As we remarked in our earlier paper, "it is entirely unnecessary to identify the quantity that individuals are to be interpreted by maximizing with a quantity that should be given special importance in public policy."[19] The ethical precept that society "should" promote the "welfare" of individuals is meaningless until "welfare" is given content. Any identification of "welfare" attained by individuals with "utility" as defined by the special theory of choice described above is itself an ethical precept, to be justified on ethical grounds, not a scientific proposition.

In light of the importance of utilitarianism as a philosophical creed and of its modern resurgence, particularly in "welfare economics," it may well have promoted confusion to have used the term "utility" in a scientific theory of choice. But, even if this was an error, it hardly seems desirable to seek to correct it by denying to economists the use of the term "measurable" in the sense in which it is used in other sciences.

3. Conclusion

The hypothesis that individuals choose among alternatives involving risk as if they were seeking to maximize the expected value of some quantity, which has been called utility, is intended to be a scientific hypothesis enabling correct predictions to be made about individual behavior. It should be accepted— tentatively, of course, as all scientific hypotheses are—if it leads to "correct" predictions usually, or more frequently than any equally useful alternative; it should be rejected if its predictions are generally contradicted by observation. At the moment, the available evidence does not contradict the hypothesis, but it must be emphasized that the opportunities for contradiction have been few, so the direct evidence in its favor is meager. Confidence in the hypothesis derives largely from its coherence with the body of economic theory and, more important, from the plausibility of the postulates with which it can be shown to be equivalent rather than from repeated success in prediction.

If the hypothesis is accepted, it justifies or permits the definition of—and therewith the assignment of numerical values, unique except for origin and unit of scale, to—the quantity called "utility." These values can in principle be determined by observing the choices made by an individual among a limited class of alternatives. The hypothesis, if accepted, thus makes it possible to regard "utility" as "measurable" in the same sense in which length and tem- perature are "measurable." In all three cases this means the adoption of a convention on grounds of its convenience in using the hypotheses or theories in question. In no case does it justify regarding the particular "measure" as an unchanging "absolute" or as having any relevance for phenomena outside the range of those encompassed by the hypotheses on which the particular conventions rest. In all three cases it would be possible in principle to dispense with the convention and to adopt a more roundabout method of discourse, but only at the cost of a probably intolerable complication of known empirical regularities.

Two quite different classes of objections are made to this particular convention for assigning a "measure" to utility: (1) that the expected-utility hypothesis is not a useful or valid interpretation of actual behavior and (2) that any convention that would treat utility as measurable is undesirable or unnec- essary. The first objection is, of course, unexceptionable; it can, and should, be removed only as and if experience in applying the hypothesis demonstrates that the hypothesis is fruitful and justifies acceptance. The second objection, on the other hand, cannot be accepted. It would deny economics a mode of speaking and expressing theories that has been found useful if not indispensable in other sciences. It expresses a viewpoint that its proponents would find impossible to apply consistently; they would have to deny themselves the privilege of speaking of money income, or stock of money, or size of population as measurable. If this viewpoint seems persuasive for utility, it is, we think, partly because some hypotheses that would, if verified, have implied convenient measures of utility were actually flagrantly contradicted by experience, and partly because of a widespread confusion between positive economics and normative economics, a widespread tendency to use the same word—utility— to stand for two quite different things: on the one hand, a quantity that it is useful to regard an individual as maximizing in interpreting his behavior and predicting his reactions to changed circumstances, and, on the other hand, a quantity that he "should" maximize or that society "should" maximize or help him maximize. The identification of these two conceptually different magnitudes is a maxim for wise behavior or an ethical precept, not a scientific proposition, and is in no way required by the adoption of a particular convention for "measuring" utility.

NOTES

1. We are indebted to William J. Baumol and Jacob Marschak for helpful comments on an earlier draft of this paper.

This paper was mainly written while Savage was a fellow of the John Simon Guggenheim Memorial Foundation and a research scholar in France under the Fulbright Act (Public Law 584, 79th Cong.). His contribution is an outgrowth of work at the University of Chicago sponsored by the Office of Naval Research.

2. The maximization of such an expected value may also be regarded as a maxim for behavior. As such, it promises to have important implications for statistical theory. Cf. L. J. Savage, "The Theory of Statistical Decision," *Journal of the American Statistical Association* 46 (March 1951): 55–67. Success of the maxim in this domain, as in any other area of decisions involving uncertainty, depends, not on its empirical verification for the economic behavior of men at large, but on its acceptability, to individuals who are particularly concerned with such decisions, as a rule guiding "wise" behavior in the face of uncertainty.

3. Milton Friedman and L. J. Savage, "The Utility Analysis of Choices Involving Risk," *Journal of Political Economy* 56 (August 1948): 279–304; reprinted in American Economic Association, *Readings in Price Theory* (Chicago: Irwin, 1952), pp. 57–96. Experimental use of the hypothesis is reported in a paper by F. Mosteller and P. Nogee,

"An Experimental Measurement of Utility," *Journal of Political Economy* 59 (October 1951): 371–404.

4. William J. Baumol, "The Neumann-Morgenstern Utility Index—an Ordinalist View," *Journal of Political Economy* 59 (February 1951): 61–66. At one point, Baumol raises the question whether Bernoulli and Marshall maintained the expected-utility hypothesis or the hypothesis that "consumers always accept the actuarial value of a risky proposition as indicative of its utility" (p. 62). This question can be answered definitively. The main thesis of Bernoulli's paper is precisely the necessity of distinguishing between the two hypotheses to solve the St. Petersburg and similar paradoxes. In the original Latin text, he labels what has come to be called expected utility, "emolumentum medium." Cramer, in the passages from his letter in French to Nicholas Bernoulli that Daniel Bernoulli quotes at the end of his own paper, contrasts the "espérance mathématique" with the "espérance morale." Alfred Marshall deals explicitly with expected utility, not expected money value, in his Mathematical Note ix. See Friedman and Savage, op. cit., pp. 280–81, and the references there cited.

5. Op. cit., pp. 62, 65.

6. Ibid., pp. 64, 65.

7. Similarly, Baumol remarks approvingly of a construction of his own that "no situation can have its 'utility' inferred from that of others" (ibid., p. 66). But this simply means that his hypothesis is almost empty and hence almost incapable of adding to our ability to predict behavior; it is therefore of almost no interest at all.

On Baumol's own implicit criterion, ordinal utility analysis of the usual indifference curve variety would have to be rejected. The usual formulations are almost but not quite empty, since they imply at least transitivity. Conceivably someone might choose oranges in preference to apples, and apples in preference to nuts, but nuts in preference to oranges, which would be inconsistent with transitivity.

An analogy with physical science may help clarify the point at issue. There is nothing "pathological" about the attraction between objects varying inversely as the cube of the distance between them, nor is it introspectively obvious that the attraction should vary inversely as the square of the distance. One can readily conceive of a sequence of measurements that if observed would contradict the inverse square law. Clearly none of these statements represents a valid objection to the inverse square law; they merely mean that it has potential power.

8. Op. cit.

9. This mistake is noted and corrected in the version reprinted in *Readings in Price Theory*, p. 71.

10. The postulate system and the motivation for it presented here may be compared with the corresponding material in section 3 of J. Marschak, "Why 'Should' Statisticians and Businessmen Maximize 'Moral Expectation'?" *Proceedings of the Second Berkeley Symposium on Mathematical Statistics and Probability* (Berkeley: University of California Press, 1951), pp. 493–506, with which it is in substantial agreement.

11. Rather more is proved in the appendix of John von Neumann and Oskar Morgenstern, *Theory of Games and Economic Behavior*, 2d ed. (Princeton, N.J.: Princeton University Press, 1947).

12. See Friedman and Savage, op. cit., p. 288, n. 23, and the references therein to the dissenting view by W. E. Armstrong.

13. Op. cit., p. 61.

14. More precisely, let I be income per unit of time, and $P(I)$ the probability of receiving an income less than I. Then a prospect consists of a particular (cumulative) probability distribution, $P_f(I)$.

15. To state it more formally:

$$U(f)=U[P_f(I)]=\int_{-\infty}^{+\infty}C(I)dP_f(I).$$

16. Op. cit., p. 65.

17. Ibid.

18. Ibid., p. 62.

19. Op. cit., p. 283, n. 11.

CHOICE, CHANCE, AND THE PERSONAL DISTRIBUTION OF INCOME[1]

· 14 ·

The traditional "theory of distribution" is concerned exclusively with the pricing of factors of production—the distribution of income among cooperating resources classified by their productive function. It has little to say about the distribution of income among the individual members of the society, and there is no corresponding body of theory that does. This absence of a satisfactory theory of the personal distribution of income and of a theoretical bridge connecting the functional distribution of income with the personal distribution is a major gap in modern economic theory.

The functional distribution of income has been treated as primarily a reflection of choices made by individuals through the market: the value of factors is derived from the value of the final products that they cooperate in producing; and the value of final products in turn is determined by choices of consumers among the alternatives technically available. The personal distribution of income, on the other hand, when it has been analyzed at all, has been treated as largely independent of choices made by individuals through the market, except as these affect the price per unit of the factors of production. Differences among individuals or families in the amount of income received are generally regarded as reflecting either circumstances largely outside the control of the individuals concerned, such as unavoidable chance

Copyright 1953 by the University of Chicago. Reprinted from *Journal of Political Economy* 61, no. 4 (August 1953).

occurrences and differences in natural endowment and inherited wealth, or collective action, such as taxation and subsidies.

This sharp difference in the role assigned individual choice in two such closely related contexts seems hardly justified. Individual choice through the market can greatly modify the effect on the personal distribution of income both of circumstances outside the control of the individuals concerned and of collective actions designed to affect the distribution of income. Moreover, these collective actions are themselves primarily a manifestation of individual preferences, even if not of choice through the market.

Individual choice can affect the income distribution in two rather different ways. The first—that differences in money income may compensate for nonpecuniary advantages or disadvantages attached to the receipt of those incomes—has often been noticed, though its importance is typically underestimated, and will not be dealt with further in this paper. For example, an unpleasant occupation must be more highly rewarded than more pleasant occupations if it is to attract persons to whom the latter are equally open, incomes in unattractive localities must be higher than those in attractive localities readily accessible to the same class of people if their inhabitants are not to leave them, and so on. In these cases, differences in money income are required to produce equality in real income.[2]

The second way that individual choice can affect the distribution of income has been less frequently noticed. The alternatives open to an individual differ, among other respects, in the probability distribution of income they promise. Hence his choice among them depends in part on his taste for risk. Let the same set of alternatives be available to members of two societies, one consisting of people who have a great aversion to risk; the other, of people who "like" risk. This difference in tastes will dictate different choices from the same alternatives. These will be reflected most clearly, though by no means exclusively, in a different allocation of resources to activities devoted to manufacturing the kind of risk attractive to individuals. For example, insurance will be a major industry in the first society, lotteries in the second; income and inheritance taxes will be highly progressive in the first society, less progressive or regressive in the second. The result will be different income distributions in the two societies; the inequality of income will tend to be less in the first society than in the second. It follows that the inequality of income in a society may be regarded in much the same way as the kinds of goods that are produced, as at least in part—and perhaps in major part—a reflection of deliberate choice in accordance with the tastes and preferences of the members of the society rather than as simply an "act of God."

The following remarks illustrate and explore on an abstract level this relation between individual choice among alternatives involving risk and the distribution of individuals by size of income. For purposes of this exploratory discussion, I shall accept the expected-utility theory of choice, that is, I shall suppose that individuals choose among alternatives involving risk as if they knew the probability distribution of incomes attached to each alternative and were seeking to maximize the expected value of some quantity, called "utility," which is a function of income.[3] I shall take it for granted that utility is an increasing function of income.

1. THE ISOLATED INDIVIDUAL

As the simplest case, consider a Robinson Crusoe entirely isolated from all other human beings. To avoid the problem of measuring income, suppose that he produces only a single product or, what is equivalent, that there is a set of relative "prices" or "values" for all products that can be used to express the output in units of a single product.

At any moment, Robinson Crusoe has many courses of action open to him—that is, different ways of using his time and the resources on the island. He can cultivate the arable land intensively or extensively, make one or another kind of capital goods to assist in cultivation, hunt or fish or do both, and so on in infinite variety. Let him adopt some course of action and carry it out. The result will be some flow of income over time, say $I(t)$, where I stands for income per unit of time and t for time. At the moment he adopts the course of action, say t_0, $I(t)$ for $t > t_0$ is of course not precisely known—the actual result of the course of action adopted depends not only on what Robinson Crusoe does but also on such chance events as the weather, the number of fish in the neighborhood when he happens to fish, the quality of the seed he plants, the state of his health, and so on. We can take account of this uncertainty by supposing that a set of possible future income streams, each with known probability $p_{t_0}[I(t)]$ of occurring, corresponds to any course of action. Such a probability distribution of income streams we may call a "prospect."

The prospects among which Robinson Crusoe can choose at any time t_0 clearly depend on his own past course of action. But this in turn can be viewed as the consequence of a similar choice at an earlier stage. So we can, if we wish, think of him as making a single decision at whatever point we start our analysis, say when he lands on the island, for the rest of his life. This degree of generality may not be desirable for all purposes; for some, it may be better to consider individual "moves" rather than entire "strategies," in von Neumann's and Morgenstern's terminology. At our present stage of analysis, however, it will be well to eliminate all unnecessary complications. Adopting this point of view enables us to dispense with the subscript t_0, since there is only one set of prospects that is relevant and each prospect contains future income streams for the same period, namely, from the initial starting point to the indefinite future.

As a further, albeit more questionable, simplification, we can replace each $I(t)$ by a single number, either by assuming that the $I(t)$ are all members of a one-parameter family, say all straight lines with the same slope, or by discounting future incomes back to the initial point at some given rate of interest, adding the discounted incomes to get the present value of each income stream, and assuming that, at this rate of interest, the individual is indifferent between any two streams with the same present value.[4] Either assumption permits each $I(t)$ to be replaced by a single number, say W (for wealth), that can be calculated without knowing the individual's utility function.

These simplifying assumptions mean that any prospect can be completely described by a cumulative probability distribution, say $P(W)$, giving the probability that the result of the course of action in question will be a value of wealth less than W. Let A' be the set of all courses of action, a any particular course of action, and $P_a(W)$, the prospect corresponding to a.[5]

The assumption that utility is an increasing function of wealth (which in our present formulation replaces income) is alone enough to rule out some prospects. If

$$P_a(W) \le P_{a'}(W) \text{ for all } W$$

and   (1)

$$P_a(W) < P_{a'}(W) \text{ for some } W,$$

then a is clearly preferable to a', regardless of the precise shape of the utility function of wealth.[6] Let the (reduced) set A consist of courses of action such that no pair of prospects corresponding to these courses of action satisfies equation 1. The choice among the set A then depends on more than the first derivative of the utility function.

Let $U(W)$ be the utility function of Robinson Crusoe. He will then, on the expected-utility hypothesis, choose that prospect a for which

$$\bar{U} = \int_{w=0}^{w=\infty} U(W)dP_a(W) \qquad (2)$$

is a maximum. Beyond this restatement of the expected-utility hypothesis there is little that can be said about this special case on the present level of generality.

Suppose that there are many identical Robinson Crusoes faced with identical sets of courses of action and associated prospects and completely isolated one from the other. All would, in principle, make the same choice, say prospect a^*. If, further, the outcome of the actions of any one Robinson Crusoe (his realized W) were statistically independent of the outcome of the actions of any other Robinson Crusoe (the other's realized W) then $P_{a^*}(W)$ would be the realized cumulative distribution of wealth among them. Income "inequality" among them would be partly a product of deliberate choice, and the amount of "inequality" would depend partly on the shape of the utility function common to them. If the utility function were a straight line, each Robinson Crusoe would choose the prospect with the highest expected income; if it were everywhere concave downward (diminishing marginal utility of income), he would be willing to sacrifice some expected income for decreased variance of income; if it were everywhere concave upward (increasing marginal utility of income), he would be willing to sacrifice some expected income for increased variance of income, and so on. Given a sufficiently large and varied set of prospects, the "inequality" of income among the Robinson Crusoes would be least in the second case and greatest in the third.[7]

The realized W of any one Robinson Crusoe need not, however, be statistically independent of the realized W of others. For example, though each were ignorant of the existence of the others, all their islands might be in the same geographical area and subject to the same weather conditions. In this case, $P_{a^*}(W)$ would not be the realized cumulative distribution of wealth among them, if we suppose each to make only one choice. At the extreme of complete dependence, all would realize the same wealth, so there might be complete equality even though the utility function were everywhere concave upward. In intermediate cases the kind and degree of interdependence affects the shape of the realized distribution of income but not the general conclusion about the effect of the shape of the utility function on the degree of inequality.

2. Individuals in a Society

Redistribution Is Costless

Suppose the many identical Robinson Crusoes establish communication with one another. The considerations determining the course of action to be adopted by each are now radically changed, for it is now possible to produce new prospects by joint advance agreement among the Robinson Crusoes for a redistribution of the product obtained. Many arrangements common among individuals in our society involve this kind of redistribution, so that one need not assume collective action through "government." Private enterprises explicitly selling insurance or conducting lotteries are extreme and obvious examples. But the phenomenon is much more widespread: almost every enterprise in our society is in part an arrangement to change the probability distribution of wealth. For example, let one Robinson Crusoe set himself up as an entrepreneur guaranteeing "wages" to the others and taking the residue, but let each proceed to do what he otherwise would have done, so that the "entrepreneur" exercises none of the usual supervisory functions. The result is to change the set of prospects available to the individuals concerned. Indeed, a strong case can be made for regarding this function of "producing" new prospects, not by technical change or improvement, but by redistribution of the impact of uncertainty, as the "essential" entrepreneurial function in modern society.

In general, of course, communication changes the probability distribution of wealth corresponding to any course of action by the diffusion of knowledge and makes new courses of action available by the exchange of products, thereby giving scope to the division of labor and specialization of function. We may neglect these complications, however, since in the main they affect the attainable level of income rather than its distribution. We shall therefore assume that the mere establishment of communication or the exchange of goods does not change the set of probability distributions of income available to each Robinson Crusoe.

We cannot brush aside so blithely another complication: costs of administration and enforcement involved in redistributive arrangements. The most important of these costs is the effect of such arrangements on incentives. A man who carries insurance against the loss of his house by fire has less incentive to devote resources to preventing fire than if he himself bore the full cost of the loss. In our terminology, the course of action a and its associated probability distribution $P_a(W)$ may be achievable only if the Robinson Crusoe in question himself receives directly the resulting W. If a group agrees that each will follow the course of action a, pool the resulting product, and share it, say, equally, the actual realized wealth may be quite different from what it would have been if each had adopted a independently—that is, individuals would not in fact follow a. This is, of course, the basic reason why full insurance against loss is feasible only for hazards that are largely independent of individual action and why all attempts to divorce payment to individuals from their productive contribution have encountered great difficulty or completely failed.

We shall postpone this complication to the next section. In this one, we shall assume that redistributive arrangements involve no cost, that is, that the set of courses of actions A and associated prospects $P_a(W)$ is equally achievable whether individuals act separately or enter into redistributive arrangements, where W represents the wealth realized by an individual *before* redistribution, that is, the amount he can contribute to any redistributive pool. If we further assume that the realized W of any one Robinson Crusoe is statistically independent of the realized W of any other,[8] that the $P_a(W)$ are reasonably well behaved,[9] and that the number of Robinson Crusoes is sufficiently large, then the course of action adopted depends only on the expected value of the $P_a(W)$, and the inequality of the distribution of wealth among the identical individuals depends only on their tastes. For given independence and large numbers there is little (in the limit, no) uncertainty about the wealth per person—the average or expected wealth—that will be realized by any common course of action. In consequence, it will pay to adopt the course of action for which the wealth per person is a maximum, since this will maximize the total to be divided, and then divide it among the Robinson Crusoes in the optimum manner. More formally, suppose a^* is the course of action chosen under conditions of the preceding section, that it yields an expected wealth $\overline{W}_{a^*}$, and that the course of action a^{**} yields a higher expected wealth $\overline{W}_{a^{**}}$. Suppose an agreement to be reached that each Crusoe will follow a^{**}, contribute the resulting product to a common pool, and then draw out a first return determined by a random mechanism which gives him a probability $P_{a^*}(W)$ of getting less than W. The prospect of this first return alone is clearly as attractive to every Crusoe as a^* is without a redistributive arrangement, and $\overline{W}_{a^{**}} - \overline{W}_{a^*}$ times the number of Crusoes is now left in the common pool to provide an additional return, so a^{**} with an appropriate redistributive arrangement is clearly preferable to a^*. By the same reasoning, it is clear that there always exists a redistributive arrangement which will make a prospect with a higher expected wealth preferable to any prospect with a lower expected wealth, whether or not the latter is accompanied by a redistributive arrangement. It follows that for the special case under consideration, the opportunities offered man by "nature" determine only the mean value of the realized distribution of wealth; the inequality of wealth is entirely a man-made creation.

Suppose the utility function of wealth is everywhere concave downward. The optimum distribution of wealth is then obviously egalitarian. The Robinson Crusoes will pool their wealth and each take out a pro rata share. At the other extreme, suppose the utility function of wealth is everywhere concave upward. The optimum distribution of income is then obviously as unequal as possible. The Robinison Crusoes will pool their wealth, and each will get a lottery ticket giving an equal chance to win a single prize equal to the total wealth.

A more interesting and empirically relevant utility function to analyze is one that has the shape suggested by Savage and me to rationalize a few simple and widely accepted empirical generalizations about behavior under circumstances involving risk.[10] We suggested a function initially concave downward, then concave upward, and then finally concave downward, like the $U(W)$ curve in Figure 14.1.

Let $\overline{W}$ be the maximum expected wealth (realized when each individual follows the course of action a^{**}). Consider a prospect consisting of two values

FIGURE 14.1

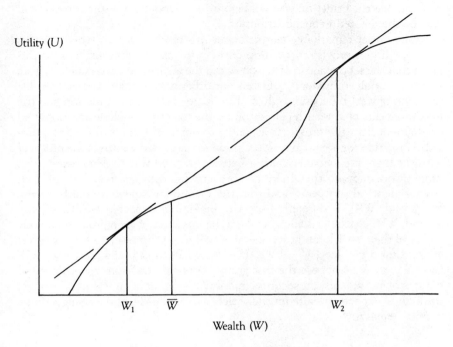

Utility (U)

W_1 $\overline{W}$ W_2

Wealth (W)

of W, say W_l and W_u, such that $W_u \geq \overline{W} \geq W_l$, and associated probabilities p and p_u such that $p_l W_l + p_u W_u = \overline{W}$. The expected utility corresponding to this prospect is given by the ordinate at $\overline{W}$ of the chord connecting $U(W_l)$ and $U(W_u)$. It is obvious geometrically that if there is a line tangent to the utility function in Figure 14.1 at two points, and if $\overline{W}$ is between the abscissae of the points of tangency, which we may designate W_1 and W_2 with $W_2 > W_1$, then this expected utility is a maximum if W_l and W_u are equal to W_1 and W_2 respectively.[11] The associated probabilities p_l and p_u are then $(W_2 - \overline{W})/(W_2 - W_1)$ and $(\overline{W} - W_1)/(W_2 - W_1)$, respectively. Call this prospect a_d (d for "double tangent").

Any more complicated prospect with the expected value $\overline{W}$ can always be expressed as a probability combination of one- or two-valued prospects each with the same expected value $\overline{W}$. The expected utility of the more complicated prospect can therefore be expressed as the expected value of the expected utilities of the one- or two-valued prospects into which it can be decomposed, hence it cannot exceed the expected utility of the component one- or two-valued prospect with the highest expected value. It follows that a_d is the optimum prospect for each member of a society composed of individuals each of whom has the utility function of Figure 14.1. Under our assumptions it will also be the realized wealth distribution.

One rather remarkable feature about this result is that it remains valid, with one minor proviso, if we drop entirely the assumption made up to this point that the set of courses of action A and the associated prospects $P_a(W)$ are identical for all individuals.[12] Given our other assumptions, the *ex post* distribution of wealth depends only on the shape of the utility function and the maximum expected wealth per person for the society as a whole and not at all on differences in the prospects available to different Robinson Crusoes, provided only that for every Robinson Crusoe the expected wealth of the prospect with the highest expected wealth is between W_1 and W_2. To demonstrate this proposition, suppose that there are two groups, with the members of each having identical prospects, and that the maximum expected wealth for the first group, $\overline{W}^{(1)}$, is different from the maximum expected wealth for the second, $\overline{W}^{(2)}$. By the preceding analysis the members of each group separately will pool their wealth, and each member will receive in return a lottery ticket giving him a chance $(W_2 - \overline{W}^{(i)})/(W_2 - W_1)$ to W_1 and a chance $(\overline{W}^{(i)} - W_1)/(W_2 - W_1)$ to W_2. Suppose the first group contains a fraction $n^{(1)}$ of the total number of individuals, the second a fraction $n^{(2)}$ so that $n^{(1)}\overline{W}^{(1)} + n^{(2)}\overline{W}^{(2)} = \overline{W}$, the highest expected wealth for the society as a whole. The final result is that a fraction equal to

$$n^{(1)}\frac{W_2 - \overline{W}^{(1)}}{W_2 - W_1} + n^{(2)}\frac{W_2 - \overline{W}^{(2)}}{W_2 - W_1} = \frac{W_2 - \overline{W}}{W_2 - W_1} \tag{3}$$

will realize a wealth of W_1, and the rest a wealth of W_2. But this is precisely the result that would have been reached if all had identical prospects, with a highest expected wealth of $\overline{W}$. More generally, the final result is that each individual adopts the course of action that has the highest expected wealth, contributes the result to a common pool, and receives in return a guarantee of a wealth W_1 plus a chance to win a single prize equal to $W_2 - W_1$, the size of the chance being equal to $(\overline{W}^{(i)} - W_1)/(W_2 - W_1)$ for the ith individual, where $\overline{W}^{(i)}$ is the expected wealth contributed by him. The chance of ending up with a wealth W_2 thus varies from individual to individual according to the brightness of his prospects, but the final distribution of realized wealth is the same as if all had identical prospects.

Neither is this result greatly affected, though it is complicated, by dropping the assumption that the realized W's (before redistribution) are statistically independent. Consider the extreme case in which knowledge of the outcome for one individual implies complete knowledge of the outcome for all individuals. Suppose, first, that all possible values of W for all individuals and any a in the set A are between W_1 and W_2. Regardless of the course of action adopted, there will then be some single actual realized value after the event, and the preceding analysis shows that the individuals will pool their W's and redistribute the total through a lottery. The realized wealth distribution will therefore consist of two groups of individuals, each member of one receiving W_1, each member of the other receiving W_2. Only the fraction of all individuals who end up in each group depends on the actual outcome. In advance, with an appropriate agreement for redistribution, expected utility increases with expected wealth, so again it is best for all to adopt the course of action that promises the highest expected wealth. And again differences among individuals in the prospects open to them do not affect the final result but only the number of lottery tickets each gets. If all possible values of W for the set A are not between W_1 and W_2, the a with the highest expected wealth may no longer be the optimum. But this much is still true: the advance arrangements will be such that if the actually realized W (before redistribution) is between W_1 and W_2, it will be redistributed so as to yield values of W_1 and W_2. In consequence, the final realized wealth distribution will under all circumstances be empty between W_1 and W_2.

The assumption that tastes (i.e., utility functions) of all individuals are identical can also be dropped without affecting our general conclusion that, so long as redistribution is costless, the inequality of wealth depends predominantly on the tastes of the members of the community and only secondarily, if at all, on the prospects available to them. Dropping this assumption does, however, change the more specific conclusion that the realized distribution of wealth will generally be two-valued. Let each individual separately have a utility function of the same general shape as that drawn in Figure 14.1, but let W_1 and W_2, the abscissae of the points of tangency of the double tangent to the utility function, vary from individual to individual (these are the only two parameters of the function that are relevant for the present problem) and designate their values for the ith individual by $W_1^{(i)}$ and $W_2^{(i)}$. For each individual separately, the optimum redistributive arrangement is essentially the same as previously: a chance $(W_2^{(i)} - \overline{W}^{(i)})/(W_2^{(i)} - W_1^{(i)})$ of a wealth $W_1^{(i)}$, and a chance $(\overline{W}^{(i)} - W_1^{(i)})/(W_2^{(i)} - W_1^{(i)})$ of a wealth $W_2^{(i)}$, where $\overline{W}^{(i)}$ is the maximum expected wealth obtainable by any course of action available to him. And there is nothing to prevent this arrangement from being adopted: each individual follows the course of action that promises the maximum expected wealth, contributes the resulting product to a common pool, and receives in return a lottery ticket giving him the above chances of receiving a wealth $W_1^{(i)}$ or $W_2^{(i)}$. Since each lottery ticket is actuarially "fair," the entire lottery is; and so long as the $P_a^{(i)}(W)$ are reasonably well behaved and the $W_2^{(i)}$ finite, the law of large numbers will still apply. So, with a sufficiently large number of individuals, the uncertainty for the lottery as a whole is negligible.[13] The realized wealth distribution in this case depends on the distribution of the $W_1^{(i)}$ and $W_2^{(i)}$ as well as on the maximum expected wealth. The effect of the difference in tastes is to introduce additional dispersion into the distribution of wealth that would be realized with identical tastes, the amount of the dispersion depending on the extent of divergence in tastes. As we shall see in the next section, the costs of redistributon have a very similar effect.

3. INDIVIDUALS IN A SOCIETY

Redistribution Involves Cost

The significant costs of redistributive arrangements, particularly through their effects on "incentives," rule out some arrangements that would otherwise be desirable, with the result that the kinds of opportunities offered by "nature," the original set of prospects $P_a(W)$, affect the shape of the distribution of wealth and not merely its mean value. The effect is to produce something of a mixture between the conclusions of section 1 for the isolated individual and of section 2 for individuals in a society in which redistribution is costless.

Perhaps the simplest model which combines these two cases (and one that, as we shall see, is capable of generating distributions of wealth or income bearing at least a family resemblance to those actually observed) is to suppose that each individual's possible actions can be divided into two independent and noncompeting sets—one set of actions, say A_s, the results of which are not accessible to redistribution, the other, say A_r, the results of which can be redistributed without cost.[14] The individual then chooses one course of action from each set. Before redistribution his realized wealth consists of two parts, W_s and W_r, after redistribution of W_s and, say, W_r'' so his final wealth is $W_s + W_r''$. Each individual is now concerned with the probability distribution of $W_s + W_r''$ not with either separately.

What is the optimum redistributive arrangement if the utility function has the shape of $U(W)$ in Figure 14.1 and, for simplicity, is the same for all individuals? It is now no longer possible to achieve the *optimum optimorum*—namely, the two-valued prospect of receiving either W_1 or W_2 with the highest expected value and appropriate probabilities. For, whatever redistributive arrangements are adopted, there is no way of averaging out or avoiding the risk attached to W_s if we suppose, as seems desirable, that W_r'' does not depend on the realized W_s, though it may depend on the anticipated $P_{a_s}(W_s)$.[15] Clearly the best choice from A_r is still the one that has the highest expected wealth—since any desired redistribution of the W_r is available, there is nothing to be lost by making the total pie as large as possible. Beyond this, it is best to adjust both the choice from the set A_s and the redistributive arrangement so as to approximate as closely as possible the *optimum optimorum*.

In order to say anything more specific about the optimum redistributive arrangements, it is almost certainly necessary to specify more precisely than we have so far done the characteristics of the set $P_{a_s}(W_s)$ and perhaps also of the utility function $U(W)$; it seems not impossible that there exists some $P_{a_s}(W_s)$ that would justify almost any kind of redistributive arrangement. I have not attempted an exhaustive analysis of this problem. But I conjecture that for a wide class of functions $P_{a_s}(W_s)$ and of utility functions $U(W)$, the optimum redistributive arrangement is identical with that of section 2, and that this is so even if the prospects differ from individual to individual.[16] Pending further analysis, I shall tentatively accept this conjecture and assume that the $P_{a_s}(W)$ and utility function $U(W)$ have the properties required to make it valid.

This redistributive arrangement can be described as the contribution of a sum by each individual, that is, the purchase of a share in a lottery, and his receiving in return some specified chance of receiving a designated sum, that is, some chance of a prize. The amount paid by each individual depends on his realized W_r and on the prospect he adopts from the set A_s—but not on the realized W_s, for this would contradict the assumption that W_s is not accessible to redistribution. If all individuals have identical sets of prospects, all will choose the same pair of prospects, and the sum paid will differ among individuals only because the realized W_r does. If, however, individuals have different sets of prospects, the amount paid depends on the particular prospect chosen from the set A_s, as well as on the realized W_r, because the aim of the payment is to put each individual in the neighborhood of W_1 if he does not win a prize. In consequence, those who have prospects promising a relatively high value of W_s will keep a smaller amount from W_r (or pay more in addition to it) than those who have prospects promising a relatively small value of W_s. These differences in payment will be compensated by differences in the chance of winning a prize (that is, in the number of lottery tickets), the former receiving a larger chance than the latter. The size of the prize will be the same for all and equal to $W_2 - W_1$, since its purpose is to put the winners in the neighborhood of W_2.

With this redistributive arrangement, the final realized wealth distribution is the probability sum of two wealth distributions. The courses of action adopted from the set A_s lead to some wealth distribution of the realized W_s, its exact form depending on the particular choices that are optimum,[17] the degree of interdependence among the W_s's realized by different individuals, and the differences among individuals in the prospects available to them. This distribution is now modified by the payments made for lottery tickets. Their effect is to shift the center of gravity of the distribution to W_1 and, in so far as the prospects available to the individuals differ, to reduce its variability, since the differences in the payments made by different individuals are designed to offset such differences in available prospects. Suppose the lottery now drawn and the winners and losers determined. This separates the wealth distribution into two distributions—one for winners and one for losers. These two distributions need not in general be the same, since individuals with generally better prospects have larger chances of winning and since the wealth distribution yielded by generally better prospects may differ systematically from that yielded by other prospects in respects other than the mean value or whatever parameter of location determines the offsetting payments into the lottery. The distribution for the winners is now shifted by the payment of a prize of $W_2 - W_1$ to each winner, and the final distribution is the sum of the distributions for the losers and for the winners.

To illustrate, let $D(W)$ be the cumulative distribution of realized wealth after payments for lottery tickets but before distribution of the prizes; that is, $D(W)$ is the fraction of individuals with a wealth less than W at this stage. Assume that the distribution at this stage is independent of the agreed-on payment into the lottery, so that the distribution is the same for winners and losers. Let g be the fraction of individuals who are to win prizes, and $W' = W_2 - W_1$ be the prize. Then the final wealth distribution is

$$F(W) = (1-g)D(W) + gD(W - W'). \qquad (4)$$

It may perhaps be worth noting explicitly that this distribution is the sum of two distributions, *not* the distribution of the sum of two random variables.

As noted in the preceding section, dropping the assumption of identical tastes does not fundamentally change these results. If there is some general similarity in tastes, the individual values of W_1 and W_2 will form two largely distinct distributions. This dispersion among the values of W_1 and W_2 is essentially added to the dispersion among the values of W_s and has the same general effect on the final distribution as an initially greater dispersion among the latter.

The relative importance of the two component distributions in equation 4, or a generalized version of it, depends on the fraction of winners, which in turn depends on the size of the mean realized wealth, $\overline{W}$, relative to W_1 and W_2. It seems reasonable that the shape and location of the utility curve is itself determined by the average wealth in the community and the distribution of wealth: we have so far treated the utility curve as simply given and as independent of the prospects available to the individuals or the realized wealth distribution, but clearly from a broader view than has been necessary for our purpose the utility curve and prospects must be regarded as interacting.[18] To fit the observed facts from which the particular shape of the utility curve in Figure 14.1 is inferred, the mean wealth in the community must be very much closer to W_1 than to W_2. This implies that g, the fraction of winners, is close to zero. If g is close to zero, the probability or frequency distribution derived by differentiating or differencing the cumulative distribution described by equation 4 is highly skewed, since the first component distribution, centered about W_1, is weighted much more heavily than the second, centered about W_2. In addition, the distribution may be unimodal, with its single mode in the neighborhood of W_1 and below $\overline{W}$; the second mode that the rising part of the second distribution tends to introduce in the neighborhood of W_2 may be swamped by the decline after W_1 in the much more heavily weighted first distribution. The effect of the second component distribution would then be to shift the mode of the combined distribution slightly to the right of the mode of the first distribution alone and to flatten and extend the tail of the distribution. The combined distribution would appear relatively peaked, with an unusually long tail in the direction of higher values of wealth. Now "considerable skewness, wide variability, and great peakedness . . . are the hallmarks of distributions of income from independent professional practice,"[19] and from other sources, as well as of observed distributions of wealth. And these are precisely the characteristics that the distributions derived from equation 4 can be expected to reveal when g is small. So the distribution function to which our theoretical analysis leads meets at least the initial test of being able to reproduce the more outstanding features of observed distributions of wealth and income.[20]

Of course, the fact that equation 4 is not patently inconsistent with observed distributions of wealth or income does not mean that it is consistent with them or that the model on which it is based isolates the central elements accounting for existing distributions of wealth or income. But, together with the plausibility of the theoretical structure, perhaps it does justify empirical study designed to see whether equation 4 in fact provides an adequate description of existing distributions of wealth or income.

4. Conclusion

The foregoing analysis is exceedingly tentative and preliminary: it contains conjectures that need to be checked, considers only highly simplified models, makes the drastic simplification of regarding the distribution of wealth as the result of a single choice and the subsequent unfolding of this choice under the impact of random events, and so on. Yet I think it goes far enough to demonstrate that one cannot rule out the possibility that a large part of the existing inequality of wealth can be regarded as produced by men to satisfy their tastes and preferences. It suggests that the link between differences in natural endowment or inherited wealth and the realized distribution of wealth or income is less direct and simple than is generally supposed and that many common economic and social arrangements—from the organizational form of economic enterprises to collectively imposed and enforced income and inheritance taxes—can be interpreted as, at least in part, devices for achieving a distribution of wealth in conformity with the tastes and preferences of the members of society. Finally, it has implications for normative judgments about the distribution of income and the arrangements producing it—inequalities resulting from deliberate decisions to participate in a lottery clearly raise very different normative issues than do inequalities imposed on individuals from the outside.

NOTES

1. This is a revised version of a paper presented in May 1952 at an international Conference on the Foundations and Applications of the Theory of Uncertainty held in Paris at the Centre d'Econométrie under the auspices of the Centre National de la Recherche Scientifique of the French government. A French translation of the original version will appear in the *Proceedings of the Conference*.

2. See George Garvy, "Inequality of Income: Causes and Measurement," in Conference on Research in Income and Wealth, *Studies in Income and Wealth*, 15 (National Bureau of Economic Research, 1952), for evidence on the possible importance of such differences in money income.

3. See Milton Friedman and L. J. Savage, "The Utility Analysis of Choices Involving Risk," *Journal of Political Economy* 56 (August 1948): 279–304, reprinted in American Economic Association, *Readings in Price Theory* (Chicago: Richard D. Irwin, 1952), pp. 57–96; and "The Expected-Utility Hypothesis and the Measurability of Utility," *Journal of Political Economy* 60 (December 1952): 463–74; chapter 13 of this volume.

4. The reason this step is questionable, even if we waive the problem of determining the "right" interest rate, is that the utility attached by an isolated individual to a given and unchangeable income stream is a function solely of its present value only for a highly special form of utility function. For any different form, the time shape of the income stream affects the utility attached to it in a more complex way, so that two streams with the same present value do not have the same utility.

The discounting process can be justified in general only by introducing the possibility of converting income streams of any one time shape into income streams of any other desired time shape at a given intertemporal rate of substitution either by productive activity, for the isolated individual, or, more generally, by borrowing and lending in a free-capital market at a market rate of interest. This justification is unobjectionable for income streams that are certain to be received. Our whole problem, however, centers precisely on streams whose receipt is uncertain, and, for these, the very notions of a free-capital market and conversion of income streams at market rates of interest are surrounded with difficulties.

It would clearly be desirable therefore to relax this simplification in a fuller analysis of the problem than is attempted in this paper.

5. It should be noted that this description takes account of deliberate action by the individual to alter the probability distribution of returns: e.g., one course of action may involve devoting time to building storage space or engaging in other activity designed to reduce the chance of an abnormally low wealth because of premature starvation.

6. This is an example of what Pierre Massé has designated in a similar context as "absolute preference."

7. I am of course using "inequality" here in a loose sense, since no precise meaning is required for present purposes.

8. This is a more stringent restriction than is necessary. Its adoption, however, simplifies the discussion without loss of essential generality.

9. To satisfy the conditions required for the law of large numbers to hold true.

10. Friedman and Savage, "The Utility Analysis of Choices Involving Risk."

11. Ibid., pp. 289–91.

12. This is equally true for a utility function everywhere concave upward, which leads to complete inequality. It is not true for a utility function everywhere concave downward. With different prospects and such a utility function, each individual adopts the course of action that has the highest expected wealth, contributes the result to a common pool, and draws out an amount equal to this highest expected wealth, so the final distribution of wealth is given by the distribution of the maximum expected wealth among individuals and is no longer egalitarian.

13. This redistributive arrangement can perhaps best be visualized concretely as consisting of two parts. (1) Each individual enters into an agreement to follow the course of action that promises the highest expected value, $\overline{W}^{(i)}$, to turn over the resulting product to a common pool, and to receive in return a guarantee of $\overline{W}^{(i)}$. He buys an insurance policy, as it were. (2) A single actuarially fair lottery offering a very large single prize is made available to the individual. He can buy any number of either whole or fractional tickets in this lottery. With such a lottery each individual can construct any actuarially fair prize distribution he wants, subject only to the limitation that the maximum prize does not exceed the single prize offered. The number of different tickets he buys determines his chance of winning a prize; the fraction of each ticket he buys determines the size of the prize he wins if that ticket is the winning ticket. For example, if there are one million tickets in a lottery with a single prize of $1,000,000, so each ticket costs one dollar, he can have one chance in 200,000 of winning $100,000 by buying one-tenth of each of five tickets; one chance in 25,000 of winning $50,000 by buying one-twentieth of each of forty tickets, and so on. With a utility function like that in Figure 14.1, he will spend $\overline{W}^{(i)} - \overline{W}_1^{(i)}$ on tickets; he will take the same fraction of each ticket he buys; and that fraction will be such as to yield a single prize of $\overline{W}_2^{(i)} - \overline{W}_1^{(i)}$. The only requirement in order that every individual be able to get his optimum prospect is that the prize offered in the lottery exceed the largest $\overline{W}_2^{(i)} - \overline{W}_1^{(i)}$.

14. The actual division between the two classes of actions will of course depend on

238 ♦ ECONOMIC THEORY

tastes (i.e., utility functions), since the cost it pays to incur depends on the gains to be achieved by improved distribution. Nonetheless, the present assumption that a hard and fast division can be made in advance does not involve any great loss at the present level of analysis.

15. To suppose the opposite is essentially to revert to the case of section 2. For making W_r' depend on realized W_s is equivalent to making W_s accessible to redistributive arrangements.

16. For example, suppose the set $P_{a_s}(W_s)$ is the same for all individuals, that every member of it is unimodal and symmetrical, with a mean value less than W_1, and that for some neighborhood around W_1 and W_2, the vertical difference between $U(W)$ and the double tangent is the same for $W_i + \Delta$ and $W_i - \Delta$ ($i = 1, 2$). Suppose further that the variance of W_s for each $P_{a_s}(W_s)$ is small compared to $W_2 - W_1$. Select any $P_{a_s}(W)$ which has a mean value $\overline{W}_s$ and combine it with a lottery involving pooling all W_r and receiving a chance $(W_2 - \overline{W}_s - \overline{W}_r)/(W_2 - W_1)$ of getting $W_1 - \overline{W}_s$ and a chance $(\overline{W}_s + \overline{W}_r - W_1)/(W_2 - W_1)$ of getting $W_2 - \overline{W}_s$. This breaks the original $P_{a_s}(W)$ into two distributions, one with its mode at W_1, the other at W_2 and combined in the proportions necessary to keep the total expected value unchanged. The expected utility of this arrangement deviates from the expected utility of the *optimum optimorum* by the expected value of the vertical differences between $U(W)$ and the double tangent. Given our assumptions, this deviation from the *optimum optimorum* is clearly less than for any alternative redistributive arrangement combined with the same $P_{a_s}(W)$, for any such arrangement would widen the variance of the two distributions at W_1 and W_2 or move their means away from W_1 and W_2 and thus increase the average value of these vertical differences. But if this is true for any $P_{a_s}(W)$ separately, it is true for the optimum $P_{a_s}(W)$.

The assumptions of the preceding paragraph are clearly stricter than are necessary. In particular, it seems likely that symmetry of the $P_{a_s}(W)$ is not necessary and that much milder restrictions on the utility function will do. Further, the $P_{a_s}(W)$ need not be the same for all individuals. Differences among them can be offset by differences in the contributions to the redistributive arrangement. All that is required is that each individual contribute $W_r^{(i)} - (W_1 - \overline{W}_s^{(i)})$ for a chance $(\overline{W}_s^{(i)} + \overline{W}_r^{(i)} - W_1)/(W_2 - W_1)$ of getting $W_2 - W_1$.

17. Note that the choice from the set A_s that is optimum to an individual is affected by the existence of the redistributive arrangement. In particular, if the redistributive arrangement affects a large enough fraction of total anticipated wealth, it will never be worth sacrificing expected W_s to increase the variance of W_s, even though it would be in the absence of the redistributive arrangement. It may be worth sacrificing expected W_s to reduce the variance of W_s, even though it would not be in the absence of the redistributive arrangement.

18. Some tentative suggestions along these lines are made in Friedman and Savage, "The Utility Analysis of Choices Involving Risk," sec. 5b, pp. 298–99.

19. Milton Friedman and Simon Kuznets, *Income from Independent Professional Practice* (New York: National Bureau of Economic Research, 1945), p. 62.

20. "Despite the great similarity among income distributions, none of the many attempts to discover a formula that describes them adequately has yet met with

occasionally gives a poor fit; the small deviations from it when it does fit reasonably well do not seem randomly distributed, and it. . . is unable to represent negative income" (ibid., pp. 66–67). The final objection would be irrelevant for distributions of wealth defined to include all sources of possible future income, including human capital, since wealth so defined cannot be negative. It is not irrelevant if, as in most statistical studies, measured wealth includes only nonhuman sources of income. Similar comments apply to various definitions of income. My offhand impression is that the addition of a second logarithmic normal curve in the way suggested by equation 4 would tend to modify a single logarithmic normal curve in the direction suggested by the systematic deviations referred to above. And it might be that the sum of two distributions would give a good fit with arithmetic normal curves, so solving the negative wealth or income problem, since the second distribution introduces the skewness which makes the logarithmic transformation or its equivalent essential when only one distribution is used.

THE THEORY OF CAPITAL
AND THE RATE OF INTEREST

· 15 ·

On an abstract level, it is instructive to view the economic system as one in which stocks of productive resources (capital) produce flows of productive services that are transformed into flows of final consumer services. The continuing flow problem is the allocation of the productive services to various uses, their combination in the process of transformation into consumer services, and the distribution of the consumer services among the ultimate consumers in the economy—problems 1, 2, 3, and 5 in Frank Knight's fivefold subdivision of the economic problem introduced in chapter 1 [of *Price Theory*]. These are the problems that have been dealt with in the preceding chapters, which can be regarded as concerned primarily with the relative prices of different service flows.

In addition to the flow problems, there is Knight's problem number 4, "provision for maintenance and progress," or the management of the stocks of productive resources, of the sources of productive services. This is the subject matter of the theory of capital with which the present chapter deals.

In practice, of course, the flow problem and the stock problem are intertwined. For example, to keep the two completely separate, we must regard consumer purchases of bread and other foods as part of the stock problem, not the flow problem. The consumer is maintaining a stock of sources of productive services, namely, his inventory of food, combining the services they render with the services from the consumer capital he uses, such as a refrigerator, stove, etc., to produce the final service of nutrition. In a physical sense, the law of conservation of energy assures that no matter can be consumed, only transformed. All consumption is the consumption of services. The food inventory is different from the refrigerator or stove only in depreciating at a much more rapid rate in the process of producing nutritive services.

For many concrete problems, nothing is gained by carrying the analysis to this point. It is often useful to assimilate goods that depreciate rapidly with services proper. But it is important to recognize that this is what we are doing.

From the broadest point of view, capital includes all sources of productive services. There are three main categories of capital: (1) material, nonhuman capital, such as buildings, machines, inventories, land, and other natural resources; (2) human beings, including their knowledge and skills; and (3) the stock of money. The main distinction between human capital and the other items is that the existing institutional and social framework and imperfections in the capital market produce a different response of human capital to economic pressures and incentives than of nonhuman capital. The stock of money differs from the other two categories because the productive services rendered by money do not depend closely on the number of physical units there are, but primarily on the mere existence of a stock. Consider two societies that are alike except that in one there are twice as many pieces of paper, each labeled one dollar, as in the other. The only effect will be that nominal prices are twice as high in the first as in the second society. The total stream of services from the stock of money is the same in the two societies.

One of the most common examples of confusion between stocks and flows is the frequently made statement that capital becomes cheap (or dear) relative to labor, and hence capital is substituted for labor (or the reverse). The statement implies that the wage rate is comparable to the interest rate. However, the wage rate is comparable to the rent per machine per unit of time, both being dollars per physical unit per unit of time, and not to the interest rate, which is dollars per dollar (a pure number) per unit of time. Put differently, a rate of wages divided by rent of a machine is entirely in physical units; it shows the rate at which man-hours can be substituted for machine-hours by purchase on the market. It is clear what it means for this ratio to go up or down, and the ratio is unaffected by a proportional change in all prices. The ratio of the wage rate to the interest rate, on the other hand, is very different; it is not wholly in physical units, but in value terms. It shows the rate of substitution between man-hours and dollar-of-capital hours, as it were, and is therefore affected by a proportional change in all prices.

An example of the usual image of the substitution of capital for labor is the use of a man operating a mechanical backhoe to dig a ditch instead of a man with a hand shovel. What is really involved is a substitution of the labor used to build the backhoe for the labor used to wield the shovel, or of the human (and other) capital used to build the backhoe for the human (and other) capital used to build the hand shovel and to wield it. Skilled labor services—of the people who build the backhoe, the engineers who design it, etc.—are substituted for unskilled labor, because skilled labor has become cheaper relative to unskilled labor. In addition, the society may have become wealthier; it may have acquired more capital in total. This is not a substitution of capital for labor, but the acquisition of more capital, generally of both more human capital and more nonhuman capital. The use of some of the existing stock of capital in the form of the man operating a backhoe instead of the form of the man wielding the hand shovel, matched by a rearrangement of other capital elsewhere, is part of the management of the existing stock of capital—Knight's "provision for maintenance." The use of current productive services to add to the stock of capital (human and nonhuman) instead of for current consumption is part of the process of saving and investment—Knight's "provision for progress."

The key price in the theory of capital is conventionally a rate of interest. However, the reciprocal of the rate of interest is in some ways a more readily grasped, basic concept. It gives the price of a source of services in terms of the service flow. Consider a piece of land yielding $1 a year indefinitely and let "the" relevant interest rate be 5 percent. Then the price of the piece of land will be $20, or in terms used more frequently in Britain than in the United States, twenty-years' purchase. This brings out the key nature of the price: the number of years' service flow from a permanent source of services that it takes to buy the source itself. Note also that there are many equivalent forms of contract. In a world of certainty, leasing the piece of land for $1 a year would be precisely equivalent to buying the piece of land by borrowing $20 indefinitely at 5 percent, or by borrowing for one year at 5 percent, intending to borrow again the next year, and so on. In a world of uncertainty, however, these would not be equivalent, which produces the coexistence of different kinds of contractual arrangements and of many quoted prices for different intertemporal transactions.

Rates of interest affect a great many decisions, such as the following:

1. The time pattern of consumption, since the terms on which income streams of varying time patterns may be exchanged depend on the rate of interest.

2. The form in which assets are held. One special problem to which recent work in monetary theory has called attention is whether to hold wealth in money or other forms. This is merely an extension of the marginal principle—the proportions of different resources held should be such as to equalize the marginal return in all directions.

3. The character and structure of production.

4. The composition of the social output, i.e., the fraction of total output that will be investment and the fraction that will be consumption goods. A decrease in the rate of interest raises the prices of sources of services and provides an incentive to produce sources of services.

5. The ratio of nonhuman wealth to total wealth and the size of contingency reserves. Since we are restricting ourselves here to relative price theory, we abstract from the possible short-run effects of the rate of interest on the level of activity.

The bewildering variety of intertemporal transactions and associated terms raises the basically arithmetic problem of how to distinguish between essential and nonessential differences in terms. We discuss this first, then turn to an analysis of the twin stock-flow problem (the pricing of stocks in terms of flows and the use of flows to add to stocks) for a particular item, using houses as an example; and finally generalize this stock-flow analysis to capital as a whole.

The Arithmetic of Interest Rates

In common parlance, the term *capital market* is used to refer to a market in which paper claims to income streams of different sizes and timings are purchased and sold. Though for our purposes, we shall want to use *capital* in a broader sense to correspond to the sources of productive services, the narrower sense is sufficient to illustrate the problems involved in comparing different income streams.

Consider, for example, the following contracts: (a) promise to pay $105 one year from date, (b) promise to pay $210 one year from date, and (c) promise to pay $525 one year from date. In all cases, for simplicity, neglect the possibility of default.

Suppose the market price for contract a is $100. We could describe that price as paying $1 for $1.05 a year from date. If the price of b were $200, of c, $500, we would say that all three are selling at the same price of $1 now for $1.05 a year from now, or at a (simple) interest rate of 5 percent per year for a one-year loan.

Note that nothing in arithmetic or economics requires that the price of b be twice that of a and the price of c five times that of a. Just as there might be quantity discounts that make the price of a dozen shirts less than twelve times the price of one shirt, so there might be quantity discounts (or the reverse) that make the price of contract c less than (or more than) five times the price of contract a. (Incidentally, the need to include in the statements for the loan contracts the parenthetical alternatives illustrates the dualism of the intertemporal contracts. Is the lender buying future funds from the borrower in return for current funds, so he could expect to pay less than five times as much for five times as much next year? Or is the borrower buying current funds from the lender in return for future funds, so he could expect to pay less than five times as much for five times as much this year? The first case leads to a higher interest rate for the larger transaction; the second to a lower interest rate for the larger transaction.) The point of reducing all the transactions to dollars a year from now for a dollar today is to be able to distinguish unessential differences from essential differences.

If there are essential differences in contracts like a, b, and c, the possibility of arbitrage arises: borrow at the terms that have the lower interest rates, lend at the terms that have the higher interest rates. This is one service of financial intermediation by such institutions as commercial banks, mutual savings banks, savings and loan associations, money market funds, etc. Such arbitrage, or financial intermediation, tends to limit essential differences to margins related to the costs that determine the supply of intermediation. In addition, it means that, as in every market in which there are middlemen, it may be necessary to distinguish between "buying" and "selling" prices for what appears to be the same contract. In general, we shall neglect this complication and speak of a single price.

Consider now a slightly different contract: (d) promise to pay $110.25 two years from date. Clearly this is a more complex situation. If its price is $100, it is a contract to pay $1.1025 two years from date for $1 today. This can be reduced to two identical one-year contracts like a. For example, it can be described as a contract promising to pay $1.05 next year for $1 this year, plus a linked contract promising to pay $1.05 two years from now for $1 next year $(1.05 \times 1.05 = 1.1025)$. However, this decomposition is not unique. Contract d is also equivalent to a contract promising to pay $1.03 next year for $1 this year, plus a linked contract promising to pay $1.07038835 two years from now for $1 next year $(1.03 \times 1.07038835 = 1.1025)$; and similarly to any other pair of linked contracts producing the same final product. Clearly, more than arithmetic is required to reduce contract d to the same terms as contracts a, b, and c.

The market will determine a price for contract d and a price for contract a, and from these two prices we can determine the separate price for two elementary contracts like a but for different years. For example, if the "two-year rate of interest compounded annually" is .05 (i.e., contract d sells for $100 currently), and the current "one-year rate of simple interest" is .05 (i.e., contract a sells for $100 also), then the (implicit) market rate of simple interest today for a one-year loan to begin a year from today is also .05. If, however, the current "one-year rate of simple interest" is $1.03 (i.e, contract a sells for $105/1.03 = 101.9417876), then the (implicit) market rate of simple interest today for a one-year loan to begin a year from today is .07038835.

Note that in making this decomposition, we have had to beg the question of quantity discounts or premiums. Note too that it is entirely feasible for individuals to make the linked contracts separately if we neglect problems of default (and hence of collateral). By simultaneously buying contract d and selling contract a—that is, lending for a two-year term and borrowing for one year—an individual is today making a loan to begin a year from now. It follows that any contract for intertemporal payments can be reduced to a series of elementary one-year contracts like contract a differing in starting dates, for all of which there can in principle be implicit market prices. And, of course, there is nothing natural about one year. The elementary contract can be for one quarter or one month or one day. The limit is continuous compounding, so that contract a can be regarded as an infinite linked sequence of instantaneous contracts at a rate of interest of the natural logarithm of 1.05 or .04879. . .

It is possible to arbitrage between contracts for the same initial and terminal dates, such as a, b, and c, or like the elementary, one-year contracts for the same year. But there is in general no way of arbitraging between two elementary contracts for different time units in the sense of entering into financial purchase and sale contracts which cancel, and so involve no risk. For example, suppose that the price of contract a is \$101.94 (rounding to two decimal places) and the price of contract d is \$100, so that the one-year simple rate of interest is .03 for the current year and .07 for the next year. It looks as if it would be desirable to borrow this year to lend next year. That can be done by, for example, selling two contracts like a and buying one contract like d, which involves borrowing net this year and lending net next year. But if you go through the arithmetic of payments and receipts, you will find that there is no assured return. The outcome depends on what the one-year interest rate turns out to be next year. The only case in which financial arbitrage proper is possible is if future interest rates are negative, in which case it pays to lend short and borrow long. At worst, the proceeds of the loan can be held in cash (yielding a zero return) to pay off the long borrowing when it becomes due.[1]

Reducing all intertemporal contracts to a succession of elementary contracts is one way, and very likely the most general way, to reduce different contracts to a common basis in terms of which essential can be distinguished from unessential differences in prices or interest rates. However, for the exposition of the basic principles of capital theory, there is an alternative, less general way that is more satisfactory.

The alternative way is to convert all patterns of intertemporal payments into constant, permanent income streams. This method was adopted by Frank Knight and also by John Maynard Keynes, in defining his concept of the *marginal efficiency of investment*. It is also the method that is used in the financial pages of newspapers in reporting the "yield to maturity" of fixed income securities.

Consider the generalized contract: (e) promise to pay R_1 (for receipts) at the end of one year from now; R_2 at the end of two years, . . . R_n at the end of n years.

Suppose this contract is selling on the market for an amount W (for wealth). Then we can write

$$W = \frac{R_1}{1+r} + \frac{R_2}{(1+r)^2} + \frac{R_3}{(1+r)^3} + \cdots + \frac{R_n}{(1+r)^n}, \tag{1}$$

i.e., the market value is the discounted value of the payment stream.[2] If W and $R_1, R_2, \ldots R_n$ are known, then the value of r that satisfies this equation is the "internal rate of return." This formula is for discontinuous data. Still more generally, let $R(t)$ be payments promised at time t. Then the capital value at time 0 can be written

$$W = \int_0^\infty e^{-\rho t} R(t) dt, \tag{2}$$

where ρ is a rate of interest compounded continuously.[3] The permanent income stream equivalent to contract e is then rW, if we use annual compounding, or ρW, if we use continuous compounding.

It will help to understand more fully what is involved in the discounting process, if we spell it out in gory detail. The essence of the process that converts a finite income stream into a permanent income stream is the division of each receipt into two parts: income and a depreciation allowance (which may be positive or negative). Take the discontinuous example of equation 1. The receipt at the end of year one is to be regarded as

Income for year 1 rW

Depreciation allowance $R_1 - rW$.

The capital value at the outset of the next year, say W_1, is then

$$W_1 = R_1 - rW + \frac{R_2}{1+r} + \frac{R_3}{(1+r)^2} + \cdots + \frac{R_n}{(1+r)^{n-1}}. \tag{3}$$

If we replace W by its value from equation 1 and collect like terms we have:

$$W_1 = R_1\left(1 - \frac{r}{1+r}\right) + R_2\left[\frac{1}{1+r} - \frac{r}{(1+r)^2}\right] + \cdots$$

$$+ R_n \left[\frac{1}{(1-r)^{n-1}} - \frac{r}{(1-r)^n} \right] \tag{4}$$

$$= \frac{R_1}{1+r} + \frac{R_2}{(1+r)^2} + \ldots + \frac{R_n}{(1+r)^n} = W,$$

establishing the proposition that rW is the income that can be consumed while keeping the capital value constant. To continue the process for future years, the depreciation allowance must be assumed to earn income at the rate r, the common discount rate.

The great virtue of this way of converting all intertemporal contracts into a comparable form is that it obviates all problems of dating. A contract is described by two numbers: total capital value and permanent income, or even more simply, by one number, yield per dollar of capital value. Of course, this does not mean that the yield may not differ depending on other characteristics of the contract, such as size, maturity of payments, etc., but at least unessential differences are eliminated.

Another virtue of this approach is that it brings out the possibility of converting income streams of one time shape into income streams of another. If a particular income stream is of one shape and the market rates of interest are constant over time, it can always be converted into any other time shape by appropriate borrowing and lending or accumulation and decumulation of depreciation allowances. Hence all that matters for describing the opportunities of the owner of the income stream is the permanent income stream to which it is equivalent.

These virtues for our subsequent theoretical presentation are paid for by a number of serious disadvantages. For one thing, as is clear from our earlier discussion, this mode of summarizing intertemporal contracts suppresses the simultaneous coexistence of different rates of interest for different future dates—an extremely important feature of actual capital markets and one to which an enormous amount of theoretical and empirical economic research has been devoted, especially in the past decade or so.

A second defect is that this mode of summarization fosters the incorrect view that a contract (or investment project) that yields a higher internal rate is preferable to one that yields a lower internal rate. This is correct, if the time pattern of receipts of the two projects are identical. It is not correct, if the time patterns of receipts are not identical and if there is a market rate of interest at which the project can be financed. For example, consider the following two projects:

	Initial cost	RECEIPTS AT END OF	
		Year 1	Year 2
(f)	100	110	—
(g)	100	—	118.81

Project f has an internal rate of return of 10 percent, project g of 9 percent, both compounded annually. Is project f preferable to project g? That depends on the conditions. If it is known now that at the end of year one another project identical to f will be available, then two such successive projects will yield $121 in year two, which is clearly preferable to $118.81. What we have done is to convert the two into projects with the same time pattern of receipts. Suppose, however, that the agent in question can borrow or lend at 5 percent in the market in general and has these two projects available to him as well. In that case, project f will have a present value of $104.76 [110/1.05], project g of $107.76, and clearly g is preferable to f. Of course, under our assumptions so far, the agent would be well advised to undertake both projects, as well as any others that have an internal rate above 5 percent. However, that may not be possible for the two projects described, since they may be alternatives, for example, correspond to different ways of building a house.

This is very far indeed from a full discussion of the principles that are relevant in choosing among investment projects, but it does bring out the important point that the objective of an economic agent engaged in undertaking projects involving converting current resources into a future income stream cannot in general be described as maximizing the internal rate of return. The agent's objective is better described as maximizing a present value calculated at an appropriate external rate of return. For an enterprise in an active capital market, that external rate of return is given by the market. For the opposite extreme, a Robinson Crusoe deciding how to use his resources, the present value he is to be interpreted as maximizing is a present value of utility, and the rate of return external to the project he considers is given by his utility function, which reveals the rate at which he is willing to substitute future income for current income.

One final comment on the arithmetic of interest rates. There is nothing in that arithmetic that requires interest rates to be positive. For example, consider a contract selling for $100 that promises to pay $90 one year hence. The internal rate of return is −10. There is something in economics that prevents negative interest rates from being more than an occasional curiosity. (This used to occur in Illinois annually at a date on which personal property tax was levied. The base included demand deposits of corporations in Illinois but not certain other financial assets. Corporations on that date would be willing to lend for brief periods at a negative rate to avoid the tax.) For nominal rates, the economic consideration is the near-zero cost of holding on to cash.[4] For real returns, the economic consideration is the existence of economically permanent assets, as we shall see more fully later.

The Relation Between Stocks and Flows: The Price of Stocks in Terms of Flows

In order to keep distinct the problem of the pricing of stocks in terms of flows and the use of flows to add to or subtract from stocks, let us start by analyzing a fixed stock that is permanent, so that it requires no maintenance expense, and that cannot be added to. A concrete example that comes close to meeting these conditions would be the stock of Old Master paintings. They cannot be added to (except by counterfeiting), but they do require maintenance expenditures, in the form of protection from theft and destruction, and occasional cleaning. However, to keep the same example for both stock-flow problems, let us take the hypothetical example of dwelling units that are homogeneous and fixed in number, say by a legal prohibition of building any additional ones. As to maintenance expenditures, we may simply assume that the stock of dwelling units is maintained physically intact and that in drawing the demand curve for dwelling units, the rent per dwelling unit is the net rent over and above the resource costs of maintaining the dwelling units intact.

On these assumptions, Figure 15.1 gives the demand curve for the services rendered by the dwelling unit. If there are A (say 100) dwelling-unit years available per unit of time, say per year, the demand price is R_A, say \$1,000, per dwelling-unit year. Total rent paid would be $A \cdot R_A$, say \$100,000, per year. If there are B (150) dwelling-unit years available, the demand price is R_B (\$800), so the total rent paid per year would be $BR_B = (\$120,000)$ per year.

The question now is, what is the demand curve, not for the services of the dwelling units but for the dwelling units themselves? If there is an exogenous market interest rate determined somehow independently of the housing market, the answer is simple. The dwelling unit will sell for the capitalized value of the permanent income stream it yields (recall that we have defined the rent as net of maintenance costs), or, if r is the rate of interest, for R/r. The demand curve drawn in Figure 15.2 will be a duplicate of the demand curve in Figure 15.1 except that the scales will be different: number of dwelling units rather than number of dwelling-unit years per year on the horizontal axis; the rent multiplied by the reciprocal of the interest rate on the vertical axis; or, if the interest rate is, say, .05, the vertical scale in Figure 15.2 will be twenty times the vertical scale on Figure 15.1.[5]

But to assume that there is an exogenous interest rate simply begs the basic

FIGURE 15.1

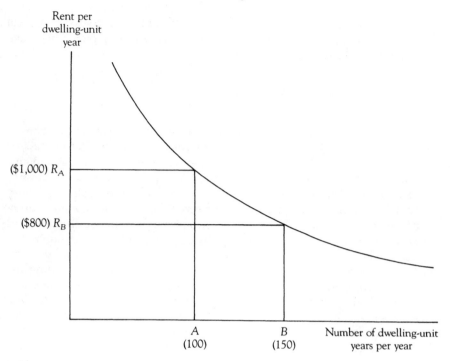

question that we are interested in. Let us suppose, therefore, that dwelling units are the only sources of income streams that can be appropriated and purchased and sold—that is, we are letting dwelling units represent all non-human capital. In that case, the interest rate must be determined simultaneously with the rent per dwelling unit. Letting the interest rate be endogenous does not alter Figure 15.1, given our explicit assumption that dwelling units cannot be added to and will not be subtracted from, and the implicit assumption that the stock of other sources of productive services is constant as well. For those assumptions rule out the use of current income, i.e., the services of the stock of productive assets, for any purpose other than current consumption. Hence the demand for dwelling units is simply a question of the allocation of a fixed total stream of consumption services among alternative uses. Once we permit the use of current productive services to add to the stock of capital, or the using up of current capital to add to the flow of consumption services, it will not be possible to treat the demand for dwelling services as independent of the determination of the rate of interest.

FIGURE 15.2

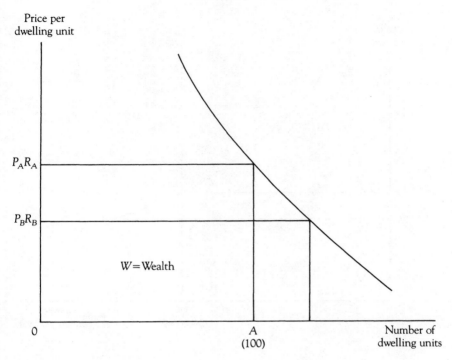

Figure 15.3 shows the demand curve that is relevant to the determination of the rate of interest. The horizontal axis gives the number of dollars per year generated by dwelling units. It corresponds to the area of the rectangles in Figure 15.1—in our example to $100,000 corresponding to point A. The vertical axis shows the price of a dollar per year. The demand for dollars per year has nothing to do with the utility derived from housing services—which is embodied in Figure 15.1. It depends rather on the utility people attach to having a stock of nonhuman wealth as a reserve for emergencies.

Consider the attitudes of individuals in the society to various prices for permanent income streams. If the price of a dollar a year were "low," few or no individuals would be willing to sell permanent income streams (i.e., a "source"), and many would be willing to buy permanent income streams. Many people would be willing to give up current consumption in order to acquire a permanent income stream. Under our assumptions, there is no way society as a whole can do this; the willingness to do so simply means that at this price people would be trying to buy more than AR_A dollars of permanent income

FIGURE 15.3

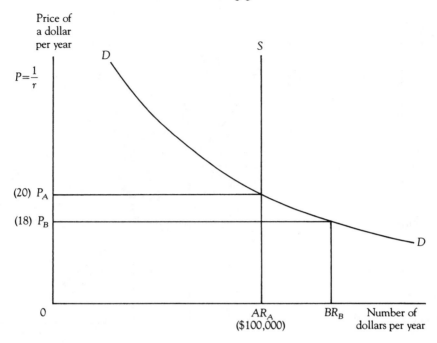

streams that are available and so would bid up the price of a permanent income stream. If the price of a dollar a year were "high," on the other hand, owners of permanent income streams would be induced to sell them—few would be interested in buying them—and the community as a whole would be seeking to convert sources of permanent income streams into current consumption. But it cannot do so under our assumptions; its willingness to do so would mean that the price would be bid down. There is some intermediate price, say OP_A, at which this market will be in equilibrium, in the sense that at this price society as a whole makes no attempt to get rid of or add to sources of income: the number some people want to sell is equal to the number others want to buy. The locus of prices like $OP_A(DD)$ for different hypothetical supplies of income streams is then a demand curve for income streams in our hypothetical society. The product of OP_A times AR_A is the total amount of wealth or the total value of all the dwelling units in our hypothetical society.

If the concept of capital were all-inclusive, including human as well as nonhuman capital, there is no reason to expect the demand curve for permanent income streams to have a negative rather than a positive slope. Perhaps the most reasonable presumption is that it would be infinitely elastic. For in such a society, income (Y) is equal to rW, where r is the interest rate and W is wealth, since all wealth has been capitalized. $1/r$, the number of time units of income that must be paid to buy a source of a permanent income stream, is then the ratio of wealth to income. This ratio of wealth to income has the dimension of time and is free from absolute units of any other kind. Why should the desired value of this ratio depend on the absolute level of either the numerator or denominator? Indeed, what standard of comparison is there by which to regard one level of wealth as "large" or "small" except *relative* to another or *relative* to income; or one level of income as "large" or "small" except *relative* to another or *relative* to wealth? But if the community desires to maintain a fixed ratio of wealth to income regardless of the absolute level of income, this implies a horizontal demand curve for permanent income streams.

If the concept of capital is not all-inclusive and refers to nonhuman wealth, and if we assume that people still wish to maintain a constant ratio between wealth and income (but in this case a constant ratio between non-human wealth and total income), then $W_{NH}/(Y_H+rW_{NH})=K$ where W_{NH} is the value of nonhuman wealth and Y_H is the income from human wealth. The fixed stock, given by AR_A, is defined by rW_{NH}. Call this Y_p. Substituting Y_p/r for W_{NH} in the preceding expression gives $[Y_p(1/r)]/(Y_H+Y_p)=K$ or $1/r=[K(Y_H+Y_p)]/Y_p$ which defines a negatively sloping demand curve for permanent income streams, for a given income from human capital. More generally, whether the desired ratio of wealth to income is a constant or not, there is in this case reason to expect a negatively sloping demand curve. For in this case an increase in nonhuman wealth, with a given income from human wealth, raises the ratio of nonhuman wealth to human wealth and the ratio of nonhuman wealth to income and so may be expected to lower the importance that individuals attach to nonhuman wealth *relative* to the importance they attach either to human wealth or to income.

The derivation of the demand curve for dwelling units in Figure 15.2 is now straightforward. For any given number of dwelling units, say A, find the rent as given by the demand curve in Figure 15.1, multiply the two together to get the total number of dollars per year, enter that in the demand curve of Figure 15.3 to get the price of a dollar per year, and multiply that by the rent per dwelling unit to get the price per dwelling unit for that number of dwelling units. The demand curve in Figure 15.2 for the stock of dwelling units is clearly a hybrid depending on two completely different sets of considerations: on the one hand, the relative utility attached to housing services compared to other consumption services; on the other, the relative utility attached to future versus current income and to a reserve of nonhuman wealth.

The demand for permanent income streams summarized in Figure 15.3 is

FIGURE 15.4

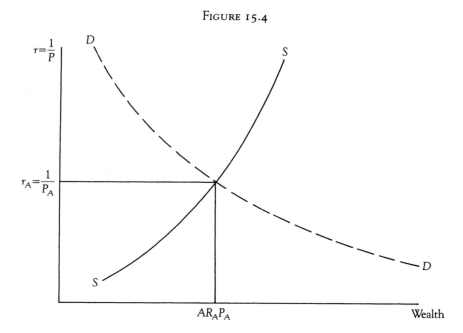

one side of a coin of which the other is the supply of capital. Owners of wealth supply capital and demand permanent income streams. Entrepreneurs building dwelling units—for a moment let us suspend the assumption that no new dwelling units can be built—demand capital and supply permanent income streams. It is natural to express the supply curve of capital as in Figure 15.4, with the interest rate viewed as the price and the stock of wealth as the quantity supplied. Note the relation between the curves in Figures 15.3 and 15.4. If the demand curve in Figure 15.3 has an elasticity of unity, that would mean that total wealth would be a constant regardless of the interest rate, which would translate into a vertical supply curve in Figure 15.4. For the supply curve in Figure 15.4 to slope positively, as seems natural, the demand curve in Figure 15.3 must be elastic. If the demand curve in Figure 15.3 were inelastic, the supply curve in Figure 15.4 would slope negatively, at the extreme being a rectangular hyperbola with elasticity equal to -1. The vertical supply curve in Figure 15.3 translates in Figure 15.4 into a unit elasticity rectangular hyperbola demand curve for capital.[6]

The two ways of looking at the determination of the interest rate bring out an essential ambiguity in the concept of a constant stock of capital. Suppose that the number of dwelling units and the demand for their services are fixed so that the number of dollars per year yielded by them is also fixed, i.e., the supply curve in Figure 15.3 is vertical. Now suppose the demand curve in Figure 15.3 were to shift upwards, as a result, say, of an increase in the demand for an emergency reserve. The price of a dollar a year would go up, and so would the wealth value of the unchanged physical stock of capital yielding an unchanged flow of services. In one sense, the stock of capital has remained unchanged; in another sense, it has risen. Much confusion has arisen as a result of the failure to keep these two senses clearly distinct. One virtue of the form of presentation in Figure 15.3 is precisely that it brings this point out very sharply.

For simplicity, let us suppose that the supply curve of capital in Figure 15.4 slopes positively, as seems reasonable, so the demand curve of permanent income streams in Figure 15.3 has an elasticity greater than unity in absolute value. We can then describe fairly simply the relation between the hybrid demand curve for dwelling units in Figure 15.2 and the two demand curves in Figures 15.1 and 15.3 on which it depends. Suppose the demand for housing services has unit elasticity. Then regardless of the number of dwelling units, total rents will be the same, which means that so will the supply curve in Figure 15.3 (and the demand curve in Figure 15.4), which means so will the interest rate. The demand for dwelling units will then also have an elasticity of unity. Increasing the physical stock of capital does not change the value attached to the flow of services from that stock, and hence does not change the wealth value of the stock. If the demand for housing services is elastic, a larger physical stock of houses will yield a higher total rent and hence a lower price per dollar of income. The value of the stock of housing will tend to increase because of the larger flow of rents but will tend to decrease because of the lower price of a dollar of rent. Our assumption that the demand curve in Figure 15.3 is elastic assumes that the first effect will more than balance the second, so the demand curve for dwelling units in Figure 15.2 will be elastic also, but less elastic than that for housing services. Likewise, if the demand for housing services is inelastic, the demand for dwelling units will also be inelastic, but less so than for housing services because a larger stock of houses, by lowering the total rents, will raise the price of a dollar of rent.

The Relation Between Stocks and Flows: The Use of Flows to Alter Stocks

We can now turn to the second stock-flow problem, the use of flows to alter stocks. To explore this problem, let us drop the assumption that the stock of dwelling units is fixed. Instead, we shall suppose that new dwelling units can be built, and old ones wear out, but we shall continue to assume that all dwelling units are homogeneous regardless of age so that we can continue to speak of *the* rent of a dwelling unit. Presumably, there will be some level of activity in the building industry that will just serve to maintain the stock of dwelling units intact. A higher level of building means an increase in the stock of dwelling units—positive net capital formation in the language of national income accounting; a lower level of building means a decrease in the stock of dwelling units—negative net capital formation.[7]

The right-hand panel of Figure 15.5 reproduces the stock demand curve for dwelling units from Figure 15.2. The left-hand panel gives a simple, and as we shall see, highly special representation of the conditions of supply of new dwelling units. The supply curve $S'S'$ of additional dwelling units extends to negative values on the horizontal axis, because the total stock can decline as well as rise. The supply curve is shown as rising throughout because the greater the rate of decline, the smaller the building industry, the greater the rate of rise, the larger the building industry, and, for simplicity, we assume rising costs throughout.

The special feature, to which we shall have to return, is that the supply curve is drawn as independent of the stock of houses, yet the stock of houses determines the size of the building industry at the point at which the supply curve cuts the vertical axis. A rationalization for such a special assumption is that long-run costs in the housing industry are constant, so the *stock* supply curve in the right-hand panel (SS) is horizontal. However, maintaining the industry at a high enough level to add to the stock of housing raises costs, because it is understood to be a temporary position; hence resources have to be compensated for entering the industry on that basis. Similarly, maintaining the industry at a low enough level to reduce the stock of housing lowers costs, because that too is understood to be a temporary position, and some resources are willing to accept temporarily lower returns because of better, long-run prospects. Even this argument suggests that while supply curves for different stocks of housing might cut the vertical axis at the same point, they might not have the same slope.

The stock demand curve DD in the right-hand panel also embodies a highly special assumption, namely, that the demand curve does not depend on the rate at which dwelling units are being added to the stock. We have already noted at least one reason why that is a dubious assumption, namely that if current resources are being used to add to the stock of housing, total current consumption will be less, which will affect the demand curve for housing services in Figure 15.1.

We shall return to these complications later. For the moment, let us carry through the analysis of the special case described in Figure 15.5. If we start from an initial stock of A dwelling units, the short-run supply of dwelling units is inelastic at A, and the price for existing houses would have to be P_A to equate demand and supply. If a new dwelling unit can be built for less than P_A, clearly it would be preferable to build new dwelling units rather than to buy existing

FIGURE 15.5

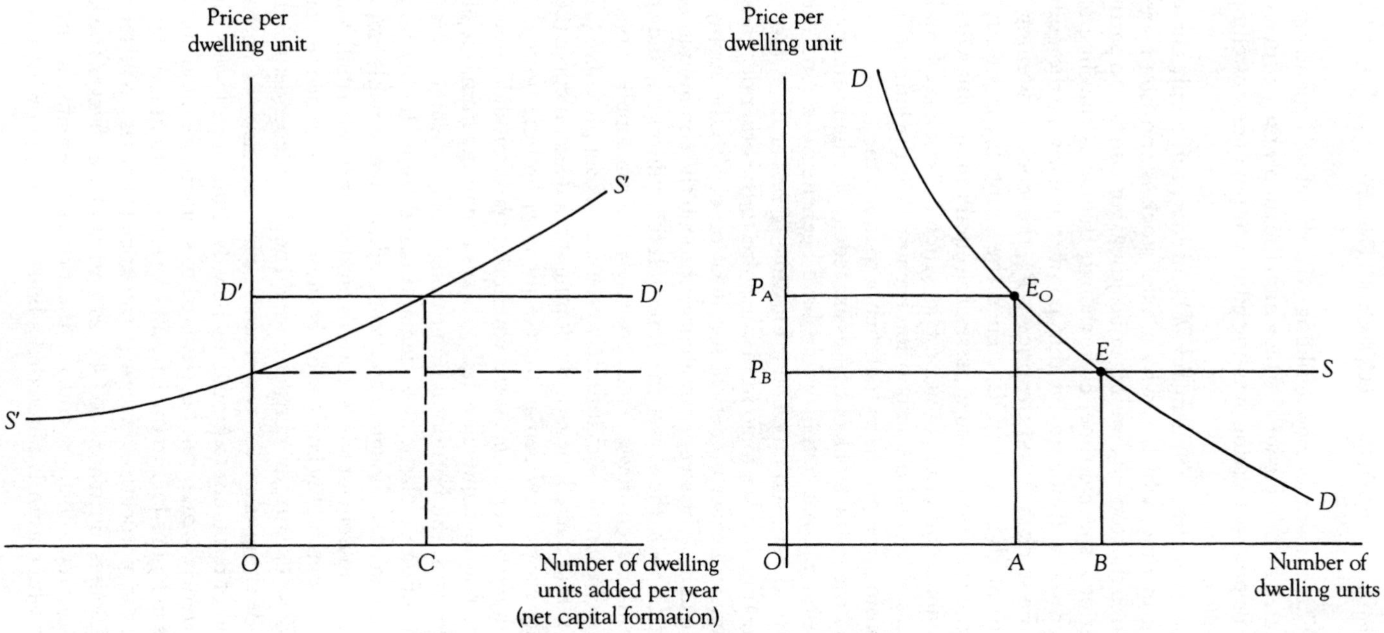
Price per dwelling unit
D'
D'
S'
S'
O
C
Number of dwelling units added per year (net capital formation)
Price per dwelling unit
D
P_A
E_O
E
P_B
S
D
O
A
B
Number of dwelling units

ones. The amount of new building will therefore expand up to the point (designated by C in Figure 15.5) at which the supply price of new dwelling units equals the price of existing dwelling units. Output of new dwelling units will be at the *rate* of OC.

Note that the stock demand DD and short-run supply curve S'S' are for a moment of time, which is why a fixed stock is consistent with any *rate* of addition to the stock of dwelling units, just as you can be at a particular point in your car at a specific time, even though the car is traveling at high speed. However, you will not stay at that point. Similarly, at the point of time for which the stock is A and the price is P_A, the stock of dwelling units is being added to at the rate of OC, hence the point E_O is strictly a temporary equilibrium position. As time passes, the equilibrium point will slide down DD to the stable equilibrium position E at which the stock is OB and the price P_B. This is a stable equilibrium position because P_B is the long-run supply price of new housing, the price at which net output is zero.

Had the initial stock of houses exceeded OB, the initial price would have been below P_B, net output would have been negative, and the equilibrium point would have slid up DD until it came to rest at E.

The time it takes to go from one point to the other depends of course on the shape and exact numerical specification of S'S', the supply curve of new dwelling units. The steeper that curve through the common intersection with the vertical axis, the slower the approach to equilibrium, and conversely.

We have seen how a fixed, positively sloping supply curve (S'S') for new dwelling units implies an infinitely elastic stock supply curve (SS). The counterpart is that a fixed, negatively sloping stock demand curve (DD) implies an infinitely elastic flow demand curve for new dwelling units (D'D'), but one which changes over time. As the equilibrium position slides down DD from E_O to E, the flow demand curve falls, always remaining infinitely elastic, until it coincides with the horizontal line through OP_B, where it comes to rest.

An infinitely elastic flow demand curve seems highly implausible as a theoretical matter, though of course it could be a reasonable empirical approximation for an item for which current production is very small compared to the stock.[8] It seems highly implausible because the price someone would be willing to pay for an existing dwelling unit would not be independent of the rate of flow of new dwelling units for two reasons. First, because, as we have seen, the diversion of resources to producing new dwelling units lowers total consumption currently, which can be expected to shift the demand curve for housing services in Figure 15.1 to the left, thus lowering current rental values. Second, because the prospective increase in the stock of houses would tend to lower the price of houses, ultimately to OP_B, as a result of the effect of the larger stock of houses on rental values and on the price of permanent income streams. Anyone who currently purchased a house at OP_A, knowing that the stock of houses was increasing, would have to look forward to bearing a future capital loss. Clearly, that prospect would reinforce the first effect. We were able to neglect these effects in discussing Figure 15.2 because that demand curve was drawn for a set of alternative, stationary worlds. But in a world in which the stock of houses is changing, the present value of a rental stream must allow for changing future rents and interest rates.

We can take these complications into account, as in Figure 15.6 by treating *DD* as valid only for alternative stocks of houses, each corresponding to a zero flow ($dH/dt=0$). This means that on the flow side, P_A is the demand price only for $dH/dt=0$. The larger the flow of new dwelling units, for the given initial stock of *OA*, the lower the demand price for both the stock and the flow. If *D'D'* in Figure 15.6 is the flow demand for new dwelling units, then the temporary equilibrium price is $P_{C'}$, and *OC'* is the rate of flow. On the right-hand side for stocks, we can express this effect by drawing a separate stock demand curve for a rate of flow equal to *OC'*. For every stock of dwelling units, the demand price will be less when $dH/dt=OC'$ than when it is zero. Between the two curves drawn in Figure 15.6 there are, of course, an infinite number of others for rates of flow between 0 and *OC'* and, similarly, still lower curves would correspond to higher rates of flow and curves above *DD* ($dH/dt=0$) to negative rates of flow.[9]

Point E'_O is now the equilibrium position. But it is obviously only a momentary one. Net output of dwelling units is positive, so the stock of housing is growing; the short-run stock supply curve moves to the right. As it does, the flow demand curve in the left-hand panel of Figure 15.6 shifts downward, its intersection on the vertical axis linked to the demand price on the stock demand curve for $dH/dt=0$. The process continues until the stock of dwelling units is *OB*, at which point the flow demand and supply curves intersect on the vertical axis. Net output is zero, and a full equilibrium is attained at *E* with the price of housing equal to P_B.[10]

So long as we stick to the assumption that the long-run stock supply curve is horizontal and the short-run flow supply curve positively sloping and independent of the stock, the price of dwelling units must be higher than the long-run price whenever output is growing and lower whenever output is falling. That is, the locus of temporary equilibrium points in the right-hand panel of Figure 15.6 must be downward sloping as it is there drawn. However, just as we have generalized the stock and flow demand curves, it is desirable to generalize the stock and flow supply curves, as in Figure 15.7. If the long-run stock supply curve is positively sloped, as in the right-hand panel of Figure 15.7, then the flow supply curve can no longer be independent of the stock of houses. The flow supply curve *S'S'*, which cuts the vertical axis at P_B is valid only when the stock is *OB*. If the stock is *OA*, the flow supply curve must cut the vertical axis

FIGURE 15.6

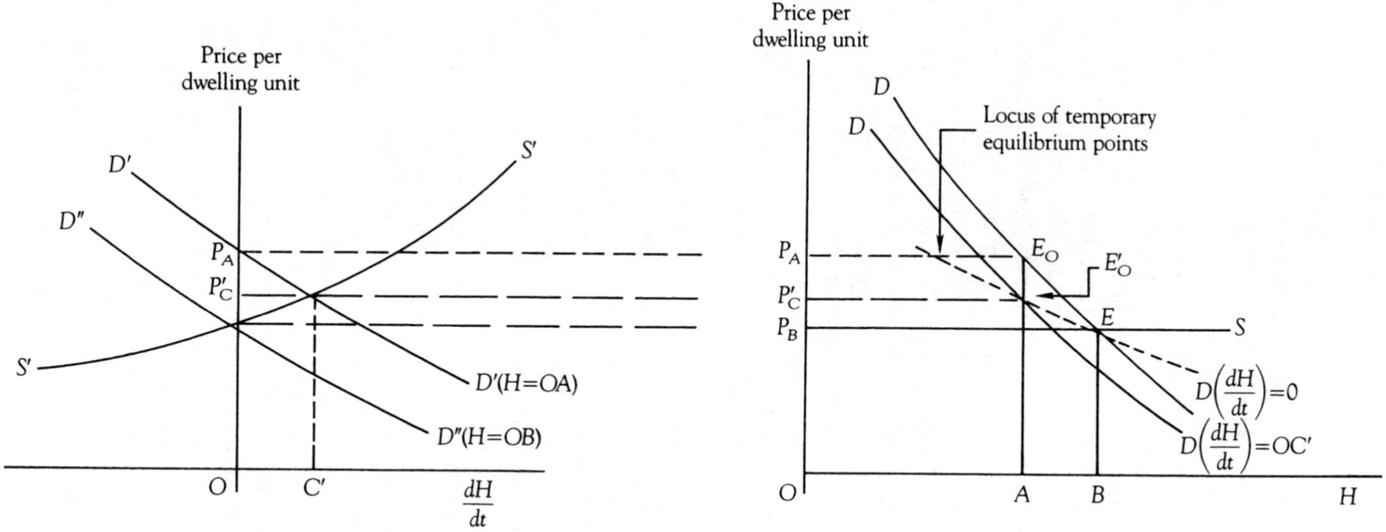
Price per dwelling unit
D′
D″
S′
P_A
P′_C
S′
D′(H=OA)
D″(H=OB)
O
C′
dH/dt
Price per dwelling unit
D
D
Locus of temporary equilibrium points
P_A
P′_C
P_B
E_O
E′_O
E
S
D(dH/dt)=0
D(dH/dt)=OC′
O
A
B
H

in the left-hand panel of Figure 15.7 at P'_A, the stock supply price of the smaller stock of dwelling units OA.

Note that the positive slope of the long-run stock supply curve in Figure 15.7 is mirrored in the left-hand panel in the points of intersection of the flow supply curves with the vertical axis, not in the slopes of the flow supply curve. The positive slope of the long-run stock supply curve reflects the rising costs attached to maintaining stationary building industries of different sizes. These rising costs reflect the need to change the proportions of factors in the industry and to attract resources less suited to the industry, the usual reasons for positively sloping, long-run supply curves. The positive slopes of the flow supply curves in the left-hand panel reflect a different, though not unrelated, set of effects, namely, the costs associated with *temporarily* expanding or contracting the building industry to above or below its usual size.

From the stock demand and supply curves in the right-hand panel, we know that the price must be between the demand price P_A and the supply price P'_A, which correspond to zero net output. If it were P_A, the price of a dwelling unit would exceed the cost of building one, and builders would have an incentive to add to the stock of dwelling units, so that is not an equilibrium position. If it were P'_A, the price of a dwelling unit would just correspond to the cost of building one, so builders would have no incentive to add to the stock, but owners and potential owners of dwelling units would want to own a larger stock at that price and so would tend to bid up the price, hence that is not an equilibrium position. As the rate of addition to the stock increases, the demand price falls and the supply price rises, as shown by the flow demand curve ($D'D'$) and flow supply curve ($S''S''$) in the left-hand panel of Figure 15.7 for a stock of OA. Just where the temporary equilibrium price will be depends on the elasticity of these flow curves. I have drawn them in Figure 15.7 in such a way as to produce an equilibrium price, $P_{C''}$, which is less than the long-run equilibrium price, in order to illustrate the possibility drawn in the right-hand panel that the temporary equilibrium price will rise, rather than fall, in the process of going from the initial stock of OA to the final stock of OB. But of course this is not necessary. Let the flow demand curve be flatter and the flow supply curve be steeper and the temporary equilibrium price could be above the final equilibrium price as it was in our earlier example.

Just as, in Figure 15.6, we were led to draw different stock demand curves for different rates of flow, so we are now led in Figure 15.7 to draw different stock supply curves for different rates of flow. The temporary equilibrium position at a price of $P_{C''}$ is at the intersection of the stock supply curve for the rate of flow of C'' and the corresponding stock demand curve (which is lower than the one drawn in Figure 15.6 for $dH/dt=OC'$ because dH/dt is here larger). As the stock increases, the stock demand curve rises, the stock supply curve falls; the flow demand curve falls and the flow supply curve rises, until

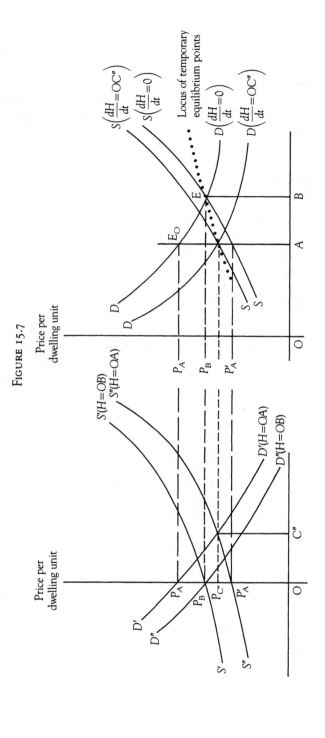

FIGURE 15.7

ultimately the two stock curves intersect at point *E*, and the two flow curves intersect on the vertical axis of the left-hand panel at a net output of zero and a price of P_B.

Generalization of the Stock-Flow Analysis

The generalization of the example of dwelling units to capital in general and the determination of the interest rate is straightforward. Instead of starting with the stock demand curve for dwelling units in Figure 15.2, we start with the stock demand for permanent income streams in Figure 15.3. Instead of introducing the supply curve for building dwelling units, we introduce the costs of providing dollars of permanent income not alone by building dwelling units but by any addition to the stock of sources of productive services or consumption services. This shift transfers the effect of an increase in the capital stock on the prices of the services it yields from the demand side to the supply side, since a decline in rents, for example, as the stock of houses increases, now shows up as a higher cost of providing a dollar of income since more physical dwelling units need to be built to produce the same permanent income stream. And as we saw earlier, the demand curve for income streams in Figure 15.3 does not depend on the demand curve for the services of dwelling units in Figure 15.1. But that is the only change of substance. As a result, Figure 15.8, which summarizes the situation for capital in general, is a direct counterpart of Figure 15.7, except for changes in labeling and except that, to illustrate a different possibility, the locus of points of temporary equilibrium in the right-hand panel is downward sloping.

In Figure 15.8, *S* stands for saving, *I* for investment. The long-run stock demand curve for permanent income streams corresponds to savings equal zero ($S=0$); the long-run stock supply curve, to investment equals zero ($I=0$). We have expressed savings and investment as fractions of income, to make them independent of units. If society has a stock of capital denoted by Q_1, then it cannot be on either the supply curve with $I=0$ or the demand curve with $S=0$. If it were on the former, owners of resources would try to buy more sources than are available and so raise their price; if it were on the latter, producing enterprises would be seeking to offer for sale more sources than are demanded and so lower their price. Somewhere between P_A and P_B, at a price here designated as P_C, is a price at which quantity of additional sources demanded is equal to the quantity of additional sources supplied. The demand price is lower because of the lessened desirability of additional sources relative to current consumption as the fraction of income devoted to buying sources increases; the supply price is higher because of the increased cost of producing additional sources as the fraction of productive services devoted to producing sources instead of current consumption increases. In the particular case on the graph,

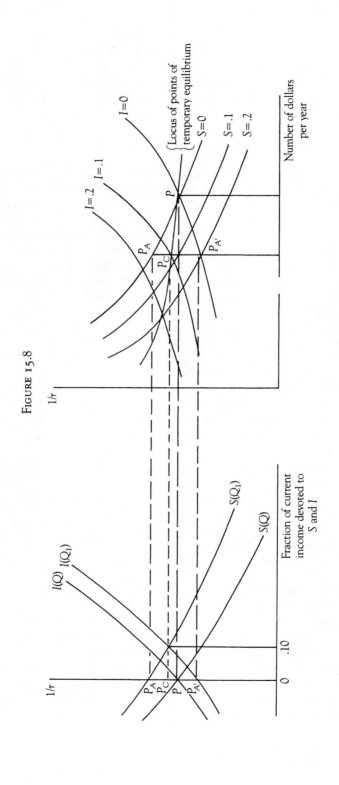

FIGURE 15.8

FIGURE 15.9

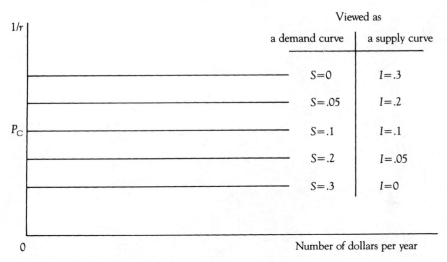

the demand price and supply price are equal when .1 of productive services are being devoted to producing additional sources and .1 of income to buying additional sources; i.e., $S=I=.1$. At this point, the stock of sources is growing. Thus point P_C is a temporary position, implying a movement along the line drawn through P_C and P in the direction of P.

Suppose we used an all-inclusive concept of capital. Then just as we saw earlier that we could expect the stock demand curve for permanent income streams to be infinitely elastic, we could also expect the stock supply curve for permanent income streams to be infinitely elastic. To use Knight's terminology, we should expect no diminishing returns from investment. The height of this curve would be determined by whatever happens to be the cost of producing a capital source capable of yielding a dollar a year indefinitely (the reciprocal of the marginal productivity of capital, according to one interpretation of that ambiguous term). The figure corresponding to Figure 15.8 might then look like Figure 15.9. All the curves could be horizontal, so any horizontal curve would correspond to a demand curve for some level of savings and a supply curve for some level of investment. If the demand curve for $S=0$ is above the supply curve for $I=0$, as in this diagram, the picture describes an indefinitely progressive state—there is no level of capital stock that will be consistent with stationary state equilibrium. As the figure is drawn, a kind of "moving equilibrium" emerges, in which the price of a dollar a year is P_C, investment and saving proceed indefinitely at a rate of .1 of income, and the stock of capital continuously grows.

FIGURE 15.10

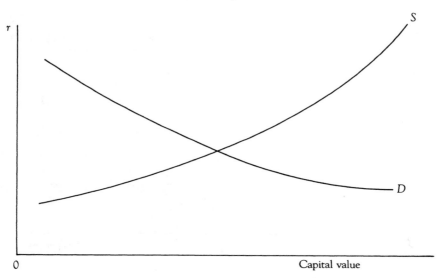

We shall now translate the preceding analysis into terms of wealth. Instead of talking about the demand for and supply of permanent income streams in terms of the price of a permanent income stream, we shall talk about the demand for and supply of capital values with the rate of interest as the independent variable. The chief advantage of the previous mode of expression (which is also the chief disadvantage of the present mode of expression) is the presentation of a constant stock of capital. Of the two ways of measuring the stock of capital, one of them is affected by the interest rate and the other is not. If capital stock is measured in terms of capitalized value of the permanent income stream, this measure will vary inversely with the rate of interest. A given set of sources yields a given income stream, and a constant stock of capital yielding a constant permanent income stream will be represented by a rectangular hyperbola. On the other hand, if we measure the stock of capital in terms of the permanent income streams it yields, this measure will not be affected by the interest rate, and hence this measure of the stock of capital will be a vertical line.

To get the demand for and supply of capital values using this second approach, we must remember that the demand for capital will be the demand of producing enterprises—what was formerly regarded as the supply of permanent income streams. The supply of capital will be the supply on the part of savers of capital sums—what was formerly regarded as the demand for income

FIGURE 15.11

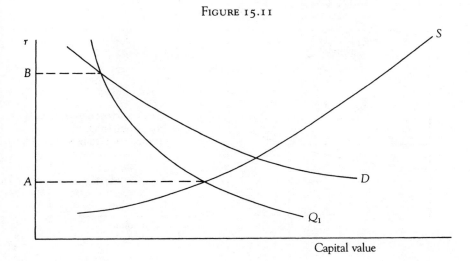

streams. Again, it is to be noted that these two curves refer to stocks and do not measure rates of flow per unit of time. The intersection of the two curves, as in Figure 15.10, will give us the long-run, stationary equilibrium stock of capital and rate of interest. As before, the curves have the shapes they do have because the concept of capital used is not all-inclusive. Consider the demand curve in this terminology that corresponds to the previous supply curve. Following the Knightian argument, we see that because the capital concept is restricted by institutional or other reasons, diminishing returns accrue to investment. The more inclusive concept of capital with no diminishing returns would imply an infinitely elastic demand for capital. The height of the demand curve or the rate of interest would be determined by the "marginal productivity of capital." Similarly, if we assume that people wish to maintain a certain constant ratio of wealth to income and if all income is derived from wealth (i.e., no distinction is necessary between human and nonhuman wealth), the supply curve would be infinitely elastic. The height of the supply curve is given by $1/K$ where K is W/Y.

In any particular stage in society there exists a stock of capital that may not be the equilibrium stock. The curve in Figure 15.11 labeled Q_1 is a rectangular hyperbola and represents the capital value of a stock of capital yielding a permanent income stream of Q_1. If producing enterprises had no incentive to change this stock of capital at any interest rate—i.e., had no incentive to pay interest on a larger stock of capital—the Q_1 curve would represent the demand for capital. In a given state of technology, the incentive for producing enter-

FIGURE 15.12

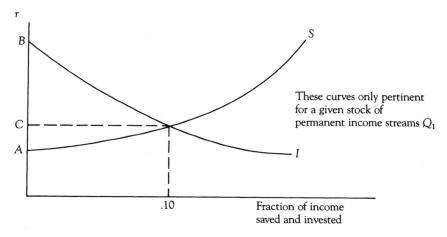

These curves only pertinent for a given stock of permanent income streams Q_1

prises to increase the stock of capital is greater the lower the rate of interest. Hence the lower the rate of interest, the higher the D curve should be relative to the Q_1 curve. If the rate of interest were at B, producing enterprises would have no incentive to try to increase the stock of capital on which they are paying interest. However, savers would have an incentive to seek to lend more. Likewise, if the rate of interest were at A, savers would have no incentive to lend more, but producing enterprises would have an incentive to borrow more. Savers will force the rate of interest below its level at B; investors will force the rate of interest above its level at A.

Therefore, the rate of interest can be at neither A nor B. Where it will be depends on the propensities of people to save and invest, i.e., on the savings and investment curves as in Figure 15.12. These curves determine the rate at which society moves away from the stock of capital corresponding to Q_1 to the equilibrium stock. As before, the demand curves for capital in Figure 15.11 consist of a locus of the combination of r and capital sums for which investment would be zero. Likewise, the supply curve of capital is the locus of combinations of r and capital sums for which savings would be zero. These two behavior functions enable us to define the long-run value of the equilibrium stock of capital. On the other hand, the savings and investment functions that are drawn in Figure 15.12 relating r to the rates of flow of savings and investment as percentages of national income, are drawn for given stocks of capital. These curves enable us to trace the dynamic path to long-run equilibrium.

This can all be summarized in Figure 15.13, which is the counterpart of

FIGURE 15.13

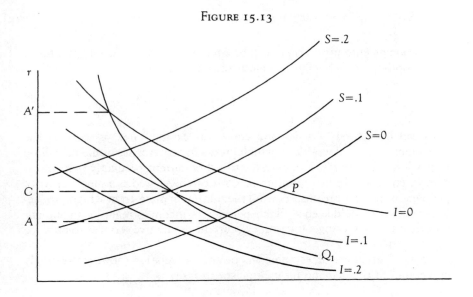

Figure 15.8. The $S=0$ and $I=0$ curves represent the supply of and demand for capital values. The intersection of these curves tells us about long-run equilibrium. The other curves have to do with direction. They give the various combinations of capital values and interest rates that must occur in order to maintain different rates of flow of savings and investment. We have assumed society to possess a given stock of capital whose value is represented by the rectangular hyperbola Q_1, so the interest rate must lie between A' and A; from the savings and investment functions which obtain when society has this given stock of capital, we have determined that the rate of interest would be C with a rate of investment and saving of .1. This rate of interest C and rate of investment and saving of .1 are temporary, because as the stock of capital of society grows, there will be a new rate of saving and investment and a new rate of interest, leading eventually to the stable equilibrium position designated by P.

This analysis can be summarized in the form of a system of simultaneous equations. Let W=total real wealth of the kind being considered,

r=interest rate,
Y_W=income per unit time from W (so that $Y_W=rW$),
I="investment" per unit time, and

S="savings" per unit time.

For producing enterprises, there will be a relation showing the rate of interest corresponding to each value of wealth and investment, say

$$r=f(W, I). \tag{5}$$

This can be viewed as a demand curve for "capital," i.e., as showing the maximum amount of wealth on which producing enterprises would be willing to pay a rate of interest r when a fraction I of current productive services is being used to add to the capital stock. Or it can be viewed as a supply curve of permanent income streams, showing the minimum price $1/r$ at which producing enterprises would keep available permanent income streams of an amount rW when they are using a fraction I of current productive services to produce income streams.

For owners of resources, there will be another relation showing the supply of "capital" or the demand for income streams, say

$$r=g(W, S). \tag{6}$$

In the short run, we suppose Y_W fixed, say at Y_{W_o}. Short-run equilibrium is then given by equations 5 and 6 plus

$$S=I \tag{7}$$

$$rW=Y_W \tag{8}$$

$$Y_W=Y_{W_o} \tag{9}$$

This is a system of five equations in the five unknowns, r, W, S, I, Y_W.

In the long run, the relevant system is equations 5 and 6 plus

$$S=0 \tag{10}$$

$$I=0 \tag{11}$$

$$Y_W=rW. \tag{12}$$

This is a system of five equations in the same five unknowns.

FIGURE 15.14

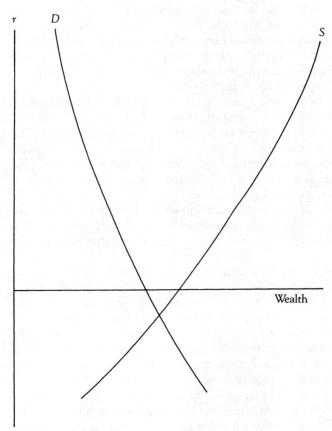

A Negative Equilibrium Interest Rate

As long as we restrict ourselves to a barter economy, nothing we have said so far imposes very many restrictions on the shape of the $S=0$, $I=0$ curves. In particular, it is possible for the curves to intersect at a negative rate of interest, as in Figure 15.14. This would mean that society would be in long-run equilibrium with a given stock of capital at a negative rate of interest.

What conditions must be satisfied in order for a result such as this to occur? Consider first the S curve, showing the stock of wealth of the limited kind that is appropriable and capable of purchase and sale and that ultimate wealth-holders are willing to hold at various rates of interest. Suppose that the rate of interest were zero—that is, that there were no way of holding wealth that would yield a return. No wealth-holders would then hold wealth as a source of current (pecuniary) income. But individuals and families would still want to hold wealth as a reserve against emergencies. Clearly, that would remain true even if wealth imposed costs rather than gave returns. For example, suppose the only way people could hold wealth was in the form of stocks of foodstuffs, which imposed carrying costs in the form of making good deterioration and wastage. People would clearly still want to hold some wealth in that form to protect themselves against fluctuations in the supply of food. The wealth-value shown by the stock supply curve in Figure 15.14 for negative interest rates corresponds to such holdings. Of course, the actual stock held would not be constant year after year, so the amount depicted is to be treated as the average value over a considerable period.[11]

In practice, negative returns on capital to wealth-holders could arise not only from such physical circumstances as those just exemplified but also from capital taxes that converted before-tax, positive returns into after-tax, negative returns.

Let us now consider the demand curve. At first, this seems to conflict with our earlier analysis that described a fixed stock of capital in the sense of a constant stream of permanent income as generating a unit elastic demand curve for wealth. The constant income stream would be the maximum total amount that the producing enterprises holding the capital would be willing to pay as interest on the wealth value of the capital. How can the demand curve be less elastic than that? Clearly, it cannot be if there is any capital source yielding an economically permanent income stream. Let there be one acre of land yielding an economically permanent stream of rent of $1 a year, and its capital value would approach infinity as the rate of interest became lower and lower. Putting it differently, if there is any way of producing an economically permanent income stream of any size at any finite cost—say by filling in swamps—it will be profitable, at a low enough interest rate, to borrow that sum to produce that stream.

Note the stress on *economically* permanent. As in the discussion of the supply of capital, there may be no economically permanent source of income for physical reasons. The only capital sources capable of being produced, appropriated, and transferred might be inventories of depreciating foodstuffs. Alternatively, there may be sources of physically or technically permanent income streams, like land areas, but taxation or other institutional arrangements like ownership rights of limited duration may make them not economically permanent.

The essential condition, therefore, for the long-run equilibrium interest rate to be negative is that there exist no capital item included in the category of

wealth to which Figure 15.14 applies that can yield an economically permanent income stream. The negative interest rate corresponds to the owners of
wealth paying caretakers to maintain the wealth intact. In order for such a
situation to persist, the owners of wealth must have some other source from
which to get the sums they pay (the negative interest rate times the value of
wealth). There must exist some forms of capital (human capital, nontransfera-
ble, nonhuman capital) that yield a permanent income stream. Otherwise, the
society could not be stationary. It would simply run down. A negative equilibrium interest rate is therefore not conceivable for an all-inclusive concept of
capital.

The conditions required for the long-run stationary state interest rate to
be negative are highly special. It is nonetheless worth spelling them out,
because a negative equilibrium interest rate is very closely connected with
Keynes's proposition that there may not be a long-run stationary state equilibrium at full employment. One insightful way of interpreting that proposition consists of the following subpropositions:

1. In a nonmonetary, barter economy, the equilibrium interest rate may
   be negative.
2. In a monetary economy, the market interest rate cannot be negative.
3. Therefore, in a monetary economy, it may not be possible to reach full
   equilibrium.

The preceding analysis shows that 1 is correct, though only under very
special conditions. We have already seen, in discussing the arithmetic of
interest rates, the sense in which 2 is correct. But 3 is a non sequitur from 1 and
2 unless the equilibrium interest rate in a monetary economy is the same as in a
nonmonetary economy. But that is not the case. The contrast that Keynes
drew between "market" and equilibrium rates is misleading. Neither can be
negative in the kind of money economy that underlay his analysis. In order to
see why that is so we must introduce money explicitly into our analysis.

Introduction of Money

Once money is introduced into an economy, it is essential to distinguish
between the *nominal* interest rate—the number of dollars per dollar after
maintaining the dollar amount of capital intact—and the *real* interest rate—
the number of dollars per dollar after maintaining the real amount of capital
intact. For continuous compounding, the real interest rate is the nominal rate
minus the rate of change of prices:

$$\rho = r - \frac{1}{P}\frac{dP}{dt}, \qquad (13)$$

where ρ is the real interest rate, r the nominal rate, and $(1/P)(dP/dt)$ the instantaneous rate of change of prices. For monetary analysis, it is essential to distinguish between the realized real rate, which treats $(1/P)(dP/dt)$ as the actual rate of price change, and the anticipated real rate, which treats $(1/P)(dP/dt)$ as the anticipated rate of change of prices. But for our purposes of analyzing stationary state equilibrium, we may neglect this distinction and treat the realized and anticipated real rates as identical.

For simplicity, we shall first consider alternative stationary states in each of which the price level is stable so $(1/P)(dP/dt)=0$. This is the case implicitly considered by Keynes and most of his followers. We shall then introduce the possibility of changing prices. We shall throughout regard money as the counterpart of currency or its equivalent, i.e., as an asset that pays zero nominal interest.

Once we introduce money, the nominal rate of interest can never be negative, since the costs of simply holding cash are essentially zero. Hence if the rate of interest approached zero, people would hold all their wealth in the form of money. In terms of the preceding section, money now becomes a form of wealth that yields a permanent income stream of zero and so dominates any form of wealth that yields a negative permanent income stream.

Figure 15.15 incorporates this feature into our long-run stationary equilibrium diagram. The S curve in Figure 15.15 is the supply curve of capital (for $S=0$) previously defined. The S' curve shows the amount of each corresponding level of wealth that owners of resources would desire to hold in forms other than money, so the horizontal distance between the S' and S curves measures the amount that owners of resources would want to hold in the form of money. The S' curve then gives the supply of wealth available for "renting" to productive enterprises at each interest rate, and its intersection with the demand curve (for $I=0$) previously defined gives the long-run equilibrium position (c in Figure 15.15).

However, producing enterprises would use part of the wealth on which they pay interest to finance the holding of cash. These "business balances" are indicated in Figure 15.15 by the horizontal distance between the D and D' curves. In equilibrium, then, bd is the equilibrium "real" amount of money of which cd is held directly by owners of resources and bc as "working" capital by producing enterprises. The equilibrium price level is then whatever is necessary to make the real value of the existing nominal quantity of money equal to bd. This assertion is one way of stating compactly the quantity theory of money.

We can now see why, once money is introduced into the system, the

FIGURE 15.15

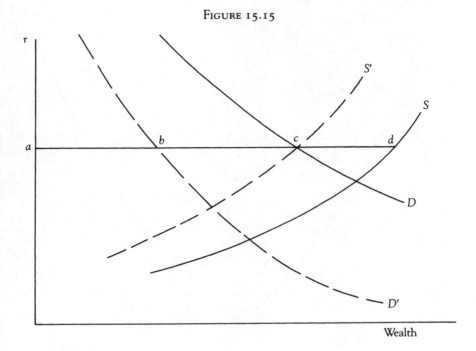

equilibrium rate of interest cannot be negative. In Figure 15.16, the S and D curves, reproduced from Figure 15.14, intersect at a negative interest rate. This intersection gives the equilibrium solution for a barter economy. But once money is introduced, equilibrium is given by the intersection of the S' curve and the D curve, and the S' curve necessarily cuts the D curve at a positive interest rate so long as the cost of holding money can be regarded as zero. This is one way to state the essence of the so-called Pigou effect, which demonstrated the non sequitur in Keynes's proposition 3.

If the price level is not constant, we can no longer use r as in Figures 15.15 and 15.16 to refer to both the nominal and the real interest rate. Suppose prices are rising at a constant rate so that the nominal rate exceeds the real rate. This will affect all of the curves in Figure 15.16. Whereas before the nominal and real return from holding a dollar of cash was zero, now it is negative. Hence for a given real rate (say a of Figure 15.15), assets yielding that real rate are more attractive relative to cash. This will be true for both ultimate wealth-holders and for business enterprises, so the distances bc and cd in Figure 15.15 will both contract as in Figure 15.17, which reproduces the curves from Figure 15.15 and adds the curves designated by an asterisk relevant to the new

FIGURE 15.16

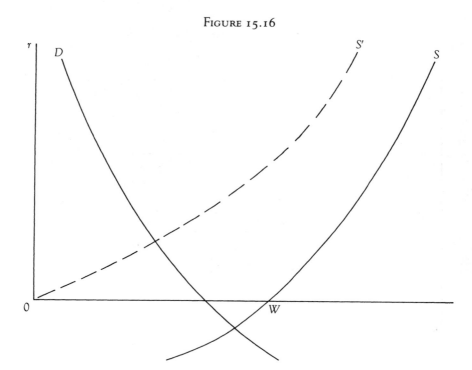

situation with prices rising. Both business enterprises and ultimate wealth-holders will be induced to substitute real wealth for cash balances, so both curves D' and S' will move to the right. However, the collection of wealth is now less productive for business enterprises and yields less utility for ultimate wealth-holders, so both curves D and S will shift to the left. The new equilibrium real rate is now defined by the intersection of the D and S' curves designated by an asterisk and is lower than the earlier real rate. However, the decline in the real rate must be less than the rate of change of prices, because it is produced by the simultaneously higher nominal rate. As a theoretical proposition, nothing more can be said about the division of the price rise between a higher nominal rate and a lower real rate. As an empirical proposition, the major effect appears to be on the nominal rate, the real rate being essentially unchanged. The implication is that the demand and supply curves D' and S' are highly elastic or that the real quantity of money is small compared to the total wealth value of all capital.

    Figure 15.17 contains the essence of what has sometimes been labeled the *Mundell effect*.[12]

FIGURE 15.17

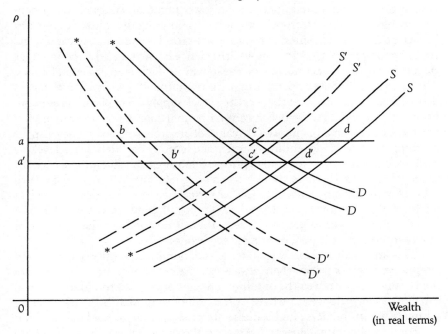

If prices were falling at a constant rate, the effects would be reversed: the real interest rate would be higher than with constant prices and the nominal rate lower.[13]

A digression will help relate this analysis to the more usual discussion of the Keynesian proposition about the possibility that there may not exist an equilibrium at full employment of resources. For such an equilibrium to exist, the amount business enterprises want to add to the stock of capital, net capital formation, or net investment, must, Keynes argued, be equal to the amount ultimate wealth-holders want to add to their stock of wealth, net savings, when all resources are employed. But suppose the yield on capital is so low that business enterprises do not want to invest as much as the community wants to save at full employment. In a barter economy, that would be resolved, Keynes implicitly argues, by a negative interest rate. But in a money economy, the nominal rate cannot be negative. The conflict will be resolved by a reduction in employment that will reduce the amount people desire to save to the amount enterprises desire to invest.

But this situation, Keynes recognizes, is not a stable equilibrium: the unemployed resources will compete for employment, driving down their nominal prices. However, he argues, there is no end to this process; lower nominal costs mean lower nominal prices, mean lower nominal values of investment and savings, but do not introduce any force eliminating the initial discrepancy between the amount business enterprises want to add to productive capital and the community wants to add to its wealth. Hence he introduced price and wage rigidity as a deus ex machina to stop the indefinite decline in prices and wages.

Pigou argued that the public's desire is not ultimately to save but to have a desired stock of wealth, that there exists a stock supply curve of capital as in our figures corresponding to $S=0$. For a given nominal quantity of money (which is what Keynes assumed), the wealth value of that quantity of money can be anything whatsoever depending on the price level. For a "high" price level, its wealth value will be low, for a "low" price level, its wealth value will be high. In terms of Figure 15.16, there always exists a price level that will make the wealth value of money balances equal to OW. At this price level, the desired stock of wealth will be attained and desired saving at full employment will be zero; hence even if desired investment is zero, there is no conflict. The equilibrium rate of interest is at least zero in a money economy.

This argument is entirely valid for a fixed nominal quantity of money and alternative levels of prices: there always exists a low enough price level to sate the community with wealth, or a high enough price level to reduce the real value of money balances to whatever fraction of total wealth the community (ultimate wealth-holders plus business enterprises) wishes to hold in that form.

For a fixed nominal quantity of money, there is an even more far-reaching answer to Keynes's propositions that renders them invalid even if the public had an insatiable desire to add to (nonhuman) wealth while there was a limit to the physical productivity of capital. That answer derives from distinguishing income defined as the value of productive resources from income defined as the sum of what individuals separately regard their incomes as being. The latter includes not only payments for productive services but also capital gains or losses. Suppose the Keynesian dilemma were to arise, and prices and wages started falling. Declining prices would add to the real value of wealth. Holders of cash would realize capital gains. Incomes as they perceived them would exceed the value of productive resources. Consumption would equal the value of productive resources, so net investment by entrepreneurs would be zero, yet wealth-holders could be saving at any desired rate. There always exists, with a fixed nominal quantity of money, a rate of price decline sufficiently great to reconcile at full employment the desires of producing enterprises to invest and of wealth-holders to save, no matter how stubborn both are.

This answer is not incorporated in our diagrams because the underlying assumptions contradict the notion that there exists a supply curve of wealth that has a finite desired level of wealth for an interest rate of zero.

Figure 15.17 shows that the Pigovian argument can readily be extended to

FIGURE 15.18

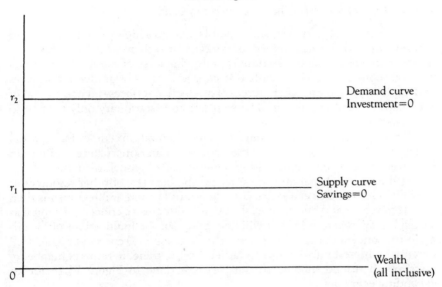

encompass a changing nominal quantity of money and an associated changing price level. The stationary picture it depicts for a positive rate of price rise corresponds to a rate of monetary growth equal to the rate of price rise. For that rate of growth of prices and money there exists at each point of time a price level and a real interest rate that will simultaneously equate the nominal amount of money available to the nominal quantity demanded and the amount of wealth on which producing enterprises are willing to pay interest to the amount of wealth ultimate wealth-holders want to hold in interest-bearing form.

Finally, the more far-reaching argument that depends on the rate of price change rather than the level of prices can also be extended to encompass a changing quantity of money. If wealth-holders stubbornly insist on saving at full employment more than producing enterprises wish to invest, then prices must fall sufficiently more rapidly than the quantity of money is falling to enable the wealth-holders to achieve their objectives in the form of increasing real value of cash balances.

The Pigovian and the more far-reaching answer to Keynes's proposition have been extremely important on a theoretical level in assuring that there is no basic flaw in our theoretical analysis. But I hasten to add that in my opinion neither corresponds to effects that are empirically important in the kind of economic fluctuations that actual economies experience.

A Final Note on an All-Inclusive Concept of Capital

The concept of stationary state equilibrium has a highly unrealistic ring in a world that has been accustomed to economic growth over centuries. Hence it is worth stressing that the stationary state character of our analysis derives from our considering mostly only one class of sources of productive services and implicitly assuming other sources of productive services (human capital in the main) as fixed in amount. The equilibrium is stationary only relative to that fixed amount.

If the quantity of other resources grows, then all our curves for a partial concept of capital keep shifting to the right, so the stationary state equilibrium becomes a moving equilibrium as in many so-called growth models.

Still more fundamentally, if we regard the quantity of other resources as altering in response to economic considerations by more indirect means than market purchase and sale, we can shift to an all-inclusive concept of capital as we did briefly in Figure 15.9. It will help bring out the implications of the all-inclusive concept of capital to express the $S=0$ and $I=0$ curves of Figure 15.9 in terms of interest rate and wealth rather than, as there, in terms of number of years' purchase and income streams. This is done in Figure 15.18 for an expanding economy.

Note that the supply curve of capital includes the part of the vertical axis below r_1, the demand curve, the part above r_2. At any (real) interest rate above r_1, there is no limit to the amount of wealth the community would be willing to accumulate in all forms, though of course at each point of time there is a limit to how rapidly they would be willing to accumulate it. At any (real) interest rate below r_2, there is no limit to the amount of sources of productive services on which it would be worth paying that interest, though of course there is a limit on how rapidly it would be worth producing the additional sources. In this conception, r_1 deserves to be called *the internal rate of discount* or *time preference*; r_2 deserves to be called *the marginal productivity of capital*. There is nothing that requires the internal rate of discount and the marginal productivity of capital to be a numerical constant for all levels of wealth, as in the special case depicted in Figure 15.18, but, as noted earlier, there is no presumption as to whether they will be higher or lower for higher quantities of capital. So long as the marginal productivity of capital is higher than the internal rate of discount, the economy will be growing.

If r_2 were less than r_1, the economy would be declining, and a similar figure could be drawn for such an economy.

NOTES

1. The reason for emphasis on "financial" arbitrage proper is, of course, because of the distinction between "real" and "nominal" yield.

2. Note that some of the values of R can be negative. E.g., equation 1 may be used for a contract that requires the purchaser to pay additional amounts for some years, as in the example of a purchaser of an unfinished building.

3. More generally still, the value of ρ can be allowed to vary, giving

$$W = \int_0^\infty e - \int_0^t \rho(\tau) d\tau R(t) dt, \tag{2a}$$

where $\rho(\tau)$ is a continuous rate applicable to time τ. However, for given W and $R(t)$, there is no unique $\rho(\tau)$, as was indicated in the text earlier.

4. Even in this case, the willingness of people to pay fees for safety-deposit boxes in bank vaults to hoard cash is an example of a negative interest rate.

5. As drawn, the horizontal scales would be numerically identical. But this is misleading. Suppose the horizontal scale of Figure 15.1 had been "number of dwelling-unit years per month." Then the horizontal scale on Figure 15.2 would be twelve times the horizontal scale on Figure 15.1, since one dwelling unit can provide only one-twelfth of a dwelling-unit year per month.

6. Note that even if the supply curve in Figure 15.4 slopes negatively, at its extreme it only approaches the rectangular hyperbola; hence, there is always a stable equilibrium in Figure 15.4.

7. One pitfall in this way of putting the matter should be made explicit because it explains why the widely used figures on gross capital formation and gross national product are conceptually arbitrary. If dwelling units were like the fabled "one-hoss shay," requiring no maintenance over a finite period during which they gave homogeneous housing services and then collapsed, it would be straightforward to count the total number of houses built each year and to specify the number that had to be built to maintain the stock of dwelling units intact. In practice, this is clearly not the case. There are alternative ways of maintaining the stock of dwelling units intact: by maintaining existing dwelling units and by letting them deteriorate and building new ones. How draw the line? Which expenditures should be regarded as ongoing current expenditures of operation, and which expenditures, as making good capital consumption and hence as includable in "gross capital formation"? The line is arbitrary both in concept and in practice. (In practice, it is defined by the durability of the items produced, the line being drawn at items having an expected durability of three years. Items that have an expected durability longer than that are treated as capital items, the production of which enters into gross capital formation; items that have a shorter expected durability are treated on an inventory basis and only net changes in stocks included in gross capital formation.) On the other hand, *net* capital formation is a logically rigorous concept, referring to the change in the stock of capital, though it is extremely difficult to measure accurately in practice.

8. For example, suppose houses have an average useful life of fifty years and that we can approximate them by the one-horse shay model. If the stock is constant, gross output per year will be 2 percent of the stock and doubling current output will add only

282 • ECONOMIC THEORY

2 percent to the stock after a year. Even if stock demand were highly elastic, the price would fall only a little over a year.

9. In principle, the stock demand curves for nonzero rates of flow depend on the whole anticipated future course of net additions to the stock of dwelling units and not solely on the current rate of flow. Treating them as a function of the current rate of flow implicitly assumes that the alternative future time paths of additions to the stock of dwelling units are a one-parameter family.

10. Obviously, the whole analysis is readiliy modified for a world in which the stock of housing is growing at a steady rate along with resources in general.

11. Also, the yield is negative in physical terms, in terms of own-interest rate, but not in utility terms, since the reserves are used to supplement deficient production when their utility value is high and are replenished when production is ample and hence its utility value is low.

12. From Robert Mundell, "Inflation and Real Interest," *Journal of Political Economy* 71 (June 1963): 280–83.

13. See Milton Friedman, "The Optimum Quantity of Money," in *The Optimum Quantity of Money and Other Essays* (Chicago: Aldine, 1969).

MONETARY
ANALYSIS

◆ ◆ ◆ ◆

◆ *PART* ◆ *FOUR* ◆

THE QUANTITY THEORY
OF MONEY—A RESTATEMENT

· 16 ·

The quantity theory of money is a term evocative of a general approach rather than a label for a well-defined theory. The exact content of the approach varies from a truism defining the term "velocity" to an allegedly rigid and unchanging ratio between the quantity of money—defined in one way or another—and the price level—also defined in one way or another. Whatever its precise meaning, it is clear that the general approach fell into disrepute after the crash of 1929 and the subsequent Great Depression and only recently has been slowly re-emerging into professional respectability.

The present volume is partly a symptom of this re-emergence and partly a continuance of an aberrant tradition. Chicago was one of the few academic centers at which the quantity theory continued to be a central and vigorous part of the oral tradition throughout the 1930s and 1940s, where students continued to study monetary theory and to write theses on monetary problems. The quantity theory that retained this role differed sharply from the atrophied and rigid caricature that is so frequently described by the proponents of the new income-expenditure approach—and with some justice, to judge by much of the literature on policy that was spawned by quantity theorists. At Chicago, Henry Simons and Lloyd Mints directly, Frank Knight and Jacob

Viner at one remove, taught and developed a more subtle and relevant version, one in which the quantity theory was connected and integrated with general price theory and became a flexible and sensitive tool for interpreting movements in aggregate economic activity and for developing relevant policy prescriptions.

To the best of my knowledge, no systematic statement of this theory as developed at Chicago exists, though much can be read between the lines of Simons's and Mints's writings. And this is as it should be, for the Chicago tradition was not a rigid system, an unchangeable orthodoxy, but a way of looking at things. It was a theoretical approach that insisted that money does matter—that any interpretation of short-term movements in economic activity is likely to be seriously at fault if it neglects monetary changes and repercussions and if it leaves unexplained why people are willing to hold the particular nominal quantity of money in existence.

The purpose of this introduction is not to enshrine—or, should I say, inter—a definitive version of the Chicago tradition. To suppose that one could do so would be inconsistent with that tradition itself. The purpose is rather to set down a particular "model" of a quantity theory in an attempt to convey the flavor of the oral tradition which nurtured the remaining essays in this volume. In consonance with this purpose, I shall not attempt to be exhaustive or to give a full justification for every assertion.

1. The quantity theory is in the first instance a theory of the *demand* for money. It is not a theory of output, or of money income, or of the price level. Any statement about these variables requires combining the quantity theory with some specifications about the conditions of supply of money and perhaps about other variables as well.

2. To the ultimate wealth-owning units in the economy, money is one kind of asset, one way of holding wealth. To the productive enterprise, money is a capital good, a source of productive services that are combined with other productive services to yield the products that the enterprise sells. Thus the theory of the demand for money is a special topic in the theory of capital; as such, it has the rather unusual feature of combining a piece from each side of the capital market, the supply of capital (points 3 through 8 that follow) and the demand for capital (points 9 through 12).

3. The analysis of the demand for money on the part of the ultimate wealth-owning units in the society can be made formally identical with that of the demand for a consumption service. As in the usual theory of consumer choice, the demand for money (or any other particular asset) depends on three major sets of factors: (a) the total wealth to be held in various forms—the analogue of the budget restraint; (b) the price of and return on this form of wealth and alternative forms; and (c) the tastes and preferences of the wealth-owning units. The substantive differences from the analysis of the demand for a

consumption service are the necessity of taking account of intertemporal rates of substitution in (b) and (c) and of casting the budget restraint in terms of wealth.

4. From the broadest and most general point of view, total wealth includes all sources of "income" or consumable services. One such source is the productive capacity of human beings, and accordingly this is one form in which wealth can be held. From this point of view, "the" rate of interest expresses the relation between the stock which is wealth and the flow which is income, so if Y be the total flow of income, and r, "the" interest rate, total wealth is

$$W = \frac{Y}{r}. \tag{1}$$

Income in this broadest sense should not be identified with income as it is ordinarily measured. The latter is generally a "gross" stream with respect to human beings, since no deduction is made for the expense of maintaining human productive capacity intact; in addition, it is affected by transitory elements that make it depart more or less widely from the theoretical concept of the stable level of consumption of services that could be maintained indefinitely.

5. Wealth can be held in numerous forms, and the ultimate wealth-owning unit is to be regarded as dividing his wealth among them (point [a] of 3), so as to maximize "utility" (point [c] of 3), subject to whatever restrictions affect the possibility of converting one form of wealth into another (point [b] of 3). As usual, this implies that he will seek an apportionment of his wealth such that the rate at which he *can* substitute one form of wealth for another is equal to the rate at which he is just willing to do so. But this general proposition has some special features in the present instance because of the necessity of considering flows as well as stocks. We can suppose all wealth (except wealth in the form of the productive capacity of human beings) to be expressed in terms of monetary units at the prices of the point of time in question. The rate at which one form can be substituted for another is then simply $1 worth for $1 worth, regardless of the forms involved. But this is clearly not a complete description, because the holding of one form of wealth instead of another involves a difference in the composition of the income stream, and it is essentially these differences that are fundamental to the "utility" of a particular structure of wealth. In consequence, to describe fully the alternative combinations of forms of wealth that are available to an individual, we must take account not only of their market prices—which except for human wealth can be done simply by expressing them in units worth $1—but also of the form and size of the income streams they yield.

It will suffice to bring out the major issues that these considerations raise to consider five different forms in which wealth can be held: (i) money (M), interpreted as claims or commodity units that are generally accepted in payment of debts at a fixed nominal value; (ii) bonds (B), interpreted as claims to time streams of payments that are fixed in nominal units; (iii) equities (E), interpreted as claims to stated pro rata shares of the returns of enterprises; (iv) physical nonhuman goods (G); and (v) human capital (H). Consider now the yield of each.

(i) Money may yield a return in the form of money, for example, interest on demand deposits. It will simplify matters, however, and entail no essential loss of generality, to suppose that money yields its return solely in kind, in the usual form of convenience, security, etc. The magnitude of this return in "real" terms per nominal unit of money clearly depends on the volume of goods that unit corresponds to, or on the general price level, which we may designate by P. Since we have decided to take $1 worth as the unit for each form of wealth, this will be equally true for other forms of wealth as well, so P is a variable affecting the "real" yield of each.

(ii) If we take the "standard" bond to be a claim to a perpetual income stream of constant nominal amount, then the return to a holder of the bond can take two forms: one, the annual sum he receives—the "coupon"; the other, any change in the price of the bond over time, a return which may of course be positive or negative. If the price is expected to remain constant, then $1 worth of a bond yields r_b per year, where r_b is simply the "coupon" sum divided by the market price of the bond, so $1/r_b$ is the price of a bond promising to pay $1 per year. We shall call r_b the market bond interest rate. If the price is expected to change, then the yield cannot be calculated so simply, since it must take account of the return in the form of expected appreciation or depreciation of the bond, and it cannot, like r_b, be calculated directly from market prices (so long, at least, as the "standard" bond is the only one traded in).

The nominal income stream purchased for $1 at time zero then consists of

$$r_b(0)+r_b(0)d\frac{\left(\frac{1}{r_b(t)}\right)}{dt}=r_b(0)-\frac{r_b(0)}{r_b^2(t)}\cdot\frac{dr_b(t)}{dt}, \tag{2}$$

where t stands for time. For simplicity, we can approximate this functional by its value at time zero, which is

$$r_b-\frac{1}{r_b}\frac{dr_b}{dt}. \tag{3}$$

This sum, together with P already introduced, defines the real return from holding $1 of wealth in the form of bonds.

(iii) Analogously to our treatment of bonds, we may take the "standard" unit of equity to be a claim to a perpetual income stream of constant "real" amount; that is, to be a standard bond with a purchasing-power escalator clause, so that it promises a perpetual income stream equal in nominal units to a constant number times a price index, which we may, for convenience, take to be the same price index P introduced in (i).[1] The nominal return to the holder of the equity can then be regarded as taking three forms: the constant nominal amount he would receive per year in the absence of any change in P; the increment or decrement to this nominal amount to adjust for changes in P; and any change in the nominal price of the equity over time, which may of course arise from changes either in interest rates or in price levels. Let r_e be the market interest rate on equities defined analogously to r_b, namely, as the ratio of the "coupon" sum at any time (the first two items above) to the price of the equity, so $1/r_e$ is the price of an equity promising to pay \$1 per year if the price level does not change, or to pay

$$\frac{P(t)}{P(0)} \cdot 1$$

if the price level varies according to $P(t)$. If $r_e(t)$ is defined analogously, the price of the equity selling for $1/r_e(0)$ at time 0 will be

$$\frac{P(t)}{P(0)r_e(t)}$$

at time t, where the ratio of prices is required to adjust for any change in the price level. The nominal stream purchased for \$1 at time zero then consists of

$$r_e(0) \cdot \frac{P(t)}{P(0)} + \frac{r_e(0)}{P(0)} \cdot d\frac{\left[\dfrac{P(t)}{r_e(t)}\right]}{dt} = r_e(0) \cdot \frac{P(t)}{P(0)}$$

$$+ \frac{r_e(0)}{r_e(t)} \cdot \frac{1}{P(0)} \cdot \frac{dP(t)}{dt} - \frac{P(t)}{P(0)} \cdot \frac{r_e(0)}{r_e^2(t)} \cdot \frac{dr_e(t)}{dt}.$$

(4)

Once again we can approximate this functional by its value at time zero, which is

$$r_e + \frac{1}{P}\frac{dP}{dt} - \frac{1}{r_e}\frac{dr_e}{dt}.$$

(5)

This sum, together with P already introduced, defines the "real" return from holding \$1 of wealth in the form of equities.

(iv) Physical goods held by ultimate wealth-owning units are similar to equities except that the annual stream they yield is in kind rather than in money. In terms of nominal units, this return, like that from equities, depends on the behavior of prices. In addition, like equities, physical goods must be regarded as yielding a nominal return in the form of appreciation or depreciation in money value. If we suppose the price level P, introduced earlier, to apply equally to the value of these physical goods, then, at time zero,

$$\frac{1}{P}\frac{dP}{dT} \tag{6}$$

is the size of this nominal return per \$1 of physical goods.[2] Together with P, it defines the "real" return from holding \$1 in the form of physical goods.

(v) Since there is only a limited market in human capital, at least in modern nonslave societies, we cannot very well define in market prices the terms of substitution of human capital for other forms of capital and so cannot define at any time the physical unit of capital corresponding to \$1 of human capital. There are some possibilities of substituting nonhuman capital for human capital in an individual's wealth holdings, as, for example, when he enters into a contract to render personal services for a specified period in return for a definitely specified number of periodic payments, the number not depending on his being physically capable of rendering the services. But, in the main, shifts between human capital and other forms must take place through direct investment and disinvestment in the human agent, and we may as well treat this as if it were the only way. With respect to this form of capital, therefore, the restriction or obstacles affecting the alternative compositions of wealth available to the individual cannot be expressed in terms of market prices or rates of return. At any one point in time there is some division between human and nonhuman wealth in his portfolio of assets; he may be able to change this over time, but we shall treat it as given at a point in time. Let w be the ratio of nonhuman to human wealth or, equivalently, of income from nonhuman wealth to income from human wealth, which means that it is closely allied to what is usually defined as the ratio of wealth to income. This is, then, the variable that needs to be taken into account so far as human wealth is concerned.

6. The tastes and preferences of wealth-owning units for the service streams arising from different forms of wealth must in general simply be taken for granted as determining the form of the demand function. In order to give the theory empirical content, it will generally have to be supposed that tastes are constant over significant stretches of space and time. However, explicit allowance can be made for some changes in tastes in so far as such changes are

linked with objective circumstances. For example, it seems reasonable that, other things the same, individuals want to hold a larger fraction of their wealth in the form of money when they are moving around geographically or are subject to unusual uncertainty than otherwise. This is probably one of the major factors explaining a frequent tendency for money holdings to rise relative to income during wartime. But the extent of geographic movement, and perhaps of other kinds of uncertainty, can be represented by objective indexes, such as indexes of migration, miles of railroad travel, and the like. Let u stand for any such variables that can be expected to affect tastes and preferences (for "utility" determining variables).

7. Combining 4, 5, and 6 along the lines suggested by 3 yields the following demand function for money:

$$M = f\left(P, \ r_b - \frac{1}{r_b}\frac{dr_b}{dt}, \ r_e + \frac{1}{P}\frac{dP}{dt} - \frac{1}{r_e}\frac{dr_e}{dt}, \ \frac{1}{P}\frac{dP}{dt}; \ w; \ \frac{Y}{r}; \ u\right). \tag{7}$$

A number of observations are in order about this function.

(i) Even if we suppose prices and rates of interest unchanged, the function contains three rates of interest: two for specific types of assets, r_b and r_e, and one intended to apply to all types of assets, r. This general rate, r, is to be interpreted as something of a weighted average of the two special rates plus the rates applicable to human wealth and to physical goods. Since the latter two cannot be observed directly, it is perhaps best to regard them as varying in some systematic way with r_b and r_e. On this assumption, we can drop r as an additional explicit variable, treating its influence as fully taken into account by the inclusion of r_b and r_e.

(ii) If there were no differences of opinion about price movements and interest-rate movements, and bonds and equities were equivalent except that the former are expressed in nominal units, arbitrage would of course make

$$r_b - \frac{1}{r_b}\frac{dr_b}{dt} = r_e + \frac{1}{P}\frac{dP}{dt} - \frac{1}{r_e}\frac{dr_e}{dt}, \tag{8}$$

or, if we suppose rates of interest either stable or changing at the same percentage rate,

$$r_b = r_e + \frac{1}{P}\frac{dP}{dt}, \tag{9}$$

that is, the "money" interest rate equal to the "real" rate plus the percentage rate of change of prices. In application the rate of change of prices must be interpreted as an "expected" rate of change and differences of opinion cannot be neglected, so we cannot suppose equation (9) to hold; indeed, one of the most consistent features of inflation seems to be that it does not.[3]

(iii) If the range of assets were to be widened to include promises to pay specified sums for a finite number of time units—"short-term" securities as well as "consols"—the rate of change of r_b and r_e would be reflected in the difference between long and short rates of interest. Since at some stage it will doubtless be desirable to introduce securities of different time duration (see point 23 below), we may simplify the present exposition by restricting it to the case in which r_b and r_e are taken to be stable over time. Since the rate of change in prices is required separately in any event, this means that we can replace the cumbrous variables introduced to designate the nominal return on bonds and equities simply by r_b and r_e.

(iv) Y can be interpreted as including the return to all forms of wealth, including money and physical capital goods owned and held directly by ultimate wealth-owning units, and so Y/r can be interpreted as an estimate of total wealth, only if Y is regarded as including some imputed income from the stock of money and directly owned physical capital goods. For monetary analysis the simplest procedure is perhaps to regard Y as referring to the return to all forms of wealth other than the money held directly by ultimate wealth-owning units, and so Y/r as referring to total remaining wealth.

8. A more fundamental point is that, as in all demand analyses resting on maximization of a utility function defined in terms of "real" magnitudes, this demand equation must be considered independent in any essential way of the nominal units used to measure money variables. If the unit in which prices and money income are expressed is changed, the amount of money demanded should change proportionately. More technically, equation (7) must be regarded as homogeneous of the first degree in P and Y, so that

$$f\left(\lambda P, r_b, r_e, \frac{1}{P}\frac{dP}{dt}; w; \lambda Y; u\right)=\lambda f\left(P, r_b, r_e, \frac{1}{P}\frac{dP}{dt}; w; Y; u\right). \quad (10)$$

where the variables within the parentheses have been rewritten in simpler form in accordance with comments 7(i) and 7(iii).

This characteristic of the function enables us to rewrite it in two alternative and more familiar ways.

(i) Let $\lambda = 1/P$. Equation (7) can then be written

$$\frac{M}{P}=f\left(r_b, r_e, \frac{1}{P}\frac{dP}{dt}; w; \frac{Y}{P}; u\right). \quad (11)$$

In this form the equation expresses the demand for real balances as a function of "real" variables independent of nominal monetary values.

(ii) Let $\lambda = 1/Y$. Equation (7) can then be written

$$\frac{M}{Y} = f\left(r_b, r_e, \frac{1}{P}\frac{dP}{dt}, w, \frac{P}{Y}, u\right) = \frac{1}{v\left(r_b, r_e, \frac{1}{P}\frac{dP}{dt}, w, \frac{Y}{P}, u\right)}, \qquad (12)$$

or

$$Y = v\left(r_b, r_e, \frac{1}{P}\frac{dP}{dt}, w, \frac{Y}{P}, u\right) \cdot M. \qquad (13)$$

In this form the equation is in the usual quantity theory form, where v is income velocity.

9. These equations are, to this point, solely for money held directly by ultimate wealth-owning units. As noted, money is also held by business enterprises as a productive resource. The counterpart to this business asset in the balance sheet of an ultimate wealth-owning unit is a claim other than money. For example, an individual may buy bonds from a corporation, and the corporation use the proceeds to finance the money holdings which it needs for its operations. Of course, the usual difficulties of separating the accounts of the business and its owner arise with unincorporated enterprises.

10. The amount of money that it pays business enterprises to hold depends, as for any other source of productive services, on the cost of the productive services, the cost of substitute productive services, and the value product yielded by the productive service. Per dollar of money held, the cost depends on how the corresponding capital is raised—whether by raising additional capital in the form of bonds or equities, by substituting cash for real capital goods, etc. These ways of financing money holdings are much the same as the alternative forms in which the ultimate wealth-owning unit can hold its nonhuman wealth, so that the variables r_b, r_e, P, and $(1/P)(dP/dt)$ introduced into equation (7) can be taken to represent the cost to the business enterprise of holding money. For some purposes, however, it may be desirable to distinguish between the rate of return received by the lender and the rate paid by the borrower; in which case it would be necessary to introduce an additional set of variables.

Substitutes for money as a productive service are numerous and varied, including all ways of economizing on money holdings by using other resources to synchronize more closely payments and receipts, reduce payment periods, extend use of book credit, establish clearing arrangements, and so on in infinite variety. There seem no particularly close substitutes whose prices deserve to be singled out for inclusion in the business demand for money.

The value product yielded by the productive services of money per unit of output depends on production conditions: the production function. It is likely to be especially dependent on features of production conditions affecting the smoothness and regularity of operations as well as on those determining the size and scope of enterprises, degree of vertical integration, etc. Again there seem no variables that deserve to be singled out on the present level of abstraction for special attention; these factors can be taken into account by interpreting u as including variables affecting not only the tastes of wealth-owners but also the relevant technological conditions of production. Given the amount of money demanded per unit of output, the total amount demanded is proportional to total output, which can be represented by Y.

11. One variable that has traditionally been singled out in considering the demand for money on the part of business enterprises is the volume of transactions, or of transactions per dollar of final products; and, of course, emphasis on transactions has been carried over to the ultimate wealth-owning unit as well as to the business enterprise. The idea that renders this approach attractive is that there is a mechanical link between a dollar of payments per unit time and the average stock of money required to effect it—a fixed technical coefficient of production, as it were. It is clear that this mechanical approach is very different in spirit from the one we have been following. On our approach, the average amount of money held per dollar of transactions is itself to be regarded as a resultant of an economic equilibrating process, not as a physical datum. If, for whatever reason, it becomes more expensive to hold money, then it is worth devoting resources to effecting money transactions in less expensive ways or to reducing the volume of transactions per dollar of final output. In consequence, our ultimate demand function for money in its most general form does not contain as a variable the volume of transactions or of transactions per dollar of final output; it contains rather those more basic technical and cost conditions that affect the costs of conserving money, be it by changing the average amount of money held per dollar of transactions per unit time or by changing the number of dollars of transactions per dollar of final output. This does not, of course, exclude the possibility that, for a particular problem, it may be useful to regard the transactions variables as given and not to dig beneath them and so to include the volume of transactions per dollar of final output as an explicit variable in a special variant of the demand function.

Similar remarks are relevant to various features of payment conditions, frequently described as "institutional conditions," affecting the velocity of circulation of money and taken as somehow mechanically determined—such items as whether workers are paid by the day or week or month; the use of book credit; and so on. On our approach these, too, are to be regarded as resultants of an economic equilibrating process, not as physical data. Lengthening the pay period, for example, may save bookkeeping and other costs to the employer, who is therefore willing to pay somewhat more than in proportion for a longer than a shorter pay period; on the other hand, it imposes on employees the cost of holding larger cash balances or providing substitutes for cash, and they therefore want to be paid more than in proportion for a longer pay period. Where these will balance depends on how costs vary with length of pay period. The cost to the employee depends in considerable part on the factors entering into his demand curve for money for a fixed pay period. If he would in any event be holding relatively large average balances, the additional costs imposed by a lengthened pay period tend to be less than if he would be holding relatively small average balances, and so it will take less of an inducement to get him to accept a longer pay period. For given cost savings to the employer, therefore, the pay period can be expected to be longer in the first case than in the second. Surely, the increase in the average cash balance over the past century in this country that has occurred for other reasons has been a factor producing a lengthening of pay periods and not the other way around. Or, again, experience in hyperinflations shows how rapidly payment practices change under the impact of drastic changes in the cost of holding money.

12. The upshot of these considerations is that the demand for money on the part of business enterprises can be regarded as expressed by a function of the same kind as equation (7), with the same variables on the right-hand side. And, like (7), since the analysis is based on informed maximization of returns by enterprises, only "real" quantities matter, so it must be homogeneous of the first degree in Y and P. In consequence, we can interpret equation (7) and its variants (11) and (13) as describing the demand for money on the part of a business enterprise as well as on the part of an ultimate wealth-owning unit, provided only that we broaden our interpretation of u.

13. Strictly speaking, the equations (7), (11), and (13) are for an individual wealth-owning unit or business enterprise. If we aggregate (7) for all wealth-owning units and business enterprises in the society, the result, in principle, depends on the distribution of the units by the several variables. This raises no serious problem about P, r_b, and r_e, for these can be taken as the same for all, or about u, for this is an unspecified portmanteau variable to be filled in as the occasion demands. We have been interpreting $(1/P)(dP/dt)$ as the expected rate of price rise, so there is no reason why this variable should be the same for all, and w and Y clearly differ substantially among units. An approximation is to neglect these difficulties and take equation (7) and the associated (11) and (13) as applying to the aggregate demand for money, with $(1/P)(dP/dt)$ interpreted as some kind of an average expected rate of change of prices, w as the ratio of total income from nonhuman wealth to income from human wealth, and Y as aggregate income. This is the procedure that has generally been followed, and it seems the right one until serious departures between this linear approxima-

tion and experience make it necessary to introduce measures of dispersion with respect to one or more of the variables.

14. It is perhaps worth noting explicitly that the model does not use the distinction between "active balances" and "idle balances" or the closely allied distinction between "transaction balances" and "speculative balances" that is so widely used in the literature. The distinction between money holdings of ultimate wealth-owners and of business enterprises is related to this distinction but only distantly so. Each of these categories of money-holders can be said to demand money partly from "transaction" motives, partly from "speculative" or "asset" motives, but dollars of money are not distinguished according as they are said to be held for one or the other purpose. Rather, each dollar is, as it were, regarded as rendering a variety of services, and the holder of money as altering his money holdings until the value to him of the addition to the total flow of services produced by adding a dollar to his money stock is equal to the reduction in the flow of services produced by subtracting a dollar from each of the other forms in which he holds assets.

15. Nothing has been said above about "banks" or producers of money. This is because their main role is in connection with the supply of money rather than the demand for it. Their introduction does, however, blur some of the points in the above analysis: the existence of banks enables productive enterprises to acquire money balances without raising capital from ultimate wealth-owners. Instead of selling claims (bonds or equities) to them, it can sell its claims to banks, getting "money" in exchange: in the phrase that was once so common in textbooks on money, the bank coins specific liabilities into generally acceptable liabilities. But this possibility does not alter the preceding analysis in any essential way.

16. Suppose the supply of money in nominal units is regarded as fixed or more generally autonomously determined. Equation (13) then defines the conditions under which this nominal stock of money will be the amount demanded. Even under these conditions, equation (13) alone is not sufficient to determine money income. In order to have a complete model for the determination of money income, it would be necessary to specify the determinants of the structure of interest rates, of real income, and of the path of adjustment in the price level. Even if we suppose interest rates determined independently—by productivity, thrift, and the like—and real income as also given by other forces, equation (13) only determines a unique equilibrium level of money income if we mean by this the level at which prices are stable. More generally, it determines a time path of money income for given initial values of money income.

In order to convert equation (13) into a "complete" model of income determination, therefore, it is necessary to suppose either that the demand for money is highly inelastic with respect to the variables in v or that all these variables are to be taken as rigid and fixed.

17. Even under the most favorable conditions, for example, that the demand for money is quite inelastic with respect to the variables in v, equation (13) gives at most a theory of money income: it then says that changes in money income mirror changes in the nominal quantity of money. But it tells nothing about how much of any change in Y is reflected in real output and how much in prices. To infer this requires bringing in outside information, as, for example, that real output is at its feasible maximum, in which case any increase in money would produce the same or a larger percentage increase in prices; and so on.

18. In light of the preceding exposition, the question arises what it means to say that someone is or is not a "quantity theorist." Almost every economist will accept the general lines of the preceding analysis on a purely formal and abstract level, although each would doubtless choose to express it differently in detail. Yet there clearly are deep and fundamental differences about the importance of this analysis for the understanding of short- and long-term movements in general economic activity. This difference of opinion arises with respect to three different issues: (i) the stability and importance of the demand function for money; (ii) the independence of the factors affecting demand and supply; and (iii) the form of the demand function or related functions.

(i) The quantity theorist accepts the empirical hypothesis that the demand for money is highly stable—more stable than functions such as the consumption function that are offered as alternative key relations. This hypothesis needs to be hedged on both sides. On the one side, the quantity theorist need not, and generally does not, mean that the real quantity of money demanded per unit of output, or the velocity of circulation of money, is to be regarded as numerically constant over time; he does not, for example, regard it as a contradiction to the stability of the demand for money that the velocity of circulation of money rises drastically during hyperinflations. For the stability he expects is in the functional relation between the quantity of money demanded and the variables that determine it, and the sharp rise in the velocity of circulation of money during hyperinflations is entirely consistent with a stable functional relation, as Cagan so clearly demonstrates in his essay.[4] On the other side, the quantity theorist must sharply limit, and be prepared to specify explicitly, the variables that it is empirically important to include in the function. For to expand the number of variables regarded as significant is to empty the hypothesis of its empirical content; there is indeed little if any difference between asserting that the demand for money is highly unstable and asserting that it is a perfectly stable function of an indefinitely large number of variables.

The quantity theorist not only regards the demand function for money as stable; he also regards it as playing a vital role in determining variables that he regards as of great importance for the analysis of the economy as a whole, such as the level of money income or of prices. It is this that leads him to put greater emphasis on the demand for money than on, let us say, the demand for pins, even though the latter might be as stable as the former. It is not easy to state this point precisely, and I cannot pretend to have done so. (See item [iii] below for an example of an argument against the quantity theorist along these lines.)

The reaction against the quantity theory in the 1930s came largely, I believe, under this head. The demand for money, it was asserted, is a will-o'-the-wisp, shifting erratically and unpredictably with every rumor and expectation; one cannot, it was asserted, reliably specify a limited number of variables on which it depends. However, although the reaction came under this head, it was largely rationalized under the two succeeding heads.

(ii) The quantity theorist also holds that there are important factors affecting the supply of money that do not affect the demand for money. Under some circumstances these are technical conditions affecting the supply of specie; under others, political or psychological conditions determining the policies of monetary authorities and the banking system. A stable demand function is useful precisely in order to trace out the effects of changes in supply, which means that it is useful only if supply is affected by at least some factors other than those regarded as affecting demand.

The classical version of the objection under this head to the quantity theory is the so-called real-bills doctrine: that changes in the demand for money call forth corresponding changes in supply and that supply cannot change otherwise, or at least cannot do so under specified institutional arrangements. The forms which this argument takes are legion and are still widespread. Another version is the argument that the "quantity theory" cannot "explain" large price rises, because the price rise produced both the increase in demand for nominal money holdings and the increase in supply of money to meet it; that is, implicitly that the same forces affect both the demand for and the supply of money, and in the same way.

(iii) The attack on the quantity theory associated with the Keynesian underemployment analysis is based primarily on an assertion about the form of equation (7) or (11). The demand for money, it is said, is infinitely elastic at a "small" positive interest rate. At this interest rate, which can be expected to prevail under underemployment conditions, changes in the real supply of money, whether produced by changes in prices or in the nominal stock of money, have no effect on anything. This is the famous "liquidity trap." A rather more complex version involves the shape of other functions as well: the magnitudes in equation (7) other than "the" interest rate, it is argued, enter into other relations in the economic system and can be regarded as determined there; the interest rate does not enter into these other functions; it can therefore be regarded as determined by this equation. So the only role of the stock of money and the demand for money is to determine the interest rate.

19. The proof of this pudding is in the eating; and the essays in this book contain much relevant food, of which I may perhaps mention three particularly juicy items.

One cannot read Lerner's description of the effects of monetary reform in the Confederacy in 1864 without recognizing that at least on occasion the supply of money can be a largely autonomous factor and the demand for money highly stable even under extraordinarily unstable circumstances.[5] After three years of war, after widespread destruction and military reverses, in the face of impending defeat, a monetary reform that succeeded in reducing the stock of money halted and reversed for some months a rise in prices that had been going on at the rate of 10 percent a month most of the war! It would be hard to construct a better controlled experiment to demonstrate the critical importance of the supply of money.

On the other hand, Klein's examination of German experience in World War II is much less favorable to the stability and importance of the demand for money.[6] Though he shows that defects in the figures account for a sizable part of the crude discrepancy between changes in the recorded stock of money and in recorded prices, correction of these defects still leaves a puzzlingly large discrepancy that it does not seem possible to account for in terms of the variables introduced into the above exposition of the theory. Klein examined German experience precisely because it seemed the most deviant on a casual examination. Both it and other wartime experience will clearly repay further examination.

Cagan's examination of hyperinflations is another important piece of evidence on the stability of the demand for money under highly unstable conditions. It is also an interesting example of the difference between a numerically stable velocity and a stable functional relation: the numerical value of the velocity varied enormously during the hyperinflations, but this was a predictable response to the changes in the expected rate of changes of prices.

20. Though the essays in this book contain evidence relevant to the issues discussed in point 18, this is a byproduct rather than their main purpose, which is rather to add to our tested knowledge about the characteristics of the demand function for money. In the process of doing so, they also raise some questions about the theoretical formulation and suggest some modifications it might be desirable to introduce. I shall comment on a few of those without attempting to summarize at all fully the essays themselves.

21. Selden's material covers the longest period of time and the most "normal" conditions.[7] This is at once a virtue and a vice—a virtue because it means that his results may be applicable most directly to ordinary peacetime

experience; a vice because "normality" is likely to spell little variation in the fundamental variables and hence a small base from which to judge their effect. The one variable that covers a rather broad range is real income, thanks to the length of the period. The secular rise in real income has been accompanied by a rise in real cash balances per unit of output—a decline in velocity—from which Selden concludes that the income elasticity of the demand for real balances is greater than unity—cash balances are a "luxury" in the terminology generally adopted. This entirely plausible result seems to be confirmed by evidence for other countries as well.

22. Selden finds that for cyclical periods velocity rises during expansions and falls during contractions, a result that at first glance seems to contradict the secular result just cited. However, there is an alternative explanation entirely consistent with the secular result. It will be recalled that Y was introduced into equation (7) as an index of wealth. This has important implications for the measure or concept of income that is relevant. What is required by the theoretical analysis is not usual measured income—which in the main corresponds to current receipts corrected for double counting—but a longer term concept, "expected income," or what I have elsewhere called "permanent income."[8] Now suppose that the variables in the v function of equation (13) are unchanged for a period. The ratio of Y to M would then be unchanged, provided Y is *permanent* income. Velocity as Selden computes it is the ratio of *measured* income to the stock of money and would not be unchanged. When measured income was above permanent income, measured velocity would be relatively high, and conversely. Now measured income is presumably above permanent income at cyclical peaks and below permanent income at cyclical troughs. The observed positive conformity of measured velocity to cyclical changes of income may therefore reflect simply the difference between measured income and the concept relevant to equation (13).

23. Another point that is raised by Selden's work is the appropriate division of wealth into forms of assets. The division suggested above is, of course, only suggestive. Selden finds more useful the distinction between "short-term" and "long-term" bonds; he treats the former as "substitutes for money" and calls the return on the latter "the cost of holding money." He finds both to be significantly related to the quantity of money demanded. It was suggested above that this is also a way to take into account expectations about changes in interest rates.

Similarly, there is no hard-and-fast line between "money" and other assets, and for some purposes it may be desirable to distinguish between different forms of "money" (e.g., between currency and deposits). Some of these forms of money may pay interest or may involve service charges, in which case the positive or negative return will be a relevant variable in determining the division of money holdings among various forms.

24. By concentrating on hyperinflations, Cagan was able to bring into sharp relief a variable whose effect is generally hard to evaluate, namely, the rate of change of prices. The other side of this coin is the necessity of neglecting practically all the remaining variables. His device for estimating expected rates of change of prices from actual rates of change, which works so well for his data, can be carried over to other variables as well and so is likely to be important in fields other than money. I have already used it to estimate "expected income" as a determinant of consumption,[9] and Gary Becker has experimented with using this "expected income" series in a demand function for money along the lines suggested above (in point 22).

Cagan's results make it clear that changes in the rate of change of prices, or in the return to an alternative form of holding wealth, have the expected effect on the quantity of money demanded: the higher the rate of change of prices, and thus the more attractive the alternative, the less the quantity of money demanded. This result is important not only directly but also because it is indirectly relevant to the effect of changes in the returns to other alternatives, such as rates of interest on various kinds of bonds. Our evidence on these is in some way less satisfactory because they have varied over so much smaller a range; tentative findings that the effect of changes in them is in the expected direction are greatly strengthened by Cagan's results.

One point which is suggested by the inapplicability of Cagan's relations to the final stages of the hyperinflations he studies is that it may at times be undesirable to replace the whole expected pattern of price movements by the rate of change expected at the moment, as Cagan does and as is done in point 5 above. For example, a given rate of price rise, expected to continue, say, for only a day, and to be followed by price stability, will clearly mean a higher (real) demand for money than the same rate of price rise expected to continue indefinitely; it will be worth incurring greater costs to avoid paying the latter than the former price. This is the same complication as occurs in demand analysis for a consumer good when it is necessary to include not only the present price but also past prices or future expected prices. This point may help explain not only Cagan's findings for the terminal stages but also Selden's findings that the inclusion of the rate of change of prices as part of the cost of holding money worsened rather than improved his estimated relations, though it may be that this result arises from a different source, namely, that it takes substantial actual rates of price change to produce firm enough and uniform enough expectations about price behavior for this variable to play a crucial role.

Similar comments are clearly relevant for expected changes in interest rates.

25. One of the chief reproaches directed at economics as an allegedly empirical science is that it can offer so few numerical "constants," that it has

isolated so few fundamental regularities. The field of money is the chief example one can offer in rebuttal: there is perhaps no other empirical relation in economics that has been observed to recur so uniformly under so wide a variety of circumstances as the relation between substantial changes over short periods in the stock of money and in prices; the one is invariably linked with the other and is in the same direction; this uniformity is, I suspect, of the same order as many of the uniformities that form the basis of the physical sciences. And the uniformity is in more than direction. There is an extraordinary empirical stability and regularity to such magnitudes as income velocity that cannot but impress anyone who works extensively with monetary data. This very stability and regularity contributed to the downfall of the quantity theory, for it was overstated and expressed in unduly simple form; the numerical value of the velocity itself, whether income or transactions, was treated as a natural "constant." Now this it is not; and its failure to be so, first during and after World War I and then, to a lesser extent, after the crash of 1929, helped greatly to foster the reaction against the quantity theory. The studies in this volume are premised on a stability and regularity in monetary relations of a more sophisticated form than a numerically constant velocity. And they make, I believe, an important contribution toward extracting this stability and reg-ularity, toward isolating the numerical "constants" of monetary behavior. It is by this criterion at any rate that I, and I believe also their authors, would wish them to be judged.

I began by referring to the tradition in the field of money at Chicago and to the role of faculty members in promoting it. I think it is fitting to end by emphasizing the part which students have played in keeping that tradition alive and vigorous. The essays that follow are one manifestation. Unpublished doctoral dissertations on money are another. In addition, I wish especially to express my own personal appreciation to the students who have participated with me in the workshop in money and banking, of which this volume is the first published fruit. I owe a special debt to David I. Fand, Phillip Cagan, Gary Becker, David Meiselman, and Raymond Zelder, who have at various times helped me to conduct it.

We all of us are indebted also to the Rockefeller Foundation for financial assistance to the workshop in money and banking. This assistance helped to finance some of the research reported in this book and has made possible its publication.

NOTES

1. This is an oversimplification, because it neglects "leverage" and therefore sup-poses that any monetary liabilities of an enterprise are balanced by monetary assets.

2. In principle, it might be better to let *P* refer solely to the value of the services of physical goods, which is essentially what it refers to in the preceding cases, and to allow for the fact that the prices of the capital goods themselves must vary also with the rate of capitalization, so that the prices of services and their sources vary at the same rate only if the relevant interest rate is constant. I have neglected this refinement for simplicity; the neglect can perhaps be justified by the rapid depreciation of many of the physical goods held by final wealth-owning units.

3. See Reuben Kessel, "Inflation: Theory of Wealth Distribution and Application in Private Investment Policy," unpublished doctoral dissertation, University of Chicago.

4. Phillip Cagan, "The Monetary Dynamics of Hyperinflation," in Milton Friedman, ed., *Studies in the Quantity Theory of Money* (Chicago: University of Chicago Press, 1973), chap. 2.

5. Eugene M. Lerner, "Inflation in the Confederacy, 1861–65," in Friedman, ed., *Studies in the Quantity Theory of Money*, chap. 4.

6. John J. Klein, "German Money and Prices, 1932–44," in Friedman, ed., *Studies in the Quantity Theory of Money*, chap 3.

7. Richard T. Selden, "Monetary Velocity in the United States," in Friedman, ed., *Studies in the Quantity Theory of Money*, chap. 5.

8. See Milton Friedman, *A Theory of the Consumption Function* (Princeton, N.J.: Princeton University Press, 1957).

9. See ibid.

THE SUPPLY OF MONEY
AND CHANGES IN
PRICES AND OUTPUT

· 17 ·

This paper deals with two broad issues that have arisen again and again in connection with movements in the general level of prices. One issue is the connection between such price movements and changes in the supply of money. The other is the relation between price changes and changes in output.

The course of economic history is replete with substantial price disturbances. Whenever such disturbances have occurred, two different explanations have been offered. One, common to all disturbances, is that the price movements reflect changes in the quantity of money, though the source of the monetary changes has varied widely—from clipping of currency to gold discoveries to changes in the monetary standard to the printing of paper money to the creation or destruction of deposit money by central banks and commercial banks. The other explanation has been in terms of some special circumstances of the particular occasion: good or bad harvests; disruptions in international trade; lack of confidence; the activities of "profiteers" or "monopolists" selling goods or of employers seeking to hold down wages; the activities of workers or unions pushing wages up; and so on in great variety. Perhaps the one common core of such explanations is that they generally attribute the price

From Milton Friedman, *The Optimum Quantity of Money and Other Essays* (Chicago: Aldine Publishing Co., 1969). Initially published in *The Relationship of Prices to Economic Stability and Growth*, Joint Economic Committee Print (Washington, D.C.: U.S. Government Printing Office, 1957).

movements to the (socially) misguided behavior of particular individuals or groups. My own view is that these alternative explanations play little or no role in either long-run or large movements in prices, though they may in short and minor movements, except indirectly as they affect the supply of money. It is clearly impossible to argue this view in detail within the compass of this paper. My reason for stating it is to make clear that I am putting such explanations to one side and concentrating instead on the monetary forces at work.

The relation between the supply of money and prices has been explored so frequently and thoroughly that I can hardly hope to add much that is new on an analytical level. My reason for dealing with it nonetheless is twofold: on the one hand, though it is the essence of the problem of long-run and large price movements, it tends to be pushed to one side and neglected—partly, perhaps, because of the desire to be novel; on the other hand, extensive empirical work that is currently underway puts flesh on the analytical skeleton to an extent that has not heretofore been possible. One of the major aims and justifications of this paper is to summarize some of the broad findings of this work.[1] I shall do so in section 1 for the longer term changes in money and prices, in section 2, for the shorter term changes.

Discussion of public policy with respect to prices necessarily involves the issue what kind of movements are socially desirable. One major problem is the relation of price movements to economic growth. Is a rising price level favorable or unfavorable to rapid growth in output? No conclusive answer can be given to this question in the present state of our knowledge. Some analysis and evidence to justify this assertion are given in section 3.

The final section of this paper presents some implications for policy that are suggested by the relation between monetary and price change and between price change and output change.

1. Relation of Stock of Money to Prices over Longer Periods

There is perhaps no empirical regularity among economic phenomena that is based on so much evidence for so wide a range of circumstances as the connection between substantial changes in the stock of money and in the level of prices.[2] To the best of my knowledge there is no instance in which a substantial change in the stock of money per unit of output has occurred without a substantial change in the level of prices in the same direction.[3] Conversely, I know of no instance in which there has been a substantial change in the level of prices without a substantial change in the stock of money per unit of output in the same direction. And instances in which prices and the stock of money have moved together are recorded for many centuries of history, for countries in every part of the globe, and for a wide diversity of monetary arrangements.

There can be little doubt about this statistical connection. The statistical connection itself, however, tells nothing about direction of influence, and it is on this question that there has been the most controversy. It could be that a rise or fall in prices, occurring for whatever reasons, produces a corresponding rise or fall in the stock of money, so that the monetary changes are a passive consequence. Alternatively, it could be that changes in the stock of money produce changes in prices in the same direction, so that control of the stock of money would imply control of prices. The variety of monetary arrangements for which a connection between monetary and price movements has been observed supports strongly the second interpretation, namely, that substantial changes in the stock of money are both a necessary and a sufficient condition for substantial changes in the general level of prices. But of course this does not exclude a reflex influence of changes in prices on the stock of money. This reflex influence is often important, almost always complex, and, depending on the monetary arrangements, may be in either direction.[4]

This general evidence is reinforced by much historical evidence of a more specific character demonstrating that changes in the stock of money, at least when they are fairly large, can exert an independent influence on prices. One dramatic example is from the experience of the Confederacy during the Civil War. In 1864, "after 3 years of war, after widespread destruction and military reverses, in the face of impending defeat, a monetary reform that succeeded in reducing the stock of money halted and reversed for some months a rise in prices that had been going on at the rate of 10 percent a month most of the war. It would be hard to construct a better controlled experiment to demonstrate the critical importance of the supply of money."[5] The effect of discoveries of precious metals in the New World in the sixteenth century and of gold in California and Australia in the 1840s, of the development of the cyanide process for extracting ore plus gold discoveries in South Africa in the 1890s, and of the printing of money in various hyperinflations, including our own Revolutionary War experience and the experience of many countries after World War I and World War II, are other striking examples of increases in the stock of money producing increases in prices. The long price decline in the second half of the nineteenth century in many parts of the world is a less dramatic example of a decline in the stock of money per unit of output producing a decline in prices.[6]

The relationship between changes in the stock of money and changes in prices, while close, is not of course precise or mechanically rigid. Two major factors produce discrepancies: changes in output, and changes in the amount of money that the public desires to hold relative to its income.

For the moment, we shall treat output as if it were determined independently of monetary and price changes, postponing to section 3 the relation between them. This is clearly a simplification that is to some extent contrary to fact, but certainly for the longer periods and larger changes that are discussed in this section, the simplification neither does serious violence to the facts nor leads to any significant errors in conclusions.

Suppose the stock of money were to remain unchanged for a period of years but total output over the same period were to double. Clearly, one would expect prices to fall—other things remaining the same—to something like half their initial level. The total amount of "work" for the money stock to do, as it were, is doubled, and the same nominal quantity of money could perform the "work" only at lower levels of prices. Roughly speaking, this is what happened in the United States in the period from the end of the Civil War in 1865 to the resumption of specie payments in 1879. The stock of money was roughly the same in 1879 as in 1865—if anything, some 10 percent higher; output grew very rapidly over the period, probably more than doubling; and wholesale prices were half their initial level.[7] Thus, for price movements, the relevant variable is the stock of money per unit of output, not simply the global stock of money.

The second major factor that can introduce a discrepancy between movements in money and in prices is a change in the ratio that the public desires to maintain between its cash balances and its income[8]—the public including individuals, business enterprises other than banks, nonprofit institutions, and the like. The number of dollars an individual wants to keep in cash depends of course on the price level—at twice the price level he will want to hold something like twice the number of dollars—and on his income—the higher his income presumably the larger cash balances he will want to hold. But the price level is what we are trying to explain, and we have already taken account of the effect of changes in output. This is why we express this factor in terms of the ratio that the public desires to maintain between its cash balances and its income, rather than in terms of the number of dollars it desires to hold.

Broadly speaking, the public as a whole cannot by itself affect the total number of dollars available to be held—this is determined primarily by the monetary institutions. To each individual separately, it appears that he can do so; in fact an individual can reduce or increase his cash balance in general only through another individual's increasing or reducing his. If individuals as a whole, for example, try to reduce the number of dollars they hold, they cannot as an aggregate do so. In trying to do so, however, they will raise the flow of expenditures and hence of money income and in this way will reduce the ratio of their cash balances to their income; since prices will tend to rise in the process, they will thereby reduce the real value of their cash balances, that is, the quantity of goods and services that the cash balances will command; and the process will continue until this ratio or this real value is in accord with their desires.

A wide range of empirical evidence suggests that the ratio which people desire to maintain between their cash balances and their income is relatively stable over fairly long periods of time aside from the effect of two major factors: (1) the level of real income per capita, or perhaps of real wealth per capita; (2) the cost of holding money.[9]

(1) Apparently, the holding of cash balances is regarded as a "luxury," like education and recreation. The amount of money the public desires to hold not only goes up as its real income rises but goes up more than in proportion. Judged by evidence for the past 75 years in the United States, a 1 percent rise in real income per capita tends to be accompanied by nearly a 2 percent increase in the real amount of money held and thus by nearly a 1 percent increase in the ratio of cash balances to income. This tendency is highly regular over the long sweep of time from 1875 to World War II; it has not been operative since the end of World War II but it is yet too soon to judge whether this is a fundamental change or simply a reaction to the abnormally high ratio of cash balances that was reached during the war.

(2) The cost of holding cash balances depends mainly on the rate of interest that can be earned on alternative assets—thus if a bond yields 4 percent while cash yields no return, this means that an individual gives up $4 a year if he holds $100 of cash instead of a bond—and on the rate of change of prices—if prices rise at 5 percent per year, for example, $100 in cash will buy at the end of the year only as much as $95 at the beginning so that it has cost the individual $5 to hold $100 of cash instead of goods. The empirical evidence suggests that while the first factor—the interest rate—has a systematic effect on the amount of money held, the effect is rather small. The second factor, the rate of change of prices, has no discernible effect in ordinary times when price changes are small—on the order of a few percent a year. On the other hand, it has a clearly discernible and major effect when price change is rapid and long continued, as during extreme inflations or deflations.[10] A rapid inflation produces a sizable decline in the desired ratio of cash balances to income; a rapid deflation, a sizable rise.

Of course even after allowance is made for changes in real income per capita and in the cost of holding money, the ratio of cash balances to income is not perfectly steady. But the remaining fluctuations in it are minor, certainly far smaller than those that occur in the stock of money itself.

Some idea of the quantitative magnitude of the changes in the United States over long periods of time can be obtained by comparing average values of various items over the most recent complete business cycle—that running from a trough in 1949 to a peak in 1953 to a trough in 1954—with those over the earliest for which we have the relevant data—that running from a trough in

1878 to a peak in 1882 to a trough in 1885. The money stock multiplied 67-fold over these seven decades, and real income ninefold, so the money stock per unit of output rose about 7.5-fold. Prices something less than tripled, so the ratio of the money stock to money income roughly tripled. In the initial cycle, the stock of money averaged about 24 percent of one year's money income—that is, cash balances were equal to the income of about three months; in the terminal cycle, the stock of money averaged about 67 percent of one year's income—that is, cash balances were equal to the income of about eight months. Over the period as a whole, the money stock rose at an average rate of 6 percent per year, money income at nearly 5 percent per year, prices at nearly 1.5 percent per year, total output at about 3 percent per year, and population at about 1.5 percent per year.

Of course, these changes did not occur smoothly. Figure 17.1 shows the more detailed behavior based on average values for each of the nineteen business cycles that we have experienced since 1879. It is clear that there is an exceedingly close connection between movements in the stock of money per unit of output and in prices. The only major difference is the more rapid long-term growth in the stock of money which in turn reflects the effect of the long-term growth in per capita real income and the associated rise in the desired ratio of money stock to money income.

2. RELATION OF STOCK OF MONEY TO PRICES OVER SHORTER PERIODS

Over the longer periods considered in the preceding section, changes in the stock of money per unit of output tend to dominate price changes, allowance being made for the effect of the growth of real income per head. This is less so over the shorter periods involved in the fluctuations we term business cycles, though the general and average relationship is very similar. The reason for the looser connection in such periods presumably is that movements in both the stock of money and in prices are smaller. Over longer periods, these movements cumulate and tend to swamp any disturbance in the relation between desired cash balances, real income, and the cost of holding money; in the ordinary business cycle, the disturbances, though perhaps no more important in an absolute sense, are much more important relative to the movements in money and prices.

On the average, prices rise during an expansion phase of a business cycle, and fall during the contraction phase. In the usual fairly mild cycle of peacetime since 1879, wholesale prices have on the average risen about 10 percent from trough to peak, and have fallen by somewhat less than half that amount from peak to trough. The general pattern has not changed much

FIGURE 17.1

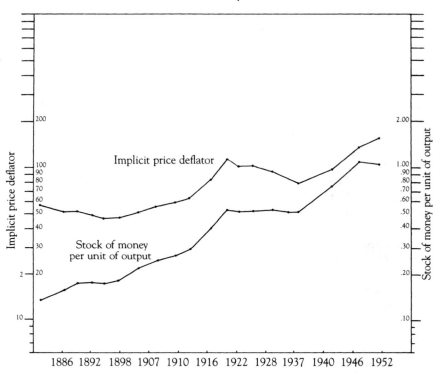

except for the relation of the rise to the fall. During the period of generally declining prices from the 1880s to the mid-1890s, prices tended to fall more during the contraction than they rose during expansion; during the subsequent period of generally rising prices, the reverse was the case and in some instances prices continued to rise during part of the contraction; in the 1920s, the rise and fall were roughly the same; in the two postwar cycles the rise was decidedly larger than the fall, as in the pre-1914 period.

Taken as a whole, these mild cycles would have imparted a generally upward drift to prices. The failure of such a drift to develop during peacetime was a consequence of the more severe depressions that occurred from time to time. In the five business cycles for which the contractions were most serious and can be designated deep depressions (1891–1894, 1904–1908, 1919–1921, 1927–1933, and 1933–1938), wholesale prices on the average rose about 10 percent during expansions, about the same as in the mild cycles, but then fell during the contractions over twice as much, ending up on the average some 12 percent below their level at the start of the cycle. It was the price declines during these deep depressions that, as a matter of experience, offset the upward tendency during mild cycles—"creeping inflation" in this sense is by no means a unique post-World War II phenomenon.

The stock of money shows the same relation to these cyclical price movements as that depicted in Figure 17.1 for longer periods. During the mild cycles, the stock of money almost invariably rose during both expansion and contraction, but at a faster rate during expansions than during contractions. On the other hand, during the deep depression cycles listed above, the stock of money invariably fell during the course of the contraction, and there is only one other cycle during which there is an appreciable absolute decline during any part of the contraction (1894–1897). This resemblance between the cyclical movement in the stock of money and in prices holds not only on the average but also from cycle to cycle, though of course with more variability for the individual cycles.[11]

There can be little doubt on the basis of this evidence that there is a close link between monetary changes and price changes over the shorter periods within which business cycles run their course as well as over longer periods and during major wartime episodes. But three important considerations must be borne in mind if this fact is not to be a misleading guide to policy.

The first is that the direction of influence between the money stock and income and prices is less clear-cut and more complex for the business cycle than for the longer movements. The character of our monetary and banking system means that an expansion of income contributes to expansion in the money stock, partly through inducing banks to trim more closely their cash reserve position, partly through a tendency for currency in public hands to decline relative to deposits; similarly, a contraction of income contributes to a reduction or a slower rate of rise in the money stock by having the opposite effects on bank reserve ratios and the public's currency ratio. Thus changes in the money stock are a consequence as well as an independent cause of changes in income and prices, though once they occur they will in their turn produce still further effects on income and prices. This consideration blurs the relation between money and prices but does not reverse it. For there is much evidence—one important piece on timing will be presented in the next paragraph—that even during business cycles the money stock plays a largely independent role. This evidence is particularly direct and clear for the deep depression periods. There can be little doubt, for example, that Federal Reserve action in sharply raising discount rates in January 1920 and again in June 1920 (five months after the onset of the contraction in January 1920) played an important role in the subsequent decline in the money supply and unprecedentedly rapid fall in prices or that Federal Reserve policy in the early 1930s played an important role in producing a decline of a third in the stock of money from 1929 to 1933—by far the largest decline in the whole period covered by our data.[12]

A second, and perhaps more important, consideration has to do with the timing of the changes in the money supply and in income and prices. The generally upward trend in the money supply which accounts for its continuing to rise, though at a slower rate, during most contractions in economic activity as well as during expansions makes it difficult to judge timing relations from ups and downs in the money supply itself. For this and other reasons, we have found it most useful to examine instead the ups and downs in the rate at which the money supply is changing. The rate of change of the money supply shows well-marked cycles that match closely those in economic activity in general and precede the latter by a long interval. On the average, the rate of change of the money supply has reached its peak nearly sixteen months before the peak in general business and has reached its trough over twelve months before the trough in general business.[13]

This is strong though not conclusive evidence for the independent influence of monetary change. But it also has a very different significance. It means that it must take a long time for the influence of monetary changes to make themselves felt—apparently what happens now to the rate of change of the money supply may not be reflected in prices or economic activity for twelve to sixteen months, on the average. Moreover, the timing varies considerably from cycle to cycle—since 1907, the shortest time span by which the money peak preceded the business cycle peak was thirteen months, the longest, twenty-four months; the corresponding range at troughs is five months to twenty-one months.[14] From the point of view of scientific analysis directed at establishing economic regularities on the basis of the historical record—the purpose for which the measures were computed—this is highly consistent behavior; it justifies considerable confidence in the reliability of the averages cited and means that they cannot easily be attributed simply to the accident of chance variation. But from the point of view of policy directed at controlling a particular movement such as the current recession, the timing differences are disturbingly large—they mean that monetary action taken today may, on the basis of past experience, affect economic activity within six months or again perhaps not for over a year and six months; and of course past experience is not exhaustive; the particular episode may establish a new limit in either direction.

The long time lag has another important effect. It leads to misinterpretation and misconception about the effects of monetary policy, as well as to consequent mistakes in monetary policy. Because the effects of monetary change do not occur instantaneously, monetary policy is regarded as ineffective. The most recent example is the tight money policy of 1956 and 1957 which coexisted with rising prices but whose delayed effects are with us in the current recession. A similar and even more dramatic example is the tight money policy from early 1928 on and the associated lack of growth in the money supply which coexisted with economic expansion but contributed to both the occurrence and the severity of the 1929 downturn. The fact that these policies had a delayed effect in turn misled the monetary authorities; on these occasions, and even more clearly in 1920, they were induced to believe that still stronger measures were required and so tended to overdo a repressive policy. On other occasions, notably in 1932 as well as earlier in that major catastrophe, the failure of tentative movements toward easy money to have an immediate effect led them to regard their actions as ineffective and to permit and contribute to the sharp decline in the stock of money which occurred and which played so crucial a role in that episode.

The third consideration is in some ways a different aspect of the one just discussed. The variation in timing means that there is considerable leeway in the precise relation between changes in the stock of money and in prices over short periods of time—there are other factors at work that lead to these variations and mean that even if the stock of money were to change in a highly regular and consistent fashion, economic activity and prices would nonetheless fluctuate. When the money changes are large, they tend to dominate these other factors—or perhaps one might better say, they will force these factors to work in a particular direction. Thus there seems little doubt that a large change in the money supply within a relatively short period will force a change in the same direction in income and prices and, conversely, that a large change in income and prices in short periods—a substantial short-period inflation or deflation—is most unlikely to occur without a large change in money supply. This is certainly the conclusion suggested by the evidence for the deep depression cycles and for sizable inflations. But when the money changes are moderate, the other factors come into their own. If we knew enough about them and about the detailed effects of monetary changes, we might be able to counter these other effects by monetary measures. But this is utopian given our present level of knowledge. There are thus definite limits to the possibility of any fine control of the general level of prices by a fine adjustment of monetary change.

3. CHANGES IN PRICES AND CHANGES IN OUTPUT OVER LONGER PERIODS

Over the cycle, prices and output tend to move together—both tend to rise during expansions and to fall during contractions. Both are part of the cyclical process and anything, including a monetary change, that promotes a vigorous expansion is likely to promote a vigorous rise in both and conversely. The preceding section implicitly assumes this connection.

Over the longer period, the relation between price changes and output changes is much less clear and in the first section we took the behavior of output for granted. Now this seems clearly valid, not only as an expository device but also as a first approximation to reality. What happens to a nation's output over long periods of time depends in the first instance on such basic factors as resources available, the industrial organization of the society, the growth of knowledge and technical skills, the growth of population, the accumulation of capital, and so on. This is the stage on which money and price changes play their parts as the supporting cast.

One proposition about the effect of changes in the stock of money and in prices that is widely accepted and hardly controversial is that large and unexpected changes in prices are adverse to the growth of output—whether these changes are up or down. At one extreme, the kind of price rise that occurs during hyperinflation seriously distorts the effective use of resources.[15] At the other extreme, sharp price declines such as occurred from 1920 to 1921 and again from 1929 to 1933 certainly produce a widespread and tragic waste of resources.

So much is agreed. The more controversial issue is the effect of moderate change in prices. One view that is widely held is that slowly rising prices stimulate economic output and produce a more rapid rate of growth than would otherwise occur. A number of reasons have been offered in support of this view. (1) Prices, and particularly wages, are, it is said, sticky. In a market economy, the reallocation of resources necessitated by economic growth and development requires changes in relative prices and relative wages. It is much easier, it is argued, for these to come about without friction and resistance if they can occur through rises in some prices and wages without declines in others. If prices were stable, some changes in relative wages could still come about in this way, since economic growth means that wages tend to rise relative to prices, but changes in relative prices could not, and, of course, there would not be as much scope even for relative wage changes. (2) Costs, and in particular wages, are, it is argued, stickier than selling prices. Hence generally rising prices will tend to raise profit margins, giving enterprises both a bigger incentive to raise output and to add to capital and the means to finance the capital needed. (3) The most recently popular variant of the preceding point is that costs are not only sticky against declines but in addition have a tendency to be pushed up with little reference to the state of demand as a result of strong trade unions. If the money stock is kept from rising, the result, it is claimed, will be unemployment as profit margins are cut, and also a higher level of prices, though not necessarily a rising level of prices. Gently rising prices, it is argued, will tend to offset this upward pressure by permitting money wages to rise without real wages doing so. (4) Interest rates are particularly slow to adapt to price rises. If prices are rising at, say, 3 percent a year, a 6 percent interest rate on a money loan is equivalent to a 3 percent rate when prices are stable. If lenders adjusted fully to the price rise, this would simply mean that interest rates would be 3 percentage points higher in the first case than in the second. But in fact this does not happen, so that productive enterprises find the cost of borrowing to be relatively low, and again have a greater incentive than otherwise to invest, and the associated transfer from creditors to debtors gives them greater means to do so.

In opposition to this view, it has been argued that generally rising prices reduce the pressure on enterprises to be efficient, stimulate speculative relative to industrial activity, reduce the incentives for individuals to save, and make it more difficult to maintain the appropriate structure of relative prices, since individual prices have to change in order to stay the same relative to others. Furthermore, it is argued that once it becomes widely recognized that prices are rising, the advantages cited in the preceding paragraph will disappear: escalator clauses or their economic equivalent will eliminate the stickiness of prices and wages and the greater stickiness of wages than of prices; strong unions will increase still further their wage demands to allow for price increases; and interest rates will rise to allow for the price rise. If the advantages are to be obtained, the rate of price rise will have to be accelerated and there is no stopping place short of runaway inflation. From this point of view, there may clearly be a major difference between the effects of a superficially similar price rise, according as it is an undesigned and largely unforeseen effect of such impersonal events as the discovery of gold, or a designed result of deliberative policy action by a public body.

Some who believe that slowly rising prices are adverse to economic growth regard stable product prices with slowly rising wage rates as most favorable, combining the advantages of stable price expectations with some easing of frictions involved in relative wage adjustments. Others view gently falling prices and stable wages as most favorable, arguing that additional problems in wage adjustments would be balanced by the stimulus to thrift and accumulation.

Historical evidence on the relation between price changes and output changes is mixed and gives no clear support to any one of these positions. (1) In the United States, the period from 1865 to 1879 was a period of exceedingly rapid progress; and, during the same period, prices were cut in half. True, neither price changes nor output changes proceeded regularly within the period. Output apparently grew most rapidly during the cyclical expansions in the period when prices rose mildly or were roughly stable; most of the price declines occurred during cyclical contractions. Yet the problem at issue is less the cyclical relation than the longer period relation and there can be no doubt that during the period as a whole prices fell sharply and output rose sharply. (2) The period from 1880 to 1897 was a period of generally declining prices, from

1897 to 1913, of generally rising prices; taken as a whole, the second period has generally been regarded as displaying more rapid growth than the first. But it is not clear that this is a satisfactory interpretation. The period of great monetary uncertainty in the early 1890s was associated with generally depressed conditions and was followed by a rapid rebound. If both are excluded, the remaining periods show about the same rates of growth in real output per head, although prices were generally falling during the 1880s and rising after the turn of the century. Moreover, the period from 1908–1914 is one of relatively slow growth despite rising prices. (3) The decade of the 1920s, after the recovery from the deep depression of 1920–1921, was a decade of rapid growth and prices were relatively stable. (4) In Great Britain, output per head apparently grew at a definitely higher rate during the period of generally falling prices before the mid-1880s than during the subsequent period of rising prices up to World War I.[16] (5) On the other hand, the attempt to achieve mildly falling prices in Britain in the 1920s was associated with considerable economic difficulties and something close to stagnation.

All in all, perhaps the only conclusion that is justified is that either rising prices or falling prices are consistent with rapid economic growth, provided that the price changes are fairly steady, moderate in size, and reasonably predictable. The mainsprings of growth are presumably to be sought elsewhere. But unpredictable and erratic changes of direction in prices are apparently as disturbing to economic growth as to economic stability.

4. POLICY IMPLICATIONS

The preceding account of the relation of money to prices over long and short periods and of price changes to output changes has some fairly direct and immediate implications for public policy with respect both to growth and stability.

(1) In order for the price level to be reasonably stable over the decades ahead, the total stock of money will have to grow to accommodate itself to the growth in output and in population. In addition, if past patterns continue, it will have to grow to satisfy the desire of the public to increase the ratio of cash balances to income as their real income rises. Past experience suggests that something like a 3 to 5 percent per year increase in the stock of money is required for long-term price stability.[17]

(2) An essential requirement for the avoidance of either substantial inflation or substantial deflation over the coming decades is the avoidance of a substantially more rapid or a substantially less rapid increase in the stock of money than the 3 to 5 percent per year required for price stability. A substantially more rapid rate of growth in the money supply will inevitably mean

inflation; conversely, continued inflation of substantial magnitude cannot occur without such a large rate of growth in the money supply. A substantially slower rate of growth in the money supply, let alone an absolute decline, will inevitably mean deflation; conversely, continued deflation of substantial magnitude cannot occur without such a small or negative rate of growth in the money supply.

(3) A highly fluctuating price level is as disturbing to economic growth as to economic stability. Given that this is avoided, it is not clear what pattern of long-term price behavior is optimum for economic stability—whether a roughly stable price level, a gently rising price level, or a gently falling price level. It does seem clear that any of these is consistent with rapid economic growth. If it is necessary to state objectives in terms of a price level goal, then a stable price level has the very great advantages of (a) ease of public understanding, (b) definiteness rendering successive alterations in the precise goal less likely, and (c) probably the closest approach to equitable treatment of the various members of the community. However, the difficulty of assuring the close attainment of any price level goal suggests that it might be better to express the immediate policy goal in terms of some variable other than the price level, for example the attainment of a steady 4 percent per year rise in the stock of money, and then to let the price level be whatever would be consistent with this money goal. The resulting price level behavior could hardly depart much from relative stability and would certainly not be violently unstable.

(4) For cyclical movements, a major problem is to prevent monetary changes from being a source of disturbance. If the stock of money can be kept growing at a relatively steady rate, without erratic fluctuations in short periods, it is highly unlikely if not impossible that we would experience either a sharp price rise—like that during World Wars I and II and after World War I—or a substantial price or output decline—like those experienced from 1920–1921, 1929–1933, 1937–1938.

(5) A steady rate of growth in the money supply will not mean perfect stability even though it would prevent the kind of wide fluctuations that we have experienced from time to time in the past. It is tempting to try to go farther and to use monetary changes to offset other factors making for expansion and contraction. Though the available evidence demonstrates a close connection between monetary change and price and income change in the course of business cycles as over larger periods, it also casts grave doubts on the possibility of producing any fine adjustments in economic activity by fine adjustments in monetary policy—at least in the present state of knowledge. The evidence suggests that monetary changes take a fairly long time to exert their influence and that the time taken varies considerably. In terms of past experience, for example, action taken now to offset the current recession may affect economic activity in six months or not for over a year and six months.

The tight money policy of late 1956 and most of 1957, which was taken to offset the then existing inflationary pressure, almost surely had little effect on that situation and is only now exerting its influence and contributing to the current recessionary tendencies; the inflationary pressures in 1956 may well themselves have been in part a delayed consequence of the expansionary monetary policy taken to offset the 1953–1954 recession. There are thus serious limitations to the possibility of a discretionary monetary policy and much danger that such a policy may make matters worse rather than better. Federal Reserve policy since 1951 has been distinctly superior to that followed during any earlier period since the establishment of the system, mainly because it has avoided wide fluctuations in the rate or growth of the money supply. At the same time, I am myself inclined to believe that in our present state of knowledge and with our present institutions, even this policy has been decidedly inferior to the much simpler policy of keeping the money supply growing at a predesignated rate month in and month out with allowance only for seasonal influences and with no attempt to adjust the rate of growth to monetary conditions.[18]

(6) To avoid misunderstanding, it should be emphasized that the problems just discussed are in no way peculiar to monetary policy. Fiscal action also involves lags. Indeed, the lag between the recognition of need for action and the taking of action is undoubtedly longer for discretionary fiscal than for discretionary monetary action: the monetary authorities can act promptly, fiscal action inevitably involves serious delays for congressional consideration. It has been argued that this defect of fiscal action is counterbalanced by a shorter lag between the action and its effects. This may well be, though there is little concrete empirical evidence that I know of; the belief is based on general considerations of plausibility, which can be a misleading guide. And there are certainly no reasons for believing and no empirical evidence to show that the lag, whatever its average length, is any less variable for fiscal than for monetary action. Hence, the basic difficulties and limitations of monetary policy apply with equal force to fiscal policy.

(7) Political pressures to "do something" in the face of either relatively mild price rises or relatively mild price and employment declines are clearly very strong indeed in the existing state of public attitudes. The main moral to be drawn from the two preceding points is that yielding to these pressures may frequently do more harm than good. There is a saying that the best is often the enemy of the good, which seems highly relevant. The goal of an extremely high degree of economic stability is certainly a splendid one; our ability to attain it, however, is limited; we can surely avoid extreme fluctuations; we do not know enough to avoid minor fluctuations; the attempt to do more than we can will itself be a disturbance that may increase rather than reduce instability. But like all such injunctions, this one too must be taken in moderation. It is a plea for a

sense of perspective and balance, not for irresponsibility in the face of major problems or for failure to correct past mistakes.

NOTES

1. These are based partly on the preliminary results of an extensive study by Anna J. Schwartz and myself under the auspices of the National Bureau of Economic Research on the secular and cyclical behavior of the stock of money in the United States, partly on a series of studies done in the workshop in money and banking at the University of Chicago. The views expressed in this paper are of course my own and are not necessarily those of the organizations sponsoring these studies or of the other participants in them.

2. "The stock of money" is not of course an unambiguous concept. There is a wide range of assets possessing to a greater or lesser degree the qualities of general acceptability and fixity in nominal value that are the main characteristics of "money." It is somewhat arbitrary just where the line is drawn which separates "money" from "near-money" or "securities" or "other financial claims." For most of what follows, the precise line drawn will not affect the analysis. For the United States at present, I shall treat as "money in the hands of the public" the sum of "currency outside banks," "demand deposits adjusted," and "adjusted time deposits in commercial banks," as these terms are defined in Federal Reserve monetary statistics. I shall note explicitly any point at which the precise definition adopted affects the statements made.

3. The nearest thing to an exception I know of is German experience from the mid-1930s to 1944. See John J. Klein, "German Money and Prices, 1932–44," in Milton Friedman, ed., *Studies in the Quantity Theory of Money* (Chicago: University of Chicago Press, 1956), pp. 121–59.

The qualification "per unit of output" is needed only to cover movements spanning long periods of time, like the long-term decline in prices in the late nineteenth century. For moderately short periods, even this qualification is unnecessary.

4. For example, under a gold standard, a rising level of prices discourages gold production and so, after a lag, tends to produce a decline in the stock of money. On the other hand, under a fractional reserve banking system, if rising prices lead banks to reduce the ratio of cash to liabilities, rising prices may tend to produce a rise in the stock of money.

5. Milton Friedman, "The Quantity Theory of Money—a Restatement," in *Studies in the Quantity Theory of Money*, p. 17. Also see chapter 16 of this volume. The quotation summarizes one item from a study by Eugene M. Lerner, summarized in his article "Inflation in the Confederacy, 1861–65," in *Studies in the Quantity Theory of Money*, pp. 163–75.

6. The decline in the stock of money per unit of output occurred as a result of (1) exhaustion of then known gold mines; (2) the shift of many countries from a silver to a gold standard; (3) the rapid increase in output.

7. The basic data underlying this statement are from the National Bureau study mentioned in note 1 above. They will appear in a monograph by Anna J. Schwartz and myself that is now in preparation.

8. The reciprocal of this ratio is termed "the income velocity of circulation."

9. On this subject, see Phillip Cagan, "The Monetary Dynamics of Hyperinflation," and Richard T. Selden, "Monetary Velocity in the United States," in *Studies in the Quantity Theory of Money*. The statements that follow are based also on additional work done in connection with the National Bureau study referred to in note 1.

For shorter periods, an additional factor enters. Cash balances are apparently adjusted to longer term income expectations ("permanent income") rather than to current income as measured on a monthly or annual basis. This introduces additional changes in the ratio of cash balances to current measured income. (See section 2.)

10. Evidence for this is presented in Cagan, op. cit., and is available also from work by John Deaver on monetary changes in Chile.

11. One difference between the comparison made here and in the preceding section is that the money series used is the stock of money, not the stock of money per unit of output. The reason for this is the problem referred to in note 9 above. Over the longer periods, the stock of money rises more rapidly than money income; an increase in real income per capita leads to a more than proportional increase in real money balances—income velocity falls with a rise in real income. Over the cycle, the reverse relation holds, if money income is measured by a figure like the regularly published national income or net national product estimates. Money stock falls relative to measured money income during expansion and rises during contraction—income velocity rises during expansion and falls during contraction. It turns out that this apparent contradiction can be accounted for, both qualitatively and quantitatively, by distinguishing between measured income and a longer term concept that I have called permanent income and also between measured prices and permanent prices. One implication of this interpretation of the behavior of velocity is that division of the money stock by measured national income in constant prices would yield estimates of the stock of money per unit of output that were formally comparable to those plotted in Figure 17.1 but did not have the same significance and meaning; the latter use an average output figure that is closer to permanent output or income than to annual measured income. Unfortunately, full analysis of this issue is impossible within the confines of the present paper. The forthcoming annual report for 1957 of the National Bureau of Economic Research will contain a somewhat fuller summary; and the monograph referred to in note 7 above, a full analysis.

12. The other deep depression episodes are a bit more complex. The decline in the stock of money from 1893 to 1894 seems connected with the uncertainty about silver; in 1907, quite clearly with the banking panic which was of course in part a consequence of a prior decline in economic activity but not through the particular channels described above and which once begun very likely served as an important factor in making the contraction as deep as it was; in 1937–1938, with the doubling of reserve requirements by the Federal Reserve System in two steps in 1936 and in 1937—the first step coincides with a sharp reduction in the rate of growth of the money stock, the second with the beginning of decline.

13. The average at peaks is based on eighteen observations, at troughs on nineteen. Of course, instead of interpreting the cycles in the rate of change as conforming positively with a lead, they could be interpreted as conforming inversely with a lag. A number of pieces of statistical evidence, however, argue strongly for the former interpretation.

14. These are for the period since 1907 because our money data prior to that date are annual or semiannual. While the annual and semiannual observations give the same average timing as the monthly, individual observations are not comparable.

15. However, even open hyperinflations are less damaging to output than suppressed inflations in which a wide range of prices are held well below the levels that would clear the market. The German hyperinflation after World War I never caused anything like the reduction of production that was produced in Germany from 1945 to the monetary reform of 1948 by the suppression of inflation. And the inflationary pressure suppressed in the second case was a small fraction of that manifested in the first.

16. See James B. Jeffreys and Dorothy Walters, "National Income and Expenditure of the United Kingdom, 1870–1952," *Income and Wealth*, series 5, table 3.

17. This range is for the stock of money as defined in note 2, namely, currency outside banks plus adjusted deposits, demand and time, of commercial banks. For a narrower definition, currency outside banks plus adjusted demand deposits, the required rate of growth is less; for a broader definition, the preceding plus all time deposits, in mutual savings banks and the postal savings system as well as commercial banks, the required rate of growth is greater. The reason is that time deposits have been growing relative to demand deposits and currency, and, until 1957, mutual savings deposits relative to other time deposits.

18. This is not intended to be a full statement of the optimum monetary structure. I would prefer automatic arrangements that would reduce the area of discretion. One particular set of such arrangements is suggested in my "A Monetary and Fiscal Framework for Economic Stability," reprinted in my *Essays in Positive Economics* (Chicago: University of Chicago Press, 1953), pp. 133–56.

The extensive empirical work that I have done since that article was written has given me no reason to doubt that the arrangements there suggested would produce a high degree of stability; it has, however, led me to believe that much simpler arrangements would do so also; that something like the simple policy suggested above would produce a very tolerable amount of stability. This evidence has persuaded me that the major problem is to prevent monetary changes from themselves contributing to instability rather than to use monetary changes to offset other forces.

On the issues in question, see also my "The Effects of a Full Employment Policy on Economic Stability: A Formal Analysis," reprinted in the same book, pp. 117–32.

A Monetary History
of the United States:
A Summing Up

· *18* ·

The monetary history of the United States during the century since the Civil War has been colorful and varied. In tracing its tortuous course, we have found it necessary to delve into domestic politics, international economic arrangements, the functioning of large administrative organizations, the role of personality in shaping events, and other matters seemingly far removed from the counting house. The varied character of U.S. monetary history renders this century of experience particularly valuable to the student of economic change. He cannot control the experiment, but he can observe monetary experience under sufficiently disparate conditions to sort out what is common from what is adventitious and to acquire considerable confidence that what is common can be counted on to hold under still other circumstances.

Throughout the near-century examined in detail we have found that:

1. Changes in the behavior of the money stock have been closely associated with changes in economic activity, money income, and prices.

2. The interrelation between monetary and economic change has been highly stable.

Milton Friedman and Anna Jacobson Schwartz, *A Monetary History of the United States 1867–1960*. Copyright ©1963 by National Bureau of Economic Research. Excerpt, pp. 676–700, reprinted here by permission of Princeton University Press.

3. Monetary changes have often had an independent origin; they have not been simply a reflection of changes in economic activity.

These common elements of monetary experience can be expected to characterize our future as they have our past. In addition, we can expect the future like the past to give further examples of the less specific generalization that:

4. In monetary matters, appearances are deceiving; the important relationships are often precisely the reverse of those that strike the eye.

1. Relation Between the Stock of Money and Other Economic Variables

From 1867 to 1960, the 93 years for which we have estimates of the money stock, there have been two major price inflations: a more than doubling of prices from 1914 to 1920 and again from 1939 to 1948, the periods during and after each of the two world wars. In both wars, there was also a more than doubling in the money stock. So large a rise in the money stock in a correspondingly brief time did not occur in any other period.

A substantial and fairly long-continued peacetime rise in prices occurred during only one period: from 1897 to 1914, when prices rose by 40 to 50 percent. The average annual rate of rise in the stock of money from 1897 to 1914 was higher than during any other period of comparable length that excludes the two world wars. It is widely feared that the post–World War II period may ultimately turn out to be another such period of long-continued rise in prices. However, as of 1960 it clearly was not. The major price rises since 1945 have been either a carryover from World War II or connected with the Korean War.

We have characterized four segments of the 93 years as displaying a relatively high degree of economic stability: 1882–1892, 1903–1913, 1923–1929, 1948–1960. Each has also displayed a high degree of stability of the year-to-year change in the stock of money; the remaining periods have shown appreciably greater instability of the year-to-year change in both money and income.

In 93 years, there have been six periods of severe economic contraction that produced widespread distress and unemployment. Historians of business cycles classify those contractions as of a different order of magnitude if not of a different species than the milder contractions that have come on the average some four years apart (see Figure 18.1). The most severe contraction was the one from 1929 to 1933. The others were 1873–1879, 1893–1894—or better, perhaps the whole period 1893 to 1897, which contained two business cycle contractions separated by a brief and incomplete expansion—1907–1908, 1920–1921, and 1937–1938. Each of those severe contractions was accompanied by an appreciable decline in the stock of money, the most severe decline accompanying the 1929–1933 contraction. The only other decline at all comparable in magnitude to the six was in the first year of the series, 1867 to 1868, the final stage of the liquidation of some of the Civil War monetary expedients. There have been only two other periods in the whole 93 years in which the stock of money has declined appreciably for more than an isolated few months, 1948–1949 and 1959–1960, and the declines in both those periods were decidedly smaller in magnitude than in any of the six severe contractions. The remaining contractions have left their impress in the form of a slower rate of growth of the stock of money during contractions than during expansions, rather than in an absolute decline.

Of the six severe contractions, four were characterized by major banking or monetary disturbances: 1873–1879, by controversy over the greenbacks and resumption of specie payments and by a banking crisis in 1873; the 1890s, by controversy over the role of silver, a banking crisis in 1890, and a more severe banking crisis in 1893 involving concerted restriction by the banks of the convertibility of deposits into currency; 1907–1908, by a banking panic also involving restriction; and 1929–1933, by collapse of the banking system involving the disappearance through failure or merger of one-third of the banks and terminating in a nationwide banking holiday and complete cessation of banking activities for a week. Only one other banking crisis at all comparable in severity to the four has occurred during the whole period: the banking crisis of 1884, an episode in the course of the third longest contraction in our period (1882 to 1885), which is on the borderline for inclusion in our list of severe contractions.

In the two other severe contractions, 1920–1921 and 1937–1938, the decline in the money stock was a consequence of policy actions of the Federal Reserve System: in 1920–1921, a sharp rise in the discount rate in early 1920 followed by another such rise some four and a half months later; in 1937–1938, a doubling of reserve requirements in 1936 and early 1937. In both cases, the subsequent decline in the money stock was associated with a severe economic decline, but in neither did it lead to a banking crisis.

Of relationships revealed by our evidence, the closest are between, on the one hand, secular and cyclical movements in the stock of money and, on the other, corresponding movements in money income and prices. Since real income tends to vary over the cycle in the same direction as money income does, we have also observed a close relation between cyclical movements in the money stock and in real income or business activity. The relation between secular movements in the money stock and in real income is much less close.

Real income grew at much the same rate during each of the four periods of stability listed earlier. Yet the money stock and prices grew at quite different rates, prices declining by 1 percent a year in one period, rising by 2 percent a year in another. Apparently, the forces determining the long-run rate of growth of real income are largely independent of the long-run rate of growth of the stock of money, so long as both proceed fairly smoothly. But marked instability of money is accompanied by instability of economic growth.

2. STABILITY OF MONETARY RELATIONS

The relation between money and other economic variables has been not only close but also highly stable in form and character. One striking example of the stability of basic economic relations is the behavior of relative prices in the United States and Great Britain adjusted for changes in the exchange rate between the dollar and the pound. We have a reasonably continuous series from 1871 on (Figure 18.2). In the 79 years from 1871 to 1949, vast changes occurred in the economic structure and development of the United States, the place of Britain in the world economy, the internal monetary structures of both the United States and Britain, and the international monetary arrangements linking them. Yet, despite these changes, despite two world wars, and despite the statistical errors in the price-index numbers, the adjusted price ratio expressed on a base which makes 1929=100 was between 84 and 111 in all but one of the 79 years. The exception was 1932. It reflected the disruption of international monetary relations that followed Britain's devaluation in the fall of 1931, which made Britain temporarily unrepresentative of the world outside the sterling area with which the United States traded. Within a year, the ratio was back in the earlier range. Moreover, almost the extremes of the range were experienced in the very first decade, during which the ratio ranged from 111 in 1871 to 86 in 1876. In 1950, after Britain had again devalued in the fall of 1949, the ratio, as in 1932, shot outside the prior range, this time by a much more sizable amount, to 143. That deviation was longer lasting, partly because of the smaller role Britain had come to play in the world economy, but even more, we believe, because of the development of more effective techniques for suppressing the expression of price rises or their equivalent in computed price-index numbers. Yet, year by year, the ratio declined until 1958, when it reached 118, only slightly outside the earlier range; it remained at roughly that level through 1960.

Even though we are accustomed to regard the United States as nearly self-sufficient, the economic integration of the Western world has been sufficiently close to leave U.S. prices little leeway relative to external prices when both are expressed in a common currency. There has been more leeway in how the price

Figure 18.2

U.S. Net International Capital Movement as a Ratio
to National Income, and Purchasing Power Parity, 1871–1960

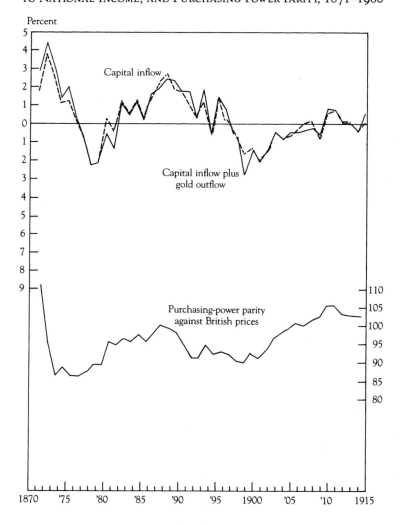

relation was achieved—whether through changes in internal prices or in exchange rates—than in what relation could be achieved. Wide variations in tariffs, a major gold-purchase program, vast shifts in the direction of capital movements (see Figure 18.2), or imposition by our trading partners of extensive

FIGURE 18.2 (*continued*)

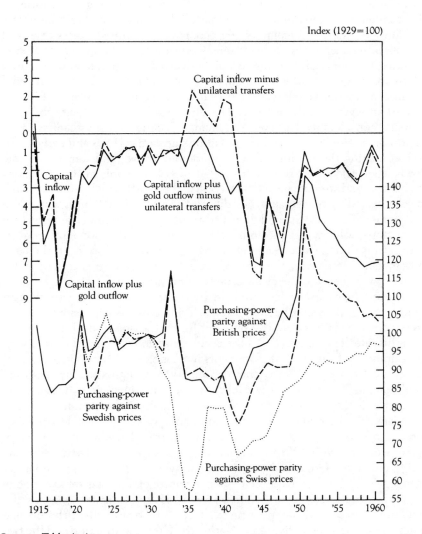

SOURCE: Table A–4.

NOTE: Calendar years are shown. Movements in a fiscal year are plotted at the beginning of the calendar year. Capital inflow, minus unilateral transfers to foreign countries, is plotted as plus. Gold outflow is plotted as plus. Both are for fiscal years 1871–1897, calendar years 1897–1960. Capital movements are in gold values, 1871–1878. Unilateral transfers are not subtracted from capital inflow before 1919, because they were small and hence departure from the usual treatment of the balance of payments did not seem worthwhile.

exchange controls—none of these has altered radically the price relationships required to yield some measure of equilibrium in international payments.

The velocity of money, which reflects the money-holding propensities of the community, offers another example of the stability of basic monetary relations. As the real income of the people of the United States rose, and perhaps also as deposits were made more convenient by the spread of banking facilities, the community came to hold a decidedly larger amount of money relative to its income, which is to say, the velocity of money declined. In 1869, the stock of money amounted to less than three months' income; in 1960, to more than seven months' income. The numerical value of velocity therefore changed considerably. However, the change occurred rather steadily: somewhat more rapidly when prices were falling during the 1880s and early 1890s and so making the holding of money more attractive; and somewhat more slowly when prices were rising from 1897 to 1914. The only major exceptions were during and after the great contraction of the 1930s, which saw a major fall in velocity and then a rebound, and during and after World War II, which also saw a major fall in velocity and then a postwar rebound. In response to cyclical fluctuations, velocity has shown a systematic and stable movement about its trend, rising during expansion and falling during contraction. Even the large movement accompanying the Great Contraction partly fits this pattern; it was so large partly because the cyclical movement was so large.

During the nine decades ending in 1960, the velocity of money fell by an average of slightly over 1 percent a year. During business expansions it either rose or declined at less than this rate; during contractions it declined at more than this rate. The amplitudes of the cyclical rise and fall tended to vary with the amplitude of the cyclical movements in economic activity. Since many of the cyclical movements in economic activity had approximately the same amplitude, so did many of the cyclical movements in velocity. Despite the secular trend, the consistent cyclical pattern, and the sizable margin of error in our estimates, the observed year-to-year change in velocity was less than 10 percent in 78 out of the 91 year-to-year changes from 1869, when our velocity figures start, to 1960. Of the thirteen larger changes, more than half came during either the Great Contraction or the two world wars, and the largest change was 17 percent. Expressed as a percentage of a secular trend, velocity was within the range 90 to 110 in 53 years, 85 to 115 in 66 years. Of the remaining 26 years, 12 were during the first 15 years, for which the income figures are seriously defective, and 7 during the Great Contraction and the two world wars.

One other monetary relation that has been highly stable is the relation between changes in the stock of money and cyclical movements in economic activity. On the average, the stock of money rose at a higher rate than money income; this is the other side of the secular decline in velocity. The rise was more rapid than usual during cyclical expansions and less rapid than usual during cyclical contractions. The rate of rise tended to slow down well before the peak in business and to speed up well before the trough. This pattern prevails throughout the period, in the very earliest cycle our data cover and also in the most recent.

The careful reader of our narrative will have come across many another detailed example of stable monetary relations to supplement these very broad ones: the similar effects of the gold-purchase programs undertaken in 1878 to prepare for resumption and after 1933 to raise domestic prices; the reliability of the deposit-currency ratio as a signal of a liquidity problem; the similar initial movements of U.S. wholesale prices following the outbreak of World Wars I and II—in both cases in a direction opposite to that which prevailed later; and so on.

These uniformities have persisted despite radical changes in monetary arrangements. From 1862 to 1879, the United States had an independent national money, convertible into neither gold nor silver nor the money of any other country at any fixed ratio. The stock of money could therefore be determined internally. From 1879 to 1914, U.S. money was convertible into gold at a fixed ratio specified by law and maintained in practice. The stock of money and internal prices had to be at levels that would produce a rough balance in international payments without abnormal gold movements. The stock of money was a dependent, not an independent, variable, though, of course, there was some leeway in short periods. Both before and after 1879, until the Reserve System was established, the U.S. unit banking system was divided between national and nonnational banks, each having roughly half of total deposits, and neither subject to any central control except as the Treasury from time to time undertook central banking functions.

From 1914 to 1933, U.S. money continued to be rigidly linked to gold, but the number of other national moneys so linked had diminished. The United States had achieved a far more important role in the world economy, and foreign trade had become a smaller part of U.S. economic activity. The links between U.S. money and international trade were therefore far looser than in earlier years. In addition, the Federal Reserve Act not only established central control over most of the banking system but also provided an agency that could deliberately intervene to alter or even to reverse the relation between international payments and the domestic stock of money.

In early 1933, the rigid link between U.S. money and gold was severed. A year later, a rigid link was reestablished at a different ratio. However, the gold standard then reestablished and legally prevailing ever since was very different from the pre-1933 standard. Gold was eliminated from circulation, and ownership of monetary gold by private citizens was made illegal, so that the national money was no longer freely convertible into gold at a fixed ratio. The loosening of the links between money and gold and, consequently, between money and international trade was completed by other countries, many of which went even further in severing all connection between the national money and gold. Today gold is primarily a commodity whose price is pegged rather than the keystone of the world or the U.S. monetary system. However, the legacy of history and the use of gold as a vehicle for fixing exchange rates still give it a monetary significance possessed by no other commodity subject to government price-fixing.

A major change occurred in the banking system in 1934 as a result of the inception of federal insurance of bank deposits. It appears to have succeeded, as the Federal Reserve Act did not, in making impossible the mushrooming of a loss of public confidence in some banks into a banking panic arising out of a widespread attempt on the part of the public to convert deposits into currency.

These changes in monetary arrangements have altered markedly the forces determining the stock of money. As a result, they have altered also the behavior of the stock of money. For example, in the 46 years from 1914 to 1960, when a government agency had explicit responsibility for the behavior of the stock of money, the year-to-year change in the stock was a more variable magnitude than in the prior 35 years, when it was determined by the quasi-automatic mechanism of the gold standard. On the other hand, in the period since the end of World War II, it has been a much less variable magnitude than it was in any earlier period of comparable length.

The changing monetary arrangements have affected in diverse ways the three variables we have found useful to regard as the arithmetic determinants of the stock of money: the stock of high-powered money; the ratio of the public's deposits to its currency holdings; and the ratio of the deposit liabilities of the commercial banking system to its reserves, which we have defined as equal to its total holdings of high-powered money (Figure 18.3).

The stock of high-powered money was the major factor accounting arithmetically for changes in the stock of money. Changes in high-powered money were, however, produced by different forces at different times: in the greenback period, mainly by changes in government fiduciary issues; from 1879 to 1914, mainly by gold flows, though to some extent also by changes in national bank notes and currency issued in exchange for silver; from 1914 to 1960, mainly by changes in Federal Reserve credit outstanding, with the notable exception of the years from 1934 to 1940 when gold flows dominated.

The deposit-currency ratio has been of major importance primarily during periods of financial difficulties. In each such period, the public's loss of confidence in banks led to an attempt to convert deposits into currency which produced a sharp decline in the ratio of deposits to currency and strong downward pressure on the stock of money. The establishment of the Federal Reserve System was expected to deprive such shifts in the deposit-currency ratio of monetary significance by providing a means of increasing the absolute volume of currency available for the public to hold, when the public desired to substitute currency for deposits, without requiring a multiple contraction of deposits. In practice, it did not succeed in achieving that objective. The most notable shift in the deposit-currency ratio in the 93 years from 1867 to 1960 occurred from 1930 to 1933, when the ratio fell to less than half its initial value and in three years erased the secular rise of three decades. Though the absolute volume of currency held by the public rose, it did so only at the expense of a very much larger decline in deposits, the combined effect being a decline of one-third in the total stock of money. The inception of federal insurance of bank deposits in 1934 finally changed decisively the behavior of the deposit-currency ratio. Since then it has not been subject to drastic changes in short periods, and it is not likely to be in the future.

The ratio of deposits to reserves, like the deposit-currency ratio, has been of major importance at times of financial difficulties, though it has played a more consistent minor role by generally rising during business expansions and falling during business contractions. Whenever the public has shown distrust of banks by seeking to lower the deposit-currency ratio, banks have reacted by seeking to strengthen their reserves. After a brief interval, they have succeeded in doing so, which is to say, in lowering the deposit-reserve ratio, thereby adding further to the downward pressure on the stock of money.

The deposit-reserve ratio has also varied over longer periods in response to changes in monetary arrangements. It rose notably in the greenback period as a result of the maturing of national banks and an increase in the relative importance of nonnational banks. It rose again in the decade from 1897 to 1907, partly as a result of the assumption by the Treasury of wider central banking functions. It rose again after the establishment of the Federal Reserve System, which both lowered legal requirements and gave banks confidence that, in case of need, they had a ready "lender of last resort" to fall back on. The monetary collapse from 1930 to 1933 changed the picture profoundly. It produced a decline in the deposit-reserve ratio from its all-time high in 1929 to a level, a decade later, not much above the level at the start of our series in 1867. The 1930–1933 experience taught banks not to rely on the Federal Reserve System for liquidity; it took them some three years to adjust their reserves to the associated shift in their preferences for liquidity. Successive increases in reserve requirements in 1936–1937 produced another shift in their preferences; again it took the banks some three years to adjust. Since then, the deposit-reserve ratio has risen as the role of deposit insurance in eliminating the danger of runs on banks has been recognized, and the effects of the earlier experiences have worn off. If adjustment is made for changes in legal requirements, the ratio is back to its level of the late 1920s.

Despite these marked alterations in the forces affecting the stock of money, there has been, as we have seen, little alteration in the relation between the changes, once determined, in the stock of money and other economic variables. The external forces impinging on the stock of money have changed radically. At the same time, the impact of changes in the stock of money on the rest of the economy appears to have been highly stable.

3. INDEPENDENCE OF MONETARY CHANGES

The close relation between changes in the stock of money and changes in other economic variables, alone, tells nothing about the origin of either or the direction of influence. The monetary changes might be dancing to the tune called by independently originating changes in the other economic variables; the changes in income and prices might be dancing to the tune called by independently originating monetary changes; the two might be mutually interacting, each having some elements of independence; or both might be dancing to the common tune of still a third set of influences. A great merit of the examination of a wide range of qualitative evidence, so essential in a monetary history, is that it provides a basis for discriminating between these possible explanations of the observed statistical covariation. We can go beyond the numbers alone and, at least on some occasions, discern the antecedent circumstances whence arose the particular movements that become so anonymous when we feed the statistics into the computer.

One thing is abundantly clear from our narrative. Monetary changes have in fact often been independent, in the sense that they have often not been an immediate or necessary consequence of contemporaneous changes in business conditions.

The clearest example is perhaps the monetary expansion from 1897 to 1914, which was worldwide and reflected an increased output of gold. The increased output of gold was partly a consequence of earlier decades of declining prices, which encouraged gold production, and so speaks also for a mutual interaction between monetary and economic changes. But clearly the monetary expansion cannot be attributed to the contemporary rise in money income and prices. By itself, the rise in money income and prices made for a reduced output of gold in the world at large and for an outflow of gold from any single country in a gold-standard world. If the common movement of money and income was not purely coincidental, the direction of influence must run from money to income.

The two major rises in the stock of money during World Wars I and II are about equally clear. In the early stages of both wars, the rise reflected an inflow of gold into the United States, as belligerent nations used the resources they could readily mobilize to purchase war material in the United States. The inflows of gold were not byproducts of contemporary changes in economic activity in this country or abroad, as gold flows had been in the years before 1914. They were a consequence of the outbreak of the two wars and the deliberate policy decisions of the political authorities in the countries at war. In the later stages of both wars, the rise reflected political decisions of U.S. authorities about the financing of war expenditures. Those decisions involved a major expansion in high-powered money which continued the work begun by gold inflows. Again, if the common movement of the stock of money and of money income and prices is not coincidental or the consequence of a common cause, the direction of influence must run from money to income.

The resumption and silver episodes display a substantial independence in the monetary changes that occurred and also a rather complex action and interaction between monetary and business changes. The pressures for and against resumption in the 1870s and the drive for free silver in the 1890s were major elements that shaped the course of events. Both were in some measure independent of the contemporary course of economic activity, though not of course of longer run economic developments. Both were also much affected by the course of events, the pressures against resumption and for free silver being greatly strengthened by a slowing down or decline in the pace of business activity or a decline in agricultural prices. More important, such contemporaneous events as the state of the harvests at home and abroad, developments in the railroad industry in the 1870s and in the London money market in the 1890s had important effects on the particular dates at which those political pressures produced monetary disturbances, which in their turn reacted on business conditions and political attitudes.

The establishment of the Federal Reserve System provides the student of money a closer substitute for the controlled experiment to determine the direction of influence than the social scientist can generally obtain. The system was at times simply a means through which other forces operated—as during the two world wars, and much of the 1930s when it followed a largely passive course, and after World War II when its policy of supporting the prices of government securities left it little independent initiative. But the establishment of the system gave a small body of individuals the power, which they exercised from time to time, to alter the course of events in significant and identifiable ways through a deliberative process—a sequence parallel with the conduct of a controlled experiment. True, the actions of the monetary authorities were greatly affected by the climate of opinion and knowledge in which they operated. Their attitudes, the experiments they undertook, and the interpretation they placed on the results were to a large extent determined by the contemporary course of events and the contemporary state of knowledge about monetary phenomena. This has also been true of physical scientists in deciding what experiments to undertake and in interpreting the results in light of preceding experiments and the contemporary body of knowledge. In either case, such dependence on the existing state of knowledge does not alter the scientific independence from the prior or contemporary course of events of the changes introduced into the controlled variables. What it means in both cases is simply that later students may reinterpret the results of the experiments in light of the changed body of knowledge and draw conclusions that are different from those drawn by the original experimenters.

True, also, it is often impossible and always difficult to identify accurately the effects of the actions of the monetary authorities. Their actions are taken amidst many other circumstances, and it may not be at all clear whether their actions or some of the other circumstances produced the results observed. This is equally true of the experiments of physical scientists. No experiment is completely controlled, and most experiments add little to tested and confirmed knowledge about the subject of experiment. It is the rare crucial experiment that throws a flood of light on its subject—a light that blinds us to many less important experiments that were necessary before the one crucial experiment could be made.

Three counterparts of such crucial experiments stand out in the monetary record since the establishment of the Federal Reserve System. On three occasions the system deliberately took policy steps of major magnitude which cannot be regarded as necessary or inevitable economic consequences of contemporary changes in money income and prices. Like the crucial experiments of the physical scientist, the results are so consistent and sharp as to leave little doubt about their interpretation. The dates are January–June 1920, October 1931, and July 1936–January 1937. These are the three occasions— and the only three—when the Federal Reserve System engaged in acts of commission that were sharply restrictive: in January 1920, by raising the rediscount rate from 4.75 percent to 6 percent and then in June 1920, to 7 percent, at a time when member banks were borrowing from the reserve banks more than the total of their reserve balances; in October 1931, by raising the rediscount rate from 1.5 percent to 3.5 percent within a two-week period, at a time when a wave of failures was engulfing commercial banks, as in the preceding year, and indebtedness to the system was growing; in July 1936 and January 1937, by announcing the doubling of reserve requirements in three stages, the last effective on May 1, 1937, at a time when the Treasury was engaged in gold sterilization, which was the equivalent of a large-scale restrictive open market operation. There is no other occasion in Federal Reserve history when it has taken explicit restrictive measures of comparable magnitude—we cannot even suggest possible parallels.

The strictly monetary changes associated with those actions were equally sharp and distinctive. The actions were followed after some months in 1920 and 1936–1937, immediately in 1931, by sharp declines in the stock of money, the three sharpest declines within a twelve-month period in the history of the Federal Reserve System: declines of 9 percent (1920), 14 percent (1931), and 3 percent (1937), respectively. And for the first and third declines, the numbers understate the severity of the monetary reaction. In 1919 and again in 1936, the money stock was growing at a rapid rate, so the subsequent declines represented a deceleration from an unusually high rate of growth to an unusually high rate of decline. The 1931 decline—the severest absolute decline of the three—was the mildest in terms of deceleration; the money stock in the preceding year had been falling at a slightly lower rate, so the increase in the rate of decline in the year beginning October 1931 was only about one percentage point.

The economic changes associated with those monetary actions were equally sharp and equally distinctive. Each was followed by sharp contractions in industrial production, after some months in 1920 and 1936–1937, and immediately in 1931: declines within a twelve-month period of 30 percent (1920), 24 percent (1931), and 34 percent (1937), respectively. There are only two other comparably severe declines in industrial production: during 1929–1931, dealt with further below; and 1945, when the sharp decline represented a shift in the composition of output away from military products after the end of the war, rather than a general contraction in economic activity, as at the other four dates. Other indicators confirm the story told by industrial production. Whether one looks at wholesale prices, freight car loadings, common stock prices, or department stores' sales, the downturns that followed the three monetary actions are the severest by a wide margin in the history of the Federal Reserve System, except only the 1929–1931 decline.[1]

The strength of the evidence furnished by those three quasi-controlled experiments can perhaps be made clearer by an analogy. Suppose we had medical records of 42 married couples (to match the 42 years of Federal Reserve history from 1919 to 1960, excluding World War I because the system was not effectively in control). Suppose three men and four women were found to have a specified illness; suppose that three of the four women turned out to be the wives of the three men with the same illness. The presumption that the illness was contagious would certainly be very strong—especially so, if it were discovered that the husband of the fourth woman was the only remaining man to have a biologically related but not identical illness. Similarly, the three episodes described above establish a comparably strong presumption that the economic changes were the consequence of the deliberately undertaken monetary actions, and hence that our finding of a close covariation between the stock of money and income reflects the existence of an influence running from money to income. Indeed, in one respect the analogy seriously understates the strength of the evidence. It takes no account of the time sequence of events.[2]

The presumption that the economic changes were the consequence of the monetary changes is greatly strengthened by examination of the one sharp economic contraction not associated with explicit restrictive measures by the Federal Reserve System—the 1929–1931 contraction, which was the first part of the great contraction from 1929 to 1933. That contraction has served perhaps more than any other experience to strengthen the view that money dances to the tune of business. The reason is that the Federal Reserve System did not, in fact, stem the decline of one-third in the stock of money—by far the largest in the course of a cyclical contraction at least since 1892–1894—or the accompanying contraction in economic activity. The system pleaded impotence, arguing explicitly that the nonmonetary forces making for contraction were so strong and violent that it was powerless to stem the tide, and implicitly that the depth of the decline in the money stock was due to the depth of the decline in business activity, rather than, as the evidence cited above suggests, the reverse. Many others, recognizing the good intentions of the monetary authorities and the ability of many individuals in the system, while independently holding a wide variety of views about the role of money in economic affairs, accepted the system's plea. In addition, a revolution in economic theory, having quite different origins and by no means necessarily implying the impotence of monetary policy, offered a theoretical structure that at one and the same time could rationalize the impotence of monetary policy and provide an intellectually satisfying alternative explanation of the economic debacle.

There is one sense—and, so far as we can see, only one—in which a case can be made for the proposition that the monetary decline was a consequence of the economic decline. That sense is not relevant to our main task of seeking to understand economic interrelations, since it involves relying primarily on psychological and political factors. The system was operating in a climate of opinion that in the main regarded recessions and depressions as curative episodes, necessary in order to purge the body economic of the aftereffects of its earlier excesses. The prevailing opinion also confused money and credit; confused the elasticity of one component of the money stock relative to another with the elasticity of the total stock; regarded it as desirable that the stock of money should respond to the "needs of trade," rising in expansions and falling in contractions; and attached much greater importance to the maintenance of the gold standard and the stability of exchanges than to the maintenance of internal stability. Most of those attitudes characterized the public at large and not merely the financial community or the Federal Reserve System in particular. Given that milieu, it can be argued that the system followed an inevitable policy; that it could not have been expected to prevent the appreciable decline in the stock of money during 1930, because it and others as well regarded the decline as a desirable offset to earlier speculative excess; and that its failure to react vigorously, after banks began failing on a large scale in late 1930 and the public sought to convert deposits into currency, reflected the attitude that it was desirable to liquidate "bad" banks, to let "nature take its course" rather than to support the financial system "artificially." Certainly, the assignment of priority to the maintenance of the gold standard was in a proximate sense the reason for the sharp rise in discount rates in October 1931 following Britain's departure from gold and a gold outflow from the United States—the restrictive action described above as one of the system's crucial experiments.

This account portrays accurately an important part of the situation. It helps to explain how able and public-spirited men could have acted in a manner which in retrospect appears misguided, why there was so notable an absence of economic statesmanship outside the system and hence no steady informed pressure on the system for different action. But even on that level, the account is seriously incomplete. We are inclined to believe that the particular course of action followed by the Federal Reserve System owed less to the climate of opinion—though it was certainly a necessary condition—than to a sequence of more or less accidental events and the running conflict for power within the system. Benjamin Strong's death in 1928 unleashed an active phase of conflict which dominated policy throughout 1929, producing a deadlock between the board and the New York bank—acting as leader of all the reserve banks—about the proper policy to adopt in face of the stock market boom. The result was a policy that, in our view, was too easy to break the bull market and too tight to permit vigorous business expansion. The conflict plus the reaction by the rest of the system to the New York bank's independent (and effective) operations in the wake of the stock market crash in October 1929 indirectly led to a shift of power over open market operations. A five-man committee, dominated by the New York bank, was replaced by a twelve-man committee of the twelve Federal Reserve bank governors in which New York played a less important role. That shift stacked the cards heavily in favor of a policy of inaction and drift.

We share the view expressed by Carl Snyder, for many years associated with the New York bank as a statistician and economist, that if Benjamin Strong could "have had twelve months more of vigorous health, we might have ended the depression in 1930, and with this the long drawn out world crisis that so profoundly affected the ensuing political developments."[3] As it was, Strong's successor at New York, George L. Harrison, vigorously advocated expansionary action in 1930, but was unable to prevail over the combined opposition of the board and the other bank governors. Harrison was in favor of expansionary action in 1931, that time with the support of the new governor of the board, Eugene Meyer, but the pattern of deadlock and inaction had been set, to be broken only temporarily in 1932 under the pressure of congressional prodding. Despite the general climate of opinion, the technical personnel of the New York bank—and it must be recalled that under Strong the New York bank dominated system policy almost completely—were consistently in favor of the policies which seem to us in retrospect the ones that should have been followed.

In any event, what is relevant to our present purpose is neither praise nor blame, nor even a full understanding of the reasons for the system's behavior under the difficult and trying circumstances it faced. Even if its behavior was psychologically or politically inevitable under the circumstances, that would explain only why the quasi-controlled experiment was conducted. It would not explain the results of the experiment. The question would remain whether the monetary changes were the inevitable result of the economic changes, so that, if the system had not been the intermediary, some other mechanism would have enforced the same monetary changes; or whether the monetary changes can be regarded as an economically independent factor which accounted in substantial measure for the economic changes. There is little doubt about the answer. At all times throughout the 1929–1933 contraction, alternative policies were available to the system by which it could have kept the stock of money from falling, and indeed could have increased it at almost any desired rate. Those policies did not involve radical innovations. They involved measures of a kind the system had taken in earlier years, of a kind explicitly contemplated by the founders of the system to meet precisely the kind of banking crisis that developed in late 1930 and persisted thereafter. They involved measures that were actually proposed and very likely would have been adopted under a slightly different bureaucratic structure or distribution of power, or even if the men in power had had somewhat different personalities. Until late 1931—and we believe not even then—the alternative policies involved no conflict with the maintenance of the gold standard. Until September 1931, the problem that recurrently troubled the system was how to keep the gold inflows under control, not the reverse.

To consider still another alternative: if the pre-1914 banking system rather than the Federal Reserve System had been in existence in 1929, the money stock almost certainly would not have undergone a decline comparable to the one that occurred. Comparison of the 1907 banking panic under the earlier system and the closely similar liquidity crisis which began in late 1930 offers strong evidence for this judgment. If the earlier system had been in operation, and if everything else had proceeded as it did up to December 1930, the experience of 1907 strongly suggests that there would have been a more severe initial reaction to the bank failures than there was in 1930, probably involving concerted restriction by banks of the convertibility of deposits into currency. The restriction might have had more severe initial effects toward deepening the economic contraction than the persistent pressure on the banking system that characterized late 1930 and early 1931 had. But it also would have cut short the spread of the crisis, would have prevented cumulation of bank failures, and would have made possible, as it did in 1908, economic recovery after a few months.

While, therefore, the actions of the Federal Reserve System in 1929–1933 may be understandable under the circumstances, even psychologically and politically inevitable, the contraction is additional strong evidence for the economic independence of monetary changes from the contemporary course of income and prices, even during the early phase of the contraction, from 1929 to 1931, when the decline in the stock of money was not the result of explicit restrictive measures taken by the system. It can indeed be regarded as a fourth crucial experiment, making the matching of independent monetary decline and subsequent economic decline 4 to 4.[4]

The existence of an important independent influence running from money to income explains the contrast we have noted between the variability in monetary arrangements during the near-century we have studied and the stability of the relation between changes in money and in other economic variables. The variability of monetary arrangements has produced, as we have seen, a corresponding variation in the movements of money itself. But, given that the major channel of influence is from money to business, there is no reason the changes in monetary arrangements should have altered the relation between movements in money and in business. That relation is determined primarily by the channels through which money affects business. So long as they remain the same, as apparently they have, so also should the relation between money and business. Suppose, however, the major channel of influence had been from business to money. Changes in monetary institutions would then have affected not only the behavior of money but also the relation between money and other economic variables, since a change in business would have had different effects on the stock of money under the different monetary arrangements. Under the pre-1914 gold standard, for example, a business expansion in the United States tended to generate a deficit in the balance of payments, which in turn tended to produce an outflow of gold and hence downward pressure on the stock of money. That particular link in the sequence was largely severed by the gold-sterilization policy followed by the Federal Reserve in the 1920s and by the Treasury in part of the 1930s, and was greatly weakened by the change in the character of the gold standard during the rest of the period after 1914. Both before and after 1914, business expansion raised interest rates and stimulated banks to expand. However, before 1914 a rise in interest rates could raise the stock of money only through a rise in the deposit-reserve ratio or through the attraction of capital and thereby gold from abroad. After 1914, a rise in interest rates could also raise the stock of money by inducing banks to borrow more heavily from the Federal Reserve System. If the predominant direction of influence had been from business to money, these and other changes in the links between business and money would very likely have produced an appreciably different relation between movements in the two before and after 1914, and perhaps also for further subdivisions of those periods.

While the influence running from money to economic activity has been predominant, there have clearly also been influences running the other way, particularly during the shorter run movements associated with the business cycle. The cyclical pattern of the deposit-reserve ratio is one example. The resumption and silver episodes, the 1919 inflation, and the 1929–1933 contraction reveal clearly other aspects of the reflex influence of business on money. Changes in the money stock are therefore a consequence as well as an independent source of change in money income and prices, though, once they occur, they produce in their turn still further effects on income and prices. Mutual interaction, but with money rather clearly the senior partner in longer-run movements and in major cyclical movements, and more nearly an equal partner with money income and prices in shorter-run and milder movements—this is the generalization suggested by our evidence.

4. DECEPTIVENESS OF APPEARANCES

Money is a fascinating subject of study because it is so full of mystery and paradox. The piece of green paper with printing on it is little different, as paper, from a piece of the same size torn from a newspaper or magazine, yet the one will enable its bearer to command some measure of food, drink, clothing, and the remaining goods of life; the other is fit only to light the fire. Whence the difference? The piece of green paper reads, "The United States of America will pay to the bearer on demand . . . dollars," or words to that effect, plus an assertion that it is "legal tender." But under current circumstances, the promise amounts only to a commitment to exchange one piece of green paper for one or several other pieces of green paper or for coins which, if melted down, will sell on the market as metal for less than the amount of paper money they serve to redeem. The legal-tender quality means only that the government will accept the pieces of paper in discharge of debts due to itself, and that the courts will regard them as discharging debts stated in dollars. Why should they also be accepted by private persons in private transactions for goods and services?

The short answer—yet the right answer—is that each accepts them because he is confident others will. The pieces of green paper have value because everybody thinks they have value, and everybody thinks they have value because in his experience they have had value. Our economy could not operate at more than a small fraction of its present level of productivity without a common and widely accepted medium of exchange; yet that common and widely accepted medium of exchange is, at bottom, a social convention which owes its very existence to the mutual acceptance of what from one point of view is a fiction.

The social convention or the fiction or what you will is no fragile thing. On the contrary, the social value of a common money is so great that people will stick to the fiction even under extreme provocation—whence, of course, comes part of the gains that can be obtained from inflation by the issuers of the money and hence also the temptation to inflate. But neither is the fiction indestructible: extreme variation in the quantity of the green paper—as in the U.S. Revolutionary War or in the hyperinflations in various countries after World Wars I and II—or moderate variation in its quantity plus legally and effectively enforced ceilings on nominal prices—as in Germany after World War II—can render the paper formerly serving as money worthless and induce people to seek substitutes—like the cigarettes and cognac which for a time became the medium of exchange in Germany after World War II.

Money is a veil. The "real" forces are the capacities of the people, their industry and ingenuity, the resources they command, their mode of economic and political organization, and the like. As John Stuart Mill wrote more than a century ago:

> There cannot, in short, be intrinsically a more insignificant thing, in the economy of society, than money; except in the character of a contrivance for sparing time and labor. It is a machine for doing quickly and commodiously what would be done, though less quickly and commodiously, without it: and like many other kinds of machinery, it only exerts a distinct and independent influence of its own when it gets out of order.[5]

Perfectly true. Yet also somewhat misleading, unless we recognize that there is hardly a contrivance man possesses which can do more damage to a society when it goes amiss.

Each man believes he can determine how much of his wealth he will hold in money; yet the total amount of money available for all to hold is outside the control of all holders of money taken together. Each bank thinks it can determine how much of its assets it will hold in the form of currency, plus deposits at Federal Reserve banks, to meet legal reserve requirements and for precautionary purposes. Yet the total amount available for all banks to hold is outside the control of all banks together. If any one bank receives an accession to its cash, it can therewith acquire additional noncash assets equal at most to that accession; yet if all banks together receive an accession to cash, the banking system can therewith acquire additional assets equal to a multiple of that accession.

This deceptiveness of appearances has recurred again and again in the course of our narrative. The price of gold in terms of greenbacks during the Civil War may have fluctuated from day to day in accordance with the changing fortunes of war; but the fortunes of war affected to only a minor extent the level about which the fluctuations occurred—only as they affected the willingness of foreigners to hold greenbacks or securities expressed in terms of greenbacks. The level reflected rather the drastic decline in cotton exports and the rising internal prices in the North as money was issued to help finance the war.

One measure taken to foster resumption, which is to say, to raise the value of the dollar in terms of foreign currencies, was identical with a measure taken by Franklin D. Roosevelt to achieve precisely the opposite purpose, to lower the value of the dollar in terms of foreign currency. In both cases, the Treasury undertook to buy gold abroad. The New Deal's economics was correct, at least in this respect; so the adoption of the same measure during the greenback period meant that the mechanical effects of the purchase of gold abroad made resumption more rather than less difficult.

Although resumption was a major political issue for a decade and a half, its successful achievement owed little to the measures taken in its name. The main governmental contribution was a minor reduction in high-powered money—granted, no mean achievement on a purely political level, in view of the pressure to expand the issue of greenbacks. Resumption succeeded because the rapid growth of output brought a halving of the price level despite a mild rise in the stock of money. The governmental measures that had the greatest effect on resumption were not the explicitly monetary measures but the acts of omission and commission that contributed to the rapid growth of output.

The proponents of free silver were attacked by "sound money" forces on the ground that free silver would produce an unduly rapid expansion in the money stock and thereby breed price inflation. The limited purchases of silver made by the Treasury were deplored because it was believed they raised unduly the stock of money and were thus harbingers of the inflation that would be unleashed by unlimited purchases. In fact, given that the gold standard was not abandoned, the main economic harm done by the silver agitation was that it enforced an unduly slow rate of increase in the money stock and thereby produced deflation. It did so because the fear that the United States would abandon gold reduced capital inflows which would otherwise have been larger, or fostered capital flights. In turn, these required lower prices in the United States than would otherwise have been necessary in order to balance international payments at the exchange rates fixed by official prices of gold in the United States and abroad.

Bryan's defeat in 1896 marked the crest of the silver agitation. It was the crest, not because Bryan lost his silver tongue, nor because the advocates of "sound money" persuaded the advocates of free silver by their arguments, but because gold discoveries and improvements in gold mining and refining made gold the effective vehicle for the inflation that Bryan and his followers had sought to achieve with silver.

The banking panic of 1907 produced apparently irresistible pressure for banking reform. Yet we have found reason to believe that at least the final step of that panic, the concerted restriction by banks of the convertibility of deposits into currency, was a therapeutic measure which cut short the liquidity crisis, prevented good banks from failing in droves as victims of mass hysteria and, at the cost of severe but brief difficulties, enabled recovery and expansion to come after a short-lived contraction.

The reform measure finally enacted—the Federal Reserve System—with the aim of preventing any such panics or any such restriction of convertibility in the future did not in fact stem the worst panic in American economic history and the severest restrictions of convertibility, the collapse of the banking system from 1930 to 1933 terminating in the banking holiday of March 1933. That same reform, intended to promote monetary stability, was followed by about 30 years of relatively greater instability in the money stock than any experienced in the pre-Federal Reserve period our data cover, and possibly than any experienced in the whole of U.S. history, the Revolutionary War alone excepted.

The stock market boom and the afterglow of concern with World War I inflation have led to a widespread belief that the 1920s were a period of inflation and that the collapse from 1929 to 1933 was a reaction to that. In fact, the 1920s were, if anything, a time of relative deflation: from 1923 to 1929—to compare peak years of business cycles and so avoid distortion from cyclical influences—wholesale prices fell at the rate of 1 percent per year and the stock of money rose at the annual rate of 4 percent per year, which is roughly the rate required to match expansion of output. The business cycle expansion from 1927 to 1929 was the first since 1891–1893 during which wholesale prices fell, even if only a trifle, and there has been none since.

The monetary collapse from 1929 to 1933 was not an inevitable consequence of what had gone before. It was a result of the policies followed during those years. As already noted, alternative policies that could have halted the monetary debacle were available throughout those years. Though the Federal Reserve System proclaimed that it was following an easy-money policy, in fact it followed an exceedingly tight policy.

The proponents of the New Deal were strongly in favor of easy money. And there was rapid monetary expansion during the late 1930s, produced primarily by two things: the rise in the price of gold and the rise of Hitler to power, which stimulated a capital flow to the United States. The rapid monetary expansion owed nothing to monetary actions other than the rise in the price of gold. Though that rise had the direct effect intended, some of the measures accompanying it—in particular the nationalization of gold, the abrogation of gold clauses, and the New Deal's program aside from monetary policy—had the opposite effects by discouraging business investment. The one major monetary action of the Federal Reserve during that period was the doubling of reserve requirements in 1936 and 1937 under newly acquired powers. The action was not intended to have significant contemporary deflationary effects; it was taken primarily as a "precautionary" step; the Federal Reserve System satisfied itself that excess reserves were ample and widely distributed. In the event, in combination with Treasury gold sterilization, it had a serious deflationary impact.

The silver-purchase program of the 1930s was undertaken with the ostensible objective of raising the proportion of silver in the nation's monetary reserves from one-sixth to one-third, in large part to aid silver miners. The program involved aggregate expenditures of $2 billion from 1933 to 1960, amounting to at least $5 for each dollar of benefit to U.S. silver miners. Yet the increase in the proportion of silver to one-third was never achieved. But the silver-purchase program in the 1930s did impose several years of drastic deflation on China, drove China permanently and Mexico temporarily off the silver standard, and must be counted as a major factor weakening China both economically and politically.

World War II was widely expected to be followed by severe unemployment. The Federal Reserve System girded itself for the possibility and welcomed the bond-support program, because the system thought it would be consistent with easy-money policies which would be required after the war. In the event, inflation rather than deflation loomed as the greater danger and, under the added impetus to inflation given by the Korean War, the Federal Reserve was finally led to divest itself of the self-imposed chains of the bond-support program.

What happened in the United States happened also abroad. The quantity of money, it had come to be widely believed, was of little economic significance except as control over it might be the means of keeping long-term interest rates lower than otherwise, which, in turn, might contribute a mite to the level of aggregate demand, which would otherwise be deficient. Easy money was the near-uniform prescription. Inflation was the near-uniform result. It was stemmed only as easy money was given up. One result has been to restore a healthy respect for the role of money in economic affairs.

Velocity has been rising throughout almost the whole of the postwar period in contrast to its decline in the preceding three-quarters of a century. A large part of the rise was clearly a reaction to the wartime decline. But the rise has been too large and too long continued to be accounted for in this way alone. Numerous explanations have been offered, ranging from the wider availability and better quality of substitutes for money to the rise in interest rates, to fear of inflation. We are inclined to believe that, while these may all have played a part, the rise over and above the reaction to the wartime decline has been mainly produced by increasing confidence on the part of the public at large in the stability of the economy. In accordance with this interpretation, we expect the secular decline to be resumed. But we are still too close to the appearances to be at all sure in what way they are deceptive. We shall have to wait for experience to unfold before discriminating finally among the alternative explanations.

One thing of which we are confident is that the history of money will continue to have surprises in store for those who follow its future course— surprises that the student of money and the statesman alike will ignore at their peril.

Notes

1. In addition to the three restrictive actions, three expansionary actions by the Federal Reserve System—apart from those it took in the two world wars—were associated with correspondingly sharp monetary and economic changes. [See Table 18.1.]

TABLE 18.1

Monetary Action	Associated Change in Money Stock	Associated Change in Industrial Production
Dec. 1923–Oct. 1924 F. R. purchase of $0.5 billion of governments	Feb. 1924–Feb. 1925 19 percent increase	July 1924–July 1925 22.5 percent increase
Apr.–Aug. 1932 F. R. purchase of $1 billion of governments	Apr. 1932–Jan. 1933 Shift from 14 percent annual rate of decline to 1.75 percent annual rate of rise	July–Nov. 1932 14 percent increase
Mar.–Dec. 1958 F. R. purchase of $3 billion of governments; $4.6 billion increase in F. R. credit	Dec. 1957–Dec. 1958 6.6 percent increase	Apr. 1958–Apr. 1959 23 percent increase

We regard these episodes as less striking and decisive than the three cited in the text, because the associated monetary and economic changes are less distinctive: e.g., from June 1933 to June 1936, there was no Federal Reserve action, yet the stock of money rose by 44 percent and industrial production by 31 percent.

2. This reflects the one respect in which the analogy is inexact. Time is continuous. There is no particular reason for taking the year instead of the quarter or the biennium as the unit of analysis, and for regarding 42 discrete observations as containing the same information as our time series covering 42 years. It is not at all clear whether the appropriate number is larger or smaller than 42. Serial correlation among successive years points toward a smaller number, say, 10, the number of complete reference cycles in the period from March 1919 to February 1961. The possibility of identifying turns and timing relations monthly argues for a larger number, since the continuous data give information not available from the discrete unordered data.

If the four ill wives and three ill husbands were distributed at random among 42 wives and 42 husbands, the probability that the three husbands would be married to three of the wives is 1 in 2,870. The corresponding probability for the same number of ill wives and husbands distributed among a total of ten couples is 1 in 30.

3. Carl Snyder, *Capitalism the Creator* (New York: Macmillan, 1940), p. 203.

4. For 42 married couples, the probability that four ill husbands and four ill wives chosen at random would constitute four married couples is 1 in 111,930. For the alternative of ten (see note 2, above) as the total number of couples, 1929–1931 and October 1931 cannot be regarded as two separate observations, since both fall within a single reference cycle. It is therefore necessary to change the number of ill individuals. The simplest counterpart is to suppose ten married couples, three ill husbands and three ill wives. The probability that the ill husbands and wives would constitute three married couples if chosen at random is then 1 in 120.

5. Ashley, ed., *Principles of Political Economy* (New York: Longmans, Green & Co., 1929), p. 488.

INFLATION AND UNEMPLOYMENT

· 19 ·

When the Bank of Sweden established the prize for Economic Science in memory of Alfred Nobel (1968), there doubtless was—as there doubtless still remains—widespread skepticism among both scientists and the broader public about the appropriateness of treating economics as parallel to physics, chemistry, and medicine. These are regarded as "exact sciences" in which objective, cumulative, definitive knowledge is possible. Economics, and its fellow social sciences, are regarded more nearly as branches of philosophy than of science properly defined, enmeshed with values at the outset because they deal with human behavior. Do not the social sciences, in which scholars are analyzing the behavior of themselves and their fellow men, who are in turn observing and reacting to what the scholars say, require fundamentally different methods of investigation than the physical and biological sciences? Should they not be judged by different criteria?

I. SOCIAL AND NATURAL SCIENCES

I have never myself accepted this view. I believe that it reflects a misunderstanding not so much of the character and possibilities of social science as of the character and possibilities of natural science. In both, there is no "certain"

From 1976 Nobel lecture. ©The Nobel Foundation 1977. Reprinted by permission.

substantive knowledge; only tentative hypotheses that can never be "proved," but can only fail to be rejected, hypotheses in which we may have more or less confidence, depending on such features as the breadth of experience they encompass relative to their own complexity and relative to alternative hypotheses, and the number of occasions on which they have escaped possible rejection. In both social and natural sciences, the body of positive knowledge grows by the failure of a tentative hypothesis to predict phenomena the hypothesis professes to explain; by the patching up of that hypothesis until someone suggests a new hypothesis that more elegantly or simply embodies the troublesome phenomena, and so on ad infinitum. In both, experiment is sometimes possible, sometimes not (witness meteorology). In both, no experiment is ever completely controlled, and experience often offers evidence that is the equivalent of controlled experiment. In both, there is no way to have a self-contained closed system or to avoid interaction between the observer and the observed. The Gödel theorem in mathematics, the Heisenberg uncertainty principle in physics, the self-fulfilling or self-defeating prophecy in the social sciences all exemplify these limitations.

Of course, the different sciences deal with different subject matter, have different bodies of evidence to draw on (for example, introspection is a more important source of evidence for social than for natural sciences), find different techniques of analysis most useful, and have achieved differential success in predicting the phenomena they are studying. But such differences are as great among, say, physics, biology, medicine, and meteorology as between any of them and economics.

Even the difficult problem of separating value judgments from scientific judgments is not unique to the social sciences. I well recall a dinner at a Cambridge University college when I was sitting between a fellow economist and R. A. Fisher, the great mathematical statistician and geneticist. My fellow economist told me about a student he had been tutoring on labor economics, who, in connection with an analysis of the effect of trade unions, remarked, "Well surely, Mr. X (another economist of a different political persuasion) would not agree with that." My colleague regarded this experience as a terrible indictment of economics because it illustrated the impossibility of a value-free positive economic science. I turned to Sir Ronald and asked whether such an experience was indeed unique to social science. His answer was an impassioned "no," and he proceeded to tell one story after another about how accurately he could infer views in genetics from political views.

One of my great teachers, Wesley C. Mitchell, impressed on me the basic reason why scholars have every incentive to pursue a value-free science, whatever their values and however strongly they may wish to spread and promote them. In order to recommend a course of action to achieve an objective, we must first know whether that course of action will in fact promote the objective. Positive scientific knowledge that enables us to predict the consequences of a possible course of action is clearly a prerequisite for the normative judgment whether that course of action is desirable. The road to hell is paved with good intentions, precisely because of the neglect of this rather obvious point.

This point is particularly important in economics. Many countries around the world are today experiencing socially destructive inflation, abnormally high unemployment, misuse of economic resources, and in some cases, the suppression of human freedom not because evil men deliberately sought to achieve these results, nor because of differences in values among their citizens, but because of erroneous judgments about the consequences of government measures: errors that at least in principle are capable of being corrected by the progress of positive economic science.

Rather than pursue these ideas in the abstract (I have discussed the methodological issues more fully in my *Methodology*),[1] I shall illustrate the positive scientific character of economics by discussing a particular economic issue that has been a major concern of the economics profession throughout the postwar period; namely, the relation between inflation and unemployment. This issue is an admirable illustration because it has been a controversial political issue throughout the period, yet the drastic change that has occurred in accepted professional views was produced primarily by the scientific response to experience that contradicted a tentatively accepted hypothesis— precisely the classical process for the revision of a scientific hypothesis.

I cannot give here an exhaustive survey of the work that has been done on this issue or of the evidence that has led to the revision of the hypothesis. I shall be able only to skim the surface in the hope of conveying the flavor of that work and that evidence and of indicating the major items requiring further investigation.

Professional controversy about the relation between inflation and unemployment has been intertwined with controversy about the relative role of monetary, fiscal, and other factors in influencing aggregate demand. One issue deals with how a change in aggregate nominal demand, however produced, works itself out through changes in employment and price levels; the other, with the factors accounting for the changes in aggregate nominal demand.

The two issues are closely related. The effects of a change in aggregate nominal demand on employment and price levels may not be independent of the source of the change, and conversely, the effect of monetary, fiscal, or other forces on aggregate nominal demand may depend on how employment and price levels react. A full analysis will clearly have to treat the two issues jointly. Yet there is a considerable measure of independence between them. To a first approximation, the effects on employment and price levels may depend only on the magnitude of the change in aggregate nominal demand, not on its source. On both issues, professional opinion today is very different than it was just after World War II because experience contradicted tentatively accepted hypotheses. Either issue could therefore serve to illustrate my main thesis. I have chosen to deal with only one in order to keep this lecture within reasonable bounds. I have chosen to make that one the relation between inflation and unemployment, because recent experience leaves me less satisfied with the adequacy of my earlier work on that issue than with the adequacy of my earlier work on the forces producing changes in aggregate nominal demand.

II. Stage 1: Negatively Sloping Phillips Curve

Professional analysis of the relation between inflation and unemployment has gone through two stages since the end of World War II and is now entering a third. The first stage was the acceptance of a hypothesis associated with the name of A. W. Phillips that there is a stable negative relation between the level of unemployment and the rate of change of wages—high levels of unemployment being accompanied by falling wages, low levels of unemployment by rising wages.[2] The wage change in turn was linked to price change by allowing for the secular increase in productivity and treating the excess of price over wage cost as given by a roughly constant markup factor.

Figure 19.1 illustrates this hypothesis, where I have followed the standard practice of relating unemployment directly to price change, short-circuiting the intermediate step through wages.

This relation was widely interpreted as a causal relation that offered a stable trade-off to policymakers. They could choose a low unemployment target, such as U_L. In that case they would have to accept an inflation rate of A. There would remain the problem of choosing the measures (monetary, fiscal, perhaps other) that would produce the level of aggregate nominal demand required to achieve U_L, but if that were done, there need be no concern about maintaining that combination of unemployment and inflation. Alternatively, the policymakers could choose a low inflation rate or even deflation as their target. In that case they would have to reconcile themselves to higher unemployment: U_0 for zero inflation, U_H for deflation.

Economists then busied themselves with trying to extract the relation depicted in Figure 19.1 from evidence for different countries and periods, to eliminate the effect of extraneous disturbances, to clarify the relation between wage change and price change, and so on. In addition, they explored social gains and losses from inflation on the one hand and unemployment on the other, in order to facilitate the choice of the "right" trade-off.

Unfortunately for this hypothesis, additional evidence failed to conform

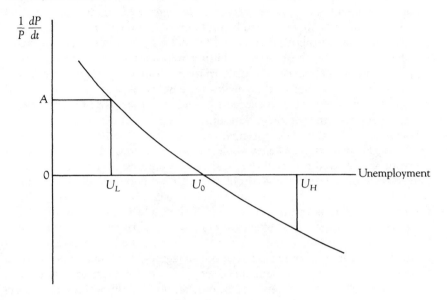

FIGURE 19.1
SIMPLE PHILLIPS CURVE

to it. Empirical estimates of the Phillips curve relation were unsatisfactory. More important, the inflation rate that appeared to be consistent with a specified level of unemployment did not remain fixed: in the circumstances of the post–World War II period, when governments everywhere were seeking to promote "full employment," it tended in any one country to rise over time and to vary sharply among countries. Looked at the other way, rates of inflation that had earlier been associated with low levels of unemployment were experienced along with high levels of unemployment. The phenomenon of simultaneous high inflation and high unemployment increasingly forced itself on public and professional notice, receiving the unlovely label of "stagflation."

Some of us were skeptical from the outset about the validity of a stable Phillips curve, primarily on theoretical rather than empirical grounds.[3] What mattered for employment, we argued, was not wages in dollars or pounds or kronor but real wages—what the wages would buy in goods and services. Low unemployment would, indeed, mean pressure for a higher real wage—but real wages could be higher even if nominal wages were lower, provided that prices were still lower. Similarly, high unemployment would, indeed, mean pressure for a lower real wage—but real wages could be lower, even if nominal wages were higher, provided prices were still higher.

There is no need to assume a stable Phillips curve in order to explain the apparent tendency for an acceleration of inflation to reduce unemployment. That can be explained by the impact of *unanticipated* changes in nominal demand on markets characterized by (implicit or explicit) long-term commitments with respect to both capital and labor. Long-term labor commitments can be explained by the cost of acquiring information by employers about employees and by employees about alternative employment opportunities plus the specific human capital that makes an employee's value to a particular employer grow over time and exceed his value to other potential employers.

Only surprises matter. If everyone anticipated that prices would rise at, say, 20 percent a year, then this anticipation would be embodied in future wage (and other) contracts, real wages would then behave precisely as they would if everyone anticipated no price rise, and there would be no reason for the 20 percent rate of inflation to be associated with a different level of unemployment than a zero rate. An unanticipated change is very different, especially in the presence of long-term commitments—themselves partly a result of the imperfect knowledge whose effect they enhance and spread over time. Long-term commitments mean, first, that there is not instantaneous market clearing (as in markets for perishable foods) but only a lagged adjustment of both prices and quantity to changes in demand or supply (as in the house rental market); second, that commitments entered into depend not only on current observable prices, but also on the prices expected to prevail throughout the term of the commitment.

III. Stage 2: The Natural-Rate Hypothesis

Proceeding along these lines, we (in particular, E. S. Phelps and myself)[4] developed an alternative hypothesis that distinguished between the short-run and long-run effects of unanticipated changes in aggregate nominal demand. Start from some initial stable position and let there be, for example, an unanticipated acceleration of aggregate nominal demand. This will come to each producer as an unexpectedly favorable demand for his product. In an environment in which changes are always occurring in the relative demand for different goods, he will not know whether this change is special to him or pervasive. It will be rational for him to interpret it as at least partly special and to react to it, by seeking to produce more to sell at what he now perceives to be a higher than expected market price for future output. He will be willing to pay higher nominal wages than he had been willing to pay before in order to attract additional workers. The real wage that matters to him is the wage in terms of the price of his product, and he perceives that price as higher than before. A higher nominal wage can therefore mean a lower *real* wage as perceived by him.

To workers, the situation is different: what matters to them is the purchasing power of wages not over the particular good they produce but over all goods in general. Both they and their employers are likely to adjust more slowly their perception of prices in general—because it is more costly to acquire information about that—than their perception of the price of the particular good they produce. As a result, a rise in nominal wages may be perceived by workers as a rise in real wages and hence call forth an increased supply, at the same time that it is perceived by employers as a fall in real wages and hence calls forth an increased offer of jobs. Expressed in terms of the average of perceived future prices, real wages are lower; in terms of the perceived future average price, real wages are higher.

But this situation is temporary: let the higher rate of growth of aggregate nominal demand and of prices continue, and perceptions will adjust to reality. When they do, the initial effect will disappear, and then even be reversed for a time as workers and employers find themselves locked into inappropriate contracts. Ultimately, employment will be back at the level that prevailed before the assumed unanticipated acceleration in aggregate nominal demand.

This alternative hypothesis is depicted in Figure 19.2. Each negatively sloping curve is a Phillips curve like that in Figure 19.1 except that it is for a particular anticipated or perceived rate of inflation, defined as the perceived average rate of price change, *not* the average of perceived rates of individual price change (the order of the curves would be reversed for the second concept). Start from point E and let the rate of inflation for whatever reason move from A to B and stay there. Unemployment would initially decline to U_L at point F, moving along the curve defined for an anticipated rate of inflation $(1/P)(dP/dt)^*$ of A. As anticipations adjusted, the short-run curve would move upward, ultimately to the curve defined for an anticipated inflation rate of B. Concurrently unemployment would move gradually over from F to G. (For a fuller discussion, see *Price Theory*.)[5]

This analysis is, of course, oversimplified. It supposes a single unanticipated change, whereas, of course, there is a continuing stream of unanticipated changes; it does not deal explicitly with lags, or with overshooting; or with the process of formation of anticipations. But it does highlight the key points: what matters is not inflation per se, but unanticipated inflation; there is no stable trade-off between inflation and unemployment; there is a "natural rate of unemployment" (U_N), which is consistent with the real forces and with accurate perceptions; unemployment can be kept below that level only by an accelerating inflation; or above it, only by accelerating deflation.

The "natural rate of unemployment," a term I introduced to parallel Knut Wicksell's "natural rate of interest," is not a numerical constant but depends on

FIGURE 19.2

EXPECTATIONS-ADJUSTED PHILLIPS CURVE

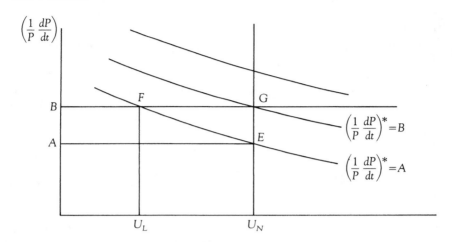

"real" as opposed to monetary factors—the effectiveness of the labor market, the extent of competition or monopoly, the barriers or encouragements to working in various occupations, and so on.

For example, the natural rate has clearly been rising in the United States for two major reasons. First, women, teenagers, and part-time workers have been constituting a growing fraction of the labor force. These groups are more mobile in employment than other workers, entering and leaving the labor market, shifting more frequently between jobs. As a result, they tend to experience higher average rates of unemployment. Second, unemployment insurance and other forms of assistance to unemployed persons have been made available to more categories of workers, and have become more generous in duration and amount. Workers who lose their jobs are under less pressure to look for other work, will tend to wait longer in the hope, generally fulfilled, of being recalled to their former employment, and can be more selective in the alternatives they consider. Further, the availability of unemployment insurance makes it more attractive to enter the labor force in the first place, and so may itself have stimulated the growth that has occurred in the labor force as a percentage of the population and also its changing composition.

The determinants of the natural rate of unemployment deserve much fuller analysis for both the United States and other countries. So also do the meaning of the recorded unemployment figures and the relation between the recorded figures and the natural rate. These issues are all of the utmost importance for public policy. However, they are side issues for my present limited purpose.

The connection between the state of employment and the level of efficiency or productivity of an economy is another topic that is of fundamental importance for public policy but is a side issue for my present purpose. There is a tendency to take it for granted that a high level of recorded unemployment is evidence of inefficient use of resources and conversely. This view is seriously in error. A low level of unemployment may be a sign of a forced-draft economy that is using its resources inefficiently and is inducing workers to sacrifice leisure for goods that they value less highly than the leisure, under the mistaken belief that their real wages will be higher than they prove to be. Or a low natural rate of unemployment may reflect institutional arrangements that inhibit change. A highly static rigid economy may have a fixed place for everyone whereas a dynamic, highly progressive economy, which offers ever-changing opportunities and fosters flexibility, may have a high natural rate of unemployment. To illustrate how the same rate may correspond to very different conditions: both Japan and the United Kingdom had low average rates of unemployment from, say, 1950 to 1970, but Japan experienced rapid growth, the United Kingdom, stagnation.

The "natural-rate" or "accelerationist" or "expectations-adjusted Phillips curve" hypothesis—as it has been variously designated—is by now widely accepted by economists, though by no means universally. A few still cling to the original Phillips curve; more recognize the difference between short-run and long-run curves but regard even the long-run curve as negatively sloped, though more steeply so than the short-run curves; some substitute a stable relation between the acceleration of inflation and unemployment for a stable relation between inflation and unemployment—aware of, but not concerned about, the possibility that the same logic that drove them to a second derivative will drive them to ever higher derivatives.

Much current economic research is devoted to exploring various aspects of this second stage—the dynamics of the process, the formation of expectations, and the kind of systematic policy, if any, that can have a predictable effect on real magnitudes. We can expect rapid progress on these issues. (Special mention should be made of the work on "rational expectations," especially the seminal contributions of John Muth, Robert Lucas, and Thomas Sargent.)[6]

IV. Stage 3: A Positively Sloped Phillips Curve?

Although the second stage is far from having been fully explored, let alone fully absorbed into the economic literature, the course of events is already producing a move to a third stage. In recent years, higher inflation has often been accompanied by higher not lower unemployment, especially for periods of several years in length. A simple statistical Phillips curve for such periods seems to be positively sloped, not vertical. The third stage is directed at accommodating this apparent empirical phenomenon. To do so, I suspect that it will have to include in the analysis the interdependence of economic experience and political developments. It will have to treat at least some political phenomena not as independent variables—as exogenous variables in econometric jargon—but as themselves determined by economic events—as endogenous variables.[7] The second stage was greatly influenced by two major developments in economic theory of the past few decades—one, the analysis of imperfect information and of the cost of acquiring information, pioneered by George Stigler; the other, the role of human capital in determining the form of labor contracts, pioneered by Gary Becker. The third stage will, I believe, be greatly influenced by a third major development—the application of economic analysis to political behavior, a field in which pioneering work has also been done by Stigler and Becker as well as by Kenneth Arrow, Duncan Black, Anthony Downs, James Buchanan, Gordon Tullock, and others.

The apparent positive relation between inflation and unemployment has been a source of great concern to government policymakers. Let me quote from a recent speech by Prime Minister Callaghan of Great Britain:

> We used to think that you could spend your way out of a recession, and increase employment by cutting taxes and boosting government spending. I tell you, in all candor, that that option no longer exists, and that, insofar as it ever did exist, it only worked by . . . injecting bigger doses of inflation into the economy, followed by higher levels of unemployment as the next step . . . That is the history of the past twenty years.[8]

The same view is expressed in a Canadian government white paper: "Continuing inflation, particularly in North America, has been accompanied by an increase in measured unemployment rates."[9]

These are remarkable statements, running as they do directly counter to the policies adopted by almost every Western government throughout the postwar period.

Some Evidence

More systematic evidence for the past two decades is given in Table 19.1 and Figures 19.3 and 19.4, which show the rates of inflation and unemployment in seven industrialized countries over the past two decades. According to the five-year averages in Table 19.1, the rate of inflation and the level of

FIGURE 19.3

RATES OF INFLATION AND UNEMPLOYMENT, 1956–1975,
BY QUINQUENNIA; UNWEIGHTED AVERAGE FOR SEVEN COUNTRIES

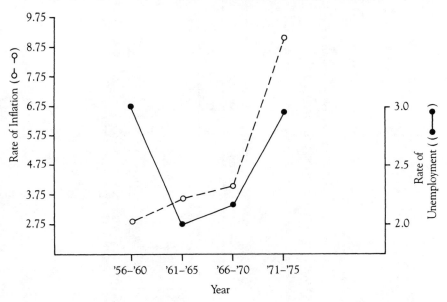

unemployment moved in opposite directions—the expected simple Phillips curve outcome—in five out of seven countries between the first two quinquennia (1956–1960, 1961–1965); in only four out of seven countries between the second and third quinquennia (1961–1965 and 1966–1970); and in only one of seven countries between the final two quinquennia (1966–1970 and 1970–1975). And even the one exception—Italy—is not a real exception. True, unemployment averaged a shade lower from 1971 to 1975 than in the prior five years, despite a more than tripling of the rate of inflation. However, since 1973, both inflation and unemployment have risen sharply.

The averages for all seven countries plotted in Figure 19.3 bring out even more clearly the shift from a negatively sloped simple Phillips curve to a positively sloped one. The two curves move in opposite directions between the first two quinquennia; in the same direction thereafter.

The annual data in Figure 19.4 tell a similar, though more confused, story. In the early years, there is wide variation in the relation between prices and unemployment, varying from essentially no relation, as in Italy, to a fairly clear-cut year-to-year negative relation, as in the United Kingdom and the

Table 19.1

Inflation and Unemployment in Seven Countries, 1956–1975: Average Values for Successive Quinquennia
(DP = Rate of Price Change, Percent per Year; U = Unemployment, Percentage of Labor Force)

Years	France DP	France U	Germany DP	Germany U	Italy DP	Italy U	Japan DP	Japan U	Sweden DP	Sweden U	United Kingdom DP	United Kingdom U	United States DP	United States U	Unweighted Average Seven Countries DP	Unweighted Average Seven Countries U
1956 through 1960	5.6	1.1	1.8	2.9	1.9	6.7	1.9	1.4	3.7	1.9	2.6	1.5	2.0	5.2	2.8	3.0
1961 through 1965	3.7	1.2	2.8	0.7	4.9	3.1	6.2	0.9	3.6	1.2	3.5	1.6	1.3	5.5	3.7	2.0
1966 through 1970	4.4	1.7	2.4	1.2	3.0	3.5	5.4	1.1	4.6	1.6	4.6	2.1	4.2	3.9	4.1	2.2
1971 through 1975	8.8	2.5	6.1	2.1	11.3	3.3	11.4	1.4	7.9	1.8	13.0	3.2	6.7	6.1	9.3	2.9

Note.—DP is rate of change of consumer prices compounded annually from calendar year 1955 to 1960; 1960 to 1965; 1965 to 1970; 1970 to 1975; U is average unemployment during five indicated calendar years. As a result, DP is dated a half year prior to associated U.

United States. In recent years, however, France, the United States, the United Kingdom, Germany, and Japan all show a clearly marked rise in both inflation and unemployment—though for Japan, the rise in unemployment is much smaller relative to the rise in inflation than in the other countries, reflecting the different meaning of unemployment in the different institutional environment of Japan. Only Sweden and Italy fail to conform to the general pattern.

Of course, these data are at most suggestive. We do not really have seven independent bodies of data. Common international influences affect all countries so that multiplying the number of countries does not multiply proportionately the amount of evidence. In particular, the oil crisis hit all seven countries at the same time. Whatever effect the crisis had on the rate of inflation, it directly disrupted the productive process and tended to increase unemployment. Any such increases can hardly be attributed to the acceleration of inflation that accompanied them; at most the two could be regarded as at least partly the common result of a third influence.[10]

Both the quinquennial and annual data show that the oil crisis cannot wholly explain the phenomenon described so graphically by Mr. Callaghan. Already before the quadrupling of oil prices in 1973, most countries show a clearly marked association of rising inflation and rising unemployment. But this too may reflect independent forces rather than the influence of inflation on unemployment. For example, the same forces that have been raising the natural rate of unemployment in the United States may have been operating in other countries and may account for their rising trend of unemployment, independently of the consequences of inflation.

Despite these qualifications, the data strongly suggest that, at least in some countries, of which Britain, Canada, and Italy may be the best examples, rising inflation and rising unemployment have been mutually reinforcing, rather than the separate effects of separate causes. The data are not inconsistent with the stronger statement that, in all industrialized countries, higher rates of inflation have some effects that, at least for a time, make for higher unemployment. The rest of this paper is devoted to a preliminary exploration of what some of these effects may be.

A Tentative Hypothesis

I conjecture that a modest elaboration of the natural-rate hypothesis is all that is required to account for a positive relation between inflation and unemployment, though of course such a positive relation may also occur for other reasons. Just as the natural-rate hypothesis explains a negatively sloped Phillips curve over short periods as a temporary phenomenon that will disappear as economic agents adjust their expectations to reality, so a positively sloped Phillips curve over somewhat longer periods may occur as a transitional

FIGURE 19.4
INFLATION AND UNEMPLOYMENT IN SEVEN COUNTRIES, ANNUALLY, 1956–1975
(SOLID LINE=RATE OF INFLATION; DASHED LINE=RATE OF UNEMPLOYMENT)

FIGURE 19.4
INFLATION AND UNEMPLOYMENT IN SEVEN COUNTRIES, ANNUALLY, 1956–1975
(SOLID LINE=RATE OF INFLATION; DASHED LINE=RATE OF UNEMPLOYMENT)

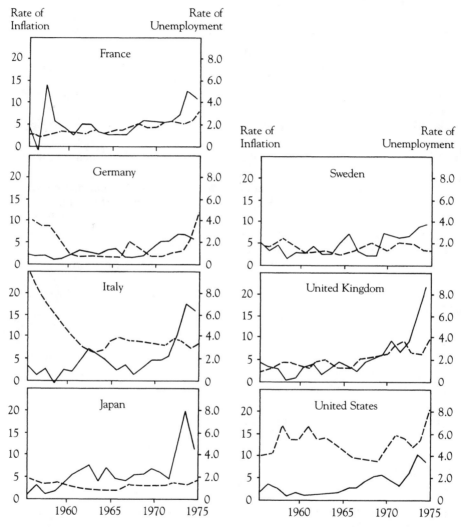

phenomenon that will disappear as economic agents adjust not only their expectations but their institutional and political arrangements to a new reality. When this is achieved, I believe that—as the natural-rate hypothesis suggests—the rate of unemployment will be largely independent of the average rate of inflation, though the efficiency of utilization of resources may not be. High inflation need not mean either abnormally high or abnormally low unemployment. However, the institutional and political arrangements that accompany it, either as relics of earlier history or as products of the inflation itself, are likely to prove antithetical to the most productive use of employed resources—a special case of the distinction between the state of employment and the productivity of an economy referred to earlier.

Experience in many Latin American countries that have adjusted to chronically high inflation rates—experience that has been analyzed most perceptively by some of my colleagues, particularly Arnold Harberger and Larry Sjaastad[11]—is consistent, I believe, with this view.

In the version of the natural-rate hypothesis summarized in Figure 19.2, the vertical curve is for alternative rates of fully anticipated inflation. Whatever that rate—be it negative, zero, or positive—it can be built into every decision if it is fully anticipated. At an anticipated 20 percent per year inflation, for example, long-term wage contracts would provide for a wage in each year that would rise relative to the zero-inflation wage by just 20 percent per year; long-term loans would bear an interest rate 20 percentage points higher than the zero-inflation rate, or a principal that would be raised by 20 percent a year; and so on—in short, the equivalent of a full indexing of all contracts. The high rate of inflation would have some real effects, by altering desired cash balances, for example, but it need not alter the efficiency of labor markets, or the length or terms of labor contracts and, hence, it need not change the natural rate of unemployment.

This analysis implicitly supposes, first, that inflation is steady or at least no more variable at a high rate than at a low—otherwise, it is unlikely that inflation would be as fully anticipated at high as at low rates of inflation; second, that the inflation is, or can be, open, with all prices free to adjust to the higher rate, so that relative price adjustments are the same with a 20 percent inflation as with a zero inflation; third, really a variant of the second point, that there are no obstacles to indexing of contracts.

Ultimately, if inflation at an average rate of 20 percent per year were to prevail for many decades, these requirements could come fairly close to being met, which is why I am inclined to retain the long-long-run vertical Phillips curve. But when a country initially moves to higher rates of inflation, these requirements will be systematically departed from. And such a transitional period may well extend over decades.

Consider, in particular, the United States and the United Kingdom. For two centuries before World War II for the United Kingdom, and a century and a half for the United States, prices varied about a roughly constant level, showing substantial increases in time of war, then postwar declines to roughly prewar levels. The concept of a "normal" price level was deeply embedded in the financial and other institutions of the two countries and in the habits and attitudes of their citizens.

In the immediate post-World War II period, prior experience was widely expected to recur. The fact was postwar inflation superimposed on wartime inflation; yet the expectation in both the United States and the United Kingdom was deflation. It took a long time for the fear of postwar deflation to dissipate—if it still has—and still longer before expectations started to adjust to the fundamental change in the monetary system. That adjustment is still far from complete.[12]

Indeed, we do not know what a complete adjustment will consist of. We cannot know now whether the industrialized countries will return to the pre–World War II pattern of a long-term stable price level, or will move toward the Latin American pattern of chronically high inflation rates—with every now and then an acute outbreak of super- or hyperinflation, as occurred recently in Chile and Argentina[13]—or will undergo more radical economic and political change leading to a still different resolution of the present ambiguous situation.

This uncertainty—or, more precisely, the circumstances producing this uncertainty—leads to systematic departures from the conditions required for a vertical Phillips curve.

The most fundamental departure is that a high inflation rate is not likely to be steady during the transition decades. Rather, the higher the rate, the more variable it is likely to be. That has been empirically true of differences among countries in the past several decades.[14] It is also highly plausible on theoretical grounds—both about actual inflation and, even more clearly, the anticipations of economic agents with respect to inflation. Governments have not produced high inflation as a deliberate announced policy but as a consequence of other policies—in particular, policies of full employment and welfare state policies raising government spending. They all proclaim their adherence to the goal of stable prices. They do so in response to their constituents, who may welcome many of the side-effects of inflation, but are still wedded to the concept of stable money. A burst of inflation produces strong pressure to counter it. Policy goes from one direction to the other, encouraging wide variation in the actual and anticipated rate of inflation. And, of course, in such an environment, no one has single-valued anticipations. Everyone recognizes that there is great uncertainty about what actual inflation will turn out to be over any specific future interval.[15]

The tendency for inflation that is high on the average to be highly variable is reinforced by the effect of inflation on the political cohesiveness of a country in which institutional arrangements and financial contracts have been adjusted to a long-term "normal" price level. Some groups gain (e.g., homeowners); others lose (e.g., owners of savings accounts and fixed-interest securities). "Prudent" behavior becomes in fact reckless, and "reckless" behavior in fact prudent. The society is polarized; one group is set against another. Political unrest increases. The capacity of any government to govern is reduced at the same time that the pressure for strong action grows.

An increased variability of actual or anticipated inflation may raise the natural rate of unemployment in two rather different ways.

First, increased volatility shortens the optimum length of unindexed commitments and renders indexing more advantageous.[16] But it takes time for actual practice to adjust. In the meantime, prior arrangements introduce rigidities that reduce the effectiveness of markets. An additional element of uncertainty is, as it were, added to every market arrangement. In addition, indexing is, even at best, an imperfect substitute for stability of the inflation rate. Price indexes are imperfect; they are available only with a lag, and generally are applied to contract terms only with a further lag.

These developments clearly lower economic efficiency. It is less clear what their effect is on recorded unemployment. High average inventories of all kinds is one way to meet increased rigidity and uncertainty. But that may mean labor-hoarding by enterprises and low unemployment or a larger force of workers between jobs and so high unemployment. Shorter commitments may mean more rapid adjustment of employment to changed conditions and so low unemployment, or the delay in adjusting the length of commitments may lead to less satisfactory adjustment and so high unemployment. Clearly, much additional research is necessary in this area to clarify the relative importance of the various effects. About all one can say now is that the slow adjustment of commitments and the imperfections of indexing may contribute to the recorded increase in unemployment.

A second related effect of increased volatility of inflation is to render market prices a less efficient system for coordinating economic activity. A fundamental function of a price system, as Hayek emphasized so brilliantly,[17] is to transmit compactly, efficiently, and at low cost the information that economic agents need in order to decide what to produce and how to produce it, or how to employ owned resources. The relevant information is about *relative* prices—of one product relative to another, of the services of one factor of production relative to another, of products relative to factor services, of prices now relative to prices in the future. But the information in practice is transmitted in the form of *absolute* prices—prices in dollars or pounds or kronor. If the price level is on the average stable or changing at a steady rate, it is relatively easy to extract the signal about relative prices from the observed absolute prices. The more volatile the rate of general inflation, the harder it becomes to extract the signal about relative prices from the absolute prices: the broadcast about relative prices is, as it were, being jammed by the noise coming from the inflation broadcast.[18] At the extreme, the system of absolute prices becomes nearly useless, and economic agents resort either to an alternative currency, or to barter, with disastrous effects on productivity.

Again, the effect on economic efficiency is clear, on unemployment less so. But, again, it seems plausible that the average level of unemployment would be raised by the increased amount of noise in market signals, at least during the period when institutional arrangements are not yet adapted to the new situation.

These effects of increased volatility of inflation would occur even if prices were legally free to adjust—if, in that sense, the inflation were open. In practice, the distorting effects of uncertainty, rigidity of voluntary long-term contracts, and the contamination of price signals will almost certainly be reinforced by legal restrictions on price change. In the modern world, governments are themselves producers of services sold on the market: from postal services to a wide range of other items. Other prices are regulated by government, and require government approval for change: from air fares to taxicab fares to charges for electricity. In these cases, governments cannot avoid being involved in the price-fixing process. In addition, the social and political forces unleashed by volatile inflation rates will lead governments to try to repress inflation in still other areas: by explicit price and wage control, or by pressuring private business or unions "voluntarily" to exercise "restraint," or by speculating in foreign exchange in order to alter the exchange rate.

The details will vary from time to time and from country to country, but the general result is the same: reduction in the capacity of the price system to guide economic activity; distortions in relative prices because of the introduction of greater friction, as it were, in all markets; and, very likely, a higher recorded rate of unemployment.[19]

The forces I have just described may render the political and economic system dynamically unstable and produce hyperinflation and radical political change—as in many defeated countries after World War I, or in Chile and Argentina more recently. At the other extreme, before any such catastrophe occurs, policies may be adopted that will achieve a relatively low and stable rate of inflation and lead to the dismantling of many of the interferences with the price system. That would reestablish the preconditions for the straightforward natural-rate hypothesis and enable that hypothesis to be used to predict the course of the transition.

An intermediate possibility is that the system will reach stability at a fairly constant though high average rate of inflation. In that case, unemployment should also settle down to a fairly constant level decidedly lower than during the transition. As the preceding discussion emphasizes, *increasing* volatility and *increasing* government intervention with the price system are the major factors that seem likely to raise unemployment, not *high* volatility or a *high* level of intervention.

Ways of coping with both volatility and intervention will develop: through indexing and similar arrangements for coping with volatility of inflation; through the development of indirect ways of altering prices and wages for avoiding government controls.

Under these circumstances, the long-run Phillips curve would again be vertical, and we would be back at the natural-rate hypothesis, though perhaps for a different range of inflation rates than that for which it was first suggested.

Because the phenomenon to be explained is the coexistence of high inflation and high unemployment, I have stressed the effect of institutional changes produced by a transition from a monetary system in which there was a "normal" price level to a monetary system consistent with long periods of high, and possibly highly variable, inflation. It should be noted that once these institutional changes were made, and economic agents had adjusted their practices and anticipations to them, a reversal to the earlier monetary framework or even the adoption in the new monetary framework of a successful policy of low inflation would in its turn require new adjustments, and these might have many of the same adverse transitional effects on the level of employment. There would appear to be an intermediate-run negatively sloped Phillips curve instead of the positively sloped one I have tried to rationalize.

V. Conclusion

One consequence of the Keynesian revolution of the 1930s was the acceptance of a rigid absolute wage level, and a nearly rigid absolute price level, as a starting point for analyzing short-term economic change. It came to be taken for granted that these were essentially institutional data and were so regarded by economic agents, so that changes in aggregate nominal demand would be reflected almost entirely in output and hardly at all in prices. The age-old confusion between absolute prices and relative prices gained a new lease on life.

In this intellectual atmosphere it was understandable that economists would analyze the relation between unemployment and *nominal* rather than *real* wages and would implicitly regard changes in anticipated *nominal* wages as equal to changes in anticipated *real* wages. Moreover, the empirical evidence that initially suggested a stable relation between the level of unemployment and the rate of change of nominal wages was drawn from a period when, despite sharp short-period fluctuations in prices, there was a relatively stable long-run price level and when the expectation of continued stability was widely shared. Hence these data flashed no warning signals about the special character of the assumptions.

The hypothesis that there is a stable relation between the level of unemployment and the rate of inflation was adopted by the economics profession with alacrity. It filled a gap in Keynes's theoretical structure. It seemed to be the "one equation" that Keynes himself had said "we are . . . short."[20] In addition, it seemed to provide a reliable tool for economic policy, enabling the economist to inform the policymaker about the alternatives available to him.

As in any science, so long as experience seemed to be consistent with the reigning hypothesis, it continued to be accepted, although, as always, a few dissenters questioned its validity.

But as the 1950s turned into the 1960s, and the 1960s into the 1970s, it became increasingly difficult to accept the hypothesis in its simple form. It seemed to take larger and larger doses of inflation to keep down the level of unemployment. Stagflation reared its ugly head.

Many attempts were made to patch up the hypothesis by allowing for special factors such as the strength of trade unions. But experience stubbornly refused to conform to the patched-up version.

A more radical revision was required. It took the form of stressing the importance of surprises—of differences between actual and anticipated magnitudes. It restored the primacy of the distinction between "real" and "nominal" magnitudes. There is a "natural rate of unemployment" at any time determined by real factors. This natural rate will tend to be attained when expectations are on the average realized. The same real situation is consistent with any absolute level of prices or of price change, provided allowance is made for the effect of price change on the real cost of holding money balances. In this respect, money is neutral. On the other hand, unanticipated changes in aggregate nominal demand and in inflation will cause systematic errors of perception on the part of employers and employees alike that will initially lead unemployment to deviate in the opposite direction from its natural rate. In this respect, money is not neutral. However, such deviations are transitory, though it may take a long chronological time before they are reversed and finally eliminated as anticipations adjust.

The natural-rate hypothesis contains the original Phillips curve hypothesis as a special case and rationalizes a far broader range of experience, in particular the phenomenon of stagflation. It has by now been widely though not universally accepted.

However, the natural-rate hypothesis in its present form has not proved rich enough to explain a more recent development—a move from stagflation to slumpflation. In recent years, higher inflation has often been accompanied by higher unemployment—not lower unemployment, as the single Phillips curve would suggest, nor the same unemployment, as the natural-rate hypothesis would suggest.

This recent association of higher inflation with higher unemployment may reflect the common impact of such events as the oil crisis, or independent forces that have imparted a common upward trend to inflation and unemployment.

However, a major factor in some countries and a contributing factor in others may be that they are in a transitional period—this time to be measured by quinquennia or decades, not years. The public has not adapted its attitudes or its institutions to a new monetary environment. Inflation tends not only to be higher but also increasingly volatile and to be accompanied by widening government intervention into the setting of prices. The growing volatility of inflation and the growing departure of relative prices from the values that market forces alone would set combine to render the economic system less efficient, to introduce frictions in all markets, and, very likely, to raise the recorded rate of unemployment.

On this analysis, the present situation cannot last. It will either degenerate into hyperinflation and radical change; or institutions will adjust to a situation of chronic inflation; or governments will adopt policies that will produce a low rate of inflation and less government intervention into the fixing of prices.

I have told a perfectly standard story of how scientific theories are revised. Yet it is a story that has far-reaching importance.

Government policy about inflation and unemployment has been at the center of political controversy. Ideological war has raged over these matters. Yet the drastic change that has occurred in economic theory has not been a result of ideological warfare. It has not resulted from divergent political beliefs or aims. It has responded almost entirely to the force of events: brute experience proved far more potent than the strongest of political or ideological preferences.

The importance for humanity of a correct understanding of positive economic science is vividly brought out by a statement made nearly two hundred years ago by Pierre S. du Pont, a deputy from Nemours to the French National Assembly, speaking, appropriately enough, on a proposal to issue additional *assignats*—the fiat money of the French Revolution:

> Gentlemen, it is a disagreeable custom to which one is too easily led by the harshness of the discussions, to assume evil intentions. It is necessary to be gracious as to intentions; one should believe them good, and apparently they are; but we do not have to be gracious at all to inconsistent logic or to absurd reasoning. Bad logicians have committed more involuntary crimes than bad men have done intentionally. [September 25, 1790.]

NOTES

1. Milton Friedman, "The Methodology of Positive Economics," *Essays in Positive Economics* (Chicago: University of Chicago Press, 1953); also see chapter 11 of this volume.

2. A. W. Phillips, "The Relationship between Unemployment and the Rate of Change of Money Wage Rates in the United Kingdom, 1861–1957," *Economica* (November 1958): 283–99.

3. Milton Friedman, "What Price Guideposts?" in G. P. Shultz and R. Z. Aliber, eds., *Guidelines: Informal Contracts and the Market Place* (Chicago: University of Chicago Press, 1966), pp. 17–39 and 55–61; idem, "An Inflationary Recession," *Newsweek* (October 17, 1966); idem, "The Role of Monetary Policy," *American Economic Review* 58 (March 1968): 1–17, also see chapter 21 of this volume; idem, *Inflation: Causes and Consequences* (Bombay: Asia Publishing House, 1963), reprinted in *Dollars and Deficits* (Englewood Cliffs, N.J.: Prentice-Hall, 1968), pp. 21–71.

4. Friedman, "Role of Monetary Policy"; E. S. Phelps, "Phillips Curve, Expectations of Inflation and Optimal Unemployment Over Time," *Economica* 34 (August 1967): 254–81; idem, "Money Wage Dynamics and Labour Market Equilibrium," in E. S. Phelps, ed., *Microeconomic Foundations of Employment and Inflation Theory* (New York: Norton, 1970).

5. Milton Friedman, *Price Theory* (Chicago: Aldine Publishing Co., 1976), chap. 12.

6. Robert J. Gordon, "Recent Developments in the Theory of Inflation and Unemployment," *Journal of Monetary Economics* 2 (1976): 185–219; John Muth, "Rational Expectations and the Theory of Price Movements," *Econometrica* 29 (July 1961): 315–33.

7. Robert J. Gordon, "The Demand and Supply of Inflation," *Journal of Law and Economics* 18 (December 1975): 807–36.

8. Speech to Labor Party Conference, September 28, 1976.

9. "The Way Ahead: A Framework for Discussion," *Government of Canada Working Papers* (October 1976).

10. Robert J. Gordon, "Alternative Responses of Policy to External Supply Shocks," *Brookings Papers on Economic Activity*, no. 1 (1975): 183–206.

11. Arnold C. Harberger, "The Inflation Problem in Latin America," a report prepared for the Buenos Aires (March 1966) meeting of the Inter-American Committee of the Alliance for Progress, *Boletin Mensual* (June 1966): 253–69; reprinted in Economic Development Institute, *Trabajos sobre desarrollo economico* (Washington, D.C.: IBRD, 1967). Larry A. Sjaastad, "Monetary Policy and Suppressed Inflation in Latin America," in R. Z. Aliber, ed., *National Monetary Policies and the International Financial System* (Chicago: University of Chicago Press, 1974), pp. 127–38.

12. Benjamin Klein, "Our New Monetary Standard: The Measurement and Effects of Price Uncertainty, 1880–1973," *Economic Inquiry* (December 1975): 461–83.

13. Arnold C. Harberger, "Inflation," *The Great Ideas Today, 1976* (Chicago: Encyclopaedia Brittanica, Inc., 1976), pp. 95–106.

14. Dwight Jaffe and Ephraim Kleiman, "The Welfare Implications of Uneven Inflation," seminar paper no. 50, Institute for International Economic Studies, University of Stockholm, November 1975. Dennis E. Logue and Thomas D. Willett, "A Note on the Relation between the Rate and Variability of Inflation," *Economica* (May 1976): 151–58.

15. Jaffe and Kleiman, "Welfare Implications"; David Meiselman, "Capital Formation, Monetary and Financial Adjustments," *Proceedings*, 27th National Conference of Tax Foundation, 1976, pp. 9–15.

16. Jo Anna Gray, "Essays on Wage Indexation," unpublished Ph.D. dissertation, University of Chicago, 1976.

17. F. A. Hayek, "The Use of Knowledge in Society," *American Economic Review* 35 (September 1945): 519–30.

18. Robert E. Lucas, "Some International Evidence on Output-Inflation Trade-offs," *American Economic Review* 63 (June 1973): 326–34; idem, "An Equilibrium Model of the Business Cycle," *Journal of Political Economy* 83 (December 1975): 1113–144; Harberger, "Inflation."

19. Friedman, *Price Theory*, chap. 12.

20. J. M. Keynes, *General Theory of Employment, Interest, and Money* (London: Macmillan, 1936), p. 276.

NOTES ON THE QUANTITY THEORY OF MONEY

· 20 ·

These notes first discuss a recent theoretical development, then summarize empirical evidence on the quantity theory, and conclude with a discussion of policy implications, giving special attention to the likely implications of the worldwide fiat money standard that has prevailed since 1971.

THE THEORY OF RATIONAL EXPECTATIONS

A subsequent theoretical development was the belated flowering of a seed planted in 1961 by John F. Muth in a long-neglected article on "Rational Expectations and the Theory of Price Movements."[1] The theory of rational expectations offers no special insight into stationary-state or long-run equilibrium analysis. Its contribution is to dynamics—short-run change, and hence potentially to stabilization policy.

It has long been recognized by writers of all persuasions that, as Abraham Lincoln put it over a century ago, "you can't fool all of the people all of the time." The tendency for the public to learn from experience and to adjust to it underlies David Hume's view that monetary expansion "is favorable to indus-

Adapted from Milton Friedman, "Quantity Theory of Money," in John Eatwell, Murray Millgate, and Peter Newman, eds., *The New Palgrave: A Dictionary of Economics*, 4 volumes (London: Macmillan; New York: Stockton Press, 1987). Reprinted by permission.

try" only in its initial stages, but that if it continues, it will come to be anticipated and will affect prices and nominal interest rates but not real magnitudes. It also underlies the companion view associated with the natural-rate hypothesis that a "full employment" policy in which monetary, or for that matter fiscal, measures are used to counteract any increase in unemployment will almost inevitably lead not simply to uneven inflation but to uneven inflation around a rising trend—a conclusion often illustrated by analogizing inflation to a drug of which the addict must take larger and larger doses to get the same kick.

Nonetheless, the importance of anticipations and how they are formed in determining the dynamic response to changes in money and other magnitudes remained largely implicit until Lucas and Sargent applied the Muth rational-expectations idea explicitly to the reliability of econometric models of the economy and to stabilization policies.[2]

The theory of rational expectations asserts that economic agents should be treated as if their anticipations fully incorporate both currently available information about the state of the world and a correct theory of the inter-relationships among the variables. Anticipations formed in this way will on the average tend to be correct (a statement whose simplicity conceals fundamental problems of interpretation).[3]

The rational-expectations hypothesis has far-reaching implications for the validity of econometric models. Suppose a statistician were able to construct a model that predicted highly accurately for a past period all relevant variables; also, that a monetary rule could be devised that if used during that past period with that model could have achieved a particular objective—say keeping unemployment between 4 and 5 percent. Suppose now that that policy rule were adopted for the future. It would be nearly certain that the model for which the rule was developed would no longer work. The economic equivalent of the Heisenberg indeterminacy principle would take over. The model was for an economy without that monetary rule. Put the rule into effect and it will alter rational expectations and hence behavior. Even without putting the rule in effect, the model would very likely continue to work only so long as its existence could be kept secret because if market participants learned about it they would use it in forming their rational expectations and thereby falsify it to a greater or lesser extent. Little wonder that every major econometric model is always being sent back to the drawing board as experience confounds it, or that their producers have reacted so strongly to the theory of rational expectations.

The implication of one variant of the theory that has received the most attention and generated the most controversy is the so-called neutrality hypothesis about stabilization policy—in particular, about discretionary monetary policy directed at promoting economic stability. Correct rational expectations of economic agents will include correct anticipation of any systematic monetary policy; hence such policy will be allowed for by economic agents in determining their behavior. Given further the natural-rate hypothesis, it follows that any systematic monetary policy will affect the behavior only of nominal magnitudes and not of such real magnitudes as output and employment. The authorities can affect the course of events only by "fooling" the participants, that is, by acting in an unpredictable ad hoc way. But, in general, such strictly ad hoc interventions will destabilize the economy, not stabilize it, serving simply to introduce another series of random shocks into the economy to which participants must adapt and which reduce their ability to form precise and accurate expectations.

This is a highly oversimplified account of the rational-expectations hypothesis and its implications. All otherwise valid models of the economy will not be falsified by being known. All real effects of systematic and announced governmental policies will not be rendered nugatory. Serious problems have arisen in formulating the hypothesis in a logically satisfactory way, and in giving it empirical content, especially in incorporating multivalued rather than single-valued expectations and allowing for nonindependence of events over time. Research in this area is exploding; rapid progress and many changes in received opinion can confidently be anticipated before the rational-expectations revolution is fully domesticated.

EMPIRICAL EVIDENCE

There is perhaps no empirical regularity among economic phenomena that is based on so much evidence for so wide a range of circumstances as the connection between substantial changes in the quantity of money and in the level of prices. There are few if any instances in which a substantial change in the quantity of money per unit of output has occurred without a substantial change in the level of prices in the same direction. Conversely, there are few if any instances in which a substantial change in the level of prices has occurred without a substantial change in the quantity of money per unit of output in the same direction. And instances in which prices and the quantity of money have moved together are recorded for many centuries of history, for countries in every part of the globe, and for a wide diversity of monetary arrangements.

The statistical connection itself, however, tells nothing about direction of influence, and this is the question about which there has been the most controversy. A rise or fall in prices, occurring for whatever reason, could produce a corresponding rise or fall in the quantity of money, so that the monetary changes are a passive consequence. Alternatively, changes in the quantity of money could produce changes in prices in the same direction, so that control of the quantity of money implies control of prices. The second interpretation—that substantial changes in the quantity of money are both a necessary and a sufficient condition for substantial changes in the general level of prices—is strongly supported by the variety of monetary arrangements for which a connection between monetary and price movements has been observed. But of course this interpretation does not exclude a reflex influence of changes in prices on the quantity of money. The reflex influence is often important, almost always complex, and, depending on the monetary arrangements, may be in either direction.

Evidence from specie standards. Until modern times, money was mostly metallic—copper, brass, silver, gold. The most notable changes in its nominal quantity were produced by sweating and clipping, by governmental edicts changing the nominal values attached to specified physical quantities of the metal, or by discoveries of new sources of specie. Economic history is replete with examples of the first two and their coincidence with corresponding changes in nominal prices.[4] The specie discoveries in the New World in the sixteenth century are the most important example of the third. The association between the resulting increase in the quantity of money and the price revolution of the sixteenth and seventeenth centuries has been well documented.[5]

Despite the much greater development of deposit money and paper money, the gold discoveries in Australia and the United States in the 1840s were followed by substantial price rises in the 1850s.[6] When growth of the gold stock slowed, and especially when country after country shifted from silver to gold (Germany in 1871–1873, the Latin Monetary Union in 1873, the Netherlands in 1875–1876) or returned to gold (the United States in 1879), world prices in terms of gold fell slowly but fairly steadily for about three decades. New gold discoveries in the 1880s and 1890s, powerfully reinforced by improved methods of mining and refining, particularly commercially feasible methods of using the cyanide process to extract gold from low-grade ore, led to much more rapid growth of the world gold stock. Further, no additional important countries shifted to gold. As a result, world prices in terms of gold rose by 25 to 50 percent from the mid-1890s to 1914.[7]

Evidence from great inflations. Periods of great monetary disturbances provide the most dramatic evidence on the role of the quantity of money. The most striking such periods are the hyperinflations after World War I in Germany, Austria, and Russia, and after World War II in Hungary and Greece, and the rapid price rises, if not hyperinflations, in many South American and some other countries both before and after World War II. These twentieth-century episodes have been studied more systematically than earlier ones. The studies demonstrate almost conclusively the critical role of changes in the quantity of money.[8]

Substantial inflations following a period of relatively stable prices have often had their start in wartime, though recently they have become common under other circumstances. What is important is that something, generally the financing of extraordinary governmental expenditures, produces a more rapid growth of the quantity of money. Prices start to rise, but at a slower pace than the quantity of money, so that for a time the real quantity of money increases. The reason is twofold: first, it takes time for people to readjust their money balances; second, initially there is a general expectation that the rise in prices is temporary and will be followed by a decline. Such expectations make money a desirable form in which to hold assets, and therefore lead to an increase in desired money balances in real terms.

As prices continue to rise, expectations are revised. Holders of money come to expect prices to continue to rise, and reduce desired balances. They also take more active measures to eliminate the discrepancy between actual and desired balances. The result is that prices start to rise faster than the stock of money, and real balances start to decline (that is, velocity starts to rise). How far this process continues depends on the rate of rise in the quantity of money. If it remains fairly stable, real balances settle down at a level that is lower than the initial level but roughly constant—a constant expected rate of inflation implies a roughly constant level of desired real balances; in this case, prices ultimately rise at the same rate as the quantity of money. If the rate of money growth declines, inflation will follow suit, which will in turn lead to an increase in actual and desired real balances as people readjust their expectations; and conversely. Once the process is in full swing, changes in real balances follow with a lag changes in the rate of change of the stock of money. The lag reflects the fact that people apparently base their expectations of future rates of price change partly on an average of experience over the preceding several years, the period of averaging being shorter the more rapid the inflation.

In the extreme cases, those that have degenerated into hyperinflation and a complete breakdown of the medium of exchange, rates of price change have been so high and real balances have been driven down so low as to lead to the widespread introduction of substitute moneys, usually foreign currencies. At that point completely new monetary systems have had to be introduced.

A similar phenomenon has occurred when inflation has been effectively suppressed by price controls, so that there is a substantial gap between the prices that would prevail in the absence of controls and the legally permitted prices. This gap prevents money from functioning as an effective medium of exchange and also leads to the introduction of substitute moneys, sometimes rather bizarre ones like the cigarettes and cognac used in post–World War II Germany.

Other evidence. The past two decades have witnessed a literal flood of literature dealing with monetary phenomena. Expressed in broad terms, the literature has been of two overlapping types—qualitative and econometric—and has dealt with two overlapping sets of issues—static or long-term effects of monetary change and dynamic or cyclical effects.

Some broad findings are:

1. For both long and short periods there is a consistent though not precise relation between the rate of growth of the quantity of money and the rate of growth of nominal income. If the quantity of money grows rapidly, so will nominal income, and conversely. This relation is much closer for long than for short periods.

Two recent econometric studies have tested the long-run effects using comparisons among countries for the post–World War II period. Lothian concludes his study for twenty countries for the period 1956–1980: "In this paper I have examined three sets of hypotheses associated with the quantity theory of money: the classical neutrality proposition [i.e., changes in the nominal quantity of money do not affect real magnitudes in the long run], the monetary approach to exchange rates [i.e., changes in exchange rates between countries reflect primarily changes in money per unit of output in the several countries], and the Fisher equation [i.e., differences in sustained rates of inflation produce corresponding differences in nominal interest rates]. The data are completely consistent with the first two and moderately supportive of the last."[9]

Duck concludes his study for 33 countries and the period 1962 to 1982—which uses overlapping data but substantially different methods: "Its [the study's] findings suggest that (i) the real demand for money is reasonably well explained by a small number of variables, principally real income and interest rates; (ii) nominal income is closely related to the quantity of money, but is also related to the behavior of other variables, principally interest rates; (iii) most changes in nominal income or its determinants are absorbed by price increases; (iv) even over a 20-year period some nominal income growth is to a significant degree absorbed by real output growth; (v) the evidence that expectations are rational is weak."[10]

2. These findings for the long run reflect a long-run real demand function for money involving, as Duck notes, a small number of variables, that is highly stable and very similar for different countries. The elasticity of this function with respect to real income is close to unity, occasionally lower, generally higher, especially for countries that are growing rapidly and in which the scope of the money economy is expanding. The elasticity with respect to interest rates is, as expected, negative but relatively low in absolute value. The real quantity demanded is not affected by the price level [i.e., there is no "monetary illusion"].[11]

3. Over short periods, the relation between growth in money and in nominal income is often concealed from the naked eye partly because the relation is less close for short than long periods but mostly because it takes time for changes in monetary growth to affect income, and how long it takes is itself variable. Today's income growth is not closely related to today's monetary growth; it depends on what has been happening to money in the past. What happens to money today affects what is going to happen to income in the future.

4. For most major Western countries, a change in the rate of monetary growth produces a change in the rate of growth of nominal income about six to nine months later. This is an average that does not hold in every individual case. Sometimes the delay is longer, sometimes shorter. In particular, it tends to be shorter under conditions of high and highly variable rates of monetary growth and of inflation.

5. In cyclical episodes the response of nominal income, allowing for the time delay, is greater in amplitude than the change in monetary growth, so that velocity tends to rise during the expansion phase of a business cycle and to fall during the contraction phase. This reaction appears to be partly a response to the procyclical pattern of interest rates; partly to the linkage of desired cash balances to permanent rather than measured income.

6. The changed rate of growth of nominal income typically shows up first in output and hardly at all in prices. If the rate of monetary growth increases or decreases, the rate of growth of nominal income and also of physical output tends to increase or decrease about six to nine months later, but the rate of price rise is affected very little.

7. The effect on prices, like that on income and output, is distributed over time, but comes some twelve to eighteen months later, so the total delay between a change in monetary growth and a change in the rate of inflation averages something like two years. That is why it is a long row to hoe to stop an inflation that has been allowed to start. It cannot be stopped overnight.

8. Even after allowance for the delayed effect of monetary growth, the relation is far from perfect. There's many a slip over short periods 'twixt the monetary change and the income change.

9. In the short run, which may be as long as three to ten years, monetary changes affect primarily output. Over decades, on the other hand, as already noted, the rate of monetary growth affects primarily prices. What happens to output depends on real factors: the enterprise, ingenuity, and industry of the people; the extent of thrift; the structure of industry and government; the relations among nations, and so on.[12]

10. One major finding has to do with severe depressions. There is strong evidence that a monetary crisis, involving a substantial decline in the quantity of money, is a necessary and sufficient condition for a major depression.

Fluctuations in monetary growth are also systematically related to minor ups and downs in the economy, but do not play as dominant a role compared to other forces. As Friedman and Schwartz put it, "Changes in the money stock are...a consequence as well as an independent source of change in money income and prices, though, once they occur, they produce in their turn still further effects on income and prices. Mutual interaction, but with money rather clearly the senior partner in longer run movements and in major cyclical movements, and more nearly an equal partner with money income and prices in shorter run and milder movements—this is the generalization suggested by our evidence."[13]

11. A major unsettled issue is the short-run division of a change in nominal income between output and price. The division has varied widely over space and time and there exists no satisfactory theory that isolates the factors responsible for the variability.[14]

12. It follows from these propositions that *inflation is always and everywhere a monetary phenomenon* in the sense that it is and can be produced only by a more rapid increase in the quantity of money than in output. Many phenomena can produce temporary fluctuations in the rate of inflation, but they can have lasting effects only insofar as they affect the rate of monetary growth. However, there are many different possible reasons for monetary growth, including gold discoveries, financing of government spending, and financing of private spending. Hence, these propositions are only the beginning of an answer to the causes and cures for inflation. The deeper question is why excessive monetary growth occurs.

13. Government spending may or may not be inflationary. It clearly will be inflationary if it is financed by creating money, that is, by printing currency or creating bank deposits. If it is financed by taxes or by borrowing from the public, the main effect is that the government spends the funds instead of the taxpayer or instead of the lender or instead of the person who would otherwise have borrowed the funds. Fiscal policy is extremely important in determining what fraction of total national income is spent by government and who bears the burden of that expenditure. It is also extremely important in determining monetary policy and, via that route, inflation. Essentially all major inflations, especially hyperinflations, have resulted from resort by governments to the printing press to finance their expenditures under conditions of great stress such as defeat in war or internal revolution, circumstances that have limited the ability of governments to acquire resources through explicit taxation.

14. A change in monetary growth affects interest rates in one direction at first but in the opposite direction later on. More rapid monetary growth at first tends to lower interest rates. But later on, the resulting acceleration in spending and still later in inflation produces a rise in the demand for loans which tends to raise interest rates. In addition, higher inflation widens the

difference between real and nominal interest rates. As both lenders and borrowers come to anticipate inflation, lenders demand, and borrowers are willing to offer, higher nominal rates to offset the anticipated inflation. That is why interest rates are highest in countries that have had the most rapid growth in the quantity of money and also in prices—countries like Brazil, Chile, Israel, South Korea. In the opposite direction, a slower rate of monetary growth at first raises interest rates but later on, as it decelerates spending and inflation, lowers interest rates. That is why interest rates are lowest in countries that *have had* the slowest rate of growth in the quantity of money—countries like Switzerland, Germany, and Japan.

15. In the major Western countries, the link to gold and the resultant long-term predictability of the price level meant that, until some time after World War II, interest rates behaved as if prices were expected to be stable and both inflation and deflation were unanticipated; the so-called Fisher effect was almost completely absent. Nominal returns on nominal assets were relatively stable; real returns unstable, absorbing almost fully inflation and deflation.

16. Beginning in the 1960s, and especially after the end of Bretton Woods in 1971, interest rates started to parallel rates of inflation. Nominal returns on nominal assets became more variable; real returns on nominal assets, less variable.[15]

POLICY IMPLICATIONS

On a very general level the implications of the quantity theory for economic policy are straightforward and clear. On a more precise and detailed level they are not.

Acceptance of the quantity theory means that the quantity of money is a key variable in policies directed at controlling the level of prices or of nominal income. Inflation can be prevented if and only if the quantity of money per unit of output can be kept from increasing appreciably. Deflation can be prevented if and only if the quantity of money per unit of output can be kept from decreasing appreciably. This implication is by no means trivial. Monetary authorities have more frequently than not taken conditions in the credit market—rates of interest, availability of loans, and so on—as criteria of policy and have paid little or no attention to the quantity of money per se. The emphasis on credit as opposed to the quantity of money accounts both for the great contraction in the United States from 1929 to 1933, when the Federal Reserve System allowed the stock of money to decline by one-third, and for many of the post–World War II inflations.

The quantity theory has no such clear implication, even on this general level, about policies concerned with the growth of real income. Both inflation and deflation have proved consistent with growth, stagnation, or decline.

Passing from these general and vague statements to specific prescriptions for policy is difficult. It is tempting to conclude from the close average relation between changes in the quantity of money and changes in money income that control over the quantity of money can be used as a precision instrument for offsetting other forces making for instability in money income. Unfortunately the loose relation between money and income over short periods, the long and variable lag between changes in the quantity of money and other variables, and the often conflicting objectives of policymakers preclude precise offsetting control.

An international specie standard leaves only limited scope for an independent monetary policy. Over any substantial period, the quantity of money is determined by the balance of payments. Capital movements plus time delays in the transmission of monetary and other impulses leave some leeway, which may be more or less extensive, depending on the importance of foreign transactions for a country and the sluggishness of response. As a result, monetary policy under an effective international specie standard has consisted primarily of banking policy, directed toward avoiding or relieving banking and liquidity crises.[16]

Until 1971, departures from an international specie standard, at least by major countries, took place infrequently and only at times of crisis. Surveying such episodes, Fisher concluded in 1911 that "irredeemable paper money has almost invariably proved a curse to the country employing it,"[17] a generalization that has applied equally to most of the period since, certainly up to 1971, and that explains why such episodes were generally transitory.

The declining importance of the international specie standard and its final termination in 1971 have changed the situation drastically. "Irredeemable paper money" is no longer an expedient grasped at in times of crisis; it is the normal state of affairs in countries at peace, facing no domestic crises, political or economic, and with governments fully capable of obtaining massive resources through explicit taxes. This is an unprecedented situation. We are in unexplored terrain.

As Keynes pointed out in 1923, monetary authorities cannot serve two masters. As he put it, "We cannot keep *both* our own price level *and* our exchanges stable. And we are compelled to choose."[18] Experience since has converted his dilemma into a trilemma. In principle, monetary authorities can achieve any two of the following three objectives: control of exchange rates, control of the price level, freedom from exchange controls. In practice, it has in fact proved impossible to achieve the first two by accepting exchange controls. Such controls have proved extremely costly and ultimately ineffective. The Bretton Woods system was ultimately wrecked on this trilemma. The attempts by many countries to pursue an independent monetary policy came into conflict with the attempt to maintain pegged exchange rates, leading to the imposition of exchange controls, repeated monetary crises, accompanied by large, discontinuous changes in exchange rates, and ultimately to the abandonment of the system in 1971.

Since then, most countries have had no formal commitment about exchange rates, which have been free to fluctuate and have fluctuated widely. Nonetheless, Keynes's dilemma is still alive and well. Monetary authorities have tried to influence the exchange rates of their currency and, at the same time, achieve internal objectives. The result has been what has been described as a system of managed floating.

One recent strand of policy discussions has consisted of attempts to devise a substitute for the Bretton Woods arrangements that would somehow combine the virtues of exchange rate stability with internal monetary stability. For example, one proposal, by McKinnon,[19] is for the United States, Germany, and Japan to fix exchange rates among their currencies and set a joint target for the rate of increase of the total quantity of money (or high-powered money) issued by the three countries together. So far, no such proposal has gained wide support among either economists or a wider public.

A different strand of policy discussions has been concerned with the instruments, targets, and objectives of monetary authorities. One element of the quantity theory approach that has had considerable influence is emphasis on the quantity of money as the appropriate intermediate target for monetary policy. Most major countries now (1985) follow the practice of announcing in advance their targets for monetary growth. That is so for the United States, Great Britain, Germany, Japan, Switzerland, and many others. The record of achievement of the announced targets varies greatly—from excellent to terrible. Recently, a considerable number of economists have favored the use of nominal income (usually nominal gross national product) as the intermediate target. The common feature is the quantity theory emphasis on nominal magnitudes.

A more abstract strand of policy discussions has been concerned with the optimum quantity of money: what rate or pattern of monetary growth would in principle promote most effectively the long-run efficiency of the economic system—meaning by that a Pareto welfare optimum. This issue turns out to be closely related to a number of others, in particular the optimum behavior of the price level; the optimum rate of interest; the optimum stock of capital, and the optimum structure of capital.[20]

One widely accepted answer is based on the observation that no real resource cost need be incurred in increasing the real quantity of money since that can be done by reducing the price level. The implication is that the optimum quantity of money is that at which the marginal benefit from increasing the real quantity is also zero. Various arrangements are possible that will achieve such an objective, of which perhaps the simplest, if money pays no interest, is a pattern of monetary growth involving a decline in the price level at a rate equal to the real interest rate.[21]

This answer, despite its great theoretical interest, has had little practical consequence. Short-run considerations have understandably been given precedence to such a highly abstract long-run proposition.

Finally, there has been a literal explosion of discussion of the basic structure of the monetary system. One component derives from the belief that Fisher's generalization about irredeemable paper money will continue to hold for the present world fiat money system and that we are headed for a world monetary collapse ending in hyperinflation unless a specie (gold) standard is promptly restored. In the United States, this monetary belief was powerful enough to lead Congress to establish a Commission on the Role of Gold. In its final report, "the Commission concludes that, under present circumstances, restoring a gold standard does not appear to be a fruitful method for dealing with the continuing problem of inflation. . . We favor no change in the flexible exchange rate system."[22] The testimony before the commission revealed that agreement on a "gold standard" concealed wide differences in the precise meaning of the phrase, varying from a system in which money consisted of full-bodied gold or warehouse receipts for gold to one in which the monetary authorities were instructed to regard the price of gold as one factor affecting their policy.

A very different component of the discussion has to do with possible alternatives to gold as a long-term anchor to the price level. This includes proposals for subjecting monetary authorities to more specific legislative or constitutional guidelines, varying from guidelines dealing with their objectives (price stability, rate of growth of nominal income, real interest rate, etc.) to guidelines specifying a specific rate of growth in money or high-powered money. Perhaps the most widely discussed proposal along this line is the proposal for imposing on the authorities the obligation to achieve a constant rate of growth in a specified monetary aggregate.[23] Other proposals include freezing the stock of base money and eliminating discretionary monetary policy, and denationalizing money entirely, leaving it to the private market and a free banking system.[24]

Finally, a still more radical series of proposals is that the unit of account be separated from the medium of exchange function, in the belief that financial innovation will establish an efficient payment system dispensing entirely with the use of cash. The specific proposals are highly sophisticated and complex, and have been sharply criticized. So far, their value has been primarily as a stimulus to a deeper analysis of the meaning and role of money.[25]

One thing is certain: the quantity theory of money will continue to generate agreement, controversy, repudiation, and scientific analysis, and will continue to play a role in government policy during the next century as it has for the past three.

NOTES

1. John F. Muth, "Rational Expectations and the Theory of Price Movements," *Econometrica* (July 1961), reprinted in R. E. Lucas, Jr., and T. J. Sargent, eds., *Rational Expectations and Economic Practice*, vols. 1 and 2 (Minneapolis: University of Minnesota Press, 1981).

2. S. Fischer, ed., *Rational Expectations and Economic Policy* (Chicago: University of Chicago Press, 1980); R. E. Lucas, Jr., "Econometric Policy Evaluation: A Critique," *Journal of Monetary Economics*, supplementary series (1976); Lucas and Sargent, *Rational Expectations and Economic Practice*.

3. Milton Friedman and Anna J. Schwartz, *Monetary Trends in the United States and the United Kingdom: Their Relation to Income, Prices, and Interest Rates, 1867–1975* (Chicago: University of Chicago Press, 1982), pp. 556–57.

4. C. M. Cipolla, *Money, Prices, and Civilization in the Mediterranean World, Fifth to Seventeenth Century* (Princeton, N.J.: Princeton University Press, 1956); A. E. Feavearyear, *The Pound Sterling: A History of English Money* (Oxford: Clarendon, 1931), 2d ed. (Oxford: Clarendon, 1963).

5. E. J. Hamilton, *American Treasure and the Price of Revolution in Spain, 1501–1650*, Harvard Economic Studies, vol. 43 (1934) (New York: Octagon, 1965).

6. J. E. Cairnes, "Essays on the Gold Question," in *Essays in Political Economy* (London: Macmillan, 1873); W. S. Jevons, "A Serious Fall in the Value of Gold," in *Investigations in Currency and Finance* (n.p., 1863), 2d ed. (London: Macmillan, 1909).

7. M. D. Bordo and A. J. Schwartz, eds., *A Retrospective on the Classical Gold Standard, 1821–1931* (Chicago: University of Chicago Press, 1984).

8. P. Cagan, *Determinants and Effects of Changes in the Stock of Money, 1875–1960* (New York: Columbia University Press, 1965); D. Meiselman, ed., *Varieties of Monetary Experience* (Chicago: University of Chicago Press, 1970); T. J. Sargent, "The Ends of Four Big Inflations," in R. E. Hall, ed., *Inflation: Causes and Effects* (Chicago: University of Chicago Press, 1982).

9. J. R. Lothian, "Equilibrium Relationships between Money and Other Economic Variables," *American Economic Review* (September 1985): 835.

10. N. W. Duck, *Money, Output and Prices: An Empirical Study Using Long-Term Cross Country Data*, Working Paper, University of Bristol (1985), p. 33.

11. Friedman and Schwartz, *Monetary Trends*; D. Laidler, *The Demand for Money: Theories, Evidence, and Problems*, 3d ed. (New York: Harper & Row, 1985).

12. In connection with points 3 through 9, see Milton Friedman and Anna J. Schwartz, "Money and Business Cycles," *Review of Economics and Statistics*, supplement (February 1963), reprinted in Milton Friedman, *The Optimum Quantity of Money and*

Other Essays (Chicago: Aldine Publishing Co., 1969); idem, *A Monetary History of the United States, 1867–1960* (Princeton, N.J.: Princeton University Press, 1963); Milton Friedman, "The Lag in Effect of Monetary Policy," *Journal of Political Economy* (October 1961), reprinted in Friedman, *Optimum Quantity of Money*; idem, "Inflation and Unemployment," *Journal of Political Economy* (June 1977); idem, "Monetary Policy for the 1980s," in J. H. Moore, ed., *To Promote Prosperity: U.S. Domestic Policy in the mid-1980s* (Stanford: Hoover Institution Press, 1984), also see chapter 22 of this volume; J. F. Judd and J. L. Scadding, "The Search for a Stable Money Demand Function," *Journal of Economic Literature* (September 1982).

13. Friedman and Schwartz, *A Monetary History*, p. 695; idem, "Money and Business Cycles"; Cagan, *Changes in the Stock of Money*, pp. 296–98.

14. R. J. Gordon, "A Consistent Characterization of a Near-Century of Price Behavior," *American Economic Review* (May 1980); idem, "Output Fluctuations and Gradual Price Adjustment," *Journal of Economic Literature* (June 1981); idem, "Price Inertia and Policy Ineffectiveness in the United States, 1890–1980," *Journal of Political Economy* 90 (December 1982); Friedman and Schwartz, *Monetary Trends*, pp. 59–62.

15. Friedman and Schwartz, *Monetary Trends*, pp. 10–11.

16. W. Bagehot, *Lombard Street* (London: Henry S. King, 1873).

17. I. Fisher, *The Purchasing Power of Money* (n.p., 1911), 2d rev. ed. (New York: Macmillan, 1929), p. 131.

18. J. M. Keynes, *A Tract on Monetary Reform* (n.p., 1923), reprinted (London: Macmillan, 1971), p. 126.

19. R. McKinnon, *An International Standard for Monetary Stabilization* (Cambridge: MIT Press, 1984).

20. Friedman, *Optimum Quantity of Money*, pp. 1–50.

21. M. Mussa, "The Welfare Cost of Inflation and the Role of Money as a Unit of Account," *Journal of Money, Credit, and Banking* (May 1977); T. Ihori, "On the Welfare Cost of Permanent Inflation," *Journal of Money, Credit, and Banking* (May 1985).

22. Commission on the Role of Gold in the Domestic and International Monetary Systems, *Report to the Congress*, vol. 1 (March 1982), pp. 17, 20.

23. Milton Friedman, *A Program for Monetary Stability* (New York: Fordham University Press, 1960), pp. 92–95; Commission on Gold, *Report*, vol. 1, p. 17.

24. Friedman, "Monetary Policy for 1980s"; Milton Friedman and Anna J. Schwartz, "Has Government Any Role in Money?" *Journal of Monetary Economics* (January 1986), also see chapter 26 of this volume; F. A. Hayek, *Denationalization of Money* (1976), 2d extended ed. (London: Institute of Economic Affairs, 1978); L. H. White, *Free Banking in Britain: Theory, Experience, and Debate, 1800–1845* (New York: Cambridge University Press, 1984).

25. The proposals are found in F. Black, "Banking and Interest Rates in a World without Money: The Effects of Uncontrolled Banking," *Journal of Bank Research* (Autumn 1970); E. F. Fama, "Banking in the Theory of Finance," *Journal of Monetary Economics* (January 1980); idem, "Fiduciary Currency and Commodity Standards," unpublished paper (January 1982); R. E. Hall, "Explorations in the Gold Standard and

Related Policies for Stabilizing the Dollar," in R. E. Hall, ed., *Inflation: Causes and Effects* (Chicago: University of Chicago Press, 1982); idem, "Monetary Trends in the United States and the United Kingdom: A Review from the Perspective of New Developments in Monetary Economics," *Journal of Economic Literature* (December 1982); R. L. Greenfield and L. B. Yeager, "A Laissez Faire Approach to Monetary Stability," *Journal of Money, Credit, and Banking* (August 1983). The criticisms are found in L. H. White, "Competitive Payment Systems and the Unit of Account," *American Economic Review* (September 1984); B. McCallum, "Bank Deregulation, Accounting Systems of Exchange and the Unit of Account: A Critical Review," Carnegie-Rochester Conference Series on Public Policy, vol. 23 (Autumn 1985).

MONETARY
POLICY

♦ ♦ ♦ ♦ ♦

• PART • FIVE •

THE ROLE OF
MONETARY POLICY

· 21 ·

There is wide agreement about the major goals of economic policy: high employment, stable prices, and rapid growth. There is less agreement that these goals are mutually compatible or, among those who regard them as incompatible, about the terms at which they can and should be substituted for one another. There is least agreement about the role that various instruments of policy can and should play in achieving the several goals.

My topic for tonight is the role of one such instrument—monetary policy. What can it contribute? And how should it be conducted to contribute the most? Opinion on these questions has fluctuated widely. In the first flush of enthusiasm about the newly created Federal Reserve System, many observers attributed the relative stability of the 1920s to the system's capacity for fine tuning—to apply an apt modern term. It came to be widely believed that a new era had arrived in which business cycles had been rendered obsolete by advances in monetary technology. This opinion was shared by economist and layman alike, though, of course, there were some dissonant voices. The Great Contraction destroyed this naive attitude. Opinion swung to the other extreme. Monetary policy was a string. You could pull on it to stop inflation but

Copyright 1968 by the American Economic Association.
Milton Friedman, "The Role of Monetary Policy," *American Economic Review* 58, no. 1 (March 1968): 1–17. Reprinted by permission.
Presidential address delivered at the 80th Annual Meeting of the American Economic Association, Washington, D.C., December 29, 1967.

you could not push on it to halt recession. You could lead a horse to water but you could not make him drink. Such theory by aphorism was soon replaced by Keynes's rigorous and sophisticated analysis.

Keynes offered simultaneously an explanation for the presumed impotence of monetary policy to stem the depression, a nonmonetary interpretation of the depression, and an alternative to monetary policy for meeting the depression and his offering was avidly accepted. If liquidity preference is absolute or nearly so—as Keynes believed likely in times of heavy unemployment—interest rates cannot be lowered by monetary measures. If investment and consumption are little affected by interest rates—as Hansen and many of Keynes's other American disciples came to believe—lower interest rates, even if they could be achieved, would do little good. Monetary policy is twice damned. The contraction, set in train, on this view, by a collapse of investment or by a shortage of investment opportunities or by stubborn thriftiness, could not, it was argued, have been stopped by monetary measures. But there was available an alternative—fiscal policy. Government spending could make up for insufficient private investment. Tax reductions could undermine stubborn thriftiness.

The wide acceptance of these views in the economics profession meant that for some two decades monetary policy was believed by all but a few reactionary souls to have been rendered obsolete by new economic knowledge. Money did not matter. Its only role was the minor one of keeping interest rates low, in order to hold down interest payments in the government budget, contribute to the "euthanasia of the rentier," and maybe, stimulate investment a bit to assist government spending in maintaining a high level of aggregate demand.

These views produced a widespread adoption of cheap money policies after the war. And they received a rude shock when these policies failed in country after country, when central bank after central bank was forced to give up the pretense that it could indefinitely keep "the" rate of interest at a low level. In this country, the public denouement came with the Federal Reserve–Treasury Accord in 1951, although the policy of pegging government bond prices was not formally abandoned until 1953. Inflation, stimulated by cheap money policies, not the widely heralded postwar depression, turned out to be the order of the day. The result was the beginning of a revival of belief in the potency of monetary policy.

This revival was strongly fostered among economists by the theoretical developments initiated by Haberler but named for Pigou that pointed out a channel—namely, changes in wealth—whereby changes in the real quantity of money can affect aggregate demand even if they do not alter interest rates. These theoretical developments did not undermine Keynes's argument against the potency of orthodox monetary measures when liquidity preference is

absolute since under such circumstances the usual monetary operations involve simply substituting money for other assets without changing total
wealth. But they did show how changes in the quantity of money produced in
other ways could affect total spending even under such circumstances. And,
more fundamentally, they did undermine Keynes's key theoretical proposition,
namely, that even in a world of flexible prices, a position of equilibrium at full
employment might not exist. Henceforth, unemployment had again to be
explained by rigidities or imperfections, not as the natural outcome of a fully
operative market process.

The revival of belief in the potency of monetary policy was fostered also by
a reevaluation of the role money played from 1929 to 1933. Keynes and most
other economists of the time believed that the Great Contraction in the
United States occurred despite aggressive expansionary policies by the monetary authorities—that they did their best but their best was not good enough.[1]
Recent studies have demonstrated that the facts are precisely the reverse: the
U.S. monetary authorities followed highly deflationary policies. The quantity
of money in the United States fell by one-third in the course of the contraction. And it fell not because there were no willing borrowers—not because the
horse would not drink. It fell because the Federal Reserve System forced or
permitted a sharp reduction in the monetary base, because it failed to exercise
the responsibilities assigned to it in the Federal Reserve Act to provide
liquidity to the banking system. The Great Contraction is tragic testimony to
the power of monetary policy—not, as Keynes and so many of his contempo-
raries believed, evidence of its impotence.

In the United States the revival of belief in the potency of monetary policy
was strengthened also by increasing disillusionment with fiscal policy, not so
much with its potential to affect aggregate demand as with the practical and
political feasibility of so using it. Expenditures turned out to respond sluggishly
and with long lags to attempts to adjust them to the course of economic
activity, so emphasis shifted to taxes. But here political factors entered with a
vengeance to prevent prompt adjustment to presumed need, as has been so
graphically illustrated in the months since I wrote the first draft of this talk.
"Fine tuning" is a marvelously evocative phrase in this electronic age, but it has
little resemblance to what is possible in practice—not, I might add, an
unmixed evil.

It is hard to realize how radical has been the change in professional
opinion on the role of money. Hardly an economist today accepts views that
were the common coin some two decades ago. Let me cite a few examples.

In a talk published in 1945, E. A. Goldenweiser, then director of the
research division of the Federal Reserve Board, described the primary objective
of monetary policy as being to "maintain the value of Government bonds. . .
This country" he wrote, "will have to adjust to a 2.5 percent interest rate as the

return on safe, long-time money, because the time has come when returns on pioneering capital can no longer be unlimited as they were in the past."[2]

In a book on *Financing American Prosperity*, edited by Paul Homan and Fritz Machlup and published in 1945, Alvin Hansen devotes nine pages of text to the "savings-investment problem" without finding any need to use the words "interest rate" or any close facsimile thereto.[3] In his contribution to this volume, Fritz Machlup wrote, "Questions regarding the rate of interest, in particular regarding its variation or its stability, may not be among the most vital problems of the postwar economy, but they are certainly among the perplexing ones."[4] In his contribution, John H. Williams—not only professor at Harvard but also a long-time adviser to the New York Federal Reserve bank—wrote, "I can see no prospect of revival of a general monetary control in the postwar period."[5]

Another of the volumes dealing with postwar policy that appeared at this time, *Planning and Paying for Full Employment*, was edited by Abba P. Lerner and Frank D. Graham and had contributors of all shades of professional opinion— from Henry Simons and Frank Graham to Abba Lerner and Hans Neisser.[6] Yet Albert Halasi, in his excellent summary of the papers, was able to say, "Our contributors do not discuss the question of money supply . . . The contributors make no special mention of credit policy to remedy actual depressions . . . Inflation . . . might be fought more effectively by raising interest rates . . . But . . . other anti-inflationary measures . . . are preferable."[7] A *Survey of Contemporary Economics*, edited by Howard Ellis and published in 1948, was an "official" attempt to codify the state of economic thought of the time. In his contribution, Arthur Smithies wrote, "In the field of compensatory action, I believe fiscal policy must shoulder most of the load. Its chief rival, monetary policy, seems to be disqualified on institutional grounds. This country appears to be committed to something like the present low level of interest rates on a long-term basis."[8]

These quotations suggest the flavor of professional thought some two decades ago. If you wish to go further in this humbling inquiry, I recommend that you compare the sections on money—when you can find them—in the *Principles* texts of the early postwar years with the lengthy sections in the current crop even, or especially, when the early and recent *Principles* are different editions of the same work.

The pendulum has swung far since then, if not all the way to the position of the late 1920s, at least much closer to that position than to the position of 1945. There are of course many differences between then and now, less in the potency attributed to monetary policy than in the roles assigned to it and the criteria by which the profession believes monetary policy should be guided. Then, the chief roles assigned monetary policy were to promote price stability and to preserve the gold standard; the chief criteria of monetary policy were the state of the "money market," the extent of "speculation," and the movement of gold. Today, primacy is assigned to the promotion of full employment, with the prevention of inflation a continuing but definitely secondary objective. And there is major disagreement about criteria of policy, varying from emphasis on money market conditions, interest rates, and the quantity of money to the belief that the state of employment itself should be the proximate criterion of policy.

I stress nonetheless the similarity between the views that prevailed in the late 1920s and those that prevail today because I fear that, now as then, the pendulum may well have swung too far, that, now as then, we are in danger of assigning to monetary policy a larger role than it can perform, in danger of asking it to accomplish tasks that it cannot achieve, and, as a result, in danger of preventing it from making the contribution that it is capable of making.

Unaccustomed as I am to denigrating the importance of money, I therefore shall, as my first task, stress what monetary policy cannot do. I shall then try to outline what it can do and how it can best make its contribution, in the present state of our knowledge—or ignorance.

I. What Monetary Policy Cannot Do

From the infinite world of negation, I have selected two limitations of monetary policy to discuss: (1) It cannot peg interest rates for more than very limited periods. (2) It cannot peg the rate of unemployment for more than very limited periods. I select these because the contrary has been or is widely believed, because they correspond to the two main unattainable tasks that are at all likely to be assigned to monetary policy, and because essentially the same theoretical analysis covers both.

Pegging of Interest Rates

History has already persuaded many of you about the first limitation. As noted earlier, the failure of cheap money policies was a major source of the reaction against simple-minded Keynesianism. In the United States, this reaction involved widespread recognition that the wartime and postwar pegging of bond prices was a mistake, that the abandonment of this policy was a desirable and inevitable step, and that it had none of the disturbing and disastrous consequences that were so freely predicted at the time.

The limitation derives from a much misunderstood feature of the relation between money and interest rates. Let the Federal Reserve set out to keep interest rates down. How will it try to do so? By buying securities. This raises their prices and lowers their yields. In the process, it also increases the quantity of reserves available to banks, hence the amount of bank credit and, ultimately, the total quantity of money. That is why central bankers in particular, and the financial community more broadly, generally believe that an increase in the quantity of money tends to lower interest rates. Academic economists accept the same conclusion, but for different reasons. They see, in their mind's eye, a negatively sloping liquidity preference schedule. How can people be induced to hold a larger quantity of money? Only by bidding down interest rates.

Both are right, up to a point. The *initial* impact of increasing the quantity of money at a faster rate than it has been increasing is to make interest rates lower for a time than they would otherwise have been. But this is only the beginning of the process not the end. The more rapid rate of monetary growth will stimulate spending, both through the impact on investment of lower market interest rates and through the impact on other spending and thereby relative prices of higher cash balances than are desired. But one man's spending is another man's income. Rising income will raise the liquidity preference schedule and the demand for loans; it may also raise prices, which would reduce the real quantity of money. These three effects will reverse the initial downward pressure on interest rates fairly promptly, say, in something less than a year. Together they will tend, after a somewhat longer interval, say, a year or two, to return interest rates to the level they would otherwise have had. Indeed, given the tendency for the economy to overreact, they are highly likely to raise interest rates temporarily beyond that level, setting in motion a cyclical adjustment process.

A fourth effect, when and if it becomes operative, will go even farther, and definitely mean that a higher rate of monetary expansion will correspond to a higher, not lower, level of interest rates than would otherwise have prevailed. Let the higher rate of monetary growth produce rising prices, and let the public come to expect that prices will continue to rise. Borrowers will then be willing to pay and lenders will then demand higher interest rates—as Irving Fisher pointed out decades ago. This price expectation effect is slow to develop and also slow to disappear. Fisher estimated that it took several decades for a full adjustment and more recent work is consistent with his estimates.

These subsequent effects explain why every attempt to keep interest rates at a low level has forced the monetary authority to engage in successively larger and larger open market purchases. They explain why, historically, high and rising nominal interest rates have been associated with rapid growth in the quantity of money, as in Brazil or Chile or in the United States in recent years, and why low and falling interest rates have been associated with slow growth in the quantity of money, as in Switzerland now or in the United States from 1929 to 1933. As an empirical matter, low interest rates are a sign that monetary policy *has been* tight—in the sense that the quantity of money has grown slowly; high interest rates are a sign that monetary policy *has been* easy—in the sense that the quantity of money has grown rapidly. The broadest facts of experience run in precisely the opposite direction from that which the financial community and academic economists have all generally taken for granted.

Paradoxically, the monetary authority could assure low nominal rates of interest—but to do so it would have to start out in what seems like the opposite direction, by engaging in a deflationary monetary policy. Similarly, it could assure high nominal interest rates by engaging in an inflationary policy and accepting a temporary movement in interest rates in the opposite direction.

These considerations not only explain why monetary policy cannot peg interest rates; they also explain why interest rates are such a misleading indicator of whether monetary policy is "tight" or "easy." For that, it is far better to look at the rate of change of the quantity of money.[9]

Employment as a Criterion of Policy

The second limitation I wish to discuss goes more against the grain of current thinking. Monetary growth, it is widely held, will tend to stimulate employment; monetary contraction, to retard employment. Why, then, cannot the monetary authority adopt a target for employment or unemployment—say, 3 percent unemployment; be tight when unemployment is less than the target; be easy when unemployment is higher than the target; and in this way peg unemployment at, say, 3 percent? The reason it cannot is precisely the same as for interest rates—the difference between the immediate and the delayed consequences of such a policy.

Thanks to Wicksell, we are all acquainted with the concept of a "natural" rate of interest and the possibility of a discrepancy between the "natural" and the "market" rate. The preceding analysis of interest rates can be translated fairly directly into Wicksellian terms. The monetary authority can make the market rate less than the natural rate only by inflation. It can make the market rate higher than the natural rate only by deflation. We have added only one wrinkle to Wicksell—the Irving Fisher distinction between the nominal and the real rate of interest. Let the monetary authority keep the nominal market rate for a time below the natural rate by inflation. That in turn will raise the nominal natural rate itself, once anticipations of inflation become widespread, thus requiring still more rapid inflation to hold down the market rate. Similarly, because of the Fisher effect, it will require not merely deflation but more and more rapid deflation to hold the market rate above the initial "natural" rate.

This analysis has its close counterpart in the employment market. At any moment of time, there is some level of unemployment which has the property that it is consistent with equilibrium in the structure of *real* wage rates. At that level of unemployment, real wage rates are tending on the average to rise at a "normal" secular rate, i.e., at a rate that can be indefinitely maintained so long as capital formation, technological improvements, etc., remain on their long-run trends. A lower level of unemployment is an indication that there is an excess demand for labor that will produce upward pressure on real wage rates. A higher level of unemployment is an indication that there is an excess supply of labor that will produce downward pressure on real wage rates. The "natural rate of unemployment," in other words, is the level that would be ground out by the Walrasian system of general equilibrium equations, provided there is imbedded in them the actual structural characteristics of the labor and commodity markets, including market imperfections, stochastic variability in demands and supplies, the cost of gathering information about job vacancies and labor availabilities, the costs of mobility, and so on.[10]

You will recognize the close similarity between this statement and the celebrated Phillips curve. The similarity is not coincidental. Phillips's analysis of the relation between unemployment and wage change is deservedly celebrated as an important and original contribution. But, unfortunately, it contains a basic defect—the failure to distinguish between *nominal* wages and *real* wages—just as Wicksell's analysis failed to distinguish between *nominal* interest rates and *real* interest rates. Implicitly, Phillips wrote his article for a world in which everyone anticipated that nominal prices would be stable and in which that anticipation remained unshaken and immutable whatever happened to actual prices and wages. Suppose, by contrast, that everyone anticipates that prices will rise at a rate of more than 75 percent a year—as, for example, Brazilians did a few years ago. Then wages must rise at that rate simply to keep real wages unchanged. An excess supply of labor will be reflected in a less rapid rise in nominal wages than in anticipated prices,[11] not in an absolute decline in wages. When Brazil embarked on a policy to bring down the rate of price rise, and succeeded in bringing the price rise down to about 45 percent a year, there was a sharp initial rise in unemployment because under the influence of earlier anticipations, wages kept rising at a pace that was higher than the new rate of price rise, though lower than earlier. This is the result experienced, and to be expected, of all attempts to reduce the rate of inflation below that widely anticipated.[12]

To avoid misunderstanding, let me emphasize that by using the term "natural" rate of unemployment, I do not mean to suggest that it is immutable and unchangeable. On the contrary, many of the market characteristics that determine its level are man-made and policy-made. In the United States, for example, legal minimum wage rates, the Walsh-Healy and Davis-Bacon Acts, and the strength of labor unions all make the natural rate of unemployment higher than it would otherwise be. Improvements in employment exchanges, in availability of information about job vacancies and labor supply, and so on, would tend to lower the natural rate of unemployment. I use the term "natural" for the same reason Wicksell did—to try to separate the real forces from monetary forces.

Let us assume that the monetary authority tries to peg the "market" rate of unemployment at a level below the "natural" rate. For definiteness, suppose that it takes 3 percent as the target rate and that the "natural" rate is higher than 3 percent. Suppose also that we start out at a time when prices have been stable and when unemployment is higher than 3 percent. Accordingly, the authority increases the rate of monetary growth. This will be expansionary. By making nominal cash balances higher than people desire, it will tend initially to lower interest rates and in this and other ways to stimulate spending. Income and spending will start to rise.

To begin with, much or most of the rise in income will take the form of an increase in output and employment rather than in prices. People have been expecting prices to be stable, and prices and wages have been set for some time in the future on that basis. It takes time for people to adjust to a new state of demand. Producers will tend to react to the initial expansion in aggregate demand by increasing output, employees by working longer hours, and the unemployed, by taking jobs now offered at former nominal wages. This much is pretty standard doctrine.

But it describes only the initial effects. Because selling prices of products typically respond to an unanticipated rise in nominal demand faster than prices of factors of production, real wages received have gone down—though real wages anticipated by employees went up, since employees implicitly evaluated the wages offered at the earlier price level. Indeed, the simultaneous fall *ex post* in real wages to employers and rise *ex ante* in real wages to employees is what enabled employment to increase. But the decline *ex post* in real wages will soon come to affect anticipations. Employees will start to reckon on rising prices of the things they buy and to demand higher nominal wages for the future. "Market" unemployment is below the "natural" level. There is an excess demand for labor so real wages will tend to rise toward their initial level.

Even though the higher rate of monetary growth continues, the rise in real wages will reverse the decline in unemployment, and then lead to a rise, which will tend to return unemployment to its former level. In order to keep unemployment at its target level of 3 percent, the monetary authority would have to raise monetary growth still more. As in the interest rate case, the "market" rate can be kept below the "natural" rate only by inflation. And, as in the interest rate case, too, only by accelerating inflation. Conversely, let the monetary authority choose a target rate of unemployment that is above the natural rate, and they will be led to produce a deflation, and an accelerating deflation at that.

What if the monetary authority chose the "natural" rate—either of interest or unemployment—as its target? One problem is that it cannot know what the "natural" rate is. Unfortunately, we have as yet devised no method to estimate accurately and readily the natural rate of either interest or unemployment. And the "natural" rate will itself change from time to time. But the basic problem is that even if the monetary authority knew the "natural" rate, and attempted to peg the market rate at that level, it would not be led to a determinate policy. The "market" rate will vary from the natural rate for all sorts of reasons other than monetary policy. If the monetary authority responds to these variations, it will set in train longer term effects that will make any monetary growth path it follows ultimately consistent with the rule of policy. The actual course of monetary growth will be analogous to a random walk, buffeted this way and that by the forces that produce temporary departures of the market rate from the natural rate.

To state this conclusion differently, there is always a temporary trade-off between inflation and unemployment; there is no permanent trade-off. The temporary trade-off comes not from inflation per se, but from unanticipated inflation, which generally means, from a rising rate of inflation. The widespread belief that there is a permanent trade-off is a sophisticated version of the confusion between "high" and "rising" that we all recognize in simpler forms. A rising rate of inflation may reduce unemployment, a high rate will not.

But how long, you will say, is "temporary"? For interest rates, we have some systematic evidence on how long each of the several effects takes to work itself out. For unemployment, we do not. I can at most venture a personal judgment, based on some examination of the historical evidence, that the initial effects of a higher and unanticipated rate of inflation last for something like two to five years; that this initial effect then begins to be reversed; and that a full adjustment to the new rate of inflation takes about as long for employment as for interest rates, say, a couple of decades. For both interest rates and employment, let me add a qualification. These estimates are for changes in the rate of inflation of the order of magnitude that has been experienced in the United States. For much more sizable changes, such as those experienced in South American countries, the whole adjustment process is greatly speeded up.

To state the general conclusion still differently, the monetary authority controls nominal quantities—directly, the quantity of its own liabilities. In principle, it can use this control to peg a nominal quantity—an exchange rate, the price level, the nominal level of national income, the quantity of money by one or another definition—or to peg the rate of change in a nominal quantity—the rate of inflation or deflation, the rate of growth or decline in nominal national income, the rate of growth of the quantity of money. It cannot use its control over nominal quantities to peg a real quantity—the real rate of interest, the rate of unemployment, the level of real national income, the real quantity of money, the rate of growth of real national income, or the rate of growth of the real quantity of money.

II. What Monetary Policy Can Do

Monetary policy cannot peg these real magnitudes at predetermined levels. But monetary policy can and does have important effects on these real magnitudes. The one is in no way inconsistent with the other.

My own studies of monetary history have made me extremely sympathetic to the oft-quoted, much reviled, and as widely misunderstood, comment by John Stuart Mill. "There cannot...," he wrote, "be intrinsically a more insignificant thing, in the economy of society, than money; except in the character of a contrivance for sparing time and labor. It is a machine for doing quickly and commodiously, what would be done, though less quickly and commodiously, without it: and like many other kinds of machinery, it only exerts a distinct and independent influence of its own when it gets out of order."[13]

True, money is only a machine, but it is an extraordinarily efficient machine. Without it, we could not have begun to attain the astounding growth in output and level of living we have experienced in the past two centuries— any more than we could have done so without those other marvelous machines that dot our countryside and enable us, for the most part, simply to do more efficiently what could be done without them at much greater cost in labor.

But money has one feature that these other machines do not share. Because it is so pervasive, when it gets out of order, it throws a monkey wrench into the operation of all the other machines. The Great Contraction is the most dramatic example but not the only one. Every other major contraction in this country has been either produced by monetary disorder or greatly exacerbated by monetary disorder. Every major inflation has been produced by monetary expansion—mostly to meet the overriding demands of war which have forced the creation of money to supplement explicit taxation.

The first and most important lesson that history teaches about what monetary policy can do—and it is a lesson of the most profound importance— is that monetary policy can prevent money itself from being a major source of economic disturbance. This sounds like a negative proposition: avoid major mistakes. In part it is. The Great Contraction might not have occurred at all, and if it had, it would have been far less severe, if the monetary authority had avoided mistakes, or if the monetary arrangements had been those of an earlier time when there was no central authority with the power to make the kinds of mistakes that the Federal Reserve System made. The past few years, to come closer to home, would have been steadier and more productive of economic well-being if the Federal Reserve had avoided drastic and erratic changes of direction, first expanding the money supply at an unduly rapid pace, then, in early 1966, stepping on the brake too hard, then, at the end of 1966, reversing itself and resuming expansion until at least November 1967 at a more rapid pace than can long be maintained without appreciable inflation.

Even if the proposition that monetary policy can prevent money itself from being a major source of economic disturbance were a wholly negative proposition, it would be none the less important for that. As it happens, however, it is not a wholly negative proposition. The monetary machine has gotten out of order even when there has been no central authority with anything like the power now possessed by the Federal Reserve. In the United States, the 1907 episode and earlier banking panics are examples of how the monetary machine can get out of order largely on its own. There is therefore a positive and important task for the monetary authority—to suggest improvements in the machine that will reduce the chances that it will get out of order, and to use its own powers so as to keep the machine in good working order.

A second thing monetary policy can do is provide a stable background for the economy—keep the machine well oiled, to continue Mill's analogy. Accomplishing the first task will contribute to this objective, but there is more to it than that. Our economic system will work best when producers and consumers, employers and employees, can proceed with full confidence that the average level of prices will behave in a known way in the future—preferably that it will be highly stable. Under any conceivable institutional arrangements, and certainly under those that now prevail in the United States, there is only a limited amount of flexibility in prices and wages. We need to conserve this flexibility to achieve changes in relative prices and wages that are required to adjust to dynamic changes in tastes and technology. We should not dissipate it simply to achieve changes in the absolute level of prices that serve no economic function.

In an earlier era, the gold standard was relied on to provide confidence in future monetary stability. In its heyday it served that function reasonably well. It clearly no longer does, since there is scarce a country in the world that is prepared to let the gold standard reign unchecked—and there are persuasive reasons why countries should not do so. The monetary authority could operate as a surrogate for the gold standard, if it pegged exchange rates and did so exclusively by altering the quantity of money in response to balance of payment flows without "sterilizing" surpluses or deficits and without resorting to open or concealed exchange control or to changes in tariffs and quotas. But again, though many central bankers talk this way, few are in fact willing to follow this course—and again there are persuasive reasons why they should not do so. Such a policy would submit each country to the vagaries not of an impersonal and automatic gold standard but of the policies—deliberate or accidental—of other monetary authorities.

In today's world, if monetary policy is to provide a stable background for the economy it must do so by deliberately employing its powers to that end. I shall come later to how it can do so.

Finally, monetary policy can contribute to offsetting major disturbances in the economic system arising from other sources. If there is an independent secular exhilaration—as the postwar expansion was described by the proponents of secular stagnation—monetary policy can in principle help to hold it in check by a slower rate of monetary growth than would otherwise be desirable. If, as now, an explosive federal budget threatens unprecedented deficits, monetary policy can hold any inflationary dangers in check by a slower rate of monetary growth than would otherwise be desirable. This will temporarily mean higher interest rates than would otherwise prevail—to enable the government to borrow the sums needed to finance the deficit—but by preventing the speeding up of inflation, it may well mean both lower prices and lower nominal interest rates for the long pull. If the end of a substantial war offers the country an opportunity to shift resources from wartime to peacetime production, monetary policy can ease the transition by a higher rate of monetary growth than would otherwise be desirable—though experience is not very encouraging that it can do so without going too far.

I have put this point last, and stated it in qualified terms—as referring to major disturbances—because I believe that the potentiality of monetary policy in offsetting other forces making for instability is far more limited than is commonly believed. We simply do not know enough to be able to recognize minor disturbances when they occur or to be able to predict either what their effects will be with any precision or what monetary policy is required to offset their effects. We do not know enough to be able to achieve stated objectives by delicate, or even fairly coarse, changes in the mix of monetary and fiscal policy. In this area particularly, the best is likely to be the enemy of the good. Experience suggests that the path of wisdom is to use monetary policy explicitly to offset other disturbances only when they offer a "clear and present danger."

III. How Should Monetary Policy Be Conducted?

How should monetary policy be conducted to make the contribution to our goals that it is capable of making? This is clearly not the occasion for presenting a detailed "Program for Monetary Stability"—to use the title of a book in which I tried to do so.[14] I shall restrict myself here to two major requirements for monetary policy that follow fairly directly from the preceding discussion.

The first requirement is that the monetary authority should guide itself by magnitudes that it can control, not by ones that it cannot control. If, as the authority has often done, it takes interest rates or the current unemployment percentage as the immediate criterion of policy, it will be like a space vehicle that has taken a fix on the wrong star. No matter how sensitive and sophisticated its guiding apparatus, the space vehicle will go astray. And so will the monetary authority. Of the various alternative magnitudes that it can control, the most appealing guides for policy are exchange rates, the price level as defined by some index, and the quantity of a monetary total—currency plus adjusted demand deposits, or this total plus commercial bank time deposits, or a still broader total.

For the United States in particular, exchange rates are an undesirable guide. It might be worth requiring the bulk of the economy to adjust to the tiny percentage consisting of foreign trade if that would guarantee freedom from monetary irresponsibility—as it might under a real gold standard. But it is hardly worth doing so simply to adapt to the average of whatever policies monetary authorities in the rest of the world adopt. Far better to let the market, through floating exchange rates, adjust to world conditions the 5 percent or so of our resources devoted to international trade while reserving monetary policy to promote the effective use of the 95 percent.

Of the three guides listed, the price level is clearly the most important in its own right. Other things the same, it would be much the best of the alternatives—as so many distinguished economists have urged in the past. But other things are not the same. The link between the policy actions of the monetary authority and the price level, while unquestionably present, is more indirect than the link between the policy actions of the authority and any of the several monetary totals. Moreover, monetary action takes a longer time to affect the price level than to affect the monetary totals and both the time lag and the magnitude of effect vary with circumstances. As a result, we cannot predict at all accurately just what effect a particular monetary action will have on the price level and, equally important, just when it will have that effect. Attempting to control directly the price level is therefore likely to make monetary policy itself a source of economic disturbance because of false stops and starts. Perhaps, as our understanding of monetary phenomena advances, the situation will change. But at the present stage of our understanding, the long way around seems the surer way to our objective. Accordingly, I believe that a monetary total is the best currently available immediate guide or criterion for monetary policy—and I believe that it matters much less which particular total is chosen than that one be chosen.

A second requirement for monetary policy is that the monetary authority avoid sharp swings in policy. In the past, monetary authorities have on occasion moved in the wrong direction—as in the episode of the Great Contraction that I have stressed. More frequently, they have moved in the right direction, albeit often too late, but have erred by moving too far. Too late and too much has been the general practice. For example, in early 1966, it was the right policy for the Federal Reserve to move in a less expansionary direction— though it should have done so at least a year earlier. But when it moved, it went too far, producing the sharpest change in the rate of monetary growth of the postwar era. Again, having gone too far, it was the right policy for the Federal Reserve to reverse course at the end of 1966. But again it went too far, not only restoring but exceeding the earlier excessive rate of monetary growth. And this episode is no exception. Time and again this has been the course followed—as in 1919 and 1920, in 1937 and 1938, in 1953 and 1954, in 1959 and 1960.

The reason for the propensity to overreact seems clear: the failure of monetary authorities to allow for the delay between their actions and the subsequent effects on the economy. They tend to determine their actions by today's conditions—but their actions will affect the economy only six or nine or twelve or fifteen months later. Hence they feel impelled to step on the brake, or the accelerator, as the case may be, too hard.

My own prescription is still that the monetary authority go all the way in avoiding such swings by adopting publicly the policy of achieving a steady rate of growth in a specified monetary total. The precise rate of growth, like the precise monetary total, is less important than the adoption of some stated and known rate. I myself have argued for a rate that would on the average achieve rough stability in the level of prices of final products, which I have estimated would call for something like a 3 to 5 percent per year rate of growth in currency plus all commercial bank deposits or a slightly lower rate of growth in currency plus demand deposits only.[15] But it would be better to have a fixed rate that would on the average produce moderate inflation or moderate deflation, provided it was steady, than to suffer the wide and erratic perturbations we have experienced.

Short of the adoption of such a publicly stated policy of a steady rate of monetary growth, it would constitute a major improvement if the monetary authority followed the self-denying ordinance of avoiding wide swings. It is a matter of record that periods of relative stability in the rate of monetary growth have also been periods of relative stability in economic activity, both in the United States and other countries. Periods of wide swings in the rate of monetary growth have also been periods of wide swings in economic activity.

By setting itself a steady course and keeping to it, the monetary authority could make a major contribution to promoting economic stability. By making that course one of steady but moderate growth in the quantity of money, it would make a major contribution to avoidance of either inflation or deflation of prices. Other forces would still affect the economy, require change and adjustment, and disturb the even tenor of our ways. But steady monetary growth would provide a monetary climate favorable to the effective operation of those basic forces of enterprise, ingenuity, invention, hard work, and thrift that are the true springs of economic growth. That is the most that we can ask from monetary policy at our present stage of knowledge. But that much—and it is a great deal—is clearly within our reach.

NOTES

1. In Milton Friedman, "The Monetary Theory and Policy of Henry Simons," *Journal of Law and Economics* 10 (October 1967): 1–13, I have argued that Henry Simons shared this view with Keynes, and that it accounts for the policy changes that he recommended.

2. E. A. Goldenweiser, "Postwar Problems and Policies," *Federal Reserve Bulletin* 31 (February 1945): 112–21.

3. P. T. Homan and Fritz Machlup, eds., *Financing American Prosperity* (New York: n.p., 1945), pp. 218–27.

4. Ibid., p. 466.

5. Ibid., p. 383.

6. A. P. Lerner and F. D. Graham, eds., *Planning and Paying for Full Employment* (Princeton, N.J.: Princeton University Press, 1946).

7. Ibid., pp. 23–24.

8. Howard S. Ellis, ed., *A Survey of Contemporary Economics* (Philadelphia, Pa.: n.p., 1948), p. 208.

9. This is partly an empirical not theoretical judgment. In principle, "tightness" or "ease" depends on the rate of change of the quantity of money supplied compared to the rate of change of the quantity demanded excluding effects on demand from monetary policy itself. However, empirically demand is highly stable, if we exclude the effect of monetary policy, so it is generally sufficient to look at supply alone.

10. It is perhaps worth noting that this "natural" rate need not correspond to equality between the number unemployed and the number of job vacancies. For any given structure of the labor market, there will be some equilibrium relation between these two magnitudes, but there is no reason why it should be one of equality.

11. Strictly speaking, the rise in nominal wages will be less rapid than the rise in anticipated nominal wages to make allowance for any secular changes in real wages.

12. Stated in terms of the rate of change of nominal wages, the Phillips curve can be expected to be reasonably stable and well defined for any period for which the *average* rate of change of prices, and hence the anticipated rate, has been relatively stable. For such periods, nominal wages and "real" wages move together. Curves computed for different periods or different countries for each of which this condition has been satisfied will differ in level, the level of the curve depending on what the average rate of price change was. The higher the average rate of price change, the higher will tend to be the level of the curve. For periods or countries for which the rate of change of prices varies considerably, the Phillips curve will not be well defined. My

impression is that these statements accord reasonably well with the experience of the economists who have explored empirical Phillips curves.

Restate Phillips's analysis in terms of the rate of change of real wages—and even more precisely, anticipated real wages—and it all falls into place. That is why students of empirical Phillips curves have found that it helps to include the rate of change of the price level as an independent variable.

13. John Stuart Mill, *Principles of Political Economy*, Ashley, ed., vol. 3 (New York: Longmans, Green & Co., 1929), p. 488.

14. Milton Friedman, *A Program for Monetary Stability* (New York: Fordham University Press, 1960).

15. In an as yet unpublished article on "The Optimum Quantity of Money," I conclude that a still lower rate of growth, something like 2 percent for the broader definition, might be better yet in order to eliminate or reduce the difference between private and total costs of adding to real balances.

MONETARY POLICY
FOR THE 1980s

· 22 ·

Monetary policy can be discussed on two very different levels: the tactics of policy—the specific actions that the monetary authorities should take; and the strategy or framework of policy—the ideal monetary institutions and arrangements for the conduct of monetary policy that should be adopted.

Tactics are more tempting. They are immediately relevant, promise direct results, and are in most respects easier to discuss than the thorny problem of the basic framework appropriate for monetary policy. Yet long experience persuades me that, given our present institutions, a discussion of tactics is unlikely to be rewarding.

The temptation to concentrate on tactics derives in considerable part from a tendency to personalize policy: to speak of the Eisenhower, Kennedy, or Reagan economic policy and the Martin, Burns, or Volcker monetary policy. Sometimes that approach is correct. The particular person in charge may make a major difference to the course of events. For example, in *Monetary History*,[1] Anna Schwartz and I attributed considerable importance to the early death of Benjamin Strong, first governor of the Federal Reserve Bank of New York, in explaining monetary policy from 1929 to 1933. More frequently perhaps, the personalized approach is misleading. The person ostensibly in charge is like the rooster crowing at dawn. The course of events is decided by

From Milton Friedman, "Monetary Policy for the 1980s," in John H. Moore, ed., *To Promote Prosperity: U.S. Domestic Policy in the Mid-1980s* (Stanford: Hoover Institution Press, 1984).

deeper and less visible forces that determine both the character of those nominally in charge and the pressure on them.

Monetary developments during the past few decades have, I believe, been determined far more by the institutional structure of the Federal Reserve and by external pressures than by the intentions, knowledge, or personal characteristics of the persons who appeared to be in charge. Knowing the name, the background, and the personal qualities of the chairman of the Fed, for example, is of little use in judging what happened to monetary growth during his term of office.

If the present monetary structure were producing satisfactory results, we would be well advised to leave it alone. Tactics would then be the only topic. However, the present monetary structure is not producing satisfactory results. Indeed, in my opinion, no major institution in the United States has so poor a record of performance over so long a period yet so high a public reputation as the Federal Reserve.

The conduct of monetary policy is of major importance: monetary instability breeds economic instability. A monetary structure that fosters steadiness and predictability in general price level is an essential precondition for healthy noninflationary growth. That is why it is important to consider fundamental changes in our monetary institutions. Such changes may be neither feasible nor urgent now. But unless we consider them now, we shall not be prepared to adopt them when and if the need is urgent.

ECONOMIC STABILITY AND MONETARY STABILITY

Is monetary stability important? For that we turn to the evidence on the relation between stability in the rate of growth of the quantity of money, on the one hand, and stability in the economy, on the other.

The evidence consists of two parts: (1) the systematic cyclical behavior of the quantity of money and its relation, on a cycle-by-cycle basis, to the subsequent behavior of the economy; (2) the linkage over time between instability in monetary growth and instability in the economy.

Anna Schwartz and I have examined the cyclical behavior of the quantity of money in the United States for the whole period since 1867. Throughout that period, monetary growth has risen and fallen not with but before economic activity. The cyclical peak of monetary growth regularly precedes the cyclical peak of economic activity by an interval that varies a good deal, but on the average is something like six to nine months; the cyclical trough of monetary growth regularly precedes the cyclical trough of economic activity by an average interval of roughly the same length. Moreover, sizable monetary accelerations and decelerations tend to be followed by sizable expansions and contractions in economic activity; modest accelerations and decelerations, by modest expansions and contractions.

The evidence is particularly strong for such major movements in income as occur during major contractions and major booms—the contractions of 1873 to 1879, 1892 to 1894, 1895 to 1896, 1907 to 1908, 1920 to 1921, 1929 to 1932, 1937 to 1938, and all the major inflationary expansions. For these, the evidence is extremely strong that large changes in monetary growth are both a necessary and a sufficient condition for large changes in nominal income.[2]

Further evidence for the importance of monetary stability is the comparison between the variability in money and in income over more than a century presented in Figure 22.1, which plots moving standard deviations for four-year periods of annual rates of change in money and in income, as measured by the net national product. This chart slightly revises and updates a chart prepared more than two decades ago, yet the description of the earlier chart will do for this one as well:

> The two curves parallel one another with a high degree of fidelity, especially when it is borne in mind that standard deviations based on only four observations (three degrees of freedom) are subject to a good deal of sampling variation, that the net national product and money series are, so far as we know, wholly independent in their statistical construction, and that both are subject to an appreciable margin of error.[3]

For the 114 years as a whole, the correlation between the two series is .776. Omitting the years before 1898, when the statistical quality of the income data improved, gives an even higher correlation, .858. For the period since 1898, monetary variability is highly correlated with the variability both of real income (correlation = .767) and prices (correlation = .706).

In a recent paper, Robert J. Gordon presented evidence on the variability of money, nominal income, real income, and prices from 1908 to 1980.[4] His basic data are the same or closely related to those we used and hence do not represent independent additional evidence on the relation between monetary and economic variability. However, he converted the original data to deviations from trend, or, as he described them, "natural" growth rates, and calculated standard deviations for seven distinct periods, rather than moving standard deviations. Some of his results are presented in Table 22.1, as a supplement to Figure 22.1. They clearly reinforce the evidence from our correlations: periods of high monetary variability are periods of high variability in nominal and real income and, with one exception, of prices. His data also reveal an important detail that comes out less clearly in our chart: during and after World War II, the variability of nominal income was decidedly less

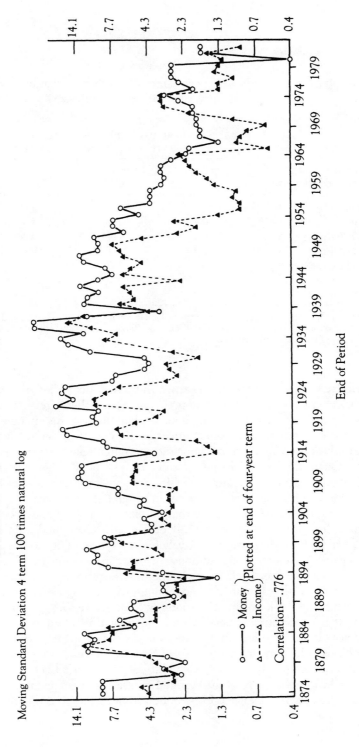

FIGURE 22.1

MONETARY AND ECONOMIC VOLATILITY: MOVING FOUR-YEAR STANDARD DEVIATIONS
OF ANNUAL RATES OF CHANGE IN MONEY AND IN INCOME, 1869–1981

Moving Standard Deviation 4 term 100 times natural log

o——o Money ⎱ Plotted at end of four-year term
△---△ Income ⎰

Correlation=.776

End of Period

TABLE 22.1

MONETARY AND ECONOMIC VARIABILITY IN SEVEN SUBPERIODS, 1908 TO 1914
(CALCULATED FROM QUARTERLY DATA)

Period (year and quarter)	STANDARD DEVIATIONS OF DEVIATIONS OF QUARTERLY GROWTH RATES FROM TREND OR NATURAL GROWTH RATE			
	Money (M2)	Nominal GNP	Real GNP	Implicit Price Index
1908:4 to 1914:4	2.9	8.3	6.4	4.3
1915:1 to 1922:4	10.1	21.4	14.4	15.4
1923:1 to 1929:3	4.1	9.9	9.0	3.7
1929:4 to 1941:4	12.3	24.1	19.4	7.8
1942:1 to 1953:4	8.5	11.6	11.4	8.1
1954:1 to 1967:2	2.6	3.9	3.8	2.0
1967:3 to 1980:4	3.5	3.9	4.0	2.2

SOURCE: Robert J. Gordon, "Price Inertia and Policy Ineffectiveness in the United States, 1890–1980," *Journal of Political Economy* 90 (1982): 1100, Table 1. Copyright 1982 by The University of Chicago Press. All rights reserved.

relative to that in money than earlier. In each earlier period, the variability of nominal income was twice or more that in money; thereafter, between one and one and a half times. I have no good explanation for this change but suspect that it may result more from changes in the statistical quality of the income data than from a structural change in economic relationships.

Quarterly data for the period since the end of World War II yield similar, though less striking, results, as Table 22.2 shows for four-quarter and twelve-quarter moving standard deviations. In general, the correlations are decidedly lower for the period as a whole than for each part separately. The reason is a sharp drop in the variability of GNP between the first period and the second—a phenomenon that I am tentatively inclined to attribute to the effect of the Korean War, which produced unusually wide movements in velocity.

The evidence is clear: variability in the rate of monetary growth is associated with variability in economic growth. High monetary variability accompanies high economic variability, and vice versa.[5]

It is important to stress two points about this relationship. First, it has persisted despite substantial changes in monetary institutions: from a fairly rigorous gold standard before World War I to a much looser gold standard followed by a purely fiduciary standard; from the period before to the period after the establishment of the Federal Reserve System. The implication is that the direction of influence is from monetary variability to economic variability, not the reverse—a conclusion that Schwartz and I have documented repeatedly on the basis of very different evidence.[6]

The second point is related to the first. The Federal Reserve has sought to use monetary policy to stabilize the economy—that is, to vary monetary growth in order to offset forces introducing disturbances into the economy. Had it succeeded, high monetary variability would have been associated with low economic variability, not with high economic variability. The correlations between the moving standard deviations that we have calculated would have been negative or zero, rather than systematically positive.[7] The implication is again that monetary variability has been a source of economic variability, not an offset.

These two points buttress a single conclusion: it is important to reduce monetary variability. In considering proposals for monetary reform, we should give that objective high priority.[8]

THE TACTICS OF MONETARY POLICY

Three issues are involved in the tactics of monetary policy: adopting a variable or variables as intermediate target or targets; choosing the desired path of the target variables; devising procedures for achieving that path as closely as possible.

The Intermediate Targets

The Federal Reserve System (herein the Fed) has vacillated between using one or more interest rates or one or more monetary aggregates as its intermediate targets. In the past decade, however, it joined monetary authorities in other countries in stressing monetary growth. Since 1975, it has been required by Congress to specify explicit numerical targets for the growth of monetary aggregates. Although many proposals have recently surfaced for the substitution of other targets—from real interest rates to sensitive commodity prices to the price of gold to nominal GNP—I shall assume that one or more monetary aggregates remains the intermediate target.[9]

In my opinion, the selection of a target or of a target path is not and has not been the problem. If the Fed had consistently achieved the targets it specified to Congress, monetary growth would have been highly stable instead of highly variable, inflation would never have become the menace it did, and the United States would have been spared the worst parts of the punishing recession (or recessions) from 1979 to 1982.

The Fed has specified targets for several aggregates primarily, as I have argued elsewhere, to obfuscate the issue and reduce accountability.[10] In gen-

TABLE 22.2

MONETARY AND ECONOMIC VARIABILITY, POST–WORLD WAR II QUARTERLY DATA

(CORRELATIONS BETWEEN LOGARITHMS OF MOVING STANDARD DEVIATIONS)

| | | CORRELATION WITH | | | | | |
| | | GNP | | REAL GNP | | IMPLICIT PRICE DEFLATOR | |
Period[a]	Item	M1	M2	M1	M2	M1	M2
Four-Quarter Moving Standard Deviations							
1947–1963	Maximum correlation	.461	.461	.468	.350	.207	.289
	Lead of M (quarters)	0	–1	0	1	9	9
1963–1982	Maximum correlation	.432	.390	.384	.378	.260	.375
	Lead of M	0	2	–1	1	4	3
1947–1982	Maximum correlation	.694	.325	.344	.265	.120	.158
	Lead of M	6	0	0	1	4	3
Twelve-Quarter Moving Standard Deviations							
1947–1963	Maximum correlation	.582	.517	.671	.541	.330	.257
	Lead of M	0	–1	0	–1	8	9
1961–1982	Maximum correlation	.505	.531	.531	.620	.104	.471
	Lead of M	0	0	0	0	7	9
1947–1982	Maximum correlation	.305	.042	.254	.221	.223	.305
	Lead of M	2	2	1	2	7	9

[a] Period refers to dates of rates of change used in calculating the moving standard deviations.

eral, the different aggregates move together. The exceptions have essentially all been due to the interest rate restrictions imposed by the Fed under Regulation Q and the associated development of new forms of deposit liabilities. And they would not have arisen if the Fed had achieved its targets for any one of the aggregates.

The use of multiple intermediate targets is undesirable. The Fed has one major instrument of monetary control: control over the quantity of high-powered money. With one instrument, it cannot independently control several aggregates. Its other instruments—primarily the discount rate and reserve requirements—are highly defective as instruments for monetary control and of questionable effectiveness in enabling it to control separately more than one aggregate.[11]

It makes far less difference which aggregate the Fed selects than that it select one and only one. For simplicity of exposition, I shall assume that the target aggregate is M1 as currently designed. Selection of another aggregate would alter the desirable numerical targets but not their temporal pattern.

The Target Path

A long-run growth rate of about 1 to 3 percent per year for M1 would be roughly consistent with zero inflation.[12] That should be our objective. Actual growth in M1 was 8.5 percent from fourth quarter 1981 to fourth quarter 1982. A crucial question is how rapidly to go from that level to the 1 to 3 percent range. In my opinion, it is desirable to proceed gradually over something like a three- to five-year period, which means that the rate of growth should be reduced by about 1 to 1.5 percentage points a year.

The Fed has consistently stated its targets in terms of a range of growth rates. For example, its initial target for M1 for 1983 was a growth rate of 4 to 8 percent from the fourth quarter of 1982 to the fourth quarter of 1983. That method of stating targets is seriously defective. It provides a widening cone of limits on the absolute money supply as the year proceeds and fosters a shift in base from year to year, thereby frustrating accountability over long periods. This is indeed what happened. In July 1983, Chairman Volker announced a new target of 5 to 9 percent for the second quarter of 1983 to the second quarter of 1984 but from the second quarter 1983 base, which is 3 percent (6 percent at an annual rate) above the top of the earlier range.

A better way to state the targets is in terms of a central target for the absolute money supply plus or minus a band of, say, 1.5 percent on either side— about the range the Fed has specified for annual growth rates.

Procedures for Hitting the Target

There is widespread agreement both inside and outside the Federal Reserve System that current procedures and reserve regulations make accurate control of monetary growth over short periods difficult or impossible. These procedures and regulations do not explain such long-sustained departures from the targets as the monetary explosions from April 1980 to April 1981 or July 1982 to July 1983 or the monetary retardations from April 1981 to October 1981 or January 1982 to July 1982. However, they do explain the wide volatility in monetary growth from week to week and month to month, which introduces undesirable uncertainty into the economy and financial markets and reduces Fed accountability for not hitting its targets.

There is also widespread agreement about the changes in procedures and regulations that would enable the Fed to come very much closer to hitting its targets over fairly short periods. The most important such change is the replacement of lagged reserve accounting, introduced in 1968, by contemporaneous reserve accounting comparable to that prevailing from 1914 to 1968. The obstacle to controlling monetary growth posed by lagged reserve accounting has been recognized since 1970 at the latest.[13] Unfortunately, the Fed did not act until 1982, when it finally decided to replace lagged by contemporary reserve requirements. However, it has delayed implementation until February 1984—the longest delay in implementing a changed regulation in the history of the Fed. There was no insuperable technical obstacle to implementing the change more promptly. However, given the Fed's past resistance to change, it cannot be taken for granted that implementation of contemporary reserves will not be further delayed, or even occur.

The other major procedural changes needed are:

1. Selection by the Fed of a single monetary target to end the Fed's juggling between targets;
2. Imposition of the same percentage reserve requirements on all deposit components of the selected target;
3. The use of total rather than nonborrowed reserves as the short-term operating instrument;
4. Linking of the discount rate to a market rate and making it a penalty rate (unfortunately, neither this change nor the preceding is feasible for technical reasons under lagged reserve accounting and hence must await the implementation of contemporaneous reserve accounting);
5. Reduction of the churning in which the Fed engages in the course of its so-called defensive open-market operations.[14]

Even without most of these changes, it would be possible for the Fed to put into effect almost instantaneously a policy that would provide a far stabler monetary environment than we have at present, even though it would by no means be ideal. The obstacle is not feasibility but bureaucratic inertia and the preservation of bureaucratic power and status.

A simple example will illustrate. Let the Fed continue to state targets for M1 growth. Let it estimate the change in its total holdings of U.S. government securities that would be required in the next six months, say, to produce the targeted growth in M1. Divide that amount by 26. Let the Fed purchase the resulting amount every week on the open market, in addition to any amount needed to replace maturing securities, and make no other purchases or sales. Finally, let it announce this schedule of purchases in advance and in full detail and stick to it.

Such a policy would assure control over the monetary aggregates, not from day to day, but over the longer period that the Fed insists is all that matters. It would enable the market to know precisely what the Fed would do and adjust its own actions accordingly. It would end the weekly guessing game that currently follows each Friday's release of figures on the money supply. The financial markets have certainly demonstrated that they have ample flexibility to handle whatever day-to-day or seasonal adjustments might be needed. It is hard to envisage any significant adverse effects from such a policy.

A few numbers will show how much difference such a policy would make to the Fed's open-market activities. In 1982, it added an average of $176 million a week to its total holdings of government securities—an unusually high amount. In the process of acquiring $176 million, it purchased each week an average of $13 *billion* of securities and sold nearly as much. About half of these transactions were on behalf of foreign central banks. But that still leaves roughly $40 of purchases or $80 of transactions for every $1 added to its portfolio—a degree of churning of a customer's account that would send a private stockbroker to jail, or at least to limbo.

Increased predictability, reduced churning, the loss of inscrutability— these are at the same time the major reasons for making so drastic a change and the major obstacle to its achievement. It would simply upset too many comfortable dovecotes.

THE FRAMEWORK OF MONETARY POLICY

The chief problem in discussing the framework of monetary policy is to set limits. The subject is old, yet immediately pertinent; numerous proposals have been made, and few, however ancient, do not have contemporary proponents. In view of my own belief that the important desiderata of structural reform are to reduce the variability of monetary growth, to limit the discretion of the monetary authorities, and to provide a stable monetary framework, I shall limit myself to proposals directed at those objectives, proceeding from the least to the most radical.

Imposing a Monetary Rule on the Fed

I have long argued that a major improvement in monetary policy could be achieved without any significant change in monetary institutions simply by imposing a monetary rule on the Fed. From an economic point of view, it would be desirable to state the rule in terms of a monetary aggregate such as M1 that has a close and consistent relation to subsequent changes in national income. However, recent years have demonstrated that the Fed has been unable or unwilling to achieve such a target, even when it sets it itself, and that it has been able to plead inability and thereby avoid accountability. Accordingly, I have reluctantly decided that it is preferable to state the rule in terms of a magnitude that has a somewhat less close relation to national income but that unquestionably can be controlled within very narrow limits within very brief time periods, namely, the Fed's own non-interest-bearing obligations, the monetary base.

In *Free to Choose*, my wife, Rose, and I proposed a specific form of rule as a constitutional amendment:

> *Congress shall have the power to authorize non-interest-bearing obligations of the government in the form of currency or book entries, provided that the total dollar amount outstanding increases by no more than 5 percent per year and no less than 3 percent.*
>
> It might be desirable to include a provision that two-thirds of each House of Congress, or some similar qualified majority, can waive the requirement in case of a declaration of war, the suspension to terminate annually unless renewed.[15]

A constitutional amendment would be the most effective way to establish confidence in the stability of the rule. However, it is clearly not the only way to impose the rule. Congress could equally well legislate it, and, indeed, proposals for a legislated monetary rule have been introduced in Congress.

This proposal has the merit that it minimizes the extent of institutional change. However, that is also its chief shortcoming. So long as the current institutional arrangements remain in being, strong pressure will be brought to bear to use them in ways that would avoid or evade the rule. Moreover, as a political matter, a constitutional amendment is unlikely to attract support sufficient for passage except under circumstances of deep and widespread dissatisfaction with monetary arrangements. Since such circumstances would also permit more far-reaching and fundamental changes, why settle for a half-measure?

I remain persuaded that a monetary rule that leads to a predictable long-run path of a specified monetary aggregate is a highly desirable goal—superior either to discretionary control of the quantity of money by a set of monetary authorities or to a commodity standard. However, I am no longer so optimistic as I once was that it can be effected by either persuading the monetary authorities to follow it or legislating its adoption. Congressional attempts in the past decade to push the Fed in that direction have repeatedly failed. The Fed has rhetorically accepted monetary targets but never a firm monetary rule. Moreover, the Fed has not been willing even to match its performance to a rhetorical acceptance of monetary targets. All this suggests that a change in our monetary institutions is required in order to make such a rule effective.

An International Monetary Rule

Some economists, in particular Ronald McKinnon, have accepted the case for a monetary rule but have argued that if applied on a national basis, it would be rendered largely ineffective by substitution of other market currencies for the one being controlled by the rule. Hence they propose the adoption of a rule by a group of countries with respect to an aggregate of their money supplies, which implies, of course, some agreement on the exchange rates at which the monies will be combined. McKinnon has suggested that Japan, the United States, and Germany should adopt such a rule for a total including the yen, the dollar, and the mark.

This proposal has received considerable attention, particularly with respect to the substantive contention that even under floating exchange rates currency substitution renders control of the U.S. money supply "increasingly inefficient for. . .stabilizing American income and prices."[16] The bulk of the evidence does not support McKinnon's contention.[17] Rather, it suggests that substitution of other currencies for the dollar is a trivial impediment to the effectiveness of a monetary rule for the dollar alone.

The economic objections to the proposal are dwarfed by the political objections. A verbal agreement is possible, but a credible and enforceable one, next to impossible.[18] But even if it were, the proposal involves giving great and essentially discretionary powers to an international body independent of any political control by citizens of each member-country short of withdrawal from the agreement. As I indicate below, I regard the independence in a democracy of a national central bank as highly objectionable on political grounds. The objection is vastly stronger to an independent world or tri-country central bank.

Separating Regulatory from Monetary Functions

A modest institutional reform that promises considerable benefits is to separate the regulatory from the monetary functions of the Fed. Currently, regulatory functions absorb most of the attention of the Fed. Moreover, they obscure accountability for monetary control by confusing the two very separate and to some extent inconsistent functions.

As has recently been proposed in a study of the Federal Deposit Insurance Corporation (FDIC), the Fed should be stripped of its regulatory functions, which would be combined with the largely overlapping functions of the FDIC, the Federal Savings and Loan Insurance Corporation (FSLIC), and the comptroller of the currency. Such a combined agency should have no monetary powers. It also might well include the operating functions of the Federal Reserve banks—the monitoring of reserve requirements, issuance of currency, clearing of checks, reporting of data, and so forth.[19]

A separate monetary control agency could be a very small body, charged solely with determining the total quantity of high-powered money through open-market operations. Its function would be clear, highly visible, and subject to effective accountability.

Ending the Independence of the Fed

An approach that need involve relatively little institutional change—although it is far more drastic than the preceding—and that could be implemented by legislation would be to end the independence of the Fed by converting it into a bureau of the Treasury Department. That would end the present division of responsibilities for monetary and fiscal policy that leads to the spectacle of chairmen of the Fed blaming all the nation's ills on the defects of fiscal policy and secretaries of the Treasury blaming them on the defects of monetary policy—a phenomenon that has prevailed for decades. There would be a single locus of authority that could be held responsible.

The immediate objection that arises is that it would make monetary policy a plaything of politics. My own examination of monetary history indicates that this judgment is correct, but that it is an argument for, not against, eliminating the central bank's independence.

I examined this issue at length in an article published more than two decades ago entitled "Should There Be an Independent Monetary Authority?"[20] I concluded that it is

> highly dubious that the United States, or for that matter any other country, has in practice ever had an independent central bank in [the] fullest sense of

the term . . . To judge by experience, even those central banks that have been nominally independent in the fullest sense of the term have in fact been closely linked to the executive authority.

But of course this does not dispose of the matter. The ideal is seldom fully realized. Suppose we could have an independent central bank in the sense of a coordinate constitutionally established, separate organization. Would it be desirable to do so? I think not, for both political and economic reasons.

The political objections are perhaps more obvious than the economic ones. Is it really tolerable in a democracy to have so much power concentrated in a body free from any kind of direct, effective political control? A "liberal" often characterizes his position as involving belief in the rule of law rather than of men. It is hard to reconcile such a view with the approval of an independent central bank in any meaningful way. True, it is impossible to dispense fully with the rule of men. No law can be specified so precisely as to avoid problems of interpretation or to cover explicitly every possible case. But the kind of limited discretion left by even the best of laws in the hands of those administering them is a far cry indeed from the kind of far-reaching powers that the laws establishing central banks generally place in the hands of a small number of men.

One [economic] defect of an independent central bank . . . is that it almost inevitably involves dispersal of responsibility . . .

Another defect . . . is the extent to which policy is . . . made highly dependent on personalities . . .

A third technical defect is that an independent central bank will almost inevitably give undue emphasis to the point of view of bankers . . .

The three defects I have outlined constitute a strong technical argument against an independent central bank. Combined with the political argument, the case against a fully independent central bank is strong indeed.[21]

The experience of the past two decades has led me to alter my views in one respect only—about the importance of personalities. They have on occasion made a great deal of difference, but additional experience and study has impressed me with the continuity of Fed policy, despite the wide differences in the personalities and backgrounds of the persons supposedly in charge.

For the rest, experience has reinforced my views. Anna Schwartz and I pointed out in *Monetary History* that subservience to congressional pressure in 1930 and 1931 would have prevented the disastrous monetary policy followed by the Fed. That is equally true for the past fifteen years. The relevant committees of Congress have generally, though by no means invariably, urged policies on the Fed that would have produced a stabler rate of monetary growth and much less inflation. Excessively rapid and volatile monetary growth from, say, 1971 to 1979 was not the result of political pressure—certainly not from Congress, although in some of these years there clearly was pressure for more rapid growth from the administration. Nonetheless, no political pressures would have prevented the Fed from increasing M1 over this period at, say, an average annual rate of 5 percent—the rate of increase during the prior eight years—instead of 6.7 percent.

Subordinating the Fed to the Treasury is by no means ideal. Yet it would be a great improvement over the existing situation, even with no other changes.

A Gold Standard

Superficially, there appears to be widespread support for a "gold standard." However, as the report of the Gold Commission demonstrated, the apparent consensus disappears when the question is what kind of gold standard.[22] Some who refer to themselves as proponents of a gold standard simply want the Fed to use the price of gold as a guide to increasing or decreasing the growth rate of the money supply without buying or selling gold and without committing itself to keeping the price of gold within any specified limits. Others want to add a commitment by the Fed to specific numerical limits on the price of gold. Still others want to fix dollar prices at which the Fed—or the Treasury—will buy and sell gold, generally with the proviso that other major countries agree to do the same in terms of their own currencies. Finally, a small minority wants a "real" gold standard in which the Fed and the Treasury would cease issuing any non-interest-bearing obligations other than, perhaps, warehouse certificates for specified physical amounts of gold, and in which gold coins or warehouse certificates, or their equivalent, would be the circulating medium.

For reasons that I have spelled out elsewhere, I regard only the last—a real gold standard—as constituting an improvement rather than a deterioration in our monetary arrangements. And that alternative, which is by no means ideal, has minuscule political support.[23]

Competitive Issue of Money

Increasing interest has been expressed in recent years in proposals to replace governmental issuance of money and control of its quality by private market arrangements. One set of proposals would end the government monopoly on the issuance of currency and permit the competitive issue of currency. Another would eliminate entirely any issuance of money by government and, instead, restrict the role of government to defining a monetary unit.

Choice in currency and a tabular standard. This set of proposals derives largely from a pamphlet by F. A. Hayek entitled *Choice in Currency: A Way to Stop Inflation.*[24] Hayek proposed that all special privileges (such as "legal tender" quality) attached to government-issued currency be removed, and that financial institutions be permitted to issue currency or deposit obligations on whatever terms were mutually acceptable to the issuer and the holder of the liabilities. He envisaged a system in which institutions would in fact issue obligations expressed in terms of purchasing power either of specific commodities, such as gold or silver, or of commodities in general through linkage to a price index. In his opinion, constant-purchasing-power moneys would come to dominate the market and largely replace both obligations denominated in dollars or pounds or other similar units and in specific commodities.

The idea of a currency unit linked to a price index is an ancient one—proposed in the nineteenth century by W. Stanley Jevons and Alfred Marshall, who named it a "tabular" standard—and repeatedly rediscovered.[25] It is part of the theoretically highly attractive idea of widespread indexation. Experience, however, has demonstrated that the theoretical attractiveness of the idea is not matched by practice. Nothing has prevented the widespread use of indexation in one form or another—indeed, the voluntary adoption of the equivalent of a tabular standard—in the United States, Britain, or other capitalist countries. Yet indexation has been extensive only when inflation has been extremely high and variable, as in some South American countries and Israel. Indexing, though frequent, is of minor importance except in labor contracts, and even in that area it is far from dominant.

I approve of Professor Hayek's proposal to remove restrictions on the issuance of private moneys to compete with government moneys. But I do not share his belief about the outcome. Private moneys now exist—traveler's and cashier's checks, bank deposits, money orders, and various forms of bank drafts and negotiable instruments. But these are almost all claims on a specified number of units of government currency (of dollars or pounds or francs or marks). Currently, they are subject to government regulation and control. But even if such regulations and controls were entirely eliminated, the advantage of a single national currency unit buttressed by long tradition will, I suspect, serve to prevent any other type of private currency unit from seriously challenging the dominant government currency, and this despite the high degree of monetary variability many countries have experienced over recent decades.

The recent explosion in financial futures markets offers a possible new road to the achievement, through private market actions, of the equivalent of a tabular standard. This possibility is highly speculative—little more than a gleam in one economist's eye. It involves the establishment of futures markets in one or more price indexes—strictly parallel to the markets that have developed in stock price indexes. Such markets, if active and covering a considerable range of future dates, would provide a relatively costless means of hedging long-term contracts against risks of changes in the price level. A combination of an orthodox dollar contract plus a properly timed set of futures in a price level would be the precise equivalent of a tabular standard, but would have the advantage that any one party to a contract, with the help of speculators and other hedgers in the futures market, could have the benefit of a tabular standard without the agreement of the other party or parties.

Recent changes in banking regulations have opened still another route to a partial tabular standard on a substantial scale. The Federal Home Loan Bank has finally authorized federally chartered savings and loan associations to offer price-level-adjusted mortgage (PLAM) loans. Concurrently, the restrictions on the interest rate that can be paid on deposits by a wide range of financial institutions have been eased and removed entirely for deposits of longer maturities.

This would permit financial institutions simultaneously to lend and borrow on a price-level-adjusted basis: to lend on a PLAM and borrow on a price-level-adjusted deposit (PLAD), both at an interest rate specified in real rather than nominal terms. By matching PLAM loans against PLAD deposits, a bank would be fully hedged against changes in inflation, covering its costs by the difference between the interest rate it charges and pays. Similarly, both borrowers and lenders would be safeguarded against changes in inflation with respect to a particular liability and asset.

As yet, I know of no financial institutions that have proceeded along these lines. I conjecture that no major development will occur unless and until inflation once again accelerates. When and if that occurs, PLAMs and PLADs may well become household words and not simply mysterious acronyms.[26]

Eliminating government money. A number of economic theorists who have been reexamining the foundations of monetary systems have recently offered a new set of proposals. The basic idea is that the government simply define a monetary unit—for example, the value of a specified basket of goods—and play no other role in the monetary system. Private institutions would issue claims denominated in the officially defined unit (as, in futures markets, they now issue promises to deliver wheat or gold or silver specified in officially defined units). The role of government would be restricted to enforcing such contracts, preventing fraud, and the like.[27]

The set of ideas underlying these proposals are intellectually exciting and will contribute to a fuller understanding of the role and value of money. But, as yet, they seem too radical, too unsupported by evidence, to be regarded as a practical proposal for institutional reform. As Robert Hall, one of the main contributors to these developments, states, "All of these proposals share a basic microeconomic goal—full deregulation of transaction services and intermediation [borrowing from some and lending to others]. None of them would rely on the concept of a money stock or its stability relative to total income. Whether their macroeconomic performance would equal that of a simple money growth rule is still a matter of controversy."[28]

Freezing High-Powered Money

The final proposal combines features from most of the preceding. It is radical and far-reaching, yet simple.

The proposal is that, after a transition period, the quantity of high-powered money—non-interest-bearing obligations of the U.S. government—be frozen at a fixed amount.[29] These non-interest-bearing obligations now take two forms: currency and deposits at the Federal Reserve System. The simplest way to envisage the change is to suppose that Federal Reserve deposit liabilities were replaced dollar for dollar by currency notes, which were turned over to the owners of those deposits. Thereafter, the government's monetary role would be limited to keeping the amount constant by replacing worn-out currency. In effect, a monetary rule of zero growth in high-powered money would be adopted. (In practice, it would not be necessary to replace deposits at the Federal Reserve with currency; they could be retained as book entries, so long as the total of such book entries plus currency notes was kept constant.)

As noted above, the Fed currently has two roles: determining the quantity of money; and regulating banking institutions and providing such services as collateralized loans, check-clearing, wire transfers, and the like. Under this proposal its first role would be eliminated. In this sense, the proposal would end the independence of the Federal Reserve System. Its second role could, if desired, be continued, preferably by combining it with the similar roles of the FDIC, the FSLIC, and the comptroller of the currency, as suggested earlier.

This proposal would be consistent with, indeed require, the continued existence of private institutions issuing claims to government currency. These could be regulated as now, with the whole paraphernalia of required reserves, bank examinations, limitations on lending, and the like. However, they could also be freed from all or most such regulations. In particular, the need for reserve requirements to enable the Fed to control the quantity of money would disappear.

Reserve requirements might still be desirable for a different though related reason. The new monetary economists argue that only the existence of such government regulations as reserve requirements and prohibition of the private issuance of currency explains the relatively stable demand for high-powered money. In the absence of such regulations, they contend, non-interest-bearing money would be completely dominated by interest-bearing assets, or, at the very least, the demand for such money would be rendered highly unstable.

I am far from persuaded by this contention. It supposes a closer approach to a frictionless world with minimal transaction costs than seems to me a useful approximation to the actual world.[30] Nonetheless, it is arguable that the elimination of reserve requirements would introduce an unpredictable and erratic element into the demand for high-powered money. For that reason, although personally I would favor the deregulation of financial institutions, thereby incorporating a major element of Hayek's proposed competitive financial system, it would seem prudent to proceed in stages: first, freeze high-powered money; then, after a period, eliminate reserve requirements and other remaining regulations, including the prohibition on the issuance of hand-to-hand currency by private institutions.

Why zero growth? Zero has a special appeal on political grounds that is not shared by any other number. If 3 percent, why not 4 percent? It is hard, as it were, to go to the political barricades to defend 3 rather than 4, or 4 rather than 5. But zero is—as a psychological matter—qualitatively different. It is what has come to be called a Schelling point—a natural point at which people tend to agree, like "splitting the difference" in a dispute over a monetary sum. Moreover, by removing any power to create money it eliminates institutional arrangements lending themselves to discretionary changes in monetary growth.

Would zero growth in high-powered money be consistent with a healthy economy? In the hypothetical long-long-run stationary economy, when the whole economy had become adjusted to the situation, and population, real output, and so on were all stationary, zero growth in high-powered money would imply zero growth in other monetary aggregates and mean stable velocities for the aggregates. In consequence, the price level would be stable. In a somewhat less than stationary state in which output was rising, if financial innovations kept pace, the money multiplier would tend to rise at the same rate as output and again prices would be stable. If financial innovations ceased but total output continued to rise, prices would decline. If output rose at about 3 percent per year, prices would tend to fall at 3 percent per year. So long as that was known and relatively stable, all contracts could be adjusted to it, and it would cause no problems and indeed would have some advantages.[31]

However, any such outcome is many decades away. The more interesting and important question is not the final stationary-state result but the intermediate dynamic process.

Once the policy was in effect, the actual behavior of nominal income and the price level would depend on what happened to a monetary aggregate like M1 relative to high-powered money and what happened to nominal income relative to M1—that is, on the behavior of the money multiplier (the ratio of M1 to high-powered money) and on the income velocity of M1 (the ratio of nominal income to M1).

Given a loosening of the financial structure through continued deregulation, there would be every reason to expect a continued flow of innovations raising the money multiplier. This process has in fact occurred throughout the past several centuries. For example, in the century from 1870 to 1970, the ratio of the quantity of money, as defined by Anna Schwartz and me in *Monetary History*, to high-powered money rose at the average rate of 1 percent per year. In the post–World War II period, the velocity of M1 has risen at about 3 percent per year, and at a relatively steady rate. This trend cannot of course continue indefinitely. Above, in specifying a desirable target for the Fed, I estimated the rise in velocity would slow to about 1 or 2 percent per year. However, a complete end to the rapid trend in velocity is not in sight.

There is no way to make precise numerical estimates, but there is every reason to anticipate that for decades after the introduction of a freeze on high-powered money, both the money multiplier and velocity would tend to rise at rates in the range of historical experience. Under these circumstances, a zero rate of growth of high-powered money would imply roughly stable prices, though ultimately, perhaps, slightly declining prices.

What of the transition? Over the three years from 1979 to 1982, high-powered money grew an average of 7.0 percent a year. It would be desirable to bring that rate to zero gradually. As for M1 growth, about a five-year period seems appropriate—or a transition that reduces the rate of growth of high-powered money by about 1.5 percentage points a year. The only other transitional problem would be to phase out the Fed's powers to create and destroy high-powered money by open-market operations and discounting. Neither transition offers any special problem. The Fed, or its successor agency, could still use part of the existing stock of high-powered money for similar purposes, particularly for lender of last resort purposes, if that function were retained.

The great advantage of this proposal is that it would end the arbitrary power of the Federal Reserve System to determine the quantity of money and would do so without establishing any comparable locus of power and without introducing any major disturbances into other existing economic and financial institutions.

I have found that few things are harder even for knowledgeable nonexperts to accept than the proposition that twelve (or nineteen) people sitting around a table in Washington, subject to neither election nor dismissal nor close administrative or political control, have the power to determine the quantity of money—to permit a reduction by one-third during the Great Depression or a near doubling from 1970 to 1980.[32] That power is too important, too pervasive, to be exercised by a few people, however public-spirited, if there is any feasible alternative.

There is no need for such arbitrary power. In the system I have just described, the total quantity of any monetary aggregate would be determined by the market interactions of many financial institutions and millions of holders of monetary assets. It would be limited by the constant quantity of high-powered money available as ultimate reserves. The ratios of various aggregates to high-powered money would doubtless change from time to time, but in the absence of rigid government controls—such as those exemplified by Regulation Q, fortunately being phased out—the ratios would change gradually and only as financial innovations or changes in business and industry altered the proportions in which the public chose to hold various monetary assets. No small number of individuals would be in a position to introduce major changes in the ratios or in the rates of growth of various monetary aggregates—to move, for example, from a 3 percent per year rate of growth in M1 for one six-month period (January to July 1982) to a 13 percent rate of growth for the next six months (July 1982 to January 1983).

CONCLUSION

Major institutional change occurs only at times of crisis. For the rest, the tyranny of the status quo limits changes in institutions to marginal tinkering— we muddle through. It took the Great Depression to produce the FDIC, the most important structural change in our monetary institutions since at least 1914, when the Federal Reserve System began operations, and to shift power over monetary policy from the Federal Reserve banks, especially that in New York, to the board in Washington. Since then, our monetary institutions have been remarkably stable. It took the severe inflation of the 1970s and accompanying double-digit interest rates—combined with the enforcement of Regulation Q—to produce money market mutual funds and thereby force a considerable measure of deregulation of banking.

Nonetheless, it is worth discussing radical changes, not in the expectation that they will be adopted promptly but for two other reasons. One is to construct an ideal goal, so that incremental changes can be judged by whether they move the institutional structure toward or away from that ideal.

The other reason is very different. It is so that if a crisis requiring or facilitating radical change does arise, alternatives will be available that have been carefully developed and fully explored. An excellent example is provided by international monetary arrangements. For decades, economists had been exploring alternatives to the system of fixed exchange rates, in particular, floating exchange rates among national currencies. The practical men of affairs derided proposals for floating rates as unrealistic, impractical, ivory tower. Yet when crisis came, when the Bretton Woods fixed-rate system had to be scrapped, the theorists' impractical proposal became highly practical and formed the basis for the new system of international monetary arrangements.

Needless to say, I hope that no crises will occur that will necessitate a drastic change in domestic monetary institutions. The most likely such crisis is continued monetary instability, a return to a roller coaster of inflation about an upward trend, with inflation accelerating to levels of 20, 30, or more percent per year. That would shake the social and political framework of the nation and would produce results none of us would like to witness. Yet, it would be burying one's head in the sand to fail to recognize that such a development is a real possibility. It has occurred elsewhere, and it could occur here. If it does, the best way to cut it short, to minimize the harm it would do, is to be ready not with Band-Aids but with a real cure for the basic illness.

As of now, I believe the best real cure would be the reform outlined in the preceding section: abolish the money-creating powers of the Federal Reserve, freeze the quantity of high-powered money, and deregulate the financial system.

The less radical changes in policy and procedures suggested in the section on tactics seem to me to offer the best chance of avoiding a crisis. They call for the Fed to change its procedures so as to enable it to control more accurately a chosen monetary aggregate; to choose a single monetary aggregate to control; and to specify in advance, and adhere to, a five-year path for the growth of that aggregate that would bring it to a rate consistent with a healthy noninflationary economy.

These tactical changes are feasible technically. However, I am not optimistic that they will be adopted. The obstacle is political. As with any bureaucratic organization, it is not in the self-interest of the Fed to adopt policies that would render it accountable. The Fed has persistently avoided doing so over a long period. None of the tactics that I have proposed is new. The proposed changes would have made just as much sense five or ten years ago— indeed, if adopted then, the inflation and volatility of the past ten years would never have occurred. They have had the support of a large fraction of monetary experts outside the Fed. The Fed has resisted them for bureaucratic and political, not technical, reasons.[33] And resistance has been in the Fed's interest. By keeping monetary policy an arcane subject that must be entrusted to "experts" and kept out of politics, incapable of being judged by nonexperts, the Fed has been able to maintain the high public reputation of which I spoke at the outset of this paper, despite its poor record of performance.

One chairman after another, in testimony to Congress, has emphasized the mystery and difficulty of the Fed's task and the need for discretion, judgment, and the balancing of many considerations. Each has stressed how well the Fed has done and proclaimed its dedication to pursuing a noninflationary policy and has attributed any undesirable outcome to forces outside the Fed's control or to deficiencies in other components of government policy— particularly fiscal policy. The testimony of the four most recent chairmen of the Fed suffice to document their pervasive concern with avoiding accountability—a concern with which it is easy to sympathize in view of the purely coincidental relation between their announced intentions and the actual outcome.

Clearly the problem is not the person who happens to be chairman, but the system.

Notes

1. Milton Friedman and Anna J. Schwartz, *A Monetary History of the United States, 1867–1960* (Princeton, N.J.: Princeton University Press, 1963).

2. For the evidence for 1867 to 1960, see Milton Friedman and Anna J. Schwartz, "Money and Business Cycles," *Review of Economics and Statistics* 45, no. 1, part 2, supplement (February 1963), reprinted in Milton Friedman, *The Optimum Quantity of Money and Other Essays* (Chicago: Aldine Publishing Co., 1969), pp. 189–235. Evidence for the more recent period is available in many publications by many authors.

3. Ibid., pp. 234–35.

4. "Price Inertia and Policy Ineffectiveness in the United States, 1890–1980," *Journal of Political Economy* 90 (1982): 1087–116.

5. Christopher A. Sims questions this proposition on the basis of evidence on the variability of money and industrial production over two decades and in five countries. However, the evidence he presents is seriously flawed. For the United States, his monetary series consists of the average of daily figures, for the other countries of figures for one day a month. As I have demonstrated elsewhere, the standard deviation of monthly growth rates (or annual averages of monthly growth rates) is more than twice as large for one-day figures as for averages of daily figures. When his estimates are corrected for this bias, the standard deviations are roughly the same for all the countries. I do not know the details of the industrial production indexes he uses and so have no judgment on their comparability among countries. His one comparison for the United States (for 1960–1971 compared with 1971–1982) seems inconsistent with the results in Table 22.1. (See Sims, "Is There a Monetary Business Cycle?" *American Economic Review: Papers and Proceedings* 73 [May 1983]: 228–33, especially Table 1, p. 231; and Milton Friedman, "Monetary Variability: U.S. and Japan," *Journal of Money, Credit, and Banking* [August 1983].)

6. See Milton Friedman, "Monetary Studies of the National Bureau," in *Optimum Quantity of Money and Other Essays*, pp. 265–77.

7. See Levis Kochin, "Judging Monetary Policy," in Federal Reserve Bank of San Francisco, *Proceedings of the Third West Coast Academic/Federal Reserve Economic Seminar* (Fall 1979), pp. 143–84.

8. A. J. Schwartz and Michael Bordo reach a similar conclusion on the basis of overlapping yet somewhat different evidence in their forthcoming paper, "The Importance of Stable Money: Theory and Evidence."

9. For a thoughtful evaluation of proposed price rules, see R. E. Hafer, "Monetary Policy and the Price Rule: The Newest Odd Couple," *Federal Reserve Bank of St. Louis Review*, February 1983, pp. 5–13.

10. See Milton Friedman, "Monetary Policy: Theory and Practice," *Journal of Money, Credit, and Banking* 14 (February 1982): 98–118.

11. See my *Program for Monetary Stability* (New York: Fordham University Press, 1960), chap. 2.

12. Over the past three decades, M1 velocity has risen about 3 percent a year. Given a long-term rate of real growth of about 3 percent per year, continued velocity growth of 3 percent a year would mean that zero M1 growth would be required for zero inflation. However, part of the velocity growth has been a reaction to rising inflation and interest rates, which have made it more costly to hold cash. Successful disinflation has the opposite effect. Since the third quarter of 1981, M1 velocity has declined (by 6 percent to the second quarter of 1983) rather than risen. In addition, technological improvements in cash management cannot continue indefinitely. It therefore seems safer to suppose that M1 velocity will cease rising as rapidly as in the past, which explains the 1 to 3 estimate in the text. It implicitly allows for about a 1 to 2 percent per year velocity growth.

13. George Kaufman warned of the problem before lagged reserve accounting was introduced. See my "Monetary Policy," pp. 110–13, for a detailed discussion of lagged reserve requirements.

14. For a fuller discussion, see my "Monetary Policy."

15. Milton and Rose Friedman, *Free to Choose* (New York: Harcourt Brace Jovanovich, 1980), p. 308.

16. Ronald I. McKinnon, "Currency Substitution and Instability in the World Dollar Standard," *American Economic Review* 72 (June 1982): 332.

17. Henry N. Goldstein and Stephen E. Haynes, "A Critical Appraisal of McKinnon's World Money Supply Hypothesis" (unpublished paper, March 1983), conclude, "In a number of important respects . . . his interpretation seems strikingly at odds with the empirical evidence." A similar negative conclusion is reached by Thomas D. Willett, "U.S. Monetary Policy and World Liquidity," *American Economic Review* 73 (May 1983): 43–47.

18. See George M. von Furstenberg, "Internationally Managed Moneys," *American Economic Review* 73 (May 1983): 54–58.

19. See Federal Deposit Insurance Corporation, *Deposit Insurance in a Changing Environment* (April 15, 1983), esp. pp. xxi–xxiv and chap. 6.

20. In Leland B. Yeager, ed., *In Search of a Monetary Constitution* (Cambridge, Mass.: Harvard University Press, 1962), chap. 8; reprinted in Milton Friedman, *Dollars and Deficits* (Englewood Cliffs, N.J.: Prentice-Hall, 1968), chap. 6; also see chapter 23 of this volume.

21. Ibid., pp. 180, 184, 186, 188, 190.

22. See *Report to the Congress of the Commission on the Role of Gold in the Domestic and International Monetary Systems* (March 1982), vols. 1 and 2.

23. See my "Real and Pseudo Gold Standards," *Dollars and Deficits*, chap. 11, also chapter 24 of this volume; and "The Role and Value of Gold," *Reason*, June 1975, pp. 87, 91–94.

24. Institute of Economic Affairs, Occasional Paper 48 (London, 1976).

25. For an interesting recent rediscovery, see the article by R. W. R. White, governor of the Reserve Bank of New Zealand, on a proposed purchasing-power-adjusted money of account that he termed the "Real" (*Reserve Bank of New Zealand Bulletin*, October 1979, pp. 371–74). This article was followed by a series of five articles in successive monthly issues of the *Bulletin* dealing with the possible effects of the Real on various aspects of the economy.

26. See J. Huston McCulloch, "PLAMs: Affordable Mortgages from Inflation-Proof Deposits," *Quarterly Review* (Federal Home Loan Bank of Cincinnati), 3 (1982): 2–6. Also see my *Newsweek* column, "PLAMs and PLADs," June 13, 1983.

27. See Robert E. Hall, "Monetary Trends in the United States and the United Kingdom: A Review from the Perspective of New Developments in Monetary Economics," *Journal of Economic Literature* 20 (December 1982): 1552–556, for a succinct and authoritative summary of recent ideas. Robert L. Greenfield and Leland B. Yeager, "A Laissez Faire Approach to Monetary Stability," *Journal of Money, Credit, and Banking* (August 1983), is an excellent analysis of the theoretical basis of this collection of proposals.

28. Hall, "New Developments in Monetary Economics," p. 1555.

29. In deference to tradition, I designate currency and deposits at the Federal Reserve as "obligations," but they are not in any meaningful sense obligations of the U.S. government, or, indeed, anyone else. They are simply pure fiat money.

30. The empirical issue is the same as that embedded in the extreme form of the rational-expectations hypothesis, which asserts the complete inability, even over short periods, of perceived changes in monetary policy to affect real magnitudes.

31. See my "The Optimum Quantity of Money," *Optimum Quantity of Money and Other Essays*, chap. 1.

32. The Open Market Investment Committee, which has the power, consists of the seven members of the Board of Governors plus five of the twelve presidents of Federal Reserve banks; hence the number twelve. However, all twelve presidents attend the meetings of the committee and engage in the discussions of policy, although only five vote; hence the number nineteen.

33. See George Kaufman, "Monetarism at the Fed," *Journal of Contemporary Studies* (Winter 1983).

SHOULD THERE BE
AN INDEPENDENT
MONETARY AUTHORITY?

· 23 ·

The text for this paper, to paraphrase the famous remark attributed to Poincaré, is, "Money is too important to be left to the central bankers." The problem that suggests this text is the one of what kind of arrangements to set up in a free society for the control of monetary policy. The believer in a free society—a "liberal" in the original meaning of the word, but unfortunately not in the meaning that is now current in this country—is fundamentally fearful of concentrated power. His objective is to preserve the maximum degree of freedom for each individual separately that is compatible with one man's freedom not interfering with other men's freedom. He believes that this objective requires power to be dispersed, that it be prevented from accumulating in any one person or group of people.

The need for dispersal of power raises an especially difficult problem in the field of money. There is widespread agreement that government must have some responsibility for monetary matters. There is also widespread recognition that control over money can be a potent tool for controlling and shaping the economy. Its potency is dramatized in Lenin's famous dictum that the most effective way to destroy a society is to destroy its money. It is exemplified in more pedestrian fashion by the extent to which control over money has always been a potent means of exacting taxes from the populace at large, very often

Reprinted by permission of the publishers, from Leland B. Yeager, ed., *In Search of a Monetary Constitution* (Cambridge, Mass.: Harvard University Press). ©1962 by the University of Virginia.

without the explicit agreement of the legislature. This has been true from early times, when monarchs clipped coins and adopted similar expedients, to the present, with our more subtle and sophisticated modern techniques for turning the printing press or simply altering book entries.

The problem is to establish institutional arrangements that will enable government to exercise responsibility for money, yet will at the same time limit the power thereby given to government and prevent the power from being used in ways that will tend to weaken rather than strengthen a free society. Three kinds of solutions have developed or have been suggested. One is an automatic commodity standard, a monetary standard which in principle requires no governmental control. A second is the control of monetary policies by an "independent" central bank. A third is the control of monetary policies by rules that are legislated in advance by the legislature, are binding upon the monetary authority, and greatly limit its initiative. This paper discusses these three alternatives with rather more attention to the solution through a central bank.

A Commodity Standard

Historically, the device that has evolved most frequently in many different places and over the course of centuries is a commodity standard, that is, the use as money of some physical commodity such as gold, silver, brass, or tin, or cigarettes, cognac, or various other commodities. If money consisted wholly of a physical commodity of this type, in principle there would be no need for control by the government at all. The amount of money in society would depend on the cost of producing the monetary commodity rather than on other things. Changes in the amount of money would depend on changes in the technical conditions of producing the monetary commodity and on changes in the demand for money.

This is an ideal that animates many believers in an automatic gold standard. In point of fact, however, as the system developed it deviated very far from this simple pattern, which required no governmental intervention. Historically, a commodity standard—such as a gold standard or a silver standard—was accompanied by the development of alternative forms of money as well, of fiduciary money of one kind or another, ostensibly convertible into the monetary commodity on fixed terms. There was a very good reason for this development. The fundamental defect of a commodity standard, from the point of view of the society as a whole, is that it requires the use of real resources to add to the stock of money. People must work hard to dig something out of the ground in one place—to dig gold out of the ground in South Africa—in order to rebury it in Fort Knox, or some similar place. The necessity of using real resources for the operation of a commodity standard establishes a strong incentive for people to find ways to achieve the same result without employing these resources. If people will accept as money pieces of paper on which is printed "I promise to pay so much of the standard commodity," these pieces of paper can perform the same functions as the physical pieces of gold or silver, and they require very much less in resources to produce. This point, which I have discussed at somewhat greater length elsewhere,[1] seems to me the fundamental difficulty of a commodity standard.

If an automatic commodity standard were feasible, it would provide an excellent solution to the liberal dilemma of how to get a stable monetary framework without the danger of irresponsible exercise of monetary powers. A full commodity standard, for example, an honest-to-goodness gold standard in which 100 percent of the money consisted literally of gold, widely supported by a public imbued with the mythology of a gold standard and the belief that it is immoral and improper for government to interfere with its operation, would provide an effective control against governmental tinkering with the currency and against irresponsible monetary action. Under such a standard, any monetary powers of government would be very minor in scope.

But such an automatic system has historically never proved feasible. It has always tended to develop in the direction of a mixed system containing fiduciary elements such as bank notes, bank deposits, or government notes in addition to the monetary commodity. And once fiduciary elements have been introduced, it has proved difficult to avoid government control over them, even when they were initially issued by private individuals. The reason is basically the difficulty of preventing counterfeiting or its economic equivalent. Fiduciary money consists of a contract to pay standard money. It so happens that there tends to be a long interval between the making of such a contract and its realization, which enhances the difficulty of enforcing the contract to pay the standard money and hence also the temptation to issue fraudulent contracts. In addition, once fiduciary elements have been introduced, the temptation for government itself to issue fiduciary money is almost irresistible. As a result of these forces, commodity standards have tended in practice to become mixed standards involving extensive intervention by the state, which leaves the problem of how intervention is to be controlled.

Despite the great amount of talk by many people in favor of the gold standard, almost no one today literally desires to see an honest-to-goodness full gold standard in operation. People who say they want a gold standard are almost invariably talking about the present kind of standard, or the kind of standard that was maintained in the 1930s, in which there is a small amount of gold in existence, held by the central monetary authority as "backing"—to use that very misleading term—for fiduciary money, and with the same authority, a central bank or other government bureau, managing the gold standard. Even during the so-called great days of the gold standard of the nineteenth century, when the Bank of England was supposedly running the gold standard skillfully, the monetary system was far from a fully automatic gold standard. It was even then a highly managed standard. And certainly the situation is now more extreme. Country after country has adopted the view that government has responsibility for internal stability. This development, plus the invention by Schacht of the widespread direct control of foreign exchange transactions, has meant that few if any countries are willing today to let the gold standard operate even as quasi-automatically as it did in the nineteenth century.

Most countries in the world currently behave asymmetrically with respect to the gold standard. They are willing to allow gold to flow in and even to inflate somewhat in response, but almost none is willing either to let gold flow out to any large extent or to adjust to the outflow by allowing or forcing internal prices to decline. Instead, they are very likely to take measures such as exchange controls, import restrictions, and the like.

My conclusion is that an automatic commodity standard is neither a feasible nor a desirable solution to the problem of establishing monetary arrangements for a free society. It is not desirable because it would involve a large cost in the form of resources used to produce the monetary commodity. It is not feasible because the mythology and beliefs required to make it effective do not exist.

An Independent Central Bank

A second device that has evolved and for which there is considerable support is a so-called independent monetary authority—a central bank—to control monetary policy and to keep it from being the football of political manipulation. The widespread belief in an independent central bank clearly rests on the acceptance—in some cases the highly reluctant acceptance—of the view I have just been expressing about a commodity standard, namely, that a fully automatic commodity standard is not a feasible way to achieve the objective of a monetary structure that is both stable and free from irresponsible governmental tinkering.

The device of an independent central bank embodies the very appealing idea that it is essential to prevent monetary policy from being a day-to-day plaything at the mercy of every whim of the current political authorities. The device is rationalized by assimilating it to a species of constitutionalism. The argument that is implicit in the views of proponents of an independent central bank—so far as I know, these views have never been fully spelled out—is that control over money is an essential function of a government comparable to the exercise of legislative or judicial or administrative powers. In all of these, it is important to distinguish between the basic structure and day-to-day operation within that structure. In our form of government, this distinction is made between the constitutional rules which set down a series of basic prescriptions and proscriptions for the legislative, judicial, and executive authorities and the detailed operation of the several authorities under these general rules. Similarly, the argument implicit in the defense of an independent central bank is that the monetary structure needs a kind of a monetary constitution, which takes the form of rules establishing and limiting the central bank as to the powers that it is given, its reserve requirements, and so on. Beyond this, the argument goes, it is desirable to let the central bank have authority largely coordinate with that of the legislature, the executive, and the judiciary to carry out the general constitutional mandate on a day-to-day basis.

In recent times, the threat of extension of government control into widening areas of economic activity has often come through proposals involving monetary expansion. Central bankers have generally been "sound money men," at least verbally, which is to say, they have tended to attach great importance to stability of the exchange rate, maintenance of convertibility of the nation's currency into other currencies and into gold, and prevention of inflation. They have therefore tended to oppose many of the proposals for extending the scope of government. This coincidence of their views in these respects with those of people like myself, who regard narrowly limited government as a requisite for a free society, is the source of much of the sympathy on the part of this group, whom I shall call "new liberals," for the notion of an independent central bank. As a practical matter, the central bankers seem more likely to impose restrictions on irresponsible monetary power than the legislative authority itself.

A first step in discussing this notion critically is to examine the meaning of the "independence" of a central bank. There is a trivial meaning that cannot be the source of dispute about the desirability of independence. In any kind of a bureaucracy, it is desirable to delegate particular functions to particular agencies. The Bureau of Internal Revenue can be described as an independent bureau within the Treasury Department. Outside the regular government departments, there are separate administrative organizations, such as the Bureau of the Budget. This kind of independence of monetary policy would exist if, within the central administrative hierarchy, there were a separate organization charged with monetary policy which was subordinate to the chief executive or officer, though it might be more or less independent in routine decisions. For our purposes, this seems to me a trivial meaning of independence, and not the meaning fundamentally involved in the argument for or against an independent central bank. This is simply a question of expediency and of the best way to organize an administrative hierarchy.

A more basic meaning is the one suggested above—that a central bank should be an independent branch of government coordinate with the legislative, executive, and judicial branches, and with its actions subject to interpretation by the judiciary. Perhaps the most extreme form of this kind of independence in practice, and the form that comes closest to the ideal type envisaged by proponents of an independent central bank, has been achieved in those historical instances where an organization that was initially entirely private and not formally part of the government at all has served as a central bank. The leading example, of course, is the Bank of England, which developed out of a strictly private bank and was not owned by or formally a part of the government until after World War II. If such a private organization strictly outside the regular political channels could not function as a central monetary authority, this form of independence would call for the establishment of a central bank through a constitutional provision which would be subject to change only by constitutional amendment. The bank would accordingly not be subject to direct control by the legislature. This is the meaning I shall assign to independence in discussing further whether an independent central bank is a desirable resolution of the problem of achieving responsible control over monetary policy.

It seems to me highly dubious that the United States, or for that matter any other country, has in practice ever had an independent central bank in this fullest sense of the term. Even when central banks have supposedly been fully independent, they have exercised their independence only so long as there has been no real conflict between them and the rest of the government. Whenever there has been a serious conflict, as in time of war, between the interests of the fiscal authorities in raising funds and of the monetary authorities in maintaining convertibility into specie, the bank has almost invariably given way, rather than the fiscal authority. To judge by experience, even those central banks that have been nominally independent in the fullest sense of the term have in fact been closely linked to the executive authority.

But of course this does not dispose of the matter. The ideal is seldom fully realized. Suppose we could have an independent central bank in the sense of a coordinate constitutionally established, separate organization. Would it be desirable to do so? I think not, for both political and economic reasons.

The political objections are perhaps more obvious than the economic ones. Is it really tolerable in a democracy to have so much power concentrated in a body free from any kind of direct, effective political control? What I have called the "new liberal" often characterizes his position as involving belief in the rule of law rather than of men. It is hard to reconcile such a view with the approval of an independent central bank in any meaningful way. True, it is impossible to dispense fully with the rule of men. No law can be specified so precisely as to avoid problems of interpretation or to cover explicitly every possible case. But the kind of limited discretion left by even the best of laws in the hands of those administering them is a far cry indeed from the kind of far-reaching powers that the laws establishing central banks generally place in the hands of a small number of men.

I was myself most fully persuaded that it would be politically intolerable to have an "independent" central bank by the memoirs of Emile Moreau, the governor of the Bank of France during the period from about 1926 to 1928, the period when France established a new parity for the franc and returned to gold. Moreau was appointed governor of the Bank of France in 1926, not long before Poincaré became premier after violent fluctuations in the exchange value of the franc and serious accompanying internal disturbances and governmental financial difficulties. Moreau's memoirs were edited and brought out in book form some years ago by Jacques Rueff, who was the leading figure in the recent French monetary reform.[2]

The book is fascinating on many counts. The particular respect that is most relevant for our present purpose is the picture that Moreau paints of Montagu Norman, governor of the Bank of England, on the one hand, and of Hjalmar Schacht, at that time governor of the Bank of Germany, on the other; they were unquestionably two of the three outstanding central bankers of the modern era, Benjamin Strong of the United States being the third. Moreau describes the views that these two European central bankers had of their functions and their roles, and implies their attitude toward other groups. The impression left with me—though it is by no means clear that Moreau drew the same conclusions from what he wrote, and it is certain that he would have expressed himself more temperately—is that Norman and Schacht were contemptuous both of the masses—of "vulgar" democracy—and of the classes—of the, to them, equally vulgar plutocracy. They viewed themselves as exercising control in the interests of both groups but free from the pressures of either. In Norman's view, if the major central bankers of the world would only cooperate with one another—and he had in mind not only himself and Schacht but also Moreau and Benjamin Strong—they could jointly wield enough power to control the basic economic destinies of the Western world in accordance with rational ends and objectives rather than with the irrational processes of either parliamentary democracy or laissez-faire capitalism. Though of course stated in obviously benevolent terms of doing the "right thing" and avoiding distrust and uncertainty, the implicit doctrine is clearly thoroughly dictatorial and totalitarian.

It is not hard to see how Schacht could later be one of the major creators of the kind of far-reaching economic planning and control that developed in Germany. Schacht's creation of extensive direct control of foreign exchange transactions is one of the few really new economic inventions of modern times. In the older literature, when people spoke of a currency as being inconvertible, they meant that it was not convertible into gold or silver or some other money at a fixed rate. To the best of my knowledge, it is only after 1934 that inconvertibility came to mean what we currently take it to mean: that it is illegal for one man to convert paper money of one country into paper money of another country at any terms he can arrange with another person.[3]

I turn now to the economic or technical aspects of an independent central bank. Clearly there are political objections to giving the group in charge of a central bank so much power independent of direct political controls, but, it has been argued, there are economic or technical grounds why it is nevertheless essential to do so. In judging this statement, much depends on the amount of leeway that the general rule governing the central bank gives to it. I have been describing an independent central bank as if it could or would be given a good deal of separate power, as clearly is currently the case. Of course, the whole notion of independence could be rendered merely a matter of words if in fact the constitutional provision setting up the bank established the limits of its authority very narrowly and controlled very closely the policies that it could follow.

In the nineteenth century, when wide support for independent central banks developed, the governing objective of the central bank was the maintenance of exchange stability. Central banks tended to develop in countries that professed to have commodity currencies, which is to say had a fixed price for the commodity serving as the monetary standard in terms of the nominal money of the country. For two countries on the same standard, this meant a fixed rate of exchange between the corresponding national currencies. In consequence, the maintenance of such fixed rates had to be the proximate aim of the central bank if it was to achieve its major aim of keeping its currency convertible into standard money. The Bank of England, for example, was narrowly limited in what it could do by the necessity of keeping England on gold.

In the same way, in the United States when the Federal Reserve System was established in 1913, it never entered into the minds of the people who were establishing it that the system would really have much effective control internally in ordinary times. The Reserve System was established when the gold standard ruled supreme, and when it was taken for granted that the major factor determining the policy of the system, and hence the behavior of the stock of money in this country, would be the necessity of maintaining external equilibrium with the currencies of other countries. So long as the maintenance of a fixed exchange rate between one country's currency and the currencies of other countries was the overriding objective of policy, the amount of leeway available to the central bank was narrowly limited. It had some leeway with respect to minor movements of a short-term character, but it ultimately had to respond to the balance of payments.

The situation has changed drastically in this respect in the course of the past few decades. In the United States, which is of most immediate concern to us, the Federal Reserve System had hardly started operations before the fundamental conditions taken for granted when it was established had changed radically. During World War I, most of the countries of the world went off gold. The United States technically remained on gold, but the gold standard on which it remained was very different from the one that had prevailed earlier. After the end of World War I, although other countries of the world gradually reestablished something they called the gold standard, the gold standard never again played the role which it had before. Prior to World War I, the United States was effectively a minor factor in the total world economy, and the necessity of maintaining external stability dominated our behavior. After the war, we had become a major factor to which other countries had to adjust. We held a very large fraction of the world's gold. Many countries never went back on gold, and those that did went back in a much diluted form. So never again has there been anything like the close domination of day-to-day policy by the gold standard that prevailed prior to 1914. Under these circumstances, "independence" of the central bank has become something meaningful, and not merely a technicality.

One defect of an independent central bank in such a situation is that it almost inevitably involves dispersal of responsibility. If we examine the monetary system in terms not of nominal institutional organization but of the economic functions performed, we find that the central bank is hardly ever the only authority in the government that has essential monetary powers. Before the Federal Reserve System was established, the Treasury exercised essential monetary powers. It operated like a central bank, and at times a very effective central bank. More recently, from 1933 to 1941, the Federal Reserve System was almost entirely passive. Such monetary actions as were taken were taken predominantly by the Treasury. The Treasury engaged in open-market operations in its debt-management operations of buying and selling securities. It created and destroyed money in its gold and silver purchases and sales. The Exchange Stabilization Fund was established and gave the Treasury yet another device for engaging in open-market operations. When the Treasury sterilized and desterilized gold, it was engaging in monetary actions. In practice, therefore, even if something called an independent central bank is established and given exclusive power over a limited range of monetary matters, in particular over the printing of pieces of paper or the making of book entries called money (Federal Reserve notes and Federal Reserve deposits), there remain other governmental authorities, particularly the fiscal authority collecting taxes and dispersing funds and managing the debt, which also have a good deal of monetary power.

If one wanted to have the substance and not merely the form of an independent monetary authority, it would be necessary to concentrate all debt-management powers as well as all powers to create and destroy governmentally issued money in the central bank. As a matter of technical efficiency, this might well be desirable. Our present division of responsibility for debt management between the Federal Reserve and the Treasury is very inefficient. It would be much more efficient if the Federal Reserve did all of the borrowing and all of the managing of the debt, and the Treasury, when it had a deficit, financed it by getting money from the Federal Reserve System, and when it had a surplus, handed the excess over to the Federal Reserve System. But while such an arrangement might be tolerable if the Federal Reserve System were part of the same administrative hierarchy as the Treasury, it is almost inconceivable that it would be if the central bank were thoroughly independent. Certainly no government to date has been willing to put that much power in the hands of a central bank even when the bank has been only partly independent. But so long as these powers are separated, there is dispersal of responsibility, with each group separately regarding the other group as responsible for what is happening and with no one willing to accept responsibility.

In the past few years, I have read through the annual reports of the Federal Reserve System from 1913 to date, seriatim. One of the few amusing dividends from that ordeal was seeing the cyclical pattern that shows up in the potency that the authorities attribute to monetary policy. In years when things are going well, the reports emphasize that monetary policy is an exceedingly potent weapon and that the favorable course of events is largely a result of the skillful handling of this delicate instrument by the monetary authority. In years of depression, on the other hand, the reports emphasize that monetary policy is but one of many tools of economic policy, that its power is highly limited, and that it was only the skillful handling of such limited powers as were available that averted disaster. This is an example of the effect of the dispersal of responsibility among different authorities, with the likely result that no one assumes or is assigned the final responsibility.

Another defect of the conduct of monetary policy through an independent central bank that has a good deal of leeway and power is the extent to which policy is thereby made highly dependent on personalities. In studying the history of American monetary policy, I have been struck by the extraordinary importance of accidents of personality.

At the end of World War I, the governor of the Federal Reserve System was W. P. G. Harding. Governor Harding was, I am sure, a thoroughly reputable and competent citizen, but he had a very limited understanding of monetary affairs, and even less backbone. Almost every student of the period is agreed that the great mistake of the Federal Reserve System in postwar monetary policy was to permit the money stock to expand very rapidly in 1919 and then to step very hard on the brakes in 1920. This policy was almost surely responsible for both the sharp postwar rise in prices and the sharp subsequent decline. It is amusing to read Harding's answer in his memoirs to criticism that was later made of the policies followed. He does not question that alternative policies might well have been preferable for the economy as a whole, but emphasizes the Treasury's desire to float securities at a reasonable rate of interest, and calls attention to a then-existing law under which the Treasury could replace the head of the Federal Reserve System. Essentially he was saying the same thing that I heard another member of the Federal Reserve Board say shortly after World War II when the bond-support program was in question. In response to the view expressed by some of my colleagues and myself that the bond-support program should be dropped, he largely agreed but said, "Do you want us to lose our jobs?"

The importance of personality is strikingly revealed by the contrast between Harding's behavior and that of Emile Moreau in France under much more difficult circumstances. Moreau formally had no independence whatsoever from the central government. He was named by the premier, and could be discharged at any time by the premier. But when he was asked by the premier to provide the treasury with funds in a manner that he considered inappropriate and undesirable, he flatly refused to do so. Of course, what happened was that Moreau was not discharged, that he did not do what the premier had asked him to, and that stabilization was rather more successful. I cite this contrast neither to praise Moreau nor to blame Harding, but simply to illustrate my main point, namely, the extent to which a system of this kind is really a system of rule by men and not by law and is extraordinarily dependent on the particular personalities involved.

Another occasion in United States history which strikingly illustrates this point is our experience from 1929 to 1933. Without doubt, the most serious mistake in the history of the Federal Reserve System was its mismanagement of monetary matters during those years. And this mismanagement, like that after World War I, can very largely be attributed to accidents of personality. Benjamin Strong, governor of the Federal Reserve bank of New York from its inception, was the dominant figure in the Federal Reserve System until his death at a rather early age in 1928. His death was followed by a shift of power in the system from New York to Washington. The people in Washington at the time happened to be fairly mediocre. Moreover, they had always played a secondary role, were not in intimate touch with the financial world, and had no background of long experience in meeting day-to-day emergencies. Further, the chairmanship changed hands just prior to the shift of power and again in mid-1931. Consequently, in the emergencies that came in 1929, 1930, and 1931, particularly in the fall of 1930, when the Bank of United States failed in New York as part of a dramatic series of bank failures, the Federal Reserve System acted timorously and passively. There is little doubt that Strong would have acted very differently. If he had still been governor, the result would almost surely have been to nip the wave of bank failures in the bud and to prevent the drastic monetary deflation that followed.

A similar situation prevails today. The actions of the Federal Reserve System depend on whether there are a few persons in the system who exert intellectual leadership, and on who these people are; its actions depend not only on the people who are nominally the heads of the system but also on such matters as the fate of particular economic advisers.

So far, I have listed two main technical defects of an independent central bank from an economic point of view: first, dispersal of responsibility, which promotes shirking responsibility in times of uncertainty and difficulty, and second, an extraordinary dependence on personalities, which fosters instability arising from accidental shifts in the particular people and the character of the people who are in charge of the system.

A third technical defect is that an independent central bank will almost inevitably give undue emphasis to the point of view of bankers. It is exceedingly important to distinguish two quite different problems that tend to be confused: the problem of credit policy and the problem of monetary policy. In our kind of monetary or banking system, money tends to be created as an incident in the extension of credit, yet conceptually the creation of money and the extension of credit are quite distinct. A monetary system could be utterly unrelated to any credit instruments whatsoever; for example, this would be true of a completely automatic commodity standard, using only the monetary commodity itself or warehouse receipts for the commodity as money. Historically, the connection between money and credit has varied widely from time to time and from place to place. It is therefore essential to distinguish policy issues connected with interest rates and conditions on the credit market from policy issues connected with changes in the aggregate stock of money, while recognizing, of course, that measures taken to affect the one set of variables may also affect the other, and that monetary measures may have credit effects as well as monetary effects proper.

It so happens that central-bank action is but one of many forces affecting the credit market. As we and other countries have seen time and again, a central bank may be able to determine the rate of interest on a narrow range of securities, such as the rate of interest on a particular category of government bonds, though even that only within limits and only at the expense of completely giving up control over the total stock of money. A central bank has never been able to determine, at all closely, rates of interest in any broader or more fundamental sense. Postwar experience in country after country that has embarked on a cheap-money policy has strikingly demonstrated that the forces which determine rates of interest broadly conceived—rates of return on equities, on real property, on corporate securities—are far too strong and widespread for the central bank to dominate. It must sooner or later yield to them, and generally rather soon.

The central bank is in a very different position in determining the quantity of money. Under systems such as that in the United States today, the central bank can make the amount of money anything it wishes. It may, of course, choose to accept some other objective and give up its power over the money supply in order to try to keep "the" or "a" rate of interest fixed, to keep "free reserves" at a particular level, or to achieve some other objective. But if it wishes, it can exercise complete control over the stock of money.

This difference between the position of the central bank in the credit markets and in determining the money supply tends to be obfuscated by the close connection between the central bank and the banking community. In the United States, for example, the reserve banks technically are owned by their member banks. One result is that the general views of the banking community exercise a strong influence on the central bank and, since the banking community is concerned primarily with the credit market, central banks are led to put altogether too much emphasis on the credit effects of their policies and too little emphasis on the monetary effects of their policies.

In recent times, this emphasis has been attributed to the effects of the Keynesian revolution and its treatment of changes in the stock of money as operating primarily through the liquidity preference function on the interest rate. But this is only a particular form of a more general and ancient tendency. The real-bills doctrine, which dates back a century and more, exemplifies the same kind of confusion between the credit and the monetary effects of monetary policy. The banking and currency controversy in Britain in the early nineteenth century is a related example. The central bank emphasized its concern with conditions in the credit market. It denied that the quantity of money it was creating was in any way an important consideration in determining price levels or the like, or that it had any discretion about how much money to create. Much the same arguments are heard today.

The three defects I have outlined constitute a strong technical argument against an independent central bank. Combined with the political argument, the case against a fully independent central bank is strong indeed.

LEGISLATED RULES

If this conclusion is valid, if we cannot achieve our objectives by giving wide discretion to independent experts, how else can we establish a monetary system that is stable, free from irresponsible governmental tinkering, and incapable of being used as a source of power to threaten economic and political freedom? A third possibility is to try to achieve a government of law instead of men literally by legislating rules for the conduct of monetary policy. The enactment of such rules would enable the public to exercise control over monetary policy through its political authorities, while at the same time preventing monetary policy from being subject to the day-to-day whim of political authorities.

The argument for legislating rules for monetary policy has much in common with a topic that seems at first altogether different, namely, the Bill of Rights to the Constitution. Whenever anyone suggests the desirability of a legislative rule for control over money, the stereotyped answer is that it makes little sense to tie the monetary authority's hands in this way because the authority, if it wants to, can always do of its own volition what the rule would require it to do, and, in addition, has other alternatives; hence "surely," it is said, it can do better than the rule. An alternative version of the same argument applies to the legislature. If the legislature is willing to adopt the rule, it is said, surely it will also be willing to legislate the "right" policy in each specific case. How then, it is said, does the adoption of the rule provide any protection against irresponsible political action?

The same argument could apply with only minor verbal changes to the first amendment to the Constitution and, equally, to the entire Bill of Rights. Is it not absurd, one might say, to have a general proscription of interference with free speech? Why not take up each case separately and treat it on its own merits? Is this not the counterpart to the usual argument in monetary policy that it is undesirable to tie the hands of the monetary authority in advance; that it should be left free to treat each case on its merits as it comes up? Why is not the argument equally valid for speech? One man wants to stand up on a street corner and advocate birth control; another, communism, a third, vegetarianism; and so on, ad infinitum. Why not enact a law affirming or denying each the right to spread his particular views? Or, alternatively, why not give the power to decide the issue to an administrative agency? It is immediately clear that if we were to take up each case separately, a majority would almost surely vote to deny free speech in most cases and perhaps even in every case. A vote on whether Mr. X should spread birth control propaganda would almost surely yield a majority saying "no"; and so would one on communism. The vegetarian might perhaps get by, although even that is by no means a foregone conclusion.

But now suppose all these cases were grouped together in one bundle, and the populace at large was asked to vote for them as a whole: to vote whether free speech should be denied in all cases or permitted in all alike. It is perfectly conceivable, if not highly probable, that an overwhelming majority would vote for free speech; that, acting on the bundle as a whole, the people would vote exactly the opposite to the way they would have voted on each case separately. Why? One reason is that each person feels much more strongly about being deprived of his right to free speech when he is in a minority than he feels about depriving somebody else of the right to free speech when he is in the majority. In consequence, when he votes on the bundle as a whole, he gives much more weight to the infrequent denial of free speech to himself when he is in the minority than to the frequent denial of free speech to others. Another reason, and one that is more directly relevant to monetary policy, is that if the bundle is viewed as a whole, it becomes clear that the policy followed has cumulative effects that tend neither to be recognized nor taken into account when each case is voted on separately. When a vote is taken on whether Mr. Jones may speak on the corner, it is not clearly affected by favorable effects of an announced general policy of free speech, and an affirmative vote will not produce these effects. In voting on the specific case, it is only peripherally relevant that a society in which people are not free to speak on the corner without special legislation is a society in which the development of new ideas, experimentation, change, and the like are all hampered in a great variety of ways. That these ways are obvious to all is due to our good fortune of having lived in a sociey that did adopt the self-denying ordinance of not considering each case of speech separately.

Exactly the same considerations apply in the monetary area. If each case is considered on its merits, the wrong decision is likely to be made in a large fraction of cases because the decision makers are examining only a limited area and are not taking into account the cumulative consequences of the policy as a whole. On the other hand, if a general rule is adopted for a group of cases as a bundle, the existence of that rule has favorable effects on people's attitudes and beliefs and expectations that would not follow even from the discretionary adoption of precisely the same policy on a series of separate occasions.

Of course, the general rule need not be explicitly written down or legislated. Unwritten constitutional limitations supported unthinkingly by the bulk of the people may be as effective in determining decisions in individual cases as a written constitution. The analogy in monetary affairs is the mythology of gold, referred to earlier as a necessary ingredient of a gold standard if it is to serve as an effective bulwark against discretionary authority.

If a rule is to be legislated, what rule should it be? The rule that has most frequently been suggested by people of a generally "new liberal" persuasion is a price-level rule; namely, a legislative direction to the monetary authorities that they maintain a stable price level. I think this is the wrong kind of rule. It is the wrong kind of rule because the objectives it specifies are ones that the monetary authorities do not have the clear and direct power to achieve by their own actions. It consequently raises the earlier problem of dispersing responsibilities and leaving the authorities too much leeway. There is unquestionably a close connection between monetary actions and the price level. But the connection is not so close, so invariable, or so direct that the objective of achieving a stable price level is an appropriate guide to the day-to-day activities of the authorities.

The issue of what rule to adopt is one that I have considered at some length elsewhere.[4] Accordingly, I will limit myself here to stating my conclusion. In the present state of our knowledge, it seems to me desirable to state the rule in terms of the behavior of the stock of money. My choice at the moment would be a legislated rule instructing the monetary authority to achieve a specified rate of growth in the stock of money. For this purpose, I would define the stock of money as including currency outside commercial banks plus all deposits of commercial banks. I would specify that the Federal Reserve System should see to it that the total stock of money so defined rises month by month, and indeed, so far as possible, day by day, at an annual rate of X percent, where X is some number between 3 and 5. The precise definition of money adopted and the precise rate of growth chosen make far less difference than the definite choice of a particular definition and a particular rate of growth.

I should like to emphasize that I do not regard this proposal as a be-all and end-all of monetary management, as a rule which is somehow to be written in tablets of gold and enshrined for all future time. It seems to me to be the rule that offers the greatest promise of achieving a reasonable degree of monetary stability in the light of our present knowledge. I would hope that as we operated with it, as we learned more about monetary matters, we might be able to devise still better rules which would achieve still better results. However, the main point of this paper is not so much to discuss the content of these or alternative rules as to suggest that the device of legislating a rule about the stock of money can effectively achieve what an independent central bank is designed to achieve but cannot. Such a rule seems to me the only feasible device currently available for converting monetary policy into a pillar of a free society rather than a threat to its foundations.

Notes

1. *A Program for Monetary Stability* (New York: Fordham University Press, 1960), pp. 4–8.

2. Emile Moreau, *Souvenirs d'un gouverneur de la Banque de France* (Paris: Génin, 1954).

3. Another feature of Moreau's book that is most fascinating but rather off the main track of the present discussion is the story it tells of the changing relations between the French and British central banks. At the beginning, with France in desperate straits seeking to stabilize its currency, Norman was contemptuous of France and regarded it as very much of a junior partner. Through the accident that the French currency was revalued at a level that stimulated gold imports, France started to accumulate gold

reserves and sterling reserves and gradually came into the position where at any time Moreau could have forced the British off gold by withdrawing the funds he had on deposit at the Bank of England. The result was that Norman changed from being a proud boss and very much the senior partner to being almost a suppliant at the mercy of Moreau. Aside from the human drama, it emphasizes how important it is whether the rate of exchange is fixed 5 percent too low or 5 percent too high. Britain went back on gold in 1925 at a price of gold in terms of the pound that was probably something like 5 or 10 percent too low, and France went back de facto at the end of 1926 and de jure in mid-1928 at a price of gold in terms of francs that was 5 or 10 percent too high. This difference meant the difference between the French being at the mercy of the British and the British being at the mercy of the French.

4. *A Program for Monetary Stability*, pp. 77–99.

REAL AND PSEUDO
GOLD STANDARDS

· 24 ·

International monetary arrangements have held a consistently important place among the topics discussed at the meetings of our Society. This is eminently fitting, since there is probably no other major facet of economic policy with respect to which liberals (in the sense of our Society) reach such divergent conclusions from the same underlying principles.

One group, of which Philip Cortney is a distinguished member, favors a continuation of the formal linking of national currencies to gold, rigid exchange rates between different national currencies, a doubling or more than doubling of the official price of gold in terms of national currencies, and an abandonment of governmental measures designed to evade the discipline of gold. This group is apparently indifferent about whether gold circulates as coin; it is satisfied with a gold bullion standard.

A second group, represented by the Economists' National Committee on Monetary Policy, also favors a continuation of the formal linking of national currencies to gold together with rigid exchange rates between different national currencies. But it emphasizes the importance of gold coinage and of a widespread use of gold coin as money in national as well as international

Copyright 1961 by the University of Chicago.
Reprinted by permission from *Journal of Law and Economics* 4 (October 1961): 66–79.
Paper written for the Mont Pelerin Society meeting in September 1961.

payments. Apparently, this group believes there is no need for a change in present official prices of gold, or, at least, in the United States price.

A third group, of which I count myself a member, favors a separation of gold policy from exchange-rate policy. It favors the abandonment of rigid exchange rates between national currencies and the substitution of a system of floating exchange rates determined from day to day by private transactions without government intervention. With respect to gold, there are some differences, but most of us would currently favor the abandonment of any commitment by governments to buy and sell gold at fixed prices and of any fixed gold reserve requirements for the issue of national currency as well as the repeal of any restrictions on private dealings in gold.

I have stated and defended my own policy views elsewhere at some length.[1] Hence, I would like to use this occasion instead to explore how it is that liberals can reach such radically different conclusions.

My thesis is that current proposals to link national currencies rigidly to gold whether at present or higher prices arise out of a confusion of two very different things: the use of gold as money, which I shall call a "real" gold standard; governmental fixing of the price of gold, whether national or international, which I shall call a "pseudo" gold standard. Though these have many surface features in common, they are at bottom fundamentally different—just as the near identity of prices charged by competitive sellers differs basically from the identity of prices charged by members of a price ring or cartel. A real gold standard is thoroughly consistent with liberal principles, and I, for one, am entirely in favor of measures promoting its development, as, I believe, are most other liberal proponents of floating exchange rates. A pseudo gold standard is in direct conflict with liberal principles, as is suggested by the curious coalition of central bankers and central planners that has formed in support of it.

It is vitally important for the preservation and promotion of a free society that we recognize the difference between a real and pseudo gold standard. War aside, nothing that has occurred in the past half-century has, in my view, done more to weaken and undermine the public's faith in liberal principles than the pseudo gold standard that has intermittently prevailed and the actions that have been taken in its name. I believe that those of us who support it in the belief that it either is or will tend to be a real gold standard are mistakenly fostering trends the outcome of which they will be among the first to deplore.

This is a sweeping charge, so let me document it by a few examples which will incidentally illustrate the difference between a real and a pseudo gold standard before turning to an explicit discussion of the difference. My examples are mostly for the United States, the country whose monetary history I have studied in most detail.

EXAMPLES OF EFFECTS OF A PSEUDO GOLD STANDARD

United States Monetary Policy after World War I

Nearly half of the monetary expansion in the United States came after the end of the war, thanks to the acquiescence of the Federal Reserve System in the Treasury's desire to avoid a fall in the price of government securities. This expansion, with its accompanying price inflation led to an outflow of gold despite the great demand for United States goods from a war-ravaged world and despite the departure of most countries from any fixed parity between their currencies and either gold or the dollar. The outflow of gold finally overcame Treasury reluctance to see the price of government securities fall. Beginning in late 1919, then more sharply in January 1920 and May 1920, the Federal Reserve System took vigorous deflationary steps that produced first a slackening of the growth in the stock of money and then a sharp decline. These brought in their train a collapse in wholesale prices and a severe economic contraction. The near-halving of wholesale prices in a twelve-month period was by all odds the most rapid price decline ever experienced in the United States before or since. It was not of course confined to the United States but spread to all countries whose money was linked to the dollar either by having a fixed price in terms of gold or by central bank policies directed at maintaining rigid or nearly rigid exchange rates. Only those countries that were to experience hyperinflation escaped the price collapse.

Under a real gold standard, the large inflow of gold up to the entry of the United States into the war would have produced a price rise to the end of the war similar to that actually experienced. But neither the postwar rise nor the subsequent collapse would have occurred. Instead, there would have been an earlier and milder price decline as the belligerent nations returned to a peacetime economy. The postwar increase in the stock of money occurred only because the Federal Reserve System had been given discretionary power to "manage" the stock of money, and the subsequent collapse occurred only because this power to manage the money had been accompanied by gold reserve requirements as one among several masters the system was instructed to serve.

Under a wholly fiduciary currency, with floating exchange rates, the initial postwar expansion might well have occurred much as it did, though the depreciating value of the dollar in terms of other currencies might have been a quicker and a more effective check than slowly declining gold reserves. But the subsequent collapse would almost surely not have occurred. And neither the initial price inflation nor the subsequent price collapse would have been communicated to the rest of the world.

The worldwide inflation and then collapse was at the time a severe blow to a belief in free trade at home and abroad, a blow whose severity we now underrate only because of the later catastrophe that overshadowed it. Either a real gold standard or a thoroughly fiduciary standard would have been preferable in its outcome to the pseudo gold standard.

United States Monetary Policy in the 1920s and Britain's Return to Gold

There is a widespread myth among gold standard advocates that the United States monetary policy during the 1920s paved the way for the Great Depression by being unduly inflationary. For example, Cortney writes, "the Federal Reserve Board succeeded in the 1920s in holding up the price level for a surprising length of time by an abnormal expansion of inflationary credit, but in so doing it helped produce the speculative boom."[2] Nothing could be farther from the truth. The United States monetary policy in the 1920s and especially in the late 1920s, judged in terms of either a real gold standard in the abstract or prior United States experience, was if anything unduly deflationary.

The sharp 1920–1921 price decline had brought prices to a level much closer to the prewar level than to the postwar peak though they were still appreciably above the prewar level. Prices rose only moderately in the subsequent cyclical expansion which reached its peak in 1923. From then until 1929, wholesale prices actually fell, at a rate of roughly 1 percent a year.

As to gold, credit, and money, the Federal Reserve System sterilized much of the gold inflow, preventing the gold from raising the stock of money anything like as much as it would have done under a real gold standard. Far from the Federal Reserve System engaging in an "abnormal expansion of inflationary credit," Federal Reserve credit outstanding in June 1929 was 33 percent lower than it had been in June 1921 and only 16 percent higher than in June 1923 although national income was nearly 25 percent higher in 1929 than in 1923 (in both money and real terms). From 1923 to 1929, to compare only peak years of business cycles and so avoid distortion from cyclical influence, the stock of money, defined to include currency, demand deposits, and commercial bank time deposits, rose at the annual rate of 4 percent per year, which is roughly the rate required to match expansion of output. On a narrower definition, excluding time deposits, the stock of money rose at the rate of only 2.5 percent per year.[3]

The deflationary pressure was particularly strong during the great bull market in stocks, which happened to coincide with the first few years after Britain returned to gold. During the business cycle expansion from 1927 to 1929, wholesale prices actually fell a trifle: one must go back to 1891–1893 to find another expansion during which prices fell and there has been none since.

The stock of money was lower at the cyclical peak in August 1929 than it had been sixteen months earlier. There is no other occasion from the time our monthly data begin in 1907 to date when so long a period elapsed during a cyclical expansion without a rise in the stock of money. The only other periods of such length which show a decline have an end point in the course of severe contractions (1920–1921, 1929–1933, 1936–1937).

So far as the United States alone was concerned, this monetary policy may have been admirable. I do not myself believe that the 1929–1933 contraction was an inevitable result of the monetary policy of the 1920s or even owed much to it. What was wrong was the policy followed from 1929 to 1933, as I shall point out in a moment. But internationally, the policy was little short of catastrophic. Much has been made of Britain's mistake in returning to gold in 1925 at a parity that overvalued the pound. I do not doubt that this was a mistake—but only because the United States was maintaining a pseudo gold standard. Had the United States been maintaining a real gold standard, the stock of money would have risen more in the United States than it did, prices would have been stable or rising instead of declining, the United States would have gained less gold or lost some, and the pressure on the pound would have been enormously eased. As it was, by sterilizing gold, the United States forced the whole burden of adapting to gold movements on other countries. When, in addition, France adopted a pseudo gold standard at a parity that undervalued the franc and proceeded also to follow a gold sterilization policy, the combined effect was to make Britain's position untenable. The adverse consequences for faith in liberal principles of the deflationary policies adopted in Britain from 1925 to 1931 in the vain effort to maintain the reestablished parity are no less obvious than they were far-reaching.

United States Policy from 1931 to 1933

United States monetary behavior from 1931 to 1933 is in some ways a repetition of that from 1920 to 1921, but on a more catastrophic scale, in less fortunate circumstances, and with less justification. As we have seen, in 1919 the Federal Reserve System deviated from the policy that would have been dictated by a real gold standard. In 1920, when it saw its gold reserves declining rapidly, it shifted rules, overreacted to the outflow, and brought on a drastic deflation. Similarly, from 1922 to 1929, the Federal Reserve sterilized gold and prevented it from exercising the influence on the money stock that it would have had under a real gold standard. And again in 1931, when Britain went off gold and the United States experienced an outflow of gold, the Federal Reserve shifted rules, overreacted to the outflow, and catastrophically intensified a deflation already two years old.

The circumstances were less fortunate in 1931 than in 1920 in two different respects, one domestic and the other foreign, and both in some measure the Federal Reserve System's own creation.

The domestic difference was that the deflationary action of 1920 came at the end of a period of expansion which was widely regarded as temporary and exceptional, and served to intensify without necessarily prolonging a recession that would probably have occurred anyway. The deflationary action of 1931 came after two years of severe contraction which had been showing some signs of terminating; probably served to nip in the bud a revival; and both greatly intensified and substantially prolonged the contraction, turning it into the most severe for nearly a century.

This difference was largely the Federal Reserve System's creation because of its inept handling of the banking difficulties that started in the fall of 1930. Until that date, the contraction, while rather severe, had shown no signs of a liquidity crisis. Widespread bank failures culminating in the failure of the Bank of United States in late 1930 changed the aspect of the contraction. This episode turned out to be the first of a series of liquidity crises, each characterized by bank failures and runs on banks by depositors anxious to convert deposits into currency, and each producing strong downward pressure on the stock of money. The Federal Reserve System had been set up with the primary aim of dealing with precisely such crises. It failed to do so effectively but not because it lacked the power or the knowledge. At all times, it had ample power to provide the liquidity that the public and the banks desperately sought and the provision of which would have cut short the vicious chain reaction of bank failures. The system failed because accidents of personality and shifts of power within the system left it with no dominant personality who could avoid the usual outcome of committee control: the evasion of responsibility by inaction, postponement, and drift. More fundamentally yet, the failure reflected the adoption of a monetary system that gave great power to a small number of men and therefore was vulnerable to such accidents of personality and shifts of power. Had the liquidity crisis been cut short at its onset in 1930 and the Bank of United States kept from failing (as very likely would have occurred before the Federal Reserve System), the economy would probably have been vigorously expanding by September 1931 instead of being precariously balanced on the verge of another liquidity crisis.

The international difference in circumstances that was less fortunate in 1931 than in 1920 was the monetary situation in other countries. In many countries, monetary arrangements in 1920 were in a state of flux, so they could adapt with some rapidity. By 1931, a new pattern of international monetary arrangements had become established, in considerable measure under the patronage of the Federal Reserve bank of New York, as well as the Banks of England and France. More serious and more directly to be laid at the Federal Reserve System's door, its gold sterilization policy had, as we have seen, increased the problem of adjustment for many other countries and so left them more vulnerable to new difficulties. In the event the monetary world split in two, one part following Britain to form the sterling area; the other, following the United States, in the gold bloc. The sterling area countries all reached bottom and began to expand in late 1931 or early 1932; most gold bloc countries experienced further deflation and did not reach bottom until 1933 or 1934.

The deflationary monetary actions had less justification in the fall of 1931 than in 1920 for two different reasons. First, in 1920, the Federal Reserve System was still in its infancy, untried and inexperienced. Set up under one set of conditions, it was operating under a drastically different set. It had no background of operation in peacetime, no experience on which to base judgments. By 1931, the system had more than a decade of experience and had developed a well-articulated body of doctrine, which underlay the gold ster-ilization policy and which called for its offsetting an outflow of gold rather than reinforcing its deflationary effect. Second, the gold situation was drastically different. By early 1920, the gold stock was declining rapidly and the Federal Reserve's gold reserve ratio was approaching its legal minimum. Prior to September 1931, the system had been gaining gold, the monetary gold stock was at an all-time high, and the system's gold reserve ratio was far above its legal minimum—a reflection of course of its not having operated in accordance with a real gold standard. The system had ample reserves to meet the gold outflow without difficulty and without resort to deflationary measures. And both its own earlier policy and the classical gold standard rules as enshrined by Bagehot called for its doing so: the gold outflow was strictly speculative and motivated by fear that the United States would go off gold; the outflow had no basis in any trade imbalance; it would have exhausted itself promptly if all demands had been met.

As it was, of course, the system behaved very differently. It reacted vigorously to the external drain as it had not to the internal drain by raising discount rates within a brief period more sharply than ever before or since. The result was a major intensification of the internal drain, and an unprecedented liquidation of the commercial banking system. Whereas the stock of money had fallen 10 percent from August 1929 to August 1931; it fell a further 28 percent from August 1931 to March 1933. Commercial bank deposits had fallen 12 percent from August 1929 to August 1931; they fell a further 35 percent from August 1931 to March 1933. Never was there a more unnecessary monetary collapse or one which did more to undermine public acceptance of liberal principles.

Once again, either a real gold standard throughout the 1920s and 1930s or a consistent adherence to a fiduciary standard would have been vastly prefera-ble to the actual pseudo gold standard under which gold inflows and minor gold outflows were offset and substantial actual or threatened gold outflows were overreacted to. And this pattern is no outmoded historical curiosity: witness the United States reaction to gold inflows in the early years after World War II and its recent reaction to gold outflows; witness the more recent German sterilization of gold inflows. The pseudo gold standard is very much a living menace.

United States Nationalization of Gold

After going off gold in March 1933, the United States reestablished a fixed official price of gold in January 1934, raising the price to $35 an ounce. Many current proponents of a rise in the official price of gold approve this action, regarding it as required to bring the value of the gold stock into line with an allegedly increased fiduciary circulation. Perhaps a rise in the price of gold was desirable in 1934 but it cannot be defended along these lines, at least for the United States itself. In 1933, the ratio of the value of the gold stock to the total stock of money was higher than it had been in 1913 or at any date between. If there be any valid argument for a rise in the price of gold along these lines, it is for 1929, not 1934.

Whatever may be the merits of the rise in the price of gold, there can be little doubt that the associated measures, which were taken in order that the rise in the price of gold should have the effect desired by the Roosevelt administration, represented a fundamental departure from liberal principles and established precedents that have returned to plague the free world. I refer, of course, to the nationalization of the gold stock, the prohibition of private possession of gold for monetary purposes, and the abrogation of gold clauses in public and private contracts.

In 1933 and early 1934, private holders of gold were required by law to turn over their gold to the federal government and were compensated at a price equal to the prior legal price, which was at the time very decidedly below the market price. To make this requirement effective, private ownership of gold within the United States was made illegal except for use in the arts. One can hardly imagine a measure more destructive of the principles of private property on which a free enterprise society rests. There is no difference in principle between this nationalization of gold at an artificially low price and Fidel Castro's nationalization of land and factories at an artificially low price. On what grounds of principle can the United States object to the one after having itself engaged in the other? Yet so great is the blindness of some supporters of free enterprise with respect to anything touching on gold that as recently as last year Henry Alexander, head of the Morgan Guaranty Trust Company, successor to J. P. Morgan and Co., proposed that the prohibition against the private ownership of gold by United States citizens be extended to cover gold held abroad! And his proposal was adopted by President Eisenhower with hardly a protest from the banking community.

Though rationalized in terms of "conserving" gold for monetary use, prohibition of private ownership of gold was not enacted for any such monetary purpose, whether itself good or bad. The circulation of gold and gold certificates had raised no monetary problems either in the 1920s or during the monetary collapse from 1930 to 1933. Except for the final weeks just preceding the banking panic, the internal drain had not been for gold but for currency of any kind in preference to deposits. And the final gold drain was the consequence of the rumors, which proved correct, that Roosevelt planned to devalue. The nationalization of gold was enacted to enable the government to reap the whole of the "paper" profit from the rise in the price of gold—or perhaps, to prevent private individuals benefiting from the rise.

The abrogation of the gold clauses had a similar purpose. And this too was a measure destructive of the basic principles of free enterprise. Contracts entered into in good faith and with full knowledge on the part of both parties to them were declared invalid for the benefit of one of the parties!

This collection of measures constituted a further step away from a real gold standard to a pseudo gold standard. Gold became even more clearly a commodity whose price was fixed by governmental purchase and sale and rationing rather than money or even a form of money.

International Monetary Fund and Postwar Exchange Policy

I agree fully with Professor Rist's criticisms of the International Monetary Fund (IMF) and the arrangements it embodied.[4] These arrangements are precisely those of a pseudo gold standard: each country is required to specify a formal price of gold in terms of its own currency and hence, by implication, to specify official exchange rates between its currency and other currencies. It is forbidden to change these prices outside narrow limits except with permission. It commits itself to maintaining these exchange rates. But there is no requirement that gold serve as money; on the contrary, many of the IMF provisions are designed to prevent it from doing so.

The results have been anything but happy from a liberal viewpoint: widespread controls over exchange transactions, restrictions on international trade in the forms of quotas and direct controls as well as tariffs; yet repeated exchange crises and numerous changes in official exchange rates. No doubt, conditions are now far better than shortly after the war, but clearly in spite of the IMF and not because of it. And the danger of foreign exchange crises and accompanying interferences with trade is hardly over. In the past year, the United States moved toward direct interferences with trade to cope with a balance of payments problem; Germany appreciated; and Britain is now in difficulties.

The Distinction Between
a Real and a Pseudo Gold Standard

Because of its succinctness and explicitness, Cortney's numbered list of prerequisites for the restoration of "monetary order by returning to an international gold standard" forms an excellent point of departure for exploring the difference between a real and a pseudo gold standard. His point number 6 concludes "the price of gold will have to be raised to at least $70 an ounce." His point number 7 is "Free markets for gold should be established in all the important countries, and trading in gold, its export and import should be absolutely free."[5] Here is the issue in a nutshell. Can one conceive of saying in one breath that worldwide free markets should be established in, say, tin, and in the next, that the price of tin should "be raised" to some specified figure? The essence of a free market is precisely that no one can "raise" or "fix" price. Price is at whatever level will clear the market and it varies from day to day as market conditions change. If we take Cortney's point 7 seriously, we cannot simultaneously take his point 6 seriously, and conversely.

Suppose we follow up the logic of his point 7 and suppose a free market to prevail in gold. There might then develop, as there has in the past, a real gold standard. People might voluntarily choose to use gold as money, which is to say, to express prices in units of gold, and to hold gold as a temporary abode of purchasing power permitting them to separate an act of barter into a sale of goods or services for money and the purchase of goods or services with money. The gold used as money might be called different things in different languages: "*or*" in French, "gold" in English; it might be measured in different units: say, in grams in France and ounces in the United States; special terms such as "napoleon" or "eagle" might develop to designate convenient amounts of gold for use in transactions, and these might differ in different countries. We might even have governments certifying to weight and fineness, as they now inspect scales in meat markets, or even coining "eagles," "double eagles," and the like. Changes in nomenclature or in units of measure, say, the shift from ounces to grams, might be made by legislation, but these would clearly have no monetary or income or redistributive effects; they would be like changing the standard units for measuring gasoline from gallons to liters; not comparable to changing the price of gold from $35 an ounce to $70 an ounce.

If such a real gold standard developed, the price of commodities in terms of gold would of course vary from place to place according to transportation costs of both the commodities and of gold. Insofar as different countries used gold, and used different units, or coins of different size, the price of one kind of gold in terms of another would be free to vary in accordance with preferences by each country's citizens for the one kind or the other. The range of variation would of course be limited by the cost of converting one kind of gold into another, just as the relative price of commodities is similarly limited.

Under such a real gold standard, private persons or governments might go into the business of offering storage facilities, and warehouse receipts might be found more convenient than the gold itself for transactions. Finally, private persons or governments might issue promises to pay gold either on demand or after a specific time interval which were not warehouse receipts but nonetheless were widely acceptable because of confidence that the promises would be redeemed. Such promises to pay would still not alter the basic character of the gold standard so long as the obligors were not retroactively relieved from fulfilling their promises, and this would be true even if such promises were not fulfilled from time to time, just as the default of dollar bond issues does not alter the monetary standard. But, of course, promises to pay that were in default or that were expected to be defaulted would not sell at face value, just as bonds in default trade at a discount. And of course this is what has happened when a system like that outlined has prevailed in practice (e.g., in much of the pre–Civil War period in the United States).

Such a system might and I believe would raise grave social problems and foster pressure for governmental prohibition of, or control over, the issue of promises to pay gold on demand.[6] But that is beside my present point, which is that it would be a real gold standard, that under it there might be different national names for the money but there would not be in any meaningful sense either national currencies or any possibility of a government legislating a change in the price of gold.

Side by side with such a standard, there could, of course, exist strictly national currencies. For example, in the United States from 1862–1879, greenbacks were such a national currency which circulated side by side with gold. Since there was a free market in gold, the price of gold in terms of greenbacks varied from day to day, that is, in modern terminology, there was a floating rate of exchange between the two currencies. Since gold was in use as money in Britain and some other countries, its main use in the United States was for foreign transactions. Most prices in the United States were quoted in greenbacks but could be paid in gold valued at the market rate. However, the situation was reversed in California, where most prices were quoted in gold but could be paid in greenbacks at the market rate. No doubt, in this historical episode, the expectation that greenbacks would some day be made promises to pay gold had an effect on their value by expanding the demand for them. But this was not essential to the simultaneous coexistence of the two currencies, so long as their relative price was freely determined in the market, just as silver and gold, or copper and silver, have often simultaneously circulated at floating rates of exchange.

If a government abjured a national currency, it might still borrow from the community in the form of securities expressed in gold (or bearing gold clauses), some of which might be demand obligations and might be non-interest-bearing. But it would thereby surrender everything that we now call monetary policy. The resources it could acquire by borrowing would depend on the interest it was willing to pay on interest-bearing securities and on the amount of non-interest-bearing demand securities the public was willing to acquire. It could not arbitrarily issue any amount of non-interest-bearing securities it wished without courting inability to meet its promises to pay gold and hence seeing its securities sink to a discount relative to gold. Of course, this limitation in governmental power is precisely what recommends a real gold standard to a liberal, but we must not make the mistake of supposing that we can get the substance by the mere adoption of the form of a nominal obeisance to gold.

The kind of gold standard we have just been describing is not the kind we have had since at least 1913 and certainly not since 1934. If the essence of a free market is that no one can "raise the price," the essence of a controlled market is that it involves restrictions of one kind or another on trade. When the government fixes the price of wheat at a level above the market price, it inevitably both accumulates stocks and is driven to control output—i.e., to ration output among producers eager to produce more than the public is willing to buy at the controlled price. When the government fixes the price of housing space at a level below the market price, it inevitably is driven to control occupancy—i.e., to ration space among purchasers eager to buy more than sellers are willing to make available at the controlled price. The controls on gold, like the related controls on foreign exchange, are a sure sign that the price is being pegged; that dollar, pound, etc., are not simply different names for different sized units of gold, but are national currencies. Insofar as the price of gold in these currencies and the price of one currency in terms of another are stable over considerable periods, it is not because of the ease of converting one quantity of gold into another and not because conditions of demand and supply make for stable prices, but because they are pegged prices in rigged markets.

The price of $35 an ounce at which gold was supported by the United States after January 1934 was initially well above the market price—like the price at which wheat is currently being supported. The evidence is in both cases the same: a rapid expansion of output and the accumulation of enormous stockpiles. From 1933 to 1940, production in the United States rose from less than 2.6 million ounces to 6 million ounces; in the world, from 25 million ounces to 41 million ounces; the gold stock in the Treasury rose from 200 million ounces to 630 million, or by 1.75 times as much as the total of world output during the intervening period. Had this pace of increase in output and stock continued, the gold purchase program might well have been limited in scope; perhaps, as the United States silver purchase program finally was, to domestic output alone.

But the war intervened, which stopped the inflow of gold and brought a major rise in the stock of money. The resultant rise in other prices with no change in the price of gold has altered the character of the fixed United States price. It is now probably below the market price (given the present monetary use of gold), like rents under rent control. The evidence is again in both cases the same; a reduction in production, a decline in stocks, and a problem of rationing demanders. The United States gold output is now less than in 1933 though world output still exceeds the level of that year. The United States gold stock has declined to roughly 500 million ounces, well below its wartime peak but still 2.5 times its level when the present price for gold was established. The restriction on the ownership of gold abroad by United States citizens is a first, and feeble, step toward still tighter rationing of demanders. The gentlemen's agreement among central banks not to press for conversion of dollar balances into gold is a more far-reaching if still rather weak additional step. The history of every attempt at government price fixing suggests that if the pegged price is far below the market price for long, such attempts are doomed to fail.

Doubling the price of gold would no doubt reverse the situation and raise the pegged price again above the market price. Gold production and United States gold stocks would no doubt rise. But to what avail? Gold would still be simply a commodity whose price is supported; countries would continue with their separate monetary policies; fixed exchange rates would freeze the only market mechanism available under such circumstances to adjust international payments; foreign exchange crises would continue to succeed one another; and direct controls of one kind or another would remain the last resort, and one often appealed to, for resolving them.

This kind of pseudo gold standard violates fundamental liberal principles in two major respects. First, it involves price fixing by government. It has always been a mystery to me how so many who oppose on principle government price fixing of all other commodities can yet approve it for this one. Second, and no less important, it involves granting discretionary authority to a small number of men over matters of the greatest importance; to the central bankers or Treasury officials who must manage the pseudo gold standard. This means the rule of men instead of law, violating one of our fundamental political tenets. Here again, I have been amazed how so many who oppose on principle the grant of wide discretionary authority to governmental officials are anxious to see such authority granted to central bankers. True, central bankers have on the whole been "sound money" men with great sympathy for private enterprise. But since when have we liberals tempered our fear of concentrated particular men who happen at a particular moment to exercise it? Surely our cry has been very different—that benevolent or not, tyranny is tyranny and the only sure defense of freedom is the dispersal of power.

CONCLUSION

Let me close by offering a proposal, not for reconciling our views, but at least for possible agreement among us on one part of the gold problem. Can we not all agree with Mr. Cortney's point 7: the establishment of a thoroughly free market in gold, with no restrictions on the ownership, purchase, sale, import, or export of gold by private individuals? This means in particular, no restrictions on the price at which gold can be bought or sold in terms of any other commodity or financial instrument, including national currencies. It means, therefore, an end to governmental price fixing of gold in terms of national currencies.

The major problem in achieving such a reform is, as for the Unites States wheat program, the transitional one of what to do with accumulated government stocks. In both cases, my own view is that the government should immediately restore a free market, and should ultimately dispose of all of its stocks. However, it would probably be desirable for the government to dispose of its stocks only gradually. For wheat, five years has always seemed to me a long enough period so I have favored the government committing itself to dispose of one-fifth of its stocks in each of five years. This period seems reasonably satisfactory for gold as well, and hence my own proposal for the United States, and also other countries, would be that the government should sell off its gold in the free market over the next five years. Perhaps the greater ratio of the accumulated stock to annual production for gold than for wheat makes a longer transitional period appropriate. This seems to me a matter of expediency not of principle.

A worldwide free market in gold might mean that the use of gold as money would become far more widespread than it is now. If so, governments might need to hold some gold as working cash balances. Beyond this, I see no reason why governments or international agencies should hold any gold. If individuals find warehouse certificates for gold more useful than literal gold, private enterprise can certainly provide the service of storing the gold. Why should gold storage and the issuance of warehouse certificates be a nationalized industry?

NOTES

1. See, in particular, "The Case for Flexible Exchange Rates" and "Commodity-Reserve Currency," in my *Essays in Positive Economics* (Chicago: University of Chicago

Press, 1953), pp. 157–203, 204–50, and A *Program for Monetary Stability* (New York: Fordham University Press, 1960), pp. 77–84. The first of these appears in chapter 25 of this volume.

2. See the introduction in Charles Rist, *The Triumph of Gold* (1961), p. 8.

3. These statements are based on estimates of the stock of money from 1867 to date constructed by Anna J. Schwartz and me in connection with a study for the National Bureau of Economic Research. Hereafter, I will use the term "stock of money" as referring to the first of these two definitions.

4. See Charles Rist, op. cit., pp. 188–93.

5. Ibid., p. 37.

6. See my *Program for Monetary Stability*, pp. 4–9.

THE CASE FOR
FLEXIBLE EXCHANGE RATES*

· 25 ·

The Western nations seem committed to a system of international payments based on exchange rates between their national currencies fixed by governments and maintained rigid except for occasional changes to new levels. This system is embodied in the statutes of the International Monetary Fund (IMF), which provides for changes in exchange rates of less than 10 percent by individual governments without approval of the IMF and for larger changes only with approval; it is implicit in the European Payments Union; and it is taken for granted in almost all discussions of international economic policy.

Whatever may have been the merits of this system for another day, it is ill suited to current economic and political conditions. These conditions make a system of flexible or floating exchange rates—exchange rates freely deter-

From Milton Friedman, *Essays in Positive Economics* (Chicago: University of Chicago Press, 1953).
* This paper had its origin in a memorandum written in the fall of 1950 when I was a consultant to the Finance and Trade Division of the Office of Special Representative for Europe, United States Economic Cooperation Administration. Needless to say, the views it expresses are entirely my own. I am grateful to Joel Bernstein and Maxwell Obst for criticism of the original memorandum and to Earl J. Hamilton and Lloyd A. Metzler for criticism of a subsequent draft. The paper owes much, also, to extensive discussion of the general problem with a number of friends, particularly Aaron Director, James Meade, Lloyd Mints, and Lionel Robbins. Unfortunately, these discussions failed to produce sufficient agreement to make a disclaimer of their responsibility unnecessary.

mined in an open market primarily by private dealings and, like other market prices, varying from day to day—absolutely essential for the fulfillment of our basic economic objective: the achievement and maintenance of a free and prosperous world community engaging in unrestricted multilateral trade. There is scarcely a facet of international economic policy for which the implicit acceptance of a system of rigid exchange rates does not create serious and unnecessary difficulties. Promotion of rearmament, liberalization of trade, avoidance of allocations and other direct controls both internal and external, harmonization of internal monetary and fiscal policies—all these problems take on a different cast and become far easier to solve in a world of flexible exchange rates and its corollary, free convertibility of currencies. The sooner a system of flexible exchange rates is established, the sooner unrestricted multilateral trade will become a real possibility. And it will become one without in any way interfering with the pursuit by each nation of domestic economic stability according to its own lights.[1]

Before proceeding to defend this thesis in detail, I should perhaps emphasize two points to avoid misunderstanding. First, advocacy of flexible exchange rates is *not* equivalent to advocacy of unstable exchange rates. The ultimate objective is a world in which exchange rates, while *free* to vary, are in fact highly stable. Instability of exchange rates is a symptom of instability in the underlying economic structure. Elimination of this symptom by administrative freezing of exchange rates cures none of the underlying difficulties and only makes adjustment to them more painful. Second, by unrestricted multilateral trade, I shall mean a system in which there are no direct quantitative controls over imports or exports, in which any tariffs or export bounties are reasonably stable and nondiscriminatory and are not subject to manipulation to affect the balance of payments, and in which a substantial fraction of international trade is in private (nongovernmental) hands. Though admittedly vague and subject to considerable ambiguity, this definition will do for our purposes. I shall take for granted without detailed examination that unrestricted multilateral trade in this sense[2] is a desirable objective of economic policy.[3] However, many of the arguments for flexible exchange rates remain valid even if this premise is not accepted.

I. ALTERNATIVE METHODS OF ADJUSTING TO CHANGES AFFECTING INTERNATIONAL PAYMENTS

Changes affecting the international trade and the balance of payments of various countries are always occurring. Some are in the "real" conditions determining international trade, such as the weather, technical conditions of production, consumer tastes, and the like. Some are in monetary conditions, such as divergent degrees of inflation or deflation in various countries.

These changes affect some commodities more than others and so tend to produce changes in the structure of relative prices—for example, rearmament by the United States impinges particularly on selected raw materials and tends to raise their prices relatively to other prices. Such effects on the relative price structure are likely to be much the same whether exchange rates are rigid or flexible and to raise much the same problem of adjustment in either case and so will receive little attention in what follows.

But, over and above these effects on particular commodities and prices, the changes in question affect each country's balance of payments, taken as a whole. Holders of foreign currencies want to exchange them for the currency of a particular country in order to purchase commodities produced in that country, or to purchase securities or other capital assets in that country, or to pay interest on or repay debts to that country, or to make gifts to citizens of that country, or simply to hold for one of these uses or for resale. The amount of currency of a particular country that is demanded per unit of time for each of these purposes will, of course, depend in the first instance on the exchange rate—the number of units of a foreign currency that must be paid to acquire one unit of the domestic currency. Other things the same, the more expensive a given currency, that is, the higher the exchange rate, the less of that currency will in general be demanded for each of these purposes. Similarly, holders of the currency of the country in question want to exchange that currency for foreign currencies for the corresponding purposes; and, again, the amount they want to exchange depends, in the first instance, on the price which they can get. The changes continuously taking place in the conditions of international trade alter the "other things" and so the desirability of using the currencies of various countries for each of the purposes listed. The aggregate effect is at one time to increase, at another to decrease, the amount of a country's currency demanded at any given rate of exchange relative to the amount offered for sale at that rate. Of course, after the event, the amount of a particular currency purchased must equal the amount sold—this is a question simply of double-entry bookkeeping. But, in advance, the amount people want to buy need not equal the amount people want to sell. The *ex post* equality involves a reconciliation of these divergent desires, either through changes in the desires themselves or through their frustration.

There is no way of avoiding this reconciliation; inconsistent desires cannot simultaneously be satisfied. The crucial question of policy is the mechanism whereby this reconciliation is brought about. Suppose the aggregate effect of changes in the conditions affecting international payments has been to increase the amount of a country's currency people want to buy with foreign currency relatively to the amount other people want to sell for foreign currency at the preexisting exchange rate—to create an incipient surplus in the balance of payments. How can these inconsistent desires be reconciled? (1) The country's currency may be bid up, or put up, in price. This increase in the exchange rate will tend to make the currency less desirable relative to the currency of other countries and so eliminate the excess demand at the preexisting rate.[4] (2) Prices within the country may rise, thus making its goods less desirable relative to goods in other countries, or incomes within the country may rise, thus increasing the demand for foreign currencies. (3) Direct controls over transactions involving foreign exchange may prevent holders of foreign balances from acquiring as much domestic exchange as they would otherwise like to; for example, they may be prevented from buying domestic goods by the inability to get a required export license. (4) The excess amount of domestic currency desired may be provided out of monetary reserves, the foreign currency acquired being added to reserves of foreign currencies—the monetary authorities (or exchange equalization fund or the like) may step in with a "desire" to buy or sell the difference between the amounts demanded and supplied by others.

Each of these four methods has its obvious counterpart if the effect of the changes is to create an incipient deficit. Aside from purely frictional frustrations of desires (the inability of a buyer to find a seller because of imperfections of the market), these are fundamentally the only four ways in which an *ex ante* divergence between the amount of a country's currency demanded and the amount supplied can be converted into the *ex post* equality that necessarily prevails. Let us consider each in turn.

Changes in Exchange Rates

Two different mechanisms whereby exchange-rate changes may be used to maintain equilibrium in the balance of payments must be sharply distinguished: (1) flexible exchange rates as defined above and (2) official changes in temporarily rigid rates.

1. *Flexible exchange rates.* Under flexible exchange rates freely determined in open markets, the first impact of any tendency toward a surplus or deficit in the balance of payments is on the exchange rate. If a country has an incipient surplus of receipts over payments—an excess demand for its currency—the exchange rate will tend to rise. If it has an incipient deficit, the exchange rate will tend to fall. If the conditions responsible for the rise or the fall in the exchange rate are generally regarded as temporary, actual or potential holders of the country's currency will tend to change their holdings in such a way as to moderate the movement in the exchange rate. If a rise in the exchange rate, for example, is expected to be temporary, there is an incentive for holders of the country's currency to sell some of their holdings for foreign currency in order to

buy the currency back later on at a lower price. By doing so, they provide the additional domestic currency to meet part of the excess demand responsible for the initial rise in the exchange rate; that is, they absorb some of what would have been surplus receipts of foreign currency at the former exchange rate. Conversely, if a decline is expected to be temporary, there is an incentive to buy domestic currency for resale at a higher price. Such purchases of domestic currency provide the foreign currency to meet some of what would have been a deficit of foreign currency at the former exchange rate. In this way, such "speculative" transactions in effect provide the country with reserves to absorb temporary surpluses or to meet temporary deficits. On the other hand, if the change in the exchange rate is generally regarded as produced by fundamental factors that are likely to be permanent, the incentives are the reverse of those listed above, and speculative transactions will speed up the rise or decline in the exchange rate and thus hasten its approach to its final position.

This final position depends on the effect that changes in exchange rates have on the demand for and supply of a country's currency, not to hold as balances, but for other purposes. A rise in the exchange rate produced by a tendency toward a surplus makes foreign goods cheaper in terms of domestic currency, even though their prices are unchanged in terms of their own currency, and domestic goods more expensive in terms of foreign currency, even though their prices are unchanged in terms of domestic currency. This tends to increase imports, reduce exports, and so offset the incipient surplus. Conversely, a decline in the exchange rate produced by a tendency toward a deficit makes imports more expensive to home consumers, and exports less expensive to foreigners, and so tends to offset the incipient deficit.

Because money imparts general purchasing power and is used for such a wide variety of purposes abroad as well as at home, the demand for and supply of any one country's currency is widely spread and comes from many sources. In consequence, broad, active, and nearly perfect markets have developed in foreign exchange whenever they have been permitted—and usually even when they have not been. The exchange rate is therefore potentially an extremely sensitive price. Changes in it occur rapidly, automatically, and continuously and so tend to produce corrective movements before tensions can accumulate and a crisis develop. For example, if Germany had had a flexible exchange rate in 1950, the crisis in the fall of that year would never have followed the course it did. The exchange rate would have been affected not later than July and would have started to produce corrective adaptations at once. The whole affair would never have assumed large proportions and would have shown up as a relatively minor ripple in exchange rates. As it was, with a rigid exchange rate, the warning of impending trouble was indirect and delayed, and the government took no action until three months later, by which time the disequilibrium had grown to crisis dimensions, requiring drastic action at home, international consultation, and help from abroad.

The recurrent foreign exchange crises of the United Kingdom in the postwar period are perhaps an even more dramatic example of the kind of crises that could not develop under a system of flexible exchange rates. In each case no significant corrective action was taken until large disequilibriums had been allowed to cumulate, and then the action had to be drastic. The rigidities and discontinuities introduced by substituting administrative action for automatic market forces have seldom been demonstrated so clearly or more impressively.

2. *Official changes in exchange rates.* These examples suggest the sharp difference between flexible exchange rates and exchange rates held temporarily rigid but subject to change by government action to meet substantial difficulties. While these exchange-rate changes have the same kind of effect on commodity trade and the like as those produced automatically under a system of flexible exchange rates, they have very different effects on speculative transactions. Partly for this reason, partly because of their innate discontinuity, each exchange-rate change tends to become the occasion for a crisis. There is no mechanism for producing changes in exchange rates of the required magnitude or for correcting mistakes, and some other mechanism must be used to maintain equilibrium during the period between exchange-rate changes— either internal price or income changes, direct controls, or monetary reserves.

Even though an exchange-rate change would not otherwise be the occasion for a crisis, speculative movements are highly likely to convert it into one, for this system practically insures a maximum of destabilizing speculation. Because the exchange rate is changed infrequently and only to meet substantial difficulties, a change tends to come well after the onset of difficulty, to be postponed as long as possible, and to be made only after substantial pressure on the exchange rate has accumulated. In consequence, there is seldom any doubt about the direction in which an exchange rate will be changed, if it is changed. In the interim between the suspicion of a possible change in the rate and the actual change, there is every incentive to sell the country's currency if devaluation is expected (to export "capital" from the country) or to buy it if an appreciation is expected (to bring in "capital"); either can be done without an exchange loss and will mean an exchange gain when and if the rate is changed. This is in sharp contrast with the situation under flexible exchange rates when the decline in the exchange rate takes place along with, and as a consequence of, the sales of a currency and so discourages or penalizes sales, and conversely for purchases. With rigid rates, if the exchange rate is not changed, the only cost to the speculators is a possible loss of interest earnings from an interest-rate differential. It is no answer to this argument to say that capital flows can be restricted by direct controls, since our ultimate objective in using this method is precisely to avoid such restrictions.

In short, the system of occasional changes in temporarily rigid exchange rates seems to me the worst of two worlds: it provides neither the stability of expectations that a genuinely rigid and stable exchange rate could provide in a world of unrestricted trade and willingness and ability to adjust the internal price structure to external conditions nor the continuous sensitivity of a flexible exchange rate.

Changes in Internal Prices or Income

In principle, changes in internal prices could produce the same effects on trade as changes in the exchange rate. For example, a decline of 10 percent in every internal price in Germany (including wages, rents, etc.) with an unchanged dollar price of the mark would clearly have identically the same effects on the relative costs of domestic and foreign goods as a decline of 10 percent in the dollar price of the mark, with all internal prices unchanged. Similarly, such price changes could have the same effects on speculative transactions. If expected to be temporary, a decline in prices would stimulate speculative purchases of goods to avoid future higher prices, thus moderating the price movement.

If internal prices were as flexible as exchange rates, it would make little economic difference whether adjustments were brought about by changes in exchange rates or by equivalent changes in internal prices. But this condition is clearly not fulfilled. The exchange rate is potentially flexible in the absence of administrative action to freeze it. At least in the modern world, internal prices are highly inflexible. They are more flexible upward than downward, but even on the upswing all prices are not equally flexible. The inflexibility of prices, or different degrees of flexibility, means a distortion of adjustments in response to changes in external conditions. The adjustment takes the form primarily of price changes in some sectors, primarily of output changes in others.

Wage rates tend to be among the less flexible prices. In consequence, an incipient deficit that is countered by a policy of permitting or forcing prices to decline is likely to produce unemployment rather than, or in addition to, wage decreases. The consequent decline in real income reduces the domestic demand for foreign goods and thus the demand for foreign currency with which to purchase these goods. In this way, it offsets the incipient deficit. But this is clearly a highly inefficient method of adjusting to external changes. If the external changes are deep-seated and persistent, the unemployment produces steady downward pressure on prices and wages, and the adjustment will not have been completed until the deflation has run its sorry course.

Despite these difficulties, the use of changes in internal prices might not be undesirable if they were called for only rarely and only as a result of changes in the real underlying conditions of trade. Such changes in underlying conditions are likely in any event to require considerable changes in relative prices of particular goods and services and only changes of a much smaller order of magnitude in the general level of internal prices. But neither condition is likely to be satisfied in the modern world. Adjustments are required continuously, and many are called for by essentially monetary phenomena, which, if promptly offset by a movement in the exchange rate, would require no change in the actual allocation of resources.

Changes in interest rates are perhaps best classified under this heading of changes in internal prices. Interest-rate changes have in the past played a particularly important role in adjustment to external changes, partly because they have been susceptible to direct influence by the monetary authorities, and partly because, under a gold standard, the initial impact of a tendency toward a deficit or surplus was a loss or gain of gold and a consequent tightening or ease in the money market. The rise in the interest rate produced in this way by an incipient deficit increased the demand for the currency for capital purposes and so offset part or all of the deficit. This reduced the rate at which the deficit had to be met by a decline in internal prices, which was itself set in motion by the loss of gold and associated decrease in the stock of money responsible for the rise in interest rates. Conversely, an incipient surplus increased the stock of gold and eased the money market. The resulting decline in the interest rate reduced the demand for the currency for capital purposes and so offset part or all of the surplus, reducing the rate at which the surplus had to be met by the rise in internal prices set in motion by the gain of gold and associated rise in the stock of money.

These interest-induced capital movements are a desirable part of a system relying primarily on changes in internal prices, since they tend to smooth out the adjustment process. They cannot, however, be relied on alone, since they come into operation only incidentally to the adjustment of internal prices.

Primary reliance on changes in internal prices and incomes was tolerable in the nineteenth century partly because the key countries of the Western world placed much heavier emphasis on freedom from government interference at home and unrestricted multilateral trade abroad than on domestic stability; thus they were willing to allow domestic economic policy to be dominated by the requirements of fixed exchange rates and free convertibility of currencies. But, equally important, this very emphasis gave holders of balances confidence in the maintenance of the system and so made them willing to let small differences in interest rates determine the currency in which they held their balances. Furthermore, the emphasis on freedom from government interference at home gave less scope to internal monetary management and so meant that most changes affecting international trade reflected real changes in underlying conditions, or else monetary changes, such as gold discoveries, more or less common to the major nations. Modern conditions, with the widespread emphasis on full employment at home and the extensive intervention of government into economic affairs, are clearly very different and much less favorable to this method of adjustment.

Direct Controls

In principle, direct controls on imports, exports, and capital movements could bring about the same effects on trade and the balance of payments as changes in exchange rates or in internal prices and incomes. The final adjustment will, after all, involve a change in the composition of imports and exports, along with specifiable capital transactions. If these could be predicted in advance, and if it were technically possible to control selectively each category of imports, exports, and capital transactions, direct controls could be used to produce the required adjustment.

It is clear, however, that the changes in imports and exports and the required capital transactions cannot be predicted; the fact that each new foreign exchange crisis in a country like Britain is officially regarded as a bolt from the blue is ample evidence for this proposition. Even if they could be predicted, direct control of imports, exports, and capital transactions by techniques other than the price system[5] necessarily means extending such control to many internal matters and interfering with the efficiency of the distribution and production of goods—some means must be found for rationing imports that are being held down in amount or disposing of increased imports and for allocating reduced exports or getting increased exports.

Aside from the many unfortunate results of such a process which are by now abundantly clear, it has a perverse effect on the foreign-payments problem itself, particularly when direct controls are used, as they have been primarily, to counter an actual or incipient deficit. The apparent deficit that has to be closed by direct controls is larger than the deficit that would emerge at the same exchange rate without the direct controls and, indeed, might be eliminated entirely or converted into a surplus if the direct controls on imports and exports and their inevitable domestic accompaniments were removed. The mere existence of the direct controls makes the currency less desirable for many purposes because of the limitations it places on what holders of the currency may do with it, and this is likely to reduce the demand for the currency more than it would be reduced by the fluctuations in exchange rates or other adaptive mechanisms substituted for the direct controls. In addition, permitted imports are generally distributed at prices lower than those that would clear the market and so are used wastefully and in the wrong places, increasing apparent import "requirements"; similarly, the composition of imports is determined by administrative decisions that tend to have the same effect. Both of

these are particularly important in hindering exports, because export industries are not likely to get so large a fraction of the imports as they would bid
away in a free market, even if the government supposedly favors export
industries, and cannot make their influence fully felt in determining the
composition of imports; and the direct controls have a tendency to make the
incentive to export lower than it would otherwise be.[6]

The considerations mentioned in the preceding paragraph may help to
reconcile—and, indeed, their elaboration was stimulated by my own need to
reconcile—the impression of casual visitors to England, and the conclusions of
some careful students of the subject, that the pound is currently (1952)
undervalued in purchasing power terms with the recurrent pressures on the
pound and the restrictive measures that seem to be required to maintain the
pound at its present rate. They show that there is no necessary inconsistency
between the following two assertions: (1) the market value of the pound would
be higher than $2.80 if all exchange restrictions and associated controls were
removed and the exchange rate were allowed to be determined by primarily
private dealings in a free market; (2) given the retention of an official exchange
rate and of the existing *system* of exchange restrictions and associated internal
controls, an *easing* of restrictions would produce pressure on the exchange rate
and require a rate lower than $2.80 to keep exchange reserves from being
depleted. Both statements may not, in fact, be correct; but there is no such
obvious contradiction between them as there appears to be at first sight.

Finally, whatever the desirability of direct controls, there are political and
administrative limits to the extent to which it is possible to impose and enforce
such controls. These limits are narrower in some countries than in others, but
they are present in all. Given sufficient incentive to do so, ways will be found to
evade or avoid the controls. A race develops between officials seeking to plug
legal loopholes and to discover and punish illegal evasions of the controls and
the ever numerous individuals whose inventive talents are directed toward
discovering or opening up new loopholes by the opportunities for large returns
or whose respect for law and fear of punishment are overcome by the same
opportunities. And the race is by no means always to the officials, even when
they are honest and able. In particular, it has proved extremely difficult in all
countries to prevent capital movements by direct controls.

Use of Monetary Reserves

Given adequate reserves, tendencies toward a surplus or a deficit can be
allowed to produce an actual surplus or deficit in transactions other than those
of the monetary authority (or exchange equalization fund, or whatever the
name may be) without a change in exchange rates, internal prices or incomes,
or direct controls, the additional domestic or foreign currency demanded being

supplied by the monetary authority. This device is feasible and not undesirable for movements that are small and temporary, though, if it is clear that the movements are small and temporary, it is largely unnecessary, since, with flexible exchange rates, private speculative transactions will provide the additional domestic or foreign currency demanded with only minor movements in exchange rates.

The exclusive use of reserves is much less desirable, if possible at all, for movements of large magnitude and long duration. If the problem is a deficit, the ability of the monetary authorities to meet the deficit is immediately limited by the size of their reserves of foreign currency or the equivalent plus whatever additional sums they can or are willing to borrow or acquire in other ways from holders of foreign currency. Moreover, if the internal price level (or level of employment) is to be kept stable, the proceeds from the sales of foreign exchange reserves must not be impounded or used in other deflationary ways. This assumes, of course, that the deficit is not itself produced by internal inflationary policies but occurs despite a stable internal price level. The proceeds must be used to retire debt or to finance a deficit in the budget to whatever extent is necessary to prevent a price decline.

If the problem is a surplus, the monetary authorities must be prepared to accumulate foreign exchange indefinitely, providing all the domestic currency that is demanded. Moreover, if the internal price level is to be maintained constant, it must obtain the domestic currency it sells for foreign currency in noninflationary ways. It can print or create the currency only to the extent that is consistent with stable prices. For the rest it must get the amount required by borrowing at whatever interest rates are necessary to keep domestic prices stable or from a surplus of the appropriate amount in the government budget. Entirely aside from the technical problems of monetary management involved, the community is unlikely to be willing to exchange indefinitely part of its product for unproductive currency hoards, particularly if the source of the surplus is monetary inflation abroad, and thus the foreign currency is decreasing in real value.

Traditionally, of course, monetary reserves have not been used as the primary method of adjusting to changes in external conditions but as a shock absorber pending changes in internal prices and incomes. A deficit has been met out of monetary reserves in the first instance, but the proceeds or even a multiple of the proceeds have been, as it were, impounded; that is, the stock of money has been allowed or made to decrease as a result of the decline of monetary reserves, with a consequent rise in interest rates and downward pressure on internal prices. Similarly, the domestic currency exchanged for a surplus of foreign currency has, as it were, been created and allowed to or made to increase the stock of money by the same amount or a multiple of that amount, with a consequent decline in interest rates and upward pressure on internal prices.[7]

Since the end of the First World War, nations have become increasingly unwilling to use reserves in this way and to allow the effect to be transmitted directly and immediately to internal monetary conditions and prices. Already during the 1920s, the United States, to cite one outstanding and critical example, refused to allow its surplus, which took the form of gold imports, to raise domestic prices in the way the supposed rules of the gold standard demanded; instead, it "sterilized" gold imports. Especially after the Great Depression completed the elevation of full employment to the primary goal of economic policy, nations have been unwilling to allow deficits to exert any deflationary effect.

The use of monetary reserves as the sole reliance to meet small and temporary strains on balances of payments and of other devices to meet larger and more extended or more basic strains is an understandable objective of economic policy and comes close to summarizing the philosophy underlying the International Monetary Fund. Unfortunately, it is not a realistic, feasible, or desirable policy. It is seldom possible to know in advance or even soon after the event whether any given strain in the balance of payments is likely to be reversed rapidly or not; that is, whether it is a result of temporary or permanent factors. Reserves must be very large indeed if they are to be the sole reliance in meeting changes in external conditions until the magnitude and probable duration of the changes can be diagnosed with confidence and more fundamental correctives undertaken in light of the diagnosis, far larger than if they serve the function they did under the classical gold standard. Except perhaps for the United States, and even for the United States only so long as gold is freely acceptable as an international currency, reserves are nothing like this large. Under the circumstances there is a strong tendency to rely on reserves too long for comfort yet not long enough for confident diagnosis and reasoned action. Corrective steps are postponed in the hope that things will right themselves until the state of the reserves forces drastic and frequently ill-advised action.

A Comparison

One or another of the methods of adjustment just described must in fact be used to meet changes in conditions affecting external trade; there is no avoiding this necessity short of the complete elimination of external trade, and even this would be an extreme form of direct controls over imports and exports. On the basis of the analysis so far, flexible exchange rates seem clearly the technique of adjustment best suited to current conditions: the use of reserves is not by itself a feasible device; direct controls are cumbrous and inefficient and,

I venture to predict, will ultimately prove ineffective in a free society; changes in internal prices and incomes are undesirable because of rigidities in internal prices, especially wages, and the emergence of full employment—or independence of internal monetary policy—as a major goal of policy.

The argument for flexible exchange rates is, strange to say, very nearly identical with the argument for daylight saving time. Isn't it absurd to change the clock in summer when exactly the same result could be achieved by having each individual change his habits? All that is required is that everyone decide to come to his office an hour earlier, have lunch an hour earlier, etc. But obviously it is much simpler to change the clock that guides all than to have each individual separately change his pattern of reaction to the clock, even though all want to do so. The situation is exactly the same in the exchange market. It is far simpler to allow one price to change, namely, the price of foreign exchange, than to rely upon changes in the multitude of prices that together constitute the internal price structure.

II. Objections to Flexible Exchange Rates

Three major criticisms have been made of the proposal to establish a system of flexible exchange rates: first, that flexible exchange rates may increase the degree of uncertainty in the economic scene; second, that flexible exchange rates will not work because they will produce offsetting changes in domestic prices; and, third, that flexible exchange rates will not produce the best attainable timing or pace of adjustment. The first objection takes many different forms, and it will promote clarity to deal with some of these separately, even though this means considerable overlapping.

Flexible Exchange Rates and Uncertainty

1. *Flexible exchange rates mean instability rather than stability.* On the naïve level on which this objection is frequently made, it involves the already-mentioned mistake of confusing the symptom of difficulties with the difficulties themselves. A flexible exchange rate need not be an unstable exchange rate. If it is, it is primarily because there is underlying instability in the economic conditions governing international trade. And a rigid exchange rate may, while itself nominally stable, perpetuate and accentuate other elements of instability in the economy. The mere fact that a rigid official exchange rate does not change while a flexible rate does is no evidence that the former means greater stability in any more fundamental sense. If it does, it is for one or more of the reasons considered in the points that follow.

2. *Flexible exchange rates make it impossible for exporters and importers to be*

certain about the price they will have to pay or receive for foreign exchange. Under flexible exchange rates traders can almost always protect themselves against changes in the rate by hedging in a futures market. Such futures markets in foreign currency readily develop when exchange rates are flexible. Any uncertainty about returns will then be borne by speculators. The most that can be said for this argument, therefore, is that flexible exchange rates impose a cost of hedging on traders, namely, the price that must be paid to speculators for assuming the risk of future changes in exchange rates. But this is saying too much. The substitution of flexible for rigid exchange rates changes the form in which uncertainty in the foreign exchange market is manifested; it may not change the extent of uncertainty at all and, indeed, may even decrease uncertainty. For example, conditions that would tend to produce a decline in a flexible exchange rate will produce a shortage of exchange with a rigid exchange rate. This in turn will produce either internal adjustments of uncertain character or administrative allocation of exchange. Traders will then be certain about the rate but uncertain about either internal conditions or the availability of exchange. The uncertainty can be removed for some transactions by advance commitments by the authorities dispensing exchange; it clearly cannot be removed for all transactions in view of the uncertainty about the total amount of exchange available; the reduction in uncertainty for some transactions therefore involves increased uncertainty for others, since all the risk is now concentrated on them. Further, such administrative allocation of exchange is always surrounded by uncertainty about the policy that will be followed. It is by no means clear whether the uncertainty associated with a flexible rate or the uncertainty associated with a rigid rate is likely to be more disruptive to trade.

3. *Speculation in foreign exchange markets tends to be destabilizing.* This point is, of course, closely related to the preceding one. It is said that speculators will take a decline in the exchange rate as a signal for further decline and will thus tend to make the movements in the exchange rate sharper than they would be in the absence of speculation. The special fear in this connection is of capital flight in response to political uncertainty or simply to movements in the exchange rate. Despite the prevailing opinion to the contrary, I am very dubious that in fact speculation in foreign exchange would be destabilizing. Evidence from some earlier experiences and from current free markets in currency in Switzerland, Tangiers, and elsewhere seems to me to suggest that, in general, speculation is stabilizing rather than the reverse, though the evidence has not yet been analyzed in sufficient detail to establish this conclusion with any confidence. People who argue that speculation is generally destabilizing seldom realize that this is largely equivalent to saying that speculators lose money, since speculation can be destabilizing in general only if speculators on the average sell when the currency is low in price and buy when

it is high.[8] It does not, of course, follow that speculation is not destabilizing; professional speculators might on the average make money while a changing body of amateurs regularly lost larger sums. But, while this may happen, it is hard to see why there is any presumption that it will; the presumption is rather the opposite. To put the same point differently, if speculation were persistently destabilizing, a government body like the Exchange Equalization Fund in England in the 1930s could make a good deal of money by speculating in exchange and in the process almost certainly eliminate the destabilizing speculation. But to suppose that speculation by governments would generally be profitable is in most cases equivalent to supposing that government officials risking funds that they do not themselves own are better judges of the likely movements in foreign exchange markets than private individuals risking their own funds.

The widespread belief that speculation is likely to be destabilizing is doubtless a major factor accounting for the cavalier rejection of a system of flexible exchange rates in the immediate postwar period. Yet this belief does not seem to be founded on any systematic analysis of the available empirical evidence.[9] It rests rather, I believe, primarily on an oversimplified interpretation of the movements of so-called hot money during the 1930s. At the time, any speculative movements which threatened a depreciation of a currency (i.e., which threatened a *change* in an exchange rate) were regarded as destabilizing, and hence these movements were so considered. In retrospect, it is clear that the speculators were "right"; that forces were at work making for depreciation in the value of most European currencies relative to the dollar independently of speculative activity; that the speculative movements were anticipating this change; and, hence, that there is at least as much reason to call them "stabilizing" as to call them "destabilizing."

In addition, the interpretation of this evidence has been marred by a failure to distinguish between a system of exchange rates held temporarily rigid but subject to change from time to time by government action and a system of flexible exchange rates. Many of the capital movements regarded as demonstrating that foreign exchange speculation is destabilizing were stimulated by the existence of rigid rates subject to change by government action and are to be attributed primarily to the absence of flexibility of rates and hence of any incentive to avoid the capital movements. This is equally true of post–World War II experience with wide swings in foreign-payments positions. For reasons noted earlier, this experience has little direct bearing on the character of the speculative movements to be expected under a regime of genuinely flexible exchange rates.

4. *Flexible exchange rates involve increased uncertainty in the internal economy.* It is argued that in many countries there is a great fear of inflation and that people have come to regard the exchange rate as an indicator of inflation

and are highly sensitive to variations in it. Exchange crises, such as would tend to occur under rigid exchange rates, will pass unnoticed, it is argued, except by people directly connected with international trade, whereas a decline in the exchange rate would attract much attention, be taken as a signal of future inflation, and produce anticipatory movements by the public at large. In this way a flexible exchange rate might produce additional uncertainty rather than merely change the form in which uncertainty is manifested. There is some merit to this argument, but it does not seem to me to be a substantial reason for avoiding a flexible exchange rate. Its implication is rather that it would be desirable, if possible, to make the transition to a flexible rate at a time when exchange rates of European countries relative to the dollar would be likely to move moderately and some to rise. It further would be desirable to accompany the transition by willingness to take prompt monetary action to counter any internal reactions. A fear of inflation has little or no chance of producing inflation, except in a favorable monetary environment. A demonstration that fears of inflation are groundless, and some experience with the absence of any direct and immediate connection between the day-to-day movements in the exchange rate and internal prices would very shortly reduce to negligible proportions any increase in uncertainty on purely domestic markets, as a result of flexible yet not highly unstable exchange rates. Further, public recognition that a substantial decline in the exchange rate is a symptom of or portends internal inflation is by no means an unmixed evil. It means that a flexible exchange rate would provide something of a barrier to a highly inflationary domestic policy.

Very nearly the opposite of this argument is also sometimes made against flexible exchange rates. It is said that, with a flexible exchange rate, governments will have less incentive and be in a less strong position to take firm internal action to prevent inflation. A rigid exchange rate, it is said, gives the government a symbol to fight for—it can nail its flag to the mast of a specified exchange rate and resist political pressure to take action that would be inflationary in the name of defending the exchange rate. Dramatic foreign exchange crises establish an atmosphere in which drastic if unpopular action is possible. On the other hand, it is said, with a flexible exchange rate, there is no definite sticking point; inflationary action will simply mean a decline in the exchange rate but no dramatic crisis, and people are little affected by a change in a price, the exchange rate, in a market in which relatively few have direct dealings.

Of course, it is not impossible for both these arguments to be valid—the first in countries like Germany, which have recently experienced hyperinflations and violently fluctuating exchange rates, the second in countries like Great Britain, which have not. But, even in countries like Britain, it is far from clear that a rigid exchange rate is more conducive under present conditions to noninflationary internal economic policy than a flexible exchange rate. A rigid exchange rate thwarts any immediate manifestation of a deterioration in the foreign-payments position as a result of inflationary internal policy. With an independent monetary standard, the loss of exchange reserves does not automatically reduce the stock of money or prevent its continued increase; yet it does temporarily reduce domestic inflationary pressure by providing goods in return for the foreign exchange reserves without any simultaneous creation of domestic income. The deterioration shows up only sometime later, in the dull tables of statistics summarizing the state of foreign exchange reserves. Even then, the authorities in the modern world have the alternative—or think they have—of suppressing a deficit by more stringent direct controls and thus postponing still longer the necessity for taking the appropriate internal measures; and they can always find any number of special reasons for the particular deterioration other than their internal policy. While the possibilities of using direct controls and of finding plausible excuses are present equally with flexible exchange rates, at least the deterioration in the foreign-payments position shows up promptly in the more readily understandable and simpler form of a decline in the exchange rates, and there is no emergency, no suddenly discovered decline in monetary reserves to dangerous levels, to force the imposition of supposedly unavoidable direct controls.

These arguments are modern versions of an argument that no longer has much merit but was at one time a valid and potent objection to flexible exchange rates, namely, the greater scope they give for government "tampering" with the currency. When rigid exchange rates were taken seriously, and when the armory of direct controls over international trade had not yet been resurrected, the maintenance of rigid rates left little scope for independent domestic monetary policy. This was the great virtue of the gold standard and the basic, albeit hidden, source of its emotional appeal; it provided an effective defense against hyperinflation, against government intervention of a kind that had time and again led to the debasement and depreciation of once-proud currencies. This argument may still be a source of emotional resistance to flexible exchange rates; it is clear that it does not deserve to be. Governments of "advanced" nations are no longer willing to submit themselves to the harsh discipline of the gold standard or any other standard involving rigid exchange rates. They will evade its discipline by direct controls over trade if that will suffice and will change exchange rates before they will surrender control over domestic monetary policy. Perhaps a few modern inflations will establish a climate in which such behavior does not qualify as "advanced"; in the meantime we had best recognize the necessity of allowing exchange rates to adjust to internal policies rather than the reverse.

Flexible Exchange Rates and Internal Prices

While I have just used the primacy of internal policy as an argument for flexible exchange rates, it has also been used as an argument against flexible exchange rates. As we have seen, flexible exchange rates promote adjustments to changes in external circumstances by producing changes in the relation between the prices of foreign and domestic goods. A decline in an exchange rate produced by a tendency toward a deficit in the balance of payments tends to make the prices of foreign goods higher in terms of domestic currency than they would otherwise have been. If domestic prices are unaffected—or affected less—this means a higher price of foreign goods relative to domestic goods, which stimulates exports and discourages imports.

The rise in prices of foreign goods will, it is argued, mean a rise in the cost of living, and this, in turn, will give rise to a demand for wage increases, setting off what is typically referred to as a "wage-price spiral"—a term that is impressive enough to conceal the emptiness of the argument that it generally adorns. In consequence, so the argument continues, prices of domestic goods rise as much as prices of foreign goods, relative prices remain unchanged, there are no market forces working toward the elimination of the deficit that initially caused the decline in the exchange rate, and so further declines in the exchange rate are inevitable until nonmarket forces are brought into play. But these might as well have been used before as after the decline in the exchange rate.

This argument clearly applies only to rather special circumstances. At most, it may be an objection to a particular country at a particular time allowing its currency to go free; it is not a general objection to a *system* of flexible exchange rates as a long-run structure. It does not apply to circumstances making for the appreciation of a currency and applies only to some circumstances making for depreciation. Suppose, for example, that the tendency toward a deficit were produced by monetary deflation in other countries. The depreciation of the currency would then prevent the fall in external prices from being transmitted to the country in question; it would prevent prices of foreign goods from being forced down in terms of domestic currency. There is no way of eliminating the effect of the lowered "real" income of other countries; flexible exchange rates prevent this effect from being magnified by monetary disturbances. Similarly, the argument has little relevance if the decline in exchange rates reflects an open inflationary movement at home; the depreciation is then an obvious result of inflation rather than a cause. The argument has perhaps most relevance in either of two cases: an inflationary situation being repressed by direct controls or a depreciation produced by a change in the "real" conditions of trade.

Even in these cases, however, the argument cannot be fully granted. The crucial fallacy is the so-called wage-price spiral. The rise in prices of foreign goods may add to the always plentiful list of excuses for wage increases; it does not in and of itself provide the economic conditions for a wage rise—or, at any rate, for a wage rise without unemployment. A general wage rise—or a general rise in domestic prices—becomes possible only if the monetary authorities create the additional money to finance the higher level of prices.[10] But if the monetary authorities are ready to do so to validate any rise in particular prices or wages, then the situation is fundamentally unstable without a change in the exchange rate, since a wage rise for any other excuse would lead to similar consequences. The assumption is that to him who asks will be given, and there is never a shortage of willingness to ask under such circumstances.

It will be answered that this innate instability is held in check by some sort of political compromise and that this compromise would be disturbed by the change in the exchange rate. This is a special case of the general argument considered earlier that the government is more likely to resist political pressure to take inflationary action if it nails its flag to the mast of a rigid exchange rate than if it lets the exchange rate fluctuate. But note that the forces leading to a changed exchange rate are not eliminated by freezing the rate; foreign exchange will have to be acquired or economized somehow. The "real" adjustment must be made in one way or another; the question is only how. Why should this way of making the adjustment destroy the compromise while other ways do not? Or, if this is true for a time, can it be expected to continue to be true? If, as we have argued, flexible exchange rates are the least costly way of making the adjustment, will not other methods be even more likely to destroy a tenuous political compromise?

Flexible Exchange Rates and the Timing of Adjustment

The ultimate adjustment to a change in external circumstances will consist of a change in the allocation of productive resources and in the composition of the goods available for consumption and investment. But this ultimate change will not be achieved immediately. It takes time to shift from the production of goods for domestic consumption to the production of goods for export, or conversely; it takes time to establish new markets abroad or to persuade consumers to substitute a foreign for a domestic good to which they have been accustomed; and so on in endless variety. The time required will vary widely: some types of adaptations can take place instantaneously (e.g., curtailment by a high price of the purchase of imported cheese, though even here the price rise required to achieve a given curtailment will be higher at first than after a time when people have had a chance to adapt their habitual pattern of consumption to the new price); other types of adaptation may take a generation (e.g., the development of a new domestic industry to produce goods formerly imported).

Suppose a substantial change in (real) external circumstances to occur and, to keep matters simple, circumstances thereafter to remain essentially unchanged for a lengthy period, so that we can (conceptually) isolate the adaptation to this one change. Suppose, further, that exchange rates are flexible and that international "capital" or "speculative" transactions are impossible, so that payments on current account must balance—a condition it is admittedly difficult to define precisely in any way susceptible to observation. It is clear that the initial change in exchange rates will be greater than the ultimate change required, for, to begin with, all the adjustment will have to be borne in those directions in which prompt adjustment is possible and relatively easy. As time passes, the slower-moving adjustments will take over part of the burden, permitting exchange rates to rebound toward a final position which is between the position prior to the external change and the position shortly thereafter. This is, of course, a highly oversimplified picture: the actual path of adjustment may involve repeated overshooting and undershooting of the final position, giving rise to a series of cycles around it or to a variety of other patterns. We are here entering into an area of economics about which we know very little, so it is fortunate that a precise discussion of the path is not essential for our purposes.

Under these circumstances it clearly might be in the interests of the community to pay something to avoid some of the initial temporary adjustments: if the exchange rate depreciates, to borrow from abroad at the going interest rate to pay for an excess of imports while the slower-moving adjustments take place rather than making the full immediate adjustment by curtailing those imports that can be readily curtailed and forcing out those exports that can be readily increased; if the exchange rate appreciates, to lend abroad at the going interest rate to finance an excess of exports while the slower-moving adjustments take place rather than making the full immediate adjustment by expanding those imports that can be readily expanded and curtailing those exports that can be readily curtailed. It would not, however, be worth doing this indefinitely, even if it were possible. For, if it were carried to the point at which the exchange rate remained unchanged, no other adjustments at all would take place. Yet the change in external circumstances makes a new allocation of resources and composition of goods optimal for the country concerned. That is, there is some optimum pace and timing of adjustment through exchange-rate–induced changes in the allocation of resources which is neither at the extreme of full immediate adjustment in this way alone nor at the other extreme of complete avoidance of adjustment.

Under a flexible exchange rate system with a reasonably broad and free market in foreign exchange and with correct foresight on the part of speculators, just such an intermediate pace and timing of adjustment is produced even if there is no explicit negotiation of foreign loans. If the exchange rate depreciates, for example, the tendency for the exchange rate to fall further initially than ultimately offers an opportunity to make a profit by buying the currency now and reselling it later at a higher price. But this is precisely equivalent to lending by speculators to the country whose currency has depreciated. The return to the speculators is equal to the rate at which the currency they hold appreciates. In a free market with correct foresight, this will tend, aside from the minor costs of buying or selling the foreign exchange, to approach the interest rate that speculators could earn in other ways. If the currency appreciates at more than this rate, speculators still have an incentive to add to their holdings; if it appreciates at less than this rate, it is costing the speculators more in foregone interest to hold the balances than they are gaining in the appreciation of the exchange rate. In this way, speculation with a flexible exchange rate produces the same effect as explicit borrowing by a country whose currency has depreciated or explicit lending by one whose currency has appreciated. In practice, of course, there will be both explicit lending or borrowing and implicit lending or borrowing through exchange speculation. Moreover, the prospect of appreciation of a currency is equivalent to a higher interest rate for loans to the country and thus serves the same function in attracting capital to that country as the rises in interest rate that took place under the gold standard when a country was losing gold. There is, however, this important difference: under flexible exchange rates the inducement to foreign lenders need involve no change in the interest rate on domestic loans; under the gold standard, it did—a particular example of the independence of domestic monetary policy under flexible exchange rates.

But is the pace and timing of adjustment achieved in this way under flexible exchange rates an approximation to the optimum? This is an exceedingly difficult question to answer, depending as it does on whether the interest rate implicitly paid in the form of the appreciation or depreciation of the currency reflects the full relevant costs of too rapid or too slow adjustment. About all one can say without much more extensive analysis, and perhaps even with such analysis, is that there seems no reason to expect the timing or pace of adjustment under the assumed conditions to be systematically biased in one direction or the other from the optimum or to expect that other techniques of adaptation—through internal price changes, direct controls, and the use of monetary reserves with rigid exchange rates—would lead to a more nearly optimum pace and timing of adjustment.

This much would probably be granted by most persons who argue that flexible exchange rates lead to an undesirable pace and timing of adjustment. But, they would maintain, the foreign exchange market is not nearly so perfect, or the foresight of speculators so good, as has been assumed to this point. The argument already considered, that speculation in foreign exchanges is destabilizing, is an extreme form of this objection. For, in that case, the immediate change in the foreign exchange rate must go far enough to produce an immediate adaptation sufficient not only to balance current transactions but also to provide payment in foreign currencies for the balances of domestic currency that speculators perversely insist on liquidating when the exchange rate falls, or to provide the domestic currency for the balances speculators perversely insist on accumulating when the exchange rate rises. The country lends, as it were, when it should be borrowing and borrows when it should be lending.

But one need not go this far. Speculation may be stabilizing on balance, yet the market for foreign exchange, it can be said, is so narrow, foresight so imperfect, and private speculation so dominated by socially irrelevant political considerations that there is an insufficient smoothing out of the adjustment process. For this to be a valid argument against flexible exchange rates, even if true, there must be some alternative that promises a better pace and timing of adjustment. We have already considered several other possibilities. We have seen that direct controls with a rigid exchange rate and the official use of monetary reserves have striking defects of their own, at least under modern conditions; they are likely to produce a highly erratic pace and timing of adjustment with alternate fits of unduly slow and unduly rapid adjustments, and direct controls are besides likely to produce the wrong kind of adjustments. Private capital movements in response to interest-rate differentials were at one time a real alternative but have been rendered largely unavailable by the unwillingness of monetary authorities to permit the required changes in interest rates, by the loss of confidence in the indefinite maintenance of the fixed exchange rates, and by the fear of restrictions on the use of exchange. In any event, such capital movements are, as we have seen, available and at least as likely to take place under flexible exchange rates.

The plausibility of the view that private exchange speculation produces too little smoothing of exchange-rate fluctuations derives, I believe, primarily from an implicit tendency to regard any slowing down of the adjustment process as an improvement; that is, implicitly to regard no adjustment at all or an indefinitely prolonged one as the ideal.[11] This is the counterpart of the tendency to believe that internal monetary policy can and should avoid all internal adjustments in the level of income.[12] And both, I suspect, are a manifestation of the urge for security that is so outstanding a feature of the modern world and that is itself a major source of insecurity by promoting measures that reduce the adaptability of our economic systems to change without eliminating the changes themselves.

III. Special Problems in the Establishment and Operation of a Flexible Exchange-Rate System

Role of Governments in the Exchange Market

The argument that private exchange speculation will not produce a sufficient smoothing of exchange fluctuations is sometimes used to justify, not rigid exchange rates, but extensive intervention by individual governments or international agencies in the exchange market to even out minor fluctuations in exchange rates and to counter capital flights.[13] Such intervention, it should be noted, is in no way necessary for the operation of a flexible exchange-rate system; the issue is solely whether it is desirable. Private traders could buy and sell exchange at prices determined entirely by private demands and offers. Arbitrageurs would keep cross-rates in line. Futures markets would exist—and should be encouraged—to provide facilities for hedging. Markets like these now exist wherever they are permitted, and there is ample experience to demonstrate that they would expand rapidly and efficiently as the area in which they were permitted to operate widened.

Two separate issues are involved in judging the desirability of government intervention:[14] first, what, if any, restrictions on governments are desirable as part of an international agreement for establishing a system of flexible exchange rates; second, what behavior is desirable for an individual nation in its own interests.

From the international point of view, the fundamental requirement is that governments not use restrictions on trade of any kind to protect exchange rates. If they wish to use their reserves to speculate in exchange markets, that is primarily their business, provided they do not use the weapons of exchange controls, trade restrictions, and the like to protect their speculations. If they make money in exchange speculations without using such weapons, they perform the useful social function of smoothing out temporary fluctuations. If they lose money, they make gifts to other speculators or traders, and the primary cost—though not quite the whole cost—is borne by them.

From the national point of view, on balance it seems to me undesirable for a country to engage in transactions on the exchange market for the purpose of affecting the rate of exchange. I see no reason to expect that government officials will be better judges than private speculators of the likely movements in underlying conditions of trade and, hence, no reason to expect that government speculation will be more successful than private speculation in promoting a desirable pace and timing of adjustment. There is every reason to expect an extensive exchange market to develop and, hence, no need for government participation to assure sufficient speculation. A positive disadvantage of government speculation is the danger that government authorities operating under strong political pressures will try to peg the exchange rate, thereby converting a flexible exchange-rate system into a system of rigid rates subject to change from time to time by official action. Even if this does not occur, the continuous possibility that it may is likely to hinder the fullest development of a private market.

At the same time one cannot be dogmatic about this issue. It may be that private speculation is at times destabilizing for reasons that would not lead government speculation to be destabilizing; for example, government officials may have access to information that cannot readily be made available, for security or similar reasons, to private speculators. In any event, it would do little harm for a government agency to speculate in the exchange market provided it held to the objective of smoothing out temporary fluctuations and not interfering with fundamental adjustments. And there should be a simple criterion of success—whether the agency makes or loses money.

There is one qualification that needs to be made to this generally negative conclusion about the desirability of government intervention: a case can be made for government speculation in response to a capital flight produced by a threat of successful invasion of one country by another, and this even if private individuals correctly assess the threat. Suppose everybody agrees that there is, say, one chance in four of a successful invasion. Private individuals will have a strong incentive separately to get capital out of the country. They cannot, of course, in the aggregate do so except in so far as they can literally ship physical goods out of the country into storage elsewhere or can induce foreigners to purchase from them physical capital (or claims to it) in the country. In the attempt to do the latter, they would drive down the rate of exchange. Suppose now that the government has reserves of foreign exchange. It can transfer these to its citizens by buying its own currency and thereby keep up the rate of exchange. If the invasion does not occur, the foreign-exchange reserves will tend to be repatriated, and the government will make money. On the other hand, if the invasion does occur and is successful, the government will lose, in a bookkeeping sense, and the expected loss will be greater than the expected gain. However, in this case the government may figure that all is lost anyway and that, if it had not transferred its reserves to its citizens, it would be forced to transfer them to the enemy. The incentives may therefore be different to the government than to its private citizens considered separately. Even this case, however, is not thoroughly clear. If there is hope of resistance, the government will want to mobilize all the foreign exchange it can to use in promoting the military effort.

Role of European Payments Union and International Monetary Fund in a System of Flexible Exchange Rates

The transition of flexible exchange rates might be organized in stages involving, first, the introduction of flexible exchange rates and free convertibility within Europe with a continuance of discrimination against the dollar and, as a later stage, free convertibility with the dollar. If this were done, the European Payments Union (EPU) would retain the extremely important function of policing such a separation. When the separation was removed, the EPU would lose its special functions. If it were continued at all, its only remaining functions would be as a check-clearing institution and as a body able to give advice to individual countries and to facilitate international consultation.

On the other hand, it is worth emphasizing that there is nothing essential in EPU arrangements that would be an obstacle to flexible exchange rates. The debits and credits could perfectly well be calculated in terms of an exchange rate changing from day to day. The only cost would be complication of the arithmetical calculations.

These comments apply equally to the International Monetary Fund, with, however, one important difference. The statutes of the IMF are designed for a world of exchange rates determined by government action and subject to major change only after consultation and discussion (changes of 10 percent are permitted without consultation); indeed, the decision to adopt this technique of exchange-rate determination is, I believe, the major mistake made in postwar international economic policy. The explicit adoption of a system of flexible exchange rates might therefore require a major rewriting of the statutes of the IMF.

There is some evidence, however, that the IMF is giving way on its former insistence on announced parities. Most recently, it has acceded to the Canadian decision to have a floating rate for the Canadian dollar—with, it is true, the qualification that the floating rate is to be regarded as a temporary expedient until a satisfactory parity rate can be determined. Given the will, it may well be that some means could be found of interpreting the present statutes so that they would offer no effective obstacle to a system of flexible rates. And the apparent success of the Canadian experiment may help to produce the will.

There remains the question what, if any, functions the IMF would have in a world of flexible rates. As implied earlier, some proponents of flexible rates would have the IMF act as an international exchange equalization fund, speculating in exchange markets under instructions to make as much money as possible. This seems to me highly undesirable; any doubts about the advisability of national equalization funds are multiplied manyfold for an international fund subject to political pressures from many governments. Could it, for example, really be in a position to sell a depreciating currency of a major country because of a belief that unwise internal policy would lead to still further depreciation?

If it is not given this function, the ones that might remain are to serve as a short-term international lender of funds along commercial lines, though I see no particular need for such an institution in a world of fully convertible currencies; to provide advice about internal monetary and fiscal policy; and possibly to serve as some kind of clearing agency.

Role of Gold in a System of Flexible Exchange Rates

A system of flexible exchange rates is incompatible with the existence in more than one country of a fixed nominal price of gold and free convertibility of currency into gold and gold into currency. The logical domestic counterpart of flexible exchange rates is a strict fiduciary currency changed in quantity in accordance with rules designed to promote domestic stability.[15] Gold could be used as part of the "backing" for such a currency, provided it was not bought and sold at a fixed price; its monetary role would then be purely fictional and psychological, designed to promote "confidence."

A fixed price for gold could, however, be maintained in one country without interfering with flexible exchange rates. The United States now has such a fixed price, and it could retain it. If it did so, other countries could use gold for the settlement of international payments, since this would be equivalent to using dollars. Insofar as the United States bought gold net, it would be providing dollars to other countries, getting in return gold to be added to its hoards in Fort Knox; and, conversely, if it sold gold. There seems no reason why the United States should follow this policy. It seems better that any dollar aid that it gives should be given directly and openly on the basis of explicit legislative authorization, without requiring other countries to use resources in acquiring gold, ultimately in digging it out of the ground so that it can be reburied in Fort Knox.

A much better alternative is to have a free gold market. There is no reason why people who want to hold gold should not be permitted to do so and no reason why speculation in gold should be discouraged. In this case, gold would lose its place in official monetary systems and become a commodity like all others. For a long time, however, it would be a rather special commodity, widely regarded as a highly safe means of keeping a liquid reserve—safer than most domestic currencies in terms of real value. Its availability for this purpose would serve the useful function of inhibiting inflationary currency issue, at the cost, however, of introducing an additional element of instability. Any fear of inflation would lead to widespread substitution of gold for currency, thereby speeding up the inflation but also reducing the resources capable of being acquired by inflationary currency issue and hence the pressure to resort to it.

These are highly dogmatic statements on an exceedingly complex issue. They are included here primarily to indicate the range of problems involved rather than as a comprehensive analysis of them.

The Sterling Area

The sterling area raises a rather special problem in connection with the establishment of flexible exchange rates, since the sterling area includes a number of different currencies linked by fixed exchange rates and convertible one into the other. Sterling could be integrated into a world of flexible exchange rates in either of two ways: (1) flexible exchange rates could be instituted within the sterling area as well as between sterling and other currencies or (2) fixed exchange rates could be retained within the sterling area.

The above analysis of a world of flexible exchange rates applies in full to the first method of handling the sterling area. However, for both financial and political reasons there is likely to be a strong and entirely understandable preference on the part of the British for the second method. As the center of the sterling area, Britain can make the most out of its banking facilities and experience, command relatively cheap credit, and exercise a considerable degree of commercial and political influence, to mention only the most obvious reasons.

In principle there is no objection to a mixed system of fixed exchange rates within the sterling area and freely flexible rates between sterling and other countries, *provided* that the fixed rates within the sterling area can be maintained without trade restrictions. There are numerous examples of such mixed systems in the past.[16] And it may well be desirable to take the attainment of such a mixed system as the immediate goal of policy. Its attainment would remove the obstacle presented by fixed exchange rates to the liberalization of trade by continental European countries and would permit observation of the operation of the two different systems side by side.

At the same time the dangers inherent in such a policy objective should be clearly recognized. These are of two kinds: (1) such a mixed system may not be viable under current political and economic conditions and (2) Britain may be unwilling to accept such a mixed system, since it may feel that freeing the exchange rate of the pound sterling would increase the difficulty of maintaining the sterling area.

The problem of maintaining fixed exchange rates within the sterling area without restrictions on trade differs only in degree from the corresponding problem for the world as a whole. In both cases the area includes a number of sovereign political units with independent final monetary and fiscal authority.

In consequence, in both cases, the permanent maintenance of a system of fixed rates without trade restrictions requires the harmonization of internal monetary and fiscal policies and a willingness and ability to meet at least substantial changes in external conditions by adjustments in the internal price and wage structure.

The differences in degree are, of course, important. The smaller extent of the area involved has somewhat divergent effects. On the one hand, it reduces the problem of harmonizing potentially divergent policies; on the other, it means that the area is subjected to larger strains from outside. The composition of the area is perhaps more important than its mere extent. It includes political units that have a long tradition of close cooperation and of mutual confidence, many of the areas are dependencies whose internal policies can be fairly well controlled from the center, and the financial relations among the members of the area are of long standing and have withstood severe strain. The preservation of these relations is considered extremely important, and, in consequence, there is a very real willingness on the part of its members to go a long way in adapting internal policies to common needs. Finally, the area has relatively large currency reserves that can be used to meet temporary strains, and its members have shown considerable willingness to accumulate balances in the currencies of other members.

Many of these differences are, of course, themselves the product of the prior existence of fixed and stable exchange rates. Whatever their cause, there can, I think, be little doubt that on balance they mean that a system of fixed exchange rates has more chance of surviving without trade restrictions in the sterling area than in the world as a whole. But, granted that the prospects are better for the sterling area than for the world as a whole, it does not follow that they are very good. There have already been substantial strains within the sterling area, most notably the drain of supposedly frozen balances and the strains within the sterling area that were among the immediate reasons for devaluation in 1949. Direct quantitative restrictions on trade have been imposed by some members on imports from others, and indirect restrictions have arisen, through some aspects of state trading and of other selective policies aimed at the foreign balance.

It is hard to see how further serious strains can be avoided in the future. Members of the sterling area are clearly not going to be willing to accumulate indefinitely balances in the currencies of other members. Reserves, no matter how large, cannot eliminate the necessity of adapting to fundamental changes in external conditions. Yet the United Kingdom and most other members of the sterling area are strongly committed to a full-employment policy which greatly limits the possibility of using changes in the internal price and wage structure as a means of adjusting to changes in external conditions. Thus within the sterling area, as in the rest of the world, if exchange-rate adjustments are ruled out, substantial strains are likely to be met sooner or later by direct controls over international trade. In consequence, I am inclined to be pessimistic about the long-run viability without trade restrictions of a sterling area with fixed exchange rates.

There remains the question whether the freeing of the pound would on balance make it more or less difficult to maintain the sterling area. The answer to this question reached in Britain is certain to be a major factor in Britain's willingness to free the pound.

The freeing of the rate for the pound, together with the removal of exchange restrictions and accompanying internal direct controls, would relieve the stress on the sterling area in some ways; in others, increase it. It would relieve the stress by insulating the sterling area as a whole from outside disturbances, and the experience of the 1930s shows how important this can be; by producing a more efficient use of imports and a better allocation of resources between the production of goods for export and for domestic use; and by making sterling a more desirable and useful currency and so increasing the willingness to hold sterling balances. On the other hand, it might increase the stress, at least initially, because of the danger that holders of the present large sterling balances would seek to convert them into dollars or other currencies and because the substitution of a flexible for a nominally fixed rate might reduce the willingness to hold balances more than the elimination of restrictions on use of balances increased the willingness to hold them. If there were any immediate widespread attempt to shift out of sterling, the rate for the pound might fall drastically unless Britain were willing to use a large part of its reserves to prevent the pound from falling.

This is an exceedingly complex problem that deserves much better-informed and more extensive analysis. The above highly tentative remarks on it are, however, perhaps sufficient to justify the qualified conclusion that, if the immediate problem of the transition could be surmounted, the longer-run effect of a floating pound would be to reduce the stress on the sterling area and thereby increase the chance that it could be viable without trade restrictions—though, even so, the chances do not seem to me to be high.

IV. Some Examples of the Importance of a System of Flexible Exchange Rates

It cannot be too strongly emphasized that the structure and method of determining exchange rates have a vital bearing on almost every problem of international economic relations. It will illustrate this basic proposition and at the same time help to bring out some of the implications of the preceding analysis if we consider the relation of flexible exchange rates to three specific problems of great current importance: (*a*) the promotion of unrestricted multilateral trade; (*b*) the harmonization of internal monetary and fiscal policies; and (*c*) the rearmament drive.

Unrestricted International Trade

We have seen that flexible exchange rates are entirely consistent with unrestricted multilateral trade. On the other hand, the absence of flexible exchange rates is almost certain to be incompatible with unrestricted multilateral trade. With rigid exchange rates, any changes in conditions of trade can be met only by changes in reserves, internal prices and monetary conditions, or direct controls over imports, exports, and other exchange transactions. With few exceptions, reserves of European countries are small, and, in any event, the use of reserves is a feasible device only for mild and temporary movements. Primary reliance on changes in the internal price level is undesirable, and, largely for this reason, there is great political reluctance to rely on such changes. Germany, Belgium, and Italy might perhaps be willing to go some way in this direction. England, France, Norway, and some other countries would almost certainly be completely unwilling to allow the level of prices and employment at home to be determined primarily by the vagaries of foreign trade.

The only other alternative to movements in exchange rates is direct control of foreign trade. Such control is therefore almost certain to be the primary technique adopted to meet substantial movements in conditions of international trade so long as exchange rates are maintained rigid. The implicit or explicit recognition of this fact is clearly one of the chief sources of difficulty in attempts to achieve a greater degree of liberalization of trade in Europe; it is reflected in the extensive escape clauses of all recent international agreements; it is dramatically demonstrated by the ultimately successful pressure on the Germans to use direct controls in the exchange crisis of the fall of 1950, despite the general belief that the crisis was temporary and would be over in a matter of months. It is part of the explanation of the pressures for direct controls produced by the rearmament drive.

Suppose that, by some fortunate turn of events, complete liberalization of trade and convertibility of currencies were achieved tomorrow and resulted in equilibrium in the balance of payments of all European countries at existing exchange rates without American aid. Suppose, in consequence, American aid and pressure were permanently removed. I have no hesitancy in predicting that, given the existing system of determination of exchange rates and the present general political and economic environment, direct controls over exports and imports would be reimposed on a large scale within two or three years at the most.

But even this understates the problem raised by fixed exchange rates. Not only is ultimate liberalization of trade almost certain to be inconsistent with rigid and fixed exchange rates in the present state of the world; equally important, the process of moving toward this objective is rendered unduly difficult. There is no way of predicting in advance the precise economic effects of meaningful reductions of trade barriers. All that is clear is that the impact of such reductions will vary from country to country and industry to industry and that many of the impacts will be highly indirect and not at all in the particular areas liberalized. The very process of liberalization will therefore add substantial and unpredictable pressures on balances of payments over and above those that would occur in any event. These pressures would make any system of rigid exchange rates appropriate to the initial position almost certainly inappropriate to the final position and to intermediate positions. And there seems no way to decide on the appropriate final exchange rates in advance; they must be reached by trial and error. Thus, even if the ultimate goal were a new system of rigid exchange rates, it seems almost essential to have flexibility in the interim period. In the absence of such flexibility, liberalization is likely to be brought to an untimely end by the very consequences of any initial successes.

The current political reluctance to use changes in internal price levels and employment to meet external changes is matched by a political reluctance to use changes in exchange rates. But I submit that the reluctance to use changes in exchange rates is on a different level and has a different basis than the reluctance to use internal changes. The reluctance to use changes in exchange rates reflects a cultural lag, the survival of a belief the bases for which have disappeared; it is a consequence of tradition and lack of understanding. The reluctance to use changes in internal price levels and employment, on the other hand, is a new development, a product of harsh experience of the recent past and, for the moment at least, in tune with current economic conditions.

Harmonization of Internal Monetary and Fiscal Policies

The positive side of the reluctance to use changes in internal price levels and employment to meet external changes is the promotion of internal monetary stability—the avoidance of either inflation or deflation. This is clearly a highly desirable objective for each country separately. But, under a system of rigid exchange rates and unrestricted trade, no country can attain this objective unless *every* other important country with which it is linked directly or indirectly by trade does so as well. If any one country inflates, for example, this tends to increase its imports and reduce its exports. Other countries now start to accumulate currency balances of the inflating country. They must either be willing to accumulate such balances indefinitely—which means they must be willing to continue shipping out goods without a return flow and thus in effect subsidize the inflating country—or they must follow the inflation themselves (or impose import controls). Hence the strong pressure to achieve harmonization of internal monetary policies.

But this pressure has understandably not been matched by a willingness of all countries to submit their internal policy to external control. Why should a country do so when the failure of any one country to cooperate or to behave "properly" would destroy the whole structure and permit it to transmit its difficulties to its neighbors? Really effective "coordination" would require essentially either that nations adopt a common commodity monetary standard like gold and agree to submit unwaveringly to its discipline or that some international body control the supply of money in each country, which in turn implies control over at least interest-rate policy and budgetary policy. The first alternative is neither currently feasible nor particularly desirable in the light of our past experience with the gold standard.[17] As to the second alternative, whether feasible or not, is it desirable that such far-reaching powers be surrendered to any authority other than an effective federal government democratically elected and responsible to the electorate?

A system of flexible exchange rates eliminates the necessity for such far-reaching coordination of internal monetary and fiscal policy in order for any country separately to follow a stable internal monetary policy. If, under such a system, any one country inflates, the primary effect is a depreciation in its exchange rate. This offsets the effect of internal inflation on its international trade position and weakens or eliminates the tendency for the inflation to be transmitted to its neighbors; and conversely with deflation. Inflation and deflation in any one country will then affect other countries primarily insofar as it affects the real income position of the initial country; there will be little or no effect through purely monetary channels.

In effect, flexible exchange rates are a means of combining interdependence among countries through trade with a maximum of internal monetary independence; they are a means of permitting each country to seek for monetary stability according to its own lights, without either imposing its mistakes on its neighbors or having their mistakes imposed on it. If all countries succeeded, the result would be a system of reasonably stable exchange rates; the substance of effective harmonization would be attained without the risks of formal but ineffective harmonization.

The chance that all countries would succeed is far greater with flexible exchange rates than with a system of rigid exchange rates that is not also a strict commodity standard. For not only do the laggards tend to call the tune under rigid exchange rates by infecting the other countries with which they are linked but also the very existence of this link gives each country an incentive to engage in inflationary action that it would not otherwise have. For, at least in the initial stages, inflationary currency issue enables the issuers to acquire resources not only from within the country but also from without: the rigid rates mean, as we have seen, that other countries accumulate balances of the currency of the inflating country. Under reasonably stable but not rigid rates, this incentive is largely removed, since the rates will remain stable only so long as countries avoid inflationary action. Once they embark on it, a decline in the exchange rates for their currency will replace the accumulation of balances that would have to take place to keep the rates rigid.

The Current Rearmament Drive

A particular example of the preceding problem is provided by the present rearmament drive. A really serious rearmament drive is almost certain to produce inflationary pressure, differing in degree from country to country because of differences in fiscal structures, monetary systems, temper of the people, the size of the rearmament effort, etc. With rigid exchange rates, these divergent pressures introduce strains and stresses that are likely to interfere with the armament effort. Country A, let us say, has more inflationary pressure than B, and B more than C. B will tend to find its exports to A expanding at the same time that its exports to C are falling and its imports from C expanding. Over all it may be in balance, but it is not in particular industries. It will be under strong pressure to impose export controls on products that it tends to export to A and at the same time import controls on products it imports from C. Under flexible exchange rates neither might have been necessary; its currency would appreciate relative to A's currency and depreciate relative to B's, thus offsetting both distortions in its trade patterns—distortions because by assumption the changes were produced primarily by differences in the rate of monetary expansion.

This kind of phenomenon is, I believe, one of the important factors that has made for resistance to the removal of import controls and for renewed pressure for export controls, though clearly there are other factors involved as well.

Of course, the rearmament drive will require changes in the structure of trade for technical and physical reasons and not merely for monetary reasons. It is essential for the efficiency of the armament effort that such changes be permitted. Under flexible exchange rates they would tend to be the primary ones. Monetary expansion in any country produces a general increase in demand for imports and a general reduction in supply of exports and so, with flexible exchange rates, is reflected primarily in exchange rates. On the other hand, the rearmament effort involves a shift of demand from some products to others and need involve no change in aggregate money demand. In consequence, particular prices rise relative to other prices, thereby providing the incentive for the required changes in production and trade. Even if the rearmament effort is financed by means that involve an increased aggregate money demand, it will mean a much greater increase in demand for some products than others and so can still lead to the required changes in *relative* prices.

V. Conclusion

The nations of the world cannot prevent changes from occurring in the circumstances affecting international transactions. And they would not if they could. For many changes reflect natural changes in weather conditions and the like; others arise from the freedom of countless individuals to order their lives as they will, which it is our ultimate goal to preserve and widen; and yet others contain the seeds of progress and development. The prison and the graveyard alone provide even a close approximation to certainty.

The major aim of policy is not to prevent such changes from occurring but to develop an efficient system of adapting to them—of using their potentialities for good while minimizing their disruptive effects. There is widespread agreement, at least in the Western world, that relatively free and unrestricted multilateral trade is a major component of such a system, besides having political advantages of a rather different kind. Yet resounding failure has so far marked repeated attempts to eliminate or reduce the extensive and complex restrictions on international trade that proliferated during and immediately after World War II. Failure will continue to mark such attempts so long as we allow implicit acceptance of an essentially minor goal—rigid exchange rates— to prevent simultaneous attainment of two major goals: unrestricted multilateral trade and freedom of each country to pursue internal stability after its own lights.

There are, after all, only four ways in which the pressures on balances of payments produced by changes in the circumstances affecting international transactions can be met: (1) by counterbalancing changes in currency reserves; (2) by adjustments in the general level of internal prices and incomes; (3) by adjustments in exchange rates; and (4) by direct controls over transactions involving foreign exchange.

The paucity of existing currency reserves makes the first impractical for all but very minor changes unless some means can be found to increase the currency reserves of the world enormously. The failure of several noble experiments in this direction is testimony to the difficulty of this solution.

The primacy everywhere attached to internal stability makes the second method one that would not be permitted to operate; the institutional rigidities in internal price structures make it undesirable that it should be the major means of adjustment.

The third—at least in the form of a thoroughgoing system of flexible rates—has been ruled out in recent years without extensive explicit consideration, partly because of a questionable interpretation of limited historical evidence; partly, I believe, because it was condemned alike by traditionalists, whose ideal was a gold standard that either ran itself or was run by international central bankers but in either case determined internal policy, and by the dominant strain of reformers, who distrusted the price system in all its manifestations—a curious coalition of the most unreconstructed believers in the price system, in all its other roles, and its most extreme opponents.

The fourth method—direct controls over transactions involving foreign exchange—has in this way, by default rather than intention, been left the only avenue whereby pressures on balances of payments can be met. Little wonder that these controls have so stubbornly resisted elimination despite the repeated protestations that they would be eliminated. Yet this method is, in my view, by all odds the least desirable of the four.

There are no major economic difficulties to prevent the prompt establishment by countries separately or jointly of a system of exchange rates freely determined in open markets, primarily by private transactions, and the simultaneous abandonment of direct controls over exchange transactions. A move in this direction is the fundamental prerequisite for the economic integration of the free world through multilateral trade.

Notes

1. Indeed, I have elsewhere argued that flexible exchange rates are the logical international counterpart of the monetary and fiscal framework for economic stability that seems to me the most promising. See "A Monetary and Fiscal Framework for Economic Stability," Friedman, *Essays in Positive Economics*, pp. 133–56.

2. And indeed in the even more extreme sense of trade free from all barriers, including tariffs and export bounties.

3. In brief, it is desirable in its own right as one of the basic freedoms we cherish; it promotes the efficient use of resources through an appropriate international division of labor and increases consumer welfare by maximizing the range of alternatives on which consumers can spend their incomes; it facilitates international political amity by removing potent sources of conflict between governments.

4. It is conceivable that, under some conditions and for some range of exchange rates, a rise in exchange rates would increase the excess demand. Though this possibility has received considerable attention, it will be neglected in what follows as of little practical relevance. As a purely theoretical matter, there will always be some set or sets of rates that will clear the market, and, in the neighborhood of at least one of these sets of rates a rise in the rate will mean a decline in excess demand (i.e., a negative

excess demand); a fall, a rise in excess demand. Exchange rates can remain in a region in which this is not true only if they are not free to move and if some nonprice mechanism is used to ration domestic or foreign currency. As a practical matter, the conditions necessary for any relevant range of rates to have the property that a rise increases excess demand seem to me highly unlikely to occur. But, if they should occur, it would merely mean that there might be two possible positions of equilibrium, one above, the other below, the existing controlled rate. If the higher is regarded as preferable, the implication for policy would be first to appreciate the controlled rate and then to set it free.

5. Note that a tariff of a uniform percentage on all imports used to pay a subsidy of a uniform percentage on all exports is equivalent to a depreciation in the exchange rate by the corresponding percentage; and, similarly, a subsidy of a uniform percentage on all imports financed by a tax of a uniform percentage on all exports is equivalent to an appreciation in the exchange rate by the corresponding percentage. Thus devices such as these should be classified under exchange-rate changes rather than direct controls.

6. Selling import licenses at a price that would clear the market would eliminate the first effect; it would not eliminate the second and third unless the permits were not for specific commodities but for foreign exchange to be used in any way desired. Even this would not eliminate the fourth unless the proceeds were used to pay a percentage subsidy to exports and other transactions leading to the acquisition of foreign exchange. This final system is, as indicated in the preceding note, identical with a change in the exchange rate. If the price of permits to use foreign exchange and the subsidy for acquiring it were determined in a free market so as to make total receipts equal total payments, the result is equivalent to or identical with a system of flexible exchange rates.

7. Under a pure gold standard, these effects follow automatically, since any international claims not settled otherwise are settled by gold, which, in case of a deficit, is bodily extracted from the monetary stock and, in case of a surplus, bodily added to it.

8. A warning is perhaps in order that this is a simplified generalization on a complex problem. A full analysis encounters difficulties in separating "speculative" from other transactions, defining precisely and satisfactorily "destabilizing speculation," and taking account of the effects of the mere existence of a system of flexible rates as contrasted with the effects of actual speculative transactions under such a system.

9. Perhaps the most ambitious attempt to summarize the evidence is that by Ragnar Nurkse, International Currency Experience (Geneva: League of Nations, 1944), pp. 117–22. Nurkse concludes from interwar experience that speculation can be expected in general to be destabilizing. However, the evidence he cites is by itself inadequate to justify any conclusion. Nurkse examines only one episode in anything approaching the required detail, the depreciation of the French franc from 1922 to 1926. For the rest, he simply lists episodes during which exchange rates were flexible and asserts that in each case speculation was destabilizing. These episodes may or may not support his conclusion; it is impossible to tell from his discussion of them; and the list is clearly highly selective, excluding some cases that seem prima facie to point in the opposite direction.

Even for the French episode, the evidence given by Nurkse does not justify any firm conclusion. Indeed, so far as it goes, it seems to me clearly less favorable to the conclusion Nurkse draws, that speculation was destabilizing, than to the opposite conclusion, that speculation was stabilizing.

In general, Nurkse's discussion of the effects of speculation is thoroughly unsatisfactory. At times, he seems to regard any transactions which threaten the existing value of a currency as destabilizing even if underlying forces would produce a changed value in the absence of speculation. At another point, he asserts that destabilizing transactions may occur on *both* capital and current account simultaneously, in a context in which these two accounts exhaust the balance of payments, so that his statement is an arithmetical impossibility (pp. 210–11). It is a sorry reflection on the scientific basis for generally held economic beliefs that Nurkse's analysis is so often cited as "the" basis or "proof" of the belief in destabilizing speculation.

10. In principle, there are other possibilities related to the "velocity of circulation" of money that I neglect to simplify the argument; they do not change its essence.

11. An interesting example is provided by an argument for 100 percent banking reserves under a gold standard given by James E. Meade, *The Balance of Payments*, vol. 1, *The Theory of International Economic Policy* (Oxford: Oxford University Press, 1951), p. 185. Meade argues correctly that with 100 percent reserves the internal adaptations consequent on an external change of any given size will be at a slower rate than with a lower reserve ratio. On this ground, he says, 100 percent reserves are better than fractional reserves. But this conclusion follows only if any slowing down in the rate of internal adaptation is an improvement, in which case 200 percent reserves or their equivalent ("sterilization" of gold imports and exports) would be better than 100 percent, and so on indefinitely. Given that there is some optimum rate of adjustment, all one can say is that there exists some reserve ratio that would tend to produce this rate of adjustment and so be optimal on these grounds alone; I see no way of knowing on the basis of the considerations Meade presents whether this ratio would be 5 percent or 500 percent.

12. See Milton Friedman, "The Effects of a Full-Employment Policy on Economic Stability: A Formal Analysis," in *Essays in Positive Economics*, pp. 117–32, for a more detailed consideration of the formal problem involved in both internal and external policy and for some examples of this tendency.

13. See Meade, op. cit., pp. 218–31.

14. I owe this distinction to Robert Triffin.

15. See Milton Friedman, "A Monetary and Fiscal Framework for Economic Stability," in *Essays in Positive Economics*, pp. 133–56, and "Commodity-Reserve Currency," pp. 204–50 of the same volume.

16. In a sense, any flexible exchange system is such a mixed system, since there are rigid rates between the different sections of one nation—between, say, the different states of the United States. The key difference for present purposes between the different states of the United States, on the one hand, and the different members of the sterling area, on the other, is that the former are, while the latter are not, all effectively subject to a single central fiscal and monetary authority—the federal government—

having ultimate fiscal and monetary powers. In addition, the former have, while the latter have not, effectively surrendered the right to impose restrictions on the movements of goods, people, or capital between one another. This is a major factor explaining why a central monetary authority is able to operate without producing serious sectional strains. Of course, these are questions of economic fact, not of political form, and of degree, not of kind. A group of politically independent nations all of which firmly adhered to, say, the gold standard would thereby in effect submit themselves to a central monetary authority, albeit an impersonal one. If, in addition, they firmly adhered to the free movement of goods, people, and capital without restrictions, and economic conditions rendered such movement easy, they would, in effect, be an economic unit for which a single currency—which is the equivalent of rigid exchange rates—would be appropriate.

17. See Friedman, "Commodity-Reserve Currency," in *Essays in Positive Economics*, pp. 204–50, for a more extensive discussion of the advantages and disadvantages of a commodity standard.

HAS GOVERNMENT
ANY ROLE IN MONEY?

· 26 ·

INTRODUCTION

In recent years there has been a burst of scholarly interest in various aspects of monetary reform—not the conduct of current monetary policy, which has for decades been the object of active scholarly work, but the institutional structure of the monetary system. This interest has centered on three separate but related topics: (1) competition versus government monopoly in the creation of or control over outside or high-powered money, (2) so-called free banking, and (3) the determination of the unit of account and its relation to media of exchange. The topics are related because they all deal with what role, if any, government has in the monetary system.

This burst of interest has been a response to mutually reinforcing developments, some internal to the discipline of economics; others, external.

The internal developments were threefold. One is the emergence of the theory of public choice, which has produced a large-scale shift from a public-interest to a private-interest interpretation of government activity. Instead of regarding civil servants and legislators as disinterestedly pursuing the public interest, as they judged it—in sharp contrast to the behavior we have attributed to participants in business enterprises—economists have increasingly

Co-authored with Anna J. Schwartz. Reprinted by permission from *Journal of Monetary Economics* 17 (1986): 37–62.

come to regard civil servants and legislators as pursuing their private interests, treated not as narrowly pecuniary or selfish but as encompassing whatever ends enter into their utility functions, not excluding concern for the public interest. This public choice perspective is extremely attractive intellectually because it aligns our interpretations of government and private activity. It has inevitably led to extensive research on the determinants of governmental behavior as well as to renewed attention to the kinds of institutions and policies, if any, that can make each participant in government as in a free market operate as if, in Adam Smith's famous phrase, he were "led by an invisible hand to promote an end that was no part of his intention," namely, the interest of the public. Monetary policy and the monetary authorities have been obvious candidates for attention.[1]

A second internal development is the rational-expectations approach, particularly its stress on the effect of the institutional structure and changes in the institutional structure on the expectations of the public. In one sense, this approach is not new. For example, the effect of the existence of central banks on the behavior of commercial banks and the public had long been explicitly recognized in the monetary literature. Yet, the coining of a new name, the application of the idea by Lucas to the validity of econometric forecasts, and the explicit modeling of the role of expectations have all had a major impact on the profession's thinking and, incidentally, have promoted greater attention to institutional structures as compared with current policy formation.

A third internal development is the renewed interest in so-called Austrian economics, with its emphasis on "invisible hand" interpretations of the origin and development of economic institutions, and its interpretation of the business cycle as largely reflecting the effect of non-neutral money. The latter in turn produced a long Austrian tradition of support for "hard" money and opposition to discretionary money management. Hayek's proposal for denationalizing money was especially influential in reviving this tradition.[2]

The key external development—the ultimate consequences of which are shrouded in uncertainty—was the emergence of a world monetary system that, we believe, is unprecedented: a system in which essentially every currency in the world is, directly or indirectly, on a pure fiat standard—directly, if the exchange rate of the currency is flexible though possibly manipulated; indirectly, if the exchange rate is effectively fixed in terms of another fiat-based currency (e.g., since 1983, the Hong Kong dollar). This system emerged gradually after World War I. From then to 1971, much of the world was effectively on a dollar standard, while the United States, though ostensibly on a gold standard (except for a brief interval in 1933–1934), was actually on a fiat standard combined with a government program for pegging the price of gold. The Bretton Woods agreement in the main simply ratified that situation, despite the lip service paid to the role of gold, and the provisions for changes in exchange rates. The end of Bretton Woods in 1971 removed both the formal links to the dollar and the pretense that the United States was on a gold standard. The stocks of gold listed on the books of the central books of the world are a relic of a bygone era, though a slim possibility remains that they will again become more than that at some future date.

The formal ending of Bretton Woods was precipitated by an inflationary surge in the United States in the 1960s and in turn helped to produce a continuation and acceleration of that surge in the 1970s. The inflation and the subsequent economic instability were more directly responsible for the burst of interest in monetary reform than the momentous change in the world's monetary system of which the inflation was both a cause and a manifestation. It did so in several ways. In the first place, it brought into sharp focus the poor performance of the monetary authorities—reinforcing the conclusions about prior policy that various scholars had reached, including ourselves in our *Monetary History*.[3] Even granted the market failures that we and many other economists had attributed to a strictly laissez-faire policy in money and banking, the course of events encouraged the view that turning to government as an alternative was a cure that was worse than the disease, at least with existing government policies and institutions. Government failure might be worse than market failure.

In the second place, the rise in nominal interest rates produced by the rise in inflation converted government control of interest rates in the United States via Regulation Q from a minor to a serious impediment to the effective clearing of credit markets. One response was the invention of money market mutual funds as a way to avoid Regulation Q. The money market funds performed a valuable social function. Yet, from a broader perspective, their invention constituted social waste. If either the inflation had not occurred or banks had been free to respond to market forces, there would have been no demand for the services of money market funds, and the entrepreneurial talent and other resources absorbed by the money market mutuals could have been employed in socially more productive activities. The money market funds proved an entering wedge to financial innovations that forced a relaxation and near-abandonment of control over the interest rates that banks could pay, as well as over other regulations that restricted their activities. The deregulation of banking that has occurred came too late and has been too incomplete to prevent a sharp reduction in the role of banks, as traditionally defined, in the financial system as a whole.

In Friedman's *Program for Monetary Stability*, published a quarter of a century ago, he asked the question "whether monetary and banking arrangements could be left to the market, subject only to the general rules applying to all other economic activity."[4]

"I am by no means certain," he wrote, "that the answer is indubitably in the negative. What is clear is that monetary arrangements have seldom been left entirely to the market, even in societies following a thoroughly liberal policy in other respects, and that there are good reasons why this should have been the case."[5] Those "good reasons" were: "(1) the resource cost of a pure commodity currency and hence its tendency to become partly fiduciary; (2) the peculiar difficulty of enforcing contracts involving promises to pay that serve as a medium of exchange and of preventing fraud in respect to them; (3) the technical monopoly character of a pure fiduciary currency which makes essential the setting of some external limit on its amount; and finally, (4) the pervasive character of money which means that the issuance of money has important effects on parties other than those directly involved and gives special importance to the preceding features. Something like a moderately stable monetary framework seems an essential prerequisite for the effective operation of a private market economy. It is dubious that the market can by itself provide such a framework. Hence, the function of providing one is an essential governmental function on a par with the provision of a stable legal framework."[6]

Of course, recognition that there are "good reasons" for government to intervene and that, as a matter of historical fact, governments, and especially modern governments, almost invariably have done so, does not mean that the actual interventions have promoted the public welfare, or that the modes of intervention have been wisely chosen. A major aim of our *Monetary History* was precisely to investigate this question for the United States for the period after the Civil War.

The evidence we assembled strongly suggests, indeed we believe demonstrates, that government intervention was at least as often a source of instability and inefficiency as the reverse, and that the major "reform" during the period, the establishment of the Federal Reserve System, in practice did more harm than good. Our personal conclusion, reinforced by the evidence in that work though not stated therein, is that a rigid monetary rule is preferable to discretionary monetary management by the Federal Reserve.

The aim of this paper is to consider whether the new evidence and new arguments that have emerged in recent years justify a revision of the earlier summary of "good reasons" why government has intervened, in particular of the conclusion that "the market itself cannot provide" a "stable monetary framework." In the most extreme form, does the evidence justify an unqualified affirmative rather than negative answer to the question "whether monetary and banking arrangements cannot [i.e., should not] be left to the market?"

This question in turn breaks down into three separate questions, the clear differentiation of which is one of the valuable contributions of recent writings:

1. Can and should the determination of a unit of account linked with a

medium of exchange and the provision of outside money itself be left to the market or do items (1), (3), and (4) of Friedman's good reasons justify a government role in defining the unit of account and providing an outside money?

2. Given a well-defined outside money involving a unit of account and a medium of exchange, can and should strict laissez-faire be the rule for banking—broadly defined to include the issuance of inside money in the form of currency as well as deposits—except only for the general rules applied to all other economic activity? This is the so-called free-banking question, which bears particularly on items (2) and (4) of Friedman's good reasons.

  In terms of institutional and legal arrangements, the major sub-issues are:

  (a) Should financial intermediaries be prohibited from issuing inside money in the form of hand-to-hand currency, i.e., should hand-to-hand currency be a government monopoly?

  (b) Are governmental limitations on lending and investing by financial intermediaries necessary or desirable?

  (c) Is a government "lender of last resort"—a central bank— necessary or desirable?

3. In the absence of legal obstacles, can, should, and would the unit of account be separated in practice from the medium of exchange function in the belief that financial innovation will render outside money unnecessary and obsolete? I.e., do financial innovations promise to make a 100 percent inside money the most efficient means of engaging in transactions?

It may be worth noting explicitly that the word "can" as used in these questions admits of two very different interpretations. One is narrowly economic: is a given set of arrangements internally consistent so far as narrowly economic conditions are concerned; that is, would it generate a stable equilibrium, both static and dynamic? The other is broader: would the set of arrangements generate a stable political as well as economic equilibrium; that is, is its existence consistent with the political constitution, or would it generate political forces leading to major changes in the arrangements?

We believe that failure to distinguish between these interpretations is responsible for much of the appearance of disagreement in the discussions of monetary reform.

Of the three questions posed, we propose to discuss the first two, since the third is much less related to our earlier work and, besides, has been dealt with recently, and in our opinion correctly, by others.[7]

The first and third questions are new in a sense in which the second is not. Essentially all participants in the nineteenth- and early twentieth-century controversies about monetary and banking matters took for granted a specie standard, in which government's role was restricted to coinage or its equivalent (i.e., provision of warehouse receipts for specie); hence they never had occasion to consider the first and third questions. Suspension of specie payments was regarded as, and in fact generally was, a temporary expedient to meet a temporary difficulty. Any government-issued money (whether notes or deposits) in excess of specie reserves was, in modern terminology, regarded as inside money, not outside money, though it clearly became the latter during periods of suspension of specie payments. This common view no doubt reflected widespread agreement that historical experience showed, as Irving Fisher put it in 1911, that "Irredeemable paper money has almost invariably proved a curse to the country employing it."[8]

The disappearance of specie standards and the emergence of a world monetary system in which, for the first time, every country is, in Fisher's terms, on an irredeemable paper standard has produced two very different streams of literature: one, scientific; the other, popular. The scientific literature is that already referred to, dealing with monetary reform and the government's role in providing outside money. The popular literature is alarmist and "hard money," essentially all of it based on the proposition that Fisher's generalization will continue to hold and that the world is inevitably condemned to runaway inflation unless and until the leading nations adopt commodity standards.

There has been some, but limited, intersection between these two streams. The scientific literature has occasionally dealt with but mostly ignored the question raised by the popular literature. Have the conditions that have produced the current unprecedented monetary system also altered the likelihood that it will go the way of earlier paper standards? We consider that question in a tentative way below.

By contrast with outside money, free banking was fully and exhaustively discussed in the nineteenth and early twentieth century. Recent literature has added much historical detail, discussed the arguments in terms of current monetary arrangements, and expressed old arguments in more formal and abstract terms. And we now have a much wider span of historical experience on which to base a judgment. Nonetheless, Vera Smith's 1936 *Rationale of Central Banking* provides, we believe, as accurate and complete a summary of recent theoretical arguments for and against free banking as it does of the earlier arguments.[9]

OUTSIDE MONEY

Whether the government has a role in providing outside money, and what that role should be, is more basic than whether government should intervene in the provision of inside money by nongovernment banking institutions. Existing banking systems rest on the foundation of an outside money, and so did those free-banking systems, such as the Scottish, Canadian, and early U.S., that have recently been subjected to reexamination and offered as object lessons. Historically, a single unit of account linked to a single dominant outside money has tended to emerge, initially via a market process of transactors settling on a particular commodity, followed almost invariably by government's exercising control over one or more aspects of the issuance of outside money—typically with the ostensible purpose of standardizing the coinage and certifying its quality (purity, fineness, etc.). Occasionally, two commodities, with a flexible rate of exchange between them, have simultaneously been outside moneys, one for small transactions, the other for large, as with silver and gold in the Middle Ages, or copper and silver in China.

Insofar as governments confined themselves to producing standardized coinage, the activity was a source of revenue because of the convenience to the public of using for transaction purposes coins with a stated face value rather than bullion. The mint could make a seigniorage charge for providing this service, and the government's visibility and authority gave it an advantage over private mints even when it did not prohibit them. However, governments have repeatedly gone farther and have used (or abused) their control over outside money to raise revenue by introducing fiat elements. Initially, this took the form of the debasement of the metallic coinage issued by the sovereign—that is, increasing the proportion of base metal in silver and gold coins, so that the stated face value of the coins exceeded the market value of the precious metal they contained. Such debasement was a source of revenue because of the lag in the adjustment of nominal prices to the lowered precious metal content of the coins. During this period, the base metal served, as it were, as inside money.

The introduction and subsequent widespread use of paper money and deposits, initially as warehouse receipts for specie, opened a broader range of possibilities, exploited both by private individuals or bankers who issued notes and deposits promising to pay specie on demand in excess of the amount of specie they held (private inside money, so long as the issuers honored the promise), and by governments that did the same (government inside money, subject to the same proviso).

As banking developed, commercial banks came to regard all non-interest-bearing government issues—in the United Kingdom, notes and deposits at the Bank of England; in the United States, U.S. notes (greenbacks), national bank notes, silver certificates, Federal Reserve notes and deposits—as outside money. However, for the system as a whole, so long as convertibility into specie was maintained, only specie was in fact outside money; the excess of government issues over the government's specie holdings was government-created inside money. All such issues, however, became true outside money—pure fiat money—when convertibility was suspended, as it now has been throughout the world.

We still refer to government-issued non-interest-bearing notes and deposits as government "liabilities" or "obligations," although that is not what they are, as is eminently clear in other contexts. We now take a pure fiat standard so much for granted that we no longer find any need to distinguish between the concepts of outside money relevant for the commercial banks and for the system as a whole. But that distinction remains important in judging proposals for monetary reform, and in interpreting historical experience.

That experience provides striking evidence of the value that communities attach to having a single unit of account and medium of exchange. The large revenue that governments have been able to extract by introducing fiat elements into outside money is one measure of the price that economic agents are willing to pay to preserve the unit of account and the medium of exchange to which they have become habituated. It takes truly major depreciation in the purchasing power of the dominant money before any substantial fraction of the community adopts alternatives, either with respect to the unit of account or the medium of exchange. Yet such alternatives have generally been available.

For example, students of money have repeatedly recommended what Alfred Marshall called a tabular standard, namely, the indexation of long-term contracts, so that for such contracts the unit of account becomes, to use one currency as an example, not the nominal dollar, but the real dollar, although the medium of exchange may remain the nominal dollar.[10] In most Western countries, nothing has prevented the private emergence of a tabular standard. Yet, a tabular standard has emerged on any widespread scale only in countries that have been subject to extreme movements in the price level, like some Latin American countries, Israel, etc. Indexation has been privately introduced on any substantial scale in the United States only with respect to labor contracts, and even there only occasionally and with respect to a minority of contracts.

Another alternative has been foreign currency, which has occasionally been resorted to both as unit of account and medium of circulation, but again only under extreme provocation.

The apparently great value to the economy of having a single unit of account linked with an (ultimate) medium of exchange does not mean that government must play any role, or that there need be a single producer of the medium of exchange. And indeed, historically, governments have entered the picture after the event, after the community had settled on a unit of account and private producers had produced media of exchange.

Two features of this history are striking. The first is that the unit of account has, invariably or nearly so, been linked to a commodity. We know of no example of an abstract unit of account—a fiduciary or fiat unit such as now prevails everywhere, having emerged spontaneously through its acceptance in private transactions. The second is how universally government has taken over, and how often it has established a monopoly in the certification or production of the outside money. In his explanation of this phenomenon, Friedman stressed considerations of economic efficiency—"can" in the narrower economic sense. But this is clearly inadequate. The theory of public choice requires attention to the political forces that have produced this result and the kind of monetary constitution, if any, that can avoid it.[11] It is not enough to document the abuses that have arisen from government control of outside money, or to demonstrate the existence of alternative arrangements that are economically more satisfactory. We shall be evading our task of explanation unless we examine the political forces that established government control under a wide range of political and economic circumstances, superseding private certification and production of outside money. And, so far as reform is concerned, we shall simply be spitting in the wind, as economists have done for 200 years with respect to tariffs, unless we explore how effective political support can be mobilized for one or another solution. We hasten to add that the latter is not the task of this paper.[12]

Item (3) of Friedman's list of good reasons, the technical monopoly character of a *"pure fiduciary* currency" (italics added) has been questioned, particularly by Benjamin Klein.[13] Klein's theoretical case, resting on the necessity for a producer of money to establish confidence in his money, and the increasing capital cost of creating such confidence, is impeccable, and has received wide acceptance. Yet it is not clear that his argument can be carried over to a pure fiduciary currency.[14] Historically, producers of money have established confidence by promising convertibility into some dominant money, generally, specie. Many examples can be cited of fairly long-continued and successful producers of private moneys convertible into specie.[15] We do not know, however, of any example of the private production of purely inconvertible fiduciary moneys (except as temporary expedients, e.g., wooden nickels, clearing house certificates), or of the simultaneous existence in the same community of private producers of moneys convertible into different ultimate media, except for the previously mentioned case when two metals circulated simultaneously at a flexible rate of exchange, and the somewhat similar case of the greenback period (1862–1878) in the United States when banks had both greenback and gold deposit liabilities. Yet Klein's argument would not seem to preclude the simultaneous existence in the same community of several dominant moneys produced by different private issuers.

Hayek, in his argument for the denationalization of money, believes that such an outcome is a real possibility, if the current legal obstacles to the production of competitive moneys were removed. In particular, he believes that private issuers who produced a medium of exchange with constant purchasing power (a "real dollar") would become dominant. He recognizes that a single dominant money might tend to develop over large areas, but anticipates that different definitions of constant purchasing power would be appropriate for different areas or groups and hence that a "number of different competitive money producers would survive, with extensive overlap in border areas."[16]

Entirely aside from the question of the political forces that such arrangements would generate, we are skeptical of his conjecture, rather agreeing with Benjamin Klein's early judgment that "I do not think that adoption of Hayek's . . . policy recommendation of complete domestic freedom of choice in currency would significantly reduce the amount of monopoly power on currency issue currently possessed by each individual European government."[17]

So far, neither Hayek's belief that privately produced constant purchasing power moneys would become dominant nor Klein's and our skepticism has any direct empirical basis, but derive rather from an interpretation of historical experience under very different monetary arrangements than those Hayek proposes. However, some direct evidence may emerge in the near future, because of developments within the present system that could facilitate the issuance of constant purchasing power money.

In the United States, the Federal Home Loan Bank Board in 1980 authorized federal savings and loan associations to make price-level-adjusted mortgage (or PLAM) loans and, in 1982, to accept price-level-adjusted deposits (PLADs). There seems no reason such deposits could not be readily transferable by checks or their equivalent, which would provide a medium of exchange as well as a unit of account of constant purchasing power. So far, apparently, no savings and loan has taken advantage of this possibility. However, since 1982 disinflation has been the rule, and confidence in a more stable future price level has grown rapidly. A real test will come when and if that confidence is shattered.[18]

Another U.S. development, in the course of being realized as this is written, is the introduction of futures markets in price index numbers.[19] The Coffee, Sugar & Cocoa Exchange has received permission from the Commodity Futures Trading Commission (the federal agency that regulates futures markets) to introduce a futures contract in the consumer price index. Trading in the contract began on June 21, 1985. Such futures markets would enable banks to accept deposits on a price-level-adjusted basis and hedge their risk in the futures market rather than by matching price-level-adjusted liabilities with price-level-adjusted assets. This development seems to us the most promising of the recent innovations, in terms of its potential effect on the operation of the monetary system.

An earlier U.S. development was the removal in 1974 of the prohibition against the ownership, purchase, and sale of gold by private persons. In principle, it has been possible since then for individuals in private dealings to use gold as a medium of exchange. And there have been some minor stirrings. The Gold Standard Corporation in Kansas City provides facilities for deposits denominated in gold and for the transfer of such deposits among persons by check. However, this is a warehousing operation—a 100 percent reserve bank, as it were—rather than a private currency denominated in gold and issued on a fractional reserve basis. Unfortunately, there are currently legal obstacles to any developments that would enable gold to be used not only as a store of value or part of an asset portfolio but as a unit of account or a medium of circulation. Hence, the current situation provides little evidence on what would occur if those obstacles were removed.

In the United Kingdom, the government now issues securities that link interest and principal to a price index number. Banks could use such securities as assets to match price-level-adjusted deposits.

It remains to be seen whether any of these opportunities will be exploited. Our personal view is that they will be if and only if government monetary policy produces wide fluctuations in inflation, fluctuations even wider than those that occurred in the United States or the United Kingdom in recent decades. Moreover, even if they are, we conjecture that the use of a constant purchasing power of money as a unit of account and medium of circulation will be confined to large transactions involving long time delays, not to small or current transactions.

A further qualification is that the circumstance envisaged in the preceding paragraph—wide fluctuations in inflation in major countries—is not likely to prove stable and long-lasting. It is almost certain to produce political pressures for major monetary reform—in the extreme, after it has degenerated into hyperinflation; on a more hopeful note, long before.

Until recent years, true hyperinflation has occurred only in countries undergoing revolution or severe civil unrest or that have been defeated in a major war, with the possible exception of John Law's experiment of doubling the French bank-note issue in the four-year period 1716 to 1720. However, currently, several countries seem on the verge of hyperinflation under relatively peaceful circumstances—Bolivia, Argentina, and Israel, to mention only the most prominent. The misfortune of these countries promises to provide us with some evidence on a so far rarely observed phenomenon.

Another recent hybrid development of considerable interest is the increased use of the European currency unit (ECU) in private transactions. The ECU is a composite of the separate national currencies of those Common Market countries participating in the European Monetary System—or, as it has come to be described, a basket containing specified numbers of units of each of the national currencies included in it. Its value in terms of any single national currency, including the dollar or any of the currencies composing it, is thus a weighted average of the market values in terms of that currency of the component ECU currencies. Though initially created for clearing intergovernmental balances, it has increasingly been used as a unit of account in private bond issues and other transactions,[20] and banks in some countries have been offering ECU-denominated deposits, though in others, such as Germany, they are currently not permitted to do so. So far, the ECU has been convertible into dollars and most other currencies. However, it has been in existence only since 1979, so it is still in the early stages of development. What role it will play in the future is highly uncertain.

The ECU is a governmentally created and issued currency. It is convertible only into other governmentally created and issued currencies, all of which are purely fiduciary, despite lip service still paid to gold by including gold, generally at an artificial price, as a "reserve asset" in the balance sheets of the central banks. What is unique is its composite character, resembling in this respect the fiduciary counterpart to the symmetallic proposal by Marshall and the later commodity reserve proposals.[21]

It does offer an alternative to the separate national currencies and so does enhance currency competition. However, its growth and wider use would represent joint government action in the field of money along the lines of the International Monetary Fund, rather than private action. As with national currencies, private action would take the form of producing inside money convertible into the ECU as an outside money.

Items (3) and (4) of Friedman's list of good reasons, technical monopoly and external effects, have been questioned also by Roland Vaubel in a thoughtful article.[22] He concludes that neither is a valid justification for a government monopoly in the production of base money.

With respect to natural monopoly, he concludes that "the only valid test of the natural monopoly argument is to abolish all barriers to entry and to admit free currency competition from private issuers on equal terms."[23] We agree with him entirely on this point while, as noted earlier, being highly skeptical that, given the starting point with a government currency firmly established, any private issuers would be likely to compete successfully—especially in producing a "pure fiduciary" money. As already noted, there is no historical precedent. Historical experience suggests that the only plausible alternative to a government-issued fiduciary currency is a commodity currency, with private issuers producing inside money convertible into the commodity. And we believe that even that outcome is highly unlikely unless there is a major collapse of national currencies—something approximating hyperinflation on a worldwide scale.

With respect to externalities, Vaubel's negative conclusion is a quibble with respect to the basic issue of whether government has a key role to play in the monetary system. Even if there are externalities, he says, it "does not follow that government should produce money (let alone as a monopolist) rather than introduce a mandatory deposit insurance scheme or act as a lender of last resort by borrowing and lending private money."[24] But either of these policies would be a far cry from leaving "money and banking arrangements . . . to the market."

To summarize our answer to the first question: there is no economic reason why the determination of a unit of account linked with a medium of exchange and the provision of outside money cannot be left to the market. But history suggests both that any privately generated unit of account will be linked to a commodity and that government will not long keep aloof. Under a wide variety of economic and political circumstances, a monetary system has emerged that rests on a unit of account and on outside money at least certified, and generally more than that, by government. Such a system will not easily be dislodged or replaced by a strictly private system.

FREE BANKING

A number of recent authors have argued that the historical experience with "free banking" is less unfavorable than suggested by Friedman and other authors. Lawrence White has reexamined the experience in Scotland for the period up to 1845 and concluded that it supports "the case for thorough deregulation" of banking.[25] Rockoff, Rolnick and Weber, and King have reexamined the experience in the United States prior to the Civil War and come to a similar conclusion, arguing that prior studies of this period have grossly exaggerated the quantitative importance of "wildcat banking," over-issue of depreciated bank notes, and the other ills generally associated with banking in that era.[26]

The experience of Scotland, as most recently described by White, is surely the most favorable. For more than a century and a half Scotland had a system of free banking, with completely free entry and minimal governmental regulation or restraint. Scottish banks were banks of issue as well as of deposit. Their note issues circulated widely and were in practice the dominant medium of circulation. With minor exceptions the issues of different banks—numbering as many as 29 in 1826 and 19 in 1845, just before the end of the era of free banking—circulated at par with one another, thanks to an agreement among the banks to accept one another's notes.[27] Some banks did fail, but holders of their notes suffered negligible, if any, losses. And this system developed entirely by market forces, with government intervention consisting solely in the chartering of three of the banks.

However, before accepting the relevance of this experience to our current situation, it is important to note several special features of Scottish experience: first, it dealt only with inside money. Outside money consisted of either gold or, during the period of suspension of convertibility by the Bank of England (1797–1821), Bank of England notes. Second, as White stresses, shareholders of banks assumed unlimited liability for the obligations of the banks.[28] As a result, bank depositors and holders of bank notes were sheltered from the failure of banks; the whole burden fell on the stockholders. Third, Scotland was an old, established community, with a relatively stable population, so that stockholders consisted in the main of persons who were well known, had considerable private wealth, and valued their own reputations for probity highly enough to honor their obligations.[29] Fourth, while the only equivalent in Scotland itself of a central bank was the extent to which some of the larger banks served as bankers' banks, the Scottish banks had access to the London financial market, which performed the equivalent of some modern central bank functions for Scotland.[30]

For a contrast, consider the experience of the United States from, say, 1791 to 1836, the period spanning the first and second Banks of the United States. New England perhaps came closest to matching Scotland in some of its characteristics, particularly in containing substantial communities with long-settled prominent families possessing much wealth. It was taken for granted that specie was the dominant money and provided the appropriate unit of account. In the main, laissez faire prevailed in banking, despite the existence of the two federal banks, as Hammond calls them.[31] There was nothing that prevented a system from developing along Scottish lines. Yet it did not. Numerous banks were established, which issued bank notes promising to pay specie on demand, yet a wide range of imaginative stratagems were adopted to postpone and impede redemption, and country bank notes circulated in Boston at varying discounts, leading Boston banks to adopt a succession of measures to enforce redemption. The end result was the famous Suffolk Bank system, which developed gradually from about 1820 on. As Hammond remarks: "The Suffolk was in effect the central bank of New England. . . The operators of the Suffolk Bank showed laissez faire at its best."[32] But even here, laissez faire did not lead to unlimited liability as a rule, though there must have been private bankers who subjected themselves to unlimited liability; it did not lead to the kind of orderly, efficient, monetary system that developed in Scotland.

And the experience of the rest of the country is even less favorable to regarding the Scottish experience as highly relevant to the circumstances of the United States in the early decades of the nineteenth century. Various degrees of laissez faire prevailed in the several states, but nowhere did it lead to unlimited liability, freely interconvertible bank notes, security of both note holders and depositors from loss, and the other favorable characteristics of the Scottish banking system.

Rockoff, Rolnick and Weber, and King may well be right that wildcat banking in the first half of the nineteenth century was less widespread and extensive than earlier writers made it out to be. They may also be correct that the bank failures that occurred owed far more to the legal conditions imposed on bank note issues—namely, that they be "backed" by state or U.S bonds—and the subsequent depreciation in value of the bonds of a number of states than to irresponsible wildcat banking. Yet none of their evidence is directly relevant to the question of how banking and currency issue would have developed in the absence of state legislation.

Further, conditions have changed drastically in the past century and a half in ways that are particularly relevant to the question whether financial intermediaries should be prohibited from issuing inside money in the form of hand-to-hand currency (our point 2(a) in the first section above). We are no longer dealing with a sparsely settled country in which travel is slow and communication between distant points involves long delays. We now have instant communication and rapid means of transport. Book entries have replaced the physical transfer of currency or specie as the principal means of discharging monetary obligations. From being the primary medium of exchange, currency has become the counterpart of a minor fraction of aggregate transactions. Private institutions, both banks and nonbanks, issue inside money in the form of traveler's checks redeemable on demand in outside money. The value of such traveler's checks outstanding is now included in the official estimates of all monetary aggregates broader than the monetary base (equal to outside money).[33] The possibility—and reality—of fraud by financial institutions remains, but under current conditions it seems unlikely to be more serious for hand-to-hand currency than for deposits.

What was a burning issue a century or two ago has therefore become a relatively minor issue today. Moreover, the arguments by Klein and Hayek discussed in the preceding section are far more persuasive with respect to permitting the issuance of hand-to-hand inside money than with respect to the possibility that the private market might produce fiduciary outside money, i.e., a noncommodity outside money. While we therefore see no reason currently to prohibit banks from issuing hand-to-hand currency, there is no pressure by banks or other groups to gain that privilege. The question of government monopoly of hand-to-hand currency is likely to remain a largely dead issue.

The more important questions currently are the other two under this heading: namely, the restrictions, if any, that government should impose on financial intermediaries and the necessity or desirability of a "lender of last resort." Whatever conclusions one may reach about these issues, it seems to us, would currently be valid regardless of the form of the liabilities issued by the financial intermediaries.

In respect of these questions, conditions have changed much less drastically—as the recent liquidity crises arising out of the problems of Continental Illinois Bank and the failure of Home State Savings in Ohio vividly illustrate. These liquidity crises are of the same genus as those that occurred repeatedly during the nineteenth century. Their very different outcomes—no significant spread to other institutions in the Continental Illinois episode; the permanent closing of many Ohio savings and loans and temporary closing of all of them in the quantitatively far smaller Ohio episode—reflect the different way they were handled—and that too evokes historical echoes.

Governor Celeste of Ohio would have benefited greatly from reading and following Walter Bagehot's famous advice on how to handle an "internal drain": "A panic," he wrote, "in a word, is a species of neuralgia, and according to the rules of science you must not starve it. The holders of the cash reserve must be ready not only to keep it for their own liabilities, but to advance it most freely for the liabilities of others."[34]

The run on the Ohio savings and loan associations precipitated by the failure of Home State Savings could have been promptly stemmed if Bagehot's advice had been followed. It was only necessary for Governor Celeste to arrange with the Federal Reserve bank of Cleveland and the commercial banks of Ohio—who were apparently more than willing—to lend currency and its equivalent to the savings and loans on the collateral of their temporarily illiquid but sound assets. Once the savings and loans demonstrated their ability to meet all demands of depositors for cash, the unusual demand would have evaporated—as many historical examples demonstrate, including, most recently, the stemming of the liquidity crisis following the Continental Illinois episode.

Instead, Governor Celeste blundered by declaring a savings and loan holiday, repeating the mistaken Federal Reserve policies of 1931 to 1933, ending in the 1933 bank holiday. As in that case, the final result of not recognizing the differences between a liquidity and a solvency crisis will doubtless be the failure or liquidation of many savings and loans that would have been sound and solvent in the absence of the savings and loan holiday.

These episodes show that what used to be called "the inherent instability" of a fractional reserve banking system is, unfortunately, still alive and well. What they do not show, and what is still an open question, is whether a government "lender of last resort"—a central bank—is necessary and desirable as a cure. It did not prove to be a cure in the United States in the 1930s; it did in the Continental Illinois case, as well as in some earlier episodes. And, whether a satisfactory cure or not, is the emergence of a "lender of last resort" a likely or unavoidable consequence of financial development?

In a recent paper, Charles Goodhart, after surveying a wide range of historical evidence, including the studies we have referred to earlier, concludes that the emergence of lenders of last resort in the form of central banks was a natural and desirable development arising from the very characteristics of a fractional reserve banking system. The theoretical argument is straightforward and well known. It rests on the distinction, already referred to, between a liquidity and solvency crisis. A bank or any other institution faces a problem of *solvency* if its liabilities exceed the value of its assets. The magnitude of the problem is measured by the difference between the two. That difference may be a small fraction of total liabilities, perhaps even less than the equity of the shareholders, so that if the assets could be liquidated in an orderly fashion the institution could pay off all other liabilities in full or for that matter continue as a going institution. The special feature of a fractional reserve bank is that the bulk of its liabilities are payable on demand—either by contract or usage. Hence, even in the special case assumed, it will face a *liquidity* problem if its depositors demand payment. Moreover, the bank's liquidity problem will be far larger in magnitude than its solvency problem.[35] It cannot satisfy its depositors unless it can in some way convert its temporarily illiquid assets into cash.

A liquidity problem is not likely to remain confined to a single bank. The difficulty of one bank gives rise to fears about others, whose depositors, not well informed about the banks' condition, seek to convert their deposits into cash. A full-blown liquidity crisis of major dimensions can be prevented only if depositors can somehow be reassured. An individual bank may be able to reassure its depositors by borrowing cash on the collateral of its sound assets from other banks and meeting all demands on it. But if the crisis is widespread, that recourse is not available. Some outside source of cash is necessary. A central bank with the power to create outside money is potentially such a source.

After the Federal Reserve in the early 1930s failed to perform the function for which it had been established, the United States enacted federal deposit insurance as an alternative way to reassure depositors and thereby prevent a widespread liquidity crisis. That device worked effectively for decades, so long as banks were closely regulated—and incidentally sheltered from competition—and so long as inflation remained moderate and relatively stable. It has become less and less effective as deregulation proceeded in an environment of high and variable inflation. In the Continental Illinois case, it had to be supplemented by the Federal Reserve as lender of last resort.

Insurance of depositors against bank insolvency is of a magnitude that is well within the capacity of private casualty insurance. It could allow for differences among banks in the riskiness of their assets much more effectively than government insurance.[36]

A liquidity crisis, whether or not it arises out of an insolvency crisis, as it did with Continental Illinois and Home State Savings of Ohio, and whether or not it spreads to solvent banks, is a different matter. In the United States, prior to the Federal Reserve, it was dealt with by a concerted agreement among banks to suspend convertibility of deposits into cash—to pay deposits only "through the clearing house." In some other countries, such as Canada, nationwide branch banks (subject to extensive government regulation) have preserved confidence sufficiently to avoid liquidity crises.

The United States has been almost unique in preserving a unit banking system with numerous independent banks. The current pressures for deregulation and the widening competition in financial intermediation is changing that situation. The barriers against interstate banking are weakening and very likely will ultimately fall completely. Such "nonbanks" as Sears Roebuck, Merrill-Lynch, and so on, in most respects are the equivalent of nationwide branch banks. These developments, as they mature, will simultaneously lessen the probability of liquidity crises and increase the magnitude and severity of those that occur. It is therefore far from clear what implications they have for the lender of last resort function.

Vera Smith rightly concluded: "A central bank is not a natural product of banking development. It is imposed from outside or comes into being as a result of Government favors."[37] However, as Goodhart's exhaustive survey of the historical experience indicates, a central bank or its equivalent, once established, reluctantly assumed the responsibility of serving as a lender of last resort because of the reality or possibility of a liquidity crisis.[38] What is impressive about his evidence is the wide range of circumstances—in respect of political and economic arrangements—and the long span of time for which that has proved the outcome.

In practice, the lender of last resort function has been combined with control over government outside money. Such a combination has obvious advantages. However, in principle the two functions could be separated, and some proposals for monetary reform would require such separation, if the government were to continue to serve as a lender of last resort.[39]

The existence of a lender of last resort has clearly enabled banks having access to the lender to operate on thinner margins of capital and cash reserves than they would otherwise have deemed prudent. This fact has been used as an argument both for and against the government assuming lender of last resort functions—for, as a way of lowering the cost of financial intermediation; against, as providing an implicit subsidy to financial intermediation. It has also led to the imposition of required reserve ratios, which has turned a subsidy into a tax by increasing the demand for non-interest-bearing outside money.

Deregulation of financial intermediaries so that they are free to pay whatever interest is required to obtain funds and to offer a variety of services over broad geographical areas seems clearly desirable on grounds of market efficiency. The open question is whether that is feasible or desirable without a continued role for government in such matters as requiring registration, provision of information, and the imposition of capital or reserve requirements. Moreover, certainly during a transition period, deregulation increases the danger of liquidity crises and so may strengthen the case for a governmental lender of last resort.[40] That role could perhaps be phased out if market developments provided protection through insurance or otherwise against the new risks that might arise in a deregulated financial system.

Goodhart's argument that such an outcome, whether desirable or not, is not achievable, can be put to the test, by enlarging the opportunities for private insurance of deposit liabilities. If such insurance became widespread, risk-adjusted premiums could render regulatory restrictions unnecessary. It is more difficult to envision the market arrangements that would eliminate the pressure for a government lender of last resort.

The Future of Fiat Money

As noted earlier, the nations of the world are for the first time in history essentially unanimously committed to a purely fiat monetary standard. Will Fisher's 1911 generalization that "irredeemable paper money has almost invariably proved a curse to the country employing it" hold true for the current situation? In some ways that seems to us the most interesting and important current scientific question in the monetary area. How it is answered will largely determine the relevance of the issues discussed in the preceding two sections.

We do not believe it is possible to give a confident and unambiguous answer. The experience of such countries as Argentina, Brazil, Chile, Mexico, and Israel are contemporary examples of Fisher's generalization, but they are all lesser developed countries that, except for chronology, may have more in common with the countries Fisher had in mind than with the more advanced Western countries. The experience of those more advanced countries—Japan, the United States, and the members of the Common Market—gives grounds for greater optimism. The pressures on government that led to the destruction of earlier irredeemable paper moneys are every bit as strong today in these countries as earlier—most clearly, the pressure to obtain resources for government use without levying explicit taxes. However, developments in the economy, and in financial markets in particular, have produced counter-pressures that reduce the political attractiveness of paper money inflation.

The most important such developments, we believe, are the greater sensitivity and sophistication of both the financial markets and the public at large. There has indeed been an information revolution, which has greatly reduced the cost of acquiring information and has enabled expectations to respond more rapidly and accurately to developments.

Historically, inflation has added to government resources in three ways: first, through the paper money issues themselves (i.e., the implicit inflation tax on outside money holdings); second, through the unvoted increase in explicit taxes as a result of bracket creep; third, by the reduction in the real value of outstanding debt issued at interest rates that did not include sufficient allowance for future inflation. The economic, political, and financial developments of recent decades have eroded the potency of all three sources of revenue.

Though outside money remained remarkably constant at about 10 percent of national income from the middle of the past century to the Great Depression, and then rose sharply to a peak of about 25 percent in 1946, it has been on a declining trend since the end of World War II, and is currently about 7 percent of national income. However, for a modern society, with the current level of government taxes and spending, this component is perhaps the least important of the three. Even if outside money as a fraction of income did not decline as a result of inflation, which it unquestionably would, a 10 percent per year increase in outside money would yield as revenue to the government only about seven-tenths of 1 percent of national income.

The second component of revenue has very likely been more important. Past rates of inflation have subjected low and moderate income persons to levels of personal income tax that could never have been voted explicitly. However, the result has been political pressure that has led to the indexation of the personal income tax schedule for inflation, which largely eliminates this source of revenue.

The third component has also been extremely important. At the end of World War II, the funded federal debt amounted to 6 percent more than a year's national income. By 1967 it was down to about 32 percent of national income despite repeated "deficits" in the official federal budget. Since then it has risen as deficits have continued and increased, but even so only to about 36 percent currently. The reason for the decline in the deficit ratio was partly real growth but mostly the reduction through inflation in the real value of debt that had been issued at interest rates that *ex post* proved negative in real terms.

The potency of this source of revenue has been sharply eroded by the developments in the financial markets referred to earlier. Market pressures have made it difficult for the government to issue long-term debt at low nominal rates. One result is that the average term to maturity of the federal debt has tended to decline. Except under wartime conditions, it is far more difficult to convert interest rates on short-term debt into *ex post* negative real rates by unanticipated inflation than to do so for long-term debt. And for both short- and long-term debt, producing unanticipated inflation of any magnitude for any substantial period has become far more difficult after several decades of historically high and variable inflation than it was even a decade or so ago, when the public's perceptions still reflected the effect of a relatively stable price level over long periods.

In the United Kingdom, the resort to government bonds adjusted for inflation eliminates more directly the possibility that government can benefit from *ex post* negative real interest rates. There have been pressures on the U.S. Treasury to issue similar securities. Those pressures would undoubtedly intensify if the United States were again to experience high and variable inflation.

Perhaps if, instead, we experienced several decades of a relatively stable long-run price level, asset holders would again be lulled into regarding nominal interest rates as equivalent to real interest rates. But that is certainly not the case today.

To summarize, inflation has become far less attractive as a political option. Given a voting public very sensitive to inflation, it may currently be politically profitable to establish monetary arrangements that will make the present inconvertible paper standard an exception to Fisher's generalization.

That is a source of promise; it is far from a guarantee that Fisher's generalization is obsolete. Governments have often acted under short-run pressures in ways that have had strongly adverse long-run consequences. Israel today offers a conspicuous example. It continues to resort to inflation under conditions that make inflation a poor source of revenue, if, indeed, not itself a drain.

CONCLUSION

To return to where we started, Friedman's list of the good reasons why "monetary arrangements have seldom been left to the market," what alterations are indicated by the experience and writings of the past quarter century?

Point (1), "the resource cost of a pure commodity currency and hence its tendency to become purely fiduciary," has in one sense fully worked itself out. All money is now fiduciary. Yet the resource cost has not been eliminated; it remains present because private individuals hoard precious metals and gold and silver coins as a hedge against the inflation that they fear may result from a wholly fiduciary money. To go farther afield, a new resource cost has been added because a purely fiduciary currency reduces the long-run predictability of the price level. That cost takes the form of resources employed in futures and other financial markets to provide the additional hedging facilities demanded by individuals, business enterprises, and governmental bodies. It would be a paradoxical reversal if these new forms of resource costs produced pressure for the reintroduction of commodity elements into money as a way to reduce the resource costs of the monetary system. We do not know of any study that has tried to compare the resource costs of the pre–World War I monetary system and the post-1971 monetary system. That is a challenging task for research.[41]

Point (2), "the peculiar difficulty of enforcing contracts involving promises to pay that serve as a medium of exchange and of preventing fraud in respect of them," remains alive and well, as the recent Continental Illinois and Ohio savings and loan episodes demonstrate, and, more indirectly, the much-publicized failures in the government bond market. However, the character of the difficulty has changed. It no longer seems any more serious for hand-to-hand currency than for deposits or other monetary or quasi-monetary promises to pay. Moreover, it is now taken for granted that governments (i.e., taxpayers) will completely shield holders of deposit liabilities from loss, whether due to fraud or other causes. The improvements in communication and in the extent and sophistication of financial markets have in some respects increased, in others decreased, the difficulty of enforcing contracts and preventing fraud. They have certainly made it more difficult politically for governments to remain uninvolved.

Point (3), "the technical monopoly character of a pure fiduciary currency which makes essential the setting of some external limit on its amount," has been questioned, far more persuasively, we believe, for currencies convertible into a commodity, than for a pure fiduciary currency. We continue to believe that the possibility that private issuers can (in either sense of that term) provide competing, efficient, and safe fiduciary currencies with no role for governmental monetary authorities remains to be demonstrated. As a result we believe that this is the most important challenge posed by the elimination of a commodity-based outside money.

Point (4), "the pervasive character of money" and the "important effects on parties other than those directly involved" in the issuance of money, has not been questioned. What has been questioned, and remains very much an open question, is what institutional arrangements would minimize those third-party effects. A strong case can be made that government involvement has made matters worse rather than better both directly and indirectly because the failure of monetary authorities to pursue a stable noninflationary policy renders performance by private intermediaries equally unstable. As yet, there has developed no consensus on desirable alternative arrangements, let alone any effective political movement to adopt alternative arrangements.

Our own conclusion—like that of Walter Bagehot and Vera Smith—is that leaving monetary and banking arrangements to the market would have produced a more satisfactory outcome than was actually achieved through governmental involvement. Nevertheless, we also believe that the same forces that prevented that outcome in the past will continue to prevent it in the future. Whether those forces produce or prevent major changes in monetary institutions will depend on developments in the monetary area in the next several decades—and that crystal ball is rendered even more murky than usual by our venture into largely unexplored monetary terrain.

The failure to recognize that we are in unexplored terrain gives an air of unreality and paradox to the whole discussion of private money and free banking. Its basis was well expressed by Walter Bagehot:

We are so accustomed to a system of banking, dependent for its cardinal function on a single bank, that we can hardly conceive of any other. But the natural system—that which would have sprung up if Government had let banking alone—is that of many banks of equal or not altogether unequal size...

I shall be at once asked—Do you propose a revolution? Do you propose to abandon the one-reserve system, and create anew a many-reserve system? My plain answer is, that I do not propose it: I know it would be childish...[A]n immense system of credit, founded on the Bank of England as its pivot and its basis, now exists. The English people and foreigners, too, trust it implicitly...The whole rests on an instinctive confidence generated by use and years...[I]f some calamity swept it away, generations must elapse before at all the same trust would be placed in any other equivalent. A many-reserve system, if some miracle should put it down in Lombard Street, would seem monstrous there. Nobody would understand it, or confide in it. *Credit is a power which may grow, but cannot be constructed* [italics added].[42]

Substitute "unit of account" or "outside money" for "credit" in the italicized sentence and it is directly relevant to the outside money issue. What has happened to the role of gold since Bagehot wrote, the way in which it has been replaced by a purely fiat money, is a striking application of Bagehot's proposition. It took "generations" for confidence in gold "generated by use and years" to erode and for confidence to develop in the pieces of paper which, for many years after it was meaningless, continued to contain the promise that "The United States of America will pay to the bearer on demand ___ dollars," or words to that effect. Now they simply state "Federal Reserve Note," "One Dollar" or "___ Dollars" plus the statement "This note is legal tender for all debts, public and private." And even now, a half century after the effective end of the domestic convertibility of government-issued money into gold, the Federal Reserve still lists the "Gold Stock," valued at an artificial "legal" price among the "Factors Supplying Reserve Funds." Like old soldiers, gold does not die; it just fades away.

Similarly, as already noted, there are no effective legal obstacles currently in the United States to the development of a private "real" (i.e., inflation adjusted) standard as an alternative to the paper dollar, yet, absent a major monetary catastrophe, it will take decades for such an alternative to become a serious competitor to the paper dollar, if it ever does.

The element of paradox arises particularly with respect to the views of Hayek.[43] His latest works have been devoted to explaining how gradual cultural evolution—a widespread invisible hand process—produces institutions and social arrangements that are far superior to those that are deliberately constructed by explicit human design. Yet he recommends in his recent publications on competitive currencies replacing the results of such an invisible hand process by a deliberate construct—the introduction of currency competition. This paradox affects us all. On the one hand, we are observers of the forces shaping society; on the other, we are participants and want ourselves to shape society.

If there is a resolution to this paradox, it occurs at times of crisis. Then and only then are major changes in monetary and other institutions likely or even possible. What changes then occur depend on the alternatives that are recognized as available. Decades of academic argument in favor of eliminating Regulation Q and, in a very different area, adopting flexible exchange rates had little or no impact on institutional arrangements until crises made major changes inevitable. The existence of well-articulated cases for these changes made them realistic options.

Similarly, the wide-ranging discussion of possible major monetary reforms will have little effect on the course of events if the present fiat system into which the world has drifted operates in a reasonably satisfactory manner—producing neither major inflations nor major depressions. However, the possibility that it will not do so is very real—particularly that it will fall victim to Fisher's generalization and lead to major inflation. When and if it does, what happens will depend critically on the options that have been explored by the intellectual community and have become intellectually respectable. That— the widening of the range of options and keeping them available—is, we believe, the major contribution of the burst of scholarly interest in monetary reform.

NOTES

1. K. Acheson and J. Chant, "Bureaucratic Theory and the Choice of Central Bank Goals: The Case of the Bank of Canada," *Journal of Money, Credit, and Banking* 5 (1973): 637–55; K. Brunner, "Programmatic Suggestions for a 'Political Economy of Inflation,'" *Journal of Law and Economics* 18 (1976): 851–57; J. M. Buchanan, *Can Policy Activism Succeed? A Public Choice Perspective*, paper presented at the Federal Reserve Bank of St. Louis Conference on The Monetary vs. Fiscal Policy Debate (1984); R. L. Hetzel, *The Formulation of Monetary Policy*, working paper (Federal Reserve Bank of Richmond, Va., 1984); E. J. Kane, "Politics and Fed Policymaking," *Journal of Monetary Economics* 6 (1980): 199–211.

2. F. A. Hayek, *Denationalization of Money* (London: Institute of Economic Affairs, 1976), 2d extended ed. (1978).

3. Milton Friedman and Anna J. Schwartz, *A Monetary History of the United States, 1867–1960* (Princeton, N.J.: Princeton University Press, 1963).

4. Milton Friedman, *A Program for Monetary Stability* (New York: Fordham University Press, 1960).

5. Ibid., p. 4.

6. Ibid., p. 8.

7. B. McCallum, *Bank Deregulation, Accounting Systems of Exchange and the Unit of Account: A Critical Review*, working paper (New York: National Bureau of Economic Research, 1985); L. H. White, "Competitive Payment Systems and the Unit of Account," *American Economic Review* 74 (1984): 699–712.

8. I. Fisher, *The Purchasing Power of Money*, new ed. (New York: Macmillan, 1929), p. 131.

9. Vera C. Smith, *The Rationale of Central Banking* (London: P. S. King, 1936).

10. In his rediscovery and advocacy of a tabular standard, R. W. R. White, former governor of the reserve bank of New Zealand, proposed terming the corresponding unit of account the "Real." See R. W. R. White, "Money and the New Zealand Economy," *Reserve Bank of New Zealand Bulletin* (1979): 371–74; W. Stanley Jevons, in recommending a tabular standrd of which he says, "the difficulties in the way of such a scheme are not considerable," refers to a book by Joseph Lowe (*The Present State of England*) published in 1822 which contains a similar proposal. W. S. Jevons, *Money and the Mechanism of Exchange*, 9th ed. (London: Kegan Paul, 1890).

11. See, for example, G. Brennan and J. M. Buchanan, *Monopoly in Money and Inflation* (London: Institute of Economic Affairs, 1981).

12. One of us has discussed elsewhere some of the issues involved, and possible reforms for the United States. Milton Friedman, "Monetary Policy for the 1980s," in J. H. Moore, ed., *To Promote Prosperity: U.S. Domestic Policy in the mid-1980s* (Stanford: Hoover Institution Press, 1984); also see chapter 22 of this volume.

13. Benjamin Klein, "The Competitive Supply of Money," *Journal of Money, Credit, and Banking* 6 (1974): 513–19.

14. McCallum also makes this point. Op. cit., p. 25.

15. E.g., George Smith money was a widely used medium of exchange in the Middle West of the United States in the 1840s and 1850s. However, when George Smith retired from control of the Wisconsin Marine and Fire Insurance Company, which he created to evade the state of Wisconsin's prohibition of banks of issue, George Smith money went the way of all money. His successors could not resist the temptation of dissipating for short-term gain the "brand name capital" George Smith had built up. See B. Hammond, *Banks and Politics in America* (Princeton, N.J.: Princeton University Press, 1957), p. 613. The Scottish banks discussed by White are another even more impressive example of a competitive issue of convertible money.

16. Hayek, *Denationalization of Money* (1978), p. 112.

17. Benjamin Klein, "Competing Monies," *Journal of Money, Credit, and Banking* 8 (1976): 513–19. See also A. Martino, "Toward Monetary Stability?" *Economia Internazionale* 37 (1984): 1–16.

18. See J. H. McCulloch, "The Ban on Indexed Bonds, 1973–1977," *American Economic Review* 70 (1980): 1018–21.

19. Milton Friedman, "Financial Futures Markets and Tabular Standards," *Journal of Political Economy* 92 (1984): 165–67.

20. R. Triffin, "The European Monetary System: Tombstone or Cornerstone?" in *The International Monetary System: Forty Years after Bretton Woods*, conference series no. 28 (Federal Reserve Bank of Boston, 1984), pp. 150–63.

21. Milton Friedman, "Commodity-Reserve Currency," *Journal of Political Economy* 59 (1951): 203–232. Interestingly, F. A. Hayek was an early supporter of such a proposal. F. A. Hayek, "A Commodity Reserve Currency," *Economic Journal* 53 (1943): 176–84.

22. Roland Vaubel, "The Government's Money Monopoly: Externalities or Natural Monopoly?" *Kyklos* 37 (1984): 27–58.

23. Ibid., p. 57.

24. Ibid., p. 32.

25. L. H. White, *Free Banking in Britain: Theory, Experience, and Debate, 1800–1845* (Mass.: Cambridge University Press, 1984), p. 148.

26. H. Rockoff, *The Free Banking Era: A Reexamination* (New York: Arno Press, 1975); A. J. Rolnick and W. E. Weber, "New Evidence on the Free Banking Era," *American Economic Review* 73 (1983): 1080–91; R. G. King, "On the Economics of Private Money," *Journal of Monetary Economics* 12 (1983): 127–58.

27. White, *Free Banking in Britain*, pp. 35, 37.

28. Ibid., p. 41. Except for the three chartered banks.

29. The extreme example was Adam Smith's patron, the Duke of Buccleigh, who was a stockholder in the ill-fated Ayr bank and suffered a major loss when it failed in 1772.

30. C. A. E. Goodhart, *The Evolution of Central Banks: A Natural Development?*, working paper (London School of Economics, 1985), note 3.

31. Hammond, *Banks and Politics in America*.

32. Ibid., pp. 554, 556.

33. For banks, the Federal Reserve statistics include traveler's checks with demand deposits, so no separate estimate of their amount is available. Traveler's checks of nonbank issuers total about 3 percent of total currency, less than 1 percent of total M1.

34. Walter Bagehot, *Lombard Street* (London: P. S. King, 1873), p. 51.

35. For example, Continental Illinois had total deposit liabilities of close to $30 billion as of December 31, 1983, and nonperforming loans of less than $2 billion. Its solvency problem was still smaller, given the presence of an equity cushion.

36. B. Ely, "No Deposit Reform, No Return to Stable Banking," *Wall Street Journal* (March 5, 1985); idem, *Yes—Private Sector Depositor Protection Is a Viable Alternative to Federal Deposit Insurance*, paper presented at the Conference on Bank Structure and Competition, Chicago, 1985.

37. Smith, *Rationale of Central Banking*, p. 148.

38. Goodhart, *Evolution of Central Banks* (1985).

39. For example, the proposal to freeze the amount of high-powered money. See Friedman, "Monetary Policy for the 1980s," pp. 48–52.

40. This point is stressed by Summers in his comment on King, "On the Economics

of Private Money" (1983). Summers contrasts the possible gain in micro-efficiency of private money with what he regards as the likely loss in macro-efficiency through increased economic instability. However, he simply takes it for granted that government control of money reduces rather than increases economic instability. That is, to put it mildly, far from clear on the basis of historical experience. L. H. Summers, "Comments," *Journal of Monetary Economics* 12 (1983): 159–62.

41. Milton Friedman, "The Resource Cost of Irredeemable Paper Money," *Journal of Political Economy* 94, no. 3 (June 1986): 642–47.

42. Bagehot, *Lombard Street* (1873), pp. 66–67, 68–69.

43. See especially F. A. Hayek, *Law, Legislation and Liberty*, vol. 3, *The Political Order of a Free People* (Chicago: University of Chicago Press, 1979).

Complete Bibliography[†]

OF

Milton Friedman

Books

One of the authors of *Consumer Expenditures in the United States*. Prepared for the National Resources Committee. Washington, D.C.: Government Printing Office, 1939.

With Carl Shoup and Ruth P. Mack. *Taxing to Prevent Inflation*. New York: Columbia University Press, 1943.

With Simon Kuznets. *Income from Independent Professional Practice*. New York: National Bureau of Economic Research, 1945.

Coeditor with H. A. Freeman, Frederick Mosteller, and W. Allen Wallis, and also coauthor of *Sampling Inspection*. New York: McGraw-Hill Book Co., Inc., 1948.

Essays in Positive Economics. Chicago: University of Chicago Press, 1953. Translations: Spanish, 1967; Japanese, 1977.

Editor of *Studies in the Quantity Theory of Money*. Chicago: University of Chicago Press, 1956.

A Theory of the Consumption Function. National Bureau of Economic Research General Series, no. 63. Princeton, N.J.: Princeton University Press, 1957. Translation: Japanese, 1961.

A Program for Monetary Stability. New York: Fordham University Press, 1960. Translations: Spanish, 1962; Japanese, 1963.

Capitalism and Freedom. Chicago: University of Chicago Press, 1962. Translations: Spanish, 1966; Italian, 1967; French, 1971; German, 1971, 1984 (pocketbook ed.);

---

† All publications are listed chronologically.

* Indicates a work which has been reprinted in one of Professor Friedman's books.

Swedish, 1972; Japanese, 1975; Hebrew, 1978; Icelandic, 1982; Russian, 1982; Portuguese, 1984.

Price Theory: A Provisional Text. Chicago: Aldine Publishing Co., 1962. Translations: Spanish, 1966 and 1972 (revised ed.); Portuguese, 1971; Japanese 1972.

With Anna J. Schwartz. *A Monetary History of the United States, 1867–1960*. National Bureau of Economic Research Studies in Business Cycles, no. 12. Princeton, N.J.: Princeton University Press, 1963. (Chapter 7 published separately as *The Great Contraction* in 1965 by Princeton University Press.) Translation of entire book: Italian, 1979.

*Inflation: Causes and Consequences. Bombay: Asia Publishing House, for the Council for Economic Education, 1963. Translation: Portuguese, 1969. Reprinted in *Dollars and Deficits*.

Postwar Trends in Monetary Theory and Policy. Center for Economic Research Lecture Series, no. 5. Athens, Greece: Center for Economic Research, 1963.

**With Robert V. Roosa. *The Balance of Payments: Free versus Fixed Exchange Rates*. Rational Debate Seminar. Washington, D.C.: American Enterprise Institute, 1967. Translation: Spanish, 1970. Friedman's lecture reprinted in *Dollars and Deficits* (but not discussion and rebuttals).

Dollars and Deficits: Inflation, Monetary Policy and the Balance of Payments. Englewood Cliffs, N.J.: Prentice-Hall, Inc., 1968. Translations: French, 1969; Japanese, 1970; Spanish, 1971.

The Optimum Quantity of Money and Other Essays. Chicago: Aldine Publishing Co., 1969. Translation: German, 1970.

With Walter W. Heller. *Monetary vs. Fiscal Policy*. Seventh Annual Arthur K. Salomon Lecture, Graduate School of Business Administration, New York University. New York: W. W. Norton & Co., 1969. Translations: French, 1969; Japanese, 1970.

With Anna J. Schwartz. *Monetary Statistics of the United States*. National Bureau of Economic Research Studies in Business Cycles, no. 20. New York: Columbia University Press, 1970.

*A Theoretical Framework for Monetary Analysis. National Bureau of Economic Research Occasional Paper, no. 112. New York: National Bureau of Economic Research, 1971. Reprinted (with revisions) in *Milton Friedman's Monetary Framework*.

An Economist's Protest: Columns on Political Economy. Glen Ridge, N.J.: Thomas Horton & Daughters, 1972; 2d ed., 1975. (The second edition also published in 1975 under the title *There's No Such Thing as a Free Lunch* by Open Court Publishing Co. of LaSalle, Ill.) Translations of 2d ed.: Italian (abridged), 1978; German, 1979.

With Wilbur J. Cohen. *Social Security: Universal or Selective?* Rational Debate Seminar. Washington, D.C.: American Enterprise Institute, 1972.

Money and Economic Development. New York: Greenwood Press, Praeger, 1973.

Teorija novica i monetaria politika. Belgrade, Yugoslavia: Izdavačo Preduzeće "Rad," 1973. (A collection in Serbo-Croatian translation of articles originally published in English.)

Milton Friedman's Monetary Framework: A Debate with His Critics. Edited by Robert J.

Gordon. Chicago: University of Chicago Press, 1974. Translations: Spanish, 1978; Japanese, 1978.

Contestazione liberale. Translated by Antonio Martino and Massimo del Buono. Florence: Sansoni, 1975. (Italian translation of the *Playboy* interview, a talk entitled "Doing Good," and some of chap. 8 and all of chap. 12 of the first edition of *An Economist's Protest*.)

Price Theory (revised and enlarged version of *Price Theory: A Provisional Text*). Chicago: Aldine Publishing Co., 1976. Translations: German, 1977; French, 1983.

Tax Limitation, Inflation and the Role of Government. Dallas, Texas: The Fisher Institute, 1978.

With Rose D. Friedman. *Free to Choose*. New York: Harcourt Brace Jovanovich, Inc., 1980. Translations: French, 1980; German, 1980; Japanese, 1980; Norwegian, 1980; Spanish, 1980; Swedish, 1980; Danish, 1981; Italian, 1981; Portuguese, 1981; Chinese, 1982; Finnish, 1982.

*With Anna Jacobson Schwartz. *From New Deal Banking Reform to World War II Inflation*. Princeton, N.J.: Princeton University Press, 1980. Chapters 8–10 of *A Monetary History of the United States*.

With Anna J. Schwartz. *Monetary Trends in the United States and the United Kingdom: Their Relation to Income, Prices, and Interest Rates, 1867–1975*. Chicago: University of Chicago Press, 1982.

Bright Promises, Dismal Performance: An Economist's Protest. Edited with an Introduction and Notes by William R. Allen. San Diego, New York, and London: Harcourt Brace Jovanovich, 1983. Translation: Japanese, 1984.

With Rose Friedman. *Tyranny of the Status Quo*. San Diego, New York, and London: Harcourt Brace Jovanovich, 1984. Translations: French, 1984; Japanese, 1984; Norwegian, 1984; Portuguese, 1985.

OTHER PUBLICATIONS

"Professor Pigou's Method for Measuring Elasticities of Demand from Budgetary Data." *Quarterly Journal of Economics* 1 (November 1934): 151–63.

Review of *Seasonal Variations in Industry and Trade* by Simon Kuznets. *Journal of Political Economy* 43 (December 1935): 830–32.

One of four editors of Frank H. Knight, *The Ethics of Competition*. London and New York: George Allen & Unwin, Ltd., 1935.

"Further Notes on Elasticity of Substitutions: Note on Dr. Machlup's Article." *Review of Economic Studies* 3 (February 1936): 147–48.

With Hildegarde Kneeland and Erika Schoenberg. "Plans for a Study of the Consumption of Goods and Services by American Families." *Journal of the American Statistical Association* 31 (March 1936): 135–40.

"Marginal Utility of Money and Elasticities of Demand." *Quarterly Journal of Economics* 50 (May 1936): 523–33.

Review of *Cyclical Fluctuations in Commodity Stocks* by Ralph H. Blodgett. *Journal of Political Economy* 44 (December 1936): 642–43.

Editor and minor contributor to *Studies in Income and Wealth*, vols. 1–3. New York: National Bureau of Economic Research, 1937, 1938, and 1939.

"The Use of Ranks to Avoid the Assumption of Normality Implicit in the Analysis of Variance." *Journal of the American Statistical Association* 32 (December 1937): 675–701.

"Mr. Broster on Demand Curves." *Journal of the Royal Statistical Society* 101, part 2 (1938): 450–54.

With Simon Kuznets. "Income from Independent Professional Practice, 1929–36." *National Bureau of Economic Research Bulletin*, no. 72–73 (January 1939).

Review of *The Income Structure of the United States* by Maurice Leven. *Journal of the American Statistical Association* 34 (March 1939): 224–25.

"A Comparison of Alternative Tests of Significance for the Problem of m Rankings." *Annals of Mathematical Statistics* 11 (March 1940): 86–92.

Review of *Business Cycles in the United States of America, 1919–32* by J. Tinbergen. *American Economic Review* 30 (September 1940): 657–60.

Review of *Monopolistic Competition and General Equilibrium* by Robert Triffin. *Journal of Farm Economics* 23 (February 1941): 389–90.

With W. Allen Wallis. "The Empirical Derivation of Indifference Functions." In *Studies in Mathematical Economics and Econometrics*, edited by O. Lange et al., pp. 175–89. Chicago: University of Chicago Press, 1942.

*"Discussion of 'The Inflationary Gap' by Walter Salant." *American Economic Review* 32 (June 1942): 314–20. Reprinted in *Essays in Positive Economics*.

"The Spendings Tax as a Wartime Fiscal Measure." *American Economic Review* 33 (March 1943): 50–62.

Review of *Saving, Investment, and National Income* by Oscar L. Altman. *Review of Economic Statistics* 26 (May 1944): 101–102.

*"Lange on Price Flexibility and Employment." *American Economic Review* 36 (September 1946): 613–31. Reprinted in *Essays in Positive Economics*.

With George J. Stigler. *Roofs or Ceilings? The Current Housing Problem.* Irvington-on-the-Hudson, N.Y.: Foundation for Economic Education, 1946.

*"Lerner on the Economics of Control." *Journal of Political Economy* 55 (October 1947): 405–16. Reprinted in *Essays in Positive Economics*.

"Utilization of Limited Experimental Facilities When the Cost of Each Measurement Depends on Its Magnitude." In *Techniques of Statistical Analysis*, edited by C. Eisenhart, M. W. Hastay, and W. A. Wallis, chap. 9, pp. 319–28. New York and London: McGraw-Hill Book Co., Inc., 1947.

"Planning an Experiment for Estimating the Mean and Standard Deviation of a Normal Distribution from Observations on the Cumulative Distribution." In *Techniques of Statistical Analysis*, chap. 11, pp. 339–52.

With L. J. Savage. "Planning Experiments Seeking Maxima." In *Techniques of Statistical Analysis*, chap. 13, pp. 363–72.

With Harold Hotelling, Walter Bartky, W. Edwards Deming, and Paul Hoel. "The Teaching of Statistics," a Report of the Institute of Mathematical Statistics Committee on the Teaching of Statistics. *Annals of Mathematical Statistics* 19 (March 1948): 95–115.

Review of *Cycles: The Science of Prediction* by Edward R. Dewey and Edwin F. Dakin. *Journal of the American Statistical Association* 43 (March 1948): 139–41.

Foreword to *Analysis of Wisconsin Income* by Frank A. Hanna, Joseph A. Pechman, and Sidney M. Lerner. Studies in Income and Wealth, vol. 9. New York: National Bureau of Economic Research, 1948.

*"A Monetary and Fiscal Framework for Economic Stability." *American Economic Review* 38 (June 1948): 245–64. Reprinted in *Essays in Positive Economics*.

With L. J. Savage. "The Utility Analysis of Choices Involving Risk." *Journal of Political Economy* 56 (August 1948): 270–304.

Discussion of "Liquidity and Uncertainty." *American Economic Review, Papers and Proceedings* 39 (May 1949): 196–201.

"'Rejoinder' to 'Professor Friedman's Proposal': Comment." *American Economic Review* 39 (September 1949): 949–55.

*"The Marshallian Demand Curve." *Journal of Political Economy* 57 (December 1949): 463–95. Reprinted in *Essays in Positive Economics*.

"Does Monopoly in Industry Justify Monopoly in Agriculture?" *Farm Policy Forum* 3 (June 1950): 5–8.

With Emile Despres, Albert G. Hart, P. A. Samuelson, and Donald H. Wallace. "The Problem of Economic Instability." *American Economic Review* 40 (September 1950): 505–38.

"Wesley C. Mitchell as an Economic Theorist." *Journal of Political Economy* 58 (December 1950): 465–93.

"Some Comments on the Significance of Labor Unions for Economic Policy." In *The Impact of the Union*, edited by David McCord Wright, pp. 204–34. New York: Harcourt Brace & Co., 1951.

Comment on "Research in the Size Distribution of Income," a paper by Dorothy Brady. In *Conference on Research in Income and Wealth*, pp. 55–60. Studies in Income and Wealth, vol. 13. New York: National Bureau of Economic Research, 1951.

Comment on "Postwar Changes in the Income of Identical Consumer Units," a paper by George Katona and Janet Fisher. In *Conference on Research in Income and Wealth*, pp. 119–22.

Comment on "A Test of an Econometric Model for the United States, 1921–1947." In *Conference on Business Cycles*, pp. 107–14. New York: National Bureau of Economic Research, 1951.

"Neoliberalism and Its Prospects." *Farmand* (Oslo, Norway), February 17, 1951, pp. 89–93.

*"Commodity-Reserve Currency." *Journal of Political Economy* 59 (June 1951): 203–32. Reprinted in *Essays in Positive Economics*.

*"Comments on Monetary Policy." *Review of Economic Statistics* 33 (August 1951): 186–91. Reprinted in *Essays in Positive Economics*.

*"Les Effets d'une politique de plein emploi sur la stabilité économique: Analyse formelle," trans. Jacques Mayer. *Économie Appliquée* 4 (July–December 1951): 441–56. Slightly revised English version reprinted in *Essays in Positive Economics*.

"Liberté d'enterprise aux Etats-Unis." *Société Belge d'Etudes et d'Expansion Bulletin Bimestriel*, no. 148 (November–December 1951): 783–88.

*"The 'Welfare' Effects of an Income Tax and an Excise Tax." *Journal of Political Economy* 60 (February 1952): 25–33. Reprinted in *Essays in Positive Economics*.

*"Price, Income, and Monetary Changes in Three Wartime Periods." *American Economic Review, Papers and Proceedings* 42 (May 1952): 612–25. Reprinted in *The Optimum Quantity of Money and Other Essays*.

"A Reply to C. G. Phipps, 'Friedman's "Welfare" Effects.'" *Journal of Political Economy* 60 (August 1952): 334–36.

"A Method of Comparing Incomes of Families Differing in Composition." In *Conference on Research in Income and Wealth*, pp. 9–20. Studies in Income and Wealth, vol. 15. New York: National Bureau of Economic Research, 1952.

Comments. In U.S. Congress, Joint Committee on the Economic Report, *Monetary Policy and the Management of the Public Debt: Replies to Questions*. 82d Cong., 2d sess., S. Doc. no. 123, part 2. Washington, D.C., 1952, pp. 1019–1020, 1069, 1105, 1117, 1131, and 1299–1301.

With L. J. Savage. "The Expected Utility Hypothesis and the Measurability of Utility." *Journal of Political Economy* 60 (December 1952): 463–74.

Discussion on *A Survey of Contemporary Economies*. *American Economic Review, Papers and Proceedings* 43 (May 1953): 445–48.

"Choice, Chance, and the Personal Distribution of Income." *Journal of Political Economy* 61 (August 1953): 277–92.

"Rejoinder to Henry M. Oliver, 'Economic Advice and Political Limitations.'" *Review of Economics and Statistics* 35 (August 1953): 252.

*"Why the Dollar Shortage?" *The Freeman* 4, no. 6 (December 14, 1953). Reprinted in *Dollars and Deficits*.

"A Reply to Martin J. Bailey, 'The Marshallian Demand Curve.'" *Journal of Political Economy* 62 (June 1954): 261–66.

*"Why the American Economy Is Depression Proof." *Nationalekonomiska föreningens förhandlingar* (Stockholm), no. 3 (1954): 58–77. Reprinted in *Dollars and Deficits*.

"The Reduction of Fluctuations in the Incomes of Primary Producers: A Critical Comment." *Economic Journal* 64 (December 1954): 698–703.

Comment on "Survey of the Empirical Evidence on Economies of Scale," a paper by Caleb Smith. In *Business Concentration and Price Policy*, pp. 230–38. A Report of the National Bureau of Economic Research. Princeton, N.J.: Princeton University Press, 1955.

"Liberalism, Old Style." In *1955 Collier's Year Book*, pp. 360–63. New York, 1955.

"The Role of Government in Education." In *Economics and the Public Interest*, edited by Robert A. Solo, pp. 123–44. New Brunswick, N.J.: Rutgers University Press, 1955.

"Comment." In *Income-Output Analysis: An Appraisal*, pp. 169–74. NBER Studies in Income and Wealth, vol. 18. Princeton, N.J.: Princeton University Press, 1955.

"What All Is Utility?" *Economic Journal* 65 (September 1955): 405–409.

"Comment on Lloyd Ulman, 'Marshall and Friedman on Union Strength.'" *Review of Economics and Statistics* 37 (November 1955): 401–406.

"Leon Walras and His Economic System." *American Economic Review* 45 (December 1955): 900–909.

*"The Quantity Theory of Money—A Restatement." In *Studies in the Quantity Theory of Money*, edited by M. Friedman, pp. 3–21. Chicago: University of Chicago Press, 1956. Reprinted in *The Optimum Quantity of Money and Other Essays*.

"The Indian Alternative," comment on an article by John Strachey. *Encounter* 8 (January 1957): 71–73.

"Consumer Credit Control as an Instrument of Stabilization Policy." In *Consumer Instalment Credit*, part 2, vol. 2: *Conference on Regulation*, pp. 73–103. Washington, D.C.: National Bureau of Economic Research and the Board of Governors of the Federal Reserve System, 1957.

With Gary S. Becker. "A Statistical Illusion in Judging Keynesian Models." *Journal of Political Economy* 65 (February 1957): 64–75.

"Government Control of Consumer Credit." *University of Pennsylvania Bulletin*, Symposium on Consumer Credit and Consumer Spending, 8, no. 13 (March 25, 1957): 65–75.

"Savings and the Balance Sheet." *Bulletin of the Oxford University Institute of Statistics* 19 (May 1957): 125–36.

"Minimizing Government Control over Economic Life and Strengthening Competitive Private Enterprise." In *Problems of United States Economic Development*, vol. 1, pp. 251–57. New York: Committee for Economic Development, 1958.

*"The Supply of Money and Changes in Prices and Output." In *The Relationship of Prices to Economic Stability and Growth*, pp. 241–56. 85th Cong., 2d sess., Joint Committee Print. Washington, D.C., 1958. Reprinted in *The Optimum Quantity of Money and Other Essays*.

"Capitalism and Freedom." In *Essays on Individuality*, edited by Felix Morley, pp. 168–82. Philadelphia: University of Pennsylvania Press, 1958; 2d ed., Indianapolis: The Liberty Fund, 1977, pp. 237–58.

"Reply to Comments on A *Theory of the Consumption Function*." In *Consumer*

Behavior, edited by Lincoln H. Clark, pp. 463–70. New York: Harper & Bros., 1958.

"Foreign Economic Aid: Means and Objectives." *Yale Review* 47 (Summer 1958): 500–16.

With Gary S. Becker. "Reply to Kuh and Johnston." *Review of Economics and Statistics* 40 (August 1958): 298.

With Gary S. Becker. "Reply [to Lawrence Klein]." *Journal of Political Economy* 66 (December 1958): 545–59.

"The Permanent Income Hypothesis: Comment." *American Economic Review* 48 (December 1958): 990–91.

"What Price Inflation?" (Presented at a session of the Division of Finance and Accounting, 38th Annual Meeting of the American Petroleum Institute.) *Finance and Accounting* 38, part 7 (1958): 18–27.

*"The Case for Flexible Exchange Rates." In *Essays on Positive Economics*, pp. 157–87. Excerpted in *Foreign Trade and Finance*, edited by W. R. Allen and C. L. Allen, pp. 313–42. New York: Macmillan, 1959.

"Discussion of 'Wage-Push Inflation,' by Walker A. Morton." (At the 11th Annual Meeting of the Industrial Relations Research Association, December 1958.) In *Proceedings of the Eleventh Annual Meeting of the Industrial Relations Research Association*, 1959, pp. 212–16.

Testimony (on May 25, 1959) and "The Quantity Theory of Money—A Restatement." In U.S. Congress, Joint Economic Committee, *Hearings on Employment, Growth, and Price Levels*, 86th Cong., 1st sess. pursuant to S. Con. Res. 13, part 4, pp. 605–69. Washington, D.C., 1959.

*"The Demand for Money: Some Theoretical and Empirical Results." *Journal of Political Economy* 67 (August 1959): 327–51. Also published as National Bureau of Economic Research Occasional Paper no. 68 (in 1959). Summary under the same title in *American Economic Review, Papers and Proceedings* 49 (May 1959): 525–27. Entire article reprinted in *The Optimum Quantity of Money and Other Essays*.

With T. W. Anderson. "A Limitation of the Optimum Property of the Sequential Probability Ratio Test." In *Contributions to Probability and Statistics*, edited by I. Oklin et al., pp. 57–69. Stanford: Stanford University Press, 1960.

"Comments." In *Consumption and Saving*, vol. 2, edited by Irwin Friend and Robert Jones, pp. 191–206. Philadelphia: University of Pennsylvania Press, 1960.

*"In Defense of Destabilizing Speculation." In *Essays in Economics and Econometrics*, edited by Ralph W. Pfouts, pp. 133–41. Chapel Hill: University of North Carolina Press, 1960. Reprinted in *The Optimum Quantity of Money and Other Essays*.

"Vault Cash and Free Reserves." *Journal of Political Economy* 69 (April 1961): 181–82.

"Monetary Data and National Income Estimates." *Economic Development and Cultural Change* 9 (April 1961): 267–86.

"Capitalism and Freedom." *The New Individualist Review* 1 (April 1961): 3–10.

Excerpts from "Capitalism and Freedom." *Wall Street Journal*, May 1961.

*"The Demand for Money." *Proceedings of the American Philosophical Society* 105 (June 1961): 259–64. Reprinted in *Dollars and Deficits*.

"Economic Aid Reconsidered: A Reply." *Yale Review* 50 (Summer 1961): 533–40.

*"The Lag in Effect of Monetary Policy." *Journal of Political Economy* 69 (October 1961): 447–66. Reprinted in *The Optimum Quantity of Money and Other Essays*.

*"Real and Pseudo Gold Standards." *Journal of Law and Economics* 4 (October 1961): 66–79. Reprinted in *Dollars and Deficits*.

Review of *Inflation* by Thomas Wilson. *American Economic Review* 51 (December 1961): 1051–55.

"An Alternative to Foreign Aid." *Wall Street Journal*, April 1962.

"The Report of the Commission on Money and Credit: An Essay in *petitio principii*." *American Economic Review, Papers and Proceedings* 52 (May 1962): 291–301.

"More on Archibald versus Chicago." *Review of Economic Studies* 30, no. 1 (1962): 65–67.

"The Interpolation of Time Series by Related Series." *Journal of the American Statistical Association* 57 (December 1962): 729–57. Also reprinted as National Bureau of Economic Research Technical Paper no. 16 (in 1962).

*"Should There Be an Independent Monetary Authority?" In *In Search of a Monetary Constitution*, edited by Leland B. Yeager, pp. 219–43. Cambridge: Harvard University Press, 1962. Reprinted in *Dollars and Deficits*.

With David Meiselman. "The Relative Stability of Monetary Velocity and the Investment Multiplier in the United States, 1897–1958." In *Stabilization Policies*, pp. 165–268. A Series of Studies Prepared for the Commission on Money and Credit. Englewood Cliffs, N.J.: Prentice-Hall, Inc., 1963.

"Windfalls, the 'Horizon,' and Related Concepts in the Permanent-Income Hypothesis." In K. Arrow et al., *Measurement in Economics: Studies in Mathematical Economics and Econometrics in Memory of Yehuda Grunfeld*, pp. 3–28. Stanford: Stanford University Press, 1963.

*With Anna J. Schwartz. "Money and Business Cycles." *Review of Economics and Statistics* 45, part 2, supplement (February 1963): 32–64. Reprinted in *The Optimum Quantity of Money and Other Essays*.

"Exchange Rate Policy." *Swarajya* (India), March 30, 1963.

"Price Determination in the U.S. Treasury Bill Market: A Comment." *Review of Economics and Statistics* 45 (August 1963): 318–20.

"The Present State of Monetary Theory." *Economic Studies Quarterly* 14 (September 1963): 1–15.

Statement and Testimony (on November 14, 1963). In U.S. Congress, Joint Economic Committee, *Hearings on the United States Balance of Payments*, 88th Cong., 1st sess., part 3, pp. 451–59, 500–25. Washington, D.C., 1963.

"Can a Controlled Economy Work?" In *The Conservative Papers*, pp. 162–74. Garden City, N.Y.: Doubleday & Co., Anchor Books, 1964.

Statement and Testimony (on March 3, 1964). In U.S. Congress, House, Committee on Banking and Currency, *Hearings on the Federal Reserve System after Fifty Years*, before the Subcommittee on Domestic Finance, 88th Cong., 2d sess., vol. 2, pp. 1133–178, 1220–222. Washington, D.C., 1964.

*"Post War Trends in Monetary Theory and Policy." *National Banking Review* 2 (September 1964): 1–9. Reprinted in *The Optimum Quantity of Money and Other Essays*.

"The Goldwater View of Economics." *New York Times Magazine*, October 11, 1964.

"Comment on 'Collusion in the Auction for Treasury Bills.'" *Journal of Political Economy* 72 (October 1964): 513–14.

With David Meiselman. "Keynes and the Quantity Theory: Reply to Donald Hester." *Review of Economics and Statistics* 46 (November 1964): 369–76.

*"The Monetary Studies of the National Bureau." In *The National Bureau Enters Its 45th Year*, Forty-fourth Annual Report of the National Bureau of Economic Research, 1964, pp. 7–25. Reprinted in *The Optimum Quantity of Money and Other Essays*.

"A Program for Monetary Stability." In *Readings in Financial Institutions*, edited by Marshall D. Ketchum and Leon T. Kendall, pp. 189–209. Boston: Houghton Mifflin, 1965.

Foreword to *Determinants and Effects of Changes in the Stock of Money, 1875–1960*, by Phillip Cagan. National Bureau of Economic Research Studies in Business Cycles, no. 13. New York: Columbia University Press, 1965.

"Social Responsibility: A Subversive Doctrine." *National Review*, August 24, 1965, pp. 721–24.

"Economic Libertarianism: Part 1." In *Proceedings of the Conference on Savings and Residential Financing*, 1965, pp. 10–29.

With David Meiselman. "Reply to Ando and Modigliani and to DePrano and Mayer." *American Economic Review* 55 (September 1965): 753–85.

"Transfer Payments and the Social Security System." *National Industrial Conference Board Record* (September 1965): 7–10.

*"The Lessons of U.S. Monetary History and Their Bearing on Current Policy." Memorandum prepared for Consultants Meeting, Board of Governors of the Federal Reserve System (October 7, 1965). Published in *Dollars and Deficits*.

*"What Price Guideposts?" In *Guidelines, Informal Controls and the Market Place*, edited by George P. Shultz, and Robert Z. Aliber, pp. 17–39. Chicago: University of Chicago Press, 1966. Reprinted in *Dollars and Deficits*.

With Yale Brozen. *The Minimum Wage: Who Pays?* Washington, D.C.: The Free Society Association, Inc., 1966.

———

Newsweek columns from 1966–1983 are reprinted in *There's No Such Thing as a Free Lunch* and *Bright Promises, Dismal Performance*.

Communication on "A Free Market in Education." *The Public Interest*, no. 3 (Spring 1966): 107.

"Hvofor har det fri market så dårlig presse?" *Farmand* (Oslo, Norway), February 12, 1966. English edition: "Why Does the Free Market Have Such a Bad Press?" *Human Events* (Washington, D.C.), July 2, 1966.

"A Tax Subsidy for the Poor?" *Social Service Outlook* 1 (April 1966): 13–14.

*"Current Monetary Policy." Memorandum prepared for Consultants Meeting, Board of Governors of the Federal Reserve System, June 15, 1966. Published in *Dollars and Deficits*.

*"Interest Rates and the Demand for Money." *Journal of Law and Economics* 9 (October 1966): 71–85. Reprinted in *The Optimum Quantity of Money and Other Essays*.

With Paul W. McCracken, Charls E. Walker, and C. Richard Youngdahl. *What Should Monetary and Fiscal Policy Be in the Present Situation?* A Symposium at the Twentieth Annual Conference of Bank Correspondents, First National Bank of Chicago, November 22, 1966.

The Case for the Negative Income Tax: A View from the Right. Washington, D.C.: U.S. Chamber of Commerce, 1966. Talk delivered at the National Symposium on Guaranteed Income sponsored by the U.S. Chamber of Commerce, Washington, D.C., December 9, 1966.

"Why Not a Voluntary Army?" In *The Draft: A Handbook of Facts and Alternatives*, edited by Sol Tax, pp. 200–207. Chicago: University of Chicago Press, 1967.

"Value Judgments in Economics." In *Human Values and Economic Policy*, edited by Sidney Hook, pp. 85–93. New York: New York University Press, 1967.

"L'Économie politique des accords monétaires internationaux" [The political economy of international monetary arrangements]. In *Les Fondements philosophiques des systèmes économiques* (essays in honor of Jacques Rueff), edited by Emil M. Claassen, pp. 384–94. Paris: Payot, 1967. Based on a paper presented at a Mont Pelerin meeting in Stresa, Italy, September 1965, which has not been published in English.

"The Case for the Negative Income Tax." *National Review*, March 7, 1967, pp. 239–41.

"Must We Choose between Inflation and Unemployment?" *Stanford Graduate School of Business Bulletin* 35 (Spring 1967): 10–13, 40, 42.

"Myths That Keep People Hungry." *Harper's Magazine*, April 1967, pp. 16–24.

"The Case for Abolishing the Draft—and Substituting for It an All-Volunteer Army." *New York Times Magazine*, May 14, 1967.

*"The Monetary Theory and Policy of Henry Simons." (The Third Henry Simons Lecture, delivered at the Law School, University of Chicago, May 5, 1967.) *Journal of Law and Economics* 10 (October 1967): 1–13. Reprinted in *The Optimum Quantity of Money and Other Essays*.

"Taxes, Money and Stabilization." *Washington Post*, November 5, 1967, pp. H1, H3.

Statement and Testimony (on February 1, 1968). In U.S. Congress, Senate, Committee on Banking and Currency, *Hearings on the Gold Cover* (on S. 1307, S. 2815, and S. 2857 relating to repeal of the gold reserve requirements for U.S. currency), 90th Cong., 2d sess., pp. 152–66. Washington, D.C., 1966.

"Has the New Economics Failed? An Interview with Milton Friedman." *Dun's Review*, February 1968, pp. 38–39, 93–94, 96.

*"The Role of Monetary Policy." (Presidential Address, American Economic Association Annual Meeting, December 29, 1967.) *American Economic Review* 58 (March 1968): 1–17. Reprinted in *The Optimum Quantity of Money and Other Essays*.

"Money and the Interest Rate." (Address before the University of Miami Savings Institutions Forum, March 11, 1968.) In *Proceedings of the University of Miami Savings Institutions Forum*, 1968.

"The Higher Schooling in America." *The Public Interest*, no. 11 (Spring 1968): 108–12.

"Factors Affecting the Level of Interest Rates." In *Proceedings of the Conference on Savings and Residential Financing*, 1968, pp. 11–27.

"Money: Quantity Theory." In *International Encyclopedia of the Social Sciences*, 1968 ed., pp. 432–47.

"The Case for the Negative Income Tax." In *Republican Papers*, edited by Melvin R. Laird, pp. 202–20. New York: Greenwood Press, Praeger, 1968.

With A. J. Schwartz. "The Definition of Money: Net Wealth and Neutrality as Criteria." *Journal of Money, Credit, and Banking* 1 (February 1969): 1–14.

"Worswick's Criticism of the Correlation Criterion, a Comment." *Journal of Money, Credit, and Banking* 1 (August 1969): 506.

"La política fiscal y monetaria" [Fiscal and monetary policy]. (Based on a talk delivered at the Bache Institutional 1969 Seminar, sponsored by Bache & Co., Geneva, Switzerland, April 25, 1969, which has not been published in English.) *Centro de Estudios Monetarios Latinoamericanos Boletín Mensual* (Mexico) 15 (August 1969): 382–88.

"The Euro-Dollar Market: Some First Principles." *The Morgan Guaranty Survey* (October 1969): 4–15.

"The Schizophrenic Businessman: Friend and Enemy of Free Enterprise." In *Readings in Contemporary Economics*, edited by Leonard Silk, pp. 27–35. New York: McGraw-Hill, 1970.

Statement and Testimony (on October 6, 1969), and Answers to Supplementary Questions Submitted Later. In U.S. Congress, Joint Economic Committee, *Hearings on Economic Analysis and the Efficiency of Government*, before the Subcommittee on Economy in Government, 91st Cong., 1st sess., part 3, pp. 810–29, 873–78. Washington, D.C., 1970.

Statement and Testimony on Family Assistance Programs (on November 7, 1969). In U.S. Congress, House, Committee on Ways and Means, *Hearings on Social*

Security and Welfare Proposals, 91st Cong., 1st sess., part 6, pp. 1944–57. Washington, D.C., 1970.

The Counter-Revolution in Monetary Theory. IEA Occasional Paper no. 33. London: Institute of Economic Affairs, 1970.

"The Market vs. the Bureaucrat." In *Individuality and the New Society,* edited by Abraham Kaplan, pp. 69–88. Seattle: University of Washington Press, 1970.

"Controls on Interest Rates Paid by Banks." *Journal of Money, Credit, and Banking* 2 (February 1970): 15–32.

"Monetary Policy for a Developing Society." *Bank Markazi Iran Bulletin* 9 (March–April 1970): 700–12.

*"A Theoretical Framework for Monetary Analysis." *Journal of Political Economy* 78 (March–April 1970): 193–238. Reprinted in *Milton Friedman's Monetary Framework.*

"Comment on Tobin." *Quarterly Journal of Economics* 84 (May 1970): 318–27.

"Special Interest and the Law." *Chicago Bar Record* (June 1970): 434–41.

"We Must Stand Firm Against Inflation." *Reader's Digest,* June 1970, pp. 202–204, 206.

*"Social Responsibility of Business." *New York Times Magazine,* September 13, 1970. Reprinted in *An Economist's Protest,* 1st ed.

"The New Monetarism: Comment." *Lloyds Bank Review,* no. 98 (October 1970): 52–53.

"Money, Economic Activity, Interest Rates: The Outlook." In *Savings and Loan Annals, 1970,* pp. 60–68. Chicago: U.S. Savings and Loan League, 1971.

*"A Monetary Theory of Nominal Income." *Journal of Political Economy* 79 (March–April 1971): 323–37. Reprinted in *Milton Friedman's Monetary Framework.*

A Theoretical Framework for Monetary Analysis. NBER Occasional Paper no. 112. New York: National Bureau of Economic Research, 1971; distributed by Columbia University Press.

"Is a Nation Justified in Compelling Physical Servitude from an Individual?" Interview in *The Montana Review* (University of Montana) 73 (April 16, 1971): 8–10.

"The Dollar Standard: Its Problems and Prospects." *Montana Business Quarterly* 9 (Spring 1971): 5–12.

"Government Revenue from Inflation." *Journal of Political Economy* 79 (July–August 1971): 846–56.

Statement and Testimony (on September 23, 1971). In U.S. Congress, Joint Economic Committee, *Hearings on the President's New Economic Program,* 92d Cong., 1st sess., part 4, pp. 698–706, 716–43. Washington, D.C., 1971.

*"Doing Good." *Reader's Digest,* October 1971. (Condensed version of commencement address delivered at the University of Rochester, June 6, 1971. Full address published in *An Economist's Protest,* 1st ed.)

*"Morality and Controls" (I and II). *New York Times*, October 28 and 29, 1971, p. 39M. Reprinted in *An Economist's Protest*, 1st and 2d eds.

"The Need for Futures Markets in Currencies." In *The Futures Market in Foreign Currencies*, pp. 6–12. Chicago: International Monetary Market of the Chicago Mercantile Exchange, Inc., 1972.

"A Libertarian Speaks." Interview in *Trial: The National Legal Newsmagazine*, January–February 1972, pp. 22–24.

"Monetary Trends in the United States and the United Kingdom." *The American Economist* 16 (Spring 1972): 4–17.

*"Milton Friedman Responds." Interview in *Business and Society*, no. 1 (Spring 1972), pp. 5–16. Excerpts reprinted in *An Economist's Protest*, 2d ed.

"Have Monetary Policies Failed?" *American Economic Review, Papers and Proceedings* 62 (May 1972): 11–18.

*"Social Security: The Poor Man's Welfare Payment to the Middle Class." *Washington Monthly*, May 1972, pp. 11–13. Reprinted as "Reforming Social Security: The Incongruities of the Present System," *Current*, July–August 1972, pp. 45–50. Adapted from *Social Security: Universal or Selective?*

"Monetary Policy." *Proceedings of the American Philosophical Society* 116 (June 1972): 183–96.

*"Comments on the Critics." *Journal of Political Economy* 80 (September–October 1972): 906–50. Reprinted in *Milton Friedman's Monetary Framework*.

"Monetary Policy in Developing Countries." *Liberian Economic and Management Review* 1 (1972): 3–15. Also published in *Nations and Households in Economic Growth: Essays in Honor of Moses Abramovitz*, edited by Paul A. David and Melvin W. Reder, pp. 265–78. New York: Academic Press, 1974.

"How Much Monetary Growth?" *Morgan Guaranty Survey* (February 1973): 5–10.

*"Interview: Milton Friedman." *Playboy*, February 1973. Reprinted in *An Economist's Protest*, 2d and 3d eds.

"Contemporary Monetary Problems." *Economic Notes* (Monte dei Paschi di Siena) 2 (1973): 5–18.

"See Yourself as V.I.P.'s See You: Milton Friedman." Interview in *Medical Economics*, April 16, 1973.

"Milton Friedman–Sir Dennis Robertson Correspondence." *Journal of Political Economy* 81 (July–August 1973): 1033–1039.

*"The Voucher Idea." *New York Times Magazine*, September 23, 1973. Reprinted in *An Economist's Protest*, 2d ed.

How Well Are Fluctuating Exchange Rates Working? AEI Reprint no. 18. Washington, D.C.: American Enterprise Institute, October 1973. Reprint of text of statement before the Subcommittee on International Exchange and Payments, Joint Economic Committee, U.S. Congress, June 21, 1973.

"A Simple Idea Whose Time Has Come: Proposed California Amendment Would

Allow Citizens to Limit Taxes." *Manion Forum* (South Bend, Ind.), October 28, 1973.

"Facing Inflation." Interview in *Challenge*, November–December 1973, pp. 29–37.

"Monetary Policy: A Letter (II)." Federal Reserve Bank of St. Louis *Review* 56 (March 1974): 20–23. Also published in several other Federal Reserve Bank *Reviews*.

"A Bias in Current Measures of Economic Growth." *Journal of Political Economy* 82, part 1 (March–April 1974): 431–32.

"Commentary." In *International Inflation: Four Commentaries*, pp. 12–18. Chicago: Federal Reserve Bank of Chicago, July 1974. A panel discussion with Andrew Brimmer, George Freeman, and Helmut Schlesinger at the Federal Reserve Bank of Chicago, December 3–4, 1973.

*"Using Escalators to Help Fight Inflation." *Fortune*, July 1974, pp. 94–97, 174, 176. Reprinted in *An Economist's Protest*, 2d ed.

Indexing and Inflation. Washington, D.C.: American Enterprise Institute, 1974. An AEI Round Table with Charls Walker, Robert J. Gordon, and William Fellner, held July 17, 1974.

Monetary Correction. IEA Occasional Paper no. 41. London: Institute of Economic Affairs, 1974. Translation: Spanish, 1975.

"Inflation, Taxation, Indexation." In *Inflation: Causes, Consequences, Cures*, pp. 71–88. IEA Readings no. 14. London: Institute of Economic Affairs, 1974.

"Money." In *Encyclopaedia Britannica*, 15th ed. (1974), pp. 349–56; revision forthcoming in 1987.

"Schools at Chicago." (Remarks delivered at the 54th annual Board of Trustees Dinner for Faculty, University of Chicago, January 9, 1974.) *The University of Chicago Magazine* 67, no. 1 (Autumn 1974): 11–16. Also published in *The University of Chicago Record*, 1974.

Free Markets for Free Men. Selected Paper no. 45. Chicago: University of Chicago, Graduate School of Business, November 1974.

"An Interview with Milton Friedman." *Reason*, December 1974, pp. 4–14.

Is Inflation a Curable Disease? Pittsburgh: Pittsburgh National Bank, Alex C. Walker Educational and Charitable Foundation, and University of Pittsburgh Graduate School of Business, 1975. Alex C. Walker Memorial Lecture, delivered December 5, 1974.

"The National Business Outlook for 1975." (Talk delivered at a one-day conference cosponsored by the Portland State University School of Business Administration and the Portland Chamber of Commerce in cooperation with the Harvard and Stanford Business School Associations, Portland, Oregon, December 16, 1974.) In *Proceedings of the 12th Annual Business and Economic Outlook for 1975*, pp. 1–27.

Inflation and the American Economy. Indianapolis: Economic Club, 1975. Speech delivered before the Economic Club of Indianapolis, January 9, 1975.

"Myth and Reality in Contemporary Public Opinion." (William Arthur Maddox Memorial Lecture, delivered at Rockford College, December 6, 1974.) *Widening Horizons* (Rockford College), vol. 11, no. 3 (March 1975).

Milton Friedman in Australia, 1975. Sydney: Constable & Bain and The Graduate Business Club, 1975. Transcript of two talks delivered in Sydney, Australia: "Inflation and the Management of Western Economies" (on April 1, 1975) and "Can Inflation Be Cured. . . before It Ends Free Society?" (on April 2, 1975).

Milton Friedman en Chile. Santiago: Fundación de Estudios Económicos, Banco Hipotecario de Chile, May 1975. Spanish translation of three talks delivered in Santiago in March 1975.

"Twenty-five Years after the Rediscovery of Money: What Have We Learned? Discussion." *American Economic Review, Papers and Proceedings* 65 (May 1975): 176–79.

"Rich and Poor." In *Whatever Happened to Equality?* edited by John Vaizey, pp. 67–76. London: The British Broadcasting Corporation, 1975.

With John Exter. "The Role and Value of Gold: 2 Views." *Reason*, special financial issue (June 1975), pp. 86–94. (Based on "Gold—Its Value as Money and an Inflation Hedge," remarks given at the Third Annual Monetary and Trade Outlook Conference of the International Monetary Market, Chicago Mercantile Exchange, October 16, 1974.)

*Unemployment versus Inflation? An Evaluation of the Phillips Curve. IEA Occasional Paper no. 44. London: Institute of Economic Affairs, 1975. Reprinted in *Price Theory* (1976 ed.).

"The Future of Capitalism." *SCONA* [Student Conference on National Affairs] XX *Proceedings* (Texas A&M University), 1975, pp. 6–9.

"Five Examples of Fed Double-Talk." *Wall Street Journal*, August 21, 1975.

"Regulation Foe: Milton Friedman Tells Why He Is Against [State Control of Hospital Rates]." Interview in *The Investor-Owned Hospital Review* 8 (August–September 1975): 16–17.

"Gold, Money and the Law: Comments." In *Gold, Money and the Law*, edited by Henry G. Manne and Roger LeRoy Miller, pp. 71–81. Chicago: Aldine Publishing Co., for the Center for Studies in Law and Economics of the University of Miami Law School, 1975.

Testimony and Prepared Statement (on November 6, 1975). In U.S. Congress, Senate, Committee on Banking, Housing and Urban Affairs, *Hearings on Oversight on the Conduct of Monetary Policy Pursuant to House Concurrent Resolution 133*, 94th Cong., 1st sess., pp. 34–49. Washington, D.C., 1975.

"There's No Such Thing as a Free Lunch. . . Ever!" Interview in the *Hillsdale Collegian*, December 4, 1975, pp. 6–8.

Testimony and Prepared Statement (on October 20, 1975). In U.S. Congress, Joint Economic Committee, *Hearings on Jobs and Prices in Chicago*, 94th Cong., 1st sess., pp. 46–50. Washington, D.C., 1976.

Testimony and Prepared Statement (on January 22, 1976). In U.S. Congress, House, Committee on Banking, Currency and Housing, *Hearings on Financial Institutions and the Nation's Economy (FINE): "Discussion Principles,"* before the Subcommittee on Financial Institutions, Supervision, Regulation and Insurance, 94th Cong., 1st and 2d sess., part 3, pp. 2151–192. Washington, D.C., 1976.

Comment: "Are Externalities Relevant?" In E. G. West, *Nonpublic School Aid: The Law, Economics, and Politics of American Education*, pp. 92–93. Lexington, Mass.: Lexington Books, D. C. Heath & Co., 1976.

The Future of the American Economy. Pittsburgh, Pa.: University of Pittsburgh, February 1976. A bicentennial lecture for the American Experience program, University of Pittsburgh, February 5, 1976.

With Anna J. Schwartz. "From Gibson to Fisher." *Explorations in Economic Research* 3 (Spring 1976): 288–91.

"In His Own Words: Economist Milton Friedman Calls the Income Tax 'An Unholy Mess' and Wants to Reform It." Interview in *People Weekly* 5, April 5, 1976, pp. 49–52.

Comment on "Long Run Effects of Fiscal and Monetary Policy on Aggregate Demand," by James Tobin and Willem Buiter. In *Monetarism*, edited by Jerome L. Stein, pp. 310–17. Amsterdam and New York: North-Holland Publishing Co., 1976.

Foreword to *Essays on Hayek*, edited by Fritz Machlup. New York: New York University Press, 1976.

Milton Friedman in South Africa, edited by Meyer Feldberg et al. Cape Town: University of Cape Town Graduate School of Business, and Johannesburg: The Sunday Times, 1976. Contains four lectures delivered in South Africa.

"The Milton Friedman View" (sample of comments during March 22–April 5, 1976 visit to South Africa). *University of Cape Town Graduate School of Business Journal*, 1975–76, pp. 15–18.

"The Fragility of Freedom." (Talk delivered at Brigham Young University, December 11, 1975.) *Brigham Young University Studies* 16 (Summer 1976): 561–74. Also published as "The Line We Dare Not Cross," *Encounter* (London) 47 (November 1976): 8–14. Excerpted under the title "The Path We Dare Not Take," *Reader's Digest*, March 1977, pp. 110–15, and "The Threat to Freedom in the Welfare State," *Business and Society Review*, no. 21 (Spring 1977), pp. 8–16.

"Interview with Economist Milton Friedman." *Christian Science Monitor*, August 26, 1976, p. 17.

Letter of July 11, 1976 to Senator Jesse Helms (on the Gold Clause Amendment), *Congressional Record* 122, no. 148, part 2 (September 28, 1976): S 1691.

"Strategy for Business." *Boardroom Reports* (New York), October 30, 1976, pp. 3–4.

"Homer Jones: A Personal Reminiscence." *Journal of Monetary Economics* 2 (November 1976): 433–36.

"Milton Friedman Speaks." *World Research INK* (San Diego) 1 (December 1976): 1–4.

Adam Smith's Relevance for 1976. Introduction by Joseph J. Spengler. IIER Original

Paper no. 5. Los Angeles: International Institute for Economic Research, December 1976.

From Galbraith to Economic Freedom. Preface by Arthur Seldon. IEA Occasional Paper no. 49. London: Institute of Economic Affairs, January 1977. Also published as *Friedman on Galbraith and on Curing the British Disease.* Preface by Michael Walker. Vancouver, B.C., Canada: Fraser Institute, April 1977. Reprinted in *Tax Limitation, Inflation and the Role of Government.*

"Payroll Taxes, No; General Revenue, Yes." In *The Crisis in Social Security: Problems and Prospects,* pp. 25–30. San Francisco: Institute for Contemporary Studies, 1977.

The Nobel Prize in Economics, 1976. Stanford: Hoover Institution Press, 1977. Remarks about receiving the Nobel Prize, delivered at the Income Distribution Conference sponsored by the Hoover Institution, January 29, 1977.

The Future of Capitalism. Malibu, Calif.: Pepperdine University, 1977. Talk delivered at Pepperdine University, February 9, 1977. Reprinted in *Tax Limitation, Inflation and the Role of Government.* Excerpted under the title "Which Way for Capitalism?" in *Reason,* May 1978, pp. 18–21, 61.

"Where Carter Is Going Wrong: Inteview with Nobel Prize Winner Milton Friedman." *U.S. News & World Report,* March 7, 1977, pp. 20–22.

"Containing Spending." *Society* (Transaction, Inc., Rutgers University) 14 (March–April 1977): 89–92.

"Economic Controls vs. Personal Freedom." *Commitment* (Abbott Laboratories), Spring 1977, pp. 1–3.

With Franco Modigliani. "Discussion of 'The Monetarist Controversy.'" Federal Reserve Bank of San Francisco *Economic Review,* supplement (Spring 1977), pp. 12–26.

"Cost Effectiveness in Health Care Takes Competition, Friedman Thinks." Interview in *Review: The Magazine for Hospital Management* 10, no. 2 (April 1977): 22–24.

The Source of Strength. Dallas, Tex.: Michigan General Corporation, May 1977. Speech delivered before the Presidents' Club of Michigan General Corporation, New Orleans, April 2, 1977.

"Monetary Policy and the Inflation Rate." Letter to the Editor, *The Times* (London), May 2, 1977.

"Milton Friedman, the Chilean Junta and the Matter of Their Association" (an exchange of letters among Nobel Laureates: Friedman with Baltimore and Luria, and with Wald and Pauling). *New York Times,* May 22, 1977, sec. 4, p. 18.

*"Nobel Lecture: Inflation and Unemployment." *Journal of Political Economy* 85 (June 1977): 451–72. Also published as Occasional Paper no. 51 of the Institute of Economic Affairs (London, May 1977) and in *Les Prix Nobel en 1976* (Stockholm: The Nobel Foundation, 1977). Reprinted in *Tax Limitation, Inflation and the Role of Government.*

"A Look at Carter Economics." (Talk delivered at the Alaska Pacific Bank Conference on Alaska Business Issues, June 9, 1977.) *Alaska Business Trends*, pp. 4–10. Anchorage: Alaska Pacific Bank, July 1977.

"*Reason* Interview: Milton Friedman." *Reason*, August 1977, pp. 24–29.

"The Economy and You: What Lies Ahead?" *Stanford Magazine*, Fall–Winter 1977–78, pp. 22–27.

"Liberal McCarthyism: A Personal Experience." (Excerpts of a speech delivered before the Commonwealth Club of California, San Francisco, November 11, 1977.) *The Commonwealth* 71, no. 47 (November 21, 1977): 490–94.

"Time Perspective in Demand for Money." *Scadinavian Journal of Economics* 79, no. 4 (1977): 397–417.

"Capitalism, Socialism, and Democracy: A Symposium." *Commentary* 65 (April 1978): 39–41.

"Has the Tide Turned?" (Hoover Foundation Inaugural Lecture, Strathclyde University Business School, Glasgow, Scotland, delivered April 21, 1978.) *The Listener* (London) 99 (April 27, 1978): 526–28.

*"The Limitations of Tax Limitation." *Policy Review*, Summer 1978, pp. 7–14. Reprinted in *Tax Limitation, Inflation and the Role of Government*.

"Relying on the Free Market." Letter to the Editor, *The Times* (London), August 15, 1978.

Milton Friedman Gives the Answers. Buena Park, Calif.: Americanism Educational League, August 1978.

"Milton Friedman on Floating Rates." Letter to the Editor, *Wall Street Journal*, August 28, 1978.

"Needed: An Investigative Report on Investigative Reporting." *Taxing & Spending* 1, no. 1 (October–November 1978): 15.

A special series of 12 articles in the *San Francisco Chronicle*, January 23 and 30; February 6, 13, 20, and 27; March 6, 13, 20, and 27; April 3 and 10, 1979.

Interview by Harry Farrell. *San Jose Mercury News*, February 11–13, 1979 (a three-part series).

"The Economics of Free Speech." *Ordo*, Band 30 (1979), pp. 221–27.

"Correspondence with Milton Friedman: A Debate on Britain's Policy." *Director* (London), December 1979.

"Prices of Money and Goods Across Frontiers: The £ and $ Over a Century." *The World Economy* 2 (February 1980): 497–511.

"Monetarism: A Reply to the Critics." *The Times* (London), March 3, 1980.

"The Economic Responsibility of Government." In *Milton Friedman and Paul Samuelson Discuss the Economic Responsibility of Government*, pp. 5–14. College Station, Texas: Center for Education and Research in Free Enterprise, Texas A&M University, 1980.

Memorandum to U.K. Treasury and Civil Service Committee on "Enquiry into Monetary Policy," June 11, 1980. In Great Britain, House of Commons (1979–1980), vol. 720, part 1 (July 1980), pp. 55–61.

"Japan—Free to Choose?" (A talk delivered at the Suntory Cultural Foundation's International Symposium on "Free Society and Japan," Tokyo, September 17, 1980.) *Look Japan*, November 10, 1980, pp. 6–7, 9.

"America: Its Economy and Government." (Excerpts of a speech delivered before the Commonwealth Club of California, San Francisco, October 31, 1980.) *The Commonwealth* 74, no. 45 (November 10, 1980): 243–44, 247.

"The Changing Character of Financial Markets." In *The American Economy in Transition*, edited, with an Introduction, by Martin Feldstein, pp. 78–86. Chicago and London: University of Chicago Press, 1980.

*"A Memorandum to the Fed." *Wall Street Journal*, January 30, 1981, p. 18. Reprinted in *An Economist's Protest*, 3d ed.

The Invisible Hand in Economics and Politics. Singapore: Institute of Southeast Asian Studies, 1981. Inaugural Singapore lecture delivered at the Institute of Southeast Asian Studies, October 14, 1980.

Introduction to *New Individualist Review*. A Periodical reprint. Indianapolis: Liberty Press, 1981.

Introduction to *Midnight Economist: Choices, Prices, and Public Policy*, by William R. Allen. New York: Playboy Press (distributed by Harper & Row), 1981.

Foreword to *Markets and Minorities*, by Thomas Sowell. New York: Basic Books, 1981.

Market Mechanisms and Central Economic Planning. Washington, D.C.: American Enterprise Institute, 1981. The second G. Warren Nutter Lecture in Political Economy delivered at the Hoover Institution, Stanford, March 4, 1981.

With Michael Porter, Fred Gruen, and Don Stammer. *Taxation, Inflation, and the Role of Government*. CIS Occasional Paper no. 4. St. Leonards, N.S.W., Australia: Centre for Independent Studies, June 1981. The edited proceedings of a Centre for Independent Studies Occasional Seminar at Sydney, Australia, April 8, 1981.

"Conscription Study Already Drafted." Letter to the Editor, *Wall Street Journal*, June 11, 1981.

"The Market and Human Freedom." (Excerpts of a speech delivered at the inaugural meeting of IATROS, the international organization of private and independent doctors, Sydney, Australia, April 13, 1981.) *Private Practice*, July 1981, pp. 36–37, 42–44, 46.

"Money Supply's Link to the Economy." Letter to the Editor, *Wall Street Journal*, July 30, 1981.

"Milton Friedman on Reaganomics." Interview in *Human Events*, December 5, 1981, pp. 1, 6–9.

"The Federal Reserve and Monetary Instability." *Wall Street Journal*, February 1, 1982.

"Monetary Policy: Theory and Practice." *Journal of Money, Credit, and Banking* 14 (February 1982): 98–118.

With Anna J. Schwartz. "The Effect of the Term Structure of Interest Rates on the Demand for Money in the United States." *Journal of Political Economy* 90 (February 1982): 201–12.

"Erratic Pulse of the Money Supply." Letter to the Editor, *Wall Street Journal*, June 28, 1982.

"Current Economic and Political Developments in the United States." (A speech delivered at the Annual General Meeting of the Fraser Institute, Vancouver, March 23, 1982.) *Focus* (Fraser Institute), no. 1 (July 1982), pp. 5–19.

"Monetary Policy: Theory and Practice. A Reply." *Journal of Money, Credit, and Banking* 14 (August 1982): 404–406.

"Supply-Side Policies: Where Do We Go from Here?" (Talk delivered at Conference on "Supply-Side Economics in the 1980s," sponsored by the Federal Reserve Bank of Atlanta and the Law and Economics Center of Emory University, Atlanta, March 17, 1982.) In *Supply-Side Economics in the 1980s: Conference Proceedings*, pp. 53–63. Westport, Conn.: Quorum Books, 1982.

"L'Inflation, ses causes et son traitement" [Inflation: cause and cure]. *Problèmes D'Amérique Latine*, no. 66 (November 30, 1982), pp. 103–13. French translation of a speech delivered at a conference in Lima, Peru, November 19, 1981. Also published in Spanish translation as "Causas y curas de la inflación," in *Dependencia y desarrollo en debate: Diario de un simposio*, edited by Federico Salazar Bustamante and Enrique Ghersi, pp. 21–38. Lima, Peru: Instituto Libertad y Democracia, 1983. Not published in English.

"Washington: Less Red Ink." *The Atlantic*, February 1983, pp. 18, 20–24, 26.

"A Monetarist View." In *Money Talks: Five Views of Britain's Economy*, edited by Alan Horrox and Gillian McCredie, pp. 1–17. London: Thames Television International Ltd., 1983. Adapted and reprinted in *Journal of Economic Education* 14, no. 4 (Fall 1983): 44–55.

"The Real Threat to U.S. Security." (Excerpts of a speech delivered before the Commonwealth Club of California, San Francisco, April 15, 1983.) *The Commonwealth* 72, no. 1 (April 25, 1983): 120–21, 124.

"A Monetarist Reflects," contribution to the Keynes Centenary of *The Economist*, June 4, 1983, pp. 17–19.

Away from Collectivism . . . Toward Freedom! Buena Park, Calif.: Americanism Educational League, 1983. Excerpts of a speech delivered at the First National Essay Contest Milton Friedman Awards Dinner of the AEL, Los Angeles, May 21, 1983.

"Monetary Variability: United States and Japan." *Journal of Money, Credit, and Banking* 15 (August 1983): 339–43.

"Sticking Price Tags on Job Performances in Government: Q & A's with Dr. Milton Friedman." *Management* 4, no. 1 (1983): 10–12, 32.

"Why a Surge of Inflation Is Likely Next Year." *Wall Street Journal*, September 1, 1983.

"Monetarism in Rhetoric and in Practice." (Keynote paper presented at the First

International Conference of the Institute for Monetary and Economic Studies of the Bank of Japan, Tokyo, June 22, 1983.) *Bank of Japan Monetary and Economic Studies* 1, no. 2 (October 1983): 1–14.

"Financial Futures Markets and Tabular Standards." *Journal of Political Economy* 92 (February 1984): 165–67.

"Monetary Policy for the 1980s." In *To Promote Prosperity: U.S. Domestic Policy in the Mid-1980s*, edited by John Moore with an Introduction by W. Glenn Campbell, pp. 23–60. Stanford: Hoover Institution Press, 1984.

"Spending Must Be Cut." *Socioeconomic Newsletter*, February–March 1984.

With Rose Friedman. "Inflation: Another Wild Ride Ahead?" *Across the Board* (The Conference Board Magazine), 21 (April 1984): 36–46. (Excerpted form *Tyranny of the Status Quo.*)

"Inflation Isn't Beaten." *New York Times*, April 3, 1984.

"Neomercantilism: Is There a Case for Tariffs? Comments." *National Review*, April 6, 1984, pp. 44–45.

"The Taxes Called Deficits." *Wall Street Journal*, April 26, 1984.

"Lessons from the 1979–82 Monetary Policy Experiment." *American Economic Review, Papers and Proceedings* 74 (May 1984): 397–400.

"Capitalism & the Jews." *Encounter*, June 1984, pp. 74–79.

The Suicidal Impulse of the Business Community. Stanford: Hoover Institution Press, for the Board of Trustees of the Leland Stanford Junior University, 1984. Based on remarks delivered at the Hoover Pacific Coast Seminar Dinner, October 25, 1983.

"An Interview with Milton Friedman." In *The U.S.A. in the World Economy*, pp. 40–46. San Francisco: Freeman, Cooper & Co., 1984. (Interview by Professor Arnold Heertjie of Amsterdam.)

"Currency Competition: A Sceptical View." In *Currency Competition and Monetary Union*, edited by Pascal Salin, pp. 42–46. The Hague: Martinus Nijhoff Publishers, 1984.

"The Economy: Where Are We Headed?" (Excerpts of a speech delivered before the Commonwealth Club of California, San Francisco, July 27, 1984.) *The Commonwealth* 78, no. 32 (August 6, 1984): 265–66, 269.

"Monetarist Can Be Supply-Sider, Too." Letter to the Editor, *Wall Street Journal*, August 31, 1984.

Free . . . or Fair—Which Way, America? Buena Park, Calif.: Americanism Educational League, 1984. Condensation of a speech delivered at the Second National Essay Contest Milton Friedman Awards Dinner of the AEL, Los Angeles, April 30, 1984.

"Tyranny of the Status Quo." (Address delivered at the National Dinner to Honor Milton Friedman, sponsored by the Pacific Institute for Public Policy Research, San Francisco, October 4, 1983.) In *Politics and Tyranny: Lessons in Pursuit of*

Freedom, edited, with an Introduction, by David J. Theroux, pp. 27–36. San Francisco: Pacific Institute for Public Policy Research, 1984.

With H. Robert Heller et al. "Economic Outlook." *Contemporary Policy Issues* 3, no. 1 (Fall 1984–85): 15–52. (Professor Friedman's discussion starts on p. 42.)

"Monetary Policy Structures." In *Candid Conversations on Monetary Policy*, pp. 32–50. Introduction by Congressman Jerry Lewis. Washington, D.C.: House Republican Research Committee, September 1984.

"To Tax or Not to Tax: That is NOT the Question." *San Francisco Chronicle*, September 14, 1984.

"Comment on 'The Success of Purchasing-Power Parity: Historical Evidence and Its Implications for Macroeconomics,' by Donald N. McCloskey and J. Richard Zecher." In *A Retrospective on the Classical Gold Standard, 1821–1931*. A Conference Report of the National Bureau of Economic Research. Edited by Michael D. Bordo and Anna J. Schwartz, pp. 157–62. Chicago: University of Chicago Press, 1984.

"Reining in Dollars, Import Curbs Cut Against the Grain." *Wall Street Journal*, November 27, 1984.

"Inflation: Retrospect and Prospect." (Adapted from a speech delivered at the Stanford in New York Conference, April 27, 1984.) *The Stanford Magazine*, Winter 1984, pp. 38–40.

The Meaning of Freedom. West Point, N.Y.: United States Military Academy, 1985. Edited version of the twelfth Sol Feinstone Lecture delivered at the United States Military Academy on September 26, 1984.

"How Trade Barriers Can Hurt U.S. Economy." *San Francisco Chronicle*, April 18, 1985.

"How Quotas Boomerang." *San Francisco Chronicle*, April 19, 1985.

"Comment on Leland Yeager's Paper on the Keynesian Heritage." In Leland Yeager, Milton Friedman, and Karl Brunner, *The Keynesian Heritage*, pp. 12–18. Center Symposia Series no. CS-16. Rochester, N.Y.: Center for Research in Government Policy and Business, University of Rochester Graduate School of Management, 1985. Paper first presented at Mont Pelerin Society meeting, Cambridge, September 1984.

The Greatest Threat to Freedom. Buena Park, Calif.: Americanism Educational League, 1985. Condensation of a speech delivered at the Third National Essay Contest Milton Friedman Awards Dinner of the AEL, Los Angeles, May 6, 1985.

"How to Give Monetarism a Bad Name." In *Monetarism, Inflation, and the Federal Reserve: Essays Prepared for the Use of the Joint Economic Committee, Congress of the United States* [in memory of Robert Weintraub], edited by James K. Galbraith and Dan C. Roberts, pp. 51–61. Washington, D.C.: U.S. Government Printing Office, 1985. Revision of a paper entitled "What Could Reasonably Have Been Expected from Monetarism: The United States," presented at Mont Pelerin Society meeting, Vancouver, August 29, 1983, which was first published in Italian translation as "Cosa ci si sarebbe potuto attendere dal monetarismo:

l'esperienza degli Stati Uniti," in *Quale politica monetario? Il dibattito sul monetarismo*, pp. 69–84. Rome: Centro Ricerche Economiche Applicate, 1984.

"Is Hyperinflation Inevitable?" (Excerpts of a speech delivered before the Commonwealth Club of California, San Francisco, June 28, 1985.) *The Commonwealth* 79, no. 26 (July 8, 1985): 213–14, 217.

"The Fed Hasn't Changed Its Ways." *Wall Street Journal*, August 20, 1985.

"Monetary Policy in a Fiat World." (Keynote paper presented at the Second International Conference of the Institute for Monetary and Economic Studies of the Bank of Japan, Tokyo, May 29, 1985.) *Bank of Japan Monetary and Economic Studies* 3, no. 2 (September 1985): 11–18. Reprinted in *Contemporary Policy Issues* 4, no. 1 (January 1986): 1–9, and in *Financial Innovation and Monetary Policy: Asia and the West*, Proceedings of the Second International Conference of the Institute for Monetary and Economic Studies of the Bank of Japan, edited by Yoshio Suzuki and Hiroshi Yomo, pp. 21–29 (Tokyo: University of Tokyo Press, 1986).

"The Trouble with Tax Reform Plans." *San Francisco Chronicle*, October 16, 1985.

"Trade School." Letter to the Editor, *National Review*, November 15, 1985.

"The Fed's Monetarism Was Never Anything but Rhetoric." Letter to the Editor, *Wall Street Journal*, December 18, 1985.

"Let Floating Rates Continue to Float." *New York Times*, December 26, 1985.

With Anna J. Schwartz. "Has Government Any Role in Money?" *Journal of Monetary Economics* 17 (1986): 37–62. Translation: Serbo-Croatian, 1986.

"Economists and Economic Policy." (Presidential address, Western Economic Association, July 2, 1985.) *Economic Inquiry* 24, no. 1 (January 1986): 1–10.

"A Defense of Reagan's Domestic Budget Cuts." *San Francisco Chronicle*, March 5, 1986.

"Right at Last, an Expert's Dream" (My Turn column). *Newsweek*, March 10, 1986.

With Anna J. Schwartz. "'The Failure of the Bank of United States: A Reappraisal,' [by Joseph L. Lucia]: A Reply." *Explorations in Economic History* 23 (April 1986): 199–204.

"Let the Protesters Themselves Divest." *New York Times*, May 16, 1986.

"Has Liberalism Failed?" In *The Unfinished Agenda: Essays on the Political Economy of Government Policy in Honour of Arthur Seldon*, edited by Martin J. Anderson, pp. 125–39. London: Institute of Economic Affairs, June 1986.

"The Resource Cost of Irredeemable Paper Money." *Journal of Political Economy* 94, part 1, no. 3 (June 1986): 642–47.

"What We Know That Ain't So about Economic Policy." (Excerpts of a speech delivered before the Commonwealth Club of California, San Francisco, June 13, 1986.) *The Commonwealth* 80, no. 25 (June 23, 1986): 242, 245–46.

"Tax Reform Lets Politicians Look for New Donors." *Wall Street Journal*, July 7, 1986.

"The Solomon Solution for Schools." *This World*, p. 16, *San Francisco Chronicle*, September 7, 1986.

"M1's Hot Streak Gave Keynesians a Bad Idea." *Wall Street Journal*, September 18, 1986.

"My Evolution as an Economist." In *Lives of the Laureates: Seven Nobel Economists*, edited by William Breit and Roger W. Spencer, pp. 77–92. Cambridge: MIT Press, 1986. Edited version of an address delivered at Trinity University, San Antonio, Texas, March 21, 1985.

With Michael R. Darby et al. "Recent Behavior of the Velocity of Money." (Published version of a panel session at the 61st annual Western Economic Association International Conference, San Francisco, July 1986.) *Contemporary Policy Issues* 5, no. 1 (January 1987): 1–33.

"The Advantage of Being Few." *Washington Post*, January 22, 1987, p. A21.

Review of *Rational Expectations and Inflation*, by Thomas J. Sargent. *Journal of Political Economy* 95, no. 1 (February 1987): 218–21.

"Monetary History, Not Dogma." *Wall Street Journal*, February 12, 1987.

"Free Markets and Free Speech." (Keynote address delivered at the Federalist Society National Symposium, Stanford University Law School, March 7, 1986.) *Harvard Journal of Law & Public Policy* 10, no. 1 (Winter 1987): 1–9.

"Good Ends, Bad Means." In *The Catholic Challenge to the American Economy: Reflections on the U.S. Bishops' Pastoral Letters on Catholic Social Teaching and the U.S. Economy*, edited by Thomas M. Cannon, S.J., pp. 99–106. New York: Macmillan Publishing Co., 1987. Published adaptation of a talk delivered under the auspices of the Catholic theological schools of Berkeley, April 24, 1985.

"Outdoing Smoot-Hawley." *Wall Street Journal*, April 20, 1987.

"Where Are We on the Road to Liberty?" (Adaptation of an address delivered at the Reason Foundation's Welcome-to-Los Angeles banquet, October 18, 1986.) *Reason*, June 1987, pp. 31–33.

INDEX

Germany (*continued*)
rate in, 378; and money, 299, 341, 374, 378, 380; and prices, 467
Glazer, Nathan, 48–49, 51
GNP [gross national product], 408
Gold: and a commodity standard, 430–32; controls on, 457–58, 459; and exchange rates, 446–47, 453–55, 458, 477, 486–87, 492, 496n7; and Federal Reserve System, 449, 450–52; and fluctuations/stability, 378, 398, 408, 448–53, 486–87; and free markets, 455, 457, 459; and interest rate, 468; and monetary authority, 443; and monetary policy, 381, 390–91, 408, 418, 448–55; and money supply, 328–44 *passim*, 381; and national currencies, 446–47, 456–57, 459; nationalization of, 453–54; and outside money, 508–9; and prices, 448–49; prices of, 453, 455–56, 457–58; private ownership of, 453–54; and rational expectations theory, 373; real/pseudo standards for, 446–60; views about role of, 446–47; and world monetary system, 500–501
Goldenweiser, E. A., 389–90
Gold Standard Corporation, 509
Goldstein, Henry N., 427n17
Goodhart, Charles, 514–15, 516, 517
Gordon, Robert J., 182n13, 183n25, 406
Government: and alcohol regulation, 135–36; as Big Brother, 146–47; business regulation by, 133–34; corruption, 131–33; and drug regulation, 135–36; and exchange rates, 483–84; and fiat money, 500, 517–19; and free banking, 503–4, 511–17; and outside money, 502–11; and public choice theory, 499–500; and rational expectations theory, 500; spending and inflation, 377–78. *See also* Education; Federal Reserve System; Fiscal Policy; Monetary authority; Monetary policy; Money supply
Graham, Frank D., 390
Great Britain: and capitalism and socialism, 26; and education, 95, 102, 110–11; and exchange rates, 454–55, 466, 469, 470, 476–77, 487, 488–89, 490; and free speech, 12, 14; and gold, 337, 444–45n3, 456; indexation in, 419; inflation in, 356, 357–59, 361–62, 518–19; output in, 316;

and outside money, 509; permanent income in, 195; prices in, 316, 325; and quantity theory of money, 380; and sterling, 452, 487, 488–89; unemployment in, 355–62 *passim*. *See also* Bank of England
Greece, 373
Green, Christopher, 67n6

Haberler, 388
Halasi, Albert, 390
Hall, Robert, 420
Hamilton, Alexander, 122, 132–33
Hammond, B., 512
Hansen, Alvin, 388, 390
Harberger, Arnold, 361
Harding, W. P. G., 438–39
Harlem Prep [New York City], 99–100, 108, 110
Harrison, George L., 337
Hatfield, Mark O., 70
Hayek, Friedrich A., 22, 363, 418–19, 422, 500, 507–8, 513, 521–22
Haynes, Stephen E., 427n17
Hershey, Lewis B., 69, 70, 72
Higher education, 94, 112–21, 122
High-powered money: and exchange rates, 380; and Federal Reserve System, 420–24; freezing of, 420–24; and monetary authorities, 380, 381, 416; and monetary policy, 342, 411, 420–24; stock of, 330–31, 333, 342–44
Hollister, John B., 82
Homan, 390
Home State Savings and Loan [Ohio], 513–15, 519–20
Housing, 128, 139–40, 249–70, 281–82nn7–10
Hua Guofeng, 34
Human capital, 288, 290
Humanitarianism and foreign aid, 79–80
Human rights, 137–38
Hume, David, 370–71
Hungary, 26, 373
Hyperinflation, 297, 299, 301, 314–15, 321n15, 373–74, 377, 381, 509
Hypotheses: and assumptions, 160–66, 178; and behavior, 193–96, 208–12, 219n2; construction of, 160–61, 179; and economic theory, 156, 157–66, 181n11; and experiments/experience, 158–66, 177,

Money supply (*continued*)
ratio, 331, 339–40; and economic development, 316–17; and economic variables, 323–32; experiments with, 333–36; and Federal Reserve System, 324, 330–44 *passim*, 345n1, 378, 389, 423–24, 425, 444; and fiscal policy, 318; and fluctuations, 306–13, 316–17, 320n12, 323–45 *passim*, 376–78; generalizations about, 340; and gold, 328–44 *passim*; and income, 307–9, 311–12, 316; 320nn9,11, 324–25, 328, 332–33, 339–40, 375–77, 405–8; and independence of money changes, 332–40; and interest rate, 308, 344–45, 392–93; international aspects of, 325–28, 329–30, 342; and monetary policy, 312–13, 316–19, 389–93 *passim*, 402n9; and outputs, 305, 306–7, 309, 313–16; and politics, 318–19, 336–37; and prices, 316–19, 325–28, 332, 333, 339–40, 372–78; and quantity theory of money, 296–97, 298; and rational expectations theory, 372–78; and silver, 333, 340, 342–43, 344; and timing, 305–13, 317–18, 320n11; and velocity, 328–29, 344–45. *See also* Economic stability; Monetary policy; Money; Quantity theory of money; Stocks
Moreau, Emile, 435, 439, 444n3
Morgenstern, Oskar, 206, 207–8, 210, 224
Mosteller, F., 209
Mundell effect, 276–79
Muth, John F., 370

National currencies, and gold, 446–47
National service. *See* Army, volunteer
National Student Loan Bank, 120
Natural rate hypothesis: and inflation, 352–55, 359–72 *passim*, 393–96, 402n10; and market rate, 395–96; and monetary policy, 393; and rational expectations theory, 370–72; and unemployment, 352–55, 359–72 *passim*, 393–96, 402n10
Natural selection, 165–66
Negroes. *See* Race
Neisser, Hans, 390
Netherlands, 373
Neutrality hypothesis of stabilization policy, 371–72
New Deal. *See* Contractions; Federal Reserve System

New York, Federal Reserve Bank of, 337–38, 404–5, 439–40, 451
New York City, 60, 139–40
Nobel prize in economics, 347
Non-interest-bearing obligations. *See* High-powered money
Norman, Montagu, 435, 444n3
North West Industries, 29
Norway, 490
Nurkse, Ragnar, 496–97n9
Nutter, G. Warren, 18, 20, 26, 29–30

Office of Economic Opportunity, U.S., 109
Oi, Walter, 73–74
Oil prices, 148–49, 359
Oliver, H. M., Jr., 182n13
OPEC [Oil Producing Exporting Countries], 148–49
Open Market Investment Committee [Federal Reserve System], 428n32
Outputs: and costs, 314–15; and economic development, 314, 315–16; factors influencing, 314; and fluctuations, 314–16; and incentives, 315; and income, 395; and interest rate, 314–15; and market economies, 314; and monetary policy, 316, 319; and money supply, 305, 306–7, 309, 313–16; and prices, 305, 306–7, 309; and rational expectations theory, 376; and timing, 313–14, 320n11; and wages, 314–15
Outside money, 502–12, 513, 518, 520, 521

Pakistan, 14–15
Patriotism, 24–25
Performance evaluation of capitalism and socialism, 33–34
Permanent income: and aggregate income, 190–91, 195; and consumption, 187–205; and data analysis, 188–89, 192–93; and economic development, 199–202; and economic policy, 197–99; evidence of acceptability of hypothesis of, 191–93, 198, 199, 203–5; and fluctuations, 202–4; hypothesis statement, 189–91; inappropriate concepts of, 187–89; research about, 197–99, 205. *See also* Interest rate
Personalities and economic policy, 405, 438–40, 451
Phelps, E. S., 352

Quantity theory (*continued*)
and wealth, 286–95, 300; and yield,
287–90

Race: and education, 93, 104–5, 122; and
volunteer army, 75–76
Rational expectations, theory of: empirical
evidence for, 372–78; and fluctuations,
373–74; generalizations about, 375–78;
and government, 500; implications of,
371–72; and money, 370–84, 428n30; and
natural rate hypothesis, 370–72; and
prices, 372–78; problems with, 372–73;
and stabilization policy, 371–72
Real-bills doctrine, 298, 441
Real income. *See* Income; Permanent
income
Reality: and assumptions, 161–66, 172–73,
178, 179; and capitalism and socialism,
33–34; and hypotheses, 158–66, 177; and
outputs, 314
Rearmament drive, 493–94
Redistribution of income, 226–35
Regulation Q, 411, 423–24, 501, 522
Relative income hypothesis, 200
Rent control, 128, 139–40
Reserve accounting, 412
Reserves and exchange rates, 464, 494,
497n11
Resumption of money, 342
Right to work, 137–38
Risk. *See* Expected-utility hypothesis
Rist, Charles, 454
Rivers, Mendel, 69
Rivkin, Ellis, 55n1
Robinson, Joan, 176–77
Robinson Crusoe analogy: and interest rate
arithmetic, 248; and personal income
distribution, 224–26
Rockefeller, Nelson, 121
Rockoff, H., 511, 512–13
Rolnick, A. J., 511, 512–13
Romania, 26
Roosevelt, Franklin D., 342, 453, 454
Rostow, Walter, 81
Rueff, Jacques, 435
Rumsfeld, Donald, 70
Russell, Richard, 69
Russia. *See* Soviet Union

St. John Chrysostom school [New York
City], 99
Salaries. *See* Wages
Samuelson, Paul A., 4, 210
Sargent, T. J., 371
Savage, L. J., 164–65, 210, 228. *See also*
Expected-utility hypothesis
Savings, 11, 201–2, 263–71, 389–90. *See also*
Consumption; Permanent income
Schacht, Hjalmar, 435
Schools. *See* Education
Schwartz, Anna J., 377, 404–5, 408–9, 417,
422–23
Scotland: free banking in, 511–12
Secular stagnation, 203, 399
Selden, Richard T., 299–300, 301
Services. *See* Flows; Quantity theory of
money
Short run. *See* Timing
Siegan, Bernard, 13
Silver, 333, 340, 342–43, 344, 452, 487–89
Simons, Henry, 285–86, 390, 402n1
Sims, Christopher, 426n5
Sjaastad, Larry, 361
Smith, Adam, 21–22, 40, 108–9, 115, 120,
147, 149
Smith, Vera, 504, 516, 520
Smithies, Arthur, 390
Smoking, 13–14
Snyder, Carl, 337
Socialism, 24–31, 95–96. *See also* Capitalism
and socialism; Communism
Social programs, failure of, 127–29
Social science, 347–50
Solzhenitsyn, Alexander, 9
Sombart, Werner, 47–48, 51, 53, 55n3
Soviet Union, 9–10, 14–21 *passim*, 29, 373.
See also Communism
Sowell, Thomas, 27
Specie money, 505–6
Speculation, 473–75, 480–84, 496–97nn8–9
Stabilization policy, 180n4, 371–72. *See also*
Economic stability; Monetary stability;
Rational expectations, theory of
Stagflation, 351, 366
Stagnation, secular, 203
Sterling, 452
Stigler, George J., 139, 182n13, 356
Stocks: altering of, 255–63; and capital,
249–73; and flows, 240–42, 249–70; gen-

eralizations about, 263–71; and interest
rate, 249–55, 263–70; and investments,
263–71; prices of, 249–55; and savings,
263–71. *See also* Money supply; Quantity
theory of money
Stone, Richard, 139–40
Storefront schools, 99–100
Strong, Benjamin, 337–38, 435, 439–40
Students and volunteer army, 71–72, 73
Subsidization, 33, 63–64, 66, 81, 102
Suffolk Bank system, 512
Sugarman, Stephen D., 106
Summers, L. H., 524–25n40
Supply. *See* Interest rate; Money supply;
Stocks
Sweden, 195, 359
Switzerland, 378, 380, 392, 474

Tabular standard, 418–20, 506
Tactics. *See* Monetary policy; Targets
Targets: and monetary policy, 409–13,
414–15, 425; and quantity theory of
money, 380
Taxes. *See* Income tax; Income tax, negative
Taylor, Fred M., 24
Theorists and quantity theory of money,
297–99
Theory, economic: and assumptions, 166–71,
178; criticisms of, 171–74, 178; and
economics, 171–79; and inflation, 356,
366–67; and monetary policy/theory, 179;
and price theory, 179; and unemployment,
356. *See also* Assumptions; Hypotheses;
name of theory
Thomas, Norman, 70
Thurow, Lester, 21
Timing: and exchange rates, 479–83; and
inflation, 352–65; and monetary policy,
411–13; and money supply, 305–13,
317–18, 320n11; and outputs, 313–14,
320n11; and prices, 304–14, 317–18; and
unemployment, 352–65. *See also* Rational
expectations, theory of
Trade. *See* Free trade; International trade
Treasury, U.S. Department of the, 388,
416–18, 437, 438, 439, 448
Trickle down theory, 60
Tullock, Gordon, 356

Unemployment: and demand, 349–50, 352,
395; and economic theory, 356; and
income, 395; and inflation, 347–69,
371–72, 393–96, 402n10; and information
transmission, 363–64; international aspects of, 357–59, 361–62, 367; and monetary policy, 391, 393–96; and natural rate
hypothesis, 352–55, 359–72 *passim*,
393–96, 402n10; and Phillips curve,
350–65, 366–67, 394; and politics, 356,
362–63; and prices, 349–50, 363–65; and
productivity, 355; and public policy, 356,
367; and timing, 352–65
Unions, 12, 39, 394
United Kingdom. *See* Great Britain
United States. *See* name of subject
Unit of account, 499, 502–3, 506, 511, 521
Universal national service, 70
Universal subsidization, 63–64
University of California at Los Angeles,
113–14
University of Chicago, 130, 181n11,
285–86, 302
Urban renewal, 128
Utility: definition of, 218; and expected-
utility hypothesis, 206–21; measurability
of, 206–21 [esp. 213–18]; and normative
economics, 219; and quantity theory of
money, 287, 290–91, 292; and wealth,
225, 228–32, 287, 290–91, 292; and
welfare economics, 217–18. *See also* Income distribution, personal

Value judgments: and anti-capitalism, 47–48;
and economics, 3–8, 348–49; and fiscal
policy, 4–5; and free markets, 6–7; and
free speech, 6–7; and impossibility theorem, 5; and integrative system, 5–6, 7–8;
and intellectuals, 5, 7; and Jews, 47–54;
and markets, 3, 5–7; and monetary policy,
4–5; and positive economics, 154, 348;
and prices, 7; and social sciences, 347–48;
and wages, 4–5; and welfare, 4
Vaubel, Roland, 510–11
Velocity. *See* Quantity theory of money
Vietnam, 69–70, 72
Viner, Jacob, 285–86
Voluntary cooperation, 137–38
Voluntary exchange. *See* Free markets
Volunteer army. *See* Army, volunteer

Von Neumann, John, 206, 207–8, 210, 224
Voucher plan for education, 99–112,
119–21, 122, 130

Wages: and economic miracles, 141–43; and
exchange rates, 467; and interest rate,
241; minimum, 155, 394; nominal,
402nn11–12; and outputs, 314–15; and
Phillips curve, 394, 402n12; and positive
economics, 155; and prices, 314–15, 394,
395, 402n12, 478–79; and purchasing
power, 353; and social responsibility of
business, 39; and value judgments, 4–5;
and volunteer army, 72–74, 76, 78. *See
also* Unemployment
Walton, Maurice, 111–12
Wartime: and banks, 434; and exchange
rates, 484; and inflation, 374; and money
supply, 299, 306, 317, 323, 328, 329,
332–33, 344–45; and prices, 306, 317;
and rational expectations theory, 373–74.
See also Fluctuations
Wealth: bonds as, 288, 291, 293, 300; and
capital, 253–55, 266–70; corporate,
293–95; definition of, 287; equities as,
288, 289, 291; and ethics, 134; forms of,
287–90, 300; good/bad, 133–34; human
capital as, 288, 290; and incentives, 134;
and income, 253–55, 287, 300; and inter-

est rate, 243, 271–73, 274–79; and monetary policy/theory, 242, 388–89; physical
nonhuman goods as, 288, 290; and pol-
itics, 134; and quantity theory of money,
286–95, 300; redistribution of, 226–35;
and utility, 225, 228–32, 287, 290–91,
292; yield of, 288–90. *See also* Income
distribution, personal; Quantity theory of
money
Weber, Max, 51
Weber, W. E., 511, 512–13
Welfare, 4, 60–61, 137–38, 217–18
West, Edwin G., 94, 95, 109
White, Lawrence, 511–12
White, R. W. R., 523n10
Wicksell, Knut, 353–54, 393, 394–95
Willett, Thomas D., 427n17
Williams, John H., 390
Wilson, James Q., 53, 56n13
Wirtz, Willard, 70
Work, right to, 137–38
Worker cooperatives, Yugoslavian, 28–31
World monetary system, 500–501, 504

Yield: and quantity theory of money, 287–90;
to maturity, 245
Yugoslavia, 28–31

Zacharias, Jerrold R., 119–20